Lecture Notes in Computer Science 1097

Edited by G. Goos, J. Hartmanis and J. van Leeuwen

Advisory Board: W. Brauer   D. Gries   J. Stoer

Springer
Berlin
Heidelberg
New York
Barcelona
Budapest
Hong Kong
London
Milan
Paris
Santa Clara
Singapore
Tokyo

Rolf Karlsson Andrzej Lingas (Eds.)

Algorithm Theory – SWAT '96

5th Scandinavian Workshop
on Algorithm Theory
Reykjavík, Iceland, July 3-5, 1996
Proceedings

 Springer

Series Editors

Gerhard Goos, Karlsruhe University, Germany

Juris Hartmanis, Cornell University, NY, USA

Jan van Leeuwen, Utrecht University, The Netherlands

Volume Editors

Rolf Karlsson
Andrzej Lingas
Lund University, Department of Computer Science
P.O. Box 118, S-22100 Lund, Sweden

Cataloging-in-Publication data applied for

Die Deutsche Bibliothek - CIP-Einheitsaufnahme

Algorithm theory : proceedings / SWAT '96, 5th Scandinavian
Workshop on Algorithm Theory, Reykjavik, Iceland, July 3 - 5,
1996. Rolf Karlsson ; Andrzej Lingas (ed.). - Berlin ;
Heidelberg ; New York ; Barcelona ; Budapest ; Hong Kong ;
London ; Milan ; Paris ; Santa Clara ; Singapore ; Tokyo :
Springer, 1996
  (Lecture notes in computer science ; Vol. 1097)
  ISBN 3-540-61422-2
NE: Karlsson, Rolf [Hrsg.]; SWAT <5, 1996, Reykjavik>; GT

CR Subject Classification (1991): F.1-2, E.1-2, G.2, G.3, I.3.5

ISSN 0302-9743
ISBN 3-540-61422-2 Springer-Verlag Berlin Heidelberg New York

© Springer-Verlag Berlin Heidelberg 1996
Printed in Germany

Typesetting: Camera-ready by author
SPIN 10513241   06/3142 – 5 4 3 2 1 0   Printed on acid-free paper

Foreword

The papers in this volume were presented at the Fifth Scandinavian Workshop on Algorithm Theory. The workshop, which continues the tradition of SWAT'88 to SWAT'94, and of the Workshops on Algorithms and Data Structures (WADS'89 to WADS'95), is intended as a forum for researchers in the area of design and analysis of algorithms. The SWAT conferences are coordinated by the SWAT steering committee, which consists of B. Aspvall (Bergen), S. Carlsson (Luleå), H. Hafsteinsson (Reykjavík), R. Karlsson (Lund), A. Lingas (Lund), E.M. Schmidt (Århus), and E. Ukkonen (Helsinki).

The call for papers sought contributions on original research on algorithms and data structures, in all areas, including computational geometry, parallel and distributed computing, graph theory, and combinatorics. There were 95 papers submitted, of which about two thirds were very good or good. Because of the SWAT format the program committee could select only 35 papers for presentation. In addition, invited lectures were presented by Noga Alon (Tel-Aviv), Arne Andersson (Lund), and Mike Paterson (Warwick).

SWAT'96 was held on July 3–5, 1996, in Reykjavík, Iceland, and was organized by Hjálmtýr Hafsteinsson and Magnús Halldórsson (University of Iceland).

We wish to thank all referees who helped to evaluate the papers. We are grateful to Nordic Research Courses (NorFA), the Ministry of Education of Iceland, the city of Reykjavík, Lund University, and the Swedish Research Council for Engineering Sciences (TFR) for their support.

Lund, April 1996

Rolf Karlsson
Andrzej Lingas

Table of Contents

Derandomization Via Small Sample Spaces

Noga Alon*

School of Mathematical Sciences, Raymond and Beverly Sackler Faculty of Exact Sciences, Tel Aviv University, Tel Aviv 69978, Israel. E-mail: noga@math.tau.ac.il.

Abstract

Many randomized algorithms run successfully even when the random choices they utilize are not fully independent. For the analysis some limited amount of independence, like *k-wise independence* for some fixed k, often suffices. In these cases, it is possible to replace the appropriate exponentially large sample spaces required to simulate all random choices of the algorithms by ones of polynomial size. This enables one to *derandomize* the algorithms, that is, convert them into deterministic ones, by searching the relatively small sample spaces deterministically. If a random variable attains a certain value with positive probability, then we can actually search and find a point in which it attains such a value.

The observation that $n-1$ *pairwise independent* nontrivial random variables can be defined over a sample space of size n has been mentioned already long ago, see [11], [23]. The pairwise independent case has been a crucial ingredient in the construction of efficient hashing schemes in [14], [17]. A more general construction, of small sample spaces supporting k-wise independent random variables, appeared in [19]. For the case of binary, uniform random variables this is treated under the name *orthogonal arrays* in the Coding Theory literature, see, e.g., [27]. Most constructions are based on some simple properties of polynomials over a finite field or on certain explicit error correcting codes.

Several researchers realized that constructions of this type are useful for derandomizing *parallel* algorithms, since one may simply check all points of the sample space in parallel. Papers pursuing this idea include [1], [22], [24], and papers dealing with the properties of the constructions in which the sample spaces are not necessarily uniform include [20], [21]. It can be shown that for fixed k, the minimum size of a sample space supporting n k-wise independent random variables is $\Omega(n^{\lfloor k/2 \rfloor})$. For the binary uniform case this is essentially the Rao bound [30] (see also [12], [16]), whereas for the general case it is shown in [1], where it is also observed this is tight for the binary uniform case. It follows that polynomial size sample spaces suffice only for handling k-wise independence for fixed k. There are, however, several ways to achieve a higher amount of independence. One method, developed in [9] and [26], (see also [25] for related ideas), starts with a construction of relatively small spaces which support k-wise

* Research supported in part by a USA Israeli BSF grant.

independent random variables for $k = (\log n)^{O(1)}$, and proceeds by searching in these spaces using the *conditional expectations* method of [32], [29]. Another method, suggested in [31], is based on constructing spaces in which only certain prescribed sets of random choices are independent. The third method, initiated in [28] and improved in [3] (see also [2], [8], [13], [15]) constructs sample spaces that support random variables any k of which are *nearly* independent.

The above techniques have been applied in numerous papers dealing with derandomization, and we make no attempt to list all of them here. Examples include parallelization of derandomized geometric algorithms in [10], [18], and various parallel graph algorithms [1], [9], [22], [24], [28]. It turned out that some variants of the techniques are also useful in derandomizing *sequential* algorithms [5], [7] and in designing space efficient on-line algorithms for estimating some statistical properties of a given input sequence [4].

In the talk I will survey the basic ideas in the constructions of small sample spaces and discuss some of the applications, focusing on various recent results that illustrate the somewhat surprising relevance of the techniques to the solutions of several algorithmic problems.

References

1. N. Alon, L. Babai and A. Itai. A fast and simple randomized parallel algorithm for the maximal independent set problem. *J. Alg.*, 7:567–583, 1986.
2. N. Alon, J. Bruck, J. Naor, M. Naor and R. Roth. Construction of asymptotically good, low-rate error-correcting codes through pseudo-random graphs. *IEEE Trans. Info. Theory*, 38:509–516, 1992.
3. N. Alon, O. Goldreich, J. Håstad and R. Peralta. Simple constructions of almost k–wise independent random variables. *Random Structures and Algorithms*, 3(3):289–303, 1992.
4. N. Alon, Y. Matias and M. Szegedy. The space complexity of approximating the frequency moments. In *Proc. of the 28th ACM Symp. on Theory of Computing*, 1996, in press.
5. N. Alon and M. Naor. Derandomization, witnesses for Boolean matrix multiplication and construction of perfect hash functions. To appear in *Algorithmica*.
6. N. Alon and J. H. Spencer. *The Probabilistic Method*. Wiley, 1992.
7. N. Alon, R. Yuster and U. Zwick. Color-coding. *J. ACM* 42:844–856, 1995.
8. Y. Azar, R. Motwani and J. Naor. Approximating arbitrary probability distributions using small sample spaces. Manuscript, 1990.
9. B. Berger and J. Rompel. Simulating $(\log^c n)$-wise independence in NC. *Journal of the ACM*, 38:1026–1046, 1991.
10. B. Berger, J. Rompel and P. W. Shor. Efficient NC algorithms for set cover with applications to learning and geometry. In *Proc. 30th IEEE Symposium on Foundations of Computer Science*, pages 54-59, 1989.
11. S. Bernstein. *Theory of Probability (3rd Edition)*. GTTI, Moscow, 1945.
12. B. Chor, O. Goldreich, J. Hastad, J. Friedman, S. Rudich and R. Smolensky. The Bit Extraction Problem or t-Resilient Functions. In 26th *Annual Symposium on Foundations of Computer Science, Portland, Oregon*, pages 396–407, 1985.

13. S. Chari, P. Rohatgi and A. Srinivasan. Improved algorithms via approximations of probability distributions. In *Proc. 26th ACM Symposium on Theory of Computing*, pages 584–592, 1994.

14. L. Carter and M. Wegman. Universal classes of Hash functions. *J. Computer System Sciences*, 18:143-154, 1979.

15. G. Even, O. Goldreich, M. Luby, N. Nisan and B. Veličković. Approximations of general independent distributions. In *Proc. 24th ACM Symposium on Theory of Computing*, pages 10–16, 1992.

16. J. Friedman. On the bit extraction problem. In *Proc. 33rd IEEE Symposium on Foundations of Computer Science*, pages 314–319, 1992.

17. M. Fredman, J. Komlos and E. Szemerédi. Storing a sparse table with $O(1)$ worst-case access time. In *Proc. 23rd IEEE Symposium on Foundations of Computer Science*, pages 165–169, 1982.

18. M. T. Goodrich. Geometric partitioning made easier, even in parallel. In *Proc. 9th ACM Symp. Comput. Geom.*, pages 73–82, 1993.

19. A. Joffe. On a set of almost deterministic k-independent random variables. *Annals of Probability*, 2:161–162, 1974.

20. D. Koller and N. Megiddo. Constructing small sample spaces satisfying given constraints. In *Proc. of the 25th Annual ACM Symposium on Theory of Computing*, pages 268–277, 1993.

21. H. Karloff and Y. Mansour. On construction of k-wise independent random variables. In *Proc. of the 26th Annual ACM Symposium on Theory of Computing*, pages 564–573, 1994.

22. R. Karp and A. Wigderson. A fast parallel algorithm for the maximum independent set problem. *J. ACM*, 32: 762-773, 1985.

23. H. O. Lancaster. Pairwise statistical independence. *Ann. Math. Stat.* 36: 1313-1317, 1965.

24. M. Luby. A simple parallel algorithm for the maximal independent set problem. *SIAM J. Comput.*, 15(4):1036–1053, 1986.

25. M. Luby. Removing randomness in parallel computation without a processor penalty. *J. Comput. Syst. Sci.*, 47(2):250–286, 1993.

26. R. Motwani, J. Naor and M. Naor. The probabilistic method yields deterministic parallel algorithms. *J. Comput. Syst. Sci.*, 49:478–516, 1994.

27. F. J. MacWilliams and N. J. A. Sloane. *The Theory of Error-Correcting Codes*. North Holland, Amsterdam, 1977.

28. J. Naor and M. Naor. Small–bias probability spaces: efficient constructions and applications. *SIAM J. Comput.*, 22(4):838–856, 1993.

29. P. Raghavan. Probabilistic construction of deterministic algorithms: approximating packing integer programs. *J. Comput. Syst. Sci.*, 37:130–143, 1988.

30. C. R. Rao. Factorial experiments derivable from combinatorial arrangements of arrays. *J. Royal Stat. Soc.* 9: 128–139, 1947.

31. L. J. Schulman. Sample spaces uniform on neighborhoods. In *Proceedings of the 24th Annual ACM Symposium on Theory of Computing*, pages 17–25, 1992.

32. J. Spencer. *Ten Lectures on the Probabilistic Method*. SIAM, 1987.

The Randomized Complexity of Maintaining the Minimum

Gerth Stølting Brodal,[1*]   Shiva Chaudhuri,[2**]   Jaikumar Radhakrishnan[3***]

[1] BRICS[†], Computer Science Department, Aarhus University,
Ny Munkegade, DK-8000 Århus C, Denmark
[2] Max–Planck–Institut für Informatik, Im Stadtwald, 66123 Saarbrücken, Germany
[3] Tata Institute of Fundamental Research, Mumbai, India

Abstract. The complexity of maintaining a set under the operations Insert, Delete and FindMin is considered. In the comparison model it is shown that any randomized algorithm with expected amortized cost t comparisons per Insert and Delete has expected cost at least $n/(e2^{2t}) - 1$ comparisons for FindMin. If FindMin is replaced by a weaker operation, FindAny, then it is shown that a randomized algorithm with constant expected cost per operation exists, but no deterministic algorithm. Finally, a deterministic algorithm with constant amortized cost per operation for an offline version of the problem is given.

1 Introduction

We consider the complexity of maintaining a set S of elements from a totally ordered universe under the following operations: Insert(e): inserts the element e into S, Delete(e): removes from S the element e provided it is known where e is stored, and FindMin: returns the minimum element in S without removing it. We refer to this problem as the Insert-Delete-FindMin problem. We denote the size of S by n. The analysis is done in the comparison model, i.e. the time required by an operation is the number of comparisons it makes. The input is a sequence of operations, given to the algorithm in an on-line manner, that is, the algorithm must process the current operation before it receives the next operation in the sequence. The *worst case* time for an operation is the maximum, over all such operations in all sequences, of the time taken to process the operation. The *amortized* time of an operation is the maximum, over all sequences, of the total number of comparisons performed, while processing this type of operation in the sequence, divided by the length of the sequence.

* Supported by the Danish Natural Science Research Council (Grant No. 9400044). This research was done while visiting the Max-Planck Institut für Informatik, Saabrücken, Germany. Email: gerth@daimi.aau.dk.

** This work was partially supported by the EU ESPRIT LTR project No. 20244 (AL-COM IT). Email: shiva@mpi-sb.mpg.de.

*** Email: jaikumar@tcs.tifr.res.in.

† Basic Research in Computer Science, a Centre of the Danish National Research Foundation.

Worst case asymptotic time bounds for some existing data structures supporting the above operations are listed in Table 1. The table suggests a trade-off between the worst case times of the two update operations Insert, Delete and the query operation FindMin. We prove the following lower bound on this tradeoff: any randomized algorithm with expected amortized update time at most t requires expected time $(n/e2^t) - 1$ for FindMin. Thus, if the update operations have expected amortized constant cost, FindMin requires linear expected time. On the other hand if FindMin has constant expected time, then one of the update operations requires logarithmic expected amortized time. This shows that all the data structures in Fig. 1 are optimal in the sense of the trade-off, and they cannot be improved even by considering amortized cost and allowing randomization.

For each n and t, the lower bound is tight. A simple data structure for the Insert-Delete-FindMin problem is the following. Assume Insert and Delete are allowed to make at most t comparisons. We represent a set by $\lceil n/2^t \rceil$ sorted lists. All lists except for the last contain exactly 2^t elements. The minimum of a set can be found among all the list minima by $\lceil n/2^t \rceil - 1$ comparisons. New elements are added to the last list, requiring at most t comparisons by a binary search. To perform Delete we replace the element to be deleted by an arbitrary element from the last list. This also requires at most t comparisons.

The above lower bound shows that it is hard to maintain the minimum. Is it any easier to maintain the rank of *some* element, not necessarily the minimum? We consider a weaker problem called Insert-Delete-FindAny, which is defined exactly as the previous problem, except that FindMin is replaced by the weaker operation FindAny: returns some element in S and its rank. FindAny is not constrained to return the same element each time it is invoked or to return the element with the same rank. The only condition is that the rank returned should be the rank of the element returned. We give a randomized algorithm for the Insert-Delete-FindAny problem with constant expected time per operation. Thus, this problem is strictly easier than Insert-Delete-FindMin, when randomization is allowed. However, we show that for deterministic algorithms, the two problems are essentially equally hard. We show that any deterministic algorithm with amortized update time at most t requires $n/2^{4t+3} - 1$ comparisons for some FindAny operation. This lower bound is proved using an explicit adversary argument. The adversary strategy is simple, yet surprisingly powerful. The same strategy may be used to obtain the well known $\Omega(n \log n)$ lower bound for sorting. An explicit adversary for sorting has previously been given by Atallah and Kosaraju [1].

The previous results show that maintaining any kind of rank information online is hard. However, if the sequence of instructions to be processed is known in advance, then one can do better. We give a deterministic algorithm for the offline Insert-Delete-FindMin problem which has an amortized cost per operation of at most 3 comparisons.

Our proofs use various averaging arguments which are used to derive general combinatorial properties of trees. These are presented in Sect. 2.2.

Implementation	Insert	Delete	FindMin
Doubly linked list	1	1	n
Heap [8]	$\log n$	$\log n$	1
Search tree [5, 7]	$\log n$	1	1
Priority queue [2, 3, 4]	1	$\log n$	1

Fig. 1. Worst case asymptotic time bounds for different set implementations.

2 Preliminaries

2.1 Definitions and notation

For a rooted tree T, let leaves(T) be the set of leaves of T. For a vertex, v in T, define deg(v) to be the number of children of v. Define, for $l \in$ leaves(T), depth(l) to be the distance of l from the root and path(l) to be the set of vertices on the path from the root to l, not including l.

For a random variable X, let support$[X]$ be the set of values that X assumes with non-zero probability. For any non-negative real-valued function f, defined on support$[X]$, define

$$\mathop{\mathrm{E}}_{X}[f(X)] = \sum_{x \in \text{support}[X]} \Pr[X = x]f(x), \quad \mathop{\mathrm{GM}}_{X}[f(X)] = \prod_{x \in \text{support}[X]} f(x)^{\Pr[X=x]}.$$

We will also use the notation **E** and **GM** to denote the arithmetic and geometric means of a set of values as follows: for a set R, and any non-negative real-valued function f, defined on R, define

$$\mathop{\mathrm{E}}_{r \in R}[f(r)] = \frac{1}{|R|} \sum_{r \in R} f(r), \quad \mathop{\mathrm{GM}}_{r \in R}[f(r)] = \prod_{r \in R} f(x)^{1/|R|}.$$

2.2 Some useful lemmas

Let T be the infinite complete binary tree. Suppose each element of $[n]$ is assigned to a node of the tree (more than one element may be assigned to the same node). That is, we have a function $f : [n] \to V(T)$. For $v \in V(T)$, define wt$_f(v) = |\{i \in [n] : f(i) = v\}|$, $d_f = \mathop{\mathrm{E}}_{i \in [n]}[\text{depth}(f(i))]$, $D_f = \max\{\text{depth}(f(i)) : i \in [n]\}$ and $m_f = \max\{\text{wt}_f(v) : v \in V(T)\}$.

Lemma 1. *For every assignment $f : [n] \to V(T)$, the maximum number of elements on a path starting at the root of T is at least $n2^{-d_f}$.*

Proof. Let P be a random infinite path starting from the root. Then, for $i \in [n]$, $\Pr[f(i) \in P] = 2^{-\text{depth}(f(i))}$. Then the expected number of elements of $[n]$

assigned to P is

$$\sum_{i=1}^{n} 2^{-\text{depth}(f(i))} = n \mathop{\mathbf{E}}_{i \in [n]} [2^{-\text{depth}(f(i))}] \geq n \mathop{\mathbf{GM}}_{i \in [n]} [2^{-\text{depth}(f(i))}]$$

$$= n 2^{- \mathbf{E}_{i \in [n]} [depth(f(i))]} = n 2^{-d_f}$$

Since the maximum is at least the expected value, the lemma follows.

Lemma 2. *For every assignment* $f : [n] \to V(T)$, $m_f \geq n/(2^{d_f+3})$.

Proof. Let $H = \{h : m_h = m_f\}$. Let h be the assignment in H with minimum average depth d_h (the minimum exists). Let $m = m_h = m_f$, and $D = D_h$. We claim that

$$\mathsf{wt}_h(v) = m, \quad \text{for each } v \in V(T) \text{ with } \mathsf{depth}(v) < D. \tag{1}$$

For suppose there is a vertex v with $\mathsf{depth}(v) < D$ and $\mathsf{wt}(v) < m$ (i.e. $\mathsf{wt}(v) \leq m - 1$). First, consider the case when some node w at depth D has m elements assigned to it. Consider the assignment h' which is the same as h except that it exchanges the elements assigned to v and w. Then $h' \in H$ and $d_{h'} < d_h$, contradicting the choice of h. Next, suppose that every node at depth D has less than m elements assigned to it. Now, there exists $i \in [n]$ such that $\mathsf{depth}(h(i)) = D$. Let h' be the assignment that is identical to h everywhere except at i, and for i, $h'(i) = v$. Then, $h' \in H$ and $d_{h'} < d_h$, again contradicting the choice of h. Thus (1) holds.

The number of elements assigned to nodes at depth at most $D-1$ is $m(2^D - 1)$, and the average depth of these elements is

$$\frac{1}{m(2^D - 1)} \sum_{i=0}^{D-1} mi2^i = \frac{(D-2)2^D + 2}{2^D - 1} \geq D - 2.$$

Since all other elements are at depth D, we have $d_h \geq D - 2$. The total number of nodes in the tree with depth at most D is $2^{D+1} - 1$. Hence, we have

$$m_f = m \geq \frac{n}{2^{D+1} - 1} \geq \frac{n}{2^{d_h+3} - 1} \geq \frac{n}{2^{d_f+3} - 1}.$$

For a rooted tree T, let $W_l = \prod_{v \in \mathsf{path}(l)} \deg(v)$. Then, it can be shown by induction on the height of tree that $\sum_{l \in \mathsf{leaves}(T)} 1/W_l = 1$.

Lemma 3. *For a rooted tree T with m leaves,* $\mathop{\mathbf{GM}}_{l \in \mathsf{leaves}(T)} [W_l] \geq m$.

Proof. Since the geometric mean is at most the arithmetic mean [6], we have

$$\mathop{\mathbf{GM}}_{l} [\frac{1}{W_l}] \leq \mathop{\mathbf{E}}_{l} [\frac{1}{W_l}] = \frac{1}{m} \sum_{l} \frac{1}{W_l} = \frac{1}{m}.$$

Now, $\mathbf{GM}_l[W_l] = 1/\mathop{\mathbf{GM}}_{l}[1/W_l] \geq m$.

3 Deterministic offline algorithm

We now consider an offline version of the Insert-Delete-FindMin problem. The sequence of operations to be performed is given in advance, however, the ordering of the set elements is unknown. The ith operation is performed at time i. We assume that an element is inserted and deleted at most once. If an element is inserted and deleted more than once, it can be treated as a distinct element each time it is inserted.

From the given operation sequence, the offline algorithm can compute, for each element e, the time, $t(e)$, at which e is deleted from the data structure ($t(e)$ is ∞ if e is never deleted).

The data structure maintained by the offline algorithm is a sorted (in increasing order) list $L = (e_1, \ldots, e_k)$ of the set elements that can become minimum elements in the data structure. The list satisfies that $t(e_i) < t(e_j)$ for $i < j$, because otherwise e_j could never become a minimum element.

FindMin returns the first element in L and Delete(e) deletes e from L, if L contains e. To process Insert(e), the algorithm computes two values, l and r, where $r = \min\{i : t(e_i) > t(e)\}$ and $l = \max\{i : e_i < e\}$. Notice that once e is in the data structure, none of $e_{l+1}, \ldots, e_{r-1}$ can ever be the minimum element. Hence, all these elements are deleted and e is inserted into the list between e_l and e_r. No comparisons are required to find r. Thus, Insert(e) may be implemented as follows: starting at e_r, step backwards through the list, deleting elements until the first element smaller than e is encountered.

The number of comparisons for an insertion is two plus the number of elements deleted from L. By letting the potential of L be $|L|$ the amortized cost of Insert is $|L'| - |L| +$ # of element removed during the Insert $+ 2$ which is at most 3 because the number of elements removed is at most $|L| - |L'| + 1$. Delete only decreases the potential, and the initial potential is zero. It follows that

Theorem 4. *For the offline* Insert-Delete-FindMin *problem the amortized cost of* Insert *is three comparisons. No comparisons are required for* Delete *and* FindMin.

4 Deterministic lower bound for FindAny

In this section we show that it is difficult for a deterministic algorithm to maintain any rank information at all. We prove

Theorem 5. *Let $\mathcal{A}$ be a deterministic algorithm for* Insert-Delete-FindAny *with amortized time at most $t = t(n)$ per update. Then, there exists an input, to process which $\mathcal{A}$ takes at least $n/2^{4t+3} - 1$ comparisons for one* FindAny.

The Adversary. We describe an adversary strategy for answering comparisons between a set of elements.

The adversary maintains an infinite binary tree and the elements currently in the data structure are distributed among the nodes of this tree. New elements inserted into the data structure are placed at the root. For $x \in S$ let $v(x)$

denote the node of the tree at which x is. The adversary maintains the following invariants (A) and (B). For any distribution of the elements among the nodes of the infinite tree, define the *occupancy tree* to be the finite tree given by the union of the paths from every non-empty node to the root. The invariants are (A) *If neither of $v(x)$ or $v(y)$ is a descendant of the other then $x < y$ is consistent with the responses given so far if $v(x)$ appears before $v(y)$ in an preorder traversal of the occupancy tree* and (B) *If $v(x) = v(y)$ or $v(x)$ is a descendant of $v(y)$, the responses given so far yield no information on the order of x and y.* More precisely, in this case, x and y are incomparable in the partial order induced on the elements by the responses so far.

The comparisons made by any algorithm can be classified into three types, and the adversary responds to each type of the comparison as described below. Let the elements compared be x and y. Three cases arise. *(i)* $v(x) = v(y)$: Then x is moved to the left child of $v(x)$ and y to the right child and the adversary answers $x < y$. *(ii)* $v(x)$ is a descendant of $v(y)$: Then y is moved to the unique child of $v(y)$ that is not an ancestor of $v(x)$. If this child is a left child then the adversary answers $y < x$ and if it is a right child then the adversary answers $x < y$. *(iii)* $v(x) \neq v(y)$ and neither is a descendant of the other: If $v(x)$ is visited before $v(y)$ in a preorder traversal of the occupancy tree, the adversary answers $x < y$ and otherwise the adversary answers $y < x$.

The key observation is that each comparison pushes two elements down one level each, in the worst case.

Maintaining ranks. We now give a proof of Theorem 5.

Consider the behaviour of the algorithm when responses to its comparisons are given according to the adversary strategy above. Define the sequences $S_1 \ldots S_{n+1}$ as follows. $S_1 = \mathsf{Insert}(a_1) \ldots \mathsf{Insert}(a_n)\mathsf{FindAny}$. Let b_1 be the element returned in response to the FindAny instruction in S_1. For $i = 2, 3, \ldots n$, define $S_i = \mathsf{Insert}(a_1) \ldots \mathsf{Insert}(a_n)\mathsf{Delete}(b_1) \ldots \mathsf{Delete}(b_{i-1})\mathsf{FindAny}$ and let b_i be the element returned in response to the FindAny instruction in S_i. Finally, let $S_{n+1} = \mathsf{Insert}(a_1) \ldots \mathsf{Insert}(a_n)\mathsf{Delete}(b_1) \ldots \mathsf{Delete}(b_n)$. For $1 \leq i \leq n$, b_i is well defined and for $1 \leq i < j \leq n$, $b_i \neq b_j$. The latter point follows from the fact that at the time b_i is returned by a FindAny, $b_1, \ldots, b_{i-1}$ have already been deleted from the data structure.

Let T be the infinite binary tree maintained by the adversary. Then the sequence S_{n+1} defines a function $f : [n] \to V(T)$, given by $f(i) = v$ if b_i is in node v just before the $\mathsf{Delete}(b_i)$ instruction during the processing of S_{n+1}. Since the amortized cost of an update is at most t, the total number of comparisons performed while processing S_{n+1} is at most $2tn$. A comparison pushes at most two elements down one level each. Then, writing d_i for the distance of $f(i)$ from the root, we have $\sum_{i=1}^{n} d_i \leq 4tn$. By Lemma 2 we know that there is a set $R \subseteq [n]$ with at least $n/2^{4t+3}$ elements and a vertex v of T such that for each $i \in R$, $f(b_i) = v$.

Let $j = \min R$. Then, while processing S_j, just before the FindAny instruction, each element b_i, $i \in R$ is in some node on the path from the root to $f(i) = v$. Since the element returned by the FindAny is b_j, it must be the case that after the comparisons for the FindAny are performed, b_j is the only element on the path from the root to the vertex in which b_j is. This is because invariant (B) implies that any other element that is on this path is incomparable with b_j. Hence, these comparisons move all the elements b_i, $i \in R\backslash j$, out of the path from the root to $f(j)$. A comparison can move at most one element out of this path, hence, the number of comparisons performed is at least $|R| - 1$, which proves the theorem.

4.1 Sorting

The same adversary can be used to give a lower bound for sorting. We note that this argument is fundamentally different from the usual information theoretic argument in that it gives an explicit adversary against which sorting is hard.

Consider an algorithm that sorts a set S, of n elements. The same adversary strategy is used to respond to comparisons. Then, invariant (B) implies that at the end of the algorithm, each element in the tree must be in a node by itself. Let the function $f : S \to V(T)$ indicate the node where each element is at the end of the algorithm, where T is the infinite binary tree maintained by the adversary. Then, f assigns at most one element to each path starting at the root of T. By Lemma 1 we have $1 \geq n2^{-d}$, where d is average distance of an element from the root. It follows that the sum of the distances from the root to the elements in this tree is at least $n \log n$, and this is equal to the sum of the number of levels each element has been pushed down. Since each comparison contributes at most two to this sum, the number of comparisons made is at least $(n \log n)/2$.

5 Randomized algorithm for FindAny

We present a randomized algorithm supporting Insert, Delete and FindAny using, on an average, a constant number of comparisons per operation.

5.1 The algorithm

The algorithm maintains three variables: S, e and $rank$. S is the set of elements currently in the data-structure, e is an element in S, and $rank$ is the rank of e in S. Initially, S is the empty set, and e and $rank$ are null. The algorithm responds to instructions as follows.

Insert(x): Set $S \leftarrow S \cup \{x\}$. With probability $1/|S|$ we set e to x and let $rank$ be the rank of e in S, that is the number of elements in S strictly less than e. In the other case, that is with probability $1 - 1/|S|$, we retain the old value of e; that is, we compare e and x and update $rank$ if necessary. In particular, if the set was empty before the instruction, then e is assigned x and $rank$ is set to 1.

Delete(x): Set S to $S - \{x\}$. If S is empty then set e and $rank$ to null and return. Otherwise (i.e. if $S \neq \emptyset$), if $x \equiv e$ then get the new value of e by picking an element of S randomly; set $rank$ to be the rank of e in S. On the other hand, if x is different from e, then decrement $rank$ by one if $x < e$.

FindAny: Return e and $rank$.

5.2 Analysis

Claim 6. *The expected number of comparisons made by the algorithm for a fixed instruction in any sequence of instructions is constant.*

Proof. FindAny takes no comparisons. Consider an Insert instruction. Suppose the number of elements in S just before the instruction was s. Then, the expected number of comparisons made by the algorithm is $s \cdot (1/(s+1)) + 1 \cdot (s/(s+1)) < 2$.

We now consider the expected number of comparisons performed for a Delete instruction. Fix a sequence of instructions. Let S_i and e_i be the values of S and e just before the ith instruction. Note that S_i depends only on the sequence of instructions and not on the coin tosses of the algorithm; on the other hand, e_i might vary depending on the coin tosses of the algorithm. The following invariant can be proved by a straightforward induction on i.

$$|S_i| \neq \emptyset \implies \Pr[e_i = x] = \frac{1}{|S_i|} \qquad \text{for all } x \in S_i. \tag{2}$$

Now, suppose the ith instruction is Delete(x). Then, the probability that $e_i = x$ is precisely $1/|S_i|$. Thus, the expected number of comparisons performed by the algorithm is $(|S_i| - 2) \cdot (1/|S_i|) < 1$.

6 Randomized lower bounds for FindMin

One may view the problem of maintaining the minimum as a game between two players: the algorithm and the adversary. The adversary gives instructions and supplies answers for the comparisons made by the algorithm. The objective of the algorithm is to respond to the instructions by making as few comparisons as possible, whereas the objective of the adversary is to force the algorithm to use a large number of comparisons.

Similarly, if randomization is permitted while maintaining the minimum, one may consider the randomized variants of this game. We have two cases based on whether or not the adversary is adaptive. An adaptive adversary constructs the input as the game progresses; its actions depend on the moves the algorithm has made so far. On the other hand, a non-adaptive adversary fixes the instruction sequence and the ordering of the elements before the game begins. The input it constructs can depend on the algorithm's strategy but not on its coin toss sequence.

It can be shown that against the adaptive adversary randomization does not help. In fact, if there is a randomized strategy for the algorithm against an adaptive adversary then there is a deterministic strategy against the adversary. Thus, the complexity of maintaining the minimum in this case is the same as in the deterministic case. In this section, we show lower bounds with a non-adaptive adversary.

The input to the algorithm is specified by fixing a sequence of Insert, Delete and FindMin instructions, and an ordering for the set $\{a_1, a_2, \ldots, a_n\}$, based on which the comparisons of the algorithm are answered.

Distributions. We will use two distributions on inputs. For the first distribution, we construct a random input I by first picking a random permutation σ of $[n]$; we associate with σ the sequence of instructions

$\mathsf{Insert}(a_1), \ldots, \mathsf{Insert}(a_n), \mathsf{Delete}(a_{\sigma(1)}), \mathsf{Delete}(a_{\sigma(2)}), \ldots, \mathsf{Delete}(a_{\sigma(n)}),$

and the ordering $a_{\sigma(1)} < a_{\sigma(2)} < \ldots < a_{\sigma(n)}$.

For the second distribution, we construct the random input J by picking $i \in [n]$ at random and a random permutation σ of $[n]$; the instruction sequence associated with i and σ is

$\mathsf{Insert}(a_1), \ldots, \mathsf{Insert}(a_n), \mathsf{Delete}(a_{\sigma(1)}), \ldots, \mathsf{Delete}(a_{\sigma(i-1)}), \mathsf{FindMin},$

and the ordering is given, as before, by $a_{\sigma(1)} < a_{\sigma(2)} < \ldots < a_{\sigma(n)}$.

For an algorithm $\mathcal{A}$ and an input I, let $C_U(\mathcal{A}, I)$ be the number of comparisons made by the algorithm while responding to the Insert and Delete instructions corresponding to I; let $C_F(\mathcal{A}, I)$ be the number of comparisons made by the algorithm while responding to the $\mathsf{FindMin}$ instructions.

Theorem 7. *Let $\mathcal{A}$ be a deterministic algorithm for maintaining the minimum. Suppose $\mathbf{E}_I[C_U(\mathcal{A}, I)] \leq tn$. Then $\mathbf{GM}_J[C_F(\mathcal{A}, J) + 1] \geq n/e2^t$.*

Before we discuss the proof of this result, we derive from it the lower bounds on the randomized and average case complexities of maintaining the minimum. Yao showed that a randomized algorithm can be viewed as a random variable assuming values in some set of deterministic algorithms according to some probability distribution over the set [9]. The randomized lower bound follows from this fact and Theorem 7.

Corollary 8 Randomized complexity. *Let $\mathcal{R}$ be a randomized algorithm for* $\mathsf{Insert\text{-}Delete\text{-}FindMin}$ *with expected amortized time per update at most $t = t(n)$. Then the expected time for* $\mathsf{FindMin}$ *is at least $n/(e2^{2t}) - 1$.*

Proof. We view $\mathcal{R}$ as a random variable taking values in a set of deterministic algorithms with some distribution. For every deterministic algorithm $\mathcal{A}$ in this set, let $t(\mathcal{A}) \stackrel{\text{def}}{=} \mathbf{E}_I[C_U(\mathcal{A}, I)]/n$. Then by Theorem 7 we have $\mathbf{GM}_J[C_F(\mathcal{A}, J)+1] \geq \left(\frac{n}{e}\right) \cdot 2^{-t(\mathcal{A})}$. Hence,

$$\mathbf{GM}_{\mathcal{R}}[\mathbf{GM}_J[C_F(\mathcal{R}, J) + 1] \geq \mathbf{GM}_{\mathcal{R}}[\left(\frac{n}{e}\right) \cdot 2^{-t(\mathcal{R})}] = \left(\frac{n}{e}\right) \cdot 2^{-\mathbf{E}_{\mathcal{R}}[t(\mathcal{R})]}.$$

Since the expected amortized time per update is at most t, we have $\mathbf{E}_{\mathcal{R}}[t(\mathcal{R})] \leq 2t$. Hence,

$$\mathbf{E}_{\mathcal{R},J}[C_F(\mathcal{R}, J)] + 1 = \mathbf{E}_{\mathcal{R},J}[C_F(\mathcal{R}, J) + 1] \geq \mathbf{GM}_{\mathcal{R},J}[C_F(\mathcal{R}, J) + 1] \geq \frac{n}{e2^{2t}}.$$

Thus, there exists an instance of J for which the expected number of comparisons performed by $\mathcal{A}$ in response to the last $\mathsf{FindMin}$ instruction is at least $n/(e2^{2t}) - 1$.

The average case lower bound follows from the arithmetic-geometric mean inequality and Theorem 7.

Corollary 9 Average case complexity. *Let $\mathcal{A}$ be a deterministic algorithm for* Insert-Delete-FindMin *with amortized time per update at most $t = t(n)$. Then the expected time to find the minimum for inputs with distribution J is at least $n/(e2^{2t}) - 1$.*

Proof. $\mathcal{A}$ takes amortized time at most t per update. Therefore, $\underset{I}{\mathbf{E}}[C_U(\mathcal{A}, I)] \leq 2tn$. Then, by Theorem 7 we have

$$\underset{J}{\mathbf{E}}[C_F(\mathcal{A}, J)] + 1 = \underset{J}{\mathbf{E}}[C_F(\mathcal{A}, J) + 1] \geq \underset{J}{\mathbf{GM}}[C_F(\mathcal{A}, J) + 1] \geq \frac{n}{e2^{2t}}.$$

6.1 Proof of Theorem 7

The Decision Tree representation. Consider the set of sequences in support$[I]$. The actions of a deterministic algorithm on this set of sequences can be represented by a decision tree with *comparison* nodes and *deletion* nodes. (Normally a decision tree representing an algorithm would also have *insertion* nodes, but since, in support$[I]$, the elements are always inserted in the same order, we may omit them.) Each comparison node is labelled by a comparison of the form $a_i : a_j$, and has two children, corresponding to the two outcomes $a_i > a_j$ and $a_i \leq a_j$. Each deletion node has a certain number of children and each edge, e, to a child, is labelled by some element a_e, denoting that element a_e is deleted by this delete instruction.

For a sequence corresponding to some permutation σ, the algorithm behaves as follows. The first instruction it must process is Insert(a_1). The root of the tree is labelled by the first comparison that the algorithm makes in order to process this instruction. Depending on the outcome of this comparison, the algorithm makes one of two comparisons, and these label the two children of the root. Thus, the processing of the first instruction can be viewed as following a path down the tree. Depending on the outcomes of the comparisons made to process the first instruction, the algorithm is currently at some vertex in the tree, and this vertex is labelled by the first comparison that the algorithm makes in order to process the second instruction. In this way, the processing of all the insert instructions corresponds to following a path consisting of comparison nodes down the tree. When the last insert instruction has been processed, the algorithm is at a delete node corresponding to the first delete instruction. Depending on the sequence, some element, $a_{\sigma(1)}$ is deleted. The algorithm follows the edge labelled by $a_{\sigma(1)}$ and the next vertex is labelled by the first comparison that the algorithm makes in order to process the next delete instruction. In this manner, each sequence determines a path down the tree, terminating at a leaf.

We make two simple observations. First, since, in different sequences, the elements are deleted in different orders, each sequence reaches a distinct leaf of the tree. Hence the number of leaves is exactly $n!$. Second, consider the ordering information available to the algorithm when it reaches a delete node v. This information consists of the outcomes of all the comparisons on the comparison nodes on the path from the root to v. This information can be represented as a poset, P_v, on the elements not deleted yet. For every sequence that causes the algorithm to reach v, the algorithm has obtained only the information in P_v. If a sequence corresponding to some permutation σ causes the algorithm to reach v, and deletes a_i, then a_i is a minimal element in P_v, since, in σ, a_i is the minimum among the remaining elements. Hence each of the elements labelling an edge from v to a child is a minimal element of P_v. If this Delete instruction was replaced by a FindMin, then the comparisons done by the FindMin would have to find the minimum among these minimal elements. A comparison between any two poset elements can cause at most one of these minimal elements to become non-minimal. Hence, the FindMin instruction would cost the algorithm $\deg(v) - 1$ comparisons.

The proof. Let T be the decision tree corresponding to the deterministic algorithm $\mathcal{A}$. Set $m = n!$. For $l \in \text{leaves}(T)$, let D_l be the set of delete nodes on the path from the root to l, and C_l be the set of comparison nodes on the path from the root to l.

Each input specified by a permutation σ and a value $i \in [n]$, in support$[J]$ causes the algorithm to follow a path in T upto some delete node, v, where, instead of a Delete, the sequence issues a FindMin instruction. As argued previously, the number of comparisons made to process this FindMin is at least $\deg(v) - 1$. There are exactly n delete nodes on any path from the root to a leaf and different inputs cause the algorithm to arrive at a different delete nodes. Hence

$$\text{GM}_J[C_F(\mathcal{A}, J) + 1] \geq \prod_{l \in \text{leaves}(T)} \prod_{v \in D_l} (\deg(v))^{1/nm}. \tag{3}$$

Since T has m leaves, we have using Lemma 3 that

$$m \leq \text{GM}_{l \in \text{leaves}(T)}[\prod_{v \in \text{path}(l)} \deg(v)]$$

$$= \text{GM}_{l \in \text{leaves}(T)}[\prod_{v \in C_l} \deg(v)] \cdot \text{GM}_{l \in \text{leaves}(T)}[\prod_{v \in D_l} \deg(v)]. \tag{4}$$

Consider the first term on the right. Since every comparison node v has arity at most two, we have $\prod_{v \in C_l} \deg(v) = 2^{|C_l|}$. Also, by the supposition of Theorem 7,

$$\mathop{\mathbf{E}}_{l \in \text{leaves}(T)}[|C_l|] = \mathop{\mathbf{E}}_I[C_U(\mathcal{A}, I)] \leq tn. \text{ Thus}$$

$$\text{GM}_{l \in \text{leaves}(T)}[\prod_{v \in C_l} \deg(v)] \leq \text{GM}_{l \in \text{leaves}(T)}[2^{|C_l|}] \leq 2^{\mathbf{E}_l[|C_l|]} \leq 2^{tn}.$$

From this and (4), we have $\text{GM}_{l \in \text{leaves}(T)}[\prod_{v \in D_l} \deg(v)] \geq m2^{-tn}$. Then using (3) and the inequality $n! \geq (n/e)^n$, we get

$$\text{GM}_J[C_F(\mathcal{A}, J) + 1] \geq \prod_{l \in \text{leaves}(T)} \prod_{v \in D_l} (\deg(v))^{1/nm}$$

$$= (\underset{l \in \text{leaves}(T)}{\textbf{GM}} [\prod_{v \in D_l} \deg(v)])^{1/n} \geq \frac{n}{e2^t}.$$

Remark. One may also consider the problem of maintaining the minimum when the algorithm is allowed to use an operator that enables it to compute the minimum of some m values in one step. The case $m = 2$ corresponds to the binary comparisons model considered in the proof above. Since an m-ary minimum operation can be simulated by $m - 1$ binary minimum operations, the above proof yields a bound of $n/e2^{2t(m-1)} - 1$. However, by modifying the proof one can show the better bound of $(1/m - 1) \cdot [\frac{n}{em^{2t}} - 1]$.

References

1. Mikhail J. Atallah and S. Rao Kosaraju. An adversary-based lower bound for sorting. *Information Processing Letters*, 13:55–57, 1981.
2. Gerth Stølting Brodal. Fast meldable priority queues. In *Proc. 4th Workshop on Algorithms and Data Structures (WADS)*, volume 955 of *Lecture Notes in Computer Science*, pages 282–290. Springer Verlag, Berlin, 1995.
3. Svante Carlsson, Patricio V. Poblete, and J. Ian Munro. An implicit binomial queue with constant insertion time. In *Proc. 1st Scandinavian Workshop on Algorithm Theory (SWAT)*, volume 318 of *Lecture Notes in Computer Science*, pages 1–13. Springer Verlag, Berlin, 1988.
4. James R. Driscoll, Harold N. Gabow, Ruth Shrairman, and Robert E. Tarjan. Relaxed heaps: An alternative to fibonacci heaps with applications to parallel computation. *Communications of the ACM*, 31(11):1343–1354, 1988.
5. Rudolf Fleischer. A simple balanced search tree with $O(1)$ worst-case update time. In *Algorithms and Computation: 4th International Symposium, ISAAC '93*, volume 762 of *Lecture Notes in Computer Science*, pages 138–146. Springer Verlag, Berlin, 1993.
6. G. H. Hardy, J. E. Littlewood, and G. Polya. Inequalities. Cambridge University Press, Cambridge, 1952.
7. Christos Levcopoulos and Mark H. Overmars. A balanced search tree with $O(1)$ worst-case update time. *ACTA Informatica*, 26:269–277, 1988.
8. J. W. J. Williams. Algorithm 232: Heapsort. *Communications of the ACM*, 7(6):347–348, 1964.
9. A. C-C. Yao. Probabilistic computations: Towards a unified measure of complexity. In *Proc. of the 17th Symp. on Found. of Comp. Sci.*, 222–227, 1977.

Faster Algorithms for the Nonemptiness of Streett Automata and for Communication Protocol Pruning

Monika Rauch Henzinger[1] * and Jan Arne Telle[2] **

[1] Systems Research Center, Digital Equipment Corporation, Palo Alto, CA
[2] Department of Informatics, University of Bergen, Norway

Abstract. This paper shows how a general technique, called *lock-step search*, used in dynamic graph algorithms, can be used to improve the running time of two problems arising in program verification and communication protocol design.

(1) We consider the *nonemptiness problem for Streett automata*: We are given a directed graph $G = (V, E)$ with $n = |V|$ and $m = |E|$, and a collection of pairs of subsets of vertices, called *Streett pairs*, $\langle L_i, U_i \rangle$, $i = 1..k$. The question is whether G has a cycle (not necessarily simple) which, for each $1 \leq i \leq k$, if it contains a vertex from L_i then it also contains a vertex of U_i. Let $b = \sum_{i=1..k} |L_i| + |U_i|$. The previously best algorithm takes time $O((m+b)\min\{n, k\})$. We present an algorithm that takes time $O(m \min\{\sqrt{m \log n}, k, n\} + b \min\{\log n, k\})$.

(2) In *communication protocol pruning* we are given a directed graph $G = (V, E)$ with l special vertices. The problem is to efficiently maintain the strongly-connected components of the special vertices on a restricted set of edge deletions. Let m_i be the number of edges in the strongly connected component of the ith special vertex. The previously best algorithm repeatedly recomputes the strongly-connected components which leads to a running time of $O(\sum_i m_i^2)$. We present an algorithm with time $O(\sqrt{l} \sum_i m_i^{1.5})$.

1 Introduction

Maintaining the strongly-connected components of a digraph $G = (V, E)$ efficiently under vertex or edge deletions is an unsolved problem. No data structure is known that is faster than recomputation from scratch. This is unfortunate since such a data structure would speed up various algorithms. In this paper we describe two such algorithms and show how a technique, called *lock-step search*, used in dynamic graph algorithms, can improve their running time.

* *monika@src.dec.edu.* This research was done while at the Department of Computer Science, Cornell University, Ithaca, NY and was supported by an NSF CAREER Award, Grant No. CCR-9501712.

** *telle@ii.uib.no.* This research was done while visiting the Department of Computer Science, Cornell University, Ithaca, NY and was supported by a fellowship from the Norwegian Research Council.

Nonemptiness for Streett automata

A Streett automaton with *Streett pairs* $\langle L_i, U_i \rangle$ is an automaton on infinite words where a run is accepting if for all pairs i, if the run visits infinitely many times some state in L_i then it also visits infinitely many times some state in U_i. The first problem that we consider is called the *nonemptiness problem for Streett automata*: Given a directed graph $G = (V, E)$ and a collection of pairs of subsets of vertices, called *Streett pairs*, $\langle L_i, U_i \rangle, i = 1..k$, determine if G has a cycle (not necessarily simple) which, for each $1 \leq i \leq k$, if it contains a vertex from L_i then it also contains a vertex of U_i. [3]

Nonemptiness checking of Streett automata is used in computer-aided verification. Consider, for example, the problem of checking if a strongly fair finite-state system A satisfies a specification ϕ in linear temporal logic ("model checking"). The system A can be modeled as a Streett automaton. The negated specification $\neg\phi$ can be translated into an equivalent Büchi automaton, and therefore Streett automaton, $B_{\neg\phi}$. Then model checking reduces to checking the nonemptiness of the product Streett automaton $A \times B_{\neg\phi}$ [7].

Let $|V| = n, |E| = m$ and $b = \sum_{i=1..k} |L_i| + |U_i|$. The previously best algorithms for this problem take time $O((m + b)\min\{n, k\})$ [1, 3]. We present an $O(m \min\{\sqrt{m \log n}, k, n\} + b \min\{\log n, k\})$ algorithm for the problem. The improved running time is achieved through (1) lock-step search and (2) an efficient data structure for representing the Streett pairs $\langle L_i, U_i \rangle$. In model checking, frequently G has bounded out-degree. In this case $m = O(n)$ and our algorithm has running time $O(n \min\{\sqrt{n \log n}, k\} + b \min\{\log n, k\})$.

Protocol Pruning

A communication system defines interactions between different components using exact rules, called *protocols*. Since protocol standards have become very complex, various approaches try to simplify protocols. A new technique by Lee, Netravali, and Sabnani [4] models a protocol as a collection of communicating finite state machines, and prunes the protocol without constructing the composite machine. The finite state machines are represented as a directed graph with l special vertices (start states), one per machine. Interactions between machines are modeled as dependencies among edges. Their algorithm repeatedly "prunes off" (i.e. deletes) edges of the graph and recomputes the strongly-connected components of the special vertices. Which edges are deleted in the next iteration depends on dependencies between the edges left in the current strongly-connected components of the special vertices. If the strongly-connected components have not changed between two iterations the algorithm terminates with these strongly-connected components representing the pruned protocol machine.

Let m_i be the number of edges in the strongly-connected component of the ith special vertex. Recomputing the strongly-connected components from scratch

---

[3] Note that the nonemptiness problem for Streett automata usually includes also a designated *root* vertex (the start state) and requires that the cycle asked for be reachable from the root. For ease of presentation, we assume that a simple linear preprocessing step has computed the input graph G consisting only of vertices reachable from the root, since the other vertices will not affect the solution.

in each iteration leads to a running time of $O(\sum_i m_i^2)$. We present an algorithm with time $O(\sqrt{l}\sum_i m_i^{1.5})$. For constant l our algorithm takes time $O(\sum_i m_i^{1.5})$.

Lock-Step Search

Both improved algorithms use lock-step search. Lock-step search was introduced by Even and Shiloach [2] to maintain the connected components of an *undirected* graph under edge deletions. After the deletion of the edge (u, v), they start a (depth-first) search for the resulting component "in parallel" at u and at v: the algorithm executes one step of the search at u and one step of the search at v and stops whenever one of the searches is completed.

Let C_u and C_v be the new components of u and v. *Case 1:* If $C_u \neq C_v$, then the lock-step search takes time $O(\min(|C_u|, |C_v|))$, where $|C|$ denotes the number of edges in a component. Charging this cost to the edges in the smaller of the two components charges at most $O(\log n)$ to an edge in the graph: an edge is charged only if the number of edges in its component is at least halved.

Case 2: If $C_u = C_v$ the search takes time $O(|C_u|)$. Thus, if this situation arises at almost all edge deletions, the running time for the whole algorithm is $O(m^2)$.

We use a slightly modified lock-step search on directed graphs, described below, to find strongly-connected components. Note that both the problems we consider allow the algorithm to terminate as soon as a strongly-connected component is found that fulfills their condition. Thus, instead of first finding the strongly connected components and then checking for each strongly-connected component if it fulfills the conditions, our new algorithms first guarantee that the conditions are fulfilled in the current graph and then start a lock-step search. If Case 1 holds, the costs are charged as described above and further deletions might be necessary. If Case 2 arises the traversed strongly-connected component fulfills the conditions and the algorithms terminate.

Lock-Step Search on Directed Graphs

Assume we have a strongly-connected digraph from which the set of edges F are deleted. If the resulting graph G is not strongly-connected then lock-step search can be used to find a strongly-connected component containing at most half the edges of G. Let $Heads = \{v : uv \in F\}$ be the vertices which are heads of edges in F and $Tails = \{u : uv \in F\}$ be the vertices which are tails of edges in F. Consider the condensed graph of G where strongly-connected components are condensed into single vertices. This graph is acyclic, every source vertex represents a source component which must contain a vertex in $Heads$ and every sink vertex represents a sink component which must contain a vertex of $Tails$, since before deletion of F the condensed graph had only one vertex. Lock-step searches are started on G at each vertex of $Tails$ and also on Reverse(G), where all edges are reversed, at each vertex of $Heads$. A search of G rooted at a vertex in a sink component will explore exactly this component. Likewise, a search of Reverse(G) started in a source component of G will explore exactly that component. A search started in any other component of G will eventually enter a sink component (or source component for the reverse searches), and thus terminate later than the search started in the sink (or source) component itself. By searching from all vertices of *Heads* and *Tails* simultaneously we are thus guaranteed to terminate as soon as the smallest source or sink component is discovered.

Notation

For a graph $G = (V, E)$ we denote the induced graph on $S \subseteq V$ by $G[S]$. We consider only directed graphs and may refer to a strongly connected component simply as a component. We denote the standard linear-time strongly-connected component algorithm [6] by SCC. We describe the algorithm for the Streett automata in Section 2. The protocol pruning algorithm is presented in Section 3.

2 Nonemptiness of Streett automata

The best known algorithm for checking nonemptiness of Streett automata dynamically modifies the input graph by deletion of *bad* vertices. A vertex is bad if it belongs to L_i, for some i, but there is no cycle containing both it and a vertex of U_i. Note that if a run reaches a bad vertex (bad state) then it will not be an accepting run. All other vertices are *good*, but note that they can become bad after some vertex deletions. A strongly-connected component of the current graph is said to be *good* if it contains good vertices only. The goal is then to find a non-trivial good component, or to decide that after iteratively deleting all bad vertices no non-trivial component is left. The algorithm computes the strongly-connected components of the graph, halts if a good component is found or if only trivial components remain, otherwise deletes at least one bad vertex and repeats. A straightforward implementation, using the linear-time depth-first strongly-connected component algorithm SCC [6], gives a running time of $O((m+b)\min\{n, k\})$ [1, 3], for $|V| = n, |E| = m$ and $b = \sum_{i=1..k} |L_i| + |U_i|$. We present an $O(m\min\{\sqrt{m}\log n, k, n\} + b\min\{\log n, k\})$ algorithm for the problem.

2.1 Data structure for Streett pairs

The algorithm maintains a partition of the vertex set. Each set in the partition induces a collection of strongly-connected components of the current graph. Note that for a set S of the partition, any vertices in $S \cap L_i$ are bad if $S \cap U_i = \emptyset$. For $S \subseteq V$, define $bits(S) = \sum_{i=1..k} |S \cap L_i| + |S \cap U_i|$. We need to quickly refine a set in the partition and locate and delete bad vertices. For this we use a data structure with operations:

Construct(S) returns the initialized data structure $C(S)$, for $S \subseteq V$.
Remove$(S, C(S), B)$ removes B from S and returns the data structure $C(S \setminus B)$, for $S, B \subseteq V$.
Bad$(C(S))$ returns $\{v \in S : \exists i : v \in L_i \land U_i \cap S = \emptyset\}$, for $S \subseteq V$.

Each operation need only return a pointer to the appropriate item. In section 2.3 we show the following result.

Lemma 1. *After a one-time initialization of $O(k)$ the data structure can be implemented with running time $O(bits(S) + |S|)$ for Construct(S), $O(bits(B) + |B|)$ for Remove(S, C(S), B) and $O(1)$ for Bad(C(S)).*

2.2 The Algorithm for Non-Emptiness Testing of Streett Automata

The algorithm maintains a list L of data structures $C(S)$, where $S \subseteq V$ is a vertex subset whose induced subgraph $G[S]$ contains candidates for good components. The vertex subsets on this list are disjoint and the list is initialized to contain the components of the input graph. Bad vertices are removed until only good vertices remain and only then are new components computed. Note that the statement "$C(S) := Remove(S, C(S), B)$" also updates S to $S \setminus B$. Some vertices may be labelled h (for head) or t (for tail) signifying that further exploration rooted at the vertex is necessary. The algorithm halts as soon as a good component is found. The algorithm is given on the next page. We argue separately for correctness and running time for the cases $\min\{n, k\} < \sqrt{m \log n}$ and $\min\{n, k\} \geq \sqrt{m \log n}$.

Lemma 2. *The algorithm for nonemptiness testing of Streett automata is correct when $\min\{n, k\} < \sqrt{m \log n}$.*

Proof. Line 3(e) is then: "Case 2. Else do" and Case 3 does not exist. The while loop in line 3 has the invariant: "For any $C(S)$ in the list L the vertices S have no h, t-labels, $G[S]$ is a component of the current graph and all candidates for non-trivial good components are in L". The invariant is maintained since after removal of bad vertices from S all h, t-labels are removed from S and components of $G[S]$, the new candidates, are added to L. If $Bad(C(S)) \neq \emptyset$ then after removal of bad vertices some vertex in the remainder (unless remainder is empty) has an edge to a removed vertex, since we started with a component. Thus, if $|Heads| + |Tails| = 0$ and S contains at least two vertices then $G[S]$ is a non-trivial component with no bad vertices. We conclude that the algorithm finds a good component, if it exists. $\square$

Lemma 3. *The algorithm for nonemptiness testing of Streett automata has running time $O(m \min\{k, n\} + b \min\{\log n, k\})$ when $\min\{n, k\} < \sqrt{m \log n}$.*

Proof. Each time an edge uv is involved in a call of SCC in line 3(e)ii, the component $S(uv)$ the edge belonged to had some bad vertices removed from it, in line 3(b). Since each such removal decreases both $|\{i \in \{1..k\} : L_i \cap S(uv) \neq \emptyset\}|$ and $|\{w \in V : w \in S(uv)\}|$ by at least one, the total cost of calls to SCC is bounded by $O(m \min\{k, n\})$. Deletions of bad vertices in line 3(b) take total time $O(b) = \sum_{v \in V} bits(v)$ since a vertex v is deleted at most once at a cost of $O(bits(v))$. Note that the partitioning of the data structure for $C(S)$ into $C(S_1), ..., C(S_d)$ in the for loop of line 3(e)iii avoids the cost of $bits(S_1)$ for the largest component S_1. After removing $S_i, i = 2..k$ from $C(S)$ then precisely $C(S_1)$ remains. The cost of Remove(S, C(S), S_i) and Construct(S_i)

Emptiness-Testing Algorithm for Streett Automata
Input: A digraph $G = (V, E)$ and Streett pairs $\langle L_i, U_i \rangle, i = 1..k$
Output: A good component, if it exists

1. Run SCC to find components $G[S_1], ..., G[S_d]$ of G.
2. For i=1 to d add $Construct(S_i)$ to list L.
3. **While** $L \neq \emptyset$ **do**
   (a) Get $C(S)$ from L.
   (b) **While** $Bad(C(S)) \neq \emptyset$ **do** $C(S) := Remove(S, C(S), Bad(C(S)))$.
   (c) Add label h (t) to vertices in S which have an incoming (outgoing) edge
       to a vertex just removed. Let $Heads := \{v \in S : h \in label(v)\}$ and
       $Tails := \{v \in S : t \in label(v)\}$.
   (d) Case 1. **If** $|Heads| + |Tails| = 0$ **do** /* $G[S]$ is a good component */
       i. If $|S| \geq 2$ then HALT and output $G[S]$
   (e) Case 2. **Else if** $|Heads| + |Tails| \geq \sqrt{m/\log n}$ **do** /* If $\min\{n, k\} <$
       $\sqrt{m \log n}$) change this line to: "Case 2. Else do ".*/
       i. Remove all h, t-labels from S
       ii. Run SCC to find components $G[S_1], ..., G[S_d]$ $(|S_1| \geq |S_i|)$ of $G[S]$.
       iii. For i=2 to d
            $C(S) := Remove(S, C(S), S_i)$
            Add $Construct(S_i)$ to L
       iv. Add $C(S)$ to L /* Note that $S = S_1$ */
   (f) Case 3. **Else** $0 < |Heads| + |Tails| < \sqrt{m/\log n}$ **do** /* If $\min\{n, k\} <$
       $\sqrt{m \log n}$) remove this case completely */
       i. For each $v \in Tails$ search $G[S]$ from v and for each $v \in Heads$ search
          $ReverseG[S]$ (all edges reversed) from v. Run the $|Tails| + |Heads|$
          searches in lock-step until the first search terminates with all vertices
          R reachable from its root visited.
       ii. If $R = S$ then HALT and output $G[S]$.
       iii. Remove all h, t-labels from R. Add label h (t) to vertices in $S \setminus R$
            which have an incoming (outgoing) edge to R.
       iv. Add $Remove(S, C(S), R)$ to L
       v. Add $Construct(R)$ to L
4. L empty, HALT and output: "No good components exist".

of $O(bits(S_i) + |S_i|)$ is charged to vertices of S_i or to their bit in L_j or U_j,
$2 \leq i \leq d$. When a vertex v is charged, the size of its component $S(v)$ is
therefore halved, and $|\{i \in \{1..k\} : L_i \cap S(v) \neq \emptyset\}|$ decreases. The total cost
of partitioning is then $O((b + n) \min\{\log n, k\})$, and the total running time is
$O(m \min\{k, n\} + b \min\{\log n, k\})$ for this case. $\square$

Lemma 4. *The algorithm for nonemptiness testing of Streett automata is correct
when* $\min\{n, k\} \geq \sqrt{m \log n}$.

Proof. We explain the parallel searches in line 3(f)i. Assume that $G[S \cup B]$ is a
component of the current graph from which we delete the vertices B. Let $Heads$

(*Tails*) be the vertices in S with an incoming (outgoing) edge to a vertex of B. Consider the condensed graph of $G[S]$ where strong components are condensed into single vertices. This graph is acyclic, every source component must contain a vertex in *Heads* and every sink component must contain a vertex of *Tails*, since $G[S \cup B]$ was strongly-connected. A search of $G[S]$ rooted at a vertex in a sink component will explore exactly this component, and likewise a search of Reverse$G[S]$ started in a source component will explore exactly that component. A search started in any other component will eventually enter a sink component (or source component for the reverse searches), and thus terminate later than the search started in the sink (or source) component itself. By searching from all vertices of *Heads* and *Tails* simultaneously we are thus guaranteed to terminate as soon as the smallest source or sink component is discovered. We can now state the invariant of the while loop: "For any $C(S)$ in the list L, either $G[S]$ is a component or any source (sink) component of $G[S]$ has a vertex labelled h (t). All candidates for non-trivial good components are in L". The algorithm takes a data structure from L, deletes bad vertices until only good vertices remain and adds labels h (or t) to vertices which had an incoming (or outgoing) edge removed. The invariant is maintained by Case 2 since it adds unlabelled components to the list. Case 3 searches all vertices labelled h and t simultaneously. As described above it returns the smallest source or sink component R of $G[S]$. If $R = S$ then we have a good component. Otherwise, we add the unlabelled component R to L and from S we delete vertices R and add labels h (or t) to vertices which had an incoming (or outgoing) edge to R, before adding $S \setminus R$ to L. Thus the loop invariant is maintained and the algorithm is correct. $\square$

Lemma 5. *The algorithm for nonemptiness testing of Streett automata has running time $O(m\sqrt{m\log n} + b\min\{\log n, k\})$ when $\min\{n, k\} \geq \sqrt{m\log n}$.*

Proof. The cost of all searches in Case 3 are charged to the edges of the smallest component $G[R]$. If $R = S$ then we halt and each edge is charged $O(\sqrt{m/\log n})$ units. Otherwise, the size of R is at most half the size of S. Thus, each edge is charged at most $\log n$ times. Each time it is charged $O(\sqrt{m/\log n})$ constant units, for total cost of searches in Case 3 of $O(m\sqrt{m\log n})$. Line 3(e) Case 2 occurs after deletion of at least $\sqrt{m/\log n}$ edges from the graph, which can happen at most $\sqrt{m\log n}$ times, each time invoking SCC for a total cost of $O(m\sqrt{m\log n})$. The earlier analysis of data structure operations not under Case 3 still holds. The cost of $O(bits(R) + |R|)$ for the data structure operations in Case 3 are charged to R, and as before each vertex v is charged at most $O((bits(v) + 1)\min\{\log n, k\})$ units total. The total running time for this case is therefore $O(m\sqrt{m\log n} + b\min\{\log n, k\})$. $\square$

We have shown the following theorem.

Theorem 6. *Given a directed graph on n vertices and m edges, and Streett pairs $\langle L_i, U_i \rangle, i = 1..k$, with $b = \sum_{i=1..k} |L_i| + |U_i|$, there is an $O(m\min\{\sqrt{m\log n}, k, n\} + b\min\{\log n, k\})$ time algorithm which either finds a good non-trivial component of the graph or decides that no such component exists, thereby solving the nonemptiness problem for Streett automata.*

2.3 Implementation of data structure for Streett pairs

We prove Lemma 1. Assume the Streett pairs are given by sets of circular linked lists, one for each vertex. The list of $v_i \in V = \{v_1, v_2, ..., v_n\}$ contains an entry for all sets L_j such that $v_i \in L_j$ and all sets U_j such that $v_i \in U_j$. The entry specifying that $v_i \in L_j$ (or $v_i \in U_j$) is called the *m-bit* (membership-bit) $[v_i, L_j]$ (or $[v_i, U_j]$) and specifies the data v_i and L_j (or U_j). There are thus a total of b m-bits, each one belonging to the unique *vertex list* specified by the vertex in the m-bit. The data structure we describe constructs analogous *set lists* so that each m-bit also belongs to a unique set list specified by the Streett set in the m-bit. For a given vertex set $S \subseteq V$ we maintain for each L_i such that $L_i \cap S \neq \emptyset$ and for each U_j such that $U_j \cap S \neq \emptyset$ a set list. The set list of $L_i \cap S$ is a doubly linked list of all m-bits $[v, L_i]$ where $v \in S$, in arbitrary order, and the set list for $U_i \cap S$ is defined analogously. The first element of the set list $L_i \cap S$ (or $U_i \cap S$) is called $first(L_i, S)$ (or $first(U_i, S)$). The data structure $C(S)$ for $S \subseteq V$ consists of

- a doubly linked list of vertices in S. Note that each vertex has a pointer to its vertex list.
- the doubly linked set lists $L_i \cap S$ and $U_i \cap S$.
- a doubly linked list of records $\langle first(L_i, S), first(U_i, S) \rangle$, for each i such that $L_i \cap S \neq \emptyset$, and a pointer from each $first(L_i, S)$ and $first(U_i, S)$ to the corresponding record. A record is bad if $L_i \cap S \neq \emptyset$ and $U_i \cap S = \emptyset$.
- a doubly linked list of bad records.

Bad$(C(S))$ in $O(1)$ time returns a pointer to the list of bad records.

Construct(S) is given the list of vertices in S and needs to construct $C(S)$. Every Construct operation uses the same auxiliary array $A[1..k]$, which is initialized only once at the beginning. After each use A is cleaned up in time independent of k, by keeping track of accessed indices. While constructing $C(S)$, the entry $A[i]$ stores the record $\langle first(L_i, S), first(U_i, S) \rangle$, initially $\langle nil, nil \rangle$. To construct $C(S)$, traverse the vertex list for each $v_j \in S$ and add each encountered m-bit to its corresponding set list, e.g. $[v_j, L_i]$ is added to the list with first element $first(L_i, S)$. A final traversal of the accessed indices of array A sets up the lists of records for non-empty set lists and the list of bad records. Apart from the one-time $O(k)$ initialization of the auxiliary array, the Construct(S) operation takes time $O(bits(S)+|S|)$, since there are $bits(S)$ m-bits in vertex lists of S.

Remove$(S, C(S), B)$ is given S, the data structure $C(S)$ and a list of vertices in B. To construct $C(S \setminus B)$ traverse the vertex list for each vertex in B and remove each encountered m-bit from its corresponding set list (note that set lists are doubly linked). If the last vertex of $S \cap U_i$ is removed then add the record $\langle first(L_i, S), first(U_i, S) \rangle$ to the list of bad records. If the last vertex of $S \cap L_i$ is removed then remove the record $\langle first(L_i, S), first(U_i, S) \rangle$ from the list of records and, if present, from the list of bad records. Finally, remove vertices in B from the (doubly linked) vertex list of S. The Remove$(S, C(S), B)$ operation takes time $O(bits(B) + |B|)$.

3   Protocol Pruning

A new technique called protocol pruning is given in [4] to simplify communication protocols. The input to this problem consists of

1. a labeled digraph $G = (V, E)$ with $m = |E|$ and $n = |V|$ and a labeling function $label : E \rightarrow \{1, ..., m\}$;
2. l vertices $a_1, ..., a_l$ of V marked as *special* vertices, such that each special vertex belongs to a different strongly-connected component of G;
3. a function $depends\_on : \{1, ..., m\} \rightarrow \{1, ..., m\}$;
4. an initial set D of edges that have to be deleted from G.

We call an edge e *bad* if the current graph does not contain an edge with label $depends\_on(label(e))$. An edge e is called *useless* if it is not contained in a strongly-connected component of a special vertex in the current graph. The protocol pruning approach repeatedly removes all edges in D and creates a new set D consisting of bad or useless edges. When the current graph does not contain any bad or useless edges then the components of the special vertices constitute the pruned protocol.

Let m_i be the number of edges in the strongly-connected component of a_i in the initial graph. The previously best implementation of protocol pruning, see [4], adds all bad or useless edges to D. To determine the useless edges it recomputes the strongly connected component of a vertex a_i every time the component lost an edge. Thus, this implementation takes time $O(\sum m_i^2)$.

We give an implementation of protocol pruning in time $O(\sqrt{l} \sum_i m_i^{1.5})$. Our algorithm maintains disjoint sets $S_1, ..., S_l$ of vertices of the current graph G with the special vertex $a_i \in S_i$ so that each induced graph $G[S_i]$ is a collection of strongly-connected components. As before, the algorithm maintains sets $Heads$ and $Tails$ of vertices. For each vertex v in $Heads$ ($Tails$) incoming (outgoing) edges incident to v have been deleted, and the search for the strongly-connected component of v has not yet been completed.

Before each iteration of the main loop we ensure the current graph has no bad edges. The main loop of the algorithm has two cases. If there exists an i with $|S_i \cap Heads| + |S_i \cap Tails| \geq \sqrt{m_i/l}$, then for each such i, the strongly-connected components of $G[S_i]$ are computed from scratch, and D is set to be all newly discovered useless edges. Otherwise, the algorithm starts a search at all vertices in $Heads \cup Tails$. The searches are lock-step in two levels. On the outer level the searches alternate between the different $G[S_i]$, running a fixed number of search steps in each $G[S_i]$. On the inner level all searches within a $G[S_i]$ are also done in lockstep. The search rooted at vertex v tries to determine the strongly-connected component of v. As in the previous algorithm the search for $v \in Tails$ is started in the current graph and the search for $v \in Heads$ in the reverse of the current graph. If all the searches terminate in the exact same component as they were started then there are no useless edges and we are done. Else, assume the first search to terminate is rooted in S_r reaching the vertices $R \subset S_r$. If the special vertex a_r belongs to R then we set D to be all edges of $G[S_r]$ which do not have both endpoints in R and update S_r to R. If a_r does not belong to R then D is set to be all edges with at least one endpoint in R and S_r is updated to $S_r \setminus R$. In this latter case the new $G[S_r]$ is not necessarily strongly connected, so vertices in *Heads* or *Tails* belonging to the new S_r remain in *Heads* or *Tails* to be searched in the next iteration.

Our implementation uses the following data structure.

- A first array of size m that stores for each edge label i a set of pointers to all edges in the current graph with label i and the number of such edges; each edge of label i stores i and a reverse pointer to its location in the list of i.
- A second array of size m that stores for each label i all labels j such that *depends_on*$(j) = i$.

The data structure is updated in an obvious way whenever an edge is deleted from the graph. If the number of edges with label i becomes 0, all edges with label j such that *depends_on*$(j) = i$ are marked as bad. The algorithm is given on the next page. All use of the above data structure is restricted to lines 3, 4, 6(c) and 6(d), where edges are removed from G.

Lemma 7. *The protocol pruning algorithm is correct.*

Proof. As shown below, the while loop in the algorithm has the invariant: "There are no bad edges in G and each edge has both endpoints in some S_i. For each i, $a_i \in S_i$ and if the induced graph $G[S_i]$ is not a strongly-connected component of G then any source (sink) component of $G[S_i]$ has a vertex in *Heads* (*Tails*)." Upon termination of the while loop *Heads* $\cup$ *Tails* $= \emptyset$ which together with the invariant ensures that there are neither any bad or useless edges left. The invariant holds initially since we delete all edges without both endpoints in some S_i in line 3 and all bad edges in line 4. Moreover, if after these edge deletions $G[S_i]$ is no longer strongly connected, then every one of its source (sink) components contains an endpoint of an edge removed, by an argument similar to one in the proof of Lemma 4. An execution of the loop either discovers a new component $G[S_i']$ (lines 6(a)i and 6(b)ii) or discovers some vertices R which do not belong to a strongly-connected component of a special vertex (line 6(b)iii). In the former case we remove from *Heads*, *Tails* all vertices of the involved component, while in the latter case only vertices R are removed from *Heads*, *Tails*. In either case the relevant component vertex sets are updated and useless edges added to D. These useless edges and any subsequent bad edges are then removed from G, ensuring that the first part of the loop invariant holds. Since endpoints of removed edges are added to *Heads* and *Tails* in lines 6(c), 6(d) and 6(e) the second part of the loop invariant holds as well. Note that the algorithm may also terminate if in line 6(b)i all searches from vertices in *Heads* and *Tails* terminate in the exact same component as they were started, meaning that each $G[S_i]$ is indeed a strongly-connected component. $\square$

Lemma 8. *The protocol pruning algorithm has running time $O(\sqrt{l} \sum m_i^{1.5})$.*

Protocol Pruning Algorithm

1. Run SCC to find the components $G[S_1], ..., G[S_l]$ of G such that $a_i \in S_i$.
2. Let m_i be the number of edges in the component $G[S_i]$.
3. Remove edges $D \cup \{uv \in E : \not\exists i : \{u, v\} \subseteq S_i\}$ from G.
4. **While** there exist bad edges **do** Remove all bad edges from G.
5. Set *Heads* (*Tails*) to be the vertices in $\bigcup_i S_i$ which had an incoming (outgoing) edge just removed in line 3 or 4 above.
6. **While** *Heads* $\cup$ *Tails* $\neq \emptyset$ **do**
   (a) Case 1: **If** $\exists i$ such that $|Heads \cap S_i| + |Tails \cap S_i| \geq \sqrt{m_i/l}$ **do**
       For each i such that $|Heads \cap S_i| + |Tails \cap S_i| \geq \sqrt{m_i/l}$:
       i. Run SCC on $G[S_i]$ to find the new component $G[S_i']$ containing a_i.
       ii. Add to D all edges with at least one endpoint in $S_i \setminus S_i'$.
       iii. Remove all vertices S_i from *Heads* and from *Tails* and set $S_i := S_i'$.
   (b) Case 2: **Else** For all i, $|Heads \cap S_i| + |Tails \cap S_i| < \sqrt{m_i/l}$ **do**
       i. For each $v \in$ *Tails* search G from v and for each $v \in$ *Heads* search Reverse(G) from v. Run the searches for all $1 \leq i \leq l$ in lock-step both between different $G[S_i]$ and lock-step within each $G[S_i]$ until the first search completes, say on $G[S_r]$, with all vertices R reachable from its root visited and $R \subset S_r$, but $R \neq S_r$. If no such search exists (i.e. $R \supseteq S_r$ for each search) HALT and output $G[S_1], ..., G[S_l]$.
       ii. If $a_r \in R$ then
           A. Add to D all edges with at least one endpoint in $S_r \setminus R$.
           B. Remove all vertices S_r from *Heads* and *Tails* and set $S_r := S_r'$.
       iii. If $a_r \notin R$ then
           A. Add to D all edges with at least one endpoint in R.
           B. Remove all vertices R from *Heads* and *Tails* and set $S_r := S_r \setminus R$.
   (c) Remove useless edges D from G
   (d) **While** there exist bad edges **do** Remove all bad edges from G.
   (e) Add to *Heads* (*Tails*) vertices in $\bigcup_i S_i$ which had an incoming (outgoing) edge just removed in line (c) or (d) above.
7. HALT and output $G[S_1], ..., G[S_l]$

Proof. The cost of all data structure operations is $O(\sum_i m_i)$. For each $1 \leq i \leq l$ line 6(a)i is executed $O(\sqrt{m_i l})$ times, since each time at least $\sqrt{m_i/l}$ edges incident with the component of a_i have been deleted. An invocation of SCC costs $O(m_i)$ for a total cost of $O(\sqrt{l} \sum m_i^{1.5})$.

In an execution of line 6(b)i, if all searches terminate in the exact same component as they were started, then their total cost is $O(\sqrt{l} \sum m_i^{1.5})$, since in each $G[S_i]$ there are at most $\sqrt{m_i/l}$ searches costing $O(m_i)$ each. Otherwise, let the search initiated at $v \in S_r$ be the first one to complete, after traversing vertices R and edges E_R. Note that there are at most $\sqrt{m_r/l}$ searches in S_r. Since the parallel searches are lock-step also between different S_i, we know that for each $1 \leq i \leq l$, the parallel searches in $G[S_i]$ cost at most $O(\sqrt{m_r/l}|E_R|)$, for a total cost of $O(\sqrt{l m_r}|E_R|)$ for all searches in this execution of 6(b)i. This cost is charged to the useless edges discovered, namely those with an endpoint in $S_r \setminus R$ if $a_r \in R$ or those with an endpoint in R itself if $a_r \notin R$. It is clear that in the latter case there are at least $|E_R|$ useless edges. This also holds in the former case since R is a source (or sink) component of $G[S_r]$ and there is therefore at least one sink (or source) component of $G[S_r]$, containing useless edges, in which a parallel search had not yet completed when E_R had been traversed. Therefore there is a charge of $O(\sqrt{m_r l})$ per edge in either case. Edges are charged only once for a total cost of $O(\sqrt{l} \sum_i m_i^{1.5})$. $\square$

Acknowledgements

The authors are indebted to Moshe Vardi for suggesting the nonemptiness problem for Streett automata and to David Lee for suggesting the protocol pruning problem.

References

1. E. A. Emerson and C. L. Lei. Modalities for model checking: Branching time strikes back. *Science of Computer Programming*, 8 (1987), 275–306.
2. S. Even and Y. Shiloach, "An On-Line Edge-Deletion Problem", *J. ACM* 28 (1981), 1–4.
3. R. Kurshan. Computer-Aided Verification of Coordinating Processes: The Automata-Theoretic Approach. Princeton University Press, Princeton, 1994.
4. D. Lee, A. N. Netravali, K. K. Sabnani. Protocol Pruning, *The Proceedings of IEEE*, October 1995.
5. S. Safra. On the complexity of ω-automata. *Proc. 29th IEEE Symposium on Foundations of Computer Science (FOCS)*, 1988, 319–327.
6. R.E. Tarjan. Depth-first search and linear graph algorithms, *SIAM Journal on Computing*, vol.1, no.2, June 1972, 146–160.
7. M. Y. Vardi and P. L. Wolper. An Automata-Theoretic Approach to Automatic Program Verification. *Proc. 1st IEEE Symposium on Logic in Computer Science (LICS)*, 1986, 322–331.

Service-Constrained Network Design Problems

Madhav V. Marathe[1] * and R. Ravi[2] ** and R. Sundaram[3] ***

[1] Los Alamos National Laboratory, Los Alamos NM 87545.
[2] Graduate School of Industrial Administration, CMU Pittsburgh.
[3] Lab. for Computer Science, M.I.T., Cambridge, MA 02139.

Abstract. Several practical instances of network design problems often require the network to satisfy multiple constraints. In this paper, we focus on the following problem (and its variants): find a low-cost network, under one cost function, that *services* every node in the graph, under another cost function, (i.e., every node of the graph is within a prespecified distance from the network). This study has important applications to the problems of optical network design and the efficient maintenance of distributed databases.

We utilize the framework developed in [MR+95] to formulate these problems as bicriteria network design problems. We present the first known approximation algorithms for the class of service-constrained network design problems. We provide a $(1, O(\tilde{\Delta} \ln n))$-approximation algorithm for the (Service cost, Total edge cost, Tree)-bicriteria problem (where $\tilde{\Delta}$ is the maximum service-degree of any node in the graph). We counterbalance this by showing that the problem does not have an (α, β)-approximation algorithm for any $\alpha \geq 1$ and $\beta < \ln n$ unless $NP \subseteq DTIME(n^{\log \log n})$. When both the objectives are evaluated under the same cost function we provide a $(2(1 + \epsilon), 2(1 + \frac{1}{\epsilon}))$-approximation algorithm, for any $\epsilon > 0$. In the opposite direction we provide a hardness result showing that even in the restricted case where the two cost functions are the same the problem does not have an (α, β)-approximation algorithm for $\alpha = 1$ and $\beta < \ln n$ unless $NP \subseteq DTIME(n^{\log \log n})$. We also consider a generalized Steiner forest version of the problem along with other variants involving diameter and bottleneck cost.

1 Introduction

1.1 Motivation

The maintenance of databases distributed across networks is an issue of great importance. The problem [WM91] can be stated as follows: given a set of sites in a network we wish to select a subset of the sites at which to place copies of the database. The major requirement is that each site should be able to access a copy of the database within a prespecified service time, and the chosen sites should be connected together as a minimum

---

* Email: madhav@c3.lanl.gov. Research supported by the Department of Energy under Contract W-7405-ENG-36.
** Email: ravi+@andrew.cmu.edu.
*** Email: koods@theory.lcs.mit.edu. Research supported by DARPA contract N0014-92-J-1799 and NSF 92-12184 CCR.

cost tree so that updates to one of the copies can be propagated to the other copies in an inexpensive manner (See Fig. 1).

A problem of a similar nature comes up in the area of optical network design. Developments in fiber-optic networking technology have finally reached the point where it is being considered as the most promising candidate for the next generation of wide-area backbone networks [Gr92, Ra93]. The optical network is a pure data transmission medium. All the computing and processing continues to be done in the electronic world. An important issue in interfacing these two worlds – the electronic and the optic – is that of designing the optical network subject to location-theoretic constraints imposed by the electronic world. Given a set of sites in a network we wish to select a subset of the sites at which to place optoelectronic switches and routers [KR+96]. As before, the major requirement is that every site should be within a prespecified distance from an optoelectronic access node and the chosen sites should be connected together using fiber-optic links as a minimum cost tree.

These problems can be thought of as particular instances of a more general class of "service-constrained network design problems." Informally, service-constrained network design problems involve both a location-theoretic objective and a cost-minimization objective subject to connectivity constraints. The location-theoretic objective requires that we choose a subset of nodes at which to "locate" services such that each node is within a bounded distance from at least one chosen location. The cost-minimization objective requires that the chosen locations be connected by a network minimizing parameters such as diameter or total cost. The two objectives are measured under two (possibly) different cost functions.

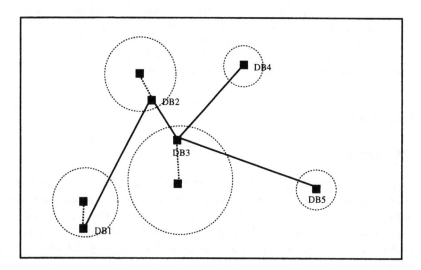

Fig. 1. The database copies are shown linked by a network. The circles represent the prespecified service times.

1.2 Our Contributions

Problem Statement The prototypical problem we consider in this paper is the following: given an undirected graph $G = (V, E)$ with two different cost functions c_e (modeling the service cost) and d_e (modeling the construction cost) for each edge $e \in E$, and a bound S_v (on the service constraint for each vertex v), find a minimum d-cost tree such that every node v in the graph is *serviced* by some node in the tree, i.e. every node v is within distance S_v (under the c-costs) of some node in the tree.

Framework for Approximation In this paper, we study the complexity and approximability of a number of service-constrained network design problems using the bicriteria framework developed in [MR+95].

A generic bicriteria network design problem, (A,B,S), is defined by identifying two minimization objectives, – **A** and **B**, – from a set of possible objectives, and specifying a membership requirement in a class of subgraphs, – **S**. The problem specifies a budget value on the first objective, **A**, under one cost function, and seeks to find a network having minimum possible value for the second objective, **B**, under another cost function, such that this network is within the budget on the first objective. The solution network must belong to the subgraph-class **S**. For example, the problem of finding low-cost service constrained networks stated above can be modeled as the (Non-uniform service cost, Total cost, Tree)-bicriteria problem.

Many of the problems considered in this paper, are NP-hard [GJ79]. Given the hardness of finding optimal solutions, we concentrate on devising approximation algorithms with worst case performance guarantees. Recall that an approximation algorithm for an optimization problem Π provides a *performance guarantee* of ρ if for every instance I of Π, the solution value returned by the approximation algorithm is within a factor ρ of the optimal value for I. Here, we use the extended version [MR+95] of this notion that is applicable to bicriteria optimization problems. An (α, β)-approximation algorithm for an (A,B,S)-bicriteria problem is defined as a polynomial-time algorithm that produces a solution in which the first objective (**A**) value, is at most α times the budget, and the second objective (**B**) value, is at most β times the minimum for any solution that is within the budget on **A**. The solution produced must belong to the subgraph-class **S**.

Problem formulations and Summary of Results The two versions of the location-theoretic or service cost objective that we consider are: (i) Non-uniform service cost and (ii) Uniform service cost. In the *Non-uniform service cost* version a service constraint S_{v_k} is specified for each vertex. The *Uniform service cost* version is a special case where $S_{v_k} = S, \forall v_k$, i.e., all vertices have the same service constraint.

For the cost-minimization objective we focus our attention on the total cost of the network. The *Total cost* objective is the sum of the costs of all the edges in the tree. We also consider the *Diameter* objective – the maximum distance between any pair of nodes in the tree – and the *Bottleneck* objective – the maximum value of any edge in the tree.

As mentioned before, the two objectives are measured with respect to different edge-cost functions. The (budgeted) service cost objective is measured using the c-cost function while the cost-minimization objective is measured using the d-cost function. As stated before, a node u is said to *service* node v if u is within distance S_v of v, under the c-cost. The *service-degree* of a node is defined to be the number of nodes it services. All our results come in two flavors: (i) Different cost functions and (ii) Identical cost functions. The *Identical cost functions* version is a special case of the *Different cost functions* case where the two cost functions are the same, i.e. $c_e = d_e, \forall e$.

We now state our main results.

Definition 1. A node u is said to **service** a node v if u is within distance S_v of v. The service-degree of a node is the number of nodes it services. The service-degree of the graph is the maximum over all nodes of the service-degree of the node and is denoted by $\tilde{\Delta}$.

Theorem 2. *There is a $(1, O(\tilde{\Delta} \cdot \ln n))$-approximation algorithm for the (Non-uniform service cost, Total cost, Tree)-bicriteria problem with different cost functions, where $\tilde{\Delta}$ is the maximum service-degree of any node in the graph.*

We provide a counterbalancing hardness of approximation result by showing that:

Theorem 3. *Unless* NP $\subseteq$ DTIME($n^{\log \log n}$), *the (Uniform service cost, Total cost, Tree)-bicriteria problem, with different cost functions, cannot be approximated to within (α, β), for any $\alpha \geq 1$ and any $\beta < \ln n$.*

We consider the identical cost functions case and show that

Theorem 4. *For any $\epsilon > 0$ there is a $(2(1+\epsilon), 2(1+\frac{1}{\epsilon}))$-approximation algorithm for the (Non-uniform service cost, Total cost, Tree)-bicriteria problem with identical cost functions.*

This is opposed by

Theorem 5. *Unless* NP $\subseteq$ DTIME($n^{\log \log n}$), *the (Uniform service cost, Total cost, Tree)-bicriteria problem, with identical cost functions, cannot be approximated to within (α, β), for $\alpha = 1$ and any $\beta < \ln n$.*

We also show that

Theorem 6. *(Non-uniform service cost, Diameter, Tree) and (Non-uniform service cost, Bottleneck, Tree)-bicriteria problems, with different cost functions, are solvable exactly in polynomial-time.*

We consider the (Uniform service cost, Total cost, Generalized Steiner forest)-bicriteria problem – a generalization that arises from its application to the optical network design problems. If we had a number of sites with connectivity requirements only among some subsets of the sites, rather than all the sites, then we need the solution subgraph to be a forest and not necessarily a tree. This motivates the service-constrained generalized Steiner forest problem. The formal statement of the (Uniform service cost, Total cost, Generalized Steiner forest)-bicriteria problem is as follows: given an undirected graph $G = (V, E)$ with two different cost functions c_e (modeling the service cost) and d_e

(modeling the construction cost) for each edge $e \in E$, a set of k site pairs (s_i, t_i), and a bound $\mathcal{S}$ (on the maximum service constraint), find a minimum d-cost forest $\mathcal{F}$ such that for each site pair (s_i, t_i) there exists a tree $T \in \mathcal{F}$ with the property that both s_i and t_i are within distance $\mathcal{S}$ of the tree.

Our main result for the service-constrained generalized Steiner forest problem is the following:

Theorem 7. *There is a* $(2(1 + \epsilon), 6(1 + \frac{1}{\epsilon}))$*-approximation algorithm for the (Uniform service cost, Total cost, Generalized Steiner forest)-bicriteria problem with identical cost functions.*

We omit the proof of the above theorem from this extended abstract due to space considerations.

1.3 Previous Work

Variants of the service-constrained *tour* problem have been considered in [AF+94, AH91, CS89]. Current and Schilling [CS89] consider the *covering salesperson problem* and present a heuristic for it without providing any performance guarantees. In this problem, nodes represent customers and the service radius represents the distance a customer is willing to travel to meet the salesperson. The goal is to find a minimum length tour connecting a subset of the nodes so that the nodes are strictly serviced. Arkin and Hassin [AH91] considered geometric versions of the problem, where the service neighborhood (i.e., the neighborhood the customer is willing to travel) is modeled as a region in the plane. For convex neighborhoods, they present heuristics that provide constant performance guarantees. They also show how their heuristics can be extended to nonconvex regions. Arkin et. al. [AF+94] considered additional geometric variations of the covering tour problem including the *lawn mower problem*, where the goal is to find a tour such that each given point is within a circle of unit radius from at least one point on the tour. They provide an approximation algorithm for this problem with a constant performance guarantee.

References [AF+94, AH91] considered only the geometric versions of the problems. In the identical cost functions case, where the edge costs satisfy the triangle inequality, our approximation algorithm for the (Non-uniform service cost, Total cost, Tree)-bicriteria problem can be used to produce a tour such that for any $\epsilon > 0$, the service constraint for each node is violated by a factor of at most $2(1 + \epsilon)$ and the cost of the tour is at most $2(1 + \frac{1}{\epsilon})$ times that of a minimum cost tour which strictly services the nodes.

The paper by Marathe et al ([MR+95]) and the references therein are an extensive source on the area of bicriteria and multicriteria network design. The framework that we employ was developed in [MR+95].

The organization of the rest of the paper is as follows: Section 2 contains the proofs of Theorems 2 and 3, where the cost functions are different; Section 3 contains the proofs of Theorems 4 and 5, where the cost functions are identical; Section 4 contains the proof of Theorem 6; Section 5 contains some concluding remarks and open problems.

2 Different Cost Functions

In this section we give a proof of Theorem 2. We provide the details of our approximation algorithm for finding a service-constrained tree with non-uniform service costs and different cost functions. The approximation algorithm guarantees a performance of $O(\tilde{\Delta} \cdot \ln n)$, where $\tilde{\Delta}$ denotes the maximum service-degree of a node in the given graph.

Before we give the details of the algorithm, we need to state two facts. The first fact is that we may assume that the graph is complete and that the edge cost functions – c and d – obey triangle inequality. The reason for this is as follows: consider the (complete) graph obtained on the same set of vertices by adding edges between every pair of vertices of c and d-costs equal to that of the shortest c and d-cost paths between the corresponding vertices in the original graph; then any solution on this new graph transforms to a solution of identical value in the original graph.

We need some more preliminaries before we can state the second fact. Given a graph G with edge weights and node weights, we define the **ratio weight** of a simple cycle C in G to be

$$\frac{\sum_{e \in C} wt_e}{\sum_{v \in C} wt_v}.$$

Here wt_e denotes the weight of an edge and wt_v denotes the weight of a vertex. In other words, the ratio weight of a cycle is the ratio of the edge weight of the cycle to the node weight of the cycle.

The following problem is NP-hard:

Definition 8. MIN-RATIO-ROOTED-CYCLE (MRRC) Problem : Given a graph $G = (V, E)$ with edge and node weights, and a distinguished vertex $r \in V$ called the root, find a simple cycle in G that contains r and has minimum ratio weight.

Now we state our second fact which is obtained by a slight modification of the ideas in [BR+96].

Theorem 9. *There is a polynomial-time approximation algorithm with performance guarantee $\rho = O(1)$ for the MRRC problem.*

Having stated the two facts we are now in a position to present the main idea behind our algorithm. To begin with, we may assume that a specific node r belongs to the optimal tree. By running over all possible r's and picking the best we find the required (approximate) tree. The algorithm runs in phases. Initially, the solution contains only the node r. At any stage only a subset of the nodes are serviced by the set of solution nodes. Each phase the algorithm finds a nearly optimal minimum ratio weight cycle that services some of the remaining unserviced nodes in the graph. The cycle is contracted to a single node and the algorithm moves to the next phase. Termination occurs when all the nodes in the graph are serviced. A logarithmic performance guarantee is obtained by assuring that the cycle added in each phase has low cost.

ALGORITHM DIFFERENT:

- *Input:* A graph $G = (V, E)$, edge cost functions c and d, service budget S_{v_k} for vertex v_k under the c-cost function.
- 1. At any point in the algorithm, for each vertex $v_k \in V$, let B_{v_k} denote the set of vertices that are within c-distance of at most S_{v_k} from v_k.
  2. For $i = 1$ to n do
     (a) Set $r = v_i$. Set $j = 0$. Set $G_0 = G - B_r + r$.
     (b) While $G_j <> r$.
         i. Set $j = j + 1$.
         ii. Compute C_j, a ρ-approximate solution to the MRRC problem on G_j where the edge weights are the d-edge-costs and the node weights are $|B_{v_k}|$ for $k \neq i$ and 0 for r.
         iii. Modify G_j by contracting C_j into a supernode. Set r to be the new supernode.
         iv. Set $G_j = G_j - B_r + r$.
     (c) Let T_i be a minimum spanning tree on $\bigcup_j C_j$ under the d-cost.
  3. Let HEU $= \min_i T_i$. Output HEU.
- *Output:* A tree HEU such that every vertex $v_i \in V$ is within a distance S_{v_i} from some node in HEU, under the c-cost, and the d-cost of HEU is at most $O(\tilde{\Delta} \cdot \ln n)$ times that of an optimal service-constrained tree.

It is easy to see that ALGORITHM DIFFERENT outputs a tree that services all the nodes. It remains to show that the d-cost of HEU is within a factor of $O(\tilde{\Delta} \cdot \ln n)$ of the optimal. We prove this in the following two lemmas.

Let OPT denote an optimal tree. In what follows, let i denote that iteration of Step 2 in which $r = v_i \in$ OPT. Let f denote the number of iterations of Step 2b for this particular value of i. Let the set of cycles chosen in Step 2(b)ii of the algorithm be $C_1, \ldots, C_f$, in order. We use C_j to denote both the cycle as well as the d-cost of the cycle. We also use OPT and HEU to denote the d-costs of the corresponding tree. Let ϕ_j denote the number of nodes in G that are not serviced by r after choosing the cycle C_j in the jth iteration of Step 2b. Alternatively, ϕ_j is the number of vertices in $G - r$ after Step 2(b)iv in the j'th iteration.. Thus, $\phi_0 \leq n$ while $\phi_f = 0$. Let cycle C_j service t_j new nodes.

Lemma 10.

$$\frac{C_j}{t_j} \leq \frac{2\rho\tilde{\Delta}\text{OPT}}{\phi_{j-1}}.$$

Proof. Focus on the graph G_j at the end of iteration $j - 1$. Since OPT services all the vertices we have that $\sum_{v_k \in \text{OPT}} |B_{v_k}| = |V(G_j)| = \phi_{j-1}$.

We first observe that OPT induces a cycle (by doing an Euler walk along the outside of the OPT tree, see [CL+90], pp 697–700) with a minimum ratio weight of $\frac{2\text{OPT}}{\phi_{j-1}}$. Hence, since in Step 2(b)ii we choose a ρ-approximate minimum ratio cycle C_j it follows that

$$\frac{C_j}{\sum_{v_k \in C_j} |B_{v_k}|} \leq \frac{2\rho\text{OPT}}{\phi_{j-1}}.$$

Since the service-degree of each vertex in G is at most $\tilde{\Delta}$, it follows that no vertex contributes more than $\tilde{\Delta}$ to the denominator of the left hand side in the above equation. Thus $\tilde{\Delta} \cdot t_j \geq \sum_{v_k \in C_j} |B_{v_k}|$. Hence

$$\frac{C_j}{\tilde{\Delta} \cdot t_j} \leq \frac{2\rho\text{OPT}}{\phi_{j-1}}.$$

The lemma follows.

Lemma 11.

$$\text{HEU} \leq 2\rho\tilde{\Delta} \, H_n \text{OPT}$$

where $H_n = 1 + \frac{1}{2} + \ldots + \frac{1}{n}$ is the harmonic function.

Proof. By definition of ϕ_j and t_j, we have that

$$\phi_j = \phi_{j-1} - t_j \tag{1}$$

and from Lemma 10, we have

$$t_j \geq \frac{C_j \phi_{j-1}}{2\rho\tilde{\Delta}\text{OPT}} \tag{2}$$

Substituting Equation (2) into (1) we get

$$C_j \leq (2\rho\tilde{\Delta}\text{OPT})\frac{t_j}{\phi_{j-1}} \leq (2\rho\tilde{\Delta}\text{OPT})(H_{\phi_{j-1}} - H_{\phi_j}).$$

Hence, since $\phi_0 \leq n$ and $\phi_f = 0$, we get

$$\sum_{j=1}^{f} C_j \leq (2\rho\tilde{\Delta}\text{OPT})(H_{\phi_0} - H_{\phi_f}) \leq (2\rho\tilde{\Delta}\text{OPT})H_n.$$

This completes the proof of the lemma since $\text{HEU} \leq \sum_{j=1}^{f} C_j$.

Since $H_n \approx \ln n$ we obtain Theorem 2.

Remark. Note that the bounds of Theorem 2 also extend to the Steiner version where only a set of terminal sites need to be serviced. The Steiner version reduces to the regular version by setting the service budgets of the nonterminal nodes to some large value, such as the diameter of the graph.

2.1 Hardness

In this section we prove Theorem 3. We show that for any $\alpha \geq 1$, if there is a polynomial-time (α, β)-approximation algorithm for the (Uniform service cost, Total cost, Tree)-bicriteria problem, then there is a polynomial-time β-approximation algorithm for the **MIN SET COVER** problem.

As an instance of the **MIN SET COVER** problem we are given a universe $Q = \{q_1, q_2, \ldots, q_n\}$ and a collection $Q_1, Q_2, \ldots, Q_m$ of subsets of Q. The problem is to find a minimum cost collection of the subsets whose union is Q. Recently Feige [Fe95] has shown the following non-approximability result:

Theorem 12. *Unless* $NP \subseteq DTIME(n^{\log \log n})$, *the* **MIN SET COVER** *problem, with a universe of size k, cannot be approximated to better than a $\ln k$ factor.*

We now present the details of the approximation preserving reduction from **MIN SET COVER** to the (Uniform service cost, Total cost, Tree)-bicriteria problem. Corresponding to an instance of **MIN SET COVER** we construct the natural bipartite graph, one partition for set nodes and the other for element nodes, with edges representing element inclusion in the sets. To this bipartite graph, we add an enforcer node with edges to all the set nodes and also a mate node attached to the enforcer. Now we complete this *skeleton-graph* by throwing in all the edges. We set the d-cost of an edge from the enforcer to a set node to be 1. We set the d-cost of all other edges to be $\beta \cdot m + 1$. We now specify the c-costs (service costs) for the edges. We set the c-cost for the edge between the enforcer and the mate and for each edge between the enforcer and a set node to be S. We set the c-cost of an edge between a set node and the element nodes contained in this set to also be S. The d-cost of all other edges is set to $\alpha \cdot S + 1$. Let G denote the resulting instance of the (Uniform service cost, Total cost, Tree)-bicriteria problem with the c and d cost functions as specified above and a uniform service budget of S.

It is easy to see that any collection of k subsets which form a set cover correspond to a tree in G that strictly services all the nodes and which has a d-cost of k. This is because the tree consisting of the enforcer and the nodes corresponding to the sets in the collection, strictly services all the nodes and has a d-cost of k.

Let OPT denote the size of a minimum set cover to the original instance. Now we show that if there exists a tree T which is an (α, β)-approximation to the resulting instance G of the (Uniform service cost, Total cost, Tree)-bicriteria problem, then from it we can derive a β-approximation to the original set cover instance. Such a tree T must satisfy the following properties:

1. The c-cost of T is at most $\beta \cdot$ OPT. This follows from the definition of β-approximation and the fact that there exists a tree in G corresponding to OPT with d-cost at most OPT.

2. The nodes of G must be serviced by T within budget S. This is because the c-cost of any edge is either S or $\alpha S + 1$, but T violates the budget constraint by at most a factor α.

3. The mate node cannot be in T. This is because the d-cost of any edge from the mate node is $\beta \cdot m + 1$ which is greater than the d-cost of T. Since only the enforcer node can service the mate node with a service cost of at most αS, the enforcer must be in T.

4. Using the same reasoning as that for the mate node, none of the nodes representing the ground elements can be in T. To service these nodes, some of the set nodes must be in T.

We thus conclude that T consists only of the enforcer node and some of the set nodes. Since the d-cost of T is at most $\beta \cdot$ OPT, it follows that the number of set nodes in T is at most $\beta \cdot$ OPT. Since the element nodes are serviced by the chosen set nodes with a service distance of at most αS, the corresponding sets must form a set cover. We thus have a β-approximation algorithm for set cover and this completes the proof.

3 Identical Cost Functions

3.1 Approximation Algorithm

In this section, we give a proof of Theorem 4. We provide the details of our approximation algorithm for finding a service-constrained tree with non-uniform service costs and identical cost functions.

ALGORITHM IDENTICAL:

- *Input:* An undirected graph $G = (V, E)$, edge cost function c, service radius $\mathcal{S}_{v_k}$ for vertex v_k, an accuracy parameter $\epsilon > 0$.
- 1. For each node $v_k \in V$, let B_{v_k} denote the set of vertices that are within distance of at most $(1 + \epsilon)\mathcal{S}_{v_k}$ from v_k.
  2. Set $\mathcal{X}' = \{v_1, v_2, \ldots, v_n\}$ the set of vertices. Set $\mathcal{X} = \emptyset$.
  3. Repeat until $\mathcal{X}' = \emptyset$.
     (a) Let i be such that $\mathcal{S}_{v_i}$ is the least among all $v_i \in \mathcal{X}'$.
     (b) Set $\mathcal{X} = \mathcal{X} \cup \{v_i\}$.
     (c) Set $\mathcal{X}' = \mathcal{X}' \setminus \{v_k | B_{v_k} \cap B_{v_i} \neq \emptyset\}$.
  4. Construct a graph on the set of vertices in $\mathcal{X}$. Let the cost of an edge in this graph be the distance of the shortest path between the two vertices in G. Construct the minimum spanning tree T of this graph. Consider the subgraph corresponding to T formed by replacing each edge in T by a shortest path of G. Let HEU be a minimum spanning tree of this subgraph. Output HEU.
- *Output:* A tree HEU such that any vertex v_k is within a distance of $2(1+\epsilon)\mathcal{S}_{v_k}$ from some node in HEU and the cost of HEU is at most $2(1 + \frac{1}{\epsilon})$ times that of any tree which contains a node within distance $\mathcal{S}_{v_k}$ of any vertex v_k.

Let OPT be an optimal solution. We also use OPT and HEU to denote the cost of the corresponding trees. We prove the performance guarantee of ALGORITHM IDENTICAL in the following lemmas. Let the vertices in $\mathcal{X}$ at the termination of ALGORITHM IDENTICAL be $v_1, v_2, \ldots, v_f$, i.e., $|\mathcal{X}| = f$.

Lemma 13. *Every vertex v_k is within a distance $2(1 + \epsilon)\mathcal{S}_{v_k}$ of some vertex in $\mathcal{X}$.*

Proof. If $v_k \in \mathcal{X}$ then the lemma follows since HEU contains v_k. If $v_k \notin \mathcal{X}$ then $\exists v_i \in$ $\mathcal{X}$ such that $B_{v_i} \cap Bv_k \neq \emptyset$ and $\mathcal{S}_{v_i} \leq \mathcal{S}_{v_k}$. In this situation, it is easy to see that v_k is within a distance $(1+\epsilon)\mathcal{S}_{v_i} + (1+\epsilon)\mathcal{S}_{v_k} \leq 2(1+\epsilon)\mathcal{S}_{v_k}$. This completes the proof.

Lemma 14. OPT $\geq \sum_{i=1}^{f} \epsilon \mathcal{S}_{v_i}$.

Proof. By definition, OPT contains at least one node from each B_{v_i} for all $v_i \in \mathcal{X}$ that is within distance $\mathcal{S}_{v_i}$ from v_i. Since the B_{v_i} for all $v_i \in \mathcal{X}$ are disjoint, any tree connecting these nodes must cross the peripheral $\epsilon \mathcal{S}_{v_i}$ width and the lemma follows.

Lemma 15. HEU $\leq 2(\text{OPT} + \sum_{i=1}^{f} \mathcal{S}_{v_i})$.

Proof. We can construct a tree Γ spanning all the $v_i \in \mathcal{X}$ as follows: for each $v_i \in \mathcal{X}$, join v_i to a vertex in OPT that is within distance $\mathcal{S}_{v_i}$ by a shortest path. The length of this path is no more than $\mathcal{S}_{v_i}$. Thus, the cost of Γ is at most OPT $+ \sum_{i=1}^{f} \mathcal{S}_{v_i}$. Note that Γ is a Steiner tree that spans all the vertices in $\mathcal{X}$. Since HEU is a minimum spanning tree on these same vertices, computed using shortest path distances between them, standard analysis of the minimum spanning tree heuristic for Steiner trees, yields that the cost of HEU is at most twice the cost of Γ. The lemma follows.

Lemma 16. HEU $\leq 2(1+\frac{1}{\epsilon})$OPT.

Proof. Follows from Lemmas 14 and 15.

Theorem 4 follows from Lemmas 13 and 16.

3.2 Hardness

In this section we prove Theorem 5. We show that if there is a $(1, \beta)$-approximation algorithm for the (Uniform service cost, Total cost, Tree)-bicriteria problem then there is a polynomial-time β-approximation algorithm for the **CONNECTED DOMINATION** problem.

As an instance of the (optimization version of the) **CONNECTED DOMINATION** problem we are given a graph $G(V, E)$ and are required to find a a dominating set D of vertices of minimum size such that the subgraph induced on D is connected.

The result of Feige [Fe95] combined in straightforward fashion with the reduction in [GJ79] yields the following non-approximability result:

Theorem 17. *Unless* NP $\subseteq$ DTIME($n^{\log \log n}$), *the* **CONNECTED DOMINATION** *problem, on a graph with n vertices cannot be approximated to better than a* $\ln n$ *factor.*

We now present the details of the approximation preserving reduction from **CONNECTED DOMINATION** to the (Uniform service cost, Total cost, Tree)-bicriteria problem. Corresponding to an instance $G = (V, E)$ of **CONNECTED DOMINATION**, we create a complete edge weighted graph $G'(V', E')$ as follows: we set $V' = V$. We set the c-cost of each edge in E' to be the length of the shortest path in G, and the uniform service budget S to be 1.

We claim that there exists a connected dominating set of size at most k in G if and only if there exists a solution to the (Uniform service cost, Total cost, Tree)-bicriteria problem with cost at most $(k-1)$. For the only if part, note that any spanning tree for connected dominating set of size k is a tree of cost $(k-1)$ that services all the nodes. Conversely, suppose we have a tree of cost $(k-1)$ servicing all the nodes in G'. Then, the tree has no more than k nodes, and all other nodes are at a distance of 1 from some node in the tree. So, the vertices in the tree form a connected dominating set for G. This completes the proof.

4 Diameter and Bottleneck

We first consider the (Non-uniform service cost, Bottleneck, Tree)-bicriteria problem – given a graph with two cost functions on the edges, and a service budget for each node, find a tree such that the service budget (under one cost function) for each node is satisfied and the tree has minimum bottleneck cost under the other cost function (i.e., the cost of the maximum edge in the tree is minimum). This problem can be solved by first sorting the edges in increasing order of the d-costs and adding the edges in that order until one of the connected components in the resulting subgraph satisfies the service constraints for all the nodes. The details are straightforward and so are omitted.

We now consider the (Non-uniform service cost, Diameter, Tree)-bicriteria problem. Using the ideas in [CG82, RS+94], we can show that the the service-constrained minimum diameter tree problem can be solved in polynomial time. In this problem, we are given a graph $G(V, E)$ and a service radius S_{v_i} for each vertex v_i. We wish to find a tree with minimum diameter (under the d-costs) such that every vertex v_i is within distance S_{v_i} (under the c-cost) from some node in the tree.

We only sketch the main idea of the algorithm below. The algorithm uses the roof graph construction in [RS+94]. Consider the case when the d-costs are integral and polynomially bounded in the size of the graph. Consider OPT – a minimum-diameter service-constrained tree. Let OPT have diameter D. Let x and y be the endpoints of a longest path (under d-cost) in the tree. The weight of this path, D, is the diameter of the tree. Consider the midpoint of this path between x and y. It either falls at a vertex or in an edge in which case we can subdivide the edge by adding a new vertex. First we guess the value of D (there are only a polynomial number of guesses). All the potential midpoints lie in half-integral points along edges of which there are only a polynomial number. From each candidate point we consider the set of nodes within distance $D/2$ and check whether they service all the vertices in the graph. We choose the the least such distance and the correspondingly suitable point and output the breadth-first tree rooted at this point appropriately truncated.

When the edge weights are arbitrary, the number of candidate midpoints are too many to check in this fashion. However, we can use a graphical representation (called the roof curve in [RS+94]) of the distance of any node from any point along a given edge to bound the search for candidate points. Thus we get the required result in the diameter case.

5 Concluding Remarks

In this paper we focused on the problem of service-constrained network design problems. We formulated a number of these problems and presented general approximation techniques along with nearly-tight hardness results. One natural open problem is to improve our approximation and the hardness results. Another extension that has many potential applications is the node-weighted version of the problems we consider.

References

[AF+94] E. M. Arkin, S. P. Fekete, J. S. B. Mitchell and C. D. Piatko, "Optimal Covering Tour Problems," *Proceedings of the 5th International Symposium on Algorithms and Computation* (1994).

[AH91] E. M. Arkin and R. Hassin, "Approximation algorithms for the geometric covering salesman problem," Technical Report #968, School of OR&IE, Cornell University, July 1991. (To appear in *Discrete Applied Mathematics*.

[AK+95] A. Agrawal, P. Klein and R. Ravi, "When trees collide: an approximation problem for the generalized Steiner problem on networks," SIAM Journal on Computing, vol. 24, pp. 440-456 (1995).

[BR+96] A. Blum, R. Ravi and S. Vempala, "A constant-factor approximation algorithm for the *k*-MST problem," To appear in the *Proceedings of the 28th Annual ACM Symposium on the Theory of Computation* (1996).

[CG82] P. M. Camerini, and G. Galbiati, "The bounded path problem," *SIAM Journal of Algebraic and Discrete Methods*, vol. 3, no. 4, pp. 474-484 (1982).

[CL+90] T. H. Cormen, C. E. Leiserson and R. Rivest, *Introduction to Algorithms*, MIT Press, Boston (1990).

[CS89] J. T. Current and D. A. Schilling, "The covering salesman problem," *Transportation Science*, vol. 23, pp 208-213 (1989).

[Fe95] U. Feige, "A threshold of ln *n* for approximating set cover," To appear in the *Proceedings of the 28th Annual ACM Symposium on the Theory of Computation* (1996).

[GJ79] M. R. Garey and D. S. Johnson, *Computers and Intractability: A guide to the theory of NP-completeness*, W. H. Freeman, San Francisco (1979).

[Gr92] P. E. Green, *Fiber-Optic Networks*, Prentice Hall (1992).

[KR+96] S. R. Kumar, A. Russell and R. Sundaram, "Faster algorithms for optical switch configuration," submitted to *IEEE Global Telecommunications Conference* (1996).

[MR+95] M. V. Marathe, R. Ravi, R. Sundaram, S. S. Ravi, D. J. Rosenkrantz and H. B. Hunt III, "Bicriteria network design problems," *Proceedings of the International Colloquium on Automata, Languages and Programming*, LNCS 944, pp. 487-498 (1995).

[Ra93] R. Ramaswami, "Multi-wavelength lightwave networks for computer communication," *IEEE Communications Magazine*, vol. 31, no. 2, pp. 78-88 (Feb. 1993).

[RS+94] R. Ravi, R. Sundaram, M. V. Marathe, D. J. Rosenkrantz, and S. S. Ravi, "Spanning trees short or small," *Proceedings of the 5th Annual ACM-SIAM Symposium on Discrete Algorithms,* pp. 546-555 (1994).

[WM91] O. Wolfson and A. Milo, "The multicast policy and its relationship to replicated data placement," *ACM Transactions on Database Systems*, vol. 16, pp 181-205 (1991).

Approximate Hypergraph Coloring

Pierre Kelsen   Sanjeev Mahajan   Hariharan Ramesh

Max-Planck-Institut für Informatik
Im Stadtwald
Saarbrücken, Germany[1]

Abstract. A coloring of a hypergraph is a mapping of vertices to colors such that no hyperedge is monochromatic. We are interested in the problem of coloring 2-colorable hypergraphs. For the special case of graphs (hypergraphs of dimension 2) this can easily be done in linear time. The problem for general hypergraphs is much more difficult since a result of Lovasz implies that the problem is NP-hard even if all hyperedges have size three.

In this paper we develop approximation algorithms for this problem. Our first result is an algorithm that colors any 2-colorable hypergraph on n vertices and dimension d with $O(n^{1-1/d} \log^{1-1/d} n)$ colors. This is the first algorithm that achieves a sublinear number of colors in polynomial time. This algorithm is based on a new technique for reducing degrees in a hypergraph that should be of independent interest. For the special case of hypergraphs of dimension three we improve on the previous result by obtaining an algorithm that uses only $O(n^{2/9} \log^{\frac{17}{8}} n)$ colors. This result makes essential use of semidefinite programming. This last result is rather surprising because we show that semidefinite programming will fail for any larger dimension.

1. Introduction. A hypergraph $H = (V, E)$ consists of a finite set V of *vertices (or nodes)* (whose number is denoted by n) and a collection E of nonempty subsets of V called *edges*. The *dimension* of H is the maximum size of an edge in E. Thus, a graph is a hypergraph of dimension 2. A k-coloring of a hypergraph is a mapping $\phi : V \to \{1, \ldots, k\}$ such that no edge of H has all vertices of the same color. A hypergraph is k-colorable if it admits a k-coloring.

We consider the problem of coloring hypergraphs that are known to be 2-colorable. Although we can 2-color a 2-colorable (or bipartite) graph in linear time using a straightforward depth-first search algorithm, the problem is NP-hard for hypergraphs even if all edges have size at most 3. (This problem is a special case of *Set Splitting* and was shown to be NP-hard by Lovasz ([9]; see also [5])).

In this paper we give the first polynomial time algorithm for coloring 2-colorable hypergraphs. Our algorithm runs in polynomial time and uses $O(n^{1-1/d} \log^{1-1/d} n)$ colors. This result is obtained by combining a simple randomized algorithm with a new technique for reducing the degrees in a hypergraph. The latter technique is inspired by a similar method that was developed by Wigderson ([11]) for coloring 3-colorable graphs. graphs.

---

[1] e-mail: kelsen@mpi-sb.mpg.de, mahajan@mpi-sb.mpg.de, ramesh@csa.iisc.ernet.in

For the special case of hypergraphs of dimension 3 we reduce the number of colors to $O(n^{2/9} \log^{\frac{17}{8}} n)$. We achieve this bound by using a powerful new technique based on semidefinite programming and pioneered by Goemans and Williamson ([6]). The technique involves relaxing an integer program (whose solution is NP-hard) into a semidefinite program (for which an approximate solution can be found in polynomial time). Using an approach based on semidefinite programming we get an algorithm that uses only $O(n^{2/9} \log^{\frac{17}{8}} n)$ colors. The degree reduction technique is also used for this result.

The semidefinite programming technique was first successfully used by Goemans and Williamson to obtain a solution to the Max-Cut problem with approximation ratio .878. The best previous ratio was $1/2$ obtained by a straightforward random cut algorithm. Using the same technique Goemans and Williamson also derived improved approximations for the MAX-2SAT problem.

Karger, Motwani and Sudan ([8]) used semidefinite programming to obtain better coloring algorithms for 3-colorable graphs. In an elegant paper they achieve a $O(n^{1/4} \log n)$ color bound for 3-colorable graph (in random polynomial time). The previous best bound was $O(n^{2/5})$ colors achieved by a deterministic polynomial time algorithm of Blum ([3]).

Frieze and Jerrum ([4]) gave a .65 approximation algorithm for MaxBisection based on semidefinite programming, improved form the .5 ratio achieved by the random bisection algorithm. Finally, Alon and Kahale ([2]) use semidefinite programming to achieve better approximations to the maximum independent set problem.

In this paper we apply the technique for the first time to a problem on hypergraphs. This application is rather surprising because we show that the technique will fail for any dimension higher than 3.

The paper is organized as follows: in the next section we present a new technique for reducing the maximum degree of a hypergraph. We present this result first because it will be used throughout the rest of the paper. In section 3 we describe an algorithm that colors 2-colorable hypergraphs with $o(n)$ colors in polynomial time. Only elementary techniques are used for this result: the key ingredients are the degree reduction technique from section 2 and a simple randomized algorithm. In sections 4 and 5 we show how semidefinite programming can be used in conjunction with the degree reduction technique to get better colorings for 2-colorable hypergraphs of dimension 3. In the concluding section 6 we argue that this algebraic technique cannot be extended to hypergraphs of higher dimensions and pose an open problem regarding the power of the semidefinite programming based approach for dimension 3 hypergraphs.

2. Degree Reduction. Wigderson ([11]) showed that by coloring some subset of vertices in a 3-colorable graph with $O(\sqrt{n})$ colors, the subgraph induced by the uncolored vertices can be made to have maximum degree $O(\sqrt{n})$. In this section we shall show a similar type of result for hypergraphs of arbitrary dimension. It may be viewed as an extension of Wigderson's technique to hypergraphs. Together with the results of the following sections it will yield polynomial time algorithms that color 2-colorable hypergraph with a sublinear number of colors.

Fix a 2-colorable hypergraph $H = (V, E)$ with n vertices. For a subset S of vertices let $N_1(S) = \{w \in V : S \cup \{w\} \in E\}$ and $d_1(S) = |N_1(S)|$. Fix an integer value $t = t(n) > 0$. Consider the following procedure:

Algorithm Reduce.
for all $S \subseteq V$ with $d_1(S) > t$:

(1) if $N_1(S)$ is an independent set (i.e., it does not completely contain an edge of E), then color the vertices of $N_1(S)$ with a new color; remove the vertices from H and all edges that contain at least one of these vertices.

(2) if $N_1(S)$ is not an independent set (i.e., it contains some edge of E), then replace all edges of H containing S with the hyperedge S.

We note that this algorithm can be made to run in polynomial time since we only have to look at those subsets S obtained by removing a single vertex from an edge (total number at most n times the number of hyperedges).

Lemma 1 *After running algorithm Reduce on hypergraph H, we obtain a hypergraph H' with the following properties: (1) in H' each subset S of vertices satisfies $d_1(S) \leq t$; (2) H' is 2-colorable; (3) any k-coloring of H' yields a $k + n/t$-coloring of H (in polynomial time).*

Proof. Property 1 is immediate from the algorithm. To verify property 2, note that step (1) of Reduce preserves 2-colorability. Now assume that the hypergraph just before an application of step (2) is 2-colorable. We observe that the fact that $N_1(S)$ is not independent implies that some two vertices in $N_1(S)$ have different colors under any 2-coloring. Thus, the subset S cannot be monochromatic under any two-coloring. Hence, replacing all edges containing S by the subset S will preserve 2-colorability. Finally, for property 3 we note that the total number of colors used by Reduce is at most n/t since each color takes care of at least t vertices. Now suppose that we color the remaining hypergraph H' with k new colors. Assign to all vertices in H that also belong to H' the new color thus chosen while all vertices not in H' get the color that they are given by Reduce (different from the k new colors). This coloring is a legal coloring of the vertices in H with at most $k + n/t$ colors. *QED* The maximum degree of a hypergraph, usually denoted by Δ, is the maximum number of edges containing the same vertex.

Theorem 1 *Suppose that we have a polynomial time algorithm that colors any 2-colorable hypergraph H of dimension d with maximum degree Δ with Δ^α colors, then we also have a polynomial time algorithm for coloring any such hypergraph on n vertices with $n^{\frac{(d-1)\alpha}{1+\alpha}}$ colors.*

Proof. Applying algorithm Reduce to H we obtain H' with maximum degree at most $n^{d-2}t$ (a more precise bound is $\binom{n-1}{d-2} \cdot t$). Thus, we can color H' with at most $(n^{d-2}t)^\alpha$ colors. The total number of colors used is then (by lemma 1) $n/t + (n^{d-2}t)^\alpha$. With $t(n) = n^{\frac{1-\alpha(d-2)}{1+\alpha}}$, we obtain the asymptotically minimum number of colors, namely $n^{\frac{(d-1)\alpha}{1+\alpha}}$) colors. *QED*

3. A Simple Randomized Algorithm. Let $H = (V, E)$ be a hypergraph of dimension $d \geq 3$ that is 2-colorable. Let Δ_k denote the maximum number of edges in H of size k that contain the same vertex and let $\Delta'_k = \Delta_k^{\frac{1}{k-1}}$. Finally, let $\Delta' = max\{\Delta'_k : 2 \leq k \leq d\}$. The following simple randomized algorithm computes an approximate coloring of H.

Algorithm Rancolor.

(1) While H is non-empty do:
  (1.1) Each vertex chooses uniformly at random a color from the same set of size $\lceil 4\Delta' \rceil$.
  (1.2) A vertex is *good* if it is not contained in any monochromatic edge. Remove all good vertices as well as the edges containing them from H. Do not reuse these colors in later rounds (i.e., remove them from the ground set).

Algorithm Rancolor does indeed produce a valid coloring of H since among all the good vertices eliminated in one round there is no monochromatic edge and each color is used in at most one round.

Theorem 2 *The expected total number of colors used is* $O(\Delta' \log n)$.

Proof. Fix a round of algorithm Rancolor. The probability that an edge of size k is monochromatic is at most $\frac{1}{4^{k-1}} \frac{1}{\Delta^{'k-1}} \leq \frac{1}{4^{k-1}} (1/\Delta'_k)^{k-1} = \frac{1}{4^{k-1}\Delta_k}$. Thus, a vertex is good with probability at least $1/2$. The expected number of good vertices removed in one round is thus at least $n/2$. We conclude that the expected total number of rounds is at most $O(\log n)$. This implies the claim of the theorem. QED We note that the claim about the expected number of colors can be transformed into a high probability claim using standard techniques (e.g., probabilistic recurrence relations; see final version).

This bound by itself is not useful since Δ' can be as large as $\Theta(n)$ making the number of colors used by Rancolor larger than n. Together with the degree reduction technique from the last section we get, however, an interesting result:

Theorem 3 *A 2-colorable hypergraph of dimension d can be colored in polynomial time with* $O(n^{1-1/d}(\log n)^{1-1/d})$ *colors.*

Proof. Applying lemma 1 we see that after running algorithm Reduce we have $\Delta_k \leq n^{k-2}t(n)$ for all k (a more precise bound would be $\binom{n-1}{k-2}t(n)$) and hence

$$\Delta' \leq max\{(n^{k-2}t(n))^{\frac{1}{k-1}} : 2 \leq k \leq d\}.$$

Fix k such that $(n^{k-2}t(n))^{\frac{1}{k-1}}$ is maximum (for $2 \leq k \leq d$). Combining this bound with the previous theorem (and applying lemma 1 once more) we see that we can color the hypergraph with $\log n(n^{k-2}t(n))^{\frac{1}{k-1}} + n/t$ colors. For $t = n^{1-1/k}/(\log n)^{1-1/k}$ we obtain the (asymptotically) minimum number of colors, namely $n^{1-1/k} \cdot (\log n)^{1-1/k}$. QED

4. Hypergraph Coloring via Semidefinite Programming. In this section we describe a better coloring algorithm for the special case where each edge of H has size at most 3. We use semidefinite programming in conjunction with our degree reduction technique to achieve this result. We interweave our exposition with a description of the semidefinite programming paradigm.

Let $H = (V, E)$ be a 2-colorable hypergraph of dimension 3. W.l.o.g., we may assume that all edges of H have size exactly three. (This assumption is not essential but simplifies the exposition.) Indeed, if there are edges of size two we can proceed as follows: in a first phase 2-color H, taking only the edges of size 2 into account. In a second phase color H as described in this section, only considering edges of size 3. Now assign to each vertex as color the pair of colors it receives in these two phases. This is clearly a legal coloring and the total number of colors is at most twice that used in the second phase.

Let ϕ denote a 2-coloring of H. For convenience we shall assume that the range of ϕ is $\{-1, 1\}$. We can express the fact that ϕ is a 2-coloring by the following set of equalities: for every edge $e = (x_1, x_2, x_3)$ we have

$$\phi(x_1)\phi(x_2) + \phi(x_2)\phi(x_3) + \phi(x_1)\phi(x_3) = -1. \tag{1}$$

Note that the validity of this equation follows from the fact that in any edge (x_1, x_2, x_3), the coloring ϕ maps exactly two x_i to one value (e.g., -1) and the remaining vertex to the other value (e.g., +1).

Write the vertex set of H as $V = \{u_1, \ldots, u_n\}$. Consider the following semidefinite optimization problem:

minimize α (*)
where $n \times n$-matrix (a_{ij}) is positive semidefinite $(1 \leq i, j \leq n)$
subject to
$$a_{ij} + a_{jk} + a_{ik} \leq \alpha \text{ if } (u_i, u_j, u_k) \in E$$
$$a_{ij} = a_{ji}$$
$$a_{ii} = 1.$$

Lemma 2 *The semidefinite optimization problem (*) above has a solution $\alpha \leq -1$.*

Proof. Recall that ϕ denotes a 2-coloring of H (with color set $\{-1, 1\}$). Fix two unit vectors u and v in R^n with[2] $u \cdot v = -1$, e.g., $u = (-1, 0, \ldots, 0)$ and $v = (1, 0, \ldots, 0)$. Define vectors $z_1, \ldots, z_n$ by $z_i = u$ if $\phi(u_i) = -1$ and $z_i = v$ if $\phi(u_i) = +1$. Since $u \cdot v = -1$, we have $z_i \cdot z_j + z_j \cdot z_k + z_i \cdot z_k = -1$ if $(u_i, u_j, u_k) \in E$. We also trivially have $z_i \cdot z_j = z_j \cdot z_i$ because of symmetry of the dot product. Finally $z_i \cdot z_i = 1$ because both u and v are unit vectors.

Define $a_{ij} = z_i \cdot z_j$ for $1 \leq i, j \leq n$. The matrix $A = (a_{ij})$ is symmetric positive definite since it is of the form $A = BB^T$. The claim of the lemma follows. QED

We can use the ellipsoid method or other interior-point methods ([7],[1]) to find a solution where $\alpha \leq -1 + \delta$ in time polynomial in n and $\log(1/\delta)$.

---

[2] We use $u \cdot v$ to denote the dot product of the two vectors u and v.

Lemma 2 tells us that we can go from the 2-coloring of H to a good solution to the semidefinite optimization problem (*). Conversely, we shall now show how to get a good coloring from a good solution to the semidefinite optimization problem. The method we describe in this section is based on separating the vectors z_i using random hyperplanes. A more sophisticated technique yielding stronger results will be developed in the next section. Both techniques were originally used in [8] in the context of graph coloring. The present paper presents the first application of these techniques to hypergraphs.

For the following discussion we fix a solution to (*) with $\alpha = -1+\delta$. Using the notation from the proof of lemma 2 we denote the corresponding (unit) vectors by $z_1, \ldots, z_n$. Thus we have

$$z_i \cdot z_j + z_j \cdot z_k + z_i \cdot z_k \leq -1 + \delta \text{ if } (u_i, u_j, u_k) \in E. \qquad (2)$$

We use the term *random hyperplane* to denote a hyperplane that is normal to a unit vector r which is uniformly distributed on the unit sphere. We need the following technical lemma.

Lemma 3 *For three vectors x_1, x_2 and x_3, the probability that they do not all lie on the same side of a random hyperplane (or equivalently, $sgn(x_1 \cdot r), sgn(x_2 \cdot r)$ and $sgn(x_3 \cdot r)$ are not all equal) is*

$$\frac{1}{2\pi}(\alpha + \beta + \gamma)$$

where $\alpha = arccos(x_1 \cdot x_2)$, $\beta = arccos(x_2 \cdot x_3)$ and $\gamma = arccos(x_1 \cdot x_3)$. Thus, if $x_1 \cdot x_2 + x_2 \cdot x_3 + x_1 \cdot x_3 \leq -1+\delta$, then this probability is at least $\frac{3}{2\pi}arccos(\frac{-1+\delta}{3})$.

Proof. The first claim of the lemma is the same as lemma 2.2 in [6]. For the second part it suffices to show that

$$\frac{1}{2\pi}(\alpha + \beta + \gamma) \geq \frac{3}{2\pi}arccos(\frac{-1+\delta}{3})$$

Elementary differential calculus shows that the expression on the left is minimized for $\alpha = \beta = \gamma$. Since $x_1 \cdot x_2 + x_2 \cdot x_3 + x_1 \cdot x_3 = -1+\delta$ we get for $\alpha = \beta = \gamma$ that $cos(\alpha)(= x_1 \cdot x_2) = \frac{-1+\delta}{3}$ or $\alpha = arccos(\frac{-1+\delta}{3})$. The claim follows. QED

Let us fix a small delta such that $\frac{-1+\delta}{3} < -.33$. Let p denote the probability that the vectors corresponding to an edge of H do not lie on the same side of a hyperplane. With lemma 3 we get $p > \frac{3}{2\pi}arccos(-0.33) > 0.91$.

Let us choose k random hyperplanes $h_1, \ldots, h_k$ with normal vectors $r_1, \ldots, r_k$ independently. Map each vertex u_i with corresponding vector z_i to the vector $y_i = (sgn(z_i \cdot r_1), sgn(z_i \cdot r_2), \ldots, sgn(z_i \cdot r_k))$.

Fix an edge e in E. Let us say that this edge is *bad* (for the given hypergraph) if the vertices in e are mapped to the same vector under the mapping just described. The probability that an edge is bad is at most $(1-p)^k < .09^k$ (since the hypergraphs are chosen independently at random).

We construct a coloring of H as follows: let $V_b \subseteq V$ denote the vertices in H that are contained in bad edges. Assign to all vertices in $V - V_b$ as colors the corresponding y vectors. Recursively color the hypergraph $H' = (V_b, E')$, where E' is the set of edges in E all of whose vertices belong to V_b, with a set of new colors. (To make sure no colors are reused, we may think of the color of a vertex as a pair (y, i) where i is the recursion depth at which a vertex was colored successfully and y is the vector that was assigned to it at that time.)

Let the random variable Z denote the number of edges that are bad w.r.t. k random hyperplanes. Note that $E[Z] < 0.09^k m$ where m denotes the number of edges in H. Let Δ denote the maximum degree[3] of H. Thus $m \leq n\Delta/3$ and $E[Z] < 0.09^k n\Delta/3$. By choosing $0.09^k < \frac{3n}{4n\Delta} = \frac{3}{4\Delta}$ or $k > .416 \ln \Delta$ we get $E[Z] < n/4$ and hence $E[|V_b|] < 3n/4$. Thus for these values of k a constant fraction of the vertices of H are colored in the current stage. The recursion will only be performed for $O(\log n)$ levels and the total number of colors is $O(2^{.416 \ln \Delta} \log n) = O(\Delta^{.289} \log n)$.

We thus have the following result:

Theorem 4 *A 2-colorable hypergraph of dimension 3 can be colored in polynomial time with $O(\Delta^{.289} \log n)$ colors.*

By applying the degree reduction technique (theorem 1) to theorem 4 we obtain the first improvement on the result from theorem 3 (which yields $n^{.66}$ for dimension 3).

Theorem 5 *There is a polynomial time algorithm that colors any 2-colorable hypergraph of dimension 3 with fewer than $n^{.45}$ colors.*

Although the algorithm is randomized, we can use the recently developed technique of Mahajan and Ramesh ([10]) to derandomize this algorithm into a deterministic polynomial time algorithm. The details will be given in the final version of this paper.

In the next section we will use a more sophisticated technique to achieve an even better bound, namely $O(n^{2/9})$.

5. The Center Method. In this method, we take t independent random vectors, called *centers* (t will turn out to be $O(\Delta^{\frac{1}{8}} \log^{9/8} n)$) and we assign to each vertex vector the center which has the largest projection on the vertex vector as its color. This method reduces the number of bad edges to $n/6$, and hence the number of bad vertices to $n/2$. Hence by iterating this method $\log n$ times, we can properly color a 2-colorable hypergraph with $O(\Delta^{\frac{1}{8}} \log^{\frac{17}{8}} n)$ colors. Ideally we would like each random center to be of unit length, but as Karger, Motwani and Sudan [8] argue, this leads to technical difficulties in the analysis. Instead we choose each coordinate of each center independently normally distributed with mean 0 and variance 1. Then each center is spherically symmetric. However the norm of such a center is now a random variable (although as the number

---

[3] The maximum degree in a hypergraph is the maximum number of edges containing any single vertex.

of dimensions tends to infinity, this norm becomes almost constant). The main contribution of this section is the analysis which requires more sophistication than the graph case.

In this case, the probability that a hyperedge (i, j, k) is bad is the probability that the same center gets assigned to all three of v_i, v_j, v_k. Or if, we call the centers $c_1, ...c_t$, then the probability that an edge is bad is t times $P(t)$ (where $P(t)$ is the probability that c_1 gets assigned to all three of v_i, v_j, v_k). Our core theorem states that $P(t)$ is $O(\frac{\log^9 t}{t^9})$. Hence the probability that an edge is bad is $O(\frac{\log^9 t}{t^8})$.

Theorem 6 $P(t)$ *is* $O(\frac{\log^9 t}{t^9})$

Before we give the proof of the core theorem, we derive the final result.

Corollary 1 *By using the center method* $O(\log n)$ *times each time reducing the number of bad vertices by half, we can properly color a 2-colorable hypergraph in* $O(\Delta^{\frac{1}{6}} \log^{\frac{17}{8}} n)$ *colors.*

Proof of the Corollary. We want the number of bad edges to be less than $n/6$. Let p denote the probability that an edge is bad. It follows from the core theorem that $p = O(\frac{\log^9 t}{t^8})$. The expected number of bad edges is at most $mp \le n\Delta p/3$. This number is less than $n/6$ provided that $p < \frac{1}{2\Delta}$. Routine algebra shows that this is satisfied by $t = \log^{9/8} n\Delta^{1/8}$. In each stage we use this many colors for a total of $O(\log n)$ stages, yielding the desired result. QED

Theorem 7 *We can color a 2-colorable hypergraph with* $O(n^{2/9} \log^{\frac{17}{8}} n)$ *colors in polynomial time.*

Proof. Straightforward application of theorem 1 in conjunction with the previous corollary. QED

Proof of the Core Theorem. We have $P(t) = Pr(c_1 \cdot v_i > \max\{c_2 \cdot v_i, ..., c_t \cdot v_i\} \wedge c_1 \cdot v_j > \max\{c_2 \cdot v_j, ..., c_t \cdot v_j\} \wedge c_1 \cdot v_k > \max\{c_2 \cdot v_k, ..., c_t \cdot v_k\})$.

Now as all of c_i's are spherically symmetric, we can rotate the coordinate system so that all but the first 3 coordinates of v_i, v_j and v_k are 0, or so that essentially we are in a 3-dimensional coordinate system. So we can assume that each of the c_i's is a 3-dimensional vector with each coordinate distributed independently with distribution $N(0,1)$. Now $c \cdot v$ (where c is a center and v a vertex vector) is $|c| \cos(< c, v >)$ (where $< c, v >$ is angle between c and v).

Also note that as $v_i \cdot v_j + v_j \cdot v_k + v_k \cdot v_i = -1$ or that $|v_i + v_j + v_k| = 1$, this implies that for any unit vector l, one of $l \cdot v_i, l \cdot v_j$ and $l \cdot v_k$ is at most $1/3$. This is because $l \cdot (v_i + v_j + v_k)$ is at most 1. So for vector c_1, the angle between either c_1 and v_i, or c_1 and v_j or c_1 and v_k is at least $\arccos(1/3)$. Let us say that this happens for v_i. Then

$$P(t) \le Pr(c_1 \cdot v_i > \max\{c_2 \cdot v_i, ..., c_t \cdot v_i\})$$

or

$$P(t) \leq Pr(|c_1|/3 > \max\{|c_2|\cos(< c_2, v_i >), ..., |c_t|\cos(< c_t, v_i >)\}$$

or

$$P(t) \leq Pr(|c_1|^2/9 > \max\|c_2|^2 \cos^2(< c_2, v_i >), ..., |c_t|^2 \cos^2(< c_t, v_i >)\}$$

Now let the conditional probability that given that there are r centers which have angle at most ϵ with v_i, the event inside the above probability ($|c_1|^2/9 > ...$) holds, be denoted by $P(t|r)$.

For a fixed vector v, the probability that a random vector is within an ϵ angle from it is $\epsilon^2/4$ for small enough ϵ. This can be seen by looking at the volume of the cone(of the unit sphere) of angle ϵ centered around v. Therefore the probability that there are r centers which have an angle at most ϵ (for small enough ϵ) with v_i is $\binom{t}{r}(\frac{\epsilon^2}{4})^r (1 - \frac{\epsilon^2}{4})^{t-r}$.

Hence $P(t) = \sum_{r=0}^{t} P(t|r)\binom{t}{r}(\frac{\epsilon^2}{4})^r (1 - \frac{\epsilon^2}{4})^{t-r}$.

We now bound $P(t|r)$. W.l.o.g. we assume that the r centers that have an angle of at most ϵ with v_i in the above conditional probability calculation are $c_2, ..., c_{r+1}$. Then

$$P(t|r) \leq Pr(|c_1|^2/9 > \max\{|c_2|^2 \cos^2(\epsilon), ..., |c_{r+1}|^2 \cos^2(\epsilon)\})$$

So we need to calculate $Pr(|c_1|^2 > q \max\{|c_2|^2, ..., |c_{r+1}|^2\})$ for $q = 9\cos^2(\epsilon)$.

Each of $|c_i|^2$ is a sum of squares of 3 independent normal random variables with mean 0 and variance 1. So we need to calculate $Pr(X_1 > q \max\{X_2, ..., X_{r+1}\})$ where each X_i is independently the sum of squares of 3 normals with mean 0 and variance 1. It is known that the probability density function $f(t)$ of each X_i is $c\sqrt{(t)}e^{-t/2}$ for some normalization constant c. The next theorem proves an appropriate upper bound on the above probability.

Theorem 8 *If $X_1..., X_{r+1}$ are independent with density function $f(t)$, then $Pr(X_1 > q \max\{X_2, ..., X_{r+1})$ is $O(\frac{1}{\binom{q+r}{r}})$, for $q \geq 1$.*

Proof. We have $Pr(X_1 > q \max\{X_2, ..., X_{r+1}\}) = c \int_0^\infty (Pr(X < t/q))^r \sqrt{t}e^{-t^2/2}dt$ where X is a random variable with density function $f(t)$.

So $Pr(X < x) = 1 - g(x)e^{\frac{-x}{2}}$ where $g(x) \geq 1$ for all x. Hence

$$Pr(X_1 > q \max\{X_2, ..., X_{r+1}\}) \leq c \int_0^\infty (1 - g(t/q)e^{\frac{-t}{2q}})^r \sqrt{t}e^{-t/2}dt.$$

As $q \geq 1$ and $g(t/q) \geq 1$ for all t, the term on the right-hand side of the above inequality is at most

$$c \int_0^\infty (1 - g(t/q)e^{\frac{-t}{2q}})^r (g(t/q))^{q-1}\sqrt{(t)}e^{-t/2}dt$$

We now make a change of variables. Let $g(t/q)e^{\frac{-t}{2q}} = z$ Then we have

$$Pr(X_1 > q\max\{X_2, ..., X_{r+1}\}) \le c'\int_0^1 (1-z)^r z^{q-1}dz$$

(where c' is some constant) because the derivative wrt t of $g(t/q)e^{\frac{-t}{2q}}$ is some constant times $\sqrt{(t)}e^{\frac{-t}{2q}}$. The term on the right-hand side of the above inequality is $\frac{c'}{q}/\binom{q+r}{r}$. Hence the required probability is $O(\frac{1}{\binom{q+r}{r}})$.

Hence $P(t|r)$ is bounded by $O(\frac{1}{\binom{q+r}{r}})$ for $q = 9\cos^2\epsilon$.

Therefore

$$P(t) \le d\sum_{r=0}^t \binom{t}{r}(\frac{\epsilon^2}{4})^r(1 - \frac{\epsilon^2}{4})^{t-r}\frac{1}{\binom{q+r}{r}}$$

for some constant d and $q = 9\cos^2\epsilon$. Manipulating algebraically the rhs, we get that $P(t)$ is $O(\epsilon^{2(\lceil q\rceil - q)}(\epsilon^2 t)^{-q})$ for $q = 9\cos^2\epsilon$. Now we set $\epsilon^2 = 1/\log t$. Then $\lceil q\rceil - q = 9 - 9\cos^2(\epsilon)$ which is $O(\epsilon^2)$. After doing some algebra, we see that $P(t) = O(\log^9 t/t^9)$. QED

6. Conclusions. In this final section we address the following two questions: can the semidefinite approach be extended to hypergraphs of higher dimension? What about dimension 3: can the bound on the number of colors be improved significantly? We also discuss a probabilistic inequality related to the center method (section 5).

We have fairly strong evidence to believe that the answer to the first question is negative. Consider the example of a 2-colorable hypergraph of dimension 4. We can write a semidefinite program very similar to the program (*) of section 4: instead of taking the sum of the dot products of three vectors we take the sum of dot products of four vectors (remember that semidefiniteness implies that each a_{ij} in (*) can be written as a dot product), i.e.,

minimize α (**)

where $n \times n$-matrix (a_{ij}) is positive semidefinite $(1 \le i, j \le n)$

subject to

$$a_{ij} + a_{jk} + a_{kl} + a_{ik} + a_{jl} + a_{il} \le \alpha \text{ if } (u_i, u_j, u_k, u_l) \in E$$
$$a_{ij} = a_{ji}$$
$$a_{ii} = 1.$$

Now consider a complete bipartite hypergraph (with n vertices on both sides) that is a maximal 2-colorable hypergraph with half the vertices of one color and half the other. As n tends to infinity, the semidefinite program is minimized for such a hypergraph at $\alpha = 0$ (intuitively, what is happening is that in a hyperedge you could have three reds and one blue, and that gives the sum of dot products to be 0, if red is +1 and blue -1). Now $\alpha = 0$ is a trivial solution, as we don't even need to solve the program to have all vectors orthogonal, and in fact for every hypergraph, $\alpha = 0$ is a feasible solution.

Let us now turn our attention to the second question. Let us say that a hypergraph H of dimension 3 is vector 2-colorable if there exist n unit vectors

v_i such that for any hyperedge $\{i, j, k\}$, $v_i \cdot v_j + v_j \cdot v_k + v_k \cdot v_i \le -1$. Notice that all vector-2-colorable hypergraphs can be colored by the number of colors given by the center method, not just 2-colorable hypergraphs. We would like to construct a hypergraph that is vector-2-colorable but has a lower bound of N^α on its chromatic number ($\alpha > 0$), where N is the number of vertices in the hypergraph. This then shows the limitation of semidefinite programming in this context.

Construct a hypergraph as follows. The vertices of the hypergraph are all strings of length n over $\{a, b, c\}$. Three vertices s_1, s_2, s_3 define a hyperedge in the hypergraph if the sum of agreements between them is at most $n/3$. We want to show an upper bound of c^n, for some $c < 3$, on the size of its independent set. This will then show a lower bound on the chromatic number of the hypergraph of the kind d^n for some $d > 1$, or in terms of number of vertices $N = 3^n$ of the hypergraph, N^α.

Why is this hypergraph vector-2-colorable? Each string of length n over $\{a, b, c\}$ is considered a vector of dimension $2n$ where a is replaced by the vector $(1, 0)/\sqrt{n}$, b by $(\frac{-1}{2}, \frac{\sqrt{3}}{2})/\sqrt{n}$ and c by $(\frac{-1}{2}, \frac{-\sqrt{3}}{2})/\sqrt{n}$. The $\sqrt{n}$ factor comes in because we wish to normalize each vector corresponding to an n-length string to a unit vector. It is now easily seen that if the sum of agreements between s_1, s_2, s_3 is at most $n/3$, the sum of dot products of the corresponding vectors is at most -1.

We conjecture that this hypergraph has an upper bound of N^α ($\alpha < 1$) on the size of an independent set, yielding a lower bound of N^β ($\beta > 0$) on the chromatic number. We leave this as an open problem:

Conjecture. The maximum number of strings of length n over $\{a, b, c\}$ such that the sum of the agreements among any three strings is greater than $n/3$ is at most c^n for some constant $c < 3$.

One last question that is a byproduct of this research is a purely probabilistic one. In the proof of the core theorem in the Center Method section, we showed an upper bound on the following probability

$$Pr(X > q \max\{X_1, ..., X_r\})$$

where $q \ge 1$ and $X, X_1, ..., X_r$ are independent random variables, each a sum of squares of three independent normals. It is "intuitively" clear that this probability should be at most the following probability

$$Pr(Y > q \max\{Y_1, ..., Y_r\})$$

where $Y, Y_1, ..., Y_r$ are independent random variables, each a sum of squares of two independent normals. However we cannot translate this intuition into a proof. Also were this true, we could simply use most of the analysis developed by [8] for the center method. In general, is the following conjecture true?

Conjecture. Let X be a random variable that only takes non-negative values. Let Y be the sum of j independent copies of X and Z be sum of $j + 1$ independent copies of X. Let $Y_1, ..., Y_r$ be independent random variables, each distributed according to Y and $Z_1, ..., Z_r$ be independent random variables, each distributed according to Z. Let $q \geq 1$. Then the following holds

$$Pr(Z \geq q \max\{Z_1, ..., Z_r\}) \leq Pr(Y \geq q \max\{Y_1, ..., Y_r\})$$

Notice that for $q = 1$, both sides of the above expression are $\frac{1}{r+1}$.

Acknowledgments. The authors would like to thank Magnus Halldorsson for helping to formulate the first conjecture in the last section.

References

1. F. Alizadeh, Interior point methods in semidefinite programming with applications to combinatorial optimization, Proc. of the 2nd MPS Conference on Integer Programming and Combinatorial Optimization, Carnegie Mellon University, 1992.
2. N. Alon, N. Kahale, Approximating Maximum Independent Sets, Manuscript, 1995.
3. A. Blum, New Approximation Algorithms for Graph Coloring, JACM, 41, pp. 470-516, 1994.
4. A. Frieze, M.Jerrum, Improved Approximation Algorithms for Max k-Cut and Max Bisection, IPCO, 1995.
5. M.R. Garey AND D.S. Johnson, *Computers and Intractability: a Guide to the Theory of NP-Completeness,* Freeman, San Francisco, CA, 1979.
6. M. Goemans, D. Williamson, 0.878 Approximation Algorithms for Max Cut and Max 2SAT, Proc. of 26th Annual Symposium on the Theory of Computing, pp. 422-431, 1993.
7. M. Grötschel, L. Lovasz, A Schrijver, The ellipsoid method and its consequences in combinatorial optimization, Combinatorica 1, pp. 169-197, 1981.
8. D. Karger, R. Motwani, M. Sudan, Approximate Graph Coloring by Semidefinite Programming, Proc. of the 35th IEEE Symposium on Foundations of Computer Science, pp. 1-10, 1994.
9. L. Lovasz, Colorings and Coverings of Hypergraphs, Proc. 4th Southeastern Conference on Combinatorics, Graph Theory, and Computing, Utilitas Mathematica Publishing, Winnipeg, pp. 3-12.
10. S. Mahajan, H. Ramesh, Derandomizing Semidefinite Programming Based Approximation Algorithms, Proc. of the 36th IEEE Symposium on Foundations of Computer Science, 1995, to appear.
11. A. Wigderson, Improving the Performance Guarantee for Approximate Graph Coloring, JACM 30(4), pp. 729-735, 1983.

Facility Dispersion and Remote Subgraphs

Barun Chandra[1]* and Magnús M. Halldórsson[2]*

[1] Department of Computer Science, Rice University, Houston, Texas
[2] Science Institute, University of Iceland, Reykjavík, Iceland.

Abstract

Dispersion problems involve arranging a set of points as far away from each other as possible. They have numerous applications in the location of facilities and in management decision science. We present several algorithms and hardness results for dispersion problems using different natural measures of remoteness, some of which have been studied previously in the literature and others which we introduce; in particular, we give the first algorithm with a non-trivial performance guarantee for the problem of locating a set of points such that the sum of their distances to their nearest neighbor in the set is maximized.

1 Introduction

As the proud and aggressive owner of the McWoofer burger chain, you are given the opportunity to build p new franchises to be located from any of n available locations. After ensuring that the available slots are all attractive in terms of cost, visibility, etc., what would your criteria be for locating the franchises *relative to each other*?

Locating two identical burger joints next to each other would not increase the number of customers, and thus halve the amount of business that either of them could do if apart. Non-competitiveness is a concern here, which can be alleviated by properly *dispersing* the facilities.

The franchise location example is one of many problems where we seek a subset of points that are, in some sense, as *remote* from each other as possible. Dispersion has found applications in diverse areas: locating undesirable or interfering facilities; aiding decision analysis with multiple objectives; marketing a set of products with different attributes; providing good starting solutions for "grand-tour" TSP heuristics. Dispersion is also of combinatorial interest, as a measure of remote subgraphs.

Which measure of remoteness should be applied? The proper measure is very much a question of the problem under study, and several of the applications we consider give rise to quite different notions of remoteness. In this paper, we present the first provably good approximation algorithms for dispersion problems under several measures of remoteness.

---

*Work of both authors performed in large part at JAIST-Hokuriku, Japan.

Applications. Location theory is a branch of management science/operations research that deals with the optimal location of facilities. Most of that work deals with desirable facilities, where nearness to users or each other is preferable. More recently, some papers have considered the opposite objective of placing the facilities far from each other.

Strategic facilities that are to be protected from simultaneous enemy attacks is one example suggested by Moon and Chaudhry [9]. This could involve oil tanks [9], missile silos, or ammunition dumps [4], which should be kept separated from each other to minimize the damage of a limited attack. Limiting the range and possible spread of fire or accidents at hazardous installations is also helped by proper spacing [8].

Non-competition is another motivation for dispersal, as in the case of the burger chain example. This may apply to other types of franchises such as gasoline stations, or to the location of radio transmitters with the objective of minimizing interference. Dispersal has also been seen to be desirable in order to obtain a more effective and/or fair coverage of a region. In fact, White [12] cites some example of government regulations to that effect, including firehouses and ambulance stations in New York City.

Yet another dispersal issue in facility location involves undesirable interaction between all facilities that grows inversely with distance [4]. This may apply to dormitories at a university, or chairs during an examination.

All of the above applications suggest a metric sensitive to the largely two-dimensional nature of our world. This is not the case, however, for the problems outside the location area.

White [12] considers dispersion problems motivated by *multiple objective analysis* in decision theory. Given a potential set of *actions* for a decision maker, we are to find a fixed-size subset of these that are as dispersed as possible, for further consideration by the decision makers. White lists several studies that have used dispersal as a filter of the possible choices, involving, for example, oil drilling, media selection, and forestry management

Dispersion also has applications in product development. The marketing of new but related products is helped by diversity [2]. From dimensions including price, quality, shape, packaging, etc., a set of products can be produced which are likely to gain greater market coverage if they are easily distinguished rather than all very similar.

Dispersion Formulations. A considerable body of work has appeared on facility dispersion problems in the management science and operations research literature [9, 2, 3, 4, 12, 8]. Most previous work has focused on either easily solvable tree networks, or empirical studies of heuristics. Only recently have some of these heuristics been analyzed analytically.

We suggest a simple formalism which lets us describe different dispersal problems in a uniform way and with a more "standardized" terminology. The input is an integer p and a network $G = (V, V \times V)$ with a distance function d on the edges satisfying the triangular inequality $d(u, v) \leq d(u, z) + d(z, v)$. The output is a set P of p vertices. The objective is a function of the subgraph induced by P, and is given by the sum of a certain set of edges within that subgraph, this edge set being chosen to be the one of minimum weight among all edge subsets satisfying a graph property Π (Π depends on the particular dispersal problem under consideration). In general, for a property Π of graphs, the objective function for Remote-Π is the weight of the minimum-weight subgraph satisfying property Π within the induced subgraph on P. The goal of the algorithm is to pick these p vertices so as to maximize the objective function.

For instance, in the Remote-tree problem, the objective function is a sum of the edge weights of a minimum-weight spanning tree over the vertex set P. The goal is to pick a subset of p vertices so as to maximize the minimum-weight spanning tree on these vertices.

We list some problems under different graph properties; most of these have been studied previously, and some are introduced in this paper.

Remote-edge	$\min_{v,u \in P} d(u,v)$
Remote-clique	$\sum_{v,u \in P} d(u,v)$
Remote-star	$\min_{v \in P} \sum_{u \in P} d(u,v)$
Remote-pseudoforest	$\sum_{v \in P} \min_{u \in P} d(u,v)$
Remote-tree	$wt(MST(P))$
Remote-cycle	$\min_T wt(T)$, where T is a TSP tour on P
Remote-matching	$\min_M wt(M)$, where M is a perfect matching on P

A *pseudo-forest* is the undirected equivalent of a directed graph where each vertex is of out-degree one and each component contains as many edges as vertices.

Observe the adversarial nature of these problems. The "algorithm" produces a vertex set P, and implicitly a graph $G[P]$. The "adversary" produces a set of edges on $G[P]$ satisfying property Π. The value of the solution is the sum of these edges.

Related work. The names used in the literature are quite different and varied. Remote-edge is known as *p-Dispersion* [2, 8] and *Max-Min Facility Dispersion* [10]; Remote-clique as *Maxisum Dispersion* [8] and *Max-Avg Facility Dispersion* [10]; Remote-star as *MaxMinSum dispersion* [4]; Remote-pseudoforest as *p-Defense* [9] and *MaxSumMin dispersion* [4].

For Remote-edge, Tamir [11], White [12, 13] and Ravi, Rosenkrantz and Tayi [10] independently showed that a simple "furthest-point greedy" algorithm is 2-approximate. This greedy algorithm, henceforth called GREEDY, works by successively selecting the next vertex so as to maximize the distance to the set of already selected vertices, till p vertices have been selected. [10] also showed that obtaining an approximation strictly less than 2 was NP-hard.

For Remote-clique, Ravi et al. gave a (different) greedy algorithm that they showed came within a factor of 4, while Hassin, Rubinstein and Tamir [6] have recently given elegant proofs of two 2-approximate algorithms. This problem has also been studied for non-metric graphs under the name Heavy Subgraph Problem by Kortsarz and Peleg [7], and they presented a sequence of algorithms that converge with a performance ratio of $O(n^{3.865})$.

No analytic bounds have been previously given for either **Remote-star** or **Remote-pseudoforest** problems. Moon and Chaudhry [9] suggested the star problem. Erkut and Neuman [4] gave branch-and-bound algorithms that solves all four of these problems.

Remote-tree and **Remote-cycle** were considered by Halldórsson, Iwano, Katoh, and Tokuyama [5], under the names *Remote-MST* and *Remote-TSP*, respectively. They showed that GREEDY approximates both problems within a factor of 4, while obtaining a ratio less than 2 is NP-hard. They proposed **Remote-matching** as an open problem.

All of the problems listed above can be seen to be NP-hard by a reduction from the maximum clique problem. The same reduction also establishes that **Remote-edge** cannot be approximated within a constant smaller than 2 [10]. Further, when the weights are not constrained to be metric, the problem is as hard to approximate as **Max Clique**, which implies that $n^{1/6}$-approximation is NP-hard [1]. Reductions from MaxClique also yield the same hardness for the pseudoforest problem [5]. On the other hand, no hardness results are known for **Remote-clique** and **Remote-star**.

Motivation. In various applications the utility of an individual facility may be directly related to its (locally measured) remoteness from the rest of the facilities. In this case, the measure of the global remoteness is the sum of the utilities of the individual points.

One example would be the average distance measure (or clique problem), in which the utility is the average distance from the other points. Note, however, that this measure is large for very clustered instances, as long as the clusters are far from each other. In many, if not most, cases, a more logical measure of utility would be the *minimum* distance to the remaining point set, i.e. the nearest neighbor distance. This gives rise to the **Remote-pseudoforest** problem.

Another meaning for a subgraph to be "remote" would be that its "nearness" measure would be high. One common nearness measure is that of a *center* : the smallest total distance from all the vertices to a single center vertex. This gives rise to the **Remote-star** problem (or alternatively **Remote 1-Median**).

Overview of paper. We review the much-studied GREEDY algorithm in section 2, and apply it to various remote problems. These involve partitions into independent segments, with the objective being the sum or maximum of the objectives on the independent segments. We also present numerous limitation results on the power of the algorithm.

In section 3 we present $O(\log p)$-approximate algorithms for **Remote-matching** and **Remote-pseudoforest** , and matching lower bounds for these algorithms.

In section 4 we use a recent result of Hassin, Rubinstein and Tamir [6] to give good approximation for **Remote-star**. We end with a summary and open problems.

1.1 Notation

For a vertex set $X \subseteq V$, let $\Pi(X)$ ($\pi(X)$) denote the maximum (minimum) weight set of edges in the induced subgraph $G[X]$ that form a graph satisfying property Π, respectively. In particular, we consider $\mathsf{star}(X)$ (min-weight spanning star), $\mathsf{pf}(X)$ (min-weight pseudoforest), $\mathsf{tree}(X)$ (min-weight spanning tree), and $\mathsf{MAT}(X)$ and $\mathsf{mat}(X)$ (max- and min-weight matching).

For a set of edges E', let $wt(E')$ denote the sum of the weights of the edges of E'. We shall also overload E' to stand for $wt(E')$ when used in expressions.

Let HEU be the vertex set selected by the algorithm in question, and let OPT be any other set of same cardinality, presumably standing for the solution that yields an optimal value. A set of p vertices is called a *p-set*.

The input is assumed to be a complete graph, with the weight of an edge (v, u), or the *distance* between v and u, denoted by $d(v, u)$. For a set of vertices X and a point v, the distance $d(v, X)$ is the shortest distance from v to some point in X, or $\min_{u \in X} d(v, u)$.

2 GREEDY algorithm

In this section we study the ubiquitous GREEDY algorithm, and obtain numerous positive and negative results. GREEDY is simple, efficient, arguably the most natural algorithm for these problems, and has been shown to be provably good for many of these problems. In addition, it is *online* (i.e. independent of p), allowing for the incremental construction of facilities that is essential in practice. As such, it warrants special attention, not only in the form of positive results but negative results as well.

2.1 The GREEDY algorithm and Anti-covers

A set X of points is said to be an *anti-cover* iff each point outside X is closer to X than the smallest distance between pairs of points in X. Namely,

$$d(v, X) \leq d(x, X - \{x\}), \quad \text{for any } v \in V, x \in X.$$

The direct way of producing an anti-cover is via the *GREEDY* algorithm. It first selects an arbitrary vertex and then iteratively selects a vertex of maximum distance from the previously selected points. We let $Y = \{y_1, y_2, \ldots, y_p\}$ denote this set of points found by GREEDY. Let Y_i be the prefix set $\{y_1, y_2, \ldots, y_i\}$, for $1 \leq i \leq p$. Let $r_i = d(y_{i+1}, Y_i)$ denote the distance of the $i + 1$-th point to the previously selected points.

Observe that every prefix Y_i of the greedy solution is an anti-cover. Thus, for each i, $1 \leq i \leq p - 1$:

$$d(v, Y_i) \leq r_i, \quad \text{for each } v \in V, \text{ and} \tag{1}$$

$$d(x, y) \geq r_i, \quad \text{for each } x, y \in Y_{i+1}. \tag{2}$$

Clearly, whenever the anti-cover property is needed, the greedy solution will suffice. However, if the additional properties of the greedy solutions are not needed, it is quite plausible that an alternative, possibly parallel, algorithm can be formulated.

GREEDY has been previously applied with success on the **edge** problem [11, 12, 13], and the **tree, cycle** and **Steiner-tree** problems [5]. It has also been shown to perform badly for a host of problems. We shall add a number of results in the remainder of this section.

2.2   Limitations of GREEDY

This subsection presents lower bounds on the performance of GREEDY on various remoteness problems. First, a general result.

Proposition 2.1 *The performance ratio of GREEDY on any remote problem is at least 2.*

Proof.   Consider an instance with two types of points: x-points of distance 1 apart and y-points of distance 2 apart, with points of different type of distance 1 apart.

GREEDY may start with some x-point, from which all points are of distance 1, and then continue choosing x-points. That is, the induced subgraph selected is complete with unit-weight edges. An optimal solution will contain only y-points, inducing a complete graph with all edge weights 2. Whatever measure used, it will be twice as large in the latter subgraph as the one chosen by GREEDY. ∎

We can generalize a result of [5] that shows that there is no upper bound on the performance ratio of GREEDY on a host of problems. Their proof applied only to graph properties where the graph was not connected but each vertex was of non-zero degree.

We are given a network with a a given partition $(S, V - S)$. Let H be an instance of the given graph property Π. The following definition counts the necessary number of cut edges of any Π-graph H that has s vertices on one side of the cut.

Definition 2.2

$$Cross(\Pi, s) = \min_{\substack{P \subseteq V \\ |S \cap P| = s}} \min_{H \in \Pi} |\{(v, w) \in H \ : \ v \in S \wedge w \in V - S\}|$$

Proposition 2.3 *Let $d_{min} = \min_s Cross(\Pi, s)$ and $d_{max} = \max_s Cross(\Pi, s)$. The performance ratio of GREEDY on* **Remote-Π-structure** *is at least arbitrarily close to d_{max}/d_{min} when $d_{min} > 0$, and unbounded when $d_{min} = 0$ and $d_{max} > 0$.*

Proof.   Let s_{min} (s_{max}) be the value of s that minimizes (maximizes) $Cross(\Pi, s)$. Without loss of generality, $s_{min}, s_{max} \leq p/2$.

Construct an instance, consisting of a block of vertices S with $p - s_{min}$ vertices and a block S' of p vertices. Vertices within S are distance ϵ apart, vertices within S' $\epsilon/2$ apart, and vertices in different partitions 1 apart, where ϵ is arbitrarily small.

GREEDY first chooses all vertices in S followed by s_{min} vertices from S'. The cost of this pointset is the sum of $Cross(\Pi, s_{min}) = d_{min}$ crossing edges of weight 1 along with a number of ϵ weights. On the other hand, the optimal solution chooses s_{max} vertices in S and the rest in S', for a cost of at least d_{max}. ∎

This shows that the performance ratio of GREEDY on the following problems is unbounded: matching, pseudoforest, degree-bounded subgraph. Also, the performance ratio is at least $\Omega(p)$ on clique, and star. We also obtain the the following lower bound for high-degree properties.

Corollary 2.4 *Suppose Π is satisfied only for structures with minimum degree at least k, for some positive integer k. Then, the performance ratio of GREEDY for* Remote-Π *is at least $k/2$.*

Some examples of Π are minimum-degree-k, clique-number-k, and k-edge-connected.

2.3 Multiple trees, tours and Steiner trees

We apply GREEDY to remote problems involving several trees or cycles. The k spanning trees problem is a generalization of the Remote-tree problem, where the adversary partitions the p vertices into k sets so that the sum of the k spanning trees is minimized; the k Steiner trees and k TSP tours problems are similarly defined. We can generalize the analysis of [5].

Proposition 2.5 *Anti-covers attains a ratio of 4 for remote problems of k spanning trees, and a ratio of $\min(5, 1 + 2p/(p - k))$ for k Steiner trees and k TSP tours.*

Proof.

We consider the k spanning tree problem. The analysis for k Steiner trees and k TSP tours is similar and is omitted.

Consider any k-partitioning of the greedy points. Let GR_j be the heuristic value on partition j. We construct a solution for OPT as follows. Divide its points among the partitions according to nearness. Thus, each optimal point is within distance r_p to some greedy point in its partition. We may assume without loss of generality that each partition contains at least one optimal point; to any empty partition we may assign an arbitrary single optimal point which will not contribute to the value of the solution.

The optimal and greedy points combined form a Steiner tree. To obtain the k-MST value, we multiply by the Steiner ratio $2 - 2/q_j$, where q_j is the number of optimal points in partition j, with the assumption that $\forall j\, q_j \geq 1$ (which also implies $\forall j\, q_j \leq p - k$). Thus, $OPT \leq \sum_j (GR_j + q_j \cdot r_p) \cdot (2 - 2/q_j)$
$= \sum_j GR_j(2 - 2/q_j) + r_p(2q_j - 2) \leq GR(2 - 2/p) + 2r_p(p - k)$. Note that the

heuristic solution contains $p - k$ edges, and so $GR \geq (p - k)r_p$. Hence, a ratio of $4 - 2/p$ follows.

∎

It is easy to construct instances to show that these bounds are tight.

3 PREFIX Algorithm

We consider the Remote-pseudoforest and Remote-matching problems, and introduce a new algorithm that approximates these problems within a logarithmic factor. As we have seen, GREEDY does not guarantee any ratio for these problems.

We first consider the problem where we want to select p vertices so as to maximize the minimum weight pseudoforest (pf). A pseudoforest is a collection of directed edges so that the outdegree of each vertex is at least one, and hence pf is the sum of the nearest neighbor distances. More formally, $wt(\mathrm{pf}(W))$ is defined to be $\sum_{x \in W} d(x, W - \{x\})$.

A related concept is that of an *edge-cover*. A set of edges covers the vertices if each vertex is incident on some edge in the set. A pseudoforest is also an edge-cover, while it can be produced from an edge-cover on the same vertex set by counting each edge at most twice. Thus, the values of these problems differ by a factor of at most two.

3.1 Upper Bounds

We present an algorithm for selecting p vertices for Remote-pseudoforest; the same algorithm (i.e. choosing the same set of vertices) works well for Remote-matching as well.

We take a two step approach to the problem. In the first step we select some number ($\leq p$) of vertices that induce a large pseudoforest. This is done by considering the sequence of vertices selected by GREEDY, and choosing some prefix of this sequence according to a simple optimality criteria. In the second step, we choose the remaining vertices in such a way that the weight of pseudoforest already accumulated does not decrease too much. This is done by ensuring that the additional vertices selected don't destroy too many of the vertices chosen in the first step by being too near.

For simplicity, we assume that $p \leq n/3$, where n is the total number of vertices. It is easy to see that the algorithm can be easily modified when this is not the case, as long as p is less than some constant fraction of n.

The PREFIX Algorithm :

Step 1 : Run the GREEDY algorithm, obtaining a set $Y = \{y_1, \ldots, y_p\}$. Recall that $r_i = \min_{j=1}^{i}\{d(y_{i+1}, y_j)\}$, $1 \leq i \leq p - 1$. Let $q \in \{1, 2, \ldots, p - 1\}$ be the value which maximizes $q \cdot r_q$. Let Y_{q+1} be a prefix subsequence of Y of length $q + 1$.

Step 2 : Let S_i be the set of vertices of distance at most $r_q/2$ from y_i, $i = 1, \ldots, q+1$. Points of distance exactly $r_q/2$ from more than one y_i are assigned arbitrarily to one sphere. The S_i are disjoint spheres centered at y_i.

Let $z = \lceil (q+1)/3 \rceil$. Let $\{S_{i_1}, S_{i_2}, \ldots, S_{i_z}\}$ be the z sparsest spheres and let $Good$ be the set of their centers $\{y_{i_1}, y_{i_2}, \ldots, y_{i_z}\}$. Let $Rest$ be any set of $p - z$ vertices from $V - \cup_j S_{i_j}$.

Let $PRE = Good \cup Rest$.

Our main result is a tight bound on **PREFIX**.

Theorem 3.1 *The performance ratio of PREFIX is $\theta(\log p)$ for* Remote-pseudoforest *and* Remote-matching.

We first prove the upper bound for pf.
Proof. First we verify that we can actually find the set $Rest$ of additional vertices. The spheres contain at most $n/(q+1)$ vertices on average, so the sparsest z of them contain at most $\lceil (q+1)/3 \rceil n/(q+1) \le 2n/3$ vertices, and at least $n/3$ can be chosen from outside the spheres as desired.

We propose that

$$\mathsf{pf}(PRE) \ge \mathsf{tree}(Y_p)/(6 \log p). \tag{3}$$

For any center $y_i \in Good$, and node z outside of S_i, $d(y_i, z) \ge r_q/2$. Hence,

$$\mathsf{pf}(PRE) \ge \sum_{x \in Good} d(x, PRE - \{x\}) \ge \sum_{x \in Good} r_q/2 \ge \frac{q+1}{3}\frac{r_q}{2} > \frac{qr_q}{6}. \tag{4}$$

Consider the spanning tree T' on Y_p which contains an edge from y_{i+1} to $Y_i = \{y_1, \ldots, y_i\}$ of weight r_i, for $i = 1, \ldots p-1$. Recall that by the choice of q, $r_i \le \frac{qr_q}{i}$. Hence,

$$\mathsf{tree}(Y_p) \le wt(T') = \sum_{i=1}^{p-1} r_i \le \sum_{i=1}^{p-1} \frac{qr_q}{i} \le qr_q \log p. \tag{5}$$

Equation 3 now follows from Equations 4 and 5.

We next show that

$$\mathsf{tree}(Y_p) \ge \mathsf{pf}(OPT)/8. \tag{6}$$

The following problem was considered in [5]: Find a set of p points F_p such that $wt(\mathsf{tree}(F_p))$ is maximized. It was shown [5, Theorem 3.1] that $\mathsf{tree}(Y_p) \ge \mathsf{tree}(F_p)/4$, and by definition $\mathsf{tree}(F_p) \ge \mathsf{tree}(OPT)$. Observe that $\mathsf{tree}(X) \ge (p-1)/p \cdot \mathsf{pf}(X) \ge \mathsf{pf}(X)/2$, for any pointset X. From these previous equations we get (6). The desired upper bound of $48 \log p$ on the approximation ratio $\mathsf{pf}(OPT)/\mathsf{pf}(HEU)$ follows from Equations 6 and 3. ∎

We now show the same upper bound for **Remote-matching** from selecting the same set PRE of vertices. We assume that p is even.

Observe that for any vertex set X, $\mathsf{tree}(X) \geq \mathsf{mat}(X)$. (It is well known that $\mathsf{tree}(X) \geq \mathsf{cycle}(X)/2$ and since a Hamilton cycle consists of two matchings, $\mathsf{cycle}(X)/2 \geq \mathsf{mat}(X)$.) Also, $\mathsf{mat}(X) \geq \mathsf{pf}(X)/2$, since doubling the edges of a matching yields a pseudoforest. Thus,

$$\mathsf{mat}(PRE) \geq \mathsf{pf}(PRE)/2 \geq \frac{\mathsf{tree}(OPT)}{48 \log p} \geq \frac{\mathsf{mat}(OPT)}{48 \log p}.$$

Same bounds hold for **Remote Cycle-Cover**, where a cycle-cover is a minimum weight subgraph that induces a collection of cycles that contain each vertex in P.

3.2 Lower Bounds

The performance analysis is tight within a constant factor.

Theorem 3.2 *The performance ratio of PREFIX for* **Remote-pseudoforest** *and* **Remote-matching** *is* $\Omega(\log n)$.

We give the construction for pseudoforest; the one for matching is similar. *Proof.* We construct a sequence of graphs G_p on $O(p^{3/2})$ vertices for which the ratio attained by PREFIX is $\log p / 20 = \Omega(\log n)$.

For simplicity, we assume that $p = 1 + 4 + \cdots + 4^t$, for integer t. The vertex set of G_p is partitioned into $t + 1$ levels, and each level i is partitioned into 4^i blocks. Each block contains 2^t vertices, each labeled with a distinct binary string of t bits. The distance between two vertices in the same block at level i is $1/4^{i+j}$, where j is the index of the first character where labels of the vertices differ. The distance between two vertices in different blocks, either at the same level i or different levels i, i', $i < i'$, is $1/4^i$.

It is easy to verify that the triangle inequality is satisfied for the edge weights of this graph. The theorem follows from the following two lemmas. ∎

Lemma 3.3 $\mathsf{pf}(OPT) \geq t + 1$.

Proof. Choose one vertex from each block. There are 4^i vertices at level i, $i = 0, 1, \ldots, t$, and each vertex at level i is at a distance 4^{-i} to its nearest neighbor in this set. ∎

Lemma 3.4 $\mathsf{pf}(PRE) \leq 10$.

Proof. Consider first the contribution of the greedy prefix Y_q. Let a be such that $r_q = 1/4^a$. Then, Y_q contains at most one vertex at level higher than a, since after that vertex is selected, other such vertices are at distance less than r_q. Y_q contains vertices from each block of level at most $a - 1$. In fact, for each block at level j, it contains at least one vertex for each value of the first

$a-1-j$ bits of the vertex label (as otherwise there would be a vertex of distance $1/4^{j+(a-1-j)} = 1/4^{a-1}$ from other selected vertices). Thus, the nearest neighbor distance of each vertex is at most $1/4^{a-1}$. On the other hand, Y_q contains at most one vertex for each value of the first $a - j$ bits. Thus, the total number q of selected vertices is at most

$$1 + \sum_{j=0}^{a} 4^j \cdot 2^{a-j} = 1 + \sum_{j=0}^{a} 2^{a+j} \leq 2 \cdot 4^a.$$

Thus, the total weight of the greedy prefix is at most $(1/4^{a-1}) \cdot 2 \cdot 4^a = 8$.

In order to bound from above the contribution of *Rest*, it suffices to supply a particular break into spheres and a choice of vertices from the dense spheres. For each vertex outside the sparse spheres, there is another vertex there of distance at most $1/4^t$. Suppose in our selection of *Rest* we ensure that for each chosen vertex, such a close neighbor be also present. Then, the contribution of rest is at most $(p - q)4^{-t} \leq 4/3$. ∎

We can also show (proof omitted in this version) that, for **Remote-pseudoforest**, no analysis of any algorithm which uses the idea of comparing the pf to the tree (as we do in the analysis of PREFIX) can hope to do any better; namely, we can construct graphs for which a large (logarithmic) gap exists between the weight of the tree of the whole graph and the pf of any subset of vertices.

4 MATCHING Algorithm

We consider the MATCHING algorithm of Hassin, Rubinstein and Tamir [6] and apply it to the **Remote-Star** problem. Recall that we seek a set of p points P that maximizes: $\min_{v \in P} \sum_{w \in P} d(v, w)$.

A *maximum-weight p-matching* is a maximum-weight set of $\lfloor p/2 \rfloor$ independent edges. It can be found efficiently via ordinary matching computation by appropriately padding the input graph [6].

The MATCHING algorithm of [6] used for the **Remote-Clique** is:

> Select the points of a maximum weight p-matching and add an arbitrary vertex if p is odd.

We consider the same algorithm for **Remote-star** i.e. the vertices for the **Remote-star** problem are the vertices selected by MATCHING.

Theorem 4.1 *The performance ratio of MATCHING for* **Remote-star** *is at most* 2.

Proof. Let HEU be the vertex set found by MATCHING. From the triangular inequality, we can see that $\text{star}(HEU) \geq \text{MAT}(HEU)$. The optimality of the p-matching tells us that $\text{MAT}(HEU) \geq \text{MAT}(OPT)$. And, the following lemma establishes that $\text{MAT}(OPT) \geq \frac{\lfloor p/2 \rfloor}{p-1}\text{star}(OPT)$. Thus, $\text{star}(OPT)/\text{star}(HEU)$ is always at most 2, and at most $2 - 2/p$ when p is even. ∎

It is easy to construct an example of an $(1, 2)$-weighted graph where this ratio is attained.

Lemma 4.2 *For any pointset X on p vertices,*

$$\frac{\text{star}(X)}{p-1} \leq \frac{MAT(X)}{\lfloor p/2 \rfloor}.$$

Proof. There are p spanning stars of X and each edge is contained in exactly two of them. The average cost of a star is $(2/p) \cdot wt(X)$ and some star is of weight at most that. Similarly, each edge appears in exactly $\lfloor p/2 \rfloor / \binom{p}{2}$ fraction of the different maximal matchings in X, and thus some matching is of weight at least the average cost of $\lfloor p/2 \rfloor / \binom{p}{2} wt(X)$. ∎

This lemma can be generalized to relate any minimum and any maximum structures for which each instance has the same number of edges (here, $p - 1$ and $\lfloor p/2 \rfloor$, respectively).

5 Discussion

We have presented a framework for studying dispersion problems, given approximation algorithm for several natural measures of remoteness, and shown several hardness results as well as limitations on the ubiquitous greedy approach.

We have considered a number of extensions of the formalism presented here. These include bottleneck problems – where the objective function is a maximum, rather than the sum, of the edge weights of a structure; Steiner problems – where the objective function may include vertices outside the selected set P; and min-max problems – where we ask for a set of points that minimizes some maximization structure.

Many threads are left open for further study. Are there constant-factor approximation algorithms for the remote pseudoforest and matching problems, or can we prove super-constant hardness results? Can we give an exhaustive classification of the approximability of a large class of remote problems, and/or can we succinctly describe those problems for which GREEDY will do well? And finally, a further study on the applied aspects from the management science viewpoint would be desirable.

We conclude with a conjecture about the complexity of (exact solutions of) remote subgraph problems: tha the remoteness operator pushes the problem exactly one level higher in the polynomial-time hierarchy.

Conjecture 5.1 *Let Π be a coNP-hard property. Then the problem of deciding whether there exists a subset S of the input of size p that forms a valid instance where Π holds is Σ_2^p-hard.*

References

[1] M. Bellare and M. Sudan. Improved non-approximability results. *STOC 1994.*

[2] E. Erkut. The discrete p-dispersion problem. *Europ. J. Oper. Res*, 46:48–60, 1990.

[3] E. Erkut and S. Neuman. Analytical models for locating undesirable facilities. *Europ. J. Oper. Res*, 40:275–291, 1989.

[4] E. Erkut and S. Neuman. Comparison of four models for dispersing facilities. *INFOR*, 29:68–85, 1990.

[5] M. M. Halldórsson, K. Iwano, N. Katoh, and T. Tokuyama. Finding subsets maximizing minimum structures. *SODA 1995*.

[6] R. Hassin, S. Rubinstein, and A. Tamir. Notes on dispersion problems. Dec. 1994.

[7] G. Kortsarz and D. Peleg. On choosing a dense subgraph. *FOCS 1993*.

[8] M. J. Kuby. Programming models for facility dispersion: The p-dispersion and maxisum dispersion problems. *Geog. Anal.*, 19(4):315–329, Oct. 1987.

[9] I. D. Moon and S. S. Chaudhry. An analysis of network location problems with distance constraints. *Mgmt. Science*, 30(3):290–307, Mar. 1984.

[10] S. S. Ravi, D. J. Rosenkrantz, and G. K. Tayi. Heuristic and special case algorithms for dispersion problems. *Op. Res*, 42(2):299–310, 1994.

[11] A. Tamir. Obnoxious facility location on graphs. *SIAM J. Disc. Math.*, 4(4):550–567, Nov. 1991.

[12] D. J. White. The maximal dispersion problem and the "first point outside the neighborhood" heuristic. *Computers Ops. Res.*, 18(1):43–50, 1991.

[13] D. J. White. The maximal dispersion problem. *J. Applic. Math. in Bus. and Ind.*, 1992.

The Constrained Minimum Spanning Tree Problem

(Extended Abstract)

R. Ravi*   M. X. Goemans[†]

Abstract

Given an undirected graph with two different nonnegative costs associated with every edge e (say, w_e for the weight and l_e for the length of edge e) and a budget L, consider the problem of finding a spanning tree of total edge length at most L and minimum total weight under this restriction. This *constrained minimum spanning tree problem* is weakly NP-hard. We present a polynomial-time approximation scheme for this problem. This algorithm always produces a spanning tree of total length at most $(1 + \epsilon)L$ and of total weight at most that of any spanning tree of total length at most L, for any fixed $\epsilon > 0$. The algorithm uses Lagrangean relaxation, and exploits adjacency relations for matroids.

Keywords: Approximation algorithm, minimum spanning trees, Lagrangean relaxation, adjacency relations.

1 Introduction

Given an undirected graph $G = (V, E)$ and nonnegative integers l_e and w_e for each edge $e \in E$, we consider the problem of finding a spanning tree that has low total cost with respect to *both* the cost functions l and w. For convenience, we will refer to l_e and w_e of an edge e as its length and weight respectively. Thus the problem we consider is that of finding a spanning tree with small total weight and small total length.

---

*GSIA, Carnegie Mellon University, 5000 Forbes Avenue, Pittsburgh PA 15213. Email: `ravi+@cmu.edu`.

[†]MIT, Department of Mathematics, Room 2-382, Cambridge, MA 02139. Email: `goemans@math.mit.edu`. Research supported in part by NSF contract 9302476-CCR, ARPA Contract N00014-95-1-1246, and a Sloan fellowship.

This is a bicriteria problem. A natural way to formulate such problems is to specify a budget on one of the cost functions and minimize the other objective under this constraint. The problem therefore becomes a capacitated problem. In this case, we can specify a budget L on the total length of the spanning tree and require a tree of minimum weight under this budget restriction. We call this problem the *Constrained Minimum Spanning Tree problem.*

Lemma 1.1 [1] The constrained minimum spanning tree problem is (weakly) NP-hard.

Define an (α, β)-approximation for this problem as a polynomial-time algorithm that always outputs a spanning tree with total length at most αL and of total weight at most βW, where W is the minimum weight of any spanning tree of G of length at most L. In other words, W is the answer to the constrained minimum spanning tree problem formulated in the previous paragraph. Observe that the definition is not completely symmetric in the two cost functions; the quantity L is given.

In this extended abstract, we first present a $(2, 1)$-approximation algorithm for the constrained minimum spanning tree problem. The algorithm is based on Lagrangean relaxation, and the proof of the performance guarantee exploits the fact that two adjacent spanning trees on the spanning tree polytope differ by exactly two edges (one in each tree). Moreover, this algorithm can be implemented in almost linear time using an elegant technique of Meggido [6].

We then refine the algorithm to derive an approximation scheme. The precise result is given below.

Theorem 1.2 For any fixed $\epsilon > 0$, there is a $(1 + \epsilon, 1)$-approximation algorithm for the constrained minimum spanning tree problem that runs in polynomial time.

The same result holds if we replace the set of spanning trees by the bases of any matroid.

Note also that the above approximation can be used to derive a $(1, 1 + \epsilon)$-approximation algorithm for the constrained minimum spanning tree problem that runs in pseudopolynomial time. This observation follows from more general arguments in [5]; we reproduce it here for completeness. In this latter problem, we must find a tree of length at most the budget L and of cost at most $(1 + \epsilon)$ times the minimum weight of any tree of length at most L. The idea is to use the weights rather than the lengths as the budgeted objective in the available algorithm. Consider running the given algorithm for all possible integral budget values on the weight of the tree to find a tree of approximately minimum length. Over all these runs, find the smallest value W' of the budget such that the length of the tree output is at most L. Since no smaller value of the budget on the weight of the tree gives a tree of length at most L, it must be the case that W' is a lower bound on the weight of any spanning tree of length at most L. But the tree obtained by running the given algorithm with a weight budget of W' must have weight at most $(1 + \epsilon)W'$, and therefore has the desired properties. Binary search can be used to speed up the determination of W' using $O(\log W_{max})$ invocations of the given approximation algorithm, where W_{max} is the sum of the largest $n - 1$ weights.

Related work

Aggarwal, Aneja and Nair [1] studied the constrained minimum spanning tree problem; they prove weak NP-hardness and describe computational experience with an approach for exact solution. Guignard and Rosenwein [3] apply a special form of Lagrangean relaxation to solve to optimality the directed version of the problem we consider here, that of finding constrained minimum arborescences.

There have not been too many approximation algorithms for bicriteria problems. This may come from the fact that capacitated problems are typically much harder than their uncapacitated counterparts. We mention here some work that is closely related; see also [9] for additional references. Lin and Vitter [4] provided approximations for the s-median problem where s median nodes must be chosen so as to minimize the sum of the distances from each vertex to its nearest median. The solution output is approximate in terms of both the number of median-nodes used and the sum of the distances from each vertex to the nearest median. Shmoys and Tardos [10] studied the problem of scheduling unrelated parallel machines with costs associated with processing a job on a given machine. Given a budget on the cost of the schedule, they presented an approximation algorithm for minimizing the makespan of the schedule. Both the papers mentioned above use a linear programming formulation of the respective problems and use different rounding methods to round a fractional solution to a feasible integral solution. Even though these methods employ linear programming, our approach is quite different.

Recently, Marathe, R. Ravi, Sundaram, S.S. Ravi, Rosenkrantz and

Hunt studied several bicriteria network design problems in [5]. They presented a $(2,2)$-approximation algorithm for the constrained minimum spanning tree problem using a parametric search method combined with a cost-scaling technique. Their method also yields approximation algorithms for several bicriteria problems for which the two criteria are similar, i.e. both the objectives are of the same type but only differ in the cost function based on which they are computed. The constrained minimum spanning tree problem is such an example. Theorem 1.2 is an improvement of the result in [5] in two ways: the performance ratio is better, and the algorithm we present is strongly polynomial and does not depend on the magnitude of the costs assigned to edges. The method in [5] uses a cost-scaling approach and hence the running time depends on the magnitudes of the costs.

In the next section, we review Lagrangean relaxation as applied to our problem. Then we present the approximation algorithm in Section 3, and describe a fast implementation in Section 4.

2 Lagrangean relaxation

Lagrangean relaxation is a classical technique to get rid of a set of "hard" constraints in an optimization problem. This gives lower bounds (for minimization problems) on the optimum value. We refer the reader to Nemhauser and Wolsey [7] for a discussion of the method. In this section, we consider the application of Lagrangean relaxation to the constrained minimum spanning tree problem. In a subsequent section, we will show how to derive from this Lagrangean relaxation a spanning tree of approximately minimum length and weight.

Given a graph $G = (V, E)$, let S denote the set of incidence vectors of spanning trees of G. The constrained minimum spanning tree problem can be formulated by the following optimization problem:

$$W \quad = \quad \text{Min} \quad \sum_{e \in E} w_e x_e$$

subject to:

(IP)
$$x \in S$$
$$\sum_{e \in E} l_e x_e \leq L. \tag{1}$$

Considering the budget constraint (1) as the complicating constraint, we can obtain a lower bound on the optimum value W by dualizing it and considering for any $z \geq 0$ the following minimum spanning tree problem:

$$l(z) \quad = \quad \text{Min} \sum_{e \in E} (w_e + z l_e) x_e - zL$$

subject to:

(P_z) $\qquad\qquad\qquad\qquad x \in S.$

The value $l(z)$ is clearly a lower bound on W since any spanning tree which satisfies the budget constraint would give an objective function value in (P_z) no higher than in (IP). We observe that (P_z) is simply a minimum spanning tree problem with respect to the costs $c_e = w_e + z l_e$. In order to get the best lower bound on W, we can maximize $l(z)$ over all $z \geq 0$ to obtain:

$$LR = \text{Max}_{z \geq 0} \ l(z).$$

We let z^* denote the value of z which maximizes $l(z)$, and let $c_e^* = w_e + z^* l_e$. It is well-known and easy to see that $l(z)$ is concave and piecewise linear. For an illustration, see Figure 1.

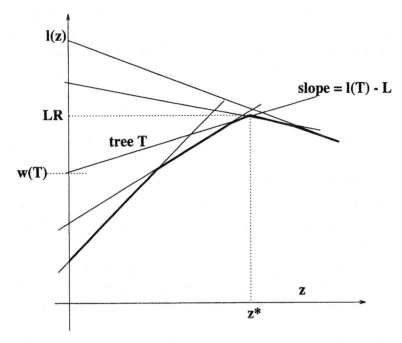

Figure 1: The plot of $l(z)$ as z varies. Every spanning tree of weight $w(T)$ and length $l(T)$ corresponds to a line with intercept $w(T)$ and slope $l(T) - L$. The plot above is the lower envelope of the lines corresponding to all spanning trees in the graph.

3 The approximation algorithm

Our algorithm is based on solving the Lagrangean relaxation and deriving a good spanning tree out of it. Our main result will follow from the following theorem.

Theorem 3.1 Let $\mathcal{O}$ denote the set of spanning trees of minimum cost with respect to c^*. There exists a spanning tree $T \in \mathcal{O}$ of weight at most $LR \leq W$ and of length less than $L + l_{max}$ where $l_{max} = \max_{e \in E} l_e$.

Proof of Theorem 3.1:

The weight $w(T)$ of any tree T in $\mathcal{O}$ is equal to

$$w(T) = [w(T) + zl(T) - zL] - z(l(T) - L) = LR - z(l(T) - L),$$

and therefore is at most LR if and only if $l(T) \geq L$.

We start by establishing a well-known and simple property of $\mathcal{O}$. If we consider $z = z^* + \epsilon$ or $z = z^* - \epsilon$ for an arbitrarily small $\epsilon > 0$, the optimum spanning trees with respect to $w_e + zl_e$ must be contained in $\mathcal{O}$. This implies that $\mathcal{O}$ must contain a spanning tree $T_\leq$ of length at most L. If not, we would have that $l(z^* + \epsilon) > l(z^*)$, contradicting the optimality of z^*. Similarly, there must exist a spanning tree $T_\geq$ of length at least L in $\mathcal{O}$.

To derive the existence of a tree in $\mathcal{O}$ of length between L and $L+l_{max}$, we use the adjacency relationship on the spanning tree polytope (the convex hull of incidence vectors of spanning trees) given in the following lemma. This adjacency relationship follows from the fact that forests of a graph define a matroid, the graphic matroid.

Lemma 3.2 The spanning trees T and T' are adjacent on the spanning tree polytope if and only if they differ by a single edge swap, i.e. there exist $e \in T$ and $e' \in T'$ such that $T - e = T' - e'$.

By considering the optimum face of the spanning tree polytope induced by the spanning trees in $\mathcal{O}$, this lemma implies that if we have two optimum spanning trees T and T' then there must exist a sequence $T = T_0, T_1, \ldots, T_k = T'$ of *optimum* spanning trees such that T_i and T_{i+1} are adjacent for $i = 0, \ldots, k - 1$. If we take $T = T_\leq$ and $T' = T_\geq$, we derive that there must exist two *adjacent* spanning trees T_i and T_{i+1} both in $\mathcal{O}$ such that $l(T_i) \leq L$ and $l(T_{i+1}) \geq L$. But T_i and T_{i+1} differ only in one edge swap. Thus $l(T_{i+1}) = l(T_i) + l_{e_{i+1}} - l_{e_i} \leq l(T_i) + l_{max}$ where $e_i \in T_i - T_{i+1}$ and $e_{i+1} \in T_{i+1} - T_i$. This shows that T_{i+1} has length at least L and less than $L + l_{max}$, completing the proof.

3.1 High-level algorithm and its performance guarantee

Theorem 3.1 and its proof motivates the following algorithm. First of all, observe that we can assume without loss of generality that $l_e \leq L$ for all edges e in G. Edges that have higher values of l_e would never be included in a feasible solution and therefore can be discarded. Then, compute the value z^* solving the Lagrangean relaxation. Among all optimum trees for the cost function $c_e = w_e + z^* l_e$, find one that satisfies the conditions of Theorem 3.1. Because we have pruned all edges with $l_e > L$, we have that $l_{max} \leq L$ and, as a result, the tree output has weight at most $LR \leq W$ and length at most $2L$. Therefore, this constitutes a $(2, 1)$-approximation algorithm, provided we can implement the various steps of the algorithm.

4 Implementation

In this section, we show that the $(2, 1)$-approximation algorithm can be implemented in almost linear time. In particular, we sketch an implementation that runs in time $O(m \log^2 n + n \log^3 n)$, where $m = |E|$ and $n = |V|$.

4.1 Solving the Lagrangean relaxation

In order to compute the value z^*, we use an algorithm of Meggido [6]. We briefly summarize his elegant method here.

For any value of z, we can compute a minimum spanning tree with respect to $c = w + zl$. We can also easily determine if $z < z^*$, $z = z^*$ or $z > z^*$. For this purpose, among all optimum trees with respect to c, we can find the two trees T_{min} and T_{max} which have smallest and largest length. This can be done by using a lexicographic ordering of the edges instead of the ordering induced by c; for example, to compute T_{min}, we use the ordering $(c_e, l_e) < (c_f, l_f)$ if $c_e < c_f$ or if $c_e = c_f$ and $l_e < l_f$. Then $z < z^*$ if $l(T_{min}) > L$, $z > z^*$ if $l(T_{max}) < L$, and z is (a possible value for) z^* otherwise.

Meggido's approach is the following. Suppose we try to find an optimum tree for the value z^*, without knowing z^*. For this purpose, we would like to sort the edges with respect to their costs at z^*. Given two edges e and f, we can determine if $c_e^* < c_f^*$, $c_e^* = c_f^*$ or $c_e^* > c_f^*$ without actually knowing z^*! Indeed, we only need to determine the breakpoint, say z_{ef}, of the two linear functions c_e and c_f as a function of z and determine if $z_{ef} < z^*$, $z_{ef} = z^*$ or $z_{ef} > z^*$. This can be done by two minimum spanning tree computations (to determine T_{min} and T_{max}) at the value z_{ef}. Therefore, if we use an algorithm which makes $O(m \log m)$ comparisons to determine the ordering of the costs at z^*, we will be able to determine z^* by $O(m \log m)$ minimum spanning tree computations.

However, Meggido proposed to do this much more efficiently. Instead of using a serial sorting algorithm, we can use a parallel sorting algorithm which takes say $O(\log m)$ rounds and in each round make $O(m \log m)$ comparisons [8]. The advantage is that in any round the $O(m \log m)$ breakpoints can be computed in advance, then sorted (this is not even necessary), and then one can use binary search to determine where z^* lies compared to all these breakpoints by doing only $O(\log(m \log m)) = O(\log m)$ minimum spanning tree computations. Over all rounds, this algorithm therefore makes $O(\log^2 m)$ minimum spanning tree computations. If we use the fastest MST algorithm available [2], this results in a total running time of $O(m \log^2 n + n \log^3 n)$.

4.2 Finding a tree satisfying the conditions of Theorem 3.1

The second part of the implementation is how to find the tree whose existence is claimed in Theorem 3.1, once z^* is known. The algorithm described in the previous section not only gives z^* but also produces two trees T_{min} and T_{max} which are optimum for z^* and such that $l(T_{min}) \leq L$ and $l(T_{max}) \geq L$.

Following the proof of Theorem 3.1, we need to compute a sequence of optimum trees $T_{min} = T_0, T_1, \cdots, T_k = T_{max}$ such that T_i and T_{i+1} are adjacent ($i = 0, \cdots, k-1$) and simply return the first tree of the sequence whose length is at least L. To compute the sequence, we simply repeatedly swap an edge e in T_{max} but not in the current tree with a maximum cost edge not in T_{max} but on the cycle closed by e. This sequence will therefore end in $k = |T_{max} - T_{min}| \leq n - 1$ steps.

If we were to implement each swap naively, this would take $O(n)$ time per swap, for a total running time of $O(n^2)$. However, using dynamic trees [11], Sleator and Tarjan show how to make this series of $O(n)$ swaps in $O(n \log n)$ time.

Summarizing, the $(2, 1)$-approximation algorithm can be implemented in $O(m \log^2 n + n \log^3 n)$ time.

5 A polynomial-time approximation scheme

The $(2,1)$-approximation algorithm can be turned into a PTAS by modifying the initial edge-pruning rule in the algorithm. Earlier, we pruned all edges with length greater then L since no such edge would be used in any feasible solution. The approximation guarantee of $2L$ on the length of the solution then followed from Theorem 3.1. To reduce this ratio, we could prune away all edges whose length is greater than ϵL for some fixed $\epsilon > 0$. Then l_{max} would be at most ϵL, resulting in a final tree of length at most $(1 + \epsilon)L$. However, we may discard edges that could possibly be used in an optimal solution. The key observation is that at most $\frac{1}{\epsilon}$ of the pruned edges can be used in any optimal solution, and there are only $O(n^{O(\frac{1}{\epsilon})})$ choices of subsets of pruned edges that may occur in any optimal solution. For each one of these polynomially many choices, we include the chosen edges in the tree, shrink the connected components, and run our algorithm on the resulting graph with a budget value of L minus the length of the chosen edges. The solution output is the tree with minimum weight among all the trees over all the choices (note that all these trees have length at most $(1 + \epsilon)L$). The proof that the weight of the tree output is at most the optimum value W is completed by considering the running of the algorithm for the same choice of the chosen edges as in some optimal solution of the constrained minimum spanning tree problem. This completes the proof of Theorem 1.2.

Acknowledgements Thanks to Philip Klein and David Williamson for discussions that led to this line of work.

References

[1] V. Aggarwal, Y. Aneja and K. Nair, "Minimal spanning tree subject to a side constraint," *Comput. Operations Res.* **9**, 287–296 (1982).

[2] T.H. Cormen, C.E. Leiserson, and R.L. Rivest, *Introduction to algorithms*, McGraw Hill (1990).

[3] M. Guignard and M.B. Rosenwein, "An application of Lagrangean decomposition to the resource-constrained minimum weighted arborescence problem," *Networks* **20**, 345–359 (1990).

[4] J.-H. Lin and J.S. Vitter, "ϵ-approximations with minimum packing constraint violation," *Proceedings of the 24th Annual ACM Symposium on the Theory of Computing*, 771–782 (1992).

[5] M.V. Marathe, R. Ravi, R. Sundaram, S.S. Ravi, D.J. Rosenkrantz, and H.B. Hunt III, "Bicriteria network design problems," *Proc. of the 22nd ICALP*, LNCS 944, 487–498 (1995).

[6] N. Meggido, "Applying parallel computation algorithms in the design of serial algorithms," *Journal of the ACM* **30**, 852–865 (1983).

[7] G.L. Nemhauser and L.A. Wolsey, *Integer and Combinatorial Optimization*, John Wiley & Sons, New York (1988).

[8] F.P. Preparata, "New parallel-sorting schemes", *IEEE Trans. Comput.* **C-27**, 669–673 (1978).

[9] R. Ravi, M.V. Marathe, S.S. Ravi, D.J. Rosenkrantz, and H.B. Hunt III, "Many birds with one stone: Multi-objective approximation algorithms," *Proceedings of the 25th Annual ACM Symposium on the Theory of Computing*, 438–447 (1993).

[10] D.B. Shmoys and E. Tardos, "Scheduling unrelated parallel machines with costs," *Proc., 4th Annual ACM-SIAM Symposium on Discrete Algorithms*, 448–454 (1993).

[11] D.D. Sleator and R.E. Tarjan, "A Data Structure fo Dynamic Trees," *Journal of Computer and System Sciences* **26**, 362–391 (1983).

Randomized Approximation of the Constraint Satisfaction Problem

(Extended Abstract)

Hoong Chuin LAU   Osamu WATANABE

Dept. of Computer Science, Tokyo Institute of Technology
2-12-1 Ookayama, Meguro-ku, Tokyo 152, Japan
{hclau,watanabe}@cs.titech.ac.jp

1   Introduction

In the Weighted Constraint Satisfaction Problem (W-CSP) we are given a set of variables and a collection of constraints (or relations) on the variables. Each variable must be assigned a value from its domain. Each constraint has a positive integer weight. A solution is an assignment of values to the variables, and it satisfies a given constraint if the values of the respective variables are related by that relation. Our objective is to find a solution that maximizes the sum of weights of satisfied constraints.

Many real-world problems can be represented as W-CSP, e.g. problems in machine vision, temporal reasoning, scheduling and timetabling. In scheduling for example, our task is to assign discrete units of resources to jobs subject to a set of constraints, some of which are more important than others. Most often, it is impossible to satisfy all constraints and so we look for an assignment that satisfies the more important constraints.

A W-CSP instance has arity t iff all its constraints are t-ary (i.e. defined on a set of t or less variables). It has domain size k iff the sizes of all domains are k or less. W-CSP with small domain size and arity contain some well-known combinatorial optimization problems. For example, the case of $k = 2$ is a generalization of the maximum satisfiability problem (MAX SAT), while the case of $k = t = 2$ is a generalization of the maximum cut problem (MAX CUT). Since it has been shown by Papadimitriou and Yannakakis [11] that unweighted MAX CUT is MAX SNP-complete, W-CSP belongs the class of MAX SNP-hard problems. This means that there exists a constant $0 \leq c < 1$ such that W-CSP cannot be approximated in polynomial time within a factor of c unless P=NP. In fact, we will prove that no $O(\log n)$ approximation algorithm is achievable for W-CSP in general since one can imbed a type of two-prover interactive proof system in the problem.

In Khanna et al.'s paper [7], one section is devoted to the approximation of W-CSP of domain size 2 and fixed arity t. They showed that the problem is approximable within a factor of $1/2^t$ by a fairly sophisticated local search technique. This means they achieve a ratio of 1/4 for W-CSP of domain size 2 and arity 2, and one of our purposes is to improve that situation. Earlier, Berman and Schnitger [3], while studying the maximum independent set problem, had obtained the same bound for a weaker version of Khanna *et al.*'s problem. More recently, Lau [8] considered W-CSP in terms of the *arc-consistency* property and obtained tight approximation via local search. That result is improved here.

In this paper, we give improved approximation of W-CSP using *randomized rounding* introduced by Raghavan and Thompson [12]. The key idea is to formulate our problem as an integer program, solve a convex mathematical programming relaxation (such as a linear program), treat the values of the optimal fractional solution as a probability distribution and obtain an integer solution using this distribution. Raghavan and Thompson showed that the values chosen under the distribution do in fact yield a solution near the expectation, thus giving good approximate solutions to the integer program. This technique yields a randomized algorithm, which can be derandomized using the *method of conditional probabilities* [4, 1].

In this paper, we are mainly concerned with binary constraints (i.e. arity 2 problems), although some of our results can be easily extended to higher arities. Unless otherwise stated, W-CSP will now refer to the class of instances with binary constraints. Our contributions are as follows:

1. By interactive proofs, we show that W-CSP in general has no $O(\log n)$ approximation ratio, even if the underlying constraint graph is bipartite, unless EXP=NEXP.

2. By representing W-CSP as a linear integer program and applying randomized rounding to its linear program relaxation, we obtain an approximation ratio of $1/(2k) + s/4$, where s is the weighted average *strength* of the constraints. The ratio can be improved to $1/k^{t-1}$ for *satisfiable* instances of arity t. These ratios are best possible in the sense that there exist instances whose expected weights match the ratios exactly.

3. By a simple rounding scheme to a semidefinite program relaxation, we obtain a constant-approximation of 0.408 for the case of $k \leq 3$. This ratio is tight in the sense that, regardless of the rounding scheme, there exists an instance whose expected weight is no more than 0.5 times the optimal value. We also analyse the hyperplane-rounding method of Goemans and Williamson [6] for the case $k = 2$ and derive a ratio of 0.634, which can be improved to 0.878 in two special cases. Derandomization of the latter rounding method was recently proposed by Mahajan and Ramesh [9]. This result improves one of Khanna *et al.*'s results in [7].

2 Preliminaries

Let $V = \{1, \ldots, n\}$ be a set of variables. For simplicity, we fix the domains of all variables to be the set $K = \{1, \ldots, k\}$, for given constant k. All results presented in this paper also hold for instances of unequal-sized domains provided that the maximum domain size is k. A constraint is a binary relation over $K \times K$. Given an assignment $\sigma : V \longrightarrow K$, a constraint between two variables i and l is *satisfied* iff the value pair (σ_i, σ_l) is an element of the relation. The definition can be extended analogously to t-ary relations. An instance of the Weighted Constraint Satisfaction Problem (W-CSP) is defined by a set V of variables, a collection E of constraints, integer k, and a weight function $w : E \longrightarrow Z^+$. The output is an assignment $\sigma : V \longrightarrow K$ such that the weighted sum of satisfied constraints (or simply weight) is maximized. W-CSP can be represented by a *constraint graph* $G = (V, E)$. Denote by W-CSP(k) the class of instances with domain size k.

Let W denote the sum of edge weights. For each constraint $j \in E$, let w_j, R_j and $s_j = \|R_j\|/k^2$ denote its weight, relation and *strength* respectively; let α_j and β_j denote the indices of the two variables incident on j; and let $c_j(u, v) \in \{0, 1\}$ indicate whether the pair (u, v) is in R_j. Let $s = \sum_{j \in E} w_j s_j / W$ denote the strength of a W-CSP instance (i.e. the weighted average strengths of all its constraints). Note that $s \geq 1/k^2$ because every constraint relation contains at least 1 out of the k^2 possible pairs. Note also that a random assignment of the variables is expected to have weight sW by definition. Hence, one can obtain an absolute ratio of s trivially by a simple derandomization techique using the method of conditional probabilities.

A W-CSP instance is termed *satisfiable* iff there exists an assignment which satisfies all constraints simultaneously. A constraint is said to be *2-consistent* iff there are at least two value pairs in the relation. Otherwise, it is said to be *selfish*. Clearly, every selfish constraint is satisfied by one unique instantiation of its variables. An instance is 2-consistent iff all its constraints are 2-consistent.

We say that a maximization problem P *can be approximated within* $0 < \epsilon \leq 1$ iff there exists a polynomial-time algorithm A such that for all input instances y of P, A computes a solution whose objective value is at least ϵ times the optimal value of y (denoted $OPT(y)$). The quantity ϵ is commonly known as the *performance guarantee* or *approximation ratio* for P. Observe that the ratio is as close to 1 as the solution is close to an optimum solution.

3 Non-Approximability of W-CSP

In this section, we prove that W-CSP is not approximable within a $O(\log n)$ multiplicative factor unless EXP=NEXP. This can be derived in a rather straightforward manner by mimicking the proof given by Feige and Lovász [5].

In a two-prover proof system, two provers P_1 and P_2 try to convince a probabilistic polynomial time verifer V that a common input x of size n belongs to a language L. The provers are not allowed to communicate with each other. The language L has a two-prover one-round multiple-prover interactive proof system (abbrev. $MIP(2, 1)$) if in one round of communication:

$$\forall x \in L, \ \exists \, P_1, P_2 \ \Pr[(V, P_1, P_2) \text{ accepts } x] = 1 \text{ and}$$

$$\forall x \notin L, \ \forall \, P_1, P_2 \ \Pr[(V, P_1, P_2) \text{ accepts } x] < 2^{-n}.^1$$

---

[1] For the acceptance probability thresholds, $(\frac{2}{3}, \frac{1}{3})$ have generally been used; but it has been shown in [5] that, for languages in NEXP, there is a 1-round protocol that guarantees the thresholds to be $(1, 2^{-n})$.

$MIP(2,1)$ can be modelled as a problem on games. Let S and T be sets of polynomial-sized messages. Let π be a probability distribution over $S \times T$. Let V be a predicate. Then $G(V, \pi)$ is the following two-person cooperative game of incomplete information: A pair of messages $(s, t) \in S \times T$ is chosen at random according to probability distribution π. The message s is sent to one player (which we call *Left*) and t is sent to the other (called *Right*). A strategy of a player is a function from messages to replies. The players' objective is to choose strategies P_1 and P_2 which maximizes the probability (over π) that $V(s, t, P_1(s), P_2(t)) = 1$. Let the value of the game, denoted $w(G)$, be the probability of success of the players' optimal strategy in the game G.

We can formulate the problem of finding the best strategy for the players as a W-CSP instance which is a bipartite constraint graph as follows. Let U and W be the sets of polynomial-sized replies returned by the Left and Right provers respectively. The set of nodes in the constraint graph is,

$$V = \{x_s \; : \; s \in S\} \bigcup \{y_t \; : \; t \in T\}.$$

Edges are connected between x_s and y_t as follows:

$$E = \{(x_s, y_t) \; : \; \pi(s, t) \neq 0\}.$$

The domain of each x_s (resp., y_t) is U (resp., W). For each constraint $(x_s, y_t) \in E$, the pair (u, v) is in the relation if $V(s, t, u, w) = 1$. Finally, define the weight of the constraint $(x_s, y_t) \in E$ as $\pi(s, t)$ scaled up to an integer.

Since each variable must be assigned to exactly one value, the assignment of variables in S and T encodes a strategy for the Left and Right players respectively. By the same argument given in Lemma 4.11 of [5], we can show that the optimum value of this W-CSP instance is exactly $w(G)$ and hence the accepting probability of the proof system.

Theorem 1. *If there is a polynomial time algorithm that approximates W-CSP within a $O(\log n)$ multiplicative factor, then* EXP = NEXP.

Proof. Consider an arbitrary language L in NEXP and an input x. In [5], it has been shown that $MIP(2, 1)$=NEXP implying that there is a two-prover one round proof system such that the acceptance probability reflects membership of x in L. This acceptance probability is the optimal value of a W-CSP instance y with $n' = O(2^{poly(n)})$ variables. Suppose there is a polynomial time algorithm which approximates y to some $c/\log n'$ factor. Then, if $x \in L$, the optimal value is at least $c/\log n' = 1/poly(n)$ and if $x \notin L$, the optimal value is less than 2^{-n}. Hence, applying the polynomial time approximation algorithm to y would give an exponential time decision procedure for L. $\square$

Trevisan pointed out to the authors that the following result is also provable by using the recent results of [2, 13]: There is no polynomial time constant approximation algorithm for W-CSP unless P = NP.

4 Randomized Rounding of Linear Program

In this section, we present randomized rounding of linear program and analyze its performance guarantee. Basically, our algorithm is as follows. First model a W-CSP instance as an integer program, then solve its linear programming (LP) relaxation and finally apply randomized rounding on the solution obtained.

Recall that α_j and β_j are the two variables connected by constraint j and $c_j(u, v)$ is the indicator function specifying whether the value pair (u, v) is in constraint j. A W-CSP instance can be formulated by the following integer linear program:

$$
\begin{aligned}
&\text{IP : maximize } \sum_{j \in E} w_j z_j \\
&\text{subject to} \quad y_{\alpha_j, u} + y_{\beta_j, v} \geq 2x_{j, u, v} \quad && \text{for } j \in E \text{ and } u, v \in K \quad [1] \\
&\qquad\qquad \sum_{u, v \in K} x_{j, u, v} \cdot c_j(u, v) \geq z_j \quad && \text{for } j \in E \quad [2] \\
&\qquad\qquad \sum_{u \in K} y_{i, u} = 1 \quad && \text{for } i \in V \quad [3] \\
&\qquad\qquad x_{j, u, v} \in \{0, 1\} \quad && \text{for } j \in E \text{ and } u, v \in K \quad [4] \\
&\qquad\qquad y_{i, u} \in \{0, 1\} \quad && \text{for } i \in V \text{ and } u \in K \quad [5] \\
&\qquad\qquad 0 \leq z_j \leq 1 \quad && \text{for } j \in E \quad [6]
\end{aligned}
$$

The 0/1 variable $y_{i, u}$ indicates whether variable i is assigned value u. The 0/1 variable $x_{j, u, v}$ indicates whether α_j is assigned to u and β_j is assigned to v. The variable z_j is used to indicate whether constraint j is satisfied. Inequality [1] ensures that $x_{j, u, v}$ is 1 only if $y_{\alpha_j, u}$ and $y_{\beta_j, v}$ are both 1. Since the edge weights are positive, inequality [2] ensures that z_j is 1 only if there exists some u and v such that $x_{j, u, v}$ and $c_j(u, v)$ are both 1. Inequality [3] ensures that each variable is assigned to exactly one value.

Given an instance of IP, solve a linear programming problem by relaxing the integrality constraints [4] and [5]. Let (x^*, y^*, z^*) denote the optimal solution obtained.

The naive form of rounding would be to assign variable i to value u with probability $y_{i, u}^*$. Call this algorithm R1. The performance of R1 is arbitrarily bad in the worst case, because there exists an instance in W-CSP such that the expected weight of the assignment obtained by R1 is 0.

We propose the following rounding procedure: assign variable i to u with probability $\frac{1}{2}\left(y_{i, u}^* + \frac{1}{k}\right)$, for all $i \in V$ and $u \in K$. Call this algorithm R2.

Theorem 2. *W-CSP(k) can be approximated within $\frac{1}{2k} + \frac{3}{4}$ by R2.*

Proof. Given an instance of W-CSP(k), let I be the corresponding instance of IP and L be its linear programming relaxation. Surely, $OPT(L) \geq OPT(I)$. The expected weight of the probabilistic assignment obtained by R2 is given by,

$$
\hat{W} = \sum_{j \in E} w_j \left(\sum_{u, v \in K} \left[\frac{1}{2}(y_{\alpha_j, u}^* + \frac{1}{k}) \cdot \frac{1}{2}(y_{\beta_j, v}^* + \frac{1}{k}) \cdot c_j(u, v) \right] \right)
$$

$$\geq \frac{1}{4} \sum_{j \in E} w_j \left(\sum_{u,v \in K} \left[\frac{y^*_{\alpha_j,u} + y^*_{\beta_j,v}}{k} + \frac{1}{k^2} \right] \cdot c_j(u,v) \right)$$

$$\geq \frac{1}{4} \sum_{j \in E} w_j \left(\sum_{u,v \in K} \frac{2}{k} x^*_{j,u,v} \cdot c_j(u,v) + \sum_{u,v \in K} \frac{1}{k^2} \cdot c_j(u,v) \right)$$

$$\geq \frac{1}{4} \left[\frac{2}{k} \sum_{j \in E} w_j z^*_j + \sum_{j \in E} w_j \frac{\|R_j\|}{k^2} \right] \geq \left(\frac{1}{2k} + \frac{s}{4} \right) OPT(I)$$

where the second inequality follows from [1], the third inequality follows from [2], and the last inequality follows by definition and the fact that $OPT(L) \geq OPT(I)$. Derandomizing using the method of conditional probabilities, we can obtain an assignment with weight at least $\hat{W}$. □

The above analysis is best possible, because there exists an instance I in W-CSP(k) such that the expected weight of the assignment obtained by R2 is no more than $\left(\frac{1}{2k} + \frac{s}{4}\right) OPT(I)$. This is shown by the following construction for the case of $s = \frac{2}{k}$ ($k > 2$). Consider two variables i and l connected by the constraint j in which all values of i are consistent with the last 2 values of l, i.e.

$$R_j = \{(u,v) : 1 \leq u \leq k, k-1 \leq v \leq k\}.$$

An optimal assignment would be to assign i to any value and l to either $k-1$ or k. On the other hand, linear programming returns an optimal solution where (i) $y_{i,u} = y_{l,u} = \frac{1}{k-2}$ and $x_{j,u,v} = \frac{1}{2(k-2)}$, for all $1 \leq u \leq k-2$ and $k-1 \leq v \leq k$; and (ii) all other x and y variables equal 0. The expected weight of the resulting probabilistic assignment is $\sum_j \left(\frac{1}{2k} + \frac{s}{4} \right) w_j$. This argument can be extended to arbitrary graphs.

Higher Arity Satisfiable Instances The above ratio can be improved for satisfiable W-CSP instances, even for higher arities.

Instead of inequality [1] defined previously, introduce the following valid inequalities [1a] and [1b]:

$$y_{\alpha_j,u} \geq \sum_{v \in K} x_{j,u,v} \cdot c_j(u,v) \text{ for } j \in E \text{ and } u \in K \text{ [1a]}$$

$$y_{\beta_j,v} \geq \sum_{u \in K} x_{j,u,v} \cdot c_j(u,v) \text{ for } j \in E \text{ and } v \in K \text{ [1b]}$$

Apply randomized rounding as in R1. Call this algorithm R3.

Lemma 3. *Let I be an instance of IP where $OPT(I) = \sum_{j \in E} w_j$ and L be the corresponding linear program. For any optimal solution of L, [1a] and [1b] are equalities.*

Lemma 4. *Given a sequence of non-negative real values $x_1, \ldots, x_k$ and positive integer t, if $\sum_{i=1}^{k} x_i = 1$, then $\sum_{i=1}^{k} x_i^t \geq \frac{1}{k^{t-1}}$.*

By applying Lemmas 3 and 4, the expected weight of the assignment obtained by R3 is derived to be at least $1/k$ of the total weight. By simple induction, one can extend the argument to t-ary constraints. Hence:

Theorem 5. *For any fixed t, satisfiable W-$CSP(k)$ of arity t can be approximated within an absolute ratio of $\frac{1}{k^{t-1}}$.*

Again, this result is best possible, because there exists a satisfiable instance I in W-CSP(k) such that the expected weight of the assignment obtained by R3 is no more than $\frac{1}{k}OPT(I)$.

By setting $k = 2$, we get a ratio of $\frac{1}{2^{t-1}}$ which improves Khanna et al.'s result by a factor of 2, albeit over satisfiable instances. Recently, Trevisan [14] has independently shown that W-CSP(2) of arity t can be approximated within a relative ratio of $\frac{1}{2^{t-1}}$.

5 Randomized Rounding of Semidefinite Program

In this section, we present constant-ratio approximation via semidefinite programming relaxations.

5.1 Simple Rounding

Recall the definitions of $c_j(u, v)$, α_j and β_j from section 2 and formulate W-CSP as a quadratic integer program (Q') as follows:

$$Q'\text{: maximize } \sum_{j \in E} w_j f'_j(x)$$
$$\text{subject to } \sum_{u \in K} x_0 x_{i,u} = -(k - 2) \text{ for } i \in V$$
$$x_{i,u} \in \{-1, +1\} \qquad \text{for } i \in V \text{ and } u \in K$$
$$x_0 = +1$$

where $f'_j(x) = \frac{1}{4} \sum_{u,v} c_j(u, v) \left(1 + x_{\alpha_j,u} x_{\beta_j,v} + x_0 x_{\alpha_j,u} + x_0 x_{\beta_j,v}\right)$ encodes the satisfiability of R_j.

Consider the following relaxation. Interpret each variable x as a 1-dimensional vector of unit length and relax it to a unit-vector X lying in the N-dimensional unit sphere S_N, where $N = kn + 1$. The resulting relaxed problem (P) is the following:

$$P\text{: maximize } \sum_{j \in E} w_j F_j(X)$$
$$\text{subject to } \sum_{u \in K} X_0 \cdot X_{i,u} = -(k - 2) \text{ for } i \in V$$
$$X_0, X_{i,u} \in S_N \qquad \text{for } i \in V \text{ and } u \in K$$

where $F_j(X) = \frac{1}{4}\sum_{u,v} c_j(u,v)\left(1 + X_{\alpha_j,u} \cdot X_{\beta_j,v} + X_0 \cdot X_{\alpha_j,u} + X_0 \cdot X_{\beta_j,v}\right)$. The notation $A \cdot B$ means the inner product of vectors A and B. Clearly, (P) is a relaxation of (Q') because any feasible solution for (Q') with $N - 1$ zeros appended form a feasible solution for (P) with the same objective value (where X_0 is $(1, 0, \ldots, 0)$). Thus, $OPT(P) \geq OPT(Q')$.

Consider the following randomized algorithm to approximate (Q') for $k = 2$ (we will extend the analysis to $k = 3$ later):

1. (Relaxation) Solve (P) to optimality and obtain optimal set of vectors X^*.
2. (Randomized Rounding) Construct an assignment for (Q') as follows. For each i, with probability $1 - \frac{\arccos(X_0^* \cdot X_{i,u}^*)}{\pi}$, assign $x_{i,u}$ to $+1$ and $x_{i,v}$ ($v \neq u$) to -1.

By [6], the Relaxation step can be solved in polynomial time (within an additive factor) by semidefinite programming. The Rounding step has the following intuitive meaning: the smaller the angle between $X_{i,u}^*$ and X_0^*, the higher the probability that $x_{i,u}$ would be assigned to $+1$ and the other $x_{i,v}$ ($v \neq u$) assigned -1. Since the vector assignment is constrained by the equation $X_0^* \cdot X_{i,1}^* + X_0^* \cdot X_{i,2}^* = 0$ for all i, the sum of angles between X_0^* and $X_{i,1}^*$ and between X_0^* and $X_{i,2}^*$ must be 180 degrees (or π). Thus, the sum of probabilities of assigning i to 1 and to 2 is exactly 1, implying that the corresponding variable assignment obtained is valid. Furthermore, the variable x_0 is always assigned to $+1$.

Lemma 6. *For all unit vectors a, b and c, $b \cdot c \leq \cos(\arccos(a \cdot b) - \arccos(a \cdot c))$.*

Proof. The vectors a, b and c span a unit 3-D sphere. By a special form of triangle inequality ([10], pages 346–347) and the fact that all angles are between 0 and π, we can conclude that $\cos(\theta(b, c)) \leq \cos(\theta(a, b) - \theta(a, c))$. $\square$

Claim 1. *The expected weight of this probabilistic assignment is 0.408... $\times$ $OPT(Q')$.*

Proof. The expected weight of the probabilistic assignment is given by,

$$\hat{W} = \sum_{j \in E} w_j \left(\sum_{u,v \in K} c_j(u,v) \left[1 - \frac{\arccos(X_0^* \cdot X_{\alpha_j,u}^*)}{\pi}\right] \left[1 - \frac{\arccos(X_0^* \cdot X_{\beta_j,v}^*)}{\pi}\right] \right)$$

$$\geq \frac{0.408}{4} \sum_{j \in E} w_j \left(\sum_{u,v \in K} c_j(u,v) \left[X_{\alpha_j,u}^* \cdot X_{\beta_j,v}^* + X_0^* \cdot X_{\alpha_j,u}^* + X_0^* \cdot X_{\beta_j,v}^* + 1\right] \right)$$

$$= 0.408 \times OPT(P).$$

Let $p = \frac{\arccos(X_0^* \cdot X_{\alpha_j,u}^*)}{\pi}$, and $q = \frac{\arccos(X_0^* \cdot X_{\beta_j,v}^*)}{\pi}$. The inequality follows if we can show that $(1-p)(1-q) \geq 0.102[X_{\alpha_j,u}^* \cdot X_{\beta_j,v}^* + \cos(p\pi) + \cos(q\pi) + 1]$. By Lemma 6, it suffices to show $(1 - p)(1 - q) \geq 0.102[\cos(p\pi - q\pi) + \cos(p\pi) + \cos(q\pi) + 1]$. This can be shown by plotting the function

$$g(p, q) = (1 - p)(1 - q) - 0.102[\cos(p\pi - q\pi) + \cos(p\pi) + \cos(q\pi) + 1]$$

for $0 \leq q \leq p \leq 1$ and observing that it is non-negative. □

Now consider the case of $k = 3$. The technical difficulty is in ensuring that the sum of probabilities of assigning a variable to the three values is exactly 1. It is possible to enforce this condition by introducing the following set of $4n$ valid equations into (Q'). For all i:

$$x_0(x_{i,1} + x_{i,2} + x_{i,3}) = -1$$
$$x_{i,1}(x_0 + x_{i,2} + x_{i,3}) = -1$$
$$x_{i,2}(x_0 + x_{i,2} + x_{i,3}) = -1$$
$$x_{i,3}(x_0 + x_{i,2} + x_{i,3}) = -1$$

Let (P) be the corresponding semidefinite program relaxation. Call two vectors X_1 and X_2 *opposite* if $X_1 = -X_2$. By simple vector calculus, one can show that (P) always returns a set of vectors with the property that for each i, there exists at least one vector $\check{X} \in \{X_{i,1}, X_{i,2}, X_{i,3}\}$ opposite to X_0 while the remaining two are opposite to each other. Noting that $1 - \frac{\arccos(X_0 \cdot \check{X})}{\pi} = 0$, the sum of probabilities of assigning i to the other two values is exactly 1. Thus, we can ignore one value and arrive at the following result after derandomization:

Theorem 7. *W-CSP(k) ($k \leq 3$) can be approximated within 0.408.*

Note that this ratio is an improvement over the linear programming bounds of 0.313 and 0.194 for $k = 2$ and 3 respectively.

5.2 Limits of Simple Rounding

The above analysis is almost best possible. We prove that, given the above formulation, regardless of the randomized rounding scheme we choose in Step 2 of the algorithm, there exists a W-CSP(2) instance such that the expected weight of the solution is no more than 0.5 times the optimal weight. Let S be the set consisting of the two constraint relations $\{(1, 1), (2, 2)\}$ and $\{(1, 2), (2, 1)\}$. Let W-CSP$_S$ be the set of W-CSP(2) instances whose constraints are drawn from the set S.

Lemma 8. *Let $\hat{X}$ be the set of vectors $\{\hat{X}_0\} \bigcup \{\hat{X}_{i,u} : i \in V, u \in K\}$ such that all $\hat{X}_{i,u}$'s are equal and orthogonal to $\hat{X}_0$. Then, $\hat{X}$ is an optimal solution for the relaxation problem (P) associated with any instance of W-CSP$_S$.*

Proof. Consider the relaxation problem (P) of an arbitrary instance of W-CSP$_S$. For any feasible solution X, the objective value is,

$$\frac{1}{4} \sum_{j \in E} w_j \left(\sum_{u,v \in \{1,2\}} c_j(u,v) \left[1 + X_0 \cdot X_{\alpha_j, u} + X_0 \cdot X_{\beta_j, v} + X_{\alpha_j, u} \cdot X_{\beta_j, v} \right] \right) \leq W$$

since $X_0 \cdot X_{i,1} = -X_0 \cdot X_{i,2}$ for all i. On the other hand, $\hat{X}$ is a feasible solution of (P) whose objective value is W. $\square$

Lemma 9. *Let $\{p_{i,u}\}$ be a fixed probabilistic distribution. There exists an instance in W-CSP$_S$ such that the expected weight of the assignment is no more than 0.5 times the optimal weight.*

Proof. Construct the following W-CSP$_S$ instance. Let the constraint graph be a simple chain connecting n variables. For each constraint j connecting variables i and l, let u_{max} (resp. u_{min}) be the value in $\{1,2\}$ such that $p_{i,u}$ is the larger (resp. smaller) quantity, ties broken arbitrarily. Let v_{max} and v_{min} be defined similarly for p_{lv}. Define the constraint relation of j to be $\{(u_{max}, v_{min}), (u_{min}, v_{max})\}$ which is an element of S. Now, one can verify by simple arithmetic that the expected weight of the solution is at most 0.5 times the sum of weights. On the other hand, there exists an assignment which can satisfy all constraints simultaneously. $\square$

Theorem 10. *Using the above semidefinite formulation, W-CSP cannot be approximated by more than 0.5 regardless of randomized rounding scheme, even for $k = 2$.*

Proof. Given a randomized rounding scheme, let $\{p_{i,u}\}$ be the fixed probability distribution associated with the fixed set of vectors $\hat{X}$. By Lemma 9, we can construct at least one instance I in W-CSP$_S$ for which the probabilistic assignment has expected weight no more than 0.5 times the optimal and by Lemma 8, $\hat{X}$ is an optimal solution of the corresponding relaxation problem (P) of I. The theorem follows if we suppose that $\hat{X}$ is returned by the Relaxation step of the algorithm. $\square$

5.3 Rounding Via Hyperplane Partitioning

The rounding scheme of Goemans and Williamson [6] for approximating MAX SAT can be extended to obtain improved ratios for W-CSP(2). Let $x_i \in \{-1, +1\}$ represent the value to be assigned to variable i. A given instance of W-CSP(2) can be modelled by the following quadratic integer program:

$$Q': \text{maximize} \sum_{i < l} [a_{il}(1 - x_i x_l) + b_{il}(1 + x_i x_l) - c_{il}]$$
$$\text{subject to } x_i \in \{-1, +1\} \qquad \text{for } i \in V \bigcup \{0\}$$

where the coefficients a_{il}, b_{il} and c_{il} are *non-negative* and x_0 is an additional variable. The details are easily derivable from the MAX SAT formulation of [6] and is omitted in this version.

Now apply the following algorithm:

1. (Relaxation) Solve the relaxation (P) optimally and obtain an optimal set of vectors X^*.
2. (Randomized Rounding) Let r be a vector uniformly distributed on unit sphere S_n. Construct an assignment for (Q') as follows:
   for each $i = 0, \ldots, n$, if $r \cdot X_i^* \geq 0$, then $x_i = +1$ else $x_i = -1$.
3. (Normalizing) If $x_0 = +1$ then return x as the assignment, else ($x_0 = -1$) return x with all values flipped as the assignment.

The Rounding step chooses a random hyperplane through the origin of unit sphere (with r as its normal) and partitions the variables into those vectors that lie on the same side of the hyperplane. The Normalizing step is needed to undo the effect of the additional variable x_0 in case it is set to -1. Let $\hat{W}$ be the expected weight of the assignment returned by the algorithm.

Claim 2. $\hat{W} \geq \gamma \left(\sum_{i<l} a_{il}(1 - X_i^* X_l^*) + \sum_{i<l} b_{il}(1 + X_i^* X_l^*) \right) - \sum_{i<l} c_{il}$, where $\gamma = 0.878....$

The proof is a direct extension of that given in [6]. From this claim, it follows that two subclasses of W-CSP, namely, *2-consistent instances* and *satisfiable instances* have approximation ratio γ. The first case follows from the observation that 2-consistent contraints have no constant terms (i.e. c_{il}). For the second case, we can iteratively satisfy all selfish constraints by uniquely fixing the values of their variables. The remaining constraint graph is 2-consistent and still satisfiable, and can be approximated within γ.

Finally, consider the general case of W-CSP(2). Observe that (i) the optimal objective value is at least $sW \geq \frac{1}{4}W$; and (ii) each coefficient c_{il} is at most half times the weight of the constraint between i and l and therefore the total contribution of the negative constant terms is at most $\frac{1}{2}W$. Hence, we have,

$$\sum_{i<l} c_{il} \leq \frac{1}{2}W \leq 2 \sum_{i<l} [a_{il}(1 - X_i^* X_l^*) + b_{il}(1 + X_i^* X_l^*) - c_{il}],$$

and therefore,

$$\hat{W} \geq \gamma \left(\sum_{i<l} [a_{il}(1 - X_i^* X_l^*) + b_{il}(1 + X_i^* X_l^*) - c_{il}] \right) - (1 - \gamma) \sum_{i<l} c_{il}$$

$$\geq (3\gamma - 2) \left(\sum_{i<l} [a_{il}(1 - X_i^* X_l^*) + b_{il}(1 + X_i^* X_l^*) - c_{il}] \right)$$

$$\geq 0.634... \times OPT(P)$$

Using the derandomization technique of Mahajan and Ramesh [9], we get:

Theorem 11. *W-CSP(2) can be approximated within 0.634, and 0.878 if instances are 2-consistent or satisfiable.*

Acknowledgements

We thank David Williamson for discovering a fatal error in an early analysis of the semidefinite programming bound; Madhu Sudan for suggesting interactive proofs to obtain the non-approximability result; Luca Trevisan for notifying us the new result of Raz [13] and its application; Magnús Halldórsson and Carlos Domingo for their constructive comments.

References

1. Noga Alon and Joe Spencer. *The Probabilistic Method.* Wiley Interscience Ser. Disc. Math. and Optimiz., 1992.
2. S. Arora, C. Lund, R. Motwani, M. Sudan, and M. Szegedy. Proof verification and hardness of approximation problems. In *Proc. 33th IEEE Symp. on Found. of Comp. Sci.*, pages 2–13, 1993.
3. P. Berman and G. Schnitger. On the complexity of approximating the independent set problem. *Infor. & Comput.*, 96:77–94, 1992.
4. P. Erdös and L. Selfridge. On a combinatorial game. *J. Comb. Theory Series A*, 14:298–301, 1989.
5. Uriel Feige and László Lovász. Two-prover one-round proof systems: Their power and their problems. In *Proc. 24th ACM Symp. on Theory of Computing*, pages 733–744, 1992.
6. Michel X. Goemans and David P. Williamson. Approximation algorithms for MAX CUT and MAX 2SAT. In *Proc. 26th ACM Symp. on Theory of Computing*, pages 422–431, 1994. Full version to appear in *J. ACM*.
7. S. Khanna, R. Motwani, M. Sudan, and U. Vazirani. On syntactic versus computational views of approximability. In *Proc. 35th IEEE Symp. on Found. of Comp. Sci.*, 1994.
8. H. C. Lau. Approximation of constraint satisfaction via local search. In *Proc. 4th Wrksp. on Algorithms and Data Structures (WADS)*, pages 461–472. Springer Verlag Lect. Notes Comp. Sci. (955), 1995.
9. S. Mahajan and H. Ramesh. Derandomizing semidefinite programming based approximation algorithms. In *Proc. 36th IEEE Symp. on Found. of Comp. Sci.*, pages 162–168, 1995.
10. Barrett O'Neill. *Elementary Differential Geometry.* Academic Press, New York, 1966.
11. Christos H. Papadimitriou and Mihalis Yannakakis. Optimization, approximation, and complexity classes. *J. Comput. Sys. Sci.*, 43:425–440, 1991.
12. P. Raghavan and C. D. Thompson. Randomized rounding: A technique for provably good algorithms and algorithmic proofs. *Combinatorica*, 7(4):365–374, 1987.
13. Ran Raz. A parallel repetition theorem. In *Proc. 27th ACM Symp. on Theory of Computing*, pages 447–456, 1995.
14. Luca Trevisan. Positive linear programming, parallel approximation and PCPs, 1996. Manuscript.

On the Hardness of Global and Local Approximation*

Hartmut Klauck

Fachbereich Informatik, Johann-Wolfgang-Goethe-Universität Frankfurt
60054 Frankfurt am Main, Germany
e-mail:klauck@thi.informatik.uni-frankfurt.de

Abstract. This paper combines local search and approximation into "approximation of local optima", i.e., an attempt to escape hardness of exact local optimization by trying to find solutions which are approximately as good as the worst local optimum. The complexity of several well known optimization problems under this approach is investigated. Our main tool is a special reduction called the "strong $\mathcal{PLS}$-reduction" which preserves cost and local search structure in a very strict sense. Completeness for the class of $\mathcal{NP}$-optimization/local search problems under this reduction allows to deduce that both approximation of global and of local optima cannot be achieved efficiently (unless $\mathcal{P} = \mathcal{NP}$ resp. $\mathcal{P} = \mathcal{PLS}$). We show that the (weighted) problems MIN 4-DNF, MAX HOPFIELD, MIN/MAX 0-1-PROGRAMMING, MIN INDEPENDENT DOMINATING SET, and MIN TRAVELING SALESMAN are all complete under the new reduction.
Moreover the unweighted MIN 3-DNF problem is shown to be complete for the class of $\mathcal{NP}$-optimization problems with polynomially bounded cost functions under an approximation preserving reduction. This implies that the logically defined class MIN Σ_0, the minimization analogue of MAX SNP, does not capture any (low) approximation degree.

1 Introduction

Combinatorial optimization is an important area of computer science. Unfortunately many interesting problems in this area are $\mathcal{NP}$-hard and are thus commonly believed to be intractable within reasonable efficiency. Therefore restrictions of these problems are considered which may yield efficient algorithms: approximation and local search are the most popular approaches that demand a guarantee for good solutions. An approximation algorithm outputs solutions for an instance of an optimization problem that have cost "near" the optimum, a local search algorithm optimizes with respect to some polynomial time computable neighborhood. Our new approach "approximation of local optima" is mainly motivated by the hope to escape hardness of both local search and global approximation, a situation that occurs e.g. for the Traveling Salesman Problem ([GJ79], [Kr89],[PapSY90]). We begin with a formal definition of $\mathcal{NP}$-optimization problems (in the spirit of [BeSc92] and [Ka92]).

---

* Research supported by DFG-grant Schn 503/1-1

Definition 1.1 *An $\mathcal{NP}$-optimization problem L is defined by a tuple $(P, C, goal)$, where P and C are polynomial time computable functions and goal $\in \{\min, \max\}$. $C : \{0,1\}^* \times \{0,1\}^* \to \mathbb{N}$ is called the "objective" (or "cost") function and $P : \{0,1\}^* \times \{0,1\}^* \to \{0,1\}$ is the "feasibility predicate".*

Solving L means to compute $opt_{P,C,goal}(x) = goal\{C(s,x)|P(s,x)$ for $s \in \{0,1\}^{poly(|x|)}\}$. x will be referred to as an "instance" of L, s with $P(s,x) = 1$ as a "feasible solution" to x.

The class of $\mathcal{NP}$-optimization problems is called $\mathcal{NPO}$, its subclass containing the problems with polynomially bounded cost function is called $\mathcal{NPO} - \mathcal{PB}$.

We will also consider a problem with an integer cost function (the Hopfield energy function), but do not formally distinguish this case. Next we define approximation algorithms in the usual way.

Definition 1.2 *Let $L = (P, C, goal)$ be some $\mathcal{NP}$-optimization problem. The "performance ratio" of a solution s to some instance x of L with global optimum $C(s_{opt}(x), x)$ is $R_L(s, x) = \max\{C(s_{opt}(x), x)/C(s, x), C(s, x)/C(s_{opt}(x), x)\}$ if $C(s, x) > 0$ and $C(s_{opt}(x), x) > 0$. Otherwise $R_L(s, x)$ is defined as $C(s, x) + C(s_{opt}(x), x) + 1$.*

Let $\mathcal{A}$ be an algorithm that produces some feasible solution $s_{\mathcal{A}}(x)$ given an instance x of L. Then $\mathcal{A}$ is called a ρ-approximation algorithm for problem L if $R_L(s_{\mathcal{A}}(x), x) \leq \rho(|x|)$ for all instances x of L ("$\mathcal{A}$ approximates L within ρ").

Showing completeness for the class $\mathcal{NPO}$ or $\mathcal{NPO} - \mathcal{PB}$ under an approximation preserving reduction is an elegant way to prove that a problem cannot be approximated efficiently. Among the few natural problems known to be complete are MIN INDEPENDENT DOMINATING SET ([Ha93] and [Ka93]), MIN 0-1-PROGRAMMING ([OM87]), MAX 0-1-PROGRAMMING ([BeSc92]) and MIN TRAVELING SALESMAN ([OM87]). Definitions of optimization problems are provided in an appendix. We investigate hard problems which cannot be approximated efficiently unless $\mathcal{P} = \mathcal{NP}$. For this we employ the E-reduction of [KMSV94].

Definition 1.3 *Let L, M be two $\mathcal{NPO}$ problems. L "E-reduces" to M if there are two polynomial time computable functions f, g and a constant c such that*

1. *f maps instances of L to instances of M. g maps pairs (y, x) [for instances x and solutions y to $f(x)$] to solutions to x.*
2. *For every instance x of L and every solution s to $f(x)$ the following holds:*

$$(R_L(g(s,x), x) - 1) \leq c \cdot (R_M(s, f(x)) - 1).$$

The complexity of local search was investigated in [JPaY88], [Kr89], and [PapSY90], leading to completeness statements for the class $\mathcal{PLS}$ as well as to $\mathcal{P}$-completeness results for unweighted local search problems. We now define local search problems analogue to [JPaY88].

Definition 1.4 *An $\mathcal{NP}$-optimization problem $L = (P, C, goal)$ together with a neighborhood structure $N(s, x)$ that maps a solution and an instance to a set of neighboring solutions, belongs to the class $\mathcal{PLS}$ (for "polynomial local search"), if the following polynomial time algorithms exist:*

1. $SOLUTION_L$. INPUT: instance x. OUTPUT: feasible solution to x.
2. $SEARCH_L$. INPUT: instance x and solution s to x. OUTPUT: if s is a local optimum of x then $SEARCH_L$ outputs s, otherwise $SEARCH_L$ produces some strictly better solution s' out of $N(s,x)$.

The algorithms allow the (obvious) design of a local search algorithm that takes polynomial time for every step. The class $\mathcal{PLS}$ is probably smaller than (functional) $\mathcal{NP}$ and larger than (functional) $\mathcal{P}$ (see [JPaY88]). The problems considered here have simple neighborhoods formalized in the following way.

Definition 1.5 *The k-Flip neighborhood for $\mathcal{PLS}$-problems with solutions in $\{0,1\}^n$ contains for each solution s all feasible solutions within Hamming-distance k from s.*

The only problem considered here that will not have the $k - Flip$ neighborhood is MIN TRAVELING SALESMAN. Here two solutions are neighboring in $k - change$, if one tour can be obtained from the other by removing k edges and inserting k edges. For the purpose of investigating hard $\mathcal{PLS}$-problems a special kind of reduction preserving local optimality was defined in [JPaY88].

Definition 1.6 *A $\mathcal{PLS}$ problem L is "$\mathcal{PLS}$-reducible" to a problem M, if there are polynomial time computable functions f and g such that*

1. *f maps instances of L to instances of M,*
2. *g maps pairs (solution to $f(x)$, x) to solutions to x,*
3. *for all instances x of L: if s is a local optimum of $f(x)$, then $g(s,x)$ is a local optimum of x.*

We introduce a new approach combining local search and approximation: a *local approximation algorithm* outputs solutions which are approximately as good as the worst local optimum. In most practical applications local search is used as a heuristic to find "good" solutions, the structural property of local optimality is seldom of interest. Approximation of local optima in contrast to exact local optimization may therefore be no severe loss with regard to applications. One could hope that this approach makes it possible to evade the hardness of local optimization as well as that of global approximation.

Definition 1.7 *Let L be a $\mathcal{PLS}$-problem. The "local performance ratio" of a solution s to an instance x of L with "worst" local optimum $C(s_{opt}(x),x)$ is defined as follows: Let $a = C(s,x)$ and $b = C(s_{opt}(x),x)$ in the case of maximization and conversely in the case of minimization. Then*

$$R_L^{loc}(s,x) = \begin{cases} 1 & \text{if } a \geq b \\ b/a & \text{if } 0 < a < b \\ b+1 & \text{if } a = 0 \leq b \end{cases}$$

Let $\mathcal{A}$ be an algorithm that produces a feasible solution $s_{\mathcal{A}}(x)$ given an instance x. $\mathcal{A}$ is called a local ρ-approximation algorithm if $R_L^{loc}(s_{\mathcal{A}}(x),x) \leq \rho(|x|)$ for all instances x.

Our goal is to investigate the structure of hard optimization and local search problems by completeness statements. The definition of the reduction we use is built up iteratively, the first step being the $\mathcal{PLS}$-reduction. The second step is the tight $\mathcal{PLS}$-reduction, which was defined in [PapSY90] to transfer $\mathcal{PSPACE}$-completeness of the so-called "standard local optimum problem" between $\mathcal{PLS}$-problems. The standard local optimum problem consists of finding the specific local optimum the algorithms of the $\mathcal{PLS}$-definition will output. The tight $\mathcal{PLS}$-reduction preserves the local search structure very strictly.

Definition 1.8 *A $\mathcal{PLS}$-reduction (f, g) is tight, if the following holds: if x is an instance, then a subset R (called the "image set") of the feasible solutions to $f(x)$ exists such that*

1. *R contains all the local optima of $f(x)$*
2. *For every feasible solution s to x a solution s' in R can be constucted in polynomial time such that $g(s', x) = s$*
3. *Let G_x be the graph of all feasible solutions to x, where (s, s') is an edge iff s' is a better neighbor of s in x. If $G_{f(x)}$ contains a path from $s \in R$ to $s' \in R$ such that all intermediate vertices are not in R, then either $g(s, x) = g(s', x)$ or $g(s', x)$ is a better neighbor of $g(s, x)$.*

To include the aspect of approximability we add another condition to the tight $\mathcal{PLS}$-reduction. The ratio of the cost functions of both problems has to be kept almost fixed along the local search paths preserved by tight $\mathcal{PLS}$-reductions. We introduce our new reduction as follows.

Definition 1.9 *A strong-$\mathcal{PLS}$-reduction (among L and M) is a tight $\mathcal{PLS}$-reduction (f, g) with the following additional property: A value t exists such that*

- *for every solution s to $f(x)$ that is contained in the image set R of the reduction: $c_L(g(s, x), x) = \lfloor \frac{c_M(s, f(x))}{t} \rfloor$.*
- *for every solution s to $f(x)$ that is not contained in the image set R of the reduction: $c_L(g(s, x), x) \geq \lfloor \frac{c_M(s, f(x))}{t} \rfloor$ in the case of maximization and $c_L(g(s, x), x) \leq \lfloor \frac{c_M(s, f(x))}{t} \rfloor$ in the case of minimization.*

It is possible to alter this definition in order to allow reductions from maximization problems to minimization problems and vice versa. We leave this generalization out, but state our results in the stronger form.

The following result can be shown with arguments similar to those in [JPaY88] for showing $\mathcal{PLS}$-completeness.

Proposition 1.1 *1. Strong $\mathcal{PLS}$-reductions are transitive.*
2. MIN CIRCUIT OUTPUT and MAX CIRCUIT OUTPUT with the 1-Flip neighborhood are $\mathcal{PLS}$-complete via strong $\mathcal{PLS}$-reductions.

The next proposition is straightforward and captures the most essential properties of complete problems under our reduction.

Proposition 1.2 *Let L be a problem that is $\mathcal{PLS}$-hard via strong $\mathcal{PLS}$-reductions.*

1. *L is $\mathcal{NPO}$-hard.*
2. *Finding local optima of L is $\mathcal{PLS}$-hard.*
3. *Solving the standard algorithm problem of L is $\mathcal{PSPACE}$-hard.*
4. *Global $2^{n^{\epsilon}}$-approximation of L solves a $\mathcal{NP}$-hard problem (for const. $\epsilon > 0$).*
5. *Local $2^{n^{\epsilon}}$-approximation of L solves a $\mathcal{PLS}$-hard problem (for const. $\epsilon > 0$).*

Up to now we have developed the machinery to show that problems are extremely expressive regarding local search and cost structure. Our main theorem points out the power of some optimization problems.

Theorem 1 *The following problems are $\mathcal{PLS}$-complete under the strong $\mathcal{PLS}$-reduction:*

1. MIN 4-DNF-*B* *with the 1-Flip neighborhood for constant B.*
2. MAX HOPFIELD *with the 1-Flip neighborhood.*
3. MIN INDEPENDENT DOMINATING SET-*B* *with the k-Flip neighborhood for constants B, k.*
4. MIN 0-1-PROGRAMMING *and* MAX 0-1-PROGRAMMING *with the k-Flip neighborhood for constant k.*
5. MIN TRAVELING SALESMAN *with the k-change neighborhood for constant k.*

A Hopfield net is a neural net with an undirected graph structure that computes local optima of the Hopfield energy function $H(x) = \sum_{i<j} w_{i,j} x_i x_j - \sum_i t_i x_i$ with $x \in \{0,1\}^n$ (see [Ho82]). Hopfield nets have been widely applied to combinatorial optimization, see [HKP91] and [HoTa85]. The problem to determine a local optimum exactly is known to be $\mathcal{P}$ resp. $\mathcal{PLS}$-complete, see [PapSY90]. We show that the problem is even complete under strong $\mathcal{PLS}$-reductions implying that local and global approximation are not efficient, too.

MIN *k*-DNF-*B* is the problem of minimizing the sum of weights on satisfied conjunctions in a *k*-DNF formula in which each variable appears at most *B* times. Up to now it was only known that unweighted MIN 3-DNF cannot be approximated globally within a constant (see [KT94]). We investigate MIN 3-DNF further by showing $\mathcal{NPO}$- resp. $\mathcal{NPO}-\mathcal{PB}$-completeness (for the weighted resp. unweighted version). Unweighted MIN *k*-DNF is a member of the logically defined class MIN Σ_0 (the minimization analogue of the class MAX SNP). The hardness of MIN 3-DNF implies that the closure of this class contains all polynomially bounded $\mathcal{NP}$-optimization problems. This is an astonishing contrast to the closure of MAX SNP which equals the set of all $\mathcal{NP}$-optimization problems with polynomially bounded cost functions that have a constant factor approximation (see [KMSV94]). The best previously known result for MIN 3-DNF was MIN Σ_0-completeness (see [KT94]). Our result of $\mathcal{NPO} - \mathcal{PB}$-completeness for MIN 3-DNF also resolves a question in [KT94] for MIN Π_1-complete problems.

In section 2 we give completeness results under the strong $\mathcal{PLS}$-reduction as stated in theorem 1. Mostly the proofs are only sketched, however. Section 3 investigates MIN 3-DNF, section 4 shows implications for logically defined classes of optimization problems. Conclusions are given in section 5. Definitions of the optimization problems considered here are provided in the appendix.

2   Proofs of Hardness Results

Lemma 2.1 MIN 4-DNF-*B* *with constant B and the 1-Flip neighborhood is* $\mathcal{PLS}$-*complete via strong* $\mathcal{PLS}$-*reductions.*

PROOF SKETCH: For the sake of simplicity we prove a weaker version, in which the number of occurences of one variable is unbounded, and the occurences of all other variables are bounded by some constant.

The inclusion statement is trivial. For the instance mapping of the reduction we have to map a circuit to a 4-DNF formula. Local search on this formula simulates the computation of two copies of the circuit recomputing one copy after the other on improved, neighboring inputs. We may assume that the given circuit consists of gates $g_s, \ldots, g_1$, where $g_s, \ldots, g_{s-n}$ are the input gates, $g_{l+n}, \ldots, g_{l+1}$ are gates which compute an improved neighboring solution to the input of the circuit as defined by the algorithm $SEARCH$ for MIN CIRCUIT OUTPUT, and $g_m, \ldots, g_1$ are the output gates of the circuit. The gates are given in reverse topological ordering, i.e., all inputs to a gate have larger numbers than this gate (all these modifications of an arbitrary circuit can be done in polynomial time).

The circuit is mapped to a formula on the following variables: for every internal and input gate g_i of the circuit we use two variables f_i and h_i (for the two simulations). Additionally we have a variable v which indicates which one of the two circuits is "verified". Errors in the verified circuit will be very costly.

There are 4 groups of conjunctions. In these groups the weights of conjunctions are decreasing geometrically by a factor of 2, so that the weight of each conjunction exceeds the weights of all "lower" conjunctions together. The groups themselves are ordered, too: there are large, medium, small, and tiny conjunctions. The large conjunctions express that the gate-variables of the verified circuit-simulation are set correctly (decreasing according to their numbers). This can be expressed by 4-conjunctions (the wrong values of the gate and its predecessors and the value of v showing that this gate should be verified). The medium conjunctions weight the variables of the output gates of the verified circuit-simulation decreasingly so that these conjunctions together weight the binary value of this output multiplied by some fixed factor t (the smallest medium weight). Here 2-conjunctions suffice. The small conjunctions punish setting the input of one circuit-simulation differently from the neighboring solution computed by the other circuit (2-conjunctions). The tiny conjunctions are analogue to the large conjunctions but with the verification variable left out, i.e., they punish wrong gate-variables in decreasing order.

Consider any assignment to the variables. Local search will proceed as follows: the verified circuit will be corrected, because the correction of a wrong gate removes more cost than it produces, since only successor gates are getting wrong by the correction. Afterwards the new neighbor will be copied to the input variables of the unverified circuit, this circuit will be corrected (due to the tiny conjunctions). Now with a single flip of v the verified circuit can be changed, so that the output conjunctions produce the improved cost of the neighboring solution evaluated by the second circuit (if the first one was not optimal). The same process can begin again (but now the verified circuit is already correct).

Clearly in a local optimum both circuit simulations compute correctly and on the same input, one of them is verified. The highest satisfied conjunctions are medium, i.e., the correct output stretched by a factor t dominates the weights.

The solution mapping g maps assignments to the formula variables to the assignments to the input variables of the verified circuit simulation. It is easy to see that this is a $\mathcal{PLS}$-reduction: local optima are mapped to local optima. Use the set of assignments, in which the verified circuit simulation computes correctly as the "image set" R. Every string s can be mapped in polynomial time to a solution in R. Two neighboring solutions in R are mapped by g either to the same string or to neighbors. We have a tight $\mathcal{PLS}$-reduction. For every solution in R the cost condition of the strong $\mathcal{PLS}$-reduction clearly holds with the factor t. For any other solution the sum of weights of the formula is very large. So this is indeed a strong $\mathcal{PLS}$-reduction. The full proof of the lemma uses chains of verification variables and push variables similar to constructions in [SchY91] and [Kr89]. □

The following can be shown by reduction from MAX CIRCUIT OUTPUT, the construction is far more complicated than that of lemma 2.1, though.

Lemma 2.2 MAX HOPFIELD *with 1-Flip is* $\mathcal{PLS}$*-complete via strong* $\mathcal{PLS}$*-reductions.*

Lemma 2.3 MIN INDEPENDENT DOMINATING SET-B *on weighted graphs with the k-Flip neighborhood (for constants B and k) is* $\mathcal{PLS}$*-complete via strong* $\mathcal{PLS}$*-reductions.*

PROOF: By reduction from MIN 4-DNF-B'. For every conjunction of a given formula take one vertex v_i. Additionally take vertices x_i and $\overline{x_i}$ for each variable and for its negation (called "literal vertices"). Connect the conjunction vertices with those literal vertices, with whom their conjunction contradicts and connect every variable vertex with its negation. The weights of the literal vertices are 0, the weights of the conjunction vertices are the weights of the respective conjunction. The degree of each literal vertex is bounded by $B' + 1$, the degree of conjunction vertices is bounded by 4. As neighborhood use k-Flip with k large enough such that switching a variable and all adjacent conjunctions is allowed.

An independent set on the defined graph contains at most one of each pair of contradicting literal vertices. If neither the variable nor its negation are contained, then possibly conjunction-vertices are contained which could be excluded by setting one of the literals, but this increases the cost of the independent set. If the independent set is dominating, then no conjunction vertex is not contained, which contradicts to none of the literals set. So the cost of an independent dominating set is at least as large as the cost of the conjunctions "satisfied" by the settings of the literal vertices. The mapping g of the reduction simply maps a vertex set s to the states of the variables induced by the literal vertices, setting uncertain variables arbitrarily. The image set R is the set of all independent dominating sets which include one of each pair of literal vertices. The cost of $g(s, x)$ for some $s \in R$ is thus always the same as the cost of s, for other solutions s the cost of $g(s, x)$ is at most as large as that of s. So this is a strong $\mathcal{PLS}$-reduction. $\square$

Lemma 2.4 MIN 0-1-PROGRAMMING *with the k-Flip neighborhood for some constant k is* $\mathcal{PLS}$-complete *via strong* $\mathcal{PLS}$-reductions, *even if the number of nonzero entries is restricted to a constant for every row and column of the matrix in the problem instances. The same holds for* MAX 0-1-PROGRAMMING.

PROOF: Reduction from MIN 4-DNF-B. Use one variable v_i for every conjunction, and variables $x_i, \overline{x_i}$ for every variable of the formula. Linear constraints express that $x_i + \overline{x_i} = 1$, and that for each v_j corresponding to $L_1 \wedge L_2 \wedge L_3 \wedge L_4$ the following holds: $v_j + \overline{L_1} + \overline{L_2} + \overline{L_3} + \overline{L_4} \geq 1$ and $v_j + \overline{L_i} \leq 1$ for $i = 1 \ldots 4$. So all variables are set consistently, and any conjunction variable is either set to 1 or contradicts to the variable setting, and no conjunction is set to 1 which contradicts to a literal. For the optimization vector c the variables v_i are weighted as in the formula, all other variables are weighted with 0. As neighborhood use $k - Flip$ with k large enough to allow changing a x_i variable, its complement variable $\overline{x_i}$ and all affected conjunction variables. Every row contains at most 5 nonzero entries, every column contains at most $2B + 2$ nonzero entries. This is a strong $\mathcal{PLS}$-reduction, because every feasible solution corresponds uniquely to a truth assignment for the formula and produces the same cost as the formula. The neighborhood allows a one to one simulation of local search.

MAX 0-1 PROGRAMMING is complete, because MIN 0-1 PROGRAMMING can be reduced to it (the proof is left out). $\square$

Lemma 2.5 MIN TRAVELING SALESMAN *with the k-change neighborhood is* $\mathcal{PLS}$-complete *via strong* $\mathcal{PLS}$-reductions.

PROOF IDEA: By a similar construction as in [Kr89] for showing $\mathcal{PLS}$-completeness for MIN TRAVELING SALESMAN with the $k - change$ neighborhood it is possible to show a strong $\mathcal{PLS}$-reduction from MIN 4-DNF-B. $\square$

An important note is that all previous reductions can be generalized to problems with polynomial weights. In this case one obtains hardness for the class of $\mathcal{PLS}$-problems with polynomially bounded cost functions and $\mathcal{NC}^1$-computable cost/feasibility/search/solution functions. This suffices to deduce $\mathcal{P}$-hardness of n^ϵ local approximation and $\mathcal{NPO} - \mathcal{PB}$-completeness from the reduction.

3 Exploring the Complexity of Min 3-DNF

Proposition 3.1 MIN CIRCUIT OUTPUT^{pol} *is* $\mathcal{NPO}-\mathcal{PB}$ *compl. via E-reductions.*

Lemma 3.2 *1. Polynomial weight* MIN 3-DNF *is* $\mathcal{NPO} - \mathcal{PB}$-complete *via E-reductions.*

2. MIN 3-DNF *with unbounded weights is* $\mathcal{NPO}$-complete *via E-reductions.*

PROOF: 1. Reduction from MIN CIRCUIT OUTPUT^{pol}. The instance mapping is as follows. Use one variable for every input and every gate of the circuit. Let w be the largest possible output of the circuit. For every internal gate of the circuit use 3-conjunction to express faulty computations, weight these with $2w$. Weight the output gates according to their position. Now in an optimum the variables corresponding to the gates are set correctly and the cost of the formula equals the output of the circuit on the assignment to the input variables. The solution mapping g maps an assignment to the variables of the formula to the values of the variables representing the input gates. Clearly the performance ratio of $g(s,x)$ is smaller than or equal to the performance ratio of s.

2. Reduction from MIN CIRCUIT OUTPUT. Use the same variables and conjunctions for the gates as in 1. This time exponential weights are necessary. □

Lemma 3.3 *For every integer $k \geq 1$ MIN k-DNF with weights of size w can be E-reduced to MIN k-DNF-3 with weights at most $2nw$.*

PROOF: The case $k = 1$ is trivial. For $k \geq 2$ a variable v appears negated in conjunctions $c_1, \ldots, c_p$ and unnegated in conjunctions $d_1, \ldots, d_q$. Replace v by variables $v_0, \ldots, v_{p+1}$ and $v'_0, \ldots, v'_{q+1}$. Use the conjunctions $(v_i, \overline{v_{i+1 \bmod p+2}})$ for every i and analogue conjunctions for the v'_i. Additionally take (v_0, v'_0) and $(\overline{v_{p+1}}, \overline{v'_{q+1}})$. These conjunctions carry weights $2nw$ (exceeding the sum of all weights on the original conjunctions). The new variables v_i and v'_i for $1 \leq i \leq p, q$ are used in the conjunctions v is involved in. Observe that one of the new conjunctions is true whenever the variables on one cycle do not have the same value and that this costs a heavy weight. The same happens if the two cycles of the v and the v' do not carry opposite values. So in an optimum the variables of each cycle have equal values, each literal-pair of cycles has opposite values. The number of occurences of each variable is bounded by 3. The solution mapping maps an assignment s to the new formula to an assignment to the original formula such that the value of a variable is the value of some variable on its v_i-cycle. If a literal pair of cycles has no consistent value then $g(s,x)$ has an improved performance ratio, else it is the same as that of s. □

Theorem 2 *1. Unweighted MIN 3-DNF is $\mathcal{NPO}-\mathcal{PB}$-compl. via E-reductions.*

2. MIN 3-DNF-3 with polynomial weights is $\mathcal{NPO}-\mathcal{PB}$-compl. via E-reductions.

3. MIN 3-DNF-3 with unbounded weights is $\mathcal{NPO}$-complete via E-reductions.

4. Unweighted MIN 3-DNF cannot be approximated within $n^{1-\epsilon}$ for any constant $\epsilon > 0$ unless $\mathcal{P} = \mathcal{NP}$.

5. MIN 3-DNF-3 with weights bounded by w cannot be approximated within w unless $\mathcal{P} = \mathcal{NP}$.

PROOF: Replacing polynomial weights in the reduction of lemma 3.2 leads to statement 1. Statements 2. and 3. follow from lemma 3.2/3.3.

It is an $\mathcal{NP}$-complete problem to decide whether a $3 - DNF$ formula is tautological (one conjunction is always satisfied) or not (the minimal number of satisfied conjunctions is 0) ([GJ79]). Let m be the number of conjunctions of a formula and $\epsilon > 0$ an arbitrarily small constant. Replacing every conjunction by m^k copies (where $k = 1/\epsilon - 1$) leads to an unweighted formula with $n = m^{k+1}$ conjunctions. A $n^{1-\epsilon}$-approximation algorithm is forced to decide an $\mathcal{NP}$-complete problem, because $n^{1-\epsilon} = m^k$.

In the case of weights choose weight w for every conjunction and such good approximation solves an $\mathcal{NP}$-complete problem. $\qquad\square$

4 Logical Definitions of Optimization Problems

An important syntactical classification of maximization problems was given in [PapY91]. The closure under E-reductions of the classes MAX SNP and MAX NP was ([KMSV94]) shown to equal the class of $\mathcal{NPO} - \mathcal{PB}$-problems that can be approximated within a constant. The definition of MAX (S)NP was generalized in [KT94].

Definition 4.1 *Consider the set of optimization problems L that can be written in the form $\max_s |\{y : \Phi_L(x, y, s)\}|$, where x is an instance of L and Φ_L a first order formula in prenex normal form. L belongs to the class MAX Σ_i (for $i \in \mathbb{N}$), if Φ_L has i alternations of quantifiers and starts with an existential quantifier. L belongs to the class MAX Π_i (for $i \in \mathbb{N}$), if Φ_L has i alternations and starts with a universal quantifier. MIN Σ_i and MIN Π_i are defined analogously.*

$\overline{\text{MIN}\Sigma_i}$ *etc. contain those problems which can be E-reduced to problems in* MIN Σ_i *etc.*

The class MAX Σ_0 is also called MAX SNP, MAX Σ_1 is known as MAX NP. These classes of optimization problems were defined in the hope to capture the degree of approximability of the problems they contain and that can be E-reduced to them. Unfortunately the following is true, because unweighted MIN 3-DNF is in MIN Σ_0.

Corollary 1 $\mathcal{NPO} - \mathcal{PB} \subseteq \overline{\text{MIN}\Sigma_0}$.

Thus the definition of MIN Σ_0 does not capture any approximation degree in contrast to corresponding definition for maximization problems (the fact that MIN 3-DNF cannot be approximated within any constant is proved in [KT94] as well as completeness of this problem for MIN Σ_0). We can also show that unweighted MIN 4-DNF is complete for the class of polynomially bounded $\mathcal{PLS}$-problems with $\mathcal{NC}^1$-computable cost/feasibility/search/solution functions via strong $\mathcal{PLS}$-reductions. So with regard to local approximation this logical definition provides no insight, too.

5 Conclusion

Approximation of local optima is an attempt to escape the hardness of exact local optimization. Unfortunately MIN 4-DNF-B, the Hopfield energy function, MIN INDEPENDENT DOMINATING SET-B, MIN/MAX 0-1 PROGRAMMING, and

MIN TRAVELING SALESMAN are not tractable in this framework. Completeness under the strong $\mathcal{PLS}$-reduction implies that a problem is able to express every optimization problem with a neighborhood structure in a way that local search paths are preserved and that the ratio of the cost function of image and original is almost fixed along these paths. It is quite astonishing that natural and simple problems like MIN 4-DNF-B or MAX HOPFIELD are complete under this reduction. The Hopfield energy function is thus extremely powerful which underlines its role as a universal "programming language" for optimization problems, but on the other hand takes away the hope that a Hopfield net may lead to efficient computation of good solutions.

6 Acknowledgement

The author would like to thank Georg Schnitger for many helpful discussions and especially for proposing the theme of approximation of local optima.

A Definitions of Optimization Problems

$\mathcal{I}$ denotes the set of instances, S the set of feasible solutions, C the cost function.

[1] CIRCUIT OUTPUT

$\mathcal{I} = \{T|T$ is circuit made of fan-in 2 and fan-out 2 AND/OR/NOT gates.$\}$

$S(T) = \{0,1\}^p$ if T has p inputs

$C(s,T) = \sum_{i=0}^{q-1} out_i^T(s)2^i$ if T has q outputs out_i^T.

The polynomial weight version CIRCUIT OUTPUT^{pol} has $O(\log n)$ outputs.

[2] k-DNF-B

$\mathcal{I} = \{(V,C,W)|V$ is a set of variables, C is a set of k-conjunctions of literals on variables in V, where each variable appears at most B times, $W : C \rightarrow \mathbb{N}$ is the weight function$\}$

$S(V,C,W) = \{0,1\}^{|V|}$

$C(x,V,C,W) = \sum_{c\in C:c \text{ is satisfied by } x} W(c)$.

[3] HOPFIELD

$\mathcal{I} = \{H|H = \langle (w_{i,j})_{1\leq i,j\leq n}, (t_i)_{1\leq i\leq n}\rangle; w_{i,j} = w_{j,i}\}$

$S(H) = \{0,1\}^n$

$C(s,H) = \sum_{i<j} w_{i,j}s_is_j - \sum_i t_is_i$

[4] INDEPENDENT DOMINATING SET-B

$\mathcal{I} = \{(G,W)|G = (V,E)$ is a graph with maximum degree B, $W : V \rightarrow \mathbb{N}\}$

$S(G) = \{x \in \{0,1\}^{|V|}|x_i=x_j=1\Rightarrow\{v_i,v_j\} \notin E; x_i=0\Rightarrow\sum_{j:\{v_i,v_j\}\in E} x_j \geq 1\}$

$C(x,G,W) = \sum_i W(v_i)x_i$

[5] TRAVELING SALESMAN

$\mathcal{I} = \{(G,W)|G = (V,E)$ is a complete graph, $W : E \rightarrow \mathbb{N}\}$

$S(G,W) = \{$permutation $\pi : [1,\ldots,|V|] \rightarrow [1,\ldots,|V|]\}$

$C(\pi,G,W) = W(v_{\pi(|V|)},v_{\pi(1)}) + \sum_{i=1}^{|V|-1} W(v_{\pi(i)},v_{\pi(i+1)})$

[6] 0-1-PROGRAMMING

$$\mathcal{I} = \{(A, b, c) | A \in \mathbb{Z}^{m \cdot n}, b \in \mathbb{Z}^m, c \in \mathbb{N}^n\}$$
$$S(A, b, c) = \{x \in \{0, 1\}^n | Ax \geq b\}$$
$$C(x, A, b, c) = c^T x$$

References

[BeSc92]   P. Berman, G. Schnitger. On the Complexity of Approximating the Independent Set Problem. *Inform. and Comp.*, vol.96, pp. 77–94, 1992.

[GJ79]   M.R. Garey, D.S. Johnson. Computers and Intractability: A Guide to the Theory of NP-Completeness. Freeman, San Francisco, 1979.

[Ha93]   M.M. Halldórson. Approximating the minimum maximal independence number. *Inf. Proc. Lett.*, Vol.46, pp. 169–172, 1993.

[HKP91]   J. Hertz, A. Krogh, R.G. Palmer. Introduction to the Theory of Neural Computation. Addison-Wesley, 1991.

[Ho82]   J.J. Hopfield. Neural Networks and Physical Systems having Emergent Collective Computational Abilities, 1982. *Reprinted in* Anderson, Rosenfeld: *Neurocomputing: Found. of Research*, Cambridge, MIT-Press, 1988.

[HoTa85]   J.J. Hopfield, D.W. Tank. "Neural" Computation of Decisions in Optimization Problems. *Biological Cybernetics*, vol.52, pp. 141–152, 1985.

[JPaY88]   D.S. Johnson, C.H. Papadimitriou, M. Yannakakis. How Easy is Local Search? *Journ. of Computer and System Sciences*, vol.37, pp. 79–100, 1988.

[Ka92]   V. Kann. On the Approximability of NP-complete Optimization Problems. Dissertation, NADA Stockholm, 1992.

[Ka93]   V. Kann. Polynomially bounded minimization problems which are hard to approximate. *Proc. 20th Int. Coll. on Automata, Lang. and Prog.*, pp. 52–63, 1993, Springer LNCS 700.

[KMSV94]   S. Khanna, R. Motwani, M. Sudhan, U. Vazirani. On Syntactic versus Computational Views of Approximability. *35th Symp. Found. Comput. Science*, pp. 819–830, 1994.

[KT94]   P.G. Kolaitis, M.N. Thakur. Logical definability of NP optimization problems. *Inform. and Comp.*, vol. 115, pp. 321–353, 1994.

[Kr89]   M.W. Krentel. Structure in locally optimal solutions. *30th Symp. Found. Comput. Science*, pp. 216–221, 1989.

[OM87]   P. Orponen, H. Mannila. On approximation preserving reductions: Complete problems and robust measures. Technical Report C-1987-28, Department of Computer Science, University of Helsinki.

[PapSY90]   C.H. Papadimitriou, A.A. Schäffer, M. Yannakakis. On the Complexity of Local Search. *Proc. 22th ACM Symp. on Theory of Comp.*, pp. 438-445, 1990.

[PapY91]   C.H. Papadimitriou, M. Yannakakis. Optimization, Approximation, and Complexity Classes. *Journ. of Computer and System Sciences*, vol.43, pp. 425–440, 1991.

[SchY91]   A.A. Schäffer, M. Yannakakis. Simple Local Search Problems that are Hard to Solve. *SIAM Journal Comput.*, vol.20, pp. 56–87, 1991.

Approximation Algorithms for the Maximum Satisfiability Problem

Takao Asano[1] Takao Ono[2] Tomio Hirata[2]

[1] Department of Information and System Engineering, Chuo University
Bunkyo-ku, Tokyo 112, Japan (asano@ise.chuo-u.ac.jp)
[2] School of Engineering, Nagoya University

Abstract. The maximum satisfiability problem (MAX SAT) is : given a set of clauses with weights, find a truth assignment that maximizes the sum of the weights of the satisfied clauses. In this paper, we present approximation algorithms for MAX SAT, including a 0.76544-approximation algorithm. The previous best approximation algorithm for MAX SAT was proposed by Goemans-Williamson and has a performance guarantee of 0.7584. Our algorithms are based on semidefinite programming and the 0.75-approximation algorithms of Yannakakis and Goemans-Williamson.

1 Introduction

We consider the maximum satisfiability problem (MAX SAT): given a set of clauses with weights, find a truth assignment that maximizes the sum of the weights of the satisfied clauses. MAX 2SAT, the restricted version of MAX SAT where each clause has at most 2 literals, is well known to be NP-complete even if the weights of the clauses are identical, and thus MAX SAT is also NP-complete. Thus, many researchers have proposed approximation algorithms and the best approximation algorithms for MAX SAT had been 0.75-approximation algorithms proposed by Yannakakis [8] and Goemans-Williamson [3]. On the other hand, Goemans-Williamson recently obtained a 0.878-approximation algorithm for MAX 2SAT based on semidefinite programming, a new and very useful technique in the approximation algorithms and noted that it leads to a 0.755-approximation algorithm for MAX SAT [2]. Then they obtained another improvement and the 0.7584-approximation algorithm is the best known algorithm [4].

In this paper, we first present a 0.75899-approximation algorithm for MAX SAT based on semidefinite programming and the 0.75-approximation algorithm of Goemans-Williamson [3]. Although this algorithm may be quite similar to the above 0.7584-approximation algorithm, in that both algorithms are based on semidefinite programming and the 0.75-approximation algorithm of Goemans-Williamson, our algorithm will not explicitly transform a MAX SAT instance into a MAX 2SAT instance.

We next present a 0.76544-approximation algorithm by combining the above 0.75899-approximation algorithm with the 0.75-approximation algorithm of Yannakakis based on the probabilistic method. Yannakakis's algorithm divides the variables of a given instance into three groups P', $(P - P') \cup Q$ and Z and sets the variables in P', $(P - P') \cup Q$ and Z to be true with probabilities $3/4$, $5/9$ and $1/2$, respectively. In our algorithm, we set the variables in P', $(P - P') \cup Q$ and Z to be true with probabilities $3/4$, 0.568729 and $1/2$, respectively (only the probability of the variables in $(P - P') \cup Q$ is changed). Combined with the 0.75899 approximation algorithm, this leads to the approximation algorithm with performance guarantee 0.76544.

2 Preliminaries

An instance of the maximum satisfiability problem (MAX SAT) is defined by a collection of boolean clauses $\mathcal{C}$ where each clause $C_j \in \mathcal{C}$ is a disjunction of literals and has a nonnegative weight w_j (a *literal* is either a variable x_i or its negation $\bar{x}_i$). Let $X = \{x_1, \ldots, x_n\}$ be the set of variables in the clauses in $\mathcal{C}$. We assume that no variable appears more than once in a clause in $\mathcal{C}$, that is, we do not allow a clause like $x_1 \vee \bar{x}_1 \vee x_2$. For each variable $x_i \in X$, we consider $x_i = 1$ ($x_i = 0$, resp.) if x_i is true (false, resp.). Then, $\bar{x}_i = 1 - x_i$ and a clause $C_j \in \mathcal{C}$ can be considered to be a function of $\boldsymbol{x} = (x_1, \ldots, x_n)$ as follows:

$$C_j = C_j(\boldsymbol{x}) = 1 - \prod_{x_i \in X_j^+} (1 - x_i) \prod_{x_i \in X_j^-} x_i \tag{1}$$

where X_j^+ (X_j^-, resp.) denotes the set of variables appearing unnegated (negated, resp.) in C_j. Thus, $C_j = C_j(\boldsymbol{x}) = 0$ or 1 for any *truth assignment* $\boldsymbol{x} \in \{0,1\}^n$ (i.e., an assignment of 0 or 1 to each $x_i \in X$), and C_j is *satisfied* (*not satisfied*, resp.) if $C_j(\boldsymbol{x}) = 1$ ($C_j(\boldsymbol{x}) = 0$, resp.). The *value* of an assignment $\boldsymbol{x}$ is defined to be

$$F(\boldsymbol{x}) = \sum_{C_j \in \mathcal{C}} w_j C_j(\boldsymbol{x}). \tag{2}$$

That is, the value of $\boldsymbol{x}$ is the sum of the weights of the clauses in $\mathcal{C}$ satisfied by $\boldsymbol{x}$. Thus, MAX SAT is to find a truth assignment of maximum value.

Let A be an algorithm for MAX SAT and let $w^A(\mathcal{C})$ be the value of a truth assignment $x^A(\mathcal{C})$ produced by A for an instance $\mathcal{C}$. If $w^A(\mathcal{C})$ is at least α times the value $w^*(\mathcal{C})$ of an optimal truth assignment $x^*(\mathcal{C})$ for any instance $\mathcal{C}$, then A is called an approximation algorithm with *performance guarantee* α. A polynomial time algorithm A with performance guarantee α is called an α-*approximation algorithm*.

The 0.75-approximation algorithm of Yannakakis is based on the probabilistic method. Let $\boldsymbol{x}^P$ be a *random* truth assignment obtained by setting independently each variable $x_i \in X$ to be true with probability p_i (i.e., $0 \leq x_i^p = p_i \leq 1$). Then the probability of the clause $C_j \in \mathcal{C}$ satisfied by the assignment $\boldsymbol{x}^P$ is

$$C_j(\boldsymbol{x}^P) = 1 - \prod_{x_i \in X_j^+} (1 - p_i) \prod_{x_i \in X_j^-} p_i . \tag{3}$$

Thus, the expected value of the random truth assignment x^p is

$$F(x^p) = \sum_{C_j \in C} w_j C_j(x^p). \tag{4}$$

The probabilistic method assures that there is a truth assignment $x^q \in \{0,1\}^n$ such that its value is at least $F(x^p)$. Such a truth assignment x^q can be obtained by the method of conditional probability ([3],[8]).

3   0.75899-Approximation Algorithm

In this section we present an approximation algorithm A for MAX SAT. The algorithm is based on semidefinite programming used first by Goemans and Williamson for MAX 2SAT [2] and if it is combined with the 0.75-approximation algorithm of Goemans-Williamson then it achieves a performance guarantee of 0.75899. The algorithm A consists of the following four steps.

1. Translate a maximization problem of $\{0,1\}$-variables into a maximization problem of $\{-1,1\}$-variables, that is, we regard MAX SAT as a maximization problem of a polynomial of variables in $\{-1,1\}$.
2. Obtain another maximization problem of a polynomial of low degree.
3. By relaxing the new maximization problem, formulate it as a semidefinite programming problem and solve it.
4. Construct a truth assignment of the original MAX SAT from a solution of the semidefinite programming problem.

We explain each of the above steps in the following subsections.

3.1   From a Maximization of $\{0,1\}$-Variables to a Maximization of $\{-1,1\}$-Variables

We translate an instance of MAX SAT of n $\{0,1\}$-variables into a polynomial of n $\{-1,1\}$-variables in the following way.

We introduce n variables $x'_1, \ldots, x'_n$ and consider

$$x_i \equiv \frac{1 + x'_i}{2}. \tag{5}$$

Thus, $\bar{x}_i = 1 - x_i = \frac{1 - x'_i}{2}$ and $x_i = 1$ ($x_i = 0$, resp.) if and only if $x'_i = 1$ ($x'_i = -1$, resp.). Let $x' = (x'_1, \ldots, x'_n)$. By this replacement, clause C_j in (1) becomes

$$C_j(x') = 1 - \prod_{x_i \in X_j^+} \frac{1 - x'_i}{2} \prod_{x_i \in X_j^-} \frac{1 + x'_i}{2}. \tag{6}$$

Thus, finding a truth assignment $x \in \{0,1\}^n$ that maximizes $F(x)$, the sum of the weights of the satisfied clauses in $\mathcal{C}$, is equivalent to finding an assignment $x' \in \{-1,1\}^n$ (assignment of -1 or 1 to each x_i') that maximizes

$$F(x') = \sum_{C_j \in \mathcal{C}} w_j C_j(x'). \tag{7}$$

$F(x')$ is called the value of x'. Thus we can regard MAX SAT as the following problem:

(P): Maximize $F(x')$ subject to $x' \in \{-1,1\}^n$.

3.2 Maximization Problem of a Polynomial of Lower Degree

Instead of maximizing $F(x')$, we will consider another maximization problem. Let C_k be the set of clauses in $\mathcal{C}$ with k literals and let $C_j = x_1 \vee x_2 \vee \cdots \vee x_k \in C_k$. Then, by (6), $C_j = C_j(x')$ is

$$\tfrac{1}{2^k} \sum_{i=1}^{k}(1 + x_i') + \tfrac{1}{2^k} \sum_{1 \le i_1 < i_2 \le k}(1 - x_{i_1}' x_{i_2}') +$$
$$\tfrac{1}{2^k} \sum_{1 \le i_1 < i_2 < i_3 \le k}(1 + x_{i_1}' x_{i_2}' x_{i_3}') + \cdots + \tfrac{1}{2^k}(1 - (-1)^k x_1' x_2' \cdots x_k').$$

For example, if $k = 3$ then $C_j = C_j(x')$ is

$$\frac{1}{2^3}(1+x_1'+1+x_2'+1+x_3') + \frac{1}{2^3}(1-x_1'x_2'+1-x_1'x_3'+1-x_2'x_3') + \frac{1}{2^3}(1+x_1'x_2'x_3').$$

We divide C_j into two parts $c_j^{(1)}$ and $c_j^{(2)}$: $c_j^{(1)}$ is the sum of the terms in C_j of forms $1 + x_i'$ and $1 - x_{i_1}' x_{i_2}'$ and $c_j^{(2)}$ is the rest, i.e.,

$$c_j^{(1)} = c_j^{(1)}(x') = \frac{1}{2^k} \sum_{i=1}^{k}(1 + x_i') + \frac{1}{2^k} \sum_{1 \le i_1 < i_2 \le k}(1 - x_{i_1}' x_{i_2}') \tag{8}$$

and

$$c_j^{(2)} = c_j^{(2)}(x') = C_j(x') - c_j^{(1)}(x').$$

Similarly, for any $C_{j'} \in \mathcal{C}$, we can define $c_{j'}^{(1)}$ and $c_{j'}^{(2)}$ in the same way even if some literal in $C_{j'}$ appears as a negation $\bar{x}_i$ (in this case we have only to replace x_i' with $-x_i'$). Note $c_j^{(1)}(x') = C_j(x')$ for any $C_j \in C_k$ with $k \le 2$, and that $1 \pm x_i' \ge 0$ and $1 \pm x_{i_1}' x_{i_2}' \ge 0$ since $x' \in \{-1,1\}^n$.

Let

$$\alpha_k = \begin{cases} \frac{4k}{(k+1)^2} & (k \text{ is odd}) \\ \frac{4k}{(k+1)^2-1} & (k \text{ is even}) \end{cases} \tag{9}$$

and define

$$G(x') = \sum_{k \ge 1} \sum_{C_j \in C_k} \frac{2^{k+1}}{4k} \alpha_k w_j c_j^{(1)}(x'). \tag{10}$$

Thus, $G(x')$ is a polynomial with nonconstant terms of degree at most 2 and we use a solution of the following problem as an approximate solution of (P).

(Q): Maximize $G(x')$ subject to $x' \in \{-1,1\}^n$.

Now we introduce new variables $y = (y_0, y_1, \ldots, y_n)$ and consider

$$x'_i \equiv y_0 y_i \text{ with } |y_0| = |y_i| = 1 \qquad (11)$$

for later use in semidefinite programming. Then $1 + x'_i$ ($1 - x'_i$, resp.) becomes $1 + y_0 y_i$ ($1 - y_0 y_i$, resp.) and $1 + x'_{i_1} x'_{i_2}$ ($1 - x'_{i_1} x'_{i_2}$, resp.) becomes $1 + y_{i_1} y_{i_2}$ ($1 - y_{i_1} y_{i_2}$, resp.). Now they are of the same form and $c_j^{(1)}(y) = c_j^{(1)}(x')$ is a linear combination of the terms $1 + y_{i_1} y_{i_2}, 1 - y_{i_1} y_{i_2}$. Thus, $G(y) = G(x')$ can be expressed by

$$G(y) = \sum_{0 \le i_1 < i_2 \le n} a_{i_1 i_2}^+ (1 + y_{i_1} y_{i_2}) + \sum_{0 \le i_1 < i_2 \le n} a_{i_1 i_2}^- (1 - y_{i_1} y_{i_2}) \qquad (12)$$

with some nonnegative numbers $a_{i_1 i_2}^+$, $a_{i_1 i_2}^-$. Note that $G(y)$ is a polynomial with nonconstant terms of degree 2. Thus, (Q) is reduced to the following problem (Q') and we use its solution as an approximate solution of (P) based on (11).

(Q'): Maximize $G(y)$ subject to $y \in \{-1,1\}^{n+1}$.

3.3 Relaxation and Semidefinite Programming Problem

Since (Q') is difficult to solve, we consider a relaxation of (Q') as described in [2]. Let v_i be an $(n+1)$-dimensional vector with norm $\|v_i\| = 1$ corresponding to y_i with $|y_i| = 1$. We replace $y_{i_1} y_{i_2}$ with an inner product $v_{i_1} \cdot v_{i_2}$. With this relaxation, (Q') is reduced to the following problem (R).

(R): Maximize $G(v) = \sum_{0 \le i_1 < i_2 \le n} a_{i_1 i_2}^+ (1 + v_{i_1} \cdot v_{i_2}) + \sum_{0 \le i_1 < i_2 \le n} a_{i_1 i_2}^- (1 - v_{i_1} \cdot v_{i_2})$ subject to $\|v_i\| = 1$ for all $i = 0, \ldots, n$.

Now let $y_{i_1 i_2} = v_{i_1} \cdot v_{i_2}$. Then, a matrix $Y = (y_{i_1 i_2})$ is symmetric and positive semidefinite. Thus, the following problem is equivalent to (R).

(R'): Maximize $G(Y) = \sum_{0 \le i_1 < i_2 \le n} a_{i_1 i_2}^+ (1 + y_{i_1 i_2}) + \sum_{0 \le i_1 < i_2 \le n} a_{i_1 i_2}^- (1 - y_{i_1 i_2})$ subject to the conditions that the matrix $Y = (y_{i_1 i_2})$ is symmetric and positive semidefinite, and that $y_{ii} = 1$ for all $i = 0, \ldots, n$.

Since (R') is a semidefinite programming problem as in [2], we can find an approximate solution $\bar{Y} = (\bar{y}_{i_1 i_2})$ within a constant error ϵ in polynomial time. An approximate solution $\bar{v} = (\bar{v}_0, \bar{v}_1, \ldots, \bar{v}_n)$ of (R) can be obtained by Cholesky decomposition of $\bar{Y} = (\bar{y}_{i_1 i_2})$. At this point we have an approximate solution of (R) in polynomial time.

3.4 Finding an Approximate Solution of MAX SAT

As described in [2], we find a randomized approximate solution $\bar{y} = (\bar{y}_0, \bar{y}_1, \ldots, \bar{y}_n)$ of (Q') and the corresonding solution of (Q) and (P) from an approximate solution $\bar{v} = (\bar{v}_0, \bar{v}_1, \ldots, \bar{v}_n)$ of (R). Taking a random vector r, let $\bar{y}_i = +1$ if $\bar{v}_i \cdot r > 0$, or $\bar{y}_i = -1$ otherwise. $\bar{x}' = (\bar{x}'_1, \ldots, \bar{x}'_n)$ is also obtained by $\bar{x}'_i = \bar{y}_0 \bar{y}_i$ based on (11).

We show in Section 4 that the expected value $F(\bar{x}')$ of $\bar{x}'$ is at least 0.75899 times the value $F(x'^*)$ of the optimal solution x'^* of (P) under some conditions. We can derandomize this method in the same way as in [2],[4],[6] and obtain an approximate solution $y^A = (y_0^A, y_1^A, \ldots, y_n^A)$ of (Q') and the corresonding approximate solution $x'^A = (x_1'^A, \ldots, x_n'^A)$ of (P) by $x_i'^A = y_0^A y_i^A$. Since $x_i = \frac{1+x_i'}{2}$ by (5) (i.e., $x_i = 1$ ($x_i =$true) if and only if $x_i' = 1$ and $x_i = 0$ ($x_i =$false) if and only if $x_i' = -1$), we have an truth assignment $x^A = (x_1^A, \ldots, x_n^A)$ which is an approximate solution of MAX SAT.

4 Analysis of the Performance Guarantee

Based on the argument in the previous section, solutions x of MAX SAT, x' of (P) and y of (Q') can be obtained from one another based on (5) and (11). Thus, we can assume, from now on, that any one solution of x, x' and y implies any other two solutions in hand even if we do not say explicitly. In this section we analyze the performance guarantee of the above algorithm. Let $x^A = (x_1, \ldots, x_n)$ be an approximate solution of MAX SAT obtained by the algorithm A described in the previous section. Let x^G be an assignment obtained by using 0.75-approximation algorithm of Goemans-Williamson. Let B be an algorithm choosing the better solution x^B between x^A and x^G. Then, roughly speaking, the performance guarantee of x^B will be 0.75899.

The following lemmas play critical roles throughout the paper.

Lemma 1. Let C_j be any clause in $\mathcal{C}$. Then, for any $x' = (x_1', \ldots, x_n') \in \{-1, 1\}^n$, $C_j(x') \neq 0$ (C_j is true) if and only if $c_j^{(1)}(x') \neq 0$. Furthermore, for any $x' \in \{-1, 1\}^n$,

$$\frac{4k}{2^{k+1}} C_j(x') \leq c_j^{(1)}(x') \leq \frac{(k+1)^2}{2^{k+1}} C_j(x') \quad (C_j \in \mathcal{C}_k \text{ and } k \text{ is odd}),$$

$$\frac{4k}{2^{k+1}} C_j(x') \leq c_j^{(1)}(x') \leq \frac{(k+1)^2 - 1}{2^{k+1}} C_j(x') \quad (C_j \in \mathcal{C}_k \text{ and } k \text{ is even}).$$

Proof. By symmetry we can assume $C_j = x_1 \lor x_2 \lor \cdots \lor x_k \in \mathcal{C}$. By equations (1), (5) and (6), if $C_j(x') \neq 0$ then $C_j(x') = 1$ since $C_j = C_j(x')$ is boolean and $x_i' = 1$ for some x_i' and thus $c_j^{(1)}(x') \neq 0$ by (8). On the other hand, if $c_j^{(1)}(x') \neq 0$, then $x_i' = 1$ for some x_i' by (8) and thus $C_j(x') = 1$ by (6). Thus, we have $C_j(x') \neq 0$ if and only if $c_j^{(1)}(x') \neq 0$. Let ℓ be the number of x_i''s with

$x_i' = 1$ $(i = 1, 2, ..., k)$. If $c_j^{(1)}(x') \neq 0$ then $1 \leq \ell \leq k$ and $c_j^{(1)}(x') = \frac{\ell + \ell(k - \ell)}{2^{k-1}}$ by (8). Since

$$\ell + \ell(k - \ell) = -(\ell - \frac{k+1}{2})^2 + \frac{(k+1)^2}{4},$$

we have the lemma. □

Lemma 2. *Let x'^A be a solution of (Q) obtained by the alogrithm A in Section 3 for an instance C. Let x'^* be any solution in $\{-1, 1\}^n$ that maximizes $F(x')$ and let $W_k^* = \sum_{C_j \in C_k} w_j C_j(x'^*)$. Then the value $w^A(C) = F(x'^A)$ of x'^A satisfies*

$$w^A(C) = F(x'^A) \geq G(x'^A) \geq \alpha \sum_{k \geq 1} \alpha_k W_k^*,$$

where $\alpha = 0.87856$ and α_k is defined in (9), i.e.,

$$\alpha_k = \begin{cases} \frac{4k}{(k+1)^2} & (k \text{ is odd }) \\ \frac{4k}{(k+1)^2 - 1} & (k \text{ is even}). \end{cases}$$

Proof. For any $C_j \in C_k$ and any $x' \in \{-1, 1\}^n$, we have

$$\frac{2^{k+1}}{4k} \alpha_k c_j^{(1)}(x') \leq C_j(x') \tag{13}$$

since $c_j^{(1)}(x') \leq \frac{(k+1)^2}{2^{k+1}} C_j(x')$ (k is odd) and $c_j^{(1)}(x') \leq \frac{(k+1)^2 - 1}{2^{k+1}} C_j(x')$ (k is even) by Lemma 1 and by the definition of α_k, and thus, we have $F(x'^A) \geq G(x'^A)$.

Let x'^*_G be any solution in $\{-1, 1\}^n$ that maximizes $G(x')$. Then, by the same analysis as in [2],[4] for $\alpha = 0.87856$, we have $G(x'^A) \geq \alpha G(x'^*_G)$ and $G(x'^*_G) \geq G(x'^*)$. On the other hand, we have $c_j^{(1)}(x') \geq \frac{4k}{2^{k+1}} C_j(x')$ for any $C_j \in C_k$ and any $x' \in \{-1, 1\}^n$ by Lemma 1 and thus

$$\frac{2^{k+1}}{4k} \alpha_k c_j^{(1)}(x') \geq \alpha_k C_j(x'). \tag{14}$$

This implies

$$G(x'^*) = \sum_{k \geq 1} \sum_{C_j \in C_k} \frac{2^{k+1}}{4k} \alpha_k w_j c_j^{(1)}(x'^*) \geq \sum_{k \geq 1} (\alpha_k \sum_{C_j \in C_k} w_j C_j(x'^*)) = \sum_{k \geq 1} \alpha_k W_k^*. \tag{15}$$

Thus, we have the lemma by

$$F(x'^A) \geq G(x'^A) \geq \alpha G(x'^*_G) \geq \alpha G(x'^*)$$

obtained above. □

The 0.75-approximation algorithm of Goemans-Williamson is obtained by choosing the better solution x^G between their original linear programming relaxation solution x^L and a solution x^J by Johnson's algorithm [5].

Let $\boldsymbol{x'}^*$ be any solution in $\{-1, 1\}^n$ that maximizes $F(\boldsymbol{x'})$ in (P) and let $\boldsymbol{x}^*$ be obtained from $\boldsymbol{x'}^*$ by setting $x_i^* = \frac{1+x_i'^*}{2}$. For $k \geq 1$, let $W_k = \sum_{C_j \in \mathcal{C}_k} w_j$ and $W_k^* = \sum_{C_j \in \mathcal{C}_k} w_j C_j(\boldsymbol{x'}^*)$. Then, the value w^J of x^J satisfies $w^J \geq \sum_{k \geq 1}(1 - \frac{1}{2^k})W_k$. On the other hand, the value w^L of x^L satisfies $w^L \geq \sum_{k \geq 1}(1 - (1 - \frac{1}{k})^k)W_k^*$. Strictly speaking, $w^L \geq \sum_{k \geq 1}(1 - (1 - \frac{1}{k})^k)W_k^{*''}$ for another optimal solution $\boldsymbol{x'}^{*''}$ in $\{-1, 1\}^n$ that maximizes $F(\boldsymbol{x'})$ and $W_k^{*''} = \sum_{C_j \in \mathcal{C}_k} w_j C_j(\boldsymbol{x'}^{*''})$. We will later show that we can assume $W_k^{*''} = W_k^*$ for all $k \geq 1$. Thus, if we let

$$\beta_k = \frac{(1 - \frac{1}{2^k}) + 1 - (1 - \frac{1}{k})^k}{2}, \tag{16}$$

then the value w^G of the better solution x^G satisfies

$$w^G \geq \sum_{k \geq 1} \beta_k W_k^*. \tag{17}$$

Now we are ready to analyze the performance guarantee of the algorithm B choosing the better one x^B between the solution x^A obtained by the algorithm A and the Goemans-Williamson's solution x^G. Thus, $w^B = \max\{w^A, w^G\}$. Let $b = \frac{\alpha(2 - \frac{1}{e})}{\frac{3}{2} - \frac{1}{e} + 2\alpha} = 0.758990...$ where e is the number e (the base of the natural logarithm). If

$$W_1^* + W_2^* \geq \frac{1}{\alpha - b} \sum_{k \geq 3}(b - \alpha\alpha_k)W_k^*, \tag{18}$$

then $w^A \geq \alpha \sum_{k \geq 1} \alpha_k W_k^* \geq b \sum_{k \geq 1} W_k^*$ by Lemma 2 and w^A (as well as w^B) has a required performance b (note that $\alpha_1 = \alpha_2 = 1$). Thus, we can assume

$$W_1^* + W_2^* < \frac{1}{\alpha - b} \sum_{k \geq 3}(b - \alpha\alpha_k)W_k^*. \tag{19}$$

On the other hand, if

$$W_1^* + W_2^* \leq \frac{1}{b - 0.75} \sum_{k \geq 3}(\beta_k - b)W_k^*,$$

then $w^G \geq \sum_{k \geq 1} \beta_k W_k^* \geq b \sum_{k \geq 1} W_k^*$ by (16) and (17) (note that $\beta_1 = \beta_2 = 0.75$) and w^G has a required performance b. Thus, we can assume

$$W_1^* + W_2^* > \frac{1}{b - 0.75} \sum_{k \geq 3}(\beta_k - b)W_k^*.$$

However, for $b = 0.75899$, it is not difficult to see

$$\frac{\beta_k - b}{b - 0.75} \geq \frac{b - \alpha\alpha_k}{\alpha - b} \qquad (k \geq 3) \tag{20}$$

and we have

$$W_1^* + W_2^* > \frac{1}{b - 0.75} \sum_{k \geq 3} (\beta_k - b) W_k^* \geq \frac{1}{\alpha - b} \sum_{k \geq 3} (b - \alpha \alpha_k) W_k^* > W_1^* + W_2^*,$$

a contradiction.

Thus, we have the following theorem.

Theorem 3. *A 0.75899-approximation algorithm can be obtained based on the algorithm A in Section 3 and the 0.75-approximation algorithm of Goemans-Williamson.*

5 Formal Formulation

In this section, we formulate MAX SAT based on the the formulation by Goemans and Williamson [3],[4] as follows.

$$(S) : \text{Maximize} \quad \sum_{C_j \in C} w_j z_j$$

$$\text{subject to:} \quad \sum_{x_i \in X_j^+} \frac{1 + y_{0i}}{2} + \sum_{x_i \in X_j^-} \frac{1 - y_{0i}}{2} \geq z_j \qquad \forall C_j \in C$$

$$\frac{2^{k+1}}{4k} c_j^{(1)}(Y) \geq z_j \qquad \forall C_j \in C_k$$

$$y_{ii} = 1 \qquad \forall 0 \leq i \leq n$$

$$0 \leq z_j \leq 1 \qquad \forall C_j \in C$$

$$Y = (y_{i_1 i_2}) \text{ is a symmetric, positive semidefinite matrix.}$$

$$(21)$$

Recall that, by (11) and $y_{i_1 i_2} = v_{i_1} \cdot v_{i_2} = y_{i_1} y_{i_2}$, the matrix $Y = (y_{i_1 i_2})$ is symmetric and positive semidefinite and $c_j^{(1)}(Y) = c_j^{(1)}(y) = c_j^{(1)}(x')$. Let (Y, z^*) is an optimal solution to (S). By fixing z^* and changing Y in the optimal solution (Y, z^*) to (S), we also solve (R') under the same constraints in (S). Let (Y^*, z^*) be an optimal solution to (S) and (R').

To achieve the bound described in the previous section, we consider Algorithm C consisting of the following three algorithms:

(1) set each variable x_i true independently with probability 0.5;

(2) set x_i true independently with probability $\frac{1 + y_{0i}}{2}$ using the optimal solution (Y, z^*) to (S);

(3) take a random unit vector r and set x_i true if and only if $\text{sgn}(\bar{v}_i^* \cdot r) = \text{sgn}(\bar{v}_0^* \cdot r)$ using the optimal solution (Y^*, z^*) to (S) and (R') $(y_{i_1 i_2}^* = v_{i_1}^* \cdot v_{i_2}^*)$.

Suppose we use algorithm (i) with probability p_i, where $p_1 + p_2 + p_3 = 1$. From the arguments in [2],[4] and the previous section, the probability that a clause $C_j \in C_k$ being satisfied by algorithm (3) is at least $\alpha\alpha_k c_j^{(1)}(Y) \geq \alpha\alpha_k z_j^*$ by Lemmas 1 and 2. Thus, the expected value W^C of the solution satisfies

$$W^C \geq \sum_{k \geq 1} (\sum_{C_j \in C_k} w_j \left[(1 - \frac{1}{2^k})p_1 + ((1 - (1 - \frac{1}{k})^k)p_2 + \alpha\alpha_k p_3)z_j^* \right]). \qquad (22)$$

Let $W_k^* = \sum_{C_j \in C_k} w_j z_j^*$. Then, by $z_j^* \leq 1$ in the constraints of (S), $W_k^* \leq \sum_{C_j \in C_k} w_j$ and thus,

$$W^C \geq \sum_{k \geq 1} \left[(1 - \frac{1}{2^k})p_1 + (1 - (1 - \frac{1}{k})^k)p_2 + \alpha\alpha_k p_3) \right] W_k^*. \qquad (23)$$

This equation also assures the arguments in the preceeding section. If we set $p_1 = p_2 = 0.4650334 = p$ and $p_3 = 0.0699332 = 1 - 2p$, then

$$W^C \geq \sum_{k \geq 1} (2\beta_k p + \alpha\alpha_k(1 - 2p))W_k^*$$

$(2\beta_k = 1 - \frac{1}{2^k} + 1 - (1 - \frac{1}{k})^k$ by (16)). Thus, we obtain Algorithm C is a 0.75899-approximation algorithm, which can be verified by checking

$$2\beta_k p + \alpha\alpha_k(1 - 2p) \geq 0.75899$$

for $k \leq 8$ and noticing $2\beta_k p + \alpha\alpha_k(1 - 2p)$ decreases as k increases, and that, for $k = \infty$, $\beta_k = 1 - \frac{1}{2e}$ and $\alpha_k = 0$ and $2\beta_k p + \alpha\alpha_k(1 - 2p) = 0.4650334(2 - \frac{1}{e}) \geq 0.75899$.

Thus Theorem 2 in the preceeding section is also obtained. For MAX kSAT where each clause has at most k literals, we can similarly obtain a 0.769 approximation algorithm for $k \leq 5$ by maximizing b in the preceeding section and appropriately fixing p_1, p_2 and p_3.

6 0.76544-Approximation Algorithm

We can improve the bound 0.75899 by using the 0.75-approximation algorithm of Yannakakis. It is based on the probabilistic method proposed by Johnson [5] and divides the variables X of a given instance C into three groups P', $(P - P') \cup Q$ and Z based on maximum network flows. Simultaneously, the set C of weighted clauses is transformed to an equivalent set of weighted clauses $\mathcal{E} \cup \mathcal{F} \cup \mathcal{G} \cup \mathcal{G}' \cup \mathcal{H}$ (two sets $\mathcal{D}, \mathcal{D}'$ of weighted clauses over the same set of variables X are *equivalent* if every truth assignment of X, $\mathcal{D}$ and $\mathcal{D}'$ have the same value). For simlicity, we assume as follows (in fact we can assume without loss of generality):

$\mathcal{E} = \{\bar{x}_1, x_1\}$ with $\bar{x}_1, x_1$ of weight K_E,

$\mathcal{G} = \{x_1, x_2, x_3, \bar{x}_1 \vee \bar{x}_2 \vee \bar{x}_3\}$ with $x_1, x_2, x_3 \in X \cup \bar{X} - \bar{P}$ of weight K_G and $\bar{x}_1 \vee \bar{x}_2 \vee \bar{x}_3$ of weight $2K_G$,

$\mathcal{G}' = \{x_{g_1}, x_{g_2}, x_{g_3}, x_{g_4}, \bar{x}_{g_1} \vee \bar{x}_{g_2} \vee \bar{x}_{g_3} \vee \bar{x}_{g_4}\}$ with $x_{g_k} \in X \cup \bar{X} - \bar{P}$ of weight $K_{G'}$ ($k = 1, 2, 3, 4$) and $\bar{x}_{i_1} \vee \bar{x}_{i_2} \vee \bar{x}_{i_3} \vee \bar{x}_{i_4}$ of weight $3K_{G'}$,

$\mathcal{H} = \{x_{h_1}, x_{h_2}, \bar{x}_{h_3}, \bar{x}_{h_1} \vee \bar{x}_{h_2} \vee x_{h_3}, x_1, \bar{x}_1\}$ with $x_{h_k} \in X \cup \bar{X} - \bar{P}$ $(k = 1, 2, 3)$ of weight $2K_H$, $\bar{x}_{h_1} \vee \bar{x}_{h_2} \vee x_{h_3}$ of weight $2K_H$ and $x_1, \bar{x}_1$ of weight $-K_H$,
$\mathcal{F} = \mathcal{F}_1 \cup \mathcal{F}_2 \cup \mathcal{F}_3 \cup \mathcal{F}_4 \cup \mathcal{F}_5 \cup \cdots$ with

$$\sum_{C_j \in \mathcal{F}_1} w_j = \sum_{C_j \in \mathcal{C}_1} w_j - 2K_E - 3K_G - 4K_{G'} - 4K_H$$

$$\sum_{C_j \in \mathcal{F}_2} w_j = \sum_{C_j \in \mathcal{C}_2} w_j$$

$$\sum_{C_j \in \mathcal{F}_3} w_j = \sum_{C_j \in \mathcal{C}_3} w_j - 2K_G - 2K_H$$

$$\sum_{C_j \in \mathcal{F}_4} w_j = \sum_{C_j \in \mathcal{C}_4} w_j - 3K_{G'}$$

$\mathcal{F}_k = \mathcal{C}_k$ for all $k \geq 5$ (weight of a clause in this class is not changed).
Furthermore, we can assume

each literal in $\mathcal{F}_1$ is contained in P',

for each clause $x \vee y \in \mathcal{F}_2$, if one of x, y is contained in $\bar{P}'$ then the other is in P', and if one of x, y is contained in $\bar{Q} \cup (\bar{P} - \bar{P}')$ then the other is in $P \vee Q$,

for each clause $x \vee y \vee z \in \mathcal{F}_3$, all x, y, z are not contained in $\bar{P}'$, and if two of x, y, z are contained in $\bar{P}'$ then the remaining one is in $P \vee Q$,

for each clause $x \vee y \vee z \vee v \in \mathcal{F}_4$, all x, y, z, v are not contained in $\bar{P}'$.
Since the set $\mathcal{C}$ and the set $\mathcal{E} \cup \mathcal{F} \cup \mathcal{G} \cup \mathcal{G}' \cup \mathcal{H}$ described above are equivalent, from now on we assume $\mathcal{C} = \mathcal{E} \cup \mathcal{F} \cup \mathcal{G} \cup \mathcal{G}' \cup \mathcal{H}$.

Then Yannakakis algorithm sets the variables in P', $(P - P') \cup Q$ and Z to be true with probabilities $3/4$, $5/9$ and $1/2$, respectively. In our algorithm we change to set the variables in $(P - P') \cup Q$ to be true with probability $p = \frac{-3+\sqrt{57}}{8} \approx 0.568729$. Let W_D^* be the value of an optimal truth assignment for $\mathcal{D}$, the sum of the weights of the satisifed clauses in $\mathcal{D}$ $(\mathcal{D} = \mathcal{E}, \mathcal{G}, \mathcal{G}', \mathcal{H})$. Then $W_E^* \leq K_E$, $W_G^* \leq 4K_G$, $W_{G'}^* \leq 6K_{G'}$ and $W_H^* \leq 5K_H$. Let $W_k' = \sum_{C_j \in \mathcal{F}_k} w_j$. Thus the probabilistic method assures that we can find a truth assignment $x^Y \in \{0,1\}^n$ of value w^Y, the sum of the weights of the satisifed clauses in $\mathcal{C}$, such that

$$w^Y \geq W_E^* + 0.770(W_G^* + W_{G'}^* + W_H^*) + \frac{3}{4}(W_1' + W_2')$$

$$+ (1 - (\frac{3}{4})^2(1-p))W_3' + (1 - (\frac{3}{4})^3 p)W_4' + \sum_{k \geq 5}(1 - (\frac{3}{4})^k)W_k'. \quad (24)$$

Now we consider an algorithm D consisting of the following four algorithms:
(1) set each variable x_i true independently with probability 0.5;
(2) set x_i true independently with probability $\frac{1+y_{0i}}{2}$ using the optimal solution (Y, z^*) to (S);
(3) take a random unit vector r and set x_i true if and only if $\text{sgn}(\bar{v}_i^* \cdot r) = \text{sgn}(\bar{v}_0^* \cdot r)$ using the optimal solution (Y^*, z^*) to (S) and (R') $(y_{i_1 i_2}^* = v_{i_1}^* \cdot v_{i_2}^*)$.
(4) set each variable x_i in P', $(P - P') \cup Q$ or Z true independently with probability $3/4$, 0.568729 or $1/2$, respectively based on the modified Yannakakis's algorithm above.

Suppose we use algorithm (i) with probability p_i, where $p_1 + p_2 + p_3 + p_4 = 1$. If we set $p_1 = p_2 = 0.3110053$, $p_3 = 0.1201425$ and $p_4 = 0.2578469$, then the expected value of $\mathcal{D}$ can be shown to be at least $0.76544 \sum_{C_j \in \mathcal{D}} w_j z_j^*$ $(\mathcal{D} =$

$\mathcal{E}, \mathcal{G}, \mathcal{G}', \mathcal{H})$. Furthermore, the expected value of $\mathcal{F}_k$ can also be shown to be at least

$$\sum_{C_j \in \mathcal{F}_k} w_j((1-\tfrac{1}{2^k})p_1 + (1-(1-\tfrac{1}{k})^k)p_2 + \alpha\alpha_k p_3 + \delta_k)z_j^* \geq 0.76544 \sum_{C_j \in \mathcal{F}_k} w_j z_j^*,$$

where $\delta_1 = \delta_2 = 0.75$ and

$$\delta_3 = 1 - 0.75^2(1-p), \quad \delta_4 = 1 - 0.75^3 p, \quad \delta_k = 1 - 0.75^k \quad (k \geq 5) \quad (25)$$

Thus, we have the following theorem.

Theorem 4. *A 0.76544-approximation algorithm can be obtained based on the algorithm A in Section 3, the Yannakakis's algorithm modified as above, and the 0.75-approximation algorithm of Goemans-Williamson.*

We have presented two approximation algorithms for MAX SAT, including a 0.76544-approximation algorithm. We believe this approach can be used to further improve the performance guarantee for MAX SAT. Note that Goemans-Williamson's 0.7584-approximation algorithm can be shown to have the same performance guantee 0.75899 by choosing $p_1 = p_2 = 0.4650334$ and $p_3 = 0.00699332$ as in this paper. Although our 0.75899-approximation algorithm is of the same performance as Geomans-Williamson's algorithm, our algorithm has better performances when applied to MAX kSAT (for example 0.769 for $k \leq 5$, while Geomans-Williamson is at most 0.765). On the other hand, Feige and Geomans recently obtained 0.931-approximation algorithm for MAX 2SAT [1] and if it is used in the Goemans-Williamson's 0.7584-approximation algorithm in place of 0.878-approximation algorithm, then the performance guarantees 0.76199 for MAX SAT and 0.770 for MAX 3SAT can be obtained. The techniques in 0.931-approximation algorithm for MAX 2SAT may also be used in our algorithms.

References

1. U. Feige and Michel X. Goemans, Approximating the value of two prover proof systems, with applications to MAX 2SAT and MAX DICUT, In *Proc. 3rd Israel Symposium on Theory of Computing and Systems*, 1995, pp.182–189.
2. Michel X. Goemans and David P. Williamson, .878-approximation algorithms for MAX CUT and MAX 2SAT, In *Proc. 26th STOC*, 1994, pp.422–431.
3. Michel X. Goemans and David P. Williamson, New 3/4-approximation algorithms for the maximum satisfiability problem, *SIAM Journal of Disc. Math.*, 7 (1994), pp.656–666.
4. Michel X. Goemans and David P. Williamson, Improved approximation algorithms for maximum cut and satisfiability problems using semidefinite programming, In *Journal of the ACM*, 42 (1995), pp.1115–1145.
5. David S. Johnson, Approximation algorithms for combinatorial problems, *Journal of Comput. and Sys. Sci.*, 9 (1974), pp.256–278.
6. S. Mahajan and H. Ramesh, Correctly derandomizing Geomans and Williamson's MAX CUT algorithm, Unpublished manuscript, 1995
7. E. Tardos, A strongly polynomial algorithm for solving combinatoral linear program, *Operations Research*, 11 (1986), pp.250-256.
8. Mihalis Yannakakis, On the approximation of maximum satisfiability, in *Proc. 3rd SODA*, 1992, pp.1–9 (and also in *J. Algorithms*, 17 (1994), pp.475-502).

On the Hardness of Approximating the Minimum Consistent OBDD Problem

Kouichi Hirata[1]   Shinichi Shimozono[2]   Ayumi Shinohara[3]

[1] *Department of Artificial Intelligence*
[2] *Department of Control Engineering and Science*
Kyushu Institute of Technology,
Kawazu 680-4, Iizuka, 820 JAPAN
E-mail: `hirata@ai.kyutech.ac.jp, sin@ces.kyutech.ac.jp`

[3] *Research Institute of Fundamental Information Science*
Kyushu University, Fukuoka 812 JAPAN
E-mail: `ayumi@rifis.kyushu-u.ac.jp`

Abstract. Ordered binary decision diagrams (OBDDs, for short) represent Boolean functions as directed acyclic graphs. The minimum consistent OBDD problem is, given an incomplete truth table of a function, to find the smallest OBDD that is consistent with the truth table with respect to a fixed order of variables. We show that this problem is NP-hard, and prove that there is a constant $\epsilon > 0$ such that no polynomial time algorithm can approximate the minimum consistent OBDD within the ratio n^ϵ unless P=NP, where n is the number of variables. This result suggests that OBDDs are unlikely to be polynomial time learnable in PAC-learning model.

1   Introduction

For a class of representations of languages, the *minimum consistent problem* is to find a representation that is as small size as possible and is consistent with given positive and negative examples. The computational complexity of the problem closely relates to the efficiency of learning with the target class. Roughly speaking, the polynomial-time learnability of a class is equivalent to the existence of a polynomial-time algorithm which can produce a consistent representation whose size is not too large compared to the smallest one. Therefore, for the minimum consistent problem that is intractable, a polynomial-time algorithm that can find an approximately small representation is undoubtedly important.

One of the minimum consistent problems that are most frequently tackled is that for deterministic finite automata (DFAs for short). The problem was first shown to be NP-hard [1, 12]. This negative result was enhanced by Li and Vazirani [14]: they showed that the minimum consistent DFA cannot be approximated within the ratio $\frac{9}{8}$ in polynomial time, unless P=NP. Pitt and Warmuth [17] improved to the ratio opt^k, where opt is the minimum number of states and k is any positive integer.

By applying recent results on non-approximabilities of combinatorial optimization problems, Hancock *et al.* [13] investigated the minimum consistent problem for decision lists and decision trees. They showed that decision lists cannot be approximated in polynomial time within a factor of n^c for some constant $c > 0$, unless P=NP. They also showed that decision trees cannot be approximated in polynomial time within a factor of n^c for any $c > 0$ unless NP is included in DTIME$[2^{poly \log n}]$.

This paper deals with the minimum consistent problem for ordered binary decision diagrams (OBDDs for short) [4]. OBDDs succinctly represent many useful Boolean functions, such as symmetric functions and threshold functions [8], as directed acyclic graphs. For a fixed order of variables, OBDDs can be regarded as acyclic DFAs whose sizes are measured by the number of only the branching states [11]. It is known that the problem of finding the optimal order that realizes the minimum size OBDD is intractable even for complete truth tables [7]. To concentrate on the complexity to deal with incomplete truth tables, we fix the order of variables in the minimum consistent OBDD problem. Our result claims that the problem cannot be approximated within the ratio n^ϵ for some $\epsilon > 0$ in polynomial time unless P = NP. This is in sharp contrast to the well-known fact that the minimum size OBDD representing the function can be computed in linear time from the *complete* truth table [19].

The remaining part of this paper is organized as follows. First, we show that the minimum consistent OBDD problem is NP-hard, even the number of either positive examples or negative examples is only one. Then, we show that there is a constant $\epsilon > 0$ such that no polynomial time algorithm can approximate the minimum consistent OBDD within the ratio n^ϵ unless P=NP. Our results suggest that any efficient algorithm for learning OBDDs would have to produce very large hypotheses.

2 Minimum Consistent OBDD Problem

We first give definitions and notations for OBDDs. Then we introduce the minimum consistent problem of OBDD as a combinatorial optimization problem, and show that the problem is NP-hard.

---

[4] Some results are known for similar problems. See Section 6.

A *binary decision diagram* over a set $X = \{x_1, \ldots, x_n\}$ of Boolean variables is a rooted, directed acyclic graph whose nodes are either *internal nodes* labeled with variables in X or *terminals* labeled with Boolean constants, 0 or 1. Every internal node has two outgoing arcs that are labeled with 0 and 1, respectively. A terminal has no outgoing arcs. The *root* is the only node with no incoming arcs.

A binary decision diagram D over n variables represents a Boolean function in the following way. An input $w = w[1] \cdots w[n] \in \{0, 1\}^n$ determines a *computation path* on D from the root to a terminal: it starts from the root, and if a reached node is labeled with x_i then it follows the arc labeled with $w[i]$. Then the output of D for w is the label of the terminal reached by the computation path for w. Terminals labeled with 1 and 0 are called 1-terminal and 0-terminal, respectively.

Let π be an order on X. We say that a binary decision diagram D is an *ordered binary decision diagram* (OBDD for short) *with respect to* π if on every path from the root to a terminal the variables are tested according to π only once. In this paper, we deal with the order $x_1 < \cdots < x_n$ on X.

We consider the following problem:

Definition 1. MINIMUM CONSISTENT OBDD
Instance: Two disjoint sets $P, N \subseteq \{0, 1\}^n$. The strings in P and N are called *positive examples* and *negative examples*, respectively.

Solution: An OBDD D over n variables that is consistent with P and N, i.e., outputs 1 for all positive examples in P and 0 for all negative examples in N.

Cost: The size $|D|$ of D, i.e., the number of internal nodes of D.
The goal is to find a solution whose cost is the minimum.

For P and N that form a complete truth table $P \cup N = \{0, 1\}^n$, the minimum consistent OBDD can be computed in polynomial time by constructing an OBDD like a complete binary tree and then applying the reduction procedure introduced by Bryant [8, 19] to it. This is one of the reasons why OBDDs are conveniently used in circuit designs of well-defined Boolean functions. However, the problem becomes intractable for incomplete examples:

Lemma 2. MINIMUM CONSISTENT OBDD *is NP-hard, even either the set of positive examples or the set of negative examples consists of only one string.*

Proof. This can be shown by a log-space reduction involving the translation of instances from MINIMUM COVER [10] to sets P, N of strings presented by Hancock *et al.* [13]. MINIMUM COVER is, given a collection C of subsets over U, to find a subcollection $C' \subseteq C$ that covers U and is as small as possible. Given an instance C, construct P, N as follows: (i) For every $i \in U$, P includes the string which is obtained by placing 1's on 0^n at all positions k for $c_k \in C$ such that $i \in c_k$, and (ii) N consists of only one string 0^n. Then by an OBDD D consistent with P and N we obtain a cover $C' = \{c_k \in C \mid x_k \in X'\}$ for U with the size $|C'| \leq |D|$, where $X' \subseteq X$ is the set of variables labeled on the nodes on the computation path for 0^n in D. □

Note that only the nodes in X' are relevant to the computations for inputs in $P \cup N$.

3 Approximate the Minimum Consistent OBDD

Since MINIMUM CONSISTENT OBDD problem is intractable, it is natural to ask whether there is an efficient approximation algorithm that produces reasonably small OBDDs for given examples. Deviations of approximate solutions from the optimum solution can be measured by the ratio of their costs. For MINIMUM CONSISTENT OBDD problem, the *performance ratio* of a solution D with respect to an instance P, N is the ratio $\frac{|D|}{|D^*|}$, where D^* is a minimum OBDD consistent with P and N. The *guaranteed performance ratio* of an approximation algorithm is the ratio r such that, for any instance, the algorithm always produces an OBDD D satisfying $\frac{|D|}{|D^*|} \leq r$.

Notice that the reduction referred in Lemma 2 preserves performance ratios between MINIMUM COVER and MINIMUM CONSISTENT OBDD. Hence, even for instances with either only one positive or one negative example, we have no polynomial-time algorithm whose performance ratio is better than $\log n$, unless NP $\subseteq$ DTIME$[n^{poly \log n}]$ [15]. The aim of this section is to show that this lower bound can be amplified by a reduction involving many both positive and negative examples.

To obtain our result, we invoke the non-approximability of GRAPH COLORING (CHROMATIC NUMBER) [10, 15]. Let $G = (V, E)$ be an undirected graph. We say that G is *k-colorable* if there is a *k*-coloring of G, that is, a mapping $f : V \to \{1, \ldots, k\}$ such that $f(u) \neq f(v)$ whenever $(u, v) \in E$. The *chromatic number* of G is the minimum number k such that G is k-colorable. We denote the chromatic number of G by $K(G)$. Then the problem GRAPH COLORING is, given a graph G, to find a k-coloring for G such that k is as small as possible. It is known in [15] that there is a constant $c > 0$ such that GRAPH COLORING cannot be approximated within the ratio n^c unless P=NP. Thus, there is $c > 0$ such that no polynomial-time algorithm can always find a k-coloring satisfying $k/K(G) < n^c$ for all G.

Let us start with introducing a translation from a graph to sets of strings for dealing with OBDDs. Let $G = (V, E)$ be a graph with the set $V = \{1, \ldots, n\}$ of nodes. For each node $i \in V$, we define the *adjacency sets* P_i and N_i as follows: (i) P_i consists of 1^n and $p_{ij} = 1^{j-1} 0 1^{n-j}$ for every $(i, j) \in E$, and (ii) N_i consists of only one string $q_i = 1^{i-1} 0 1^{n-i}$. Note that, for any $i \in V$, P_i and N_i are disjoint.

Let U be a subset of V. We denote the union $\bigcup_{i \in U} P_i$ by P_U and $\bigcup_{i \in U} N_i$ by N_U. We identify a mapping $f : V \to \{1, \ldots, k\}$ with the partition of nodes $U_1, \ldots, U_k \subseteq V$ defined by $U_i = \{v \in V \mid f(v) = i\}$.

Lemma 3. *A partition $U_1, \ldots, U_k$ of V is a k-coloring of G if and only if P_{U_i} and N_{U_i} are disjoint for all $1 \leq i \leq k$.*

Proof. This holds since there is $(i, j) \in E$ with $i, j \in U_h$ for some $1 \leq h \leq k$ if and only if there are the same strings $p_{ij} \in P_i$ and $q_j \in N_j$.

Lemma 4. *Let $G = (V, E)$ be a graph and let P_U and N_U be disjoint unions of the adjacency sets for $U \subseteq V$ of G. Then the minimum OBDD consistent with P_U and N_U has exactly $|U|$ nodes all of which are on the computation path for 1^n.*

Proof. Every string in $P_U \cup N_U$ except 1^n includes exactly one 0. This implies that any internal node can separate either one negative string or one positive string from 1^n and other strings. Since there are $|U|$ negative strings in N_U, the minimum OBDD must have exactly $|U|$ nodes. Thus the lemma holds.

The translation of graphs to strings presented here is different from those in the reductions to other problem, such as k-term DNF and k-decision list [13, 16]. This is because OBDDs can count easily the number of 0's (or 1's) in input strings.

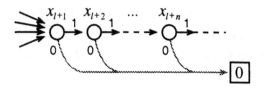

Fig. 1. A conduit detecting $\langle i \rangle 1^{j-1} 0 1^{n-j} 1^n$ for all $1 \leq j \leq n$.

Theorem 5. *There is a constant $0 < \epsilon < 1$ such that* MINIMUM CONSISTENT OBDD *cannot be approximated within a ratio n^ϵ in polynomial time unless* P = NP.

Proof. We show a reduction that preserves the performance ratio from GRAPH COLORING to MINIMUM CONSISTENT OBDD, that is, two log-space procedures ϕ and ψ such that: (i) for any graph $G = (V, E)$ with the set $V = \{1, \ldots, n\}$ of nodes, ϕ produces disjoint sets $P, N \subseteq \{0, 1\}^{2n + \lceil \log n \rceil}$; (ii) for any OBDD D consistent with P and N, ψ produces k-coloring for G satisfying $k - 1 + nk + n \leq |D|$.

First we define ϕ, the construction of strings for $G = (V, E)$. By $\langle i \rangle$ we denote the binary representation of $i - 1$ of the length $l = \lceil \log n \rceil$ for $1 \leq i \leq n$. The sets P and N of strings, which consist of three parts, are defined as follows:

$$P = \{ \langle i \rangle 1^n p \mid i \in V \wedge p \in P_i \},$$
$$N = \{ \langle i \rangle 1^n q \mid i \in V \wedge q \in N_i \} \cup \{ \langle i \rangle 1^{j-1} 0 1^{n-j} 1^n \mid i, j \in V \},$$

where P_i and N_i for $i \in V$ are the adjacency sets of G. Note that P and N are disjoint. We say the first part consisting of l symbols the *header part* and the next part consisting of n symbols the *middle part*. For the sake of brevity, we denote the sets $\{ \langle i \rangle 1^n p \mid p \in P_i \}$ and $\{ \langle i \rangle 1^n q \mid q \in N_i \}$ by P_i^* and N_i^*, respectively.

Next we define ψ that constructs a coloring for G from an OBDD D' consistent with P and N. The procedure ψ first computes from D' an OBDD D reduced with respect to P and N as follows: For each node u of D', (i) check whether there is $i \in V$ such that u is on the computation path for $\langle i \rangle 1^n 1^n \in P$; (ii) if u is not on any of those paths, then remove u and redirect the arcs into u to 0-terminal. Each path in D from the root to 1-terminal has all the nodes labeled with $x_{l+1}, \ldots, x_{l+n}$ to distinguish negative strings $\langle i \rangle 1^{j-1} 0 1^{n-j} 1^n$ for

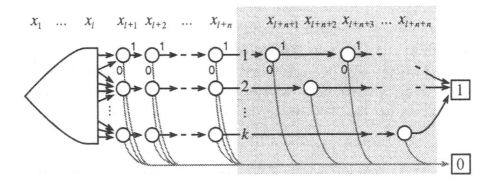

Fig. 2. The structure of D with k conduits. After the conduits, the pathes contain exactly n nodes (grey hatched area) for detecting $|V| = n$ negative strings.

$1 \leq j \leq n$ from positive string $\langle i \rangle 1^n 1^n$. This part, which examines the middle part of strings, is called a *conduit* (Fig. 1). A string s is said to be *enclosed* by a conduit C if the middle part of s is examined by nodes of C, i.e., s "flows through" C. Note that if $s \in P_i^* \cup N_i^*$ flows through C then all strings in $P_i^* \cup N_i^*$ flow through C.

For such an OBDD D, the following claim holds.

Claim 6. *Let k be the number of conduits in D, and let U_i be the set of integers expressed by headers of the strings enclosed by the ith conduit. Then the sets $P_{U_1}^*, \ldots, P_{U_k}^*$ and $N_{U_1}^*, \ldots, N_{U_k}^*$ form the partition of P and N, respectively, such that $P_{U_i}^*$ and $N_{U_i}^*$ are disjoint and thus $P_{U_i} \cap N_{U_i} = \emptyset$ for $1 \leq i \leq k$.*

This is true since if $P_{U_i} \cap N_{U_i} \neq \emptyset$ then D is not consistent with P and N.

By examining all the first l symbols in headers, $P_i^* \cup N_i^*$ can be separated from $P_j^* \cup N_j^*$ for any $i \neq j$. It is the "worst case" that the nodes referring the first l variables form a binary tree with $n - 1$ nodes. However, the number of nodes needed to make a consistent partition can be ignored: it will be considered later. From Lemma 3, the partition $U_1, \ldots, U_k$ of nodes V defined by the conduits of D is a coloring for G. So ψ produces a k-coloring for G according to the partition $U_1, \ldots, U_k$.

Now we show that if there exists a polynomial-time algorithm for MINIMUM CONSISTENT OBDD that approximates within ratio r, then with ψ and ϕ we have a polynomial-time algorithm that approximates GRAPH COLORING within ratio $\frac{1}{2}r$. Let $h(D)$ be the number of nodes that are labeled with variables $x_1, \ldots, x_l$ and needed to make the partition in D. Note that, for any case, the inequality $k - 1 \leq h(D) \leq n - 1$ holds. For each subset U_i of the partition, the path to 1-terminal after ith conduit must reject $|U_i|$ negative strings. The total number of nodes labeled with variables $x_{l+n+1}, \ldots, x_{l+n+n}$ is exactly n since $|\bigcup_{i=1}^{k} U_i| = n$ (see Fig. 2). Therefore, the size $|D|$ of D is

$$k - 1 + nk + n \leq |D| = h(D) + nk + n \leq n - 1 + nk + n.$$

For G with the chromatic number $K(G)$, there exists an OBDD D^* with $K(G)$ conduits consistent with P and N. The size of D^* is

$$K(G) - 1 + nK(G) + n \leq |D^*| \leq n - 1 + nK(G) + n.$$

Then a lower bound for the ratio r of the size $|D|$ to the size $|D^*|$ is

$$\frac{k}{2K(G)} < \frac{k - 1 + nk + n}{n - 1 + nK(G) + n} \leq \frac{|D|}{|D^*|} \leq r.$$

Since $\frac{k}{K(G)}$ is the performance ratio of a k-coloring for G, the worst case ratio r^* for any polynomial-time algorithm that produces an OBDD consistent with P and N is greater than $\frac{1}{2}n^c$ for some $c > 0$. Let t be the length of strings in P and N (so the number of variables). Then $t = l + 2n < 3n$, and thus the inequality $\frac{1}{2}(\frac{t}{3})^c < \frac{1}{2}n^c < r$ holds. Therefore, there is $0 < \epsilon < c < 1$ such that $n^\epsilon < r^*$ for sufficiently large t satisfying $(2 \cdot 3^c)^{\frac{1}{c-\epsilon}} < m$ unless P = NP. $\square$

4   Learnability of OBDDs

Valiant [21] has proposed a criterion of correct identification of a concept from examples in a stochastic setting. The idea of this model is that after randomly sampled examples and non-examples of a concept are given, an identification procedure should conjecture a concept with "high probability" that is "not too different" from the correct concept. This model is called a *probably approximately correct* (*PAC*, for short) learning model.

The MINIMUM CONSISTENT OBDD in the previous sections closely relates to the PAC-learnability of OBDDs. If OBDDs are polynomial time PAC-learnable, then a polynomial time algorithm that can produce a not too large consistent OBDD exists. In this sense, our result gives a partial negative result on the polynomial-time learnability. Our hardness results, however, *do not* imply that OBDDs are not polynomial time PAC-learnable, since an *Occam algorithm* [6] is allowed to produce an OBDD whose size is also dependent on the number of given examples.

Angluin [2, 3] has formulated another learning model which is allowed to make several types of queries. The goal of this model is *exact* identification of a concept from a concept class, that is, to succeed the algorithm must halt and output a concept which is equivalent to a target concept. By using two types of queries, *membership* and *equivalence* queries, Angluin has shown that DFAs are polynomial time learnable [2]. By regarding OBDDs as DFAs and applying this result to OBDDs, Gavaldà and Guijarro [11] have obtained the following results: (1) The OBDDs are polynomial time learnable with both membership and equivalence queries; (2) The OBDDs are not polynomial time learnable with equivalence queries alone. It is known that if a concept class is not polynomial time PAC-learnable, then it is not polynomial time learnable with equivalence queries, but the converse does not hold [3].

As a learnable subclass of OBDDs, Ergün *et al.* [9] introduced *bounded-width* OBDDs[5] and showed that, for a fixed order of variables, width-2 OBDDs are polynomial time PAC-learnable[6], although learning width-k OBDDs is as hard as learning DNF formulas for $k \geq 3$.

As another learnable subclass, we can consider OBDDs representing *symmetric* functions. Note that any n-ary symmetric functions are representable as OBDDs with $O(n^2)$ nodes. The learning algorithm works as follows: The initial internal OBDD is the OBDD with $O(n^2)$ nodes where all of the terminals are labeled by 0. When our learning algorithm receives a counterexample w from equivalence queries, the OBDD exchanges the label 0 of the terminal node in the computation path w to 1. It is obvious that the runtime of this algorithm is bounded by some polynomial with respect to n. Hence, OBDDs representing symmetric functions are polynomial time PAC-learnable.

5   Discussion

We have shown the intractability of the problem to find the minimum consistent OBDD from given examples with respect to a fixed order of variables. Our results provide some interesting contrasts to the similar results on the problems to find the minimum consistent decision lists and decision trees due to Hancock

---

[5] The paper [9] deals with the notion of branching programs instead of OBDDs.

[6] Note that the result in [9] is not a *proper* PAC-learnability.

et al. [13]. The first result, Lemma 2, is essentially the same to their result on hardness to find the shortest monomial. According to Theorem 5, however, the difficulties of finding minimum decision lists and decision trees mainly relies on choosing the optimal order of variables, while the order of variables is fixed in our problem. Thus, the proof strategy to reduce from GRAPH COLORING completely differs from theirs, although they have also reduced from the same problem.

On the other hand, since the order of variables is fixed in our setting, OBDDs can be regarded as a kind of DFAs. Pitt and Warmuth [17] have shown that finding the minimum consistent DFA cannot be approximated within opt^k states, where opt is the minimum number of states and k is any constant greater than 1. They constructed a special form of DFAs, so called *counter-like DFAs*, where the cyclic transitions play an essential role to show their hardness. In contrast to their reduction, since OBDDs cannot have any cycles, our results would suggest that finding the minimum consistent DFA is still very difficult even when the DFA is restricted to be acyclic. In future works, we will deal with the problem of finding the minimum consistent acyclic DFA directly.

6 Remarks on Related Results

Takenaga and Yajima [20] have been shown that the minimum consistent problem for quasi-reduced OBDDs, which are identical to acyclic DFAs, is NP-complete. This result corresponds to Lemma 2, although the reduction does not preserve the performance ratios and requires many both positive examples and negative examples.

Also as a remarkable result, Sauerhoff and Wegener [18] have independently investigated the complexity of approximating the minimum OBDD that is consistent with an incompletely specified function. Their problem MINIMUM OBDD COVER is, given incompletely specified OBDD D (which has terminals labeled with '*', as well as 0 and 1), to find a minimum OBDD D' that covers D, i.e., $D'(w) = D(w)$ for $w \in \{0,1\}^n$ whenever $D(w) \neq *$. They have proved that the problem has the same lower bound of the performance ratio as Theorem 5 by reducing the problem to GRAPH COLORING.

Since MINIMUM OBDD COVER takes as an instance an incompletely specified OBDD, their result does not imply our result itself. However, OBDDs constructed in their proof are similar to those in our proof of Theorem 5. Thus, if an appropriate polynomial-time procedure that produces a reduced OBDD for an incomplete truth table could be provided, then their result would also say the hardness of MINIMUM CONSISTENT OBDD. Our proof provides a direct reduction to the sets of positive and negative examples, and thus it shows an explicit hardness of the learning problem.

References

1. Angluin, D.: *On the complexity of minimum inference of regular sets*, Information and Control **39**, 337–350, 1978.
2. Angluin, D.: *Learning regular sets from queries and counterexamples*, Information and Computation **75**, 87–106, 1987.
3. Angluin, D.: *Queries and concept learning*, Machine Learning **2**, 319–342, 1988.
4. Angluin, D.: *Negative results for equivalence queries*, Machine Learning **5**, 121–150, 1990.
5. Blum, A.: *New approximation algorithms for graph coloring*, Journal of the Association for Computing Machinery **41**, 470–516, 1994.
6. Board, R. and Pitt, L.: *On the necessity of Occam algorithms*, Theoretical Computer Science **100**, 157–184, 1992.
7. Bolling, B. and Wegener, I.: *Improving the variable ordering of OBDDs is NP-complete*, Technical Report, Universität Dortmund, 1994.
8. Bryant, R. E.: *Symbolic Boolean manipulation with ordered binary-decision diagrams*, ACM Computing Surveys **24**, 293–318, 1992.
9. Ergün, F., Kumar, S. R. and Rubinfeld, R.: *On learning bounded-width branching programs*, Proc. 8th International Workshop on Computational Learning Theory, 361–368, 1995.
10. Garey, M. and Johnson, D. S.: *Computers and intractability: A guide to the theory of NP-completeness*, W. H. Freeman and Company, 1978.
11. Gavaldà, R. and Guijarro, D.: *Learning ordered binary decision diagrams*, Proc. 6th International Workshop on Algorithmic Learning Theory, 228–238, LNAI **997**, 1995.
12. Gold, E. M.: *Complexity of automaton identification from given data*, Information and Control **37**, 302–320, 1978.
13. Hancock, T., Jiang, T., Li, M. and Tromp, J.: *Lower bounds on learning decision lists and trees*, draft, 1996.
14. Li, M. and Vazirani, U.: *On the learnability of finite automata*, Proc. 1988 Workshop on Computational Learning Theory, 359–370, 1988.
15. Lund, C. and Yannakakis, M.: *On the hardness of approximating minimization problems*, Proc. 25th Annual ACM Symposium on Theory of Computing, 286–293, 1993.
16. Pitt. L and Valiant, L. G.: *Computational limitation on learning from examples*, Journal of the Association for Computing Machinery **35**, 965–984, 1988.
17. Pitt, L. and Warmuth, M. K.: *The minimum consistent DFA problem cannot be approximated within any polynomial*, Journal of the Association for Computing Machinery **40**, 95–142, 1993.
18. Sauerhoff, M. and Wegener, I.: *On the complexity of minimizing the OBDD size for incompletely specified functions*, Technical Report 560, Univ. Dortmund, 1994.
19. Sieling, D. and Wegener, I.: *Reduction of OBDDs in linear time*, Information Processing Letter **48**, 139–144, 1993.

20. Takenaga, Y. and Yajima, S.: *NP-completeness of minimum binary decision diagram identification*, Technical Report of IEICE, COMP92-99, 57–62, 1993.
21. Valiant, L. G.: *A theory of the learnable*, Communications of the ACM **27**, 1134–1142, 1984.

Computing the Unrooted Maximum Agreement Subtree in Sub-quadratic Time

T.W. Lam   W.K. Sung   H.F. Ting

Department of Computer Science, University of Hong Kong
Email: {twlam, wksung, hfting}@cs.hku.hk

Abstract. This paper presents the first sub-quadratic time algorithm for the Unrooted Maximum Agreement Subtree (UMAST) problem: Given a set A of n items (e.g., species) and two unrooted trees T and T', each with n leaves uniquely labeled by the items of A, we want to compute the largest subset B of A such that the subtrees of T and T' induced by B are isomorphic. The UMAST problem is closely related to some problems in biology, in particular, the one of finding the consensus between evolutionary trees (or phylogenies) of a set of species. The previous best algorithm for the UMAST problem requires time $O(n^{2+o(1)})$ [5]; the algorithm in this paper improves the time bound to $O(n^{1.75+o(1)})$. The rooted version of this problem has also attracted a lot of attention; the time complexity has recently been improved from $O(n^2)$ [5] to $O(n^{1.5} \log n)$ [6].

1 Introduction

In this paper, we study a fundamental problem in Computational Biology, namely the **Unrooted Maximum Agreement Subtree** (UMAST) problem. Given a set of species, scientists are interested in recovering the evolutionary relationship among them. One of the models for capturing this kind of relationship is the evolutionary tree (also known as the phylogeny). From a computational point of view, an evolutionary tree is just a labeled tree satisfying some criteria. Different sets of criteria capture different kinds of evolutionary relationship and induce different evolutionary trees [1, 8, 12]. In the Biology community there is no universal agreement on what should be the right criteria. Even worse, most of the proposed criteria turn out to be NP-hard in finding the intended evolutionary trees [2, 4]. Current practice is to apply heuristics to construct different evolutionary trees and compare the results manually in order to arrive at some consensus. As the number of species grows, finding the consensus of different evolutionary trees is non-trivial. Automating this process has given rise to a number of challenging computational problems. In particular, Finden and Gordon [9] initiated the study of the problem of computing the consensus of *two* evolutionary trees, which is formulated as follows:

Preamble: Let T be an unrooted tree of which each leaf is labeled with a distinct species chosen from a set A. For any subset B of A, let $T|_B$ denote the subtree of T induced by B, which can be constructed as follows: Discard those leaves of T not labeled with species in B, as well as those internal nodes whose degrees eventually become one; then contract every path whose intermediate nodes are each of degree two into an edge. See Figure 1 for an example. **Problem:** Given two unrooted trees T and T', both with n leaves labeled distinctly with species chosen from a set A, we say that a subset B of A is an agreement subset (*a.s.*) of T and T' if $T|_B$ and $T'|_B$ are leaf-label preserving isomorphic, i.e. there exists a 1-1 correspondence between the nodes of $T|_B$ and of $T'|_B$ such that (i) $T|_B$ has an edge (u, v) if and only if $T'|_B$ has an edge between the images

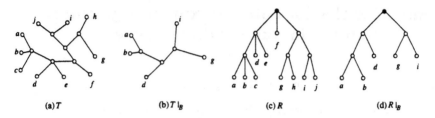

Fig. 1. The subtrees of an unrooted tree T and a rooted tree R induced by $B = \{a, b, d, g, i\}$.

of u and v; and (ii) every leaf in $T|_B$ is mapped to a leaf of $T'|_B$ with the same label. The UMAST problem asks for the maximum agreement subset ($m.a.s.$) of T and T'.

The problem has a rooted version. **Preamble:** Let R be a rooted tree of which each leaf is labeled with a distinct species chosen from a set A. For any subset B of A, let $R|_B$ denote a rooted tree whose nodes are either leaves of R labeled with species in B, or the least common ancestors of all pairs of these leaves. Notice that unlike the unrooted case, $R|_B$ may have a node of degree two (that is the root). See Figure 1 for an example. **Problem:** Given two rooted trees R and R' whose leaves are labeled with the same set A of species. The RMAST problem asks for the maximum agreement subset of R and R', i.e. the largest subset B of A such that $R|_B$ and $R'|_B$ are leaf-label preserving isomorphic.

It is believed that UMAST is harder than RMAST. There is indeed a linear time reduction from RMAST to UMAST [5], but not known for the reverse.

Previous results versus our result: Finden and Gordon gave a heuristic for finding an approximate solution to UMAST in $O(n^5)$ time. An $O(n^{(\frac{1}{2}+\epsilon)\log n})$ time algorithm which could guarantee an optimal solution was later proposed by Kubicka *et al.* [14]. Steel and Warnow [15] were the first to give a polynomial time algorithm for UMAST, as well as one for RMAST; the time complexity is $O(n^{4.5}\log n)$ in either case (the bound can be improved to $O(n^2)$ if the inputs are restricted to bounded degree trees). Subsequently, Farach and Thorup [5] improved the time complexity of UMAST to $O(n^{2+o(1)})$ and RMAST to $O(n^2)$.

Very recently, the quadratic barrier to RMAST has been broken. Farach and Thorup [6] have given an algorithm that takes $O(n^{1.5}\log n)$ time. If the inputs are restricted to bounded degree trees, Farach and Thorup's algorithm [6] only requires $O(n^{1+o(1)})$ time; moreover, Farach, Przytycka, and Thorup [7] further improved the time bound to $O(n\log^3 n)$. The case when the trees are binary has also been considered by Cole and Hariharan [3], they gave an $O(n\log n)$ time algorithm.

For the UMAST problem, the quadratic time bound seems to be more difficult to improve. No improvement has been known even for the bounded degree case. This paper presents an $O(n^{1.75+o(1)})$ time algorithm for UMAST without any restriction on the degree of the trees.

The problem of finding the consensus of three or more trees is NP-hard [13], but admits polynomial time solution if the trees have bounded degree [7, 13].

2 Preliminary

Let T and T' be two unrooted trees with n leaves, each leaf is labeled by a distinct species chosen from a fixed set A. We assume that there is no internal node of degree two. Following the previous work, we simplify the discussion by focusing on computing the size of the *m.a.s.*; the algorithm presented can be augmented to report the *m.a.s.* itself. Define $umast(T, T')$ to be the size of the *m.a.s.* of any unrooted trees T and T', and $rmast(R, R')$ the size of the *m.a.s.* of any rooted trees R and R'.

Unrooted versus rooted trees: If we pick a node u in T as the root, T becomes a rooted tree, referred to as T_u. Inside T_u, any subtree rooted at a node v is denoted by T_{uv}. The following facts reveal a reduction from UMAST to RMAST.

1. Let v and v' be any nodes chosen arbitrarily from T and T'. The *m.a.s.* of the rooted trees T_v and $T'_{v'}$ is also an *a.s.* of T and T'.
2. Let B be the *m.a.s.* of T and T'. In respect of the isomorphism between $T|_B$ and $T'|_B$, if a node u is mapped to a node u' then B is also the *m.a.s.* of the rooted trees T_u and $T'_{u'}$.

We conclude that $umast(T, T') = \max_{(u,u') \in T \times T'} rmast(T_u, T'_{u'})$. A straightforward but inefficient approach to finding $umast(T, T')$ is to use any RMAST algorithm to compute $rmast(T_u, T'_{u'})$ for all pairs of nodes (u, u'), and then report the maximum. For instance, we can compute each $rmast(T_u, T'_{u'})$ in $O(n^{1.5} \log n)$ time [6] and hence $umast(T, T')$ in $O(n^{3.5} \log n)$ time.

To get a better performance, our UMAST algorithm adopts a more sophisticated approach based on Farach and Thorup's quadratic time UMAST algorithm [5]; in particular, it makes use of their concepts, *cores* and *intervals* of *side trees*, whose definitions are given below.

A slightly generalized notion of core [5]: Consider a connected subgraph $\mathcal{K}$ of T, comprising internal nodes only. $\mathcal{K}$ is an unrooted tree itself; a node in $\mathcal{K}$ is said to be *critical* if it is a leaf or its degree is greater than two. Degree-two nodes in $\mathcal{K}$ are naturally partitioned into chains, each called a *spine*, and these nodes are also called *spine nodes* (see Figure 2). Consider the subgraph $T - \mathcal{K}$, the nodes are decomposed into a number of subtrees, each called a *side tree*. $\mathcal{K}$ is said to be a *k-core* (or simply a *core*) of T if $\mathcal{K}$ contains $\Theta(k)$ critical nodes and every side tree has at most n/k leaves. Notice that the number of spines cannot exceed the number of critical nodes, which is $O(k)$. Yet there may be $\Theta(n)$ spine nodes. We can compute a core with at most $2k$ critical nodes using a linear time algorithm by Farach and Thorup [5].

With respect to a core $\mathcal{K}$ of T, each side tree is connected through a unique edge to a core node (i.e. a node in $\mathcal{K}$). We often consider a side tree τ as a rooted tree, the root, denoted $r(\tau)$, is the node connected to the core node. We use the notation $\langle \tau \rangle$ to denote the leaf labels (i.e. species) of τ.

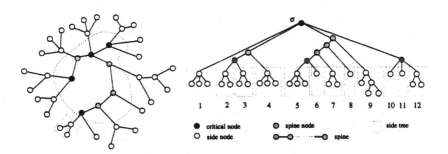

Fig. 2. A core of an unrooted tree

Intervals of side trees: In respect of a core $\mathcal{K}$ of T, we assign an ordering to the side trees as follows: Root $\mathcal{K}$ at an arbitrary critical node σ and perform a postorder traversal on $\mathcal{K}$; every time a node is visited, the side trees connected to it are labeled. Note that side trees connected to the same core node or the same spine are always labeled by consecutive integers (see Figure 2). Our algorithm often processes a group of side trees labeled by consecutive integers, say, $i_1, i_1 + 1, \cdots, i_2$, as a single unit; we denote such a group of side trees as an *interval* $I = [i_1..i_2]$.

3 Overview of the algorithm

Exact values versus realistic upper bounds: In our UMAST algorithm, we often restrict our attention to some small collection of agreement subsets of T and T', say, Σ, and would like to determine the size of the biggest agreement subset in Σ, denoted $\mu(\Sigma)$. However, computing the exact value $\mu(\Sigma)$ is very difficult in some cases; we usually resort to finding a *realistic upper bound* of $\mu(\Sigma)$, denoted $\hat{\mu}(\Sigma)$, which is any value satisfying the following conditions: **(i)** $\hat{\mu}(\Sigma) \geq \mu(\Sigma)$; and **(ii)** $\hat{\mu}(\Sigma)$ corresponds to the size of some agreement subset of T and T' (not necessarily in Σ). As a matter of fact, if Σ does contain the *m.a.s.* of T and T' then we have $\hat{\mu}(\Sigma) = umast(T, T') = \mu(\Sigma)$.

Framework: Our UMAST algorithm basically follows the framework of the quadratic time algorithm in [5]. First of all, we construct for each of T and T' a k-core with at most $2k$ critical nodes, where $k = 2^{\sqrt{\log n}}$; these cores are denoted $\mathcal{K}$ and $\mathcal{K}'$. We order the side trees of T in respect of some critical node σ in $\mathcal{K}$, and similarly for T' in respect of σ'. The actual computation of $umast(T, T')$ is divided into two parts: Part I attempts to compute $umast(T, T')$ with an assumption that there exists a *m.a.s.* B such that, in respect of the isomorphism between $T|_B$ and $T'|_B$, there is a core node in $T|_B$ mapped to a core node in $T'|_B$. When no such B exists, the value computed in Part I may underestimate $umast(T, T')$. Yet Part II computes $umast(T, T')$ correctly whenever there is a *m.a.s.* B such that no core node in $T|_B$ is mapped to a core node in $T'|_B$. The maximum of the values computed by Parts I and II always gives the correct answer.

Naively, Part I aims at computing the maximum, over all pairs of core nodes (c, c'), of the biggest agreement subset D such that $T|_D$ and $T'|_D$ involves a mapping between c and c'. Yet this would require $\Omega(n^2)$ time if we work on a pair each time (as T and T' each may contain $\Omega(n)$ core nodes). To break the quadratic barrier, we observe that it suffices to find a realistic upper bound and many pairs of core nodes can be put into groups according to some structurally relationship. We devise a new technique to process a group of such pairs efficiently without working on every individual pair. More precisely, for a group composed of all pairs of nodes (c, c') where c is chosen from a subset L of core nodes of T and c' from a subset L' of core nodes of T', we are able to find a realistic upper bound of the maximum of all the required agreement subsets using time in the order of $|L| + |L'|$ instead of $|L| \times |L'|$. As to be shown in Section 4, this leads to an $O(n^{1.5+o(1)})$ time procedure for finding the realistic upper bound of the biggest *a.s.* that involves a mapping between two core nodes.

Part II is required to compute $umast(T, T')$ correctly whenever there is a *m.a.s.* that does not induce a mapping between a pair of core nodes. Farach and Thorup [5] observed that such a *m.a.s.* B must be "small" and, in particular, $B \subseteq \langle \tau_1 \rangle \cup \langle \tau_2 \rangle$ for some side trees τ_1 and τ_2, each in either T or T'. Thus, Part II can compute $umast(T, T')$ by solving a number of subproblems recursively, each restricting T and T' to a pair of side trees. However, this recursion may generate a total of $\Theta(n^2)$ problem instances and may require $\Omega(n^2)$ time in the worst case. Luckily, we further observe that if $B \subseteq \langle \tau_1 \rangle \cup \langle \tau_2 \rangle$ where τ_1

and τ_2 do not have any species in common, we can actually find B in a straightforward manner without using recursion. This allows us to obtain a tight control on the width of the recursion tree, thus reducing the number of recursive calls to $O(n \log n)$.

In summary, Part I involves a detailed study of the structure of the core (in particular, the spine); precisely, it uses $O(k^2 n^{1.5} \log^2 n)$ time. Part II is recursive in nature and simpler conceptually, but it requires $O(k^{5.25} n^{1.75 + o(1)})$ time.

Preprocessing: To achieve the above time bound of Part I and II, our algorithm actually requires a preprocessing stage, which basically involves the computation of $rmast(T_u, T'_{u'})$ for $O(k^2)$ pairs of core nodes (u, u') chosen from $\mathcal{K}$ and $\mathcal{K}'$. The aim of the preprocessing is to enable us afterwards to determine each of the following values efficiently (more precisely, in $O(\log^2 n)$ time): (i) $rmast(T_{uv}, T'_{u'v'})$, where u, u' are any core nodes in T and T', and v and v' each are core nodes or roots of side trees; (ii)(a) $rmast^*(I, T'_{u'v'})$, defined as $\max_{\tau \in I} \{rmast(\tau, T'_{u'v'})\}$; and (b) $rmast^*(I, T'_{u'v'}, T'_{v'u'})$, defined as $\max_{\tau_1, \tau_2 \in I} \{rmast(\tau_1, T'_{u'v'}) + rmast(\tau_2, T'_{v'u'})\}$, where I is an interval of side trees of T and u', v' are distinct core nodes in T'. Details of this preprocessing will be given in the full paper. The overall time required is $O(k^5 n^{1.5} \log n)$. Most of the techniques involved are based on the work of Farach and Thorup on RMAST [6].

4 Part I—in the presence of core-core mapping

In this section, we show how to compute the value of $umast(T, T')$ when there is a maximum agreement subset B such that $T|_B$ and $T'|_B$ involve a pair of core nodes mapped to each other.

Denote $\mathcal{C}$ the set of all core node pairs (c, c') where c in T and c' in T'. For any such pair (c, c'), let $\Sigma_{cc'}$ be the collection of all agreement subsets D such that $T|_D$ and $T'|_D$ involves a mapping between c and c'; for a set $\mathcal{X}$ of core node pairs, define $\Sigma_{\mathcal{X}} = \bigcup_{(c,c') \in \mathcal{X}} \{\Sigma_{cc'}\}$. If there exists a $m.a.s.$ B of T and T' that involves a pair of core nodes mapped to each other, such B is in $\Sigma_{\mathcal{C}}$ and $umast(T, T')$ is equal to the size of the biggest $a.s.$ in $\Sigma_{\mathcal{C}}$, i.e. $\mu(\Sigma_{\mathcal{C}})$. However, finding $\mu(\Sigma_{\mathcal{C}})$ by examining every $a.s.$ in $\mathcal{C}$ requires exponential time. The contribution of this section is defining a realistic upper bound to $\mu(\Sigma_{\mathcal{C}})$, i.e. $\hat{\mu}(\Sigma_{\mathcal{C}})$, which can be computed in $o(n^2)$ time. If the above-mentioned $m.a.s.$ B exists then $umast(T, T') = \mu(\Sigma_{\mathcal{C}}) = \hat{\mu}(\Sigma_{\mathcal{C}})$.

Below, we show that $\hat{\mu}(\Sigma_{\mathcal{C}})$ can be computed by examining some kinds of matchings in some bipartite graphs. Let $V(T)$ and $V(T')$ be the set of nodes in T and T' respectively. Given any $E \subseteq V(T) \times V(T')$ and a core node pair (u, u'), let $V_1 \subseteq V(T)$ and $V_2 \subseteq V(T')$ be the set of nodes to which edges in E are incident, and denote $\langle E, (u, u') \rangle$ the weighted bipartite graph with vertex set $V_1 \cup V_2$, edge set E, and the weight of an edge $(v, w') \in E$ being $rmast(T_{uv}, T'_{u'w'})$.

There is a class of bipartite graphs very important to our analysis. Given any $(c, c') \in \mathcal{C}$, denote $G_{cc'}$ the weighted bipartite graph $\langle \mathbf{N}(c) \times \mathbf{N}(c'), (c, c') \rangle$, where $\mathbf{N}(c)$ and $\mathbf{N}(c')$ denote the neighbors of c and c' respectively. Note that any $u \in \mathbf{N}(c)$ (and any $v' \in \mathbf{N}(c')$) is either a core node or the root of a side tree. We distinguish three types of edges in $G_{cc'}$, core-core, side-side, and side-core, according to whether the end-points of the edges are core nodes or roots of side trees. Throughout this paper we consider matchings in $G_{cc'}$ comprising only edges with positive weights (since adding zero weighted edges does not increase the overall weight of the matching). Let $\text{MWM}(G_{cc'})$ denote the weight of the maximum weight matching in $G_{cc'}$, and $\text{MWM}_3(G_{cc'})$ the weight of the maximum weight matching in $G_{cc'}$ containing at least three edges. The importance of $G_{cc'}$ stems from Theorem 1, which can be deduced from the work of [6].

Theorem 1. $\mu(\Sigma_{cc'}) = \mathrm{MWM}_3(G_{cc'})$.

From the theorem, we have $\mu(\Sigma_C) = \max_{(c,c')\in C}[\mathrm{MWM}_3(G_{cc'})]$. On the other hand, as $\mathrm{MWM}_3(G_{cc'}) \leq \mathrm{MWM}(G_{cc'})$ and $\mathrm{MWM}(G_{cc'})$ also corresponds to an *a.s.* of (T, T'), we can use $\max_{(c,c')\in C}\mathrm{MWM}(G_{cc'})$ as a realistic upper bound of $\mu(\Sigma_C)$. To compute the maximum weight matching in any $G_{cc'}$, we need to determine the weight of the edges in $G_{cc'}$. As mentioned before, after the preprocessing has been done, the weight of a single edge in any $G_{cc'}$ can be determined in $O(\log^2 n)$ time. Note that $G_{cc'}$ has $\Theta(n^2)$ edges in the worst case. But many edges in $G_{cc'}$ can be ignored in the course of computing $\mathrm{MWM}(G_{cc'})$. This is captured in Lemma 2 (the proof is a generalization of the proof of Lemma 6.2 in [6]).

Lemma 2. For any $\mathcal{X} \subseteq \mathcal{C}$, we can compute $\max_{(c,c')\in\mathcal{X}}\mathrm{MWM}(G_{cc'})$ in $O(k^3|\mathcal{X}|\log^2 n + (kn)^{1.5}\log n)$ time (recall that k is chosen as $2^{\sqrt{\log n}}$).

$\mathcal{C}$ contains $\Theta(n^2)$ pairs in the worst case. Lemma 2 implies that $\max_{(c,c')\in\mathcal{C}}\mathrm{MWM}(G_{cc'})$ can be found in $O(k^3 n^2 \log^2 n)$ time. To break the n^2-barrier, we must not compute $\mathrm{MWM}(G_{cc'})$ one by one and report the maximum. We divide $\mathcal{C}$ into two sets $\mathcal{BS}$ and $\mathcal{CS}$: $\mathcal{BS}$ contains all spine node pairs (c, c') in $\mathcal{C}$ that are *boring*, i.e. the side trees connected to c and those to c' have no common species. $\mathcal{CS}$ is defined as $\mathcal{C} - \mathcal{BS}$.

We will find the realistic upper bounds $\hat{\mu}(\Sigma_{\mathcal{BS}})$ and $\hat{\mu}(\Sigma_{\mathcal{CS}})$ using different methods; $\hat{\mu}(\Sigma_\mathcal{C})$ is equal to the maximum of $\hat{\mu}(\Sigma_{\mathcal{BS}})$ and $\hat{\mu}(\Sigma_{\mathcal{CS}})$. As to be explained, there are only $o(n^2)$ pairs inside $\mathcal{CS}$; thus, we can afford to evaluate $\mathrm{MWM}(G_{cc'})$ for every (c, c') in $\mathcal{CS}$ and compute $\hat{\mu}(\Sigma_{\mathcal{CS}})$ as $\max_{(c,c')\in\mathcal{CS}}\mathrm{MWM}(G_{cc'})$. For every $(c, c') \in \mathcal{CS}$, either (c, c') is a non-boring spine node pair or one of c and c' is a critical node. There are at most n non-boring spine node pairs in $\mathcal{CS}$. There are at most $2k$ critical nodes in T and the number of pairs (c, c') with c or c' being critical is at most $4kn$. Hence, $|\mathcal{CS}| \leq 4kn + n$. Applying Lemma 2, we can find $\max_{(c,c')\in\mathcal{CS}}\mathrm{MWM}(G_{cc'})$ in time $O(k^3(4kn + n)\log^2 n + (kn)^{1.5}\log n)$, or equivalently, $O((kn)^{1.5}\log n)$.

To compute $\hat{\mu}(\Sigma_{\mathcal{BS}})$ efficiently, we need some sophisticated techniques. In the rest of this section, we show that $\hat{\mu}(\Sigma_{\mathcal{BS}})$ requires $O(k^2 n^{1.5}\log^2 n)$ time and hence conclude that it takes $O(k^2 n^{1.5}\log^2 n)$ time to compute a realistic upper bound of $\mu(\Sigma_C)$.

Because $|\mathcal{BS}| = \Omega(n^2)$ in the worst case, we cannot afford to find, for each $(c, c') \in \mathcal{BS}$, a realistic upper bound of $\mu(\Sigma_{cc'})$. Instead, we base on some structural relationship to divide $\mathcal{BS}$ into a smaller number of groups; we find the realistic upper bound for each group efficiently without computing a realistic upper bound for every pair in the group.

Given a spine S in T or T', a *segment* of S is a set of consecutive nodes on S. Given a pair of spine segments (L, L') chosen from T and T', if every pair of nodes $(c, c') \in L \times L'$ is boring, we say that (L, L') is a boring pair; in this case, we show that a realistic upper bound of $\mu(\Sigma_{L\times L'})$ can be found in time $O((|L| + |L'|)\log^2 n)$ instead of $\Omega(|L| \times |L'|)$ (see Section 4.1). Consider any pair of spines (S, S'). (S, S') may contain $\Theta(n^2)$ pairs of nodes that are boring, yet each pair of nodes can often be considered together with many others as a boring pair of segments. The following scheme partitions all boring pairs of nodes in (S, S') into $o(n^2)$ boring pairs of segments. Details are as follows:

Definition 3. A partition tree of a pair of spines (S, S') is a rooted tree of which every node is labeled by a pair of segments (L, L'). The root has the label (S, S'). As regards an internal node, the label (L, L') is a non-boring pair and one of L and L' has more than one spine node. This internal node has up to four children, each has a label in the form of (H, H') where H is either the left or the right half of L if L has more than one spine node and similarly for H'. The depth of the partition tree is at most $\lceil \log n \rceil$.

Define $\mathcal{P}(S, S')$ as the set of all (L, L') in the partition tree such that (L, L') is boring. Note that each (L, L') in $\mathcal{P}(S, S')$ corresponds to a leaf of the partition tree. It is easy to see that the partition tree contains $O(n \log n)$ nodes and hence $\mathcal{P}(S, S')$ contains only $O(n \log n)$ pairs of segments. More importantly, there is a tight upper bound on the total length of segments in $\mathcal{P}(S, S')$, it reads $\sum_{(L,L') \in \mathcal{P}(S,S')} (|L| + |L'|) = O(n^{1.5})$ (the proof will be given in the full paper). For any boring pair of spine nodes (c, c') in (S, S'), we can find a pair of segments $(L, L') \in \mathcal{P}(S, S')$ containing (c, c'). Thus,

$$BS = \bigcup_{\text{all } (S, S')} \left(\bigcup_{(L,L') \in \mathcal{P}(S,S')} L \times L' \right); \text{ and } \mu(\Sigma_{BS}) = \max_{\text{all } (S, S')} \left(\max_{(L,L') \in \mathcal{P}(S,S')} \mu(\Sigma_{L \times L'}) \right).$$

As to be shown in Section 4.1, the realistic upper bound $\hat{\mu}(\Sigma_{L \times L'})$ can be computed in $O((|L| + |L'|) \log^2 n)$ time; thus, we find a realistic upper bound of $\mu(\Sigma_{BS})$ by computing $\max_{\text{all } (S, S')} [\max_{(L,L') \in \mathcal{P}(S,S')} \hat{\mu}(\Sigma_{L \times L'})]$; the total time required is $O(k^2 \sum_{(L,L') \in \mathcal{P}(S,S')} (|L| + |L'|) \log^2 n)$, bounded by $O(k^2 n^{1.5} \log^2 n)$.

4.1 Computing $\hat{\mu}(\Sigma_{L \times L'})$ in $O((|L| + |L'|) \log^2 n)$ time

By Theorem 1, $\mu(\Sigma_{L \times L'}) = \max_{(c,c') \in L \times L'} \text{MWM}_3(G_{cc'})$. Consider any pair of nodes (c, c') in $L \times L'$ and its bipartite graph $G_{cc'}$. Let M be the maximum weight matching in $G_{cc'}$ including at least three edges (i.e. M's weight $= \text{MWM}_3(G_{cc'})$). Because (c, c') is boring, M includes no side-side edge (which has zero weight). As (c, c') is a pair of spine nodes, c and c' each have only two neighbors that are core nodes, and M consists of either (i) two core-core edges and no core-side edge; or (ii) zero or one core-core edge and some core-side edges. Since M contains at least 3 edges, case (i) is impossible.

We are going to compute a different kind of realistic upper bound of $\mu(\Sigma_{L \times L'})$. Let $\text{MWM}^\dagger(G_{cc'})$ denote the weight of the maximum weight matching in $G_{cc'}$ including no core-core edge, and $\text{MWM}^\ddagger(G_{cc'})$ including one core-core edge. Based on the discussion above, we have $\text{MWM}_3(G_{cc'}) \leq \max\{\text{MWM}^\dagger(G_{cc'}), \text{MWM}^\ddagger(G_{cc'})\} \leq \text{MWM}(G_{cc'})$, and

$$\max_{(c,c') \in L \times L'} \text{MWM}_3(G_{cc'}) \leq \max \left\{ \begin{array}{l} \max_{(c,c') \in L \times L'} \text{MWM}^\dagger(G_{cc'}) \\ \max_{(c,c') \in L \times L'} \text{MWM}^\ddagger(G_{cc'}) \end{array} \right\} \leq \max_{(c,c') \in L \times L'} \text{MWM}(G_{cc'}).$$

The structural relationship among the pairs of nodes in $L \times L'$ can enable us to compute $\max_{(c,c') \in L \times L'} \text{MWM}^\dagger(G_{cc'})$ without evaluating every $\text{MWM}^\dagger(G_{cc'})$. In particular, we can express $\text{MWM}^\dagger(G_{cc'})$ in the form $f(c) + g(c')$ for some functions f and g as follows.

Lemma 4. Let $a, \bar{a}$ be the core nodes adjacent to the two ends of L, and similarly for $a', \bar{a}'$ and L'. Then $\text{MWM}^\dagger(G_{cc'}) = rmast^*(I'_{c'}, T_{a\bar{a}}, T_{\bar{a}a}) + rmast^*(I_c, T'_{a'\bar{a}'}, T'_{\bar{a}'a'})$ where $I_c, I'_{c'}$ are the intervals comprising the side trees connected to c, c' respectively.

Lemma 4 implies that $\max_{(c,c')\in L\times L'} \text{MWM}^\dagger(G_{cc'}) = \max_{c'\in L'}\left[rmast^*(I'_{c'}, T_{a\bar{a}}, T_{\bar{a}a})\right] + \max_{c\in L}\left[rmast^*(I_c, T'_{a'\bar{a}'}, T'_{\bar{a}'a'})\right]$. To compute $\max_{(c,c')\in L\times L'}[\text{MWM}^\dagger(G_{cc'})]$, we need to solve $|L|+|L'|$ instances of $rmast^*$, each requiring $O(\log^2 n)$ time due to the preprocessing. The total time is $O((|L|+|L'|)\log^2 n)$.

For $\max_{(c,c')\in L\times L'} \text{MWM}^\ddagger(G_{cc'})$, the computation is also performed in the same spirit; details will be given in the full paper. In summary, we compute $\hat{\mu}(\Sigma_{L\times L'})$ by finding the maximum of $\max_{(c,c')\in L\times L'} \text{MWM}^\dagger(G_{cc'})$ and $\max_{(c,c')\in L\times L'} \text{MWM}^\ddagger(G_{cc'})$. In each case, we show that the time required is $O((|L|+|L'|)\log^2 n)$.

5 Part II—no core-core mapping

In this section, we show how to compute $umast(T,T')$ correctly when T and T' have a m.a.s. B such that $T|_B$ and $T'|_B$ do not involve a pair of core nodes mapped to each other. Farach and Thorup [5] have observed that such a m.a.s. B must be quite "small" and, in particular, their work implies that

if the species in B spread over three or more side trees of T, say $\tau_{i_1}, \tau_{i_2}, \cdots, \tau_{i_p}$, and they also spread over three or more side trees of T', say $\tau'_{j_1}, \tau'_{j_2}, \cdots, \tau'_{j_q}$, then, for some $h\in[1..p]$ and $l\in[1..q]$, $B\subseteq \langle\tau_{i_h}\rangle\cup\langle\tau'_{j_l}\rangle$.

In other words, either B is restricted to at most two side trees of T (or T'), or we can pick two side trees, one from each tree, to cover B. More precisely, we distinguish the following two cases.

Case 1: $B\subseteq\langle\tau\rangle\cup\langle\tau'\rangle$ for some side trees τ of T and τ' of T'; or
Case 2: Case 1 is false and $B\subseteq\langle\tau_1\rangle\cup\langle\tau_2\rangle$ for some side trees τ_1,τ_2 of T, or of T'.

Concerning Case 1, we would like to consider Σ, the collection of all agreement subsets D such that $D\subseteq\langle\tau\rangle\cup\langle\tau'\rangle$ for some side trees τ of T and τ' of T', and to compute $\mu(\Sigma)$, the size of the biggest a.s. in Σ. However, computing $\mu(\Sigma)$ in $o(n^2)$ time is not trivial. For instance, realizing that the biggest D in Σ is also the m.a.s. of the smaller trees $T|_{\langle\tau\rangle\cup\langle\tau'\rangle}$ and $T'|_{\langle\tau\rangle\cup\langle\tau'\rangle}$ for some side trees τ and τ', one may attempt to compute $\mu(\Sigma)$ recursively as

$$\max_{\tau\text{ is a side tree of } T;\ \tau'\text{ is a side tree of } T'} umast(T|_{\langle\tau\rangle\cup\langle\tau'\rangle}, T'|_{\langle\tau\rangle\cup\langle\tau'\rangle});$$

yet this naive solution involves too many sub-problems and requires $\Omega(n^2)$ time in the worst case. Our approach is again to find a realistic upper bound of $\mu(\Sigma)$, i.e. $\hat{\mu}(\Sigma)$. We require that $\hat{\mu}(\Sigma)\geq\mu(\Sigma)$ and $\hat{\mu}(\Sigma)$ always corresponds to the size of some a.s. of T and T'. If T and T' have a m.a.s. B falling into Case 1, then $umast(T,T')=\mu(\Sigma)=\hat{\mu}(\Sigma)$. More importantly, such $\hat{\mu}(\Sigma)$ can be computed in $o(n^2)$ time using a tightly-controlled recursion.

In respect of Case 2, we consider another collection Π that contains those agreement subsets D such that $D\subseteq\langle\tau_1\rangle\cup\langle\tau_2\rangle$ for some side trees τ_1,τ_2 of T or of T', and $D\not\subseteq\langle\tau\rangle\cup\langle\tau'\rangle$ for any side trees τ of T and τ' of T'. We can use a non-recursive way to compute $\hat{\mu}(\Pi)$. The time required is only $O(n\log^2 n)$. If T and T' have a m.a.s. B falling into Case 2, then $umast(T,T')=\mu(\Pi)=\hat{\mu}(\Pi)$.

In conclusion, if T and T' have a m.a.s. B such that $T|_B$ and $T'|_B$ do not involve a pair of core nodes mapped to each other, $umast(T,T')=|B|=\max\{\hat{\mu}(\Sigma),\hat{\mu}(\Pi)\}$. To ease our discussion, we first describe the details of computing $\hat{\mu}(\Pi)$. Then we study the recursion involved in finding $\hat{\mu}(\Sigma)$.

5.1 A non-recursive way to compute $\hat{\mu}(\Pi)$

The following lemma gives a clue to a non-recursive solution to compute $\hat{\mu}(\Pi)$.

Lemma 5. Let D be any a.s. in Π. Let I_0 (I_0') denote the interval composing of all side trees of T (T'). Then either T' contains two adjacent core nodes u', v' such that $|D| \leq rmast^*(I_0, T'_{u'v'}, T'_{v'u'})$ or T contains two adjacent core nodes u, v such that $|D| \leq rmast^*(I_0', T_{uv}, T_{vu})$.

By Lemma 5, we can compute $\hat{\mu}(\Pi)$ by finding the maximum over all pairs of adjacent core nodes (u, v) in T of $rmast^*(I_0', T_{uv}, T_{vu})$, as well as the similar maximum for T'. As mentioned before, we have performed a preprocessing stage so that each such $rmast^*$ can be computed in $O(\log^2 n)$ time afterwards. Each core contains $O(n)$ edges, or equivalently, $O(n)$ pairs of adjacent nodes. The time required to compute $\hat{\mu}(\Pi)$ is $O(n \log^2 n)$ time.

5.2 An efficient recursive solution for computing $\hat{\mu}(\Sigma)$

Recall that Σ denotes the collection of agreement subsets D such that $D \subseteq \langle \tau \rangle \cup \langle \tau' \rangle$ for some side trees τ of T and τ' of T'. This section shows how to compute a realistic upper bound of $\mu(\Sigma)$, i.e. $\hat{\mu}(\Sigma)$, in $o(n^2)$ time.

First of all, we use a trick from Farach and Thorup [5] to avoid operating on very small side trees individually. The side trees of each of T and T' are partitioned into $O(k)$ disjoint intervals, each containing a total of at most n/k species. Our algorithm is then based on intervals instead of side trees. Below, we give an elaborate scheme to partition the side trees of T (as well as T') into at most $8k$ intervals, each containing a total of at most n/k species. From now on, whenever we mention an interval of T (T'), we mean one of these $8k$ intervals.

Type (a) For a critical node c whose side trees contain a total of at most n/k species, we put its side trees into a single interval.

Type (b) For a critical node c or a spine node s whose side trees contain a total of more than n/k species, we divide the side trees into a minimum number of intervals such that each contains at most n/k species.

Type (c) For a (maximal) segment of contiguous spine nodes $(s_1, s_2, \cdots, s_h)$, where each s_i containing at most n/k species in its side trees, we divide the segment into sub-segments greedily such that the number of species in all the side-trees of each sub-segment just does not exceed n/k. The side trees of each sub-segment $(s_i, s_{i+1}, \cdots, s_j)$ form an interval; s_i will be called the *leading* spine node associated with the interval. Note that each of these intervals (except the last one) contains an average of at least $n/2k$.

To compute $\hat{\mu}(\Sigma)$ efficiently, we divide the agreement subsets of Σ into two categories with respect to the intervals defined above:

1. For any interval I of T or T', $\Sigma_I = \{D \in \Sigma \mid D \subseteq \langle I \rangle\}$;
2. For any intervals I of T and I' of T', $\Sigma_{I,I'} = \{D \in \Sigma \mid D \subseteq \langle I \rangle \cup \langle I' \rangle; D \not\subseteq \langle I \rangle; D \not\subseteq \langle I' \rangle\}$.

Note that $\mu(\Sigma) = \max(\{\mu(\Sigma_I) \mid I \in T \text{ or } T'\} \cup \{\mu(\Sigma_{I,I'}) \mid I \in T; I' \in T'\})$. We compute $\hat{\mu}(\Sigma_I)$ and $\hat{\mu}(\Sigma_{I,I'})$ for all possible intervals, the maximum value will be returned as $\hat{\mu}(\Sigma)$. The case for Σ_I is actually a warm-up and we compute $\hat{\mu}(\Sigma_I)$ efficiently using simple recursion. $\Sigma_{I,I'}$ captures the intricacy of Σ; we compute $\hat{\mu}(\Sigma_{I,I'})$ using a hybrid of recursive and non-recursive techniques.

A trivial case: For any interval I of T or T', every *a.s.* in Σ_I is also an *a.s.* of the subtrees $T|_{\langle I \rangle}$ and $T'|_{\langle I \rangle}$; thus we can find $\hat{\mu}(\Sigma_I)$ by computing $umast(T|_{\langle I \rangle}, T'|_{\langle I \rangle})$ recursively. There are only $16k$ such sub-problems, each of size at most n/k. The time complexity will be analyzed with other cases in Section 6.

A more general and difficult case: Next, we consider the computation of $\hat{\mu}(\Sigma_{I,I'})$ for any pair of intervals (I, I') in $T \times T'$. An *a.s.* in $\Sigma_{I,I'}$ is obviously an *a.s.* of $T|_{\langle I \rangle \cup \langle I' \rangle}$ and $T'|_{\langle I \rangle \cup \langle I' \rangle}$, and $umast(T|_{\langle I \rangle \cup \langle I' \rangle}, T'|_{\langle I \rangle \cup \langle I' \rangle})$ is a legitimate realistic upper bound of $\mu(\Sigma_{I,I'})$. However, we cannot afford to compute every $umast(T|_{\langle I \rangle \cup \langle I' \rangle}, T'|_{\langle I \rangle \cup \langle I' \rangle})$ recursively because this might involve as many as $\Theta(k^2)$ sub-problems, each of size n/k, and the overall time required would be too much. In our algorithm, we avoid computing each $umast(T|_{\langle I \rangle \cup \langle I' \rangle}, T'|_{\langle I \rangle \cup \langle I' \rangle})$; we aim at a realistic upper bound that is easier to compute. For a pair of intervals (I, I') containing no common species, we use a simple and non-recursive way to compute $\hat{\mu}(\Sigma_{I,I'})$ (Section 5.2.1). For a pair (I, I') containing some common species, we still compute $\hat{\mu}(\Sigma_{I,I'})$ recursively but using a procedure substantially simpler than that of computing $umast(T|_{\langle I \rangle \cup \langle I' \rangle}, T'|_{\langle I \rangle \cup \langle I' \rangle})$ (Section 5.2.2). The property that (I, I') contains common species will provide a basis for controlling the number of sub-problems generated in the recursive computation of $\hat{\mu}(\Sigma_{I,I'})$.

Summary: We compute $\hat{\mu}(\Sigma)$ by finding the maximum of $\{\hat{\mu}(\Sigma_I) = umast(T|_{\langle I \rangle}, T'|_{\langle I \rangle}) \mid I \in T \text{ or } T'\} \cup \{\hat{\mu}(\Sigma_{I,I'}) \mid I \in T; I' \in T'\}$.

5.2.1 Recursion can be avoided when $\langle I \rangle \cap \langle I' \rangle = \phi$

For a pair of intervals (I, I') with no common species, we can base on the following lemma to compute the exact value of $\mu(\Sigma_{I,I'})$ in a non-recursive manner.

Lemma 6. Consider any pair of intervals (I, I') with $\langle I \rangle \cap \langle I' \rangle = \phi$. Let D_0 be the biggest *a.s.* in $\Sigma_{I,I'}$. Then $|D_0| = rmast^*(I, T'_t) + rmast^*(I', T_s)$, where s and t are the unique core nodes or the leading spine nodes connected to the side trees of I and I' respectively.

By Lemma 6, we compute $\mu(\Sigma_{I,I'})$ as $rmast^*(I, T'_s) + rmast^*(I', T_t)$. It requires only $O(\log^2 n)$ time after the preprocessing.

5.2.2 A bounded-width recursion suffices when $\langle I \rangle \cap \langle I' \rangle \neq \phi$

For a pair of intervals (I, I') containing common species, we use a recursive approach to compute $\hat{\mu}(\Sigma_{I,I'})$, using $O(k^5(2n/k)^{1.75+o(1)})$ time.

Let D be any *a.s.* in $\Sigma_{I,I'}$. That is, $D \subseteq \langle I \rangle \cup \langle I' \rangle$; $D \not\subseteq \langle I \rangle$ and $D \not\subseteq \langle I' \rangle$. Consider the subtrees $P = T|_{\langle I \rangle \cup \langle I' \rangle}$ and $P' = T'|_{\langle I \rangle \cup \langle I' \rangle}$. D is also an *a.s.* of P and P' satisfying the additional constraints $D \not\subseteq \langle I \rangle$ and $D \not\subseteq \langle I' \rangle$. Obviously, $umast(P, P')$ can be a realistic upper bound of $\mu(\Sigma_{I,I'})$, but, as explained before, it is inefficient to compute such a bound. Instead, we can obtain another realistic upper bound of $\mu(\Sigma_{I,I'})$ by computing the biggest *a.s.* D_0 of P and P' satisfying the constraints $D_0 \not\subseteq \langle I \rangle$ and $D_0 \not\subseteq \langle I' \rangle$, or a realistic upper bound of D_0. The latter indeed admits an efficient solution and will be adopted as the value of $\hat{\mu}(\Sigma_{I,I'})$. The framework of computing $\hat{\mu}(\Sigma_{I,I'})$ is quite similar to that of computing $umast(P, P')$, but in the bottleneck cases, we have substantial simplification due to the above additional constraint.

First of all, we construct a k-core for P, where k remains as $2^{\sqrt{\log n}}$, such that every side tree in I (of T) induces one or more side trees of P, i.e. all the species of a side tree of P are found in a single side tree of I. The side trees of P are partitioned into intervals of types (a), (b), and (c) as before, but with an extra requirement that for every interval J of P, either $\langle J \rangle \subseteq \langle I \rangle$ or $\langle J \rangle \subseteq \langle I' \rangle - \langle I \rangle$. We can show that there are still at most $8k$ intervals in P. Let N denote the number of species in P, i.e. $|\langle I \rangle \cup \langle I' \rangle|$. Each interval contains a total of at most N/k species. We process P' similarly but with the roles of I and I' reversed. Next, we perform the preprocessing on P and P' as if on T and T'. The time required is $O(k^5 N^{1.5} \log N)$.

The computation of $\hat{\mu}(\Sigma_{I,I'})$ is then divided into two parts. First, based on the assumption that P and P' have a m.a.s. involving a core node of P mapped to a core node of P', we compute the size of the m.a.s. of P and P' using the algorithm in Section 4. It requires $O(k^2 N^{1.5} \log^2 N)$ time. Second, we consider the a.s. of P and P' involving no core node mapped to a core node; we investigate Cases 1 and 2 (as described at the beginning of Section 5) and define the collections $\tilde{\Sigma}$ and $\tilde{\Pi}$ for P and P' in the same spirit as Σ and Π for T and T'.

Case 1: $\tilde{\Sigma}$ should capture those a.s. D of P and P' such that $D \subseteq \langle \tau \rangle \cup \langle \tau' \rangle$ for some side trees τ of P and τ' of P'; moreover, in view of D should be in $\Sigma_{I,I'}$, we further impose the constraints $D \not\subseteq \langle I \rangle$ and $D \not\subseteq \langle I' \rangle$. Following the framework of computing $\hat{\mu}(\Sigma)$ for T and T', we can find $\hat{\mu}(\tilde{\Sigma})$ for P and P' by computing the maximum of $\{\hat{\mu}(\tilde{\Sigma}_J) \mid J \in P \text{ or } P'\} \cup \{\hat{\mu}(\tilde{\Sigma}_{J,J'}) \mid J \in P; J \in P'\}$. However, it is unnecessary to compute any $\hat{\mu}(\tilde{\Sigma}_J)$ because an a.s. D of P and P' included entirely in some $\langle J \rangle$ must be a subset of $\langle I \rangle$ or $\langle I' \rangle$ and out of our consideration. The way we compute each $\hat{\mu}(\tilde{\Sigma}_{J,J'})$ again depends on whether $\langle J \rangle \cap \langle J' \rangle$ is equal to empty.
  1. When $\langle J \rangle \cap \langle J' \rangle$ is empty, we use the non-recursive approach described in Section 5.2 to compute $\tilde{\Sigma}_{J,J'}$ using $O(\log^2 N)$ time.
  2. When $\langle J \rangle \cap \langle J' \rangle$ is non-empty, we have only three possible cases: (i) $\langle J \rangle \subseteq \langle I \rangle$ and $\langle J' \rangle \subseteq \langle I' \rangle$: we compute $\tilde{\Sigma}_{J,J'}$ recursively; (ii) $\langle J \rangle \subseteq \langle I \rangle$ and $\langle J' \rangle \subseteq \langle I \rangle - \langle I' \rangle$: we ignore this case because we are not interested in a.s. that is included entirely in $\langle I \rangle$; (iii) $\langle J \rangle \subseteq \langle I' \rangle - \langle I \rangle$ and $\langle J' \rangle \subseteq \langle I' \rangle$: we also ignore this case for the same reason as (ii).

Case 2: We compute $\hat{\mu}(\tilde{\Pi})$, i.e. the realistic upper bound of the biggest a.s. D_0 such that $D_0 \subseteq \langle \tau_1 \rangle \cup \langle \tau_2 \rangle$ for some side trees τ_1, τ_2 in P or P', using the non-recursive method described in Section 5.1. This requires $O(N \log^2 N)$ time.

In summary, we compute $\hat{\mu}(\Sigma_{I,I'})$ by computing $\hat{\mu}(\tilde{\Sigma}_{J,J'})$ recursively for every pair of intervals (J, J') such that $\langle J \rangle \subseteq \langle I \rangle$, $\langle J' \rangle \subseteq \langle I' \rangle$, and $\langle J \rangle \cap \langle J' \rangle \neq \phi$. We reach the base of recursion when the size of $\langle J \rangle \cup \langle J' \rangle$ is bounded by k; in this case, we find $\hat{\mu}(\tilde{\Sigma}_{J,J'})$ by computing $umast(T|_{\langle J \rangle \cup \langle J' \rangle}, T'|_{\langle J \rangle \cup \langle J' \rangle})$ using Farach and Thorup's $O(n^{2+o(1)})$ time algorithm. Regarding the recursion tree defined the computation of $\hat{\mu}(\Sigma_{I,I'})$, we observe that the number of subproblems across a level is always bounded by N (i.e. $|\langle I \rangle \cup \langle I' \rangle|$) and hence the overall number of subproblems is $O(N \log N)$. The exact time complexity of computing $\hat{\mu}(\Sigma_{I,I'})$ is stated in the following lemma.

Lemma 7. It takes $O(k^5 N^{1.75+o(1)})$ time to compute $\hat{\mu}(\Sigma_{I,I'})$, where $N = |\langle I \rangle \cup \langle I' \rangle|$.

6 Overall Time Complexity

Theorem 8. It requires $O(n^{1.75+o(1)})$ time to compute $umast(T, T')$.

Proof. Let $f(n)$ be the time required to compute $umast(T, T')$ for any two unrooted trees T and T' with at most n species each. Recall that the computation of $umast(T, T')$ is divided into the preprocessing, Part I, and Part II. The preprocessing and Part I require time $O(k^5 n^{1.5} \log n)$ and $O(k^2 n^{1.5} \log^2 n)$, respectively. For Part II, we compute the following values: (i) $\hat{\mu}(\Pi)$: it requires $O(n \log^2 n)$ time; (ii) $\hat{\mu}(\Sigma_I)$ for every interval I of T or T': they are computed through a direct recursion involving at most $2 \times 8k$ instances of $umast$, each with at most n/k species; hence, the total time required is at most $16 f(n/k)$; (iii) $\hat{\mu}(\Sigma_{I, I'})$ for all intervals I of T and I' of T': there are only $O(k^2)$ pairs of intervals, each requiring either $O(\log^2 n)$ time or $O(k^5 (2n/k)^{1.75+o(1)})$ time; they altogether require $O(k^{5.25} n^{1.75+o(1)})$ time. To sum up, we have the following recurrence formula:

$$f(n) \leq 16 k f(\frac{n}{k}) + k^{5.25} n^{1.75+\lambda}, \quad \text{where } \lambda = O(1/\log k)$$

$$\leq 2 k^{5.25} n^{1.75+\lambda}$$

Putting $k = 2^{\sqrt{\log n}}$, we have $f(n) = O(n^{1.75+\epsilon})$ where $\epsilon = O(1/\sqrt{\log n})$, i.e. $o(1)$.

References

1. R. Agarwala and D. Fernandez-Baca, A polynomial-time algorithm for the phylogeny problem when the number of character states is fixed, *FOCS*, 140-147, 1993.
2. H. Bodlaender, M. Fellows and T. Warnow, Two strikes against perfect phylogeny, *ICALP*, 273-283, 1992.
3. R. Cole and R. Hariharan, An $O(n \log n)$ algorithm for the maximum agreement subtree problem for binary trees, *SODA*, 323-332, 1996.
4. W.H.E. Day, Computational complexity of inferring phylogenies from dissimilarity matrices, *Bulletin of Mathematical Biology*, 49(4):461-467, 1987.
5. M. Farach and M. Thorup, Fast comparison of evolutionary trees, *SODA*, 481-488, 1994.
6. M. Farach and M. Thorup, Optimal evolutionary tree comparison by sparse dynamic programming, *FOCS*, 770-779, 1994.
7. M. Farach, T. Przytycka and M. Thorup, Computing the agreement of trees with bounded degrees, *ESA*, 381-393, 1995.
8. J. Felsenstein, Numerical methods for inferring evolutionary tree, *The Quarterly Review of Biology*, 57(4):379-404, 1982.
9. C. Finden and A. Gordon, Obtaining common pruned trees, *Journal of Classification*, 2:255-276, 1985.
10. H. Gabow and R. Tarjan, Faster scaling algorithms for network problems, *SIAM Journal of Computing*, 18(5): 1013-1036, 1989.
11. S. Kannan, T. Warnow and S. Yooseph, Computing the local consensus of trees, *SODA*, 68-77, 1995.
12. J. Kececioglu and D. Gusfield, Reconstructing a history of recombinations from a set of sequences, *SODA*, 471-480, 1994.
13. D. Keselman and A. Amir, Maximum agreement subtree in a set of evolutionary trees - Metrics and efficient algorithms, *FOCS*, 758-769, 1994.
14. E. Kubicka, G. Kubicki and F. McMorris, An algorithm to find agreement subtrees, *Journal of Classification*, 1994.
15. M. Steel and T. Warnow, Kaikoura tree theorems: computing the maximum agreement subtree, *Information Processing Letters*, 48:77-82, 1994.

Greedily Finding a Dense Subgraph

Yuichi Asahiro[1], Kazuo Iwama[1]*, Hisao Tamaki[2], and Takeshi Tokuyama[2]

[1] Dept of Computer Science, Kyushu Univ., Fukuoka 812, Japan,
{asahiro, iwama}@csce.kyushu-u.ac.jp
[2] IBM Tokyo Research Laboratory, Yamato 242, Japan,
{htamaki, ttoku}@trl.ibm.co.jp

Abstract. Given an n-vertex graph with non-negative edge weights and a positive integer $k \leq n$, we are to find a k-vertex subgraph with the maximum weight. We study the following greedy algorithm for this problem: repeatedly remove a vertex with the minimum weighted-degree in the currently remaining graph, until exactly k vertices are left. We derive tight bounds on the worst case approximation ratio R of this greedy algorithm: $(1/2+n/(2k))^2 - O(1/n) \leq R \leq (1/2+n/(2k))^2 + O(1/n)$ for k in the range $n/3 \leq k \leq n$ and $2(n/k-1) - O(1/k) \leq R \leq 2(n/k-1) + O(n/k^2)$ for $k < n/3$. For $k = n/2$, for example, these bounds are $9/4 \pm O(1/n)$, improving on naive lower and upper bounds of 2 and 4 respectively. The upper bound for general k shows that this simple algorithm is better than the best previously known algorithm at least by a factor of 2 when $k \geq n^{11/18}$.

1 Introduction

In the *maximum edge subgraph problem*, we are given an n-vertex graph with non-negative edge weights and a positive integer $k \leq n$, and are asked to find a k-vertex subgraph with the maximum weight. Being a generalization of the maximum clique problem, this problem is obviously NP-hard. In fact, it is known that the problem remains NP-hard even if the weight function satisfies the triangle inequality (see [RRT91]). The decision problem version of the problem for unweighted graphs, in which one is asked if there is a k-vertex graph with more than m edges, is NP-complete even if m is restricted by $m \leq k^{1+\epsilon}$ [AI95]. Naturally, we seek efficient algorithms for approximate solutions[RRT91, KP93, AKK95, AI95]. The problem is related to facility dispersion[RRT91] and to the sparsest spanner problem[KP92]. It may also find application in data mining, where diverse methods of data clustering is being actively explored.

In the following discussions, the *approximation ratio* of a solution is OPT/A, where OPT is the weight of the optimal subgraph and A is the weight of the given solution. The (*worst case*) *approximation ratio* of an algorithm is the supremum, over all inputs (and, when the algorithm is non-deterministic, over all non-deterministic choices the algorithm makes), of the approximation ratio of the solution it produces. Ravi, Rosenkrantz, and Tayi[RRT91] studied the case where the weight function satisfies the triangle inequality (in the context of the facility

---

* Research supported in part by Science Research Grant, Ministry of Education, Japan, No. 07458061

dispersion problem) and showed that a greedy algorithm achieves the approximation ratio 4. Kortsarz and Peleg[KP93] studied the problem with a general weight function and constructed an algorithm with approximation ratio $O(n^{7/18})$. Recently, Arora, Karger, and Karpinski[AKK95] have developed a framework for approximately solving dense instances of NP-hard problems and applied it to the maximum edge subgraph problem: the result is a PTAS (i.e., a polynomial time algorithm A_ϵ with approximation ratio $(1 + \epsilon)$, for each constant $\epsilon > 0$) for the special cases where the graph is unweighted and (1) the graph has $\Omega(n^2)$ edges and $k = \Omega(n)$ or (2) each vertex of the graph has degree $\Omega(n)$.

The greedy algorithm of Ravi, Rosenkrantz and Tayi starts from a heaviest edge and repeats adding a vertex to the current subgraph that maximizes the weight of the resulting new subgraph, until k vertices are chosen. Although this algorithm works well for a weight function with the triangle inequality, it fails miserably for a general weight function, as pointed out by Kortsarz and Peleg[KP93]. What we study in this paper is an alternative greedy algorithm which we call GREEDY: given G and a weight function,

1. Set $X = V(G)$.
2. If $|X| = k$ then output $G[X]$. Otherwise, find a vertex in X with the minimum weighted degree in $G[X]$ under the given weight function and remove it from X. Go to 1.

Here, $G[X]$ denotes the subgraph of G induced by X. Since this algorithm can be viewed as a derandomization (using the method of conditional probability[Rag88]) of a randomized algorithm that picks a random set of k vertices, it obviously produces a subgraph with weight at least $\frac{k(k-1)w(G)}{n(n-1)}$, where $w(G)$ is the weight of the entire graph, giving an $n^2/k^2 + o(1)$ upper bound on the approximation ratio. On the other hand, when $k = n/2$, there is a particularly simple lower bound of $2 - o(1)$: an unweighted graph consisting of $n/4$ independent edges and a path of $n/2$ vertices. When GREEDY is applied to this graph, it may leave the $n/4$ independent edges as its solution while the optimal is the path with $n/2 - 1$ edges. Our result is upper and lower bounds on the approximation ratio of GREEDY, which are tight up to an $O(n/k^2)$ additive term.

Theorem 1. *The worst case approximation ratio R of GREEDY satisfies*

$$\left(\tfrac{1}{2} + \tfrac{n}{2k}\right)^2 - O(1/n) \leq R \leq \left(\tfrac{1}{2} + \tfrac{n}{2k}\right)^2 + O(1/n) \quad \text{for } n/3 \leq k \leq n, \text{ and}$$
$$2\left(\tfrac{n}{k} - 1\right) - O(1/k) \leq R \leq 2\left(\tfrac{n}{k} - 1\right) + O(n/k^2) \quad \text{for } k < n/3.$$

For the special case $k = n/2$, the bounds are $9/4 \pm O(1/n)$ improving the naive bounds of 2 and 4. For general k, the upper bound improves the above naive analysis by a factor of $n/(2k)$. The algorithm of Kortsarz and Peleg[KP93] uses a subprocedure called LARGE, which solves the problem with approximation ratio $O(n/k)$, where the constant in the O notation is at least 4. The advantage of GREEDY lies partly in its smaller constant and mostly in its simplicity: procedure LARGE is a combination of several ideas including binary search, "expanding kernels", and the method of conditional probability. Their algorithm also includes a subprocedure that solves the unweighted version of the problem with approximation ratio $O((n/k)^{2/3})$, but only when the number of edges in the optimal solution is larger than $\sqrt{k^5/n}$.

In combinatorial optimization problems in general, greedy heuristics are particularly attractive for their simplicity and it is important to determine how well they perform in terms of approximation. Our result adds to the interesting cases where tight bounds on the approximation ratio are obtained through non-trivial analysis. See Grötschel and Lovász [GL95] for other examples and general discussion on greedy heuristics.

The rest of the paper is organized as follows. In Section 2 we describe an example that establishes the lower bound in Theorem 1. Readers who are more interested in the upper bound are advised *not* to skip this section, because the insight we obtain from the lower bound example is essential when we prove the upper bound in Section 3. The upper bound proof appeals to transformations of the given greedy execution instances into a certain canonical form, whose structure is conceptually close to the lower bound example.

2   A lower bound example

The goal of this section is to exhibit an example that establishes the lower bound in Theorem 1. In fact, the graph we construct is unweighted, i.e., every edge is assigned a unit weight, showing that the upper bound is tight even if the input is restricted to unweighted graphs. To simplify the presentation, we describe the construction assuming $k = n/2$; we will later sketch how the construction can be generalized.

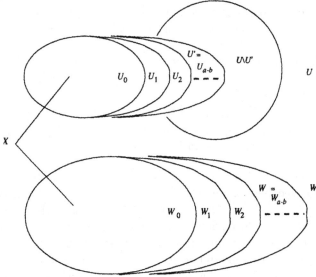

Fig. 1. Lower bound example: $|X| = |U| = |W| = n/2$, $|U_0| = n/6$, $|W_0| = n/3$, and $|U'| = n/4$

We first outline the structure of our graph G, which is illustrated in Fig 1. The construction will be made precise later. The vertex set V of G, $|V| = n$, is divided into equal halves U and W. The subset U is going to be the optimal solution, i.e., $G[U]$ will have the largest number of edges among all the $n/2$-vertex subgraphs. The greedy solution X intersects U at $n/6$ vertices and intersects W at $n/3$ vertices. Both $G[X \cap U]$ and $G[X \cap W]$ are b-regular for some integer b. $G[W]$ is roughly a-regular for $a \simeq 3b/2$. Within W is a chain of subsets $X \cap W = W_0 \subset W_1 \subset \ldots \subset W_{a-b} = W$, such that each $G[W_i]$ is roughly $(b+i)$-regular. On the other hand, U contains a subset U' of size $n/4$ which has a structure similar to W: $U \cap X = U_0 \subset U_1 \subset \ldots \subset U_{a-b} = U'$, with each $G[U_i]$ being roughly $(b+i)$-regular. From each vertex in $U \setminus U'$, there are a edges to U' in an arbitrary manner. The graph is completed by adding a small number of edges between U and W (but not between $U \cap X$ and $W \cap X$). A possible execution of the greedy algorithm first removes all the vertices in $U \setminus U'$, leaving $U_{a-b} \cup W_{a-b}$, and successively shrink the vertex set to $U_i \cup W_i$ for $i = a - b - 1, a - b - 2, \ldots, 0$. The greedy solution $G[X]$ has roughly $bn/4$ edges while $G[U]$ has $an/8$ edges within U' and $an/4$ additional edges between $U \setminus U'$ and U'. Since $a \simeq 3b/2$, the ratio $|E(G[U])|/|E(G[X])|$ is roughly $(3an/8)/(bn/4) \simeq 9/4$.

We now fill in the details to show that the parameters and the greedy execution sketched above are indeed possible. Assume n is a multiple of 24 and set $b = n/12 + 1$ and $a = n/8 + 1$. We set the sizes of the subsets U_i and W_i by $|U_i| = n/6 + 2i$ and $|W_i| = n/3 + 4i$, $0 \le i \le n/24$. Our graph G is the union of the following subgraphs.

1. b-regular graphs $G[U_0]$ and $G[W_0]$;
2. for each i, $1 \le i \le n/24$,
   (a) an arbitrary bipartite graph between vertex sets U_{i-1} and $U_i \setminus U_{i-1}$ such that the degree of each vertex of U_{i-1} is 1 and the degree of each vertex of $U_i \setminus U_{i-1}$ is $n/12 + i - 1$,
   (b) an arbitrary bipartite graph between vertex sets W_{i-1} and $W_i \setminus W_{i-1}$ such that the degree of each vertex of W_{i-1} is 1 and the degree of each vertex of $W_i \setminus W_{i-1}$ is $n/12 + i - 1$, and
   (c) a cycle on $(U_i \cup W_i) \setminus (U_{i-1} \cup W_{i-1})$;
3. an arbitrary bipartite graph between vertex sets $U' = U_{n/24}$ and $U \setminus U'$ such that the degree of each vertex in $U \setminus U'$ is a.

It is easy to confirm that $G[U_i \cup W_i]$ is $(b+i)$-regular, for $0 \le i \le n/24$. The greedy execution sequence as described above is realized as follows. We may first remove all the vertices of $U \setminus U'$ in an arbitrary order, because the minimum degree of the graph remains a throughout this process. This leaves us with $G[U_{n/24} \cup W_{n/24}]$. Proceeding by induction, suppose we are left with $G[U_i \cup W_i]$ for some i, $1 \le i \le n/24$. Since this subgraph is regular, we may choose to remove a vertex in $(U_i \cup W_i) \setminus (U_{i-1} \cup W_{i-1})$. This removal creates several vertices with one less degree, two of which are contained in $(U_i \cup W_i) \setminus (U_{i-1} \cup W_{i-1})$. We may choose one of the two for removal and, repeating in a similar fashion, may successively remove all the 6 vertices in $(U_i \cup W_i) \setminus (U_{i-1} \cup W_{i-1})$, leaving $G[U_{i-1} \cup W_{i-1}]$. Therefore, by induction, there is an execution of the greedy algorithm that leaves the vertex set $X = U_0 \cup W_0$.

Since $a = 3b/2 - 1/2$ and the number of edges between U and W is $O(n)$, our previous estimate $9/4$ of the ratio $|E(G[U])|/|E(G[X])|$ is accurate within an additive error of $O(1/n)$, establishing the lower bound in Theorem 1 for the special case $k = n/2$.

The construction for general k is essentially the same, with different parameter values. Let $r = n/k$ and $x = |U'|/|U| = |U'|/k$. Then, we have $|U \setminus U'| = (1-x)k$ and hence $|U' \cup W| = (r - 1 + x)k$. If we examine the above construction, we see that we can make a roughly equal to $b|U' \cup W|/|X| = b(r - 1 + x)$. Since $G[U]$ has roughly $akx/2$ edges among U' and $ak(1 - x)$ edges between U' and $U \setminus U'$, it has $ak(2 - x)/2 \simeq bk(2 - x)(r - 1 + x)/2$ edges in total. Therefore, we have

$$|E(G[U])|/|E(G[X])| \simeq (2 - x)(r - 1 + x). \tag{1}$$

This function of x has the maximum value $(\frac{r+1}{2})^2$ at $x = (3 - r)/2$ for $1 \le r < 3$ and the maximum value $2(r - 1)$ at $x = 0$ for $r \ge 3$. This is essentially the lower bound in Theorem 1. We omit the details of choosing appropriate integer parameters and of bounding the errors stemming from this discretization.

In passing, let us remark on the meaning of the two cases in the above bound. When $1 \le r \le 3$, i.e., $n/3 \le k \le n$, the maximum is achieved at some positive value of x. This means that the non-empty intersection of the optimal vertex set U and the greedy set X is essential in this range. On the other hand, for $k < 3/n$, the maximum is at $x = 0$, meaning that the best lower bound from our construction is achieved by making U and X disjoint.

3 Upper bound

In this section, we give an upper bound that matches the lower bound construction of the previous section. The result is for general weighted graphs. A weighted graph is a pair (G, w), where G is a graph and $w : E(G) \to \mathbf{R}^+$ is a *weight function* that assigns a non-negative real to each edge of G. For each subgraph H of G, we extend the weight function so that $w(H)$ denotes the sum of the weights of all the edges of H. For each subgraph H of G, the *weighted degree* of a vertex v in H under weight function w, denoted by $\deg_{w,H}(v)$, is defined to be the sum of $w(e)$ over all edges e incident to v in H. For each subgraph H of G and each subset U of the vertex set of H, the *average degree* of U in H under weight function w is defined to be $\sum_{v \in U} \deg_{w,H}(v)/|U|$. Then, the *average degree* of a subgraph H under w is defined to be $V(H)$ in H under w. Clearly, the average degree of H under w is equal to $2w(H)/|V(H)|$. An (n, k)-*instance* or an *execution instance*, when unambiguous, is a triple (G, w, σ), where (G, w) is a weighted graph with $V(G) = n$ and σ is a sequence of distinct $n - k$ of vertices of G. We call an (n, k)-instance $(G, w, (v_n, \dots, v_{k+1}))$ *greedy* if GREEDY may legally remove the vertices $v_n, \dots, v_{k+1}$ in this order, i.e., v_i is the vertex of $G[V_i]$ with the minimum weighted degree, where $V_i = V(G) \setminus \{v_{i+1}, \dots, v_n\}$, for $k < i \le n$.

Examining the lower bound example in the previous section, one might suspect that it is indeed the worst case example. Our upper bound proof consists in showing that this is essentially the case: given an arbitrary greedy execution instance we transform the instance (by which we roughly mean changing the weight function w) into a certain canonical form without decreasing the approximation ratio. The structure of the canonical form is very close to that of the lower bound example and thus allows us to obtain the claimed upper bound on the approximation ratio.

The objects we are going to manipulate are in fact slightly abstract versions of execution instances, which we call *scenarios*, rather than execution instances themselves. Before formally defining scenarios, let us first discuss some underlying ideas. As soon as we try to change the weight function in an execution instance in such a way to preserve greediness, we notice that it is a tricky process: simply adding some weight from one edge to another can destroy the greediness of the instance in several ways. So, let us consider relaxing the greediness condition somewhat to make transformations easier.

We call an (n, k)-instance $(G, w, (v_n, \ldots, v_{k+1}))$ *semi-greedy* if the weighted degree of v_i in $G[V_i]$ is not greater than the average degree of $G[V_i]$. Note that any greedy execution instance is semi-greedy and therefore un upper bound on the approximation ratios of semi-greedy instances will be an upper bound for greedy instances. The advantage of dealing with semi-greedy instances is that the actual weight function w is not important in deciding if the given instance is semi-greedy or not. For such a check, we only need the sequence $h(v_n), h(v_{n-1}), \ldots, h(v_{k+1})$, where $h(v_i)$ is the weighted degree of v_i in $G[V_i]$, and the average degree $\hat{h}$ of $G[V_k]$. Note that the average degree of $G[V_i]$, $k \leq i \leq n$, can be determined from these values. If we discard w from the execution instance and include h and $\hat{h}$ instead, then preserving semi-greediness in transformations would be easier than preserving greediness with full values of w. Unfortunately, by doing so we would lose information necessary to determine the approximation ratio of an execution instance: we would know the weight of the greedy solution but not the optimal solution. To keep track of the weight of the optimal solution U, we need to divide the weighted degree $h(v_i)$ into two parts: weights going into U and those going into $V(G) \setminus U$. These considerations lead to the following definition of scenarios.

An (n, k)-*scenario* is a 7-tuple $S = (V, U, \sigma, \hat{f}, \hat{g}, f, g)$, where V is a set of n vertices, U is a subset of V with $|U| = k$, σ is a sequence of distinct $n - k$ vertices of G, $\hat{f}$ and $\hat{g}$ are non-negative reals, and f, g are mappings from the set of vertices of σ to the set of non-negative reals. The following notation will be used freely whenever we refer to an (n, k)-scenario $S = (V, U, \sigma, \hat{f}, \hat{g}, f, g)$. We let $\sigma = (v_n, v_{n-1}, \ldots, v_{k+1})$, let $V_i = V \setminus \{v_{i+1}, \ldots, v_n\}$, and let $W = V \setminus U$. We set $s_i = |V_i \cap U|$ and $t_i = |V_i \cap W|$, for $k \leq i \leq n$, and $h(v_i) = f(v_i) + g(v_i)$ for $k < i \leq n$.

Given an (n, k)-instance $I = (G, w, \sigma)$ and $U \subseteq V(G)$ with $|U| = k$, we define an (n, k)-scenario $S(I, U) = (V, U, \sigma', \hat{f}, \hat{g}, f, g)$ as follows. We set $V = V(G)$, $\sigma' = \sigma$, and

1. $f(v_i)$, for $k < i \leq n$, is the total weight of the edges between v_i and $V_{i-1} \cap U$ under weight function w.
2. $g(v_i)$, for $k < i \leq n$, is the total weight of the edges between v_i and $V_{i-1} \cap W$ under w.
3. $\hat{f}$ is the average degree of $V_k \cap U$ in $G[V_k]$ under w.
4. $\hat{g}$ is the average degree of $V_k \cap W$ in $G[V_k]$ under w.

Note that 1 and 2 imply that $h(v_i) = f(v_i) + g(v_i)$ is the weighted degree of v_i in $G[V_i]$ under the weight function w. We say that an (n, k)-scenario S *corresponds to* an execution instance I if $S = S(I, U)$ for some set of vertices U.

Given an (n, k)-instance S, define $\hat{f}_i$ and $\hat{g}_i$, $k \leq i \leq n$ by

$$s_i \hat{f}_i = s_k \hat{f} + \sum_{k < j \leq i} f(v_j) + \sum_{k < j \leq i, \ v_j \in U} h(v_j),$$

$$t_i \hat{g}_i = t_k \hat{g} + \sum_{k < j \leq i} g(v_j) + \sum_{k < j \leq i, \ v_j \in W} h(v_j).$$

It is easy to verify the following proposition.

Proposition 2. *If S corresponds to $I = (G, w, \sigma)$, i.e., $S = S(I, U)$ for some $U \subseteq V(G)$, then for each i, $k < i \leq n$, $\hat{f}_i$ is the average degree of $V_i \cap U$ in $G[V_i]$ and $\hat{g}_i$ is the average degree of $V_i \cap W$ in $G[V_i]$, under weight function w.*

In view of this proposition, we call $\hat{f}_i$ ($\hat{h}_i$, resp.) the average degree of $V_i \cap U$ ($V_i \cap W$, resp.) in scenario S, even when S does not correspond to an execution instance.

We say that (n, k)-scenario S is *valid* if the following inequality is satisfied for $k < i \leq n$:

$$h(v_i) \leq \min(\hat{f}_i, \hat{g}_i) \tag{2}$$

Lemma 3. *If S corresponds to a greedy execution instance then it is valid.*

Proof. Suppose $S = S(I, U)$, where $I = (G, w, \sigma)$ is a greedy execution instance. Then, $h(v_i)$ is the weighted degree of v_i in $G[V_i]$ under w and, because I is greedy, $h(v_i)$ is not greater than the weighted degree of v in $G[V_i]$ for any vertex $v \in V_i$. Therefore, $h(v_i)$ is not greater than the average degree of any vertex set in $G[V_i]$; in particular, it is not greater than the average degree $\hat{f}_i$ of $V_i \cap U$ or the average degree $\hat{g}_i$ of $V_i \cap W$.

Define the *value* of an (n, k)-scenario S by

$$\mathrm{val}(S) = \frac{s_k \hat{f} + 2 \sum_{k < i \leq n, \ v_i \in U} f(v_i)}{s_k \hat{f} + t_k \hat{g}}.$$

Lemma 4. *Let $I = (G, w, \sigma)$ be a greedy (n, k)-instance, U be an optimal solution for (G, w), and R be the approximation ratio of this execution instance. Then $\mathrm{val}(S(I, U)) \geq R$.*

Proof. If $S = S(I, U)$, then the numerator in the definition of val(S) upper-bounds twice the weight of $G[U]$ while the denominator lower-bounds twice the weight of $G[V_k]$.

Thus, to upper-bound the approximation ratio of the greedy algorithm, it suffices to upper-bound val(S) over all valid scenarios S. In what follows, we define several transformations of scenarios that brings a given valid scenario into a certain canonical form. In doing so, it is crucial that we work on general scenarios that do not necessarily correspond to execution instances. We fully rely on the flexibility of general scenarios in defining those transformations.

We say that a valid scenario S is *saturated* if the equality holds in inequality (2), for $k < i \le n$. Our first transformation, called saturate, converts an arbitrary given scenario S into a saturated one. Fixing other components of S, it successively redefine $f(v_i)$ and $g(v_i)$, for $i = k + 1$ up to n, increasing their values by the minimum amount so as to make the equality hold in (2). It is clear that the result of saturate is a valid and saturated scenario. Moreover, this transformation never decreases the value of S, because the denominator is fixed and the numerator may only increase.

The purpose of transformation saturate is to make a scenario *monotone*: we call scenario S monotone if $h(v_i)$ is non-decreasing in i for $k < i \le n$.

Proposition 5. *If S is valid and saturated then S is monotone.*

Proof. Since S is saturated, it suffices to show that $\min(\hat{f}_i, \hat{g}_i)$ is non-decreasing in i. Fix i, $k < i \le n$, and suppose $v_i \in U$. We have $\hat{g}_i \ge \hat{g}_{i-1}$ because $t_i = t_{i-1}$. Moreover, we have $s_i \hat{f}_i \ge s_{i-1} \hat{f}_{i-1} + h(v_i)$ from the definition of $\hat{f}_i$. If we set $y = (s_{i-1} \hat{f}_{i-1} + h(v_i))/s_i$ so that $\hat{f}_i \ge y$ then y is a convex combination of $\hat{f}_{i-1}$ and $h(v_i)$ and hence either $h(v_i) \ge y \ge \hat{f}_{i-1}$ or $\hat{f}_{i-1} > y > h(v_i)$. The first case trivially implies $\hat{f}_i \ge \hat{f}_{i-1}$. The second case implies $\hat{f}_i > h(v_i)$ and hence $h(v_i) = \hat{g}_i$ since S is saturated. But then we have $\hat{f}_i > \hat{g}_i \ge \hat{g}_{i-1}$. Therefore, we have $\min(\hat{f}_i, \hat{g}_i) \ge \min(\hat{f}_{i-1}, \hat{g}_{i-1})$. To deal with the case $v_i \in W$, swap the roles of f and U with those of g and W.

Our two other transformations are defined on valid monotone scenarios. As we will see, they keep $h(v_i)$ unchanged for every v_i and hence preserve monotonicity. Note, however, that they do not necessarily preserve saturated-ness -- it is not important since saturation is only a means for achieving monotonicity in the first place.

Call scenario S *lean* if there exists some i, $k < i \le n$, such that $\hat{f}_i \le h(v_n)$. Our second transformation, called squeeze, converts an arbitrary monotone valid scenario S into a lean one: fixing other components of S, it decreases $\hat{f}$ by the minimum amount so as to make S lean. Note here that $\hat{f}_i$ for each i is an increasing function of $\hat{f}$. Let S' be the result of applying squeeze to S. If $S' \ne S$, then the definition of squeeze implies that $\hat{f}'_i \ge h(v_n)$ for every i, where $\hat{f}'_i$ is defined for S' as $\hat{f}_i$ is defined for S. Since $h(v_i) \le h(v_n)$ for every i by the monotonicity of S, and neither $h(v_i)$ nor $\hat{g}_i$ changes in the transformation, it follows that S' is valid.

Moreover, since $\hat{f}$ is common in the numerator and the denominator of val(S), we have val(S) $\leq$ val(S') provided val(S) ≥ 1 (which we can always assume for our upper-bounding purposes).

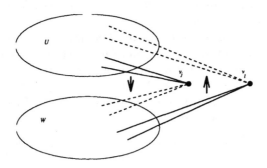

Fig. 2. Operation exchange(j, l)

Our last transformation, which is parameterized by integers j and l, $k <$ $j < l \leq n$, and is called exchange(j, l), applies to lean, monotone valid scenarios. Loosely speaking, this transformation corresponds to moving some weight from the edges between v_j and U to the edges between v_j and W while moving back the same amount of weight from the edges between v_l and W to the edges between v_l and U. See Figure 2. More formally suppose a monotone valid scenario S is given that is lean. Let $m(S)$ denote the largest integer m such that $\hat{f}_m \leq h(v_n)$. Transformation exchange(j, l) is applicable to S if $m(S) < j < l \leq n$, $f(v_j) > 0$, $g(v_l) > 0$, and $v_l \in U$. Suppose these conditions are satisfied. Keeping fixed each of $h(v_j)$, $h(v_l)$, $f(v_j) + f(v_l)$, and hence $g(v_j) + g(v_l)$, the transformation decreases $f(v_j)$ by the minimum amount such that one of the following happens: (a) $f(v_j) = 0$, (b) $g(v_l) = 0$, or (c)$\hat{f}_i \leq h(v_n)$ for some i, $j < i < l$. The result of this transformation is a valid scenario, because $\hat{g}_i$ for each i is never decreased and, although $\hat{f}_i$ may be decreased it may never become strictly smaller than $h(v_n) \geq h(v_i)$ due to condition (c). It is also clear that the scenario remains monotone (because h is not changed) and lean (because neither $\hat{f}$ nor $f(v_i)$, for any $k < i \leq m(S)$, is changed). Finally note that this transformation does not decrease val(S), because the denominator is fixed and the numerator is either unchanged (when both v_j and v_l are in U) or increased (when $v_j \in W$ and $v_l \in U$).

We call a scenario S *canonical*, if it is valid, monotone and lean and if, moreover, transformation exchange(j, l) is not applicable to S for any pair of indices j, l, i.e.,

(A) there is no pair (j, l), $m(S) < j < l \leq n$ such that $v_l \in U$, $f(v_j) > 0$, and $g(v_l) > 0$.

The following lemma summarizes the role of our transformations.

Lemma 6. *For any valid (n, k)-scenario S such that $\mathrm{val}(S) \geq 1$, there is a canonical scenario S' such that $\mathrm{val}(S') \geq \mathrm{val}(S)$.*

Proof. S can be made monotone by applying transformation **saturate**. Then, transformation **squeeze** can be applied to make it lean. Suppose S is already lean. We repeatedly apply transformation $\mathsf{exchange}(j, l)$ for some j, l until S is canonical. This process terminates in a finite number of steps, because $m(S)$ does not decrease in this process and, during the steps in which $m(S)$ is fixed (and hence only conditions (a) and (b) in the definition of $\mathsf{exchange}(j, l)$ happen) we can apply $\mathsf{exchange}(j, l)$ at most once for each fixed pair (j, l). Therefore, we eventually arrive at a canonical scenario. As we have observed, none of the transformations increases the value of the scenario.

The following property of a canonical scenario is crucial in our upper-bound proof.

Lemma 7. *Let S be a canonical scenario and let $m = m(S)$. Then,*

$$\sum_{m < i \leq n, \; v_i \in U} g(v_i) \leq h(v_n). \tag{3}$$

Proof. Let S be canonical and suppose that inequality (3) does not hold, i.e., that

$$h(v_n) < \sum_{m < i \leq n, \; v_i \in U} g(v_i), \tag{4}$$

where $m = m(S)$. Let j be the smallest integer $j > m$ such that $v_j \in U$; (4) guarantees the existence of such j. Since $g(v_j) \leq h(v_n)$ from the monotonicity of S, (4) moreover implies that there is some $l > j$ such that $v_l \in U$ and $g(v_l) > 0$. Therefore by condition (A), we must have $f(v_j) = 0$. This implies $g(v_j) > 0$ and, again by condition (A), that $f(v_i) = 0$ for every i, $m < i < j$. These facts mean that the contributions of $f(v_i)$ and $g(v_i)$, $m < i \leq j$, to $s_j \hat{f}_j$ is at most $h(v_j) \leq h(v_n)$ in total. Since $\hat{f}_m \leq h(v_n)$, it follows that $\hat{f}_j \leq h(v_n)$, contradicting the definition of $m(S)$ that it is the largest integer m satisfying $\hat{f}_m \leq h(v_n)$. Therefore, inequality (3) must hold.

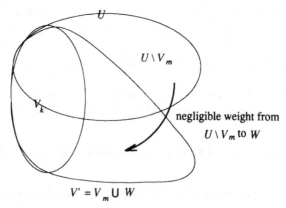

Fig. 3. Canonical scenario

The above lemma states that there is a very small weight going from the vertices in $U \setminus V_m$ to those in W. This together with the condition that a canonical scenario is monotone makes the structure of the scenario resemble that of the lower bound construction in Section 2. See Figure 3. For each scenario with fixed size of $U \setminus V_m$, the adversary tries, in order to have a maximal value of the scenario, to make the ratio of the average degree of $V_m \cup W$ (which upper-bounds $h(v_n)$) to the average degree of V_k as large as possible. Because only a small amount of weight is coming from outside, the largest possible ratio is essentially determined by the ratio of the size of $V_m \cup W$ to the size of V_k. The following lemma will be used to establish such a bound on the ratio. Our upper bound on the values of scenarios will be proved by taking a trade-off between the degree ratio and the size of $U \setminus V_m$, which the adversary also wants to make large.

For $k \leq i \leq n$, define $\hat{h}_i$ by $\hat{h}_i = (s_i \hat{f}_i + t_i \hat{g}_i)/i$. We call $\hat{h}_i$ the average degree of V_i in scenario S, since it is equal to the average degree of $G[V_i]$ when S corresponds to an execution instance on graph G. Note that $\hat{h}_i$ is determined solely by $\hat{h}_k$ and $h(v_j)$, $k < j \leq i$ namely $\hat{h}_i = (k\hat{h}_k + 2\sum_{k<j\leq i} h(v_j))/i$.

Lemma 8. *For any valid scenario S, we have*

$$\hat{h}_k \geq \frac{k-1}{n-1}\hat{h}_n.$$

Proof. First note that a valid scenario satisfies inequalities

$$h(v_i) \leq \hat{h}_i, \text{ for } k < i \leq n. \tag{5}$$

Let y_i denote the solution to the system of equations $y_i = (k\hat{h}_k + 2\sum_{k<j\leq i} y_j)/i$, $k < i \leq n$. A straightforward induction shows that $y_i = (i-1)\hat{h}_k/(k-1)$ for $k < i \leq n$ and that $h(v_i) \leq \hat{h}_i \leq y_i$, for $k < i \leq n$, for any solution h to the system of inequalities (5). $\quad\blacksquare$

We are ready to prove the main lemma for our upper bound.

Lemma 9. *For any canonical (n, k)-scenario S, $\mathrm{val}(S) \leq (1/2 + n/(2k))^2 + O(1/n)$ for $n/3 \leq k \leq n$ and $\mathrm{val}(S) \leq 2(n/k - 1) + O(n/k^2)$ for $k < n/3$.*

Proof. Let $S = (G, U, \sigma, \hat{f}, \hat{g}, f, g)$ be a canonical (n, k)-scenario. We use the notation in the definition of a canonical scenario. Let m denote the largest integer such that $\hat{f}_m \leq h(v_n)$. Since S is canonical, we have $\sum_{m<i\leq n,\, v_i \in U} g(v_i) \leq h(v_n)$. Let $V' = V_m \cup W$ and $n' = |V'|$. We claim that

$$k\hat{h}_k \geq \frac{k(k-1)h(v_n)}{n'-1} - 3h(v_n). \tag{6}$$

Suppose first that this bound holds; we will prove it later. Then, we can bound $\mathrm{val}(S)$ as follows. The numerator $s_k \hat{f} + 2\sum_{k<i\leq n,\, v_i \in U} f(v_i)$ can be decomposed into two parts $s_k \hat{f} + 2\sum_{k<i\leq m,\, v_i \in U} f(v_i) \leq s_m \hat{f}_m$ and $2\sum_{m<i\leq n,\, v_i \in U} f(v_i)$. The

first part is bounded from above by $s_m h(v_n)$ because $\hat{f}_m \leq h(v_n)$ by the choice of m. The second part is trivially bounded from above by $2h(v_n)(k - s_m)$, because $|U| = k$ and S is monotone. Therefore, the numerator is at most $h(v_n)(2k - s_m)$. On the other hand, the denominator $s_k \hat{f} + t_k \hat{g} = k\hat{h}_k$ is bounded by inequality (6). Thus, noting that $n' = n - (k - s_m)$ and putting $x = s_m/k$ and $r = n/k$, we have

$$\text{val}(S) \leq (2 - x)/\left(\frac{1 - 1/k}{r - 1 + x - 1/k} - 3/k\right)$$
$$= (2 - x)(r - 1 + x) + O(r/k),$$

since x is bounded by $0 \leq x \leq 1$, arriving at the same function of x as in equation (1) of Section 2. The claimed bound follows.

It remains to show that inequality (6) holds. The idea is to use Lemma 8 on the rate with which the average degree drops in a valid scenario. Note that a weaker bound $k\hat{h}_k \geq \frac{k(k-1)h(v_n)}{n-1}$ can be obtained from directly applying the lemma to S. To obtain (6), consider a (n', k)-scenario $S' = (V', U \cap V_m, \tau, \hat{f}', \hat{g}', f', g')$, where τ is the sequence obtained from σ by striking out each v_i not in V', $\hat{f}' = \hat{f} + 2h(v_n)/s_k$, $\hat{g}' = \hat{g} + h(v_n)/t_k$, and $f'(v) = f(v)$ and $g'(v) = g(v)$ for each $v \in \tau$. We claim that this scenario is valid. Define $\hat{f}'_i$ and $\hat{g}'_i$ analogously to $\hat{f}_i$ and $\hat{g}_i$, for each i such that $v_i \in \tau$:

$$s'_i \hat{f}'_i = s_k \hat{f}' + \sum_{k < j \leq i, \ v_j \in V'} f(v_j) + \sum_{k < j \leq i, \ v_j \in U \cap V_m} h(v_j),$$

and

$$t_i \hat{g}'_i = t_k \hat{g}' + \sum_{k < j \leq i, \ v_j \in V'} g(v_j) + \sum_{k < j \leq i, \ v_j \in W} h(v_j),$$

where $s'_i = s_i$ for $k \leq i \leq m$ and $s'_i = s_m$ for $m < i \leq n$. We need to show $h(v_i) \leq \min(\hat{f}'_i, \hat{g}'_i)$ for each i such that $v_i \in \tau$. First note that $\hat{g}'_i \geq \hat{g}_i$ for each such i, because the contributions of $g(v)$, $v \in U \setminus V_m$, that are in $\hat{g}_i$ but not in $\hat{g}'_i$ are compensated by the term $h(v_n)/t_k$ added to $\hat{g}'$. Moreover, $\hat{f}'_i > \hat{f}_i$ holds trivially for $k < i \leq m$. For the range $m < i \leq n$, first note that $\hat{f}_{m+1} > h(v_n)$. Since $s_{m+1}\hat{f}_{m+1} \leq s_m \hat{f}_m + 2h(v_n)$, it follows that $s_m \hat{f}'_m = s_m \hat{f}_m + 2h(v_n) \geq s_{m+1}\hat{f}_{m+1} \geq s_{m+1}h(v_n)$ and hence $\hat{f}'_m \geq h(v_n)$. Since $s'_i = s_m$ for $m < i \leq n$, we have $\hat{f}'_i \geq \hat{f}'_m$ and hence $\hat{f}'_i \geq h(v_n) \geq h(v_i)$. Summing up, we have $\hat{f}'_i \geq h(v_i)$ and $\hat{g}'_i \geq h(v_i)$ in the full range $k < i \leq m$, establishing that S' is valid.

Let l be the largest integer such that $v_l \in V'$, i.e., v_l is the first element of τ. Let $\hat{h}'_l = (s'_l \hat{f}'_l + t_l \hat{g}'_l)/n'$ be the average degree of V' in scenario S'. As we have shown above, we have $\hat{f}'_l \geq \hat{f}'_m \geq h(v_n)$. On the other hand, we have $t_l \hat{g}'_l \geq t_l \hat{g}_l + h(v_n) \geq t_l \hat{g}_n \geq t_l h(v_n)$, where we used condition inequality (3) to derive the second inequality. Combining these, we have $\hat{h}'_l \geq h(v_n)$. Therefore, by Lemma 8 applied to S', we have

$$\hat{h}'_k \geq \frac{(k-1)h(v_n)}{n'-1},$$

where $\hat{h}'_k = (s_k \hat{f}' + t_k \hat{g}')/k$ is the average degree of V_k in scenario S'. Inequality (6) now follows, completing the proof.

The upper bound in Theorem 1 now follows from Lemmas 4, 6, and 9.

References

[AI95]   Y. Asahiro and K. Iwama. Finding dense subgraphs. *Proc. International Symposium on Algorithms and Computation '95*, Lecture Notes in Computer Science 1004, 102-111, 1995

[AKK95] S. Arora, D. Karger, and M. Karpinski. Polynomial time approximation schemes for dense instances of NP-hard problems. *Proc. 27th ACM Symposium on Theory of Computing*, 284-293, 1995.

[GL95]   M. Grötschel and L. Lovász. Combinatorial Optimization: A Survey. In *Handbook of Combinatorics*, North-Holland, 1995.

[KP92]   G. Kortsarz and D. Peleg. Generating sparse 2-spanners. *Proc. 3rd Scandinavian Workshop on Algorithm Theory*, 73-82, 1992.

[KP93]   G. Kortsarz and D. Peleg. On choosing a dense subgraph. *Proc. 34th IEEE Symposium on Foundations of Computer Science*, 692-701, 1993.

[Rag88] P. Raghavan. Probabilistic construction of deterministic algorithms: Approximating packing integer programs. *Journal of Computer and System Sciences*, 37:130-143, 1988.

[RRT91] S.S. Ravi, D.J. Rosenkrantz, and G.K. Tayi. Facility dispersion problems: Heuristics and special cases. In *Proc. 2nd Workshop on Algorithms and Data Structures*, LNCS-519, 355-366, 1991.

Using Sparsification for Parametric Minimum Spanning Tree Problems

David Fernández-Baca[1], Giora Slutzki[1], and David Eppstein[2]

[1] Department of Computer Science, Iowa State University, Ames, IA 50011.
[2] Department of Information and Computer Science, University of California, Irvine, CA 92717.

Abstract. Two applications of sparsification to parametric computing are given. The first is a fast algorithm for enumerating all distinct minimum spanning trees in a graph whose edge weights vary linearly with a parameter. The second is an asymptotically optimal algorithm for the minimum ratio spanning tree problem, as well as other search problems, on dense graphs.

1 Introduction

In the parametric minimum spanning tree problem, one is given an n-node, m-edge undirected graph G where each edge e has a linear weight function $w_e(\lambda) = a_e + \lambda b_e$. Let $Z(\lambda)$ denote the weight of the minimum spanning tree relative to the weights $w_e(\lambda)$. It can be shown that $Z(\lambda)$ is a piecewise linear concave function of λ [Gus80]; the points at which the slope of Z changes are called *breakpoints*.

We shall present two results regarding parametric minimum spanning trees. First, we show that $Z(\lambda)$ can be constructed in $O(\min\{nm \log n, T_{MST}(2n, n) \cdot b(m, n)\})$ time, where $T_{MST}(m, n)$ is the time to compute a minimum spanning tree and $b(m, n)$ is the worst-case number of breakpoints of $Z(\lambda)$. It is known that $b(m, n) = O(m\sqrt{n})$ [Gus80, KaIb83] and $b(m, n) = \Omega(m\alpha(n))$ [Epp95], and that $T_{MST}(m, n) = O(m \log \beta(m, n))$ time [GGST86] (here $\beta(m, n) = \min\{i : \log^{(i)} n \le m/n\}$) [3]. Our algorithm improves on the Eisner-Severance method [EiSe76], which, when applied to parametric minimum spanning trees, takes $O(T_{MST}(m, n) \cdot b(m, n))$ time. For example, if $T_{MST}(m, n) = O(m \log \beta(m, n))$ and $b(m, n) = O(m\sqrt{n})$, then our algorithm runs in $O(nm \log n)$ time, while the Eisner-Severance approach takes time $O(n^{1/2}m^2 \log \beta(m, n))$; the speedup is less dramatic, but still significant, if $b(m, n)$ is, say, $O(m\alpha(n))$. Our construction procedure can be used for problems such as the stochastic spanning trees studied by Ishii et al. [ISN81], which are solved by enumerating the different solutions obtained when the parameter is varied throughout its range. Several other applications are discussed by Hassin and Tamir [HaTa89].

Our second result is an approach for solving the following closely-related parametric search problems in $O(n\sqrt{m} \log^2(n^2/m))$ time:

---

[3] Linear time (i.e., $O(m)$) algorithms can be obtained either through randomization [KKT95], or by working in less restrictive models of computation [FrWi90].

(P1) Given a value λ_1 find the first breakpoint λ^* of $Z(\lambda)$ such that $\lambda^* \geq \lambda_1$.

(P2) Find a value λ^* such that $Z(\lambda^*) = 0$. This assumes that the slopes of the edge weight functions are either all negative or all positive; we shall assume the former.

(P3) Find a λ^* such that $Z(\lambda^*) = \max_\lambda Z(\lambda)$.

Problem (P1) is a standard problem in sensitivity analysis [Gus83], (P2) arises in the solution of the *minimum-ratio spanning tree problem* (MRST) [Cha77, Meg83], and (P3) arises in Lagrangian relaxation [CMV89].

Our result should be contrasted with the fastest known algorithm for the above problems, due to Cole [Cole87], which solves them in $O(T_{MST}(m, n) \log n) = O(m \log \beta(m, n) \log n)$ time. Thus, our algorithm is faster than Cole's for all sufficiently dense graphs — i.e., $m = n^2/o(\log n)$ — and is optimal, to within a constant factor, for graphs with $\Theta(n^2)$ edges. While our search procedure is an improvement over existing methods only for the upper ranges of graph density, it constitutes what, to our knowledge, is the first non-trivial progress on the problem in many years. We hope that this result will lead to improvements in other ranges as well. We should note that, while problems (P1)–(P3) deal with with graphic matroids, counterparts for other matroids can be defined. Linear-time algorithms for an analog to (P2) for uniform matroids have been devised by Eppstein and Hirschberg [EpHi95].

Cole's parametric minimum spanning tree algorithm is a clever application of Megiddo's method of parametric search [Meg79, Meg83], a technique with numerous applications to optimization and computational geometry [CoMe93, Tol93a, CEGS92, MaSc93, ShTo94]. Indeed, MRST has the distinction of being one of the original problems to which Megiddo applied his approach. Megiddo's technique relies on the existence of an algorithm $\mathcal{E}$ for the underlying non-parametric version of the problem; for MRST, such an algorithm would solve the minimum spanning tree problem. Algorithm $\mathcal{E}$ is simulated to determine its computation path at the value λ^* being sought. Algorithm $\mathcal{E}$ is also used to implement an oracle for narrowing the search interval. This dual use of $\mathcal{E}$ tends to lead to algorithms that are, at best, a polylogarithmic factor slower than the algorithms for the underlying non-parametric problems.

The research reported here is part of an ongoing attempt to determine the conditions under which one can eliminate the slowdown that seems inherent in Megiddo's method. We have been motivated in part by Frederickson's observation [Fre90] that, as the search progresses, it is sometimes possible to compile information that can speed up subsequent oracle calls. This idea was used to devise linear-time algorithms for a variety of location problems on trees [Fre90]. Subsequently we showed that a large class of parametric optimization problems can be solved in linear time for graphs of bounded tree-width [FeSl94]. More recently, we showed that related techniques lead to linear time algorithms for several parametric minimum spanning tree problems on planar graphs [FeSl95]. The above-mentioned work and the results in the current paper suggest that a combination of certain ideas can lead to the elimination of much of the overhead implicit in Megiddo's method. Among these is the use of sampling to decide which portion of the search interval to focus our attention on, and the use of a looser variant of Megiddo's method in which, instead of attempting to maintain only one computation path of $\mathcal{E}$ at any phase of the simulation, several are maintained simultaneously; this exhibits the strong connection between construction and search problems. A crucial component of our algorithms is *sparsification* [EGIN92, EGI93], which allows us to organize computations in such a way that successive steps examine progressively less of the input. Finally, our algorithms rely critically on the processing of intersections of arrangements of lines associated with edge costs. We note that, in contrast to many of the known applications of parametric search, we do not rely explicitly on parallelism in the solution of the underlying non-parametric problem.

2 Sparsification

Sparsification relies on the observation that for many graph problems — minimum spanning trees included — the portion of the graph that actually participates in the final solution is relatively small. The same property often holds for updates as well, a fact that has been used by Eppstein et al. [EGIN92, EGI93] to solve several dynamic graph problems. We shall now summarize one of the key ideas behind sparsification: the use of *sparsification trees*, which were introduced in [EGI93] (see also Frederickson's work [Fre85a, Fre91]).

Sparsification trees are built in two steps. In the first, a *vertex partition tree* is constructed by splitting the vertex set into two equal-size parts (to within 1) and then recursively partitioning each half. This results in a complete binary tree of height at most $\log n$ where nodes at depth i have $n/2^i$ vertices. The vertex partition tree is used to build an *edge partition tree*. For any nodes α and β of the vertex partition tree at the same depth i, containing vertex sets V_α and V_β, we create a node $E_{\alpha\beta}$ in the edge partition tree containing all edges of G in $V_\alpha \times V_\beta$. The parent of $E_{\alpha\beta}$ is $E_{\gamma\delta}$, where γ and δ are, respectively, the parents of α and β in the vertex partition tree. An internal node $E_{\alpha\beta}$ will have three children if $\alpha = \beta$ and four otherwise. The *sparsification tree*, denoted T_G, is built from the edge partition tree by including only those nodes $E_{\alpha\beta}$ that contain at least one edge of $E(G)$.

Consider any node $u = E_{\alpha\beta}$ in T_G. We will denote by G_u the subgraph of G whose vertex set is $V_\alpha \cup V_\beta$ and whose edge set is $E(G) \cap (V_\alpha \times V_\beta)$. The next lemma summarizes, for future reference, properties of sparsification trees that are either straightforward or have been proved elsewhere [EGI93].

Lemma 1. *For any k between 0 and the depth of the sparsification tree, (i) there are at most 2^{2k} depth k nodes; (ii) the edge sets of the graphs associated with the nodes at depth k are disjoint and form a partition of $E(G)$; and (iii) if u is a node at depth k, $|V(G_u)| \le n/2^k$, and $|E(G_u)| \le n^2/2^{2k}$.*

3 Generating $Z(\lambda)$

We now discuss how to generate $Z(\lambda)$ in $O(mn \log n)$ time.

We assume without loss of generality that no two pairs of edge weights become equal simultaneously; this can be achieved without significantly changing $Z(\lambda)$ by perturbing the weight functions infinitesimally. Such a perturbation can be done symbolically without changing the asymptotic running time of our algorithms.

First let us discuss a simpler algorithm for the same problem, which runs in $O(m^2 \log n)$ time, and appears to be folklore. Our improved result comes from applying sparsification to this technique. The key observation (also used in previous work on the subject) is that if λ^* is a breakpoint of $Z(\lambda)$, then two edges e and f have equal weights at λ^*, and the symmetric difference of the minimum spanning trees before and after λ^* is $\{e, f\}$. The idea is to compute for each pair $\{e, f\}$ the potential breakpoint at which the two weights become equal. We then compute $Z(\lambda)$ by sweeping through the sequence of potential breakpoints, maintaining the minimum spanning tree as we do. A potential breakpoint corresponds to an actual change in the MST exactly when the edge that is heavier before the breakpoint (say e) is not already in the MST and induces a cycle in the MST containing f; this can be tested in $O(\log n)$ time per potential breakpoint using the dynamic tree data structure of Sleator and Tarjan [SlTa83].

In this $O(m^2 \log n)$ time algorithm, there are many more potential than actual breakpoints, so it seems we are wasting work testing them all. Our idea is to apply sparsification to reduce the number of breakpoints we test.

We will need some notation. Let u be any node of a sparsification tree T_G of G. Then, $Z_u(\lambda)$ will denote the minimum spanning forest function[4] for G_u, b_u will denote the number of breakpoints of Z_u, and n_u and m_u will denote, respectively, the number of vertices and edges of G_u; $F_u(\lambda)$ will denote the minimum spanning forest of G_u at λ.

We will describe our algorithm in geometric terms, following Eppstein [Epp95]. Graph the weight functions of the individual edges in G_u as lines $w = w_e(\lambda)$, drawn in a plane with coordinates (λ, w). Then the potential breakpoints discussed above occur at the vertices of this arrangement of lines. We form a line segment arrangement A_u by taking subsegments of the lines; specifically, we include those portions of the line $w_e(\lambda)$ corresponding to values of λ for which e belongs to $F_u(\lambda)$. The following fact was proved by Eppstein [Epp95].

Lemma 2. *The arrangement A_u consists of $b_u + 1$ line segments that can be grouped to form $n_u - 1$ convex chains in the (λ, w) plane.*

The proof of this lemma is given by an argument in which we assign tokens to the edges in $F_u(\lambda)$; when two edges $\{e, f\}$ are swapped we pass the token from e to f; then the convex polygons described by the lemma are traced out by the $n_u - 1$ tokens.

Lemma 3. *Let p, q, r, and s be the four children of node u in the sparsification tree, and let $\{e, f\}$ be a swap occurring at $F_u(\lambda^*)$. Then there is a pair of line*

---

[4] Since G_u need not be connected, we must consider spanning forests rather than spanning trees, but this does not lead to any additional complication.

segments $\{s_e, s_f\}$ in the line segment arrangement $A_p \cup A_q \cup A_r \cup A_s$, on the two lines $w_e(\lambda)$ and $w_f(\lambda)$ respectively, that either cross at a point $(\lambda^*, w_e(\lambda^*))$ or both have endpoints at that point.

Proof. We have already seen that the lines $w_e(\lambda)$ and $w_f(\lambda)$ cross at this point. But if e is in $F_u(\lambda^* - \epsilon)$, it is also in one of F_p, F_q, F_r, or F_s, so there is a line segment in the arrangement that goes through the points $(\lambda^* - \epsilon, w_e(\lambda^* - \epsilon))$. A symmetric argument shows that there is also a line segment corresponding to f through the points $(\lambda^* + \epsilon, w_f(\lambda^* + \epsilon))$. If one of these segments does not cross at $(\lambda^*, w_e(\lambda^*))$, it must be because the same two edges took part in a swap at a lower level of the sparsification tree, in which case both segments terminate at that point. □

Our algorithm then is to calculate $Z_u(\lambda)$, and $A_u(\lambda)$ by traversing T_G in postorder, computing these quantities at each node by combining the same information from the node's children. Specifically, we compute the line segment intersections in the arrangement $A_p \cup A_q \cup A_r \cup A_s$, sort them by their λ-coordinates, and use these as potential breakpoints in an algorithm for computing Z_u similar to the folklore one described above: we sweep through the sequence of potential breakpoints, maintaining the minimum spanning tree as we do. A potential breakpoint corresponds to an actual change in the MST exactly when the edge that is heavier before the breakpoint (say e) is not already in the MST and induces a cycle in the MST containing f; this can be tested in $O(\log n)$ time per potential breakpoint using the dynamic tree data structure of Sleator and Tarjan [SlTa83].

Lemma 4. *The number of potential breakpoints tested by the algorithm above, at node u of the sparsification tree, is $O(m_u n_u)$.*

Proof. By Lemma 3 each potential breakpoint $\{e, f\}$ occurs at a point $(\lambda, w_e(\lambda))$ where a segment on line $w_e(\lambda)$ crosses another segment in one of A_p, A_q, A_r, or A_s. In particular, it corresponds to a point where line $w_e(\lambda)$ crosses one of the at most $4(n_u - 1)$ polygons into which (by Lemma 2) these four arrangements can be grouped. Each line can only cross each polygon at most twice, so there are at most $8m_u(n_u - 1)$ crossings total. □

Theorem 5. *The algorithm described above computes $Z(\lambda)$ in $O(mn \log n)$ total time.*

Proof. It takes time $O(b_u \log b_u + m_u n_u)$ to compute the set of potential crossings [ChEd92], $O(m_u n_u \log n)$ to sort them by λ, and $O(m_u n_u \log n)$ to use the algorithm of Sleator and Tarjan to test each potential breakpoint. Thus the total time per node u is $O(m_u n_u \log n)$. The overall bound comes from summing this quantity over the nodes of the sparsification tree. □

Remark. By using the bottom-up scheme just described, but replacing the arrangement-based approach by a suitable modification of the Eisner-Severance method, $Z(\lambda)$ can be generated in $O(T_{MST}(2n, n) \cdot b(m, n))$ time; this construction will be described in the full version of the paper. Depending on b and T_{MST}, this running time will be no worse than $O(n^{3/2}m \log \log^* n)$ and no better than $O(nm\alpha(n))$.

4 Parametric search problems

We now give an algorithm for problems (P1)–(P3) of the Introduction. For concreteness, we will describe our approach in the context of problem (P2), which asks one to find the value λ^* such that $Z(\lambda^*) = 0$; a similar approach works for the other problems. Problem (P2) arises in the solution of the minimum ratio spanning tree problem, a problem that is defined as follows. Given a graph where every edge e has two weights, a_e and b_e, find a spanning tree T of G such that the ratio $\sum_{e \in T} a_e / \sum_{e \in T} b_e$ is minimized [Cha77] (the b_e's are assumed to be either all negative or all positive). MRST arises in the design of communication networks, where the number a_e represents the cost of building link e, and b_e represents the time required to build that link. The goal is to find a tree that minimizes the ratio of total cost over construction time. Other applications of MRST are given elsewhere [CMV89, Meg83]. MRST can be reduced to a problem of type (P2) by associating with each edge $e \in G$ a linear weight function $w_e(\lambda) = a_e - \lambda b_e$ and letting $Z(\lambda)$ denote the weight of the minimum spanning tree relative to the weights $w_e(\lambda)$. It can be shown [Cha77] that the minimum ratio is the root λ^* of $Z(\lambda)$.

Our algorithm resembles the construction algorithm of the previous section in that it traverses the sparsification tree T_G from the bottom up, constructing Z_u for every node u; there are, however, some key differences. First, while the construction algorithm only required postorder traversal of the nodes, the search algorithm processes nodes level by level. Second, when processing a node u, the search algorithm computes $Z_u(\lambda)$ only for a restricted interval $\mathcal{I}$ containing λ^* within which Z_u has few breakpoints.

In more detail, the search algorithm is as follows. The initialization consists of (i) constructing the sparsification tree T_G of G up to a depth D to be specified later, (ii) initializing the search interval $\mathcal{I}$ to $(-\infty, +\infty)$, and (iii) generating Z_u within $\mathcal{I}$ for every node u at depth D in T_G. Next, for every value of k from $D - 1$ down to 0, it does the following two steps. First, it narrows $\mathcal{I}$, so that, in addition to $\lambda^* \in \mathcal{I}$, the following property holds:

$$\sum_{u \in L_k} b_{\mathcal{I}}(Z_u) \le 2^{2k}, \tag{1}$$

where $b_{\mathcal{I}}(f)$ denotes the number of breakpoints of a piecewise-linear function within $\mathcal{I}$ and L_k denotes the set of nodes at depth k in T_G. The second step is to construct a representation of Z_u within $\mathcal{I}$ for every depth-k node u. This two-step processing of all nodes at depth k will be called *phase* k.

After phase 0 is complete, the root of T_G will have a complete description of $Z(\lambda)$ within $\mathcal{I}$. In the final step, the algorithm searches $Z(\lambda)$ to locate the value λ^* such that $Z_r(\lambda^*) = 0$

Next, we will describe the implementation of the main steps of the algorithm.

Constructing the Z_u's. For $u \in L_D$, Z_u is constructed using the algorithm of section 3. Nodes at depth $k < D$ are processed using a sparsification-based variant of the Eisner-Severance method [EiSe76]. The Eisner-Severance approach has the property that, for any node u of T_G, it generates a complete description of $Z_u(\lambda)$ within an interval $\mathcal{I}$ in time proportional to that required to do $b_{\mathcal{I}}(Z_u)$ evaluations of Z_u. Sparsification can be used to accelerate the evaluation of Z_u, assuming we have a suitable representation of Z_v for every child v of u. Such a representation must enable us to quickly retrieve two pieces of information for any $\lambda \in \mathcal{I}$: the value of $Z_v(\lambda)$ and the minimum spanning forest $F_u(\lambda)$ of G_u at λ. The representation can be implemented using balanced binary search trees [CLR90, FeSl94], in order to support retrieval in time logarithmic in $b_{\mathcal{I}}(Z_v)$; based on the known bounds on the number of breakpoints, the retrieval time will be $O(\log n_v)$.

Given representations of Z_p, Z_q, Z_r, Z_s for each of the children p, q, r, s of u, $Z_u(\lambda)$ can be evaluated in $O(T_{MST}(2n_u, n_u))$ time, since the minimum spanning forest of G_u is the same as the minimum spanning forest of the graph induced by $F_p(\lambda) \cup F_q(\lambda) \cup F_r(\lambda) \cup F_s(\lambda)$, which has at most $2n_u$ edges and n_u vertices. Our algorithm is then to use the Eisner-Severance method for every $u \in L_k$, but to rely on the preceding idea to ensure that the required evaluations are done on sparse graphs.

Lemma 6. *The method described above generates Z_u within $\mathcal{I}$ for every node u at depth k in total time $O(nm/2^D \log(n/2^D))$ for $k = D$ and in total time $O(n2^k \log\log^*(n/2^k))$ for $0 \le k \le D-1$.*

Proof. By Theorem 5, the total time to process all nodes at level D is

$$O\left(\sum_{u \in L_D} n_u m_u \log n_u\right) = O\left((n/2^D)\log(n/2^D) \cdot \sum_{u \in L_D} m_u\right)$$
$$= O\left((nm/2^D)\log(n/2^D)\right),$$

where the first equality follows from Lemma 1.

For each of the remaining levels, the time is proportional to that required to do $O(\sum_{u \in L_k} b_{\mathcal{I}}(Z_u))$ evaluations of Z_u on a graph with at most $n/2^{k-1}$ edges and $n/2^k$ vertices. Assuming (1), and taking $T_{MST}(m, n) = O(m \log \beta(m, n))$, this is $O(n2^k \log\log^*(n/2^k))$. $\square$

Narrowing the search interval. Narrowing requires the use of an *oracle*, a procedure that can determine the position of any λ-value λ_0 relative to λ^*; we refer to this as *resolving* λ_0. We will only describe the oracles for (P2); the other two problems can be handled analogously. Observe that any value $\lambda_0 \notin \mathcal{I}$ can be resolved in $O(1)$ time by determining its position relative to the endpoints of $\mathcal{I}$. Suppose, instead, that $\lambda_0 \in \mathcal{I}$. Assume that the slopes of all the edge costs are nonpositive (the case where they are all nonnegative is handled analogously). Then, $Z(\lambda)$ is a nonincreasing function and we have three possibilities [Meg83]: If $Z(\lambda_0) = 0$, then, $\lambda_0 = \lambda^*$. If $Z(\lambda_0) > 0$, then, $\lambda_0 < \lambda^*$. Finally, if $Z(\lambda_0) < 0$, then, $\lambda_0 > \lambda^*$. Thus, resolving a λ-value λ_0 reduces in $O(1)$ time to evaluating $Z(\lambda_0)$. We shall therefore focus on the evaluation problem.

Each phase of the search algorithm uses a different oracle; the oracle for phase k is denoted by $\mathcal{C}_k$. Oracle $\mathcal{C}_D$ evaluates Z using a minimum spanning tree algorithm with running time $T_{MST}(m, n)$. For $k < D$, oracle $\mathcal{C}_k$ computes $Z(\lambda)$ by retrieving the values of the $Z_u(\lambda)$'s for all depth $k+1$ nodes and then processing the nodes of the sparsification tree from depth $k+1$ up.

Lemma 7. *The running time of $\mathcal{C}_k$ is*

$$
t_k = \begin{cases} T_{MST}(m, n) & \text{for } k = D \\ O\left(n2^k \log\log^*\left(n/2^k\right)\right) & \text{for } 0 \le k \le D-1 \end{cases}
$$

Proof. We only need to bound the running time of $\mathcal{C}_k$ for $k \le D-1$; this is

$$
O\left(\sum_{j=k+1}^{0} \sum_{u \in L_j} T_{MST}(m_u, n_u)\right) = O\left(\sum_{j=k+1}^{0} n2^j \log\beta\left(n/2^{j-1}, n/2^j\right)\right)
$$
$$
= O\left(n2^k \log\log^*\left(n/2^k\right)\right).
$$

Note that we are using $T_{MST}(m, n) = O(m\log\beta(m, n))$. □

We now describe how to narrow $\mathcal{I}$ using the oracles. Assume that at the beginning of phase k, $\sum_{u \in L_{k+1}} b_{\mathcal{I}}(Z_u) \le 2^{2k+2}$; our objective is to find a subinterval of $\mathcal{I}$ such that (1) holds. To ensure that our assumption holds at the beginning of phase $D-1$, it will be necessary to do some narrowing immediately after the initialization step, in which the nodes at depth D are processed. By Lemma 1 and Gusfield's bound on $b(m, n)$ [Gus80], for $\mathcal{I} = (-\infty, +\infty)$, we have

$$
\sum_{u \in L_D} b_{\mathcal{I}}(Z_u) = O\left(\sum_{u \in L_D} m_u\sqrt{n_u}\right) = O\left(\sqrt{n}m/2^{D/2}\right).
$$

One can narrow $\mathcal{I}$ so that $\sum_{u \in L_D} b_{\mathcal{I}}(Z_u) \le 2^{2D}$ by making $O(\log(m\sqrt{n}/2^{5D/2}))$ calls to $\mathcal{C}_D$. The approach is standard: do a series of steps each of which halves the number of breakpoints by locating the median breakpoint within $\mathcal{I}$, and, by resolving it, decides whether to discard the part of $\mathcal{I}$ before the median, or the part after the median [FeSl95].

To understand how narrowing works, it helps to examine the relationship between breakpoints of functions associated with depth-k nodes, and those associated with nodes at depth $k+1$. Following notation similar to that of section 3, A_v will denote the arrangement of line segments associated edges appearing in the minimum spanning tree of G_v for $\lambda \in \mathcal{I}$; i.e., we include those portions of the line $w_e(\lambda)$ corresponding to values of $\lambda \in \mathcal{I}$ for which e belongs to $F_v(\lambda)$. We have the following complement to Lemma 3, which is similar to a fact proved in an earlier paper [FeSl95].

Lemma 8. *Let p, q, r, and s be the four children of node u in the sparsification tree. Then, there is a breakpoint of Z_u at $\lambda_0 \in \mathcal{I}$ only if there is a pair of line segments $\{s_e, s_f\}$ in the line segment arrangement $A_p \cup A_q \cup A_r \cup A_s$, on the two cost lines $w_e(\lambda)$ and $w_f(\lambda)$ respectively, that either cross at a point $(\lambda_0, w_e(\lambda_0))$ or both have endpoints at that point.*

Thus, when narrowing the search interval, we can focus on breakpoints of the Z_v's associated with nodes at depth $k+1$, and on the intersections between line segments associated with siblings at depth $k + 1$, in a manner similar to the approach in Section 3. Unlike what was done there, however, we cannot simply generate all intersection points, since this would be too time-consuming. We shall, instead, repeatedly use a procedure SELECT, which allows us to select specific intersection points in an arrangement of cost lines.

SELECT$(A, k, \mathcal{I})$: Given an arrangement of lines A, an integer k, and an interval $\mathcal{I}$, return the intersection point in A with the kth largest abscissa amongst those intersection points whose abscissa falls within $\mathcal{I}$.

Agarwal [Aga91] showed that SELECT can be implemented in $O(r \log r)$ time, where r is the number of lines in the arrangement.

Roughly speaking, the interval narrowing algorithm uses SELECT to generate sample points in the middle of each subinterval of $\mathcal{I}_u$; the oracle will then be used to halve these intervals. This process is repeated logarithmically-many times until the interval is small enough. The details of the algorithm are given below. In the description, we shall write l_e to denote the line on the (λ, w) plane traced by the cost of $e \in E(G)$, and we shall write $\mathcal{I}(B)$ to denote the subdivision of $\mathcal{I}$ induced by a set of λ-values B. The algorithm assumes that, prior to being called, $\lambda^* \in \mathcal{I}$ and $\sum_{u \in L_{k+1}} b_{\mathcal{I}}(Z_u) \leq 2^{2k+2}$.

NARROW$(k, \mathcal{I})$

0 $N := \binom{n/2^k}{2}$
1 **for each** $u \in L_k$ **do**
2 $B_u := \{\lambda \in \mathcal{I} : \lambda$ is a breakpoint of Z_v for some child v of $u\}$
3 **for** $i := 2$ **to** $\log N$ **do**
4 **for each** $u \in L_k$ **and each subinterval** $\mathcal{J}$ of $\mathcal{I}(B_u)$ **do**
5   $C_u := \{l_e : e \in F_v(\lambda), \lambda \in \mathcal{J},$ for some child v of $u\}$
   Comment: By definition of B_u, $F_v(\lambda)$ is the same for all $\lambda \in \mathcal{J}$
6   Add to B_u the λ-coordinate of SELECT$(C_u, N/2^i, \mathcal{J})$
7 Reduce $\mathcal{I}$ so that $\lambda^* \in \mathcal{I}$ and $|L \cap \mathcal{I}| \leq 2^{2k}$, where $L = \bigcup_{u \in L_k} B_u$
8 **return** $\mathcal{I}$

Lemma 9. NARROW *computes an interval $\mathcal{I}$ containing λ^* satisfying (1) in $O(n2^k \log^2(n/2^k))$ time.*

Proof. Suppose that, at the beginning of each iteration of the loop beginning at line 3, $|\bigcup B_u| \leq 2^{2k+2}$; by assumption this is true at the beginning of the first iteration. Thus, steps 4–6 take $O(n2^k \log(n/2^k))$ time and, in step 7, we will have $|L| \leq 2^{2k+3}$.

Step 7 can be implemented with three calls to C_k as follows. First, discard all values in L that fall outside $\mathcal{I}$. Next, in $O(|L|)$ time [CLR90], compute the median value λ_m of L, and apply C_k to resolve its position relative to λ^*. The answer allows us to either discard the portion of $\mathcal{I}$ to the left of λ_m or the portion to the right of λ_m, thereby halving the number of elements of L in $\mathcal{I}$. Repeating this process at most two additional times will ensure that $|L \cap \mathcal{I}'| \leq 2^{2k}$. Hence, the total time for Step 7, including the median computations, is $O(2^{2k} + t_k)$. Since statements 3–7 are iterated $O(\log(n/2^k))$ times, the running time of the narrowing algorithm is $O(n2^k \log^2(n/2^k) + t_k \log(n/2^k))$; the time bound follows from Lemma 7.

After the ith iteration of statements 3–7, each subinterval of $\mathcal{I}(B_u)$ will have at most $\binom{n/2^k}{2}/2^i$ intersection points of C_u. Thus, after the last iteration, for every $u \in L_k$, no subinterval of $\mathcal{I}(B_u)$ will have any such intersection points. The total size of the B_u's will be at most 2^{2k}; this, together with Lemma 8, implies that the interval returned by NARROW satisfies (1). $\qquad \square$

Analysis. We now state the main result of this section:

Theorem 10. *The search algorithm runs in $O(n\sqrt{m}\log^2(n^2/m))$ time.*

Proof. We choose $D = \lceil 0.5 \log m \rceil$. Thus, the initialization (including the processing of all nodes at depth D) takes $O(n\sqrt{m}\log(n^2/m))$. The initial narrowing prior to the beginning of phase $D - 1$ takes $O(m \log \beta(m,n) \log(n^2/m))$ time. By Lemmas 6 and 9, the total running time of phases $D - 1$ to 0 is

$$O\left(n \sum_{k=D}^{0} 2^k \log^2(n/2^k)\right) = O\left((n2^D) \log^2(n/2^D)\right)$$
$$= O\left(n\sqrt{m}\log^2(n^2/m)\right),$$

At the end of the last phase, we will have an representation of $Z(\lambda)$ within an interval $\lambda^* \in \mathcal{I}$. Since the number of breakpoints of Z is polynomially-bounded in n, a binary search on its representation will enable us to locate λ^* in $O(\log n)$ times. Thus, the total running time is $O(n\sqrt{m}\log^2(n^2/m))$. $\qquad \square$

5 Discussion

We have presented algorithms for construction and search problems arising from parametric minimum spanning trees. While our time bounds for constructing Z improve on the Eisner-Severance approach, the latter seems more output-sensitive. It is an open problem to determine if there is a faster, perhaps output-sensitive, algorithm for the construction problem. Finally, we note that our search algorithm is inefficient for non-dense graphs; whether or not it is possible to find an algorithm whose running time matches T_{MST} remains open.

Acknowledgements

David Fernández-Baca was supported in part by the National Science Foundation under grants CCR-9211262 and CCR-9520946. He also thanks Jens Lagergren for helpful discussions and Vladimir Estivill-Castro, who hosted him during a visit to LANIA, in Xalapa, Mexico, where part of the work reported here was conducted.

David Eppstein was supported in part by the National Science Foundation under grant CCR-9258355 and by matching funds from Xerox Corp.

References

[Aga91] P.K. Agarwal. *Intersection and Decomposition Algorithms for Planar Arrangements.* Cambridge University Press, Cambridge, 1991.

[CEGS92] B. Chazelle, H. Edelsbrunner, L. Guibas, and M. Sharir. Diameter, width, closest line pair, and parametric searching. In *Proceedings of the 8th Annual ACM Symposium on Computational Geometry*, pp. 120– 129 (1992).

[CMV89] P.M. Camerini, F. Maffioli, and C. Vercellis. Multi-constrained matroidal knapsack problems. *Mathematical Programming* 45:211–231, 1989.

[CoMe93] E. Cohen and N. Megiddo. Maximizing concave functions in fixed dimension. In *Complexity in Numerical Computations*, P.M. Pardalos, ed., pp. 74–87, World Scientific Press 1993.

[Cole87] R. Cole. Slowing down sorting networks to obtain faster sorting algorithms. *J. Assoc. Comput. Mach.*, 34(1):200–208, 1987.

[Cha77] R. Chandrasekaran. Minimal ratio spanning trees. *Networks*, 7: 335–342, 1977.

[ChEd92] B. Chazelle and H. Edelsbrunner. An optimal algorithm for intersecting line segments in the plane. *J. Assoc. Comput. Mach.*, 39:1–54, 1992.

[CLR90] T.H. Cormen, C.E. Leiserson, and R.L. Rivest. *Introduction to Algorithms.* MIT Press, Cambridge, Massachusetts, 1990.

[EiSe76] M.J. Eisner and D.G. Severance. Mathematical techniques for efficient record segmentation in large shared databases. *J. Assoc. Comput. Mach.*, 23:619–635, 1976.

[EGIN92] D. Eppstein, Z. Galil, G.F. Italiano, and A. Nissenzweig. Sparsification — a technique for speeding up dynamic graph algorithms. In *Proc. 33rd Annual Symposium on Foundations of Computer Science*, pp. 60–69, 1992.

[EGI93] D. Eppstein, Z. Galil, and G.F. Italiano. Improved sparsification. Tech Report 93-20, Department of Computer Science, University of Califonia, Irvine, April, 1993.

[EpHi95] D. Eppstein and D. S. Hirschberg. Choosing subsets with maximum weighted average. Tech. Rep. 95-12, Dept. Inf. and Comp. Sci., UC Irvine, 1995.

[Epp95] D. Eppstein. Geometric lower bounds for parametric matroid optimization. In *27th Annual Symp. on Theory of Computing*, pp. 662–671, 1995.

[FeSl94] D. Fernández-Baca and G. Slutzki. Optimal parametric search on graphs of bounded tree-width. In *Proc. 4th Scandinavian Workshop on Algorithm Theory*, pp. 155–166, LNCS 824, Springer-Verlag, 1994. To appear in *J. Algorithms.*

[FeSl95] D. Fernández-Baca and G. Slutzki. Linear-time algorithms for parametric minimum spanning tree problems on planar graphs. In *Proc. Latin American Conference on Theoretical Informatics*, pp. 257–271, LNCS 911, Springer-Verlag, 1995.

[Fre85a] G.N. Frederickson. Data structures for on-line updating of minimum spanning trees. *SIAM J. Comput.* 14:781–798, 1985.

[Fre90] G.N. Frederickson. Optimal algorithms for partitioning trees and locating *p*-centers in trees. Technical Report CSD-TR 1029, Department of Computer Science, Purdue University, October 1990.

[Fre91] G.N. Frederickson. Ambivalent data structures for dynamic 2-edge connectivity and *k*-smallest spanning trees. In *Proc. 32nd Annual Symp. on Foundations of Computer Science*, pp. 632–641, 1991.

[FrWi90] M. Fredman and D. Willard. Trans-dichotomous algorithms for minimum spanning trees and shortest paths. In *Proc. 31st Annual IEEE Symp. on Foundations of Computer Science*, 1990, pp. 719–725.

[GGST86] H.N. Gabow, Z. Galil, T. Spencer, and R.E. Tarjan. Efficient algorithms for finding minimum spanning trees in undirected and directed graphs. *Combinatorica*, 6:109–122, 1986.

[Gus80] D. Gusfield. *Sensitivity analysis for combinatorial optimization.* Technical Report UCB/ERL M80/22, University of California, Berkeley, May 1980.

[Gus83] D. Gusfield. Parametric combinatorial computing and a problem in program module allocation. *J. Assoc. Comput. Mach.*, 30(3):551–563, 1983.

[HaTa89] R. Hassin and A. Tamir. Maximizing classes of two-parametric objectives over matroids. *Math. Oper. Res.*, 14:362-375, 1989.

[ISN81] H. Ishii, S. Shiode, and T. Nishida. Stochastic spanning tree problem. *Discrete Applied Mathematics*, 3:263–273, 1981.

[KaIb83] N. Katoh and T. Ibaraki. On the total number of pivots required for certain parametric combinatorial optimization problems. Technical Report Working Paper 71, Inst. Econ. Res., Kobe Univ. Commerce, 1983.

[KKT95] D.R. Karger, P.N. Klein, and R.E. Tarjan. A randomized linear-time algorithm for finding minimum spanning trees. *J. Assoc. Comput. Mach.*, 42:321-329, 1995.

[MaSc93] J. Matoušek and O. Schwartzkopf. A deterministic algorithm for the three-dimensional diameter problem. In *Proceedings of 25th Annual Symposium on Theory of Computing*, pp. 478–484 (1993).

[Meg79] N. Megiddo. Combinatorial optimization with rational objective functions. *Math. Oper. Res.*, 4:414–424, 1979.

[Meg83] N. Megiddo. Applying parallel computation algorithms in the design of serial algorithms. *J. Assoc. Comput. Mach.*, 30(4):852–865, 1983.

[ShTo94] M. Sharir and S. Toledo. Extremal polygon containment problems. *Computational Geometry*, 4:99–118, 1994.

[SlTa83] D.D.K. Sleator and R.E. Tarjan. A data structure for dynamic trees. *Journal of Computer and System Sciences*, 26(3):362–391, 1983.

[Tol93a] S. Toledo. Maximizing non-linear convex functions in fixed dimension. In *Complexity in Numerical Computations*, P.M. Pardalos, ed., pp. 74–87, World Scientific Press 1993. A preliminary version appeared in FOCS 92.

Vertex Partitioning Problems
On Partial k-Trees

Arvind Gupta*, Damon Kaller*, Sanjeev Mahajan** and Tom Shermer*

Abstract. We describe a general approach to obtain polynomial-time algorithms over partial k-trees for graph problems in which the vertex set is to be partitioned in some way. We encode these problems with formulae of the *Extended Monadic Second-order* (or EMS) logic. Such a formula can be translated into a polynomial-time algorithm automatically. We focus on the problem of partitioning a partial k-tree into induced subgraphs isomorphic to a fixed *pattern* graph; a distinct algorithm is derived for each pattern graph and each value of k. We use a "pumping lemma" to show that (for some pattern graphs) this problem cannot be encoded in the "ordinary" Monadic Second-order logic—from which a linear-time algorithm over partial k-trees would be obtained. Hence, an EMS formula is in some sense the strongest possible. As a further application of our general approach, we derive a polynomial-time algorithm to determine the maximum number of *co-dominating sets* into which the vertices of a partial k-tree can be partitioned. (A co-dominating set of a graph is a dominating set of its complement graph).

1 Introduction

Many NP-hard graph problems are known to have polynomial-time (often even linear-time) algorithms over the class of partial k-trees (see Arnborg [Arn85] for a survey of early results). This class encompasses many important graph families including trees and forests ($k = 1$), series-parallel and outerplanar graphs ($k = 2$) and Halin graphs ($k = 3$). Any partial k-tree can be decomposed into a tree-like hierarchy of *basic* graphs—each with $k + 1$ or fewer vertices. This *tree decomposition* can be generated in linear time [Bod93], and provides a structure on which dynamic-programming algorithms can operate to solve a wide spectrum of graph problems. A number of different formalisms have been used to capture the problems amenable to this approach [BLW87, Bod88, MP94], including several variations of the Monadic Second-order (or MS) logic [ALS91, BPT92, Cou90b]. An MS logical statement can be automatically translated into a dynamic-programming algorithm to solve the encoded problem over partial k-trees. In this paper, we use interesting combinatorial techniques to show that

---

* School of Computing Science, Simon Fraser University, Burnaby, B.C., Canada, V5A 1S6. E-mail: {arvind, kaller, shermer}@cs.sfu.ca Research supported by the Natural Sciences and Engineering Research Council of Canada.

** Max Planck Institut für Informatik, D-66123 Saarbrücken, Germany. E-mail: mahajan@mpi-sb.mpg.de

vertex partitioning problems of a certain type can be encoded in the *Extended MS* (or EMS) logic of Arnborg *et al.* [ALS91].

An instance of PARTITION INTO ISOMORPHIC SUBGRAPHS [GJ79, Problem GT12] consists of two graphs G and H: This is a yes-instance iff the vertex set of G can be partitioned into disjoint sets, each of which induces a subgraph isomorphic to H. Kirkpatrick and Hell [KH78] have shown this problem to be NP-complete, even under the restriction that H is a fixed graph on three or more vertices. In this paper, we consider the variation PARTITION INTO FIXED ISOMORPHIC SUBGRAPHS, where the *pattern* graph H is fixed as part of the problem description. This generalizes several well-known problems: Probably the most famous is VERTEX MATCHING, where the pattern graph consists of just two adjacent vertices. Another example—in which the pattern graph consists of a constant number t of isolated vertices—has been studied under the names χ_t-COLORING [KGS95a] and PARTITION INTO BOUNDED INDEPENDENT SETS [BJ93]. For these pattern graphs, the problem has linear time-complexity over partial k-trees [KGS95a]. We will show that, for any pattern graph, the problem has polynomial time-complexity over partial k-trees. This is done by encoding the problem with a distinct EMS formula for each pattern graph and each value of k. In their seminal paper, Arnborg *et al.* [ALS91] claimed that EMS logic can encode the problem with a single formulation for every value of k; the claim has since been withdrawn [Lag94].

An MS logical statement automatically provides a *tree automaton* [GS84, Tho90] which executes tree decompositions in much the same way as strings are executed by a conventional finite-state automaton. The "ordinary" MS logic generates *finite-state* tree automata—as also does Courcelle's *Counting* MS (or CMS) logic [Cou90b]—and these machines spend only constant time at each node of a tree decomposition. In contrast, the EMS formalism generates tree automata equipped with extra machinery to perform arithmetic calculations: These "extended tree automata" (no longer finite-state machines) may spend polynomial time at each node of the tree decomposition. A tree automaton *recognizes* a particular subclass of the partial k-trees. It has been conjectured (see *e.g.* [Cou91]) that a subclass of the partial k-trees is recognizable by a finite-state tree automaton *only* if the subclass can be encoded with a CMS formula. Under this conjecture, CMS logic would elegantly characterize a large class of graph problems with linear time-complexity over partial k-trees. This conjecture is known to hold for partial 1-trees [Cou90b], partial 2-trees [Cou91] and partial 3-trees [Kal96]. In many cases, this logical characterization is very useful: Many natural graph problems can be (almost automatically) expressed in this way.

There are natural graph problems, however, that do not readily lend themselves to expression in MS logic. Some such problems can still be encoded over partial k-trees by exploiting certain properties of the graph family [KGS95a, KGS95b]. Other problems provably cannot be encoded in MS logic [Cou90a, WW89]; and in this paper, we use a *pumping lemma* (reminiscent of the pumping lemma for regular sets [HU79]) to show that CMS logic cannot always encode PARTITION INTO FIXED ISOMORPHIC SUBGRAPHS when the pattern graph is disconnected. It is often difficult to find a CMS encoding for the *complement* [KGS95a] of a CMS-encodable graph problem: If a problem Π can be expressed as the question "Does a graph G have a subgraph with some specified properties?", then the complement problem $\overline{\Pi}$ asks whether the complement $\overline{G}$ of the input graph has a subgraph with the same properties. Thus, a solution to $\overline{\Pi}$ requires there be no edge wherever a solution to Π has an edge (and *vice-versa*).

If the problem PARTITION INTO FIXED ISOMORPHIC SUBGRAPHS is defined with a *connected* pattern graph H, then it can be encoded quite easily in CMS logic: A graph $G = (V, E)$ is a yes instance iff there exists an edge subset $E' \subseteq E$ such that H is isomorphic to each maximal component of the graph $G' = (V, E')$. The complement of such a problem, then, requires a graph to be partitioned into copies of a pattern graph H whose complement graph $\overline{H}$ is connected (*i.e.* H is possibly disconnected). The disconnectedness causes difficulties in obtaining a logical encoding; and we will show that, for some disconnected pattern graphs, CMS logic cannot encode the problem—not even over the class of trees.

We will also describe how our approach can be used to encode the complement of DOMATIC NUMBER [GJ79, Problem GT3]: This problem asks whether the vertices of a graph G can be partitioned into some number r of dominating sets. (A dominating set is a vertex subset V' such that any vertex not in V' is adjacent to one or more vertices in V'.) DOMATIC NUMBER can be encoded over partial k-trees with a CMS formulation of $O(k)$ size, regardless of the value of r: A partial k-tree can have no more than $k + 1$ disjoint dominating sets; so a logical formulation need only encode "NO" for $r \geq k + 2$, and otherwise provide at most $k + 1$ sets to partition the vertex set. For the complement problem (CO-DOMATIC NUMBER), the vertices are to be partitioned into *co-dominating sets*: There is no constant bound on the number of sets in such a partition, but we will show that the partition can nevertheless be represented with a bounded-size formulation.

The rest of this paper is organized as follows: In Section 2 we review graph-theoretic notation and preliminaries. In Section 3 we describe the CMS logic, and show that PARTITION INTO FIXED ISOMORPHIC SUBGRAPHS is not always CMS-encodable; we then proceed to discuss the more powerful formalism of EMS logic. In Section 4 we develop an EMS formulation encoding PARTITION INTO FIXED ISOMORPHIC SUBGRAPHS for any pattern graph. In Section 5 we briefly describe how the same techniques can be used to encode CO-DOMATIC NUMBER. In Section 6 we examine the common features of these two different problems, and discuss a general specification of the problems that can be encoded using these techniques.

2 Preliminaries

The graphs in this paper are finite, simple and undirected. If G is a graph, then $V(G)$ is its vertex set and $E(G)$ is its edge set. If V' is a subset of $V(G)$, then $G_{[V']}$ is the subgraph of G induced by V'. If V' is a set (but not necessarily a subset of $V(G)$), then $G \backslash V'$ is the subgraph of G that is induced by $V(G) - V'$; we say that $G \backslash V'$ is obtained by *deleting* the vertices of V' from G.

If G and G' are graphs, then we write $G \sqsubseteq G'$ to indicate that G is a subgraph of G'; and $G \cong G'$ to indicate that G and G' are isomorphic. The disjoint union of G and G' is denoted by $G \sqcup G'$: this is the graph with vertex set $V(G) \cup V(G')$ and edge set $E(G) \cup E(G')$. If H and H' are vertex-disjoint subgraphs of G such that some edge of G has one endpoint in $V(H)$ and the other in $V(H')$, then we write $H \sim_G H'$ and say that H and H' are *adjacent*.

2.1 Partial k-Trees and Tree Decompositions

A k-*tree* is either the clique on k vertices, or a graph that can be obtained (recursively) from a k-tree G by adding a new vertex, and making it adjacent to any k distinct vertices that induce a clique in G. A *partial k-tree* is a subgraph of a k-tree. For example, a graph is a partial 0-tree iff its edge set is empty; a graph is a partial 1-tree iff it is a forest. Series-parallel graphs and outerplanar graphs are subclasses of the partial 2-trees; Halin graphs form a subclass of the partial 3-trees. The partial k-trees can be characterized as those graphs that admit a width-k tree decomposition [RS86]:

Definition 1. A *tree decomposition* of a graph G is a pair $(T, \mathcal{X})$ where T is a tree and $\mathcal{X} = \{X_a\}_{a \in V(T)}$ is a collection of subsets of $V(G)$, indexed by the nodes of T, such that

- $\bigcup_{a \in V(T)} X_a = V(G)$, and
- each edge of G has both its endpoints in some $X_a \in \mathcal{X}$, and
- for $v \in V(G)$, a connected subgraph of T is induced by $\{a \in V(T) | v \in X_a\}$.

We refer to the elements of $V(T)$ as *nodes*, so as not to confuse them with the vertices of G. The set X_b is called the *bag* indexed by $b \in V(T)$. We say that $(T, \mathcal{X})$ is a *width-k tree decomposition* if no bag contains more than $k+1$ vertices. If T' is a subgraph of T, then $X_{T'}$ is the union of those bags indexed by nodes of T': that is, $X_{T'} = \bigcup_{a \in V(T')} X_a$.

Lemma 2. *Suppose G is a partial k-tree; and let $V' \subseteq V(G)$. There exists a subset X of $V(G)$, with cardinality $|X| \leq k + 1$, such that $G \backslash X$ consists of two disjoint partial k-trees, neither containing more than $\lfloor \frac{2|V'|}{3} \rfloor$ vertices of V'.*

Proof. Let $n' = |V'|$; and let $(T, \mathcal{X})$ be a width-k tree decomposition of G. By deleting an edge $\{a, b\}$ from $E(T)$, we obtain two disjoint trees, say T_a and T_b, where $a \in V(T_a)$ and $b \in V(T_b)$. Suppose that this edge becomes directed from a to b if $|X_{T_b} \cap V'| > |X_{T_a} \cap V'|$. Since T has more nodes than edges, there exists a node (say c) away from which no edge may become directed in this manner. It follows that no component of $G \backslash X_c$ contains more than $\lfloor \frac{n'}{2} \rfloor$ vertices of V'. Since V' contains only n' vertices in total, we can easily group the components of $G \backslash X_c$ into two disjoint partial k-trees, neither containing more than $\lfloor \frac{2n'}{3} \rfloor$ vertices of V'. Therefore, $X = X_c$ is the subset required by the lemma. $\quad\square$

3 Monadic Second-Order Logic

A graph G can be interpreted as a logical structure over a universe consisting of a set V of vertices and a set E of edges. The structure of G is described by a predicate $Edge(e, v)$ which holds whenever $v \in V$ is an endpoint of $e \in E$. Many graph properties can then be expressed in a predicate calculus [ALS91, BPT92, Cou90b]. We follow Courcelle's *Counting Monadic Second-order* (or CMS) logic which uses the following symbols: individual variables (to represent vertices or edges); set variables (to represent sets of vertices or edges); the equality ($=$) and membership ($\in$) symbols; existential ($\exists$) and universal ($\forall$) quantifiers; the logical operators $\wedge$ ("and"), $\vee$ ("or"), $\neg$ ("not"), $\Rightarrow$ ("implies") $\Leftrightarrow$ ("if and only if"); the *Edge* predicate; and unary predicates $\mathbf{card}_{\ell,c}$ for nonnegative integer constants ℓ, c (with $\ell < c$). If S is a set, then $\mathbf{card}_{\ell,c}(S)$ is true iff S has cardinality ℓ (mod c). A *CMS statement* is a string of these symbols such that all variables are quantified, and the usual syntactic rules of logic are observed. We write $G \models \Phi$ to indicate that a CMS statement Φ is true when evaluated over a graph G. Thus, Φ defines the graph class $\{G \mid G \models \Phi\}$. A *tree automaton* [GS84, Tho90] can be used to recognize the partial k-trees that belong to this class.

Definition 3. A *tree automaton* over an alphabet Σ is a quadruple $(\mathcal{S}, S_0, \mathcal{S}_A, f)$ where $\mathcal{S}$ is a finite set of *states*; $S_0 \in \mathcal{S}$ is the *initial* state; $\mathcal{S}_A \subseteq \mathcal{S} - \{S_0\}$ is the set of *accepting* states; and $f : \mathcal{S} \times \mathcal{S} \times \Sigma \rightarrow \mathcal{S} - \{S_0\}$ is the *transition function*.

The *input* to this tree automaton is a rooted binary tree T, with a labeling function $\sigma : V(T) \rightarrow \Sigma$. Each leaf b of T is then assigned to the state $f(S_0, S_0, \sigma(b))$; and each other node b of T is assigned to the state $f(S, S', \sigma(b))$, where S and S' are the states to which the children of b are (recursively) assigned. The tree T is *accepted* iff its root is thus assigned to an accepting state.

For our purposes, the alphabet Σ is the set of graphs on $k + 1$ or fewer (labeled) vertices: These are the *basic* graphs induced by the bags of a width-k tree decomposition $(T, \mathcal{X})$. Without loss of generality, we assume T is a binary tree; an arbitrary root is chosen; and the label $\sigma(b)$ of each node b corresponds roughly to the subgraph $G_{[X_b]}$. If we say that $(T, \mathcal{X})$ is accepted by a tree automaton, we mean that T is accepted when its vertices are labeled in this way.

Lemma 4. *If Φ is a CMS statement, then (for each $k \in \mathbb{N}$) there exists a tree automaton $\mathcal{A}$ for which the input is any width-k tree decomposition $(T, \mathcal{X})$ of a graph G such that: $\mathcal{A}$ accepts $(T, \mathcal{X})$ iff $G \models \Phi$.*

Proof. See Courcelle [Cou90b]. Similar results were obtained independently by Arnborg *et al.* [ALS91], and by Borie *et al.* [BPT92]. □

The transition function of a tree automaton can be implemented with a constant-size table; so only linear time is needed to decide whether a given tree decomposition is accepted. Since tree decompositions can be generated in linear time [Bod93], it follows that any CMS-encodable decision problem has a linear-time algorithm over the class of partial k-trees.

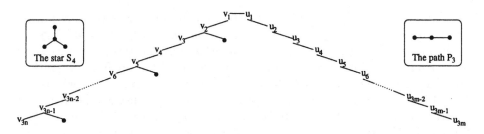

Fig. 1. The tree $G_{n,m}$

Since a tree automaton has only a finite number of states, we can use a "pumping lemma" to show that certain graph problems cannot be solved by such a machine. This approach was used by Mahajan and Peters [MP94] to show that tree automata cannot recognize sets of graph-subgraph pairs (G, S) where S is a solution to some *non-regular* problem on a partial k-tree G. The proof of Theorem 5 relies on a slightly different pumping lemma that refers only to the input graph, making no reference to the subgraph forming a putative solution. This theorem shows that, for some pattern graphs, PARTITION INTO FIXED ISOMORPHIC SUBGRAPHS is not CMS-encodable over partial k-trees. (The proof carries through even if the subgraphs need not be induced.)

Theorem 5. *For some pattern graphs, the problem* PARTITION INTO FIXED ISO-MORPHIC SUBGRAPHS *is not CMS-encodable over the class of trees.*

Proof sketch. Suppose a CMS statment Φ encodes whether or not a tree can be partitioned into (induced) copies of $P_3 \sqcup S_4$, where P_3 is the path on three vertices, and S_4 is the star on four vertices. By Lemma 4, there exists a tree automaton $\mathcal{A}$, such that $\mathcal{A}$ accepts a width-1 tree decompositions of a graph G iff $G \models \Phi$. For $n, m \geq 2$, let $G_{n,m}$ be the tree (shown in Figure 1) on $3m + 4n$ vertices, containing a path with vertex sequence $v_{3n}, v_{3n-1}, \ldots, v_1, u_1, u_2, \ldots, u_{3m}$ such that, for $i \equiv 2 \pmod 3$, the vertex v_i is adjacent to one other pendant vertex (not counting v_{3n}). So $G_{n,m} \models \Phi$ iff $m = n \geq 2$.

Let $(T, \mathcal{X})$ be a width-1 tree decomposition of $G_{n,n}$ such that T is binary; and choose the root r of T such that $X_r = \{v_1, u_1\}$. Say the subtree rooted at the right child of r is a path $P \sqsubseteq T$ on $3n - 1$ nodes, such that $\{u_i, u_{i+1}\}$ is the bag indexed by the ith node of P. Provided n is large enough, two nodes of P become assigned to the same state when $(T, \mathcal{X})$ is executed by $\mathcal{A}$. Therefore, the subtree between them can be "pumped" so that $\mathcal{A}$ will (incorrectly) accept trees $G_{n,m}$ where $m > n$. $\qquad\square$

3.1 Extended Monadic Second-Order Logic

The *Extended Monadic Second-order* (EMS) logic [ALS91] captures a large class of graph-problems that have polynomial-time algorithms over partial k-trees.

Such an algorithm is modeled by a tree automaton to which certain machinery has been added enabling set cardinalities to be evaluated. The EMS logic is defined in the more general setting of weighted graphs, but this is not necessary for our purposes. An EMS formulation consists of a CMS predicate Φ (with a constant number of free set variables) and an *evaluation relation* Ψ—which is a logical predicate that enforces equality (and inequality) conditions on polynomial functions of the cardinalities of the free set variables. When we say that a CMS formulation encodes a graph decision problem, we mean that a partial k-tree G is a yes-instance iff the free set variables can be instantiated such that $G \models \Phi$ and Ψ is true.

It is not difficult to encode in EMS the problem of whether a graph G can be partitioned into *noninduced* subgraphs isomorphic to a fixed graph H. Suppose H has c maximal components $H_1, H_2, \ldots, H_c$; and let d_i $(1 \leq i \leq c)$ be the number of vertices in H_i. An EMS formulation for this problem uses free set variables $V_1, V_2, \ldots, V_c$, as well as set variables $E_1, E_2, \ldots, E_c$ that are quantified within Φ. Now, Φ can ensure that $V_1, V_2, \ldots, V_c$ is a partition of $V(G)$, and (for $1 \leq i \leq c$) that H_i is isomorphic to each maximal component of the subgraph with vertex set V_i and edge set $E_i \subseteq E(G)$. The evaluation relation Ψ can then stipulate that the value of $\frac{|V_i|}{d_i}$ is equal over $1 \leq i \leq c$. However, if each subgraph of the partition need be vertex-induced, a difficulty arises in ensuring that the components can be grouped together such that $H_i \not\sim_G H_j$ over $1 \leq i < j \leq c$. In Section 4 we will show how this can be ensured if G is a partial k-tree.

4 Deriving an EMS Formulation

In this section we show how PARTITION INTO FIXED ISOMORPHIC SUBGRAPHS can be encoded in EMS logic over partial k-trees. Such a partition is composed of a linear number of vertex subsets; but we will show that they can be grouped into a constant number of equivalence classes so that a (constant-length) EMS formulation can represent them.

Throughout this section, G is a partial k-tree on n vertices; and H is a pattern graph with c maximal components $H_1, H_2, \ldots, H_c$. We assume that G is a yes-instance of PARTITION INTO FIXED ISOMORPHIC SUBGRAPHS, and develop an EMS formulation to represent a partition $\mathcal{P}$ of $V(G)$ to satisfy the following:

$$\exists \mathcal{P} = \{V_1, V_2, \ldots, V_r\} \text{ such that: } \mathcal{P} \text{ is a partition of } V(G), \text{ and} \atop G_{[V_i]} \cong H \text{ for } 1 \leq i \leq r \tag{1}$$

Since the partition $\mathcal{P}$ consists of an unbounded number $r = \frac{n}{h}$ of sets (where $h = |V(H)|$), an EMS formulation cannot explicitly represent each of them. We will show, however, that the r copies of H can be grouped together into a constant number of subgraphs of G in which no pair of components corresponding to H_ℓ and $H_{\ell'}$ $(\ell \neq \ell')$ are adjacent. Thus, the components of each subgraph can be "mixed and matched" arbitrarily. Any pair $H_\ell, H_{\ell'}$ $(\ell \neq \ell')$ of isomorphic components are not considered to be equivalent.

Table 1. Partition of a partial k-tree G into induced copies of $H = H_1 \sqcup H_2 \sqcup \ldots \sqcup H_c$

There Exist ...
$\left. \begin{array}{l} S_i \sqsubseteq G \\ W_{i,j,h} \subseteq V(G) \end{array} \right\} \begin{array}{l} 1 \leq i \leq c^* \\ 1 \leq j \leq c' \\ 1 \leq h \leq c_j \end{array}$ (see text)

MS Formula (Φ)
<ul><li>$V(S_1), V(S_2), \ldots, V(S_{c^*})$ is a partition of $V(G)$.</li><li>For $1 \leq i \leq c^*$: each maximal component of S_i is isomorphic to $H_1, \ldots$ or H_c.</li><li>For $1 \leq i \leq c^*$ and $1 \leq j \leq c'$: $\bigcup_{h=1}^{c_j} W_{i,j,h}$ contains exactly one vertex of each maximal component of S_i that is isomorphic to H_j.</li><li>For $1 \leq i \leq c^*$: if C and C' are maximal components of S_i that are represented in distinct "counting sets" $(W_{i,j,h}, W_{i,j',h'})$, then $C \not\sim_G C'$.</li></ul>

Evaluation Relation (Ψ)
<ul><li>For $1 \leq i \leq c^*$: $\|W_{i,j,h}\|$ has the same value for all $1 \leq j \leq c'$; $1 \leq h \leq c_j$</li></ul>

Definition 6. A *$\mathcal{P}$-component* is a maximal component in the subgraph $G_{[V]}$ for any $V \in \mathcal{P}$. A $\mathcal{P}$-component is said to have color ℓ whenever it corresponds to a copy of component H_ℓ (for some $1 \leq \ell \leq c$).

Table 1 give a high-level description of the EMS formulation; details of the translation into EMS can be inferred from Arnborg *et al.* [ALS91]. Without loss of generality, assume that $H_1, H_2, \ldots, H_{c'}$ are pairwise non-isomorphic, and that each other maximal component is isomorphic to $H_1, H_2, \ldots$ or $H_{c'}$. Suppose c_j maximal components of H are isomorphic to H_j (for $1 \leq j \leq c'$). The EMS formulation provides a constant number c^* of subgraphs $S_i \sqsubseteq G$; and each is associated with c "counting sets" $W_{i,j,h}$ ($1 \leq j \leq c'$; $1 \leq h \leq c_j$) which ensure that S_i contains the same number of each $\mathcal{P}$-component. The union $\bigcup_{h=1}^{c_j} W_{i,j,h}$ contains a "witness" for each $\mathcal{P}$-component in S_i that is isomorphic to H_j.

For each $V \in \mathcal{P}$, the subgraph $G_{[V]}$ consists of c differently-colored $\mathcal{P}$-components. In total, there are rc $\mathcal{P}$-components, r of each color. We will delete, from G, the vertices of a constant number of the sets in $\mathcal{P}$, resulting in a graph G' with "small" components. The subgraph of G induced by each deleted set may then be represented in a separate subgraph S_i of the EMS formulation. From among the remaining $\mathcal{P}$-components (in G'), an induced subgraph isomorphic to H is obtained by choosing *any* set of c $\mathcal{P}$-components with pairwise distinct colors from pairwise distinct components of G'.

Claim 7. *Suppose that G' contains a total of $r'c$ $\mathcal{P}$-components, and that each maximal component of G' contains at most $\lfloor \frac{r'}{c-1} \rfloor$ of them (for $c \geq 2$). It is possible to group the $\mathcal{P}$-components into $(c+1)!$ classes—each containing an equal number of $\mathcal{P}$-components of each color, such that no pair of differently-colored $\mathcal{P}$-components are adjacent.*

We will apply this claim after deleting the vertices of $(r-r')$ sets in $\mathcal{P}$, thereby breaking G into "small" components—none of which contains more than $\lfloor \frac{r'}{c-1} \rfloor$ $\mathcal{P}$-components. The claim then allows us to group the remaining $\mathcal{P}$-components into $(c+1)!$ equivalence classes.

Proposition 8. *Suppose G' is the subgraph of G induced by the vertices in some collection of (say n') $\mathcal{P}$-components. There exists a set $X \subseteq V(G)$, the union of $k+1$ or fewer sets in $\mathcal{P}$, such that $G'\backslash X$ consists of two disjoint partial k-trees, neither containing more than $\lfloor \frac{2n'}{3} \rfloor$ $\mathcal{P}$-components. We will say that the deletion of X is a* balanced cut *to G'.*

Proof. Let V' be a subset of $V(G')$ that contains exactly one vertex from each of the n' $\mathcal{P}$-components. By Lemma 2, there exists a set $Y \subseteq V(G')$ with cardinality $|Y| \le k+1$, such that $G'\backslash Y$ consists of two disjoint partial k-trees, neither containing more than $\lfloor \frac{2}{3}n' \rfloor$ vertices of V'. We choose the set X (to satisfy the proposition) as the union of the vertex sets of the $(k+1$ or fewer) sets in $\mathcal{P}$ that each contain one or more vertices of Y. □

Lemma 9. *For $\ell \in \mathbb{N}$, there exists a subset $X_\ell \subseteq V(G)$ for which*

C1 X_ℓ *is the union of $(k+1)(2^\ell - 1)$ or fewer of the sets in $\mathcal{P}$, and*
C2 $G_\ell = G\backslash X_\ell$ *consists of 2^ℓ disjoint partial k-trees, none of which contains more than $\lfloor (\frac{2}{3})^\ell rc \rfloor$ $\mathcal{P}$-components.*

Proof. Let $X_0 = \emptyset$; so $G\backslash X_0 = G$, and the lemma is satisfied for $\ell = 0$. For $\ell \ge 1$, let G_ℓ be obtained (inductively) by making a balanced cut (Prop. 8) to each of the 2^ℓ disjoint partial k-trees comprising $G_{\ell-1}$. For each such cut, we delete the vertices of $k+1$ or fewer sets in $\mathcal{P}$. So $G_\ell = G_{\ell-1}\backslash X$ where X is the union of $(k+1)2^\ell$ or fewer sets in $\mathcal{P}$. Inductively, $G_\ell = G_{\ell-1}\backslash X = G\backslash X_\ell$ where $X_\ell = X_{\ell-1} \cup X$ is the union of $(k+1)(2^\ell - 1)$ or fewer sets in $\mathcal{P}$ (hence **C1**). Furthermore, G_ℓ consists of $2 \cdot 2^{\ell-1} = 2^\ell$ disjoint partial k-trees, none with more than $\lfloor \frac{2n'}{3} \rfloor$ $\mathcal{P}$-components, where $n' = \lfloor (\frac{2}{3})^{\ell-1} rc \rfloor$ (hence **C2**). □

Lemma 10. *For $c \ge 2$, there is a constant c_k (dependent only on c and k) for which the following statement is true: There exists a subset $X \subseteq V(G)$, the union of $d \le c_k$ of the sets in $\mathcal{P}$, for which $G\backslash X$ has no component with more than $\frac{r-d}{c-1}$ $\mathcal{P}$-components.*

Proof. Let ℓ be a constant greater than $\lceil 2\log_{\frac{3}{2}} c \rceil$; so $c^2(\frac{2}{3})^\ell < 1$. Now, the set X_ℓ (of Lemma 9) is the union of some number $d \le (2^\ell - 1)(k+1)$ of the sets in $\mathcal{P}$; and no component of $G\backslash X_\ell$ contains more than $\lfloor (\frac{2}{3})^\ell rc \rfloor$ $\mathcal{P}$-components.

Since $c^2(\frac{2}{3})^\ell < 1$, there exists a constant c_k' (dependent only on c and k) for which the following holds whenever $r \ge c_k'$.

$$rc^2(\tfrac{2}{3})^\ell + 2^\ell(k+1) \le r$$
$$rc(\tfrac{2}{3})^\ell \le \frac{r-2^\ell(k+1)}{c} \le \frac{r-d}{c-1}$$

Therefore, the statement of lemma is satisfied by $X = X_\ell$, provided the constant c_k is chosen such that $c_k \ge \max\{c_k', (2^\ell - 1)(k+1)\}$. □

Theorem 11. *A partial k-tree G can be partitioned into subgraphs isomorphic to a pattern graph H if and only if the EMS formulation of Table 1 is satisfiable.*

Proof. Suppose the EMS formulation is satisfied by a partial k-tree G. Hence, each S_i $(1 \leq i \leq c^*)$ contains the same number of copies of each maximal component of H; and for $\ell \neq \ell'$, no copy of H_ℓ is adjacent to any copy of $H_{\ell'}$. Therefore, formulation (1) can be satisfied.

Conversely, suppose that formulation (1) is satisfied by a partial k-tree G. If $c = 1$, the EMS formulation is satisfied by letting S_1 contain all r copies of H, and letting each other S_i be the null graph. Otherwise, by Lemma 10, there exists a set X, the union of $d \leq c_k$ sets in $\mathcal{P}$, such that $G \backslash X$ contains $(r - d)c$ $\mathcal{P}$-components; and no component of $G \backslash X$ contains more than $\frac{r-d}{c-1}$ of them. By Claim 7, the $\mathcal{P}$-components of $G \backslash X$ can be represented with $(c + 1)!$ of the subgraphs S_i of the EMS formulation. Hence, at most $c^* = c_k + (c+1)!$ subgraphs S_i are required. The "counting sets" $W_{i,j,h}$ ensure that the components of H are properly distributed into these subgraphs. □

5   CO-DOMATIC NUMBER

In this section we describe how EMS logic can encode whether the vertices of a partial k-tree may be partitioned into some number of *co-dominating sets*.

Definition 12. *A co-dominating set of a graph G is a vertex subset $V' \subseteq V(G)$ such that if $v \in V(G) - V'$, then there exists a vertex in V' that is not adjacent to v. The co-domatic number of G is the maximum number of co-dominating sets into which $V(G)$ can be partitioned.*

Since EMS logic is defined within the framework of decision problems, a number r must be fixed by the problem description "Is the co-domatic number at least r?" However, only minor modifications are needed to convert the resulting decision algorithm into an optimization algorithm that finds the domatic number.

If V' is a co-dominating set of a graph G, but no proper subset of V' is, then we say that V' is a *minimal* co-dominating set of G. It is not hard to show

Lemma 13. *A minimal co-dominating set of a partial k-tree has $O(k)$ vertices.*

Theorem 14. *An EMS formulation can encode the problem of whether the vertex set of a partial k-tree can be partitioned into r co-dominating sets.*

Proof sketch. Let G be a partial k-tree. If the vertex set of G can be partitioned into r co-dominating sets, then (by Lemma 13) G has r disjoint co-dominating sets of $O(k)$ cardinality. We ignore the "left-over" vertices, and group these sets into $O(k)$ disjoint collections containing sets with some fixed cardinality. An EMS formulation can represent each such collection—using the same approach as was used to represent the $\mathcal{P}$-components in Section 4—as follows:

Let G' be the subgraph of G induced by the union of the co-dominating sets with fixed cardinality c; and let the vertices of each such set be arbitrarily assigned to c distinct color classes. Using Lemma 2, we find a set $X \subseteq V(G)$ with $O(1)$ cardinality such that each component of $G \backslash X$ contains only a "small" number of vertices of G'. If two vertices of $G' \backslash X$ are chosen from distinct components, then no vertex of $G \backslash X$ is adjacent to both of them. Furthermore, the vertices of $G' \backslash X$ can be partitioned into a constant number of families in which all vertices are adjacent to the same subset of X. Therefore, using a variation of Claim 7, we can represent the dominating sets of $G' \backslash X$ with a constant number of equivalence classes. □

6 Conclusion

We have described a general technique to encode a family of graph problems in EMS logic over partial k-trees. Such an encoding is equivalent to a polynomial-time algorithm [ALS91]. The problems amenable to this technique have solutions consisting of a (possibly unbounded) number of disjoint vertex sets—each with $O(1)$ cardinality, and each satisfying certain problem-specific conditions. This sort of problem can be encoded using our technique if these vertex sets can be partitioned into a constant number of equivalence classes of the following type: each vertex set in a given class induces the same number c of (not necessarily maximal) components $H_1, H_2, \ldots, H_c$, such that any choice of c components (one of each type) satisfies the problem-specific conditions.

PARTITION INTO FIXED ISOMORPHIC SUBGRAPHS has problem-specific conditions requiring that each copy of H_i be isomorphic to a fixed graph, and that no copy of H_i be adjacent to any copy of H_j (for $i \neq j$). These are very local conditions: only the vertices of $H_1 \sqcup H_2 \sqcup \ldots \sqcup H_c$ need be examined. CO-DOMATIC NUMBER requires that each H_i consist of a single vertex, such that the c vertices of $H_1 \sqcup H_2 \sqcup \ldots \sqcup H_c$ are not all adjacent to a common vertex of the underlying graph. Again, these conditions are local: it is only necessary to examine the vertices adjacent to the c vertices. Locality is an essential feature of the problems amenable to the technique of this paper. Since the components of each equivalence class may be recombined in an arbitrary way, we cannot force an unbounded number of distinct pairs H_i, H_j to interact in some way unless they are "close together" in the underlying graph. Indeed, if long-range interactions are necessary between different components in each set, then a bounded-size formulation will not be able to represent a solution.

Note that the "ordinary" MS logic, or the CMS logic, can be used to encode problems of this sort if each vertex set of the solution induces a connected subgraph: This encoding would then provide a linear-time algorithm over partial k-trees. The technique of this paper is of interest when disconnected subgraphs are induced by each vertex set, rendering CMS inefficacious.

References

[ALS91] S. Arnborg, J. Lagergren, and D. Seese. Easy problems for tree decomposable graphs. *J. Algorithms*, 12:308–340, 1991.

[Arn85] S. Arnborg. Efficient algorithms for combinatorial problems on graphs with bounded decomposability. *BIT*, 25:2-33, 1985.

[BJ93] H.L. Bodlaender and K. Jansen. On the complexity of scheduling incompatible jobs with unit-times. In *Lecture Notes in Computer Science (Proc. 18th MFCS)*, volume 711, pages 291-300. Springer-Verlag, 1993.

[BLW87] M.W. Bern, E.L. Lawler, and A.L. Wong. Linear-time computation of optimal subgraphs of decomposable graphs. *J. Algorithms*, 8:216-235, 1987.

[Bod88] H.L. Bodlaender. Dynamic programming on graphs with bounded treewidth. In *Lecture Notes in Computer Science (Proc. 15th ICALP)*, volume 317, pages 105-119. Springer-Verlag, 1988.

[Bod93] H.L. Bodlaender. A linear time algorithm for finding tree-decompositions of small treewidth. In *Proc. 25th STOC*, pages 226-234, 1993.

[BPT92] R.B. Borie, R.G. Parker, and C.A. Tovey. Automatic generation of linear-time algorithms from predicate calculus descriptions of problems on recursively constructed graph families. *Algorithmica*, 7:555-581, 1992.

[Cou90a] B. Courcelle. Graph rewriting: an algebraic and logic approach. In J. van Leeuwen, editor, *Handbook of Theoretical Computer Science*, volume B, pages 193-242. Elsevier, Amsterdam, 1990.

[Cou90b] B. Courcelle. The monadic second-order logic of graphs. I. Recognizable sets of finite graphs. *Information and Computation*, 85:12-75, 1990.

[Cou91] B. Courcelle. The monadic second-order logic of graphs. V. On closing the gap between definability and recognizability. *Theoret. Comput. Sci.*, 80:153-202, 1991.

[GJ79] M.R. Garey and D.S. Johnson. *Computers and Intractability: A Guide to the Theory of NP-Completeness*. W.H. Freeman and Company, New York, 1979.

[GS84] F. Gécseg and M. Steinby. *Tree Automata*. Akadémiai Kiadó, Budapest, 1984.

[HU79] J.E. Hopcroft and J.D. Ullman. *Introduction to Automata Theory, Languages, and Computation*. Addison-Wesley, 1979.

[Kal96] D. Kaller. Definability equals recognizability of partial 3-trees, 1996. To appear.

[KGS95a] D. Kaller, A. Gupta, and T. Shermer. The χ_t-coloring problem. In *Lecture Notes in Computer Science (Proc. 12th STACS)*, volume 900, pages 409-420. Springer-Verlag, 1995.

[KGS95b] D. Kaller, A. Gupta, and T. Shermer. Regular-factors in the complements of partial k-trees. In *Lecture Notes in Computer Science (Proc. 4th WADS)*, volume 955, pages 403-414. Springer-Verlag, 1995.

[KH78] D.G. Kirkpatrick and P. Hell. On the complexity of a generalized matching problem. In *Proc. 10th STOC*, pages 240-245, 1978.

[Lag94] J. Lagergren, October 1994. Personal communication.

[MP94] S. Mahajan and J.G. Peters. Regularity and locality in k-terminal graphs. *Disc. Appl. Math.*, 54:229-250, 1994.

[RS86] N. Robertson and P.D. Seymour. Graph minors. II. Algorithmic aspects of tree-width. *J. Algorithms*, 7:309-322, 1986.

[Tho90] W. Thomas. Automata on infinite objects. In J. van Leeuwen, editor, *Handbook of Theoretical Computer Science*, volume B, pages 133-191. Elsevier, Amsterdam, 1990.

[WW89] E. Wanke and M. Wiegers. Undecidability of the bandwidth problem on linear graph languages. *Inform. Process. Lett.*, 33:193-197, 1989.

Making an Arbitrary Filled Graph Minimal by Removing Fill Edges *

Jean R. S. Blair[1] and Pinar Heggernes[2] and Jan Arne Telle[2]

[1] United States Military Academy, West Point, NY
[2] Department of Informatics, University of Bergen, Norway

Abstract. We consider the problem of removing fill edges from a filled graph G' to get a minimal chordal supergraph M of the original graph G; thus $G \subseteq M \subseteq G'$. We show that a greedy strategy can be applied if fill edges are processed for removal in the reverse order of their introduction. For a filled graph with f fill edges and e original edges, we give a simple $O(f(e + f))$ algorithm which solves the problem and computes a corresponding minimal elimination ordering. We believe that in practice the runtime of our algorithm is usually better than the worst-case bound of $O(f(e + f))$.

1 Introduction

For any graph G and an ordering α of its vertices, there is an associated set of edges called the *fill* that, when added to G, results in a chordal graph $(G; \alpha)$.[3] The goal of finding orderings of the vertices that produce a small fill has been studied by researchers in many areas of computer science (*e.g.*, data-base management systems [2, 14], knowledge-based systems [5, 7], computer vision [3] and the solution of sparse symmetric systems of linear equations [8, 9, 10, 11, 12]) and remains an important problem.

In a central 1976 paper Rose, Tarjan and Lueker [13] gave an algorithm which finds a *minimal* fill of a graph G in $O(ne)$ time, where n and e are respectively the number of vertices and edges in G. To date, this algorithm, which is called LEX-M, has the best known running time for finding a minimal chordal super-graph of an arbitrary graph. An efficient parallel algorithm for the same problem is given in [4]. Yannakakis showed in [15] that finding the *minimum* fill for an arbitrary graph is $\mathcal{NP}$-hard. Several heuristics have been proposed for finding elimination orderings producing small fill. The two most famous and practically useful methods are called *minimum degree* and *nested dissection* (see [6] for a survey). For graphs of bounded maximum degree, nested dissection based on near-optimal node separators gives fill which is within a ploylogarithmic factor of the minimum fill [1].

We consider the more restricted problem of, given a graph G and an arbitrary ordering α, finding a graph M that is both a minimal chordal supergraph of

---

* This research was supported in part by the Norwegian Research Council and was conducted while the first author was visiting the University of Bergen, Norway.
[3] All terms are formally defined in Section 2.

G, and a subgraph of the filled graph $(G; \alpha)$. We also find a related minimal ordering β so that $(G; \beta) = M$. Minimal orderings are desirable since any perfect elimination ordering of the resulting filled graph, when applied to the original graph, produces the same filled graph. In other words, if β is a minimal ordering of a graph G then for any perfect elimination ordering γ of $(G; \beta)$ we have $(G; \gamma) = (G; \beta)$. The problem we consider is motivated by the fact that the minimal orderings produced by the LEX-M algorithm (and other breadth-first-search-based algorithms) typically result in a large amount of fill relative to that produced by practical low-fill heuristic algorithms such as minimum degree and nested dissection, and by the fact that these heuristic algorithms usually produce non-minimal fill. So to get a minimal low fill ordering of a graph G, first find a non-minimal low fill ordering α produced by a heuristic algorithm, and then run our algorithm which removes redundant fill until the remaining fill is minimal.

The main contributions of this paper are two-fold: First, our Theorem 7 shows that by considering the fill edges in the reverse order to that in which they were introduced, each edge need only be considered as a candidate for removal once. This property is significant since, in general, the removal of a fill edge can both add to and delete from the set of remaining "removable edges." Second, using this result, we develop an $O(f(e + f))$ time algorithm that, given both G and α, will produce an ordering β such that the filled graph $(G; \beta)$ is minimal and is a subgraph of $(G; \alpha)$. Here, f and e are respectively the number of fill edges in $(G; \alpha)$ and the number of edges in G. Furthermore, the time complexity of our algorithm depends on structural properties of the filled graph and is in many cases better than the worst-case bound of $O(f(e + f))$.

The paper is organized as follows. Section 2 formally defines terms used in the paper. Section 3 characterizes redundant fill edges. The new algorithm and its proof of correctness are found in Section 4 with an analysis of the time complexity. Section 5 contains concluding remarks and some questions raised by our results.

2 Definitions and Notation

We start with some standard graph terminology. We consider undirected, simple graphs. For a graph G, the vertex and edge sets are denoted by respectively $V(G)$ and $E(G)$. $N_G(v)$ is the set of neighbors of v in G. A *path* from v_1 to v_k is a sequence of vertices $v_1, v_2, ..., v_k$ that are connected by the edges $v_1 v_2, v_2 v_3, ..., v_{k-1} v_k$. We also use $v_1 \rightarrow v_k$ to denote a path from v_1 to v_k. A *cycle* is a path whose first and last vertices are the same. An edge in G is called a *chord* of a cycle if it joins two nonconsecutive vertices on the cycle. A graph is *chordal* if every cycle of length at least four has a chord. For a set S of vertices in G, the subgraph of G induced by S is denoted by $G[S]$. The graph $G \setminus S$ is the graph $G[V(G) \setminus S]$. For a set K of edges in G, the graph $G \setminus K$ is the result of removing the edges in K from G. A *supergraph* of G is a graph which contains G as a subgraph.

For a graph G with $|V(G)| = n$, an *elimination ordering* of G is a bijection

$\alpha : V(G) \leftrightarrow \{1, 2, ..., n\}$. For ease of presentation, we will also refer to α as a sequence, $\alpha = v_1, v_2, ..., v_n = \alpha^{-1}(1), \alpha^{-1}(2), ..., \alpha^{-1}(n)$. Thus v_i denotes the vertex v such that $\alpha(v) = i$.

Associated with α is a sequence of supergraphs of G, defined as follows. $G_0 = G$ and for $1 \leq i \leq n$, G_i is the graph obtained by adding edges to G_{i-1} so that all vertices in $N_{G_{i-1}}(v_i) \cap \{v_{i+1}, ...v_n\}$ are pairwise adjacent. This step is called the *elimination* of vertex v_i, and the whole process of obtaining G_n from G is called the *elimination process*. Note that vertices are not removed from the graph: $V(G) = V(G_i)$, $1 \leq i \leq n$. The new edges added are called *fill edges*, and $F_i = E(G_i) \setminus E(G_{i-1})$ is the set of fill edges created by the elimination of v_i. We use C_i to denote the resulting clique induced by v_i and its higher numbered neighbors. The graph G_n is the *filled graph* of G for elimination ordering α. We also use $(G; \alpha)$ to denote the filled graph G_n. All filled graphs are chordal.

An elimination ordering α on G is *minimal* if the resulting $(G; \alpha)$ is a *minimal chordal* supergraph of G, i.e., no strict subgraph of $(G; \alpha)$ containing G is chordal, equivalently for no ordering γ is $(G; \gamma)$ a strict subgraph of $(G; \alpha)$. Then $(G; \alpha)$ is also referred to as a *minimal filled graph* of G.

A vertex is *simplicial* in a graph G if its neighbors induce a clique. Note that v_i is simplicial in $G_{i-1}[\{v_i, ..., v_n\}]$ if and only if $F_i = \emptyset$. An elimination ordering on G is *perfect* if no fill edges are created, that is, if $F_i = \emptyset$ for $1 \leq i \leq n$. Chordal graphs are exactly the class of graphs that have perfect elimination orderings.

3 Greedy Removal of Redundant Fill Edges

In this section we develop some properties of fill edges related to the order of their introduction, with the goal of finding an algorithm to remove redundant fill edges. The following result (Lemma 4 of [13]) gives another characterization of fill edges.

Lemma 1. *[13] Let G be a graph and α an elimination ordering of its vertices. Then uv is an edge of $(G; \alpha)$ if and only if $uv \in E(G)$ or there exists a path $u = u_0, u_1, ..., u_{k+1} = v$ in G such that for each $1 \leq i \leq k$ we have $\alpha(u_i) < \min\{\alpha(u), \alpha(v)\}$.*

The same paper also gives (Theorem 2 of [13]) an alternative characterization of minimal elimination orderings.

Theorem 2. *[13] Let G be a graph and α an elimination ordering of its vertices. Then α is a minimal elimination ordering if and only if each fill edge is the unique chord of a 4-cycle in $(G; \alpha)$.*

We will need the following easy corollary.

Corollary 3. *Let G be a graph and $\alpha = v_1, ..., v_n$ be an elimination ordering of its vertices. If a fill edge $uv \in F_i$, created by elimination of v_i, is the unique chord of a 4-cycle in $(G; \alpha)$ then uv is the unique chord of a 4-cycle u, v_i, v, x, u in $(G; \alpha)$ with $\alpha(x) > i$, $\alpha(u) > i$ and $\alpha(v) > i$.*

Proof. Let u, y, v, x, u be a 4-cycle of $(G; \alpha)$ in which uv is the only chord. Since uv is created by elimination of v_i we must have $\alpha(u) > i$, $\alpha(v) > i$, $\alpha(y) \geq i$ and $\alpha(x) \geq i$. If either $y = v_i$ or $x = v_i$ we are done. If this is not the case, note that either yv_i or xv_i is not an edge of $(G; \alpha)$ since otherwise we would have xy a fill edge. As u and v are both neighbors of v_i, we can find a 4-cycle as stated in the corollary. $\square$

Observe that Corollary 3 and Theorem 2 can be used to easily detect if a given elimination ordering is minimal.

Definition 4. Let G' be a chordal supergraph of a graph G. A *candidate* edge is an edge $uv \in E(G') \setminus E(G)$ which is not the unique chord of any 4-cycle in G'.

Since removing a single edge from a chordal graph results in either a chordal graph or a graph with a chordless 4-cycle, it is clear that removing any candidate edge cannot destroy chordality. The following result is implicit in [13].

Proposition 5. *[13] A non-minimal chordal supergraph G' of a graph G has at least one candidate edge. Any candidate edge can be removed without destroying chordality.*

This result immediately leads to an algorithm for finding a minimal filled graph by removing fill edges from a filled graph: repeatedly remove candidate edges until no candidate edges remain. Unfortunately, the set of candidate edges changes as edges are removed, with new candidate edges being introduced and old candidate edges ceasing to be candidates. For a very simple example, consider the path on 4 vertices P_4 with edges ab, bc, cd and elimination order b, c, d, a creating the fill $F_1 = \{ac\}$ and $F_2 = \{ad\}$. The fill edge ac is not a candidate for removal but ad is. However, after removing ad the fill edge ac becomes a candidate for removal.

This non-monotonicity property of the set of candidate edges seems to be the main obstacle in obtaining an efficient implementation of this algorithm. As we show below, we can partially avoid this by processing fill edges in the reverse fill order of that in which they were introduced. In particular, the following strategy will produce a minimal chordal supergraph:

for $i = n$ **downto** 1 **do**
    while there is a candidate edge in F_i **do** remove it from the filled graph;

We first give a lemma and then a theorem that will provide the basis for the correctness of this strategy.

Lemma 6. *Let $\alpha = v_1, ..., v_n$ be an elimination order of a graph G. Let M_i be both a subgraph of G_n and a minimal chordal supergraph of G_{i-1}. Then M_i has a perfect elimination ordering $\gamma = w_1, w_2, ..., w_n$ with $(G; \gamma) = M_i$ and and $v_k = w_k$ for all $k = 1, ..., i-1$.*

Proof. Since both G_{i-1} and G_n are associated with $\alpha = v_1, ..., v_n$, we have for all $k = 1, ..., i-1$ the vertex v_k simplicial in both the graphs $G_{i-1}[\{v_k, v_{k+1}, ..., v_n\}]$ and $G_n[\{v_k, v_{k+1}, ..., v_n\}]$. Note also that v_k has the same neighbors in both these graphs.

Hence v_k is also simplicial in M_i since M_i is a supergraph of G_{i-1} and a subgraph of G_n. For chordal graphs it is well-known that the elimination order resulting from repeatedly eliminating a vertex which is simplicial in the graph induced by non-eliminated vertices, is a perfect elimination ordering. We can therefore find a perfect elimination ordering γ of M_i with $\gamma = w_1, ..., w_n$ and $v_k = w_k$ for $k = 1, ..., i-1$.

We now show that $(G; \gamma) = M_i$. Eliminating $v_1, ..., v_{i-1}$ in this order in G or G_{i-1} will in either case give us G_{i-1}. Since M_i is a minimal chordal supergraph of G_{i-1} we must have $(G_{i-1}; \gamma) = M_i$. Hence, $(G; \gamma) = M_i$ since the initial sequence of γ is $v_1, ..., v_{i-1}$. □

We can now state the main theorem of this section.

Theorem 7. *Let $\alpha = v_1, ..., v_n$ be an elimination order of a graph G. Let M_i be both a subgraph of $(G; \alpha)$ and a minimal chordal supergraph of G_{i-1}. For any graph M which is both a subgraph of M_i and a chordal supergraph of G, we have $E(M_i) \setminus E(G_{i-1}) \subseteq E(M)$.*

Proof. Observe that $G \subseteq G_{i-1} \subseteq M_i \subseteq (G; \alpha)$ and $G \subseteq M \subseteq M_i$. By Lemma 6, we know that M_i has a perfect elimination ordering $\gamma = w_1, w_2, ..., w_n$ with $v_k = w_k$ for all $k = 1, ..., i-1$ and we also know that $(G_{i-1}; \gamma) = M_i$. The statement in the theorem says that if the edge uv of M_i is a fill edge created, in the process giving $(G_{i-1}; \gamma) = M_i$ from G_{i-1}, by the elimination of some w_j with $i \le j \le n$, then uv must be an edge of M.

We prove this by contradiction. Assume that uv is the latest introduced fill edge violating the condition. In other words, uv is created in the process giving $(G_{i-1}; \gamma) = M_i$ by $w = w_j$, uv is not an edge of M, and every other fill edge of this elimination process created by any w_k with $k > j$ is an edge of M. Since M_i is a minimal chordal supergraph of G_{i-1}, and uv is a fill edge created by w, by Theorem 2 and Corollary 3 there must exist a vertex x which in M_i is not adjacent to w but is adjacent to both u and v, with $\gamma(u) > \gamma(w)$, $\gamma(v) > \gamma(w)$ and $\gamma(x) > \gamma(w)$.

We will show that there exists, in $M \subseteq M_i$, a path from w to x whose internal vertices have γ-order less than w and x. We will thereby arrive at a contradiction since, with γ being a perfect elimination ordering of M_i, such a path would imply, by Lemma 1, that wx is an edge of M_i. But w and x are not adjacent in M_i.

Since neither uv nor wx are edges in the chordal graph M, at least one of wu, ux, xv and vw is not an edge of M. But M is a supergraph of G so any of wu, ux, xv and vw which is not an edge of M must be a fill edge in the elimination process $(G; \gamma)$ giving M_i. By assumption, uv is the latest fill edge in this elimination process which is not in M, so any of wu, ux, xv and vw which is not an edge of M, must be a fill edge of M_i created earlier than uv. (Note it could not be created at the same time as uv.) Therefore, by Lemma 1 there must exist paths $w \to u, u \to x, x \to v$, and $v \to w$ in $G \subseteq M$ whose internal vertices (if any) are earlier in the γ-order than w and thus also earlier than u, x, v. Consider the combined paths $u \to w \to v$ and $u \to x \to v$. If these two paths intersect in an internal vertex y then we find a path $w \to y \to x$ giving the desired contradiction. Otherwise, consider the shortest path $u \to w' \to v$ in M from u to v using only vertices on the $u \to w \to v$ path and the shortest path $u \to x' \to v$ in M from u to v using only vertices on the $u \to x \to v$ path. These paths must have an internal vertex since uv is not an edge of M, and the vertices on these paths therefore induce a subgraph of M containing a k-cycle with $k \geq 4$. Since M is chordal, there is a chord on this cycle and this chord must connect an internal vertex y' in $u \to x' \to v$ with an internal vertex y'' in $u \to w' \to v$. But then we find a path $w \to y' \to y'' \to x$ giving the desired contradiction. (Note that this argument allows for $w = y'$ or $x = y''$.) $\square$

4 The Algorithm

In this section, we develop an algorithm which given a graph G and an elimination ordering α of G, finds a graph M which is both a minimal chordal supergraph of G and also a subgraph of $(G; \alpha)$.

After computing $G_n \equiv (G; \alpha)$, and finding C_i and F_i for $i = 1, ..., n$ from G_n in a straightforward manner, our algorithm proceeds as follows: The algorithm has n iterations. Initially, we set $M = G_n$. Starting from $i = n$ and going backwards, at each iteration i, redundant fill edges in F_i introduced by the elimination of v_i are removed. By Theorem 7, we know that the remaining edges of F_i need not be considered for removal at later iterations. The algorithm has n iterations for simplicity, but actually $n - 3$ would suffice since F_n and F_{n-1} are empty and F_{n-2} can always be removed.

The full algorithm is given in Figure 1. The subroutine that checks an edge $uv \in F_i$ for its candidacy for removal is called CandidateEdge, and is based on Corollary 3. The subroutine LEX-M is used to decide which of the candidate edges in F_i can be removed and which must stay to preserve chordality. W_i is the subgraph of C_i on which we run LEX-M to find out which edges in $Candidate(i)$ are necessary. The original LEX-M was introduced by Rose, Tarjan and Lueker in [13], and finds an elimination ordering resulting in a minimal chordal supergraph of a given graph. Our version of LEX-M(W_i) returns the set $KeepFill(i) \subseteq Candidate(i)$ of fill edges whose addition to W_i produces a minimal chordal supergraph of W_i. Note that $W_i \cup Candidate(i)$, if nonempty, is a clique and a subgraph of C_i.

Since the resulting graph M is a minimal chordal supergraph of G, every perfect elimination ordering β of M gives $(G; \beta) = M$. A linear-time algorithm for finding a perfect elimination ordering of a chordal graph is given in [13] and is called LEX-P. Figure 2 illustrates how the algorithm processes a graph on 7 edges, with details of the calls of LEX-M in Figure 3. We first prove correctness of the algorithm and then consider its time complexity.

Algorithm MinimalChordal (G, α);
Input: A graph G and an elimination ordering $\alpha = v_1, ..., v_n$ of G.
Output: 1. A chordal graph M which is both a minimal chordal supergraph of G
and a subgraph of the filled graph $(G; \alpha)$.
2. A minimal elimination order β of G s.t. M is the filled graph $(G; \beta)$.
begin
    Find $(G; \alpha)$ and C_i, F_i for $i = 1, 2, ..., n$;
    $M = (G; \alpha)$;
    for $i = n$ **downto** 1 **do**
        $Candidate(i) = \emptyset$;
        $Incident(i) = \emptyset$;
        for all edges $uv \in F_i$ **do**
            if CandidateEdge(uv, i, M) **then**
                $Candidate(i) = Candidate(i) \cup \{uv\}$;
                $Incident(i) = Incident(i) \cup \{u, v\}$;
            end-if;
        if $Candidate(i) \neq \emptyset$ **then**
            $W_i = C_i[Incident(i)] \setminus Candidate(i)$;
            $KeepFill(i) = $ LEX-M(W_i);
            $M = M \setminus (Candidate(i) \setminus KeepFill(i))$;
        end-if;
    end-for;
    return M and $\beta = $ LEX-P(M);
end;

Function CandidateEdge(uv, i, M): **boolean**;
Input: An edge $uv \in F_i$ and the graph M.
Output: Returns **true** if uv is a candidate to be removed from M, **false** o.w.
begin
    cand $=$ **true**;
    for each neighbor x of u **do**
        if $\alpha(x) > i$ and $xv \in E(M)$ and $xv_i \notin E(M)$ **then**
            cand $=$ **false**;
    return cand;
end;

Fig. 1. Algorithm MinimalChordal and Function CandidateEdge.

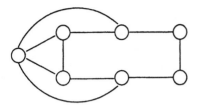

1. The original graph G.

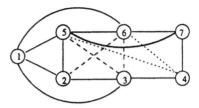

2. The filled graph of G resulting from the shown elimination ordering. The fill edges introduced by vertices 1, 3 and 4 are drawn with respectively dashed, dotted and thick lines.

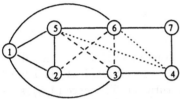

3. After removal of fill introduced by vertex 4. The edge (5,7) was a candidate edge and was removed by LEX-M.

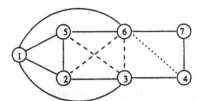

4. After removal of fill introduced by vertex 3. The edge (4,5) was a candidate edge and was removed by LEX-M, whereas (4,6) was not a candidate edge since (6,7) and (4,7) are edges, and (3,7) is not an edge.

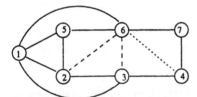

5. After removal of fill introduced by vertex 1. Edges (2,6) and (3,5) were candidate edges, whereas (3,6) was not a candidate edge since (6,4) and (3,4) are edges and (2,4) is not. One of the candidate edges can be removed by LEX-M, and (3,5) was chosen.

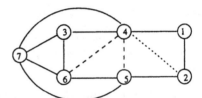

6. A perfect elimination ordering on the resulting minimal chordal supergraph of G.

Fig. 2. An example illustrating the algorithm. The calls of LEX-M in Steps 4 and 5 are shown in detail in Figure 3.

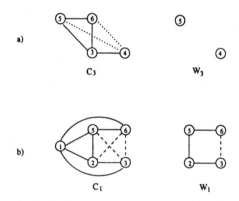

Fig. 3. Steps 4 and 5 of the previous example (Figure 2) shown in detail. a) $Candidate(3) = \{(4,5)\}$, and $Incident(3) = \{4,5\}$. The subgraph W_3 is defined as $C_3[Incident(3)] \setminus Candidate(3)$. LEX-M($W_3$) returns no fill, hence $(4,5)$ is removed from M. b) $Candidate(1) = \{(2,6),(3,5)\}$, and $Incident(1) = \{2,3,5,6\}$. LEX-M($W_1$) returns $(2,6)$ as fill, thus only $(3,5)$ can be removed from M as redundant fill.

Theorem 8. *Algorithm MinimalChordal on input G and $\alpha = v_1, ..., v_n$ finds a graph M which is both a minimal chordal supergraph of G and a subgraph of $(G;\alpha)$.*

Proof. Denote the graph M at the beginning of iteration i of the main loop of the algorithm by M_{i+1}, and at the end of iteration i by M_i. Since $M_i \subseteq M_{i+1}$ and M_{n+1} is initialized to $G_n \equiv (G;\alpha)$ it is clear that each M_i is a subgraph of $(G;\alpha)$. In addition, the algorithm has the loop invariant: "The graph M_i is a minimal chordal supergraph of G_{i-1}." We show this by reverse induction on i from $n+1$ to 1. The loop invariant is clearly true initially for the graph $M_{n+1} = G_n$. The edges $E(M_{i+1})$ are of four types:

(1) edges belonging to the original graph G.

(2) fill edges that were introduced before the elimination of v_i which will be considered for removal at later iterations.

(3) fill edges that were introduced after the elimination of v_i which have not been removed at earlier iterations.

(4) fill edges belonging to F_i.

The graphs G_i and G_{i-1} both contain all the edges of types 1 and 2, so these edges must belong to any chordal supergraph of G_{i-1}. Since M_{i+1} is a subgraph of G_n and a minimal chordal supergraph of G_i we know by Theorem 7 that no edges of Type 3 can be removed from M_{i+1} and still give a chordal supergraph of $G \subseteq G_{i-1}$.

Hence, we need only show that (A) M_i is chordal and that (B) any edge uv of F_i which remains in M_i is not a candidate for removal. Consider Case (B) first. By Theorem 2 it suffices to show that any such edge uv is the only chord of a 4-cycle in M_i. There are two cases: either (B.1) $uv \in Candidate(i)$ or (B.2) not.

(B.1) At the beginning of iteration i, the neighbors among $\{v_{i+1}, ..., v_n\}$ in M_{i+1} of vertex v_i induce a clique C_i, and the fill edges F_i are all contained in this clique. The edges in F_i that are candidates for removal are identified as $Candidate(i)$, and the vertices which are incident to at least one candidate edge, are stored in $Incident(i)$. We set W_i to be the subgraph of C_i induced by the vertices in $Incident(i)$ minus the edges in $Candidate(i)$. Candidate edges of F_i may be removed in the call of LEX-M(W_i), which gives us a set $KeepFill(i) \subseteq Candidate(i)$ of fill edges that when added to W_i gives a minimal chordal supergraph of W_i. The edges in $Candidate(i) \setminus KeepFill(i)$ are then removed from M_{i+1} to give us M_i. An edge $uv \in KeepFill(i)$ is guaranteed, by the correctness of algorithm LEX-M and Theorem 2, to be a unique chord of a 4-cycle in the graph $W_i \cup KeepFill(i)$ and therefore also in M_i, since $W_i \cup KeepFill(i)$ is an induced subgraph of M_i.

(B.2) If uv is found not to be a candidate in the call CandidateEdge(uv, i, M_{i+1}) then it is because there exists a vertex x which in M_{i+1} is a neighbor of both u and v but is not a neighbor of v_i. Note that the 4-cycle v_i, u, x, v, v_i contains only edges of Type 1, 2 or 3 and uv is therefore a unique chord of this 4-cycle also in M_i.

(A) It remains to show that M_i is chordal, which we do by contradiction. Let S be the vertices on a shortest chordless cycle of length at least 4 of M_i. We know that there must exist at least two vertices a, c in S such that $ac \in Candidate(i) \setminus KeepFill(i)$, since $M_{i+1} = M_i \cup (Candidate(i) \setminus KeepFill(i))$ is chordal. Also S must contain at least one vertex $s \notin V(C_i)$ since the graph $M_i[V(C_i)]$ is chordal ($M_i[V(C_i)]$ contains the minimal chordal supergraph of W_i computed by LEX-M and the vertices in $V(C_i) \setminus Incident(i)$ which are incident to every other vertex in $V(C_i)$.) Moreover, every vertex $x \in S$ must have $\alpha(x) \geq i$ since M_i contains all fill edges $F_1, ..., F_{i-1}$, and the cycle induced by S contains no chords. We can therefore find a path $a, b_1, ..., b_k, c$ in $M_i[S]$ with a and c in $V(C_i)$ and $ac \in Candidate(i) \setminus KeepFill(i)$ and $b_j, 1 \leq j \leq k$ not in $V(C_i)$ and $k \geq 1$. But then we have $a, b_1, ..., b_k, c, v_i, a$ inducing a chordless $k+3$-cycle in M_{i+1}, since none of b_j is in $V(C_i)$, contradicting the chordality of the graph M_{i+1}.

The loop invariant therefore holds as claimed. Note that this establishes correctness of the algorithm as upon termination the returned graph M_1 is both a minimal chordal supergraph of $G_0 = G$ and a subgraph of $G_n \equiv (G; \alpha)$. $\square$

Theorem 9. *Let $\alpha = v_1, v_2, ..., v_n$ be an elimination ordering of a connected graph G, with $n = |V(G)|$, $e = |E(G)|$ and $f = \sum_{i=1}^{n} |F_i|$. The time complexity of Algorithm MinimalChordal(G, α) is $O(f(e+f))$.*

Proof. Computing G_n (see [14]) and the call of LEX-P (see [13]) both take time linear in the size of the filled graph. From G_n, the sets F_i and C_i can be computed in time $O(nf)$ by simply examining every fill edge for every vertex. The algorithm has n iterations. At each iteration i, CandidateEdge is called $|F_i|$ times, and LEX-M is called once. The time complexity of CandidateEdge(uv, i, M) is $O(|N_G(u)|) = O(n)$. The time complexity of LEX-M(W_i) is $O(|V(W_i)||E(W_i)|)$, (see [13]). Thus for the whole algorithm, we get:

$$O\left(\sum_{i=1}^{n}(|V(W_i)||E(W_i)| + |F_i|n)\right)$$

By the definition of W_i, $|V(W_i)| = |Incident(i)| \leq 2|F_i|$. Clearly, $|E(W_i)| \leq (e+f)$. Thus, the time complexity of LEX-M(W_i) becomes $O(|F_i|(e+f))$. Since all the F_i are disjoint, $\sum_{i=1}^{n}|F_i|n = O(fn)$, and $\sum_{i=1}^{n}|F_i|(e+f) = O(f(e+f))$. Since G is connected, $n \leq (e+f)$, and the overall time complexity is $O(f(e+f))$ □

We would like to emphasize that the time complexity $O(f(e+f))$ is usually an overestimate and the sum in the proof of Theorem 9 is often less than this bound. A brief discussion about this is included in the next concluding section.

5 Conclusion

As mentioned in the Introduction, minimal low fill orderings are desirable, but minimal fill is not necessarily low fill. Practical algorithms like minimum degree and nested dissection usually produce low fill orderings, but not minimal fill orderings. Therefore we assumed a filled graph (with low fill) already given and considered the problem of removing fill edges to produce a minimal filled graph.

We have given a strategy to remove candidate fill edges so that each fill edge is checked for candidacy exactly once, avoiding backtracking. The time complexity of our algorithm is dependent on the number of fill edges we start with. In some cases this number is already low, in other cases it is high and our algorithm may remove many redundant fill edges. The upper bound given on the time complexity is met only if the subgraphs $W_1, W_2, ..., W_n$ overlap heavily so that the calls of LEX-M involve some large part of the graph several times. However, from examples we have studied it seems that these subgraphs usually do not overlap very much. In the example of Figure 3 we see that the subgraphs W_i do not overlap on edges at all.

From the results given in this paper the following questions arise:

1. Can the time complexity of our algorithm be improved if we assume that the given elimination ordering α was produced by the minimum degree algorithm? What if α was produced by the nested dissection algorithm?
2. Can the time complexity of our algorithm be expressed as a function of the number of fill edges removed?
3. Does our algorithm have an implementation which is fast enough to be useful in practice?
4. Does Theorem 7 have other interesting implications?

Acknowledgement

The authors are indebted to Barry Peyton for suggesting the problem of finding a minimal chordal supergraph from a non-minimal chordal supergraph.

References

1. A.Agrawal, P.Klein, and R.Ravi. Cutting down on fill using nested dissection: provably good elimination orderings. In J. A. George, J. R. Gilbert, and J. W. H. Liu, editors, *Sparse matrix computations: Graph theory issues and algorithms*, pages 31–55. Springer Verlag, 1993. IMA Volumes in Mathematics and its Applications, Vol. 56.

2. C. Beeri, R. Fagin, D. Maier, and M. Yannakakis. On the desirability of acyclic database systems. *J. Assoc. Comput. Mach.*, 30:479–513, 1983.

3. F. R. K. Chung and D. Mumford. Chordal completions of planar graphs. *J. Comb. Theory*, 31:96–106, 1994.

4. E. Dahlhaus and M. Karpinski. An efficient parallel algorithm for the minimal elimination ordering of an arbitrary graph. *Proceedings FOCS*, pages 454–459, 1989.

5. R. E. England, J. R. S. Blair, and M. G. Thomason. Independent computations in a probablistic knowledge-based system. Technical Report CS-90-128, Department of Computer Science, The University of Tennessee, Knoxville, Tennessee, 1991.

6. A. George and J.W-H. Liu. *Computer Solution of Large Sparse Positive Definite Systems*. Prentice-Hall Inc., Englewood Cliffs, New Jersey, 1981.

7. S. L. Lauritzen and D. J. Spiegelhalter. Local computations with probabilities on graphical structures and their applications to expert systems. *J. Royal Statist. Soc., ser B*, 50:157–224, 1988.

8. J. G. Lewis, B. W. Peyton, and A. Pothen. A fast algorithm for reordering sparse matrices for parallel factorization. *SIAM J. Sci. Stat. Comput.*, 10:1156–1173, 1989.

9. J. W-H. Liu and A. Mirzaian. A linear reordering algorithm for parallel pivoting of chordal graphs. *SIAM J. Disc. Math.*, 2:100–107, 1989.

10. T. Ohtsuki, L.K.Cheung, and T.Fujisawa. Minimal triangulation of a graph and optimal pivoting ordering in a sparse matrix. *J. Math. Anal. Appl.*, 54:622–633, 1976.

11. B. W. Peyton. *Some applications of clique trees to the solution of sparse linear systems*. PhD thesis, Dept. of Mathematical Sciences, Clemson University, 1986.

12. D. J. Rose. A graph-theoretic study of the numerical solution of sparse positive definite systems of linear equations. In R. C. Read, editor, *Graph Theory and Computing*, pages 183–217. Academic Press, 1972.

13. D.J. Rose, R.E. Tarjan, and G.S. Lueker. Algorithmic aspects of vertex elimination on graphs. *SIAM J. Comput.*, 5:266–283, 1976.

14. R. E. Tarjan and M. Yannakakis. Simple linear-time algorithms to test chordality of graphs, test acyclicity of hypergraphs, and selectively reduce acyclic hypergraphs. *SIAM J. Comput.*, 13:566–579, 1984.

15. M. Yannakakis. Computing the minimum fill-in is NP-complete. *SIAM J. Alg. Disc. Meth.*, 2:77–79, 1981.

Sorting and Searching Revisited

Arne Andersson

Department of Computer Science
Lund University
Box 118, S–221 00 Lund, Sweden
arne@dna.lth.se

Abstract. We discuss the complexity of sorting and searching from the following point of view: The n keys are binary strings (or integers) of length w and the employed computer has word size w. In this natural setting, and assuming that a traditional instruction set is available, a comparison-based algorithm is not the obvious choice. Indeed, the comparison-based algorithms are suboptimal in this model.

Rather than going into technical details, this invited talk aims at presenting some basic ideas. For more details, we give references to the literature. The following will be discussed:

1. Deterministic data structures and algorithms that use superlinear space
   - tries are used to decrease key length;
   - the resulting short keys are handled efficiently by packing them tightly.

   With these methods, the worst-case cost of sorting is $O(n \log \log n)$ and the worst-case cost of searching is $O(\sqrt{\log n})$. (Tries use superlinear space, but with randomization, i.e. hash coding, the space can be reduced to linear.)
2. Deterministic data structures and algorithms that use linear space
   - the fusion tree; with this data structure the worst-case cost of sorting is $O(n \log n / \log \log n)$ and the amortized cost of searching is $O(\log n / \log \log n)$.
   - a new data structure, the *exponential search tree*; the bounds on deterministic sorting and searching in linear space are improved to $O(n\sqrt{\log n})$ and $O(\sqrt{\log n})$, respectively.

1 Purpose of this article

Efficient sorting and searching are cornerstones in algorithm design. For a long time it was believed that comparison-based algorithms were the best choice in general. However, some recent findings give reason to question this situation. This paper contains an overview of these findings from a theoretical point of view; we show how to surpass the comparison-based algorithms in a natural model of computation.

The purpose of this survey is to give the non-expert a brief sketch of some basic methods. It should be seen as a complement to the literature and many details are ignored. For the full cascade of technicalities we refer to the research papers.

2 Model of computation

We use a RAM with word size w and we assume that the n keys to be sorted or searched for are w-bit keys that can be treated as binary strings or integers. When the problem is viewed in this way, we can allow ourselves to use other operations than comparisons, such as indirect addressing, shifting, bitwise logical operations etc.

To argue that this model of computation is natural, we note that it fits basic data types, such as strings and integers. It should also be noted that the IEEE 754 floating-point standard [13, p. 228] is also well-suited for our model.

As a matter of fact, it is quite hard to come up with a reasonable problem specification where comparisons can be computed in constant time, but where our model can not be adopted. It seems much easier to come up with a problem where the comparison-based model is questionable. Consider the following example: We wish to sort n keys, where each key occupies L words. In this case, a single comparison may take as much as $\Omega(L)$ time. Hence, the assumption of constant-time comparisons would not hold; sorting these keys with heapsort, quicksort, or mergesort would take $\Theta(Ln \log n)$ time. If, on the other hand, indirect addressing is used, the problem of sorting n strings of L words each can be reduced to the problem of sorting n words in $O(nL)$ time [6]; this reduction time is optimal since we must read the input at least once.

3 Simple algorithms using superlinear space

In this section, we study some rather simple algorithms that allows sorting and searching asymptotically faster than comparison-based algorithms. We use indirect addressing and large arrays. As a consequence, these algorithms will need much space. However, all algorithms presented here can be fit into linear space with randomization (i.e. with universal hashing [10]).

The word size of our RAM, as well as the length of our keys, is w. In our algorithms, we will also consider shorter keys. In cases when the key length may differ from w we use b, $b \leq w$, to denote the key length.

Our lemmas will be expressed as problem reductions. For this purpose, we use the notation below. For the searching problem, we assume that an ordered set is maintained and that operations like range queries and neighbour queries are supported.

Definition 1. A dictionary is ordered if neighbour queries and range queries are supported at the same cost as member queries, and if the keys can be reported in sorted order in linear time.

Definition 2. Let $F(n, b)$ be the worst-case cost of performing one search or update in an ordered dictionary storing n keys of length b.

Definition 3. Let $T(n, b)$ be the worst-case cost of sorting n keys of length b.

The methods discussed in this section are fairly simple. Furthermore, they can all be implemented with a simple instruction set. All necessary instructions are standard, they are even in AC^0. (An instruction is in AC^0 if it is implementable by a constant depth, unbounded fan-in (AND,OR,NOT)-circuit of size $w^{O(1)}$. An example of a non-AC^0 instruction is multiplication [9].)

3.1 Tries and range reduction

One way to simplify a computational problem is by *range reduction*. In this case, we replace our b-bit keys with k-bits keys, $k < b$.

Lemma 4. $F(n, b) = O(b/k) + F(n, k)$.

Hint of proof: We store the keys in a trie of height b/k. At each node, k bits are used for branching, and each node contains an array of length 2^k. A trie is illustrated in Figure 1. In this example $w = 12$ and $k = 3$. The array entries that contain pointers to subtries are marked with filled boxes. As an example: the smallest (leftmost) key is $\boxed{000}\ \boxed{100}\ \boxed{000}\ \boxed{011}$.

When searching for a key x or x's nearest neighbour, we traverse a path down the trie. At each node we use k bits in x as an address in the node's array. If x is present, the search ends at a trie node. Otherwise, the trie traversal ends when trying to reach a non-existing subtrie. In this case, we have to locate the nearest existing subtrie. Once this subtrie is found, we can find x's nearest neighbour; we may for example assume that each subtrie contains a reference to its smallest and largest keys. When k is large, the array itself can not be used to locate the nearest existing subtrie, since we then may have to scan too many empty entries. Instead, we note that the array entries (subtries) represent a set of k-bit keys which can be stored in some suitable data structure. In this way, each node contains an array used for trie traversal plus a local data structure.

The cost of traversing the trie is proportional to the height of the trie, that is $O(b/k)$. After the trie traversal, one search is made in a local data structure; the cost of this is $F(n, k)$ (the local data structure can not contain more than n keys).

Updates are rather straightforward.   □

For sorting, there is a similar lemma:

Lemma 5. $T(n, b) = O(nb/k) + T(n, k)$.

Hint of proof: We use a trie as above, with some minor differences. In each node, we use an array as before, but instead of an additional local data structure we just keep an unsorted edge-list in each node telling which array entries are being used. Then, after all keys have been inserted into the trie in $O(nb/k)$ time, we tag each list element with the node it belongs to. We collect all lists into one list which is sorted in $T(n, k)$ time. After the sorting, we traverse the list and create a sorted edge-list at each node. Then, an inorder traversal of the trie according to the edge-lists gives the sorted sequence.

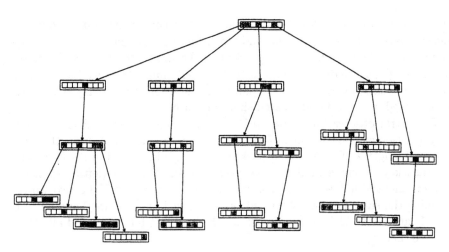

Fig. 1. *A trie.*

There is one problem with this approach: the number of list elements, corresponding to the number of edges in the trie, may be larger than n. To avoid this problem, we have to remove some edges from the lists. If we take away one element from each edge list, the total number of list elements will be less than n. In each edge list the removed edge can be inserted after the sorting, by just scanning the sorted list; the total cost for this is linear. In this way, the recursion equation of the lemma holds. □

Applying the lemmas above recursively, we can improve the complexity significantly. These reductions were first used in van Emde Boas trees [20, 21, 22] and in the sorting algorithm by Kirkpatrick and Reisch [14].

Lemma 6. $\begin{cases} F(n,b) = O(1) + F(n,b/2). \\ T(n,b) = O(n) + T(n,b/2). \end{cases}$

Hint of proof: Apply Lemmas 4 and 5, respectively, with $k = b/2$. □

Lemma 7. $\begin{cases} F(n,b) = O(\log(b/k)) + F(n,k). \\ T(n,b) = O(n\log(b/k)) + T(n,k). \end{cases}$

Hint of proof: Apply Lemma 6 recursively $\log(b/k)$ times. □

3.2 Packing keys

If the word length is small enough—like in today's computers—the range reduction technique discussed above will decrease the key length to a constant at a low cost. However, in order to make a really convincing comparison between comparison-based algorithms and algorithms based on indirect addressing, we must make the complexity independent of the word size. This can be done by combining range reduction with *packed computation*. The basic idea behind packed computation is to exploit the parallelism in a computer; many short keys can be packed in a word and treated simultaneously.

The central observation is due to Paul and Simon [17]; they observed that one subtraction can be used to perform comparisons in parallel. Assume that the keys are of length k. We may then pack $\Theta(w/k)$ keys in a word in the following way: Each key is represented by a $(k + 1)$-bit field. The first (leftmost) bit is a *test bit* and the following bits contain the key. Let X and Y be two words containing the same number of packed keys, all test bits in X are 0 and all test bits in Y are 1. Let M be a fixed mask in which all test bits are 1 and all other bits are 0. Let

$$R \leftarrow (Y - X) \text{ AND } M. \tag{1}$$

Then, the ith test bit in R will be 1 if and only if $y_i > x_i$. all other test bits, as well as all other bits, in R will be 0.

3.3 Packed searching

Lemma 8. $F(n, k) = O\left(\log(w/k) + \frac{\log n}{\log(w/k)}\right).$

Hint of proof: We use a packed B-tree [3]. The essential operation in this data structure is a multiple comparison as in Expression 1 where the keys in Y are sorted left-to-right and X contains multiple copies of one key x. Then, the rightmost p test bits in R will be 1 if and only if there are p keys in Y which are greater than x. This is illustrated in Figure 2. Hence, by finding the position of the leftmost 1-bit in R we can compute the rank of x among the keys in Y. (Finding the leftmost bit can either be done in constant time with multiplication [12] or via a lookup table [3].)

We use this technique to implement a B-tree with nodes of degree $\Theta(w/k)$. When searching for a k-bit key x in a packed B-tree, we first construct a word X containing multiple copies of x. X is created by a simple doubling technique: Starting with a word containing x in the rightmost part, we copy the word, shift the copy $k + 1$ steps and unite the words with a bitwise OR. The resulting word is copied, shifted $2k + 2$ steps and united, etc. Altogether X is generated in $O(\log(w/k))$ time.

After the word X has been constructed, we traverse the tree. At each node, we compute the rank of x in constant time with a multiple comparison. The cost of the traversal is proportional to the height of the tree, which is $O(\log n / \log(w/k))$
□

Above, we omitted a lot of details, such as how to perform updates and how pointers within the tree are represented.

```
    Y 1 00010 1 00111 1 01001 1 01110 1 10101 1 11000 1 11011 1 11110

    X 0 01011 0 01011 0 01011 0 01011 0 01011 0 01011 0 01011 0 01011

  Y − X 0 10111 0 11100 0 11110 1 00011 1 01010 1 01101 1 10000 0 10011

    M 1 00000 1 00000 1 00000 1 00000 1 00000 1 00000 1 00000 1 00000

(Y − X) AND M 0 00000 0 00000 0 00000 1 00000 1 00000 1 00000 1 00000 1 00000
```

Fig. 2. A multiple comparison in a packed B-tree

3.4 Packed sorting

Above, we compared a query key with all keys in a B-tree node in order to determine the rank of the key. This seems to be a waste of comparisons; a binary search would use less comparisons. Hence, there seems to be room for improvement. For searching, no such improvement is known, but the multiple comparisons can be utilized more efficiently when sorting.

We need a lemma by Batcher [7]. A sequence is *bitonic* if it is the concatenation of a nondecreasing and a nonincreasing sequence, or if it can be obtained as the cyclic shift of such a concatenation.

Lemma 9. *Consider a bitonic sequence* $x_1, x_2, \ldots, x_{2k}$ *and the two subsequences*

$$L = \min(x_1, x_{k+1}), \min(x_2, x_{k+2}), \ldots, \min(x_k, x_{2k})$$

and

$$R = \max(x_1, x_{k+1}), \max(x_2, x_{k+2}), \ldots, \max(x_k, x_{2k}).$$

The sequences L *and* R *are bitonic, and each element of* L *is smaller than or equal to each element of* R.

The lemma suggests a parallel algorithm for sorting a bitonic sequence of length k, where k is a power of 2, and, in particular, an algorithm for merging two sorted sequences.

- If $k = 1$ halt.
- If $k > 1$ compare the corresponding elements of the left and right half in parallel and generate the sequences L and R, then sort these bitonic sequences in parallel.

Batcher's lemma is well suited for combination with the Paul-Simon technique, as shown by Albers and Hagerup [1].

Lemma 10. $T(n, w/\log n) \leq O(n \log \log n)$.

Hint of proof:
We combine Lemma 9 (with $k = \log n$) with the Paul-Simon technique. We let a word X contain $x_1, x_2, \ldots, x_k$ and a word Y contain $x_{k+1}, x_{k+2}, \ldots, x_{2k}$.

After a subtraction as in Expression 1, the test bits will tell which keys should belong to L and R respectively. By copying and shifting test bits, we create bit masks that allow us to extract L and R respectively.

$\square$

3.5 Combining

We can now derive our first bound for sorting and searching. First, we state bounds in terms of w. The following bound holds for searching [20, 21, 22]:

Theorem 11. $F(n, w) = O(\log w)$.

Hint of proof: Apply Lemma 7 with $k = 1$. $\square$

For sorting, there is a similar bound [14]:

Theorem 12. $T(n, w) = O(n \log(w/\log n))$.

Hint of proof: Apply Lemma 7 with $k = \log n$. Keys of length $\log n$ can be sorted in linear time with bucketsort. $\square$

Next, we show how to remove the dependency of word length. For searching, we have [3]:

Theorem 13. $F(n, w) = O(\sqrt{\log n})$.

Hint of proof: If $\log w \le \sqrt{\log n}$, Theorem 11 is sufficient. Otherwise, Lemma 7 with $k = w/2^{\sqrt{\log n}}$ gives $F(n, w) = O(\sqrt{\log n}) + F(n, w/2^{\sqrt{\log n}})$. Lemma 8 gives that $F(n, w/2^{\sqrt{\log n}}) = O(\sqrt{\log n})$. $\square$

Finally, we get the following bound for sorting [4]:

Theorem 14. $T(n, w) = O(n \log \log n)$.

Hint of proof: If $\log w \le \log \log n$, Theorem 12 is sufficient. Otherwise, Lemma 7 with $k = w/\log n$ gives $T(n, w) = O(n \log \log n) + T(n, w/\log n)$. Lemma 10 gives the final bound. $\square$

4 Deterministic algorithms and linear space

The first algorithm that surpassed the comparison-based algorithms independent of word size was the fusion tree [12]. Here, we present a short overview as well as a new, faster, data structure.

The data structures in this section are more complicated than the previous ones. They also need more powerful—but standard—instructions, like multiplication.

Definition 15. Let $D(n)$ be the worst-case search cost and the amortized update cost in an ordered dictionary storing n keys in $O(n)$ space.

4.1 Fusion trees

The central part of the fusion tree [12] is a static data structure with the following properties:

Lemma 16. *For any d, $d = O\left(w^{1/6}\right)$, a static data structure containing d keys can be constructed in $O\left(d^4\right)$ time and space, such that it supports neighbour queries in $O(1)$ worst-case time.*

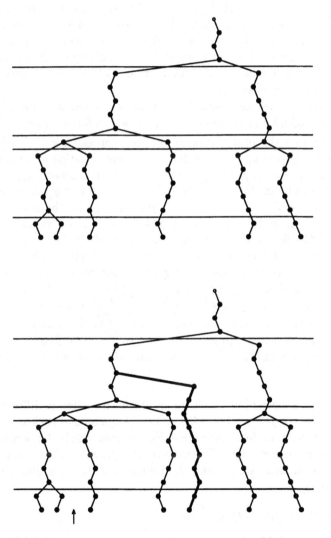

Fig. 3. *(a) Selecting bit positions in a fusion tree node. (b) Determining the rank of a query key.*

Hint of proof: The main idea behind the fusion tree is to make use of significant bit positions. We illustrate the basic mechanism with an example, shown in Figure 3. In this small example we have chosen $w = 16$ and $d = 6$. Let Y be the set of keys $y_1, \ldots, y_d$. Assume that Y is stored in a binary trie. Each key is represented as a path down the trie. In the figure, a left edge denotes a 0 and a right edge denotes a 1. For example, y_3 is $\boxed{1010010101011010}$. We get the significant bit positions by selecting the levels in the trie where there is at least one binary (that is, non-unary) node. In this example the levels are 4, 9, 10, and 15, marked by horizontal lines. Create a set Y' of compressed keys $y'_1, \ldots, y'_d$ by extracting these bits from each key. In the example the compressed keys are $\boxed{0000}$, $\boxed{0001}$, $\boxed{0011}$, $\boxed{0110}$, $\boxed{1001}$, and $\boxed{1011}$. These compressed keys are used for packed searching. Since the trie has exactly d leaves, it contains exactly $d - 1$ binary nodes. Therefore, the number of significant bit positions, and the length of a compressed key, is at most $d - 1$. This implies that we can pack the d keys, including test bits, in d^2 bits. Since $d = O\left(w^{1/6}\right)$, the packed keys fit in a constant number of words.

The d compressed keys may be used to determine the rank of a query key among the original d keys. Assume that we search for $x = \boxed{1010011001110100}$. First, we extract the proper bits to form a compressed key $x' = \boxed{0010}$. (This extraction is nontrivial; it can be done with multiplication and masking.) Then, we use packed searching to determine the rank of x' among $y'_1, \ldots, y'_d$.. In this case, the packed searching will place x' between y'_2 and y'_3. as indicated by the arrow in Figure 3(b). This is not the proper rank of the original key x, but nevertheless it is useful. The important information is obtained by finding the position of the first differing bit of x and one of the keys y_2 and y_3. In this example, the 7th bit is the first differing bit. and, since x has a 1 at this bit position, we can conclude that it is greater than all keys in Y with the same 6-bit prefix. Furthermore, the remaining bits in x are insignificant. Therefore, we can replace x by the key $\boxed{1010011111111111}$, where all the last bits are 1s. When compressed, this new key becomes $\boxed{0111}$. Making a second packed searching with this key instead, the proper rank will be found.

Hence, in constant time we can determine the rank of a query key among our d keys. $\qquad\square$

The original method by Fredman and Willard is slightly different. Instead of filling the query keys with 1s (or 0s) and making a second packed searching, they use a large lookup table in each node. Fusion trees can be implemented without multiplication, using only AC^0 instructions, provided that some simple non-standard instructions are allowed. A discussion of these possibilities is currently in progress [5].

Theorem 17. $D(n) = O(\log n / \log \log n)$.

Hint of proof: Based on Lemma 16, we use a B-tree where only the upper levels in the tree contain B-tree nodes, all having the same degree (within a constant factor). At the lower levels, traditional (i.e. comparison-based) weight-balanced trees are used. The reason for using weight-balanced trees is that the B-tree nodes are costly to reconstruct; the trees at the bottom ensure that few updates propagate to the upper levels. In this way, the amortized cost of updating a B-tree node is small.

The amortized cost of searches and updates is $O(\log n / \log d + \log d)$ for any $d = O\left(w^{1/6}\right)$. The first term corresponds to the number of B-tree levels and the second term corresponds to the height of the weight-balanced trees. Since $w \geq \log n$, the cost becomes at most $O(\log n / \log \log n)$. $\qquad\square$

4.2 Exponential search trees

Since their introduction, the fusion trees have been the only available deterministic data structure that uses linear space and supports searching in $o(\log n)$ time and sorting in $o(n \log n)$ time. Recently, an improved data structure has been developed [2].

The basic data structure is a multiway tree where the degrees of the nodes decrease exponentially down the tree.

Lemma 18. *Suppose a static data structure containing d keys can be constructed in $O\left(d^4\right)$ time and space, such that it supports neighbour queries in $O(S(d))$ worst-case time. Then,*

$$D(n) = O\left(S\left(n^{1/5}\right)\right) + D\left(n^{4/5}\right);$$

Hint of proof: We use an *exponential search tree*. It has the following properties:

- Its root has degree $\Theta(n^{1/5})$.
- The keys of the root are stored in a local (static) data structure, with the properties stated above. During a search, the local data structure is used to determine in which subtree the search is to be continued.
- The subtrees are exponential search trees of size $\Theta(n^{4/5})$.

First, we show that, given n sorted keys, an exponential search tree can be constructed in linear time and space. Since the cost of constructing a node of degree d is $O\left(d^4\right)$, the total construction cost $C(n)$ is given by

$$C(n) = O\left(\left(n^{1/5}\right)^4\right) + n^{1/5} \cdot C\left(n^{4/5}\right) \quad \Rightarrow \quad C(n) = O(n). \qquad (2)$$

Furthermore, with a similar equation, the space required by the data structure can be shown to be $O(n)$.

Balance is maintained by joining and splitting subtrees. The basic idea is the following: A join or split occurs when the size of a subtree has changed significantly, i.e. after $\Omega(n^{4/5})$ updates. Then, a constant number of subtrees will be reconstructed; according to Equation 2, the cost of this is linear in the size of the subtrees $= O(n^{4/5})$. Also, some keys will be inserted or deleted from the root, causing a reconstruction of the root; the cost of this is by definition $O(n^{4/5})$. Amortizing these two costs over the $\Omega(n^{4/5})$ updates, we get $O(1)$ amortized cost for reconstructing the root. Hence, the restructuring cost is dominated by the search cost.

Finally, the search cost follow immediately from the description of the exponential search tree. $\qquad\square$

Exponential search trees may be combined with various other data structures, as illustrated by the following two lemmas:

Lemma 19. *A static data structure containing d keys can be constructed in $O\left(d^4\right)$ time and space, such that it supports neighbour queries in $O\left(\frac{\log d}{\log w} + 1\right)$ worst-case time.*

Hint of proof: We just construct a static B-tree where each node has the largest possible degree according to Lemma 16. That is, it has a degree of $\min\left(d, w^{1/6}\right)$. This tree satisfies the conditions of the lemma. $\qquad\square$

Lemma 20. *A static data structure containing d keys and supporting neighbour queries in $O(\log w)$ worst-case time can be constructed in $O\left(d^4\right)$ time and space.*

Hint of proof: We study two cases.

Case 1: $w > d^{1/3}$. Lemma 19 gives constant query cost.

Case 2: $w \leq d^{1/3}$. The basic idea is to combine a van emde Boas tree (Theorem 11) with perfect hashing. The data structure of Theorem 11 uses much space, which can be reduced to $O(d)$ by hash coding. Since we can afford a rather slow construction, we can use the deterministic algorithm by Fredman, Komlós, and Szemerédi [11]. With this algorithm, we can construct a perfectly hashed van Emde Boas tree in $O(d^3 w) = o(d^4)$ time. $\qquad\square$

Combining these two lemmas, we get a significantly improved upper bound on deterministic sorting and searching in linear space:

Theorem 21. $D(n) = O(\sqrt{\log n})$.

Hint of proof: If we combine Lemmas 18, 19, and 20, we obtain the following equation

$$D(n) = O\left(\min\left(1 + \frac{\log n}{\log w}, \quad \log w\right)\right) + D\left(n^{4/5}\right) \qquad (3)$$

which, when solved, gives the theorem. $\qquad\square$

Theorem 21 implies that the worst-case cost of sorting n keys in linear space is $O(n\sqrt{\log n})$. This is an improvement from $O(n \log n / \log \log n)$, achieved by the fusion tree. Taking both n and w as parameters, $D(n)$ is $o(\sqrt{\log n})$ in many cases [2]. For example, it can be shown that $D(n) = O(\log w \log \log n)$.

5 Related work

In this short survey, we have concentrated on asymptotic upper bound on sorting and searching. There is much more to be said.

Thorup has shown a number of related results for priority queues [19]. In particular, he has developed a simple priority queue with a cost of $O(\log \log n)$ per operation. As a more general result, he has shown a direct correspondence between the complexity of sorting and that of maintaining a priority queu.

There is another method of doing range reduction, which has not been mentioned here. For large word sizes, a key can be divided into fields that can be hash coded simultaneously. In this way, each field will be represented by a shorter *signature*. Replacing the fields in a key by the corresponding signatures, we get fast range reduction. The hash coding will destroy the order among the keys, yet we can use the hash coded keys to construct a trie. Once the trie is constructed, we can replace the signatures with the original fields and the edges lists can be sorted as in the proof of Lemma 5. In this way, we can sort in linear time if $w \geq (\log n)^{2+\epsilon}$ [4]. With these techniques, Raman [18] has shown that, if multiplication and randomization is used, the searching problem can be solved at a cost of of $O(1 + \log n/\log w)$ per search or update.

It is intersting to note that while sorting can be done in $O(n \log \log n)$ time and a priority queue can be maintained in $O(\log \log n)$ time per operation, a corresponding bound cannot be achieved for searching. From a proof by Miltersen [16] a lower bound of $\Omega(\log^{1/3-o(1)} n)$ can be derived [15] for the searching problem. Recently, an even stronger lower bound has been shown by Beame and Fich [8]. They show a lower bound of $\Omega(\sqrt{\log n/\log \log n})$ per dictionary operation.

6 Conclusions

From Section 3 we conclude:

> *The "information-theoretic barrier"*
> *can be surpassed*
> *by simple means.*

From Section 4 we conclude:

> *Deterministic sorting and searching in linear space*
> *can be made even faster*
> *than with fusion trees.*

Finally, we claim:

> *Methods based on indirect addressing*
> *(tries, bucketing etc)*
> *are fast in theory and practice.*

References

1. S. Albers and T. Hagerup. Improved parallel integer sorting without concurrent writing. In *Proc. 3rd ACM-SIAM SODA*, pages 463–472, 1992.

2. A. Andersson. Faster deterministic sorting and searching in linear space. Tech. report LU–CS–TR:95–160, Lund University, 1995.

3. A. Andersson. Sublogarithmic searching without multiplications. In *Proc. 36th IEEE Symposium on Foundations of Computer Science*, pages 655–663. ACM Press, 1995.

4. A. Andersson, T. Hagerup, S. Nilsson, and R. Raman. Sorting in linear time? In *Proceedings 27th ACM Symposium on Theory of Computing*, pages 427–436. ACM Press, 1995.

5. A. Andersson, P.B. Miltersen, and M. Thorup. Manuscript. In preparation, 1996.

6. A. Andersson and S. Nilsson. A new efficient radix sort. In *Proc. 35th Annual IEEE Symposium on Foundations of Computer Science*, pages 714–721. IEEE Computer Society Press, 1994.

7. K. E. Batcher. Sorting networks and their applications. In *Proceedings of the AFIPS Spring Joint Computer Conference*, pages 307–314, 1968. Volume 32.

8. P. Beame and F. Fich. Manuscript. 1996.

9. P. Beame and J. Håstad. Optimal bounds for decision problems on the CRCW PRAM. *Journal of the ACM*, 36(3):643–670, 1989.

10. J. L. Carter and M. N. Wegman. Universal classes of hash functions. *Journal of Computer and System Sciences*, 18:143–154, 1979.

11. M. L. Fredman, J. Komlós, and E. Szemerédi. Storing a sparse table with $O(1)$ worst case access time. *Journal of the ACM*, 31(3):538–544, 1984.

12. M. L. Fredman and D. E. Willard. Surpassing the information theoretic bound with fusion trees. *J. Comput. Syst. Sci.*, 47:424–436, 1994.

13. J. L. Hennessy and D. A. Patterson. *Computer Organization and Design: The Hardware/Software Interface*. Morgan Kaufmann Publ., San Mateo, CA, 1994.

14. D. Kirkpatrick and S. Reisch. Upper bounds for sorting integers on random access machines. *Theoretical Computer Science*, 28:263–276, 1984.

15. P. B. Miltersen. Personal communication.

16. P. B. Miltersen. Lower bounds for union-split-find related problems on random access machines. In *Proc. 26th Ann. ACM Symp. Theory of Computing*, pages 625–634, 1994.

17. W. J. Paul and J. Simon. Decision trees and random access machines. In *Logic and Algorithmic: An International Symposium Held in Honour of Ernst Specker*, pages 331–340. L'Enseignement Mathématique, Université de Genevè, 1982.

18. R. Raman. Improved data structures for predecessor queries in integer sets. manuscript, 1995.

19. M. Thorup. On RAM priority queues. In *Proc. 7th Annual ACM-SIAM Symposium on Discrete Algorithms*, 1996.

20. P. van Emde Boas. Preserving order in a forest in less than logarithmic time. In *Proceedings of the 16th Annual IEEE Symposium on Foundations of Computer Science*, pages 75–84, 1975.

21. P. van Emde Boas. Preserving order in a forest in less than logarithmic time and linear space. *Information Processing Letters*, 6(3):80–82, 1977.

22. P. van Emde Boas, R. Kaas, and E. Zijlstra. Design and implementation of an efficient priority queue. *Math. Syst. Theory*, 10:99–127, 1977.

Lower Bounds for Dynamic Transitive Closure, Planar Point Location, and Parentheses Matching

Thore Husfeldt, Theis Rauhe, and Søren Skyum

BRICS*
Department of Computer Science, University of Aarhus
Ny Munkegade, DK–8000 Århus C, Denmark

Abstract. We give a number of new lower bounds in the cell probe model with logarithmic cell size, which entails the same bounds on the random access computer with logarithmic word size and unit cost operations.

We study the signed prefix sum problem: given a string of length n of 0s and signed 1s, compute the sum of its ith prefix during updates. We show a lower bound of $\Omega(\log n / \log \log n)$ time per operations, even if the prefix sums are bounded by $\log n / \log \log n$ during all updates. We also show that if the update time is bounded by the product of the worst-case update time and the answer to the query, then the update time must be $\Omega\big(\sqrt{(\log n / \log \log n)}\big)$.

These results allow us to prove lower bounds for a variety of seemingly unrelated dynamic problems. We give a lower bound for the dynamic planar point location in monotone subdivisions of $\Omega(\log n / \log \log n)$ per operation. We give a lower bound for dynamic transitive closure on upward planar graphs with one source and one sink of $\Omega(\log n / (\log \log n)^2)$ per operation. We give a lower bound of $\Omega\big(\sqrt{(\log n / \log \log n)}\big)$ for the dynamic membership problem of any Dyck language with two or more letters. This implies the same lower bound for the dynamic word problem for the free group with k generators. We also give lower bounds for the dynamic prefix majority and prefix equality problems.

1 Introduction

We introduce a new technique for proving lower bounds for dynamic algorithms in the cell probe model. With this, we easily derive lower bounds for half a dozen natural problems, including the following:

Computational Geometry: Dynamic planar point location in monotone subdivisions cannot be solved faster than $\Omega(\log n / \log \log n)$. The important algorithm of Preparata and Tamassia [16] achieves upper bounds of $O(\log^2 n)$ per operation.

---

* Basic Research in Computer Science, Centre of the Danish National Research Foundation

Graph algorithms: Dynamic transitive closure in planar acyclic digraphs with one source and one sink that are on the same face cannot be solved faster than $\Omega(\log n/(\log\log n)^2)$. Tamassia and Preparata [17] achieve a logarithmic upper bound for this problem.

Parentheses matching: The dynamic membership problem for the Dyck languages (alternatively, the dynamic word problem for the free group) cannot be solved faster than $\Omega(\sqrt{\log n/\log\log n})$ per operation. Frandsen et al. [7] show polylogarithmic upper bounds for this problem.

No lower bounds (in the cell probe model) for any of these problems have been published to the knowledge of the authors, even though an exponentially worse bound of $\Omega(\log\log n/\log\log\log n)$ can be seen to hold for most of them, using an unpublished result by Beame and Fich [3], that improves work of Miltersen [13]. Lower bounds for harder variants of dynamic transitive closure and dynamic planar point location follow from [9, 12].

In the rest of the paper, our nomenclature for dynamic problems omits the prefix 'dynamic' for brevity, since all our problems are of this type.

1.1 Roadmap

The Introduction contains a short presentation of our model of computation and recalls a seminal result for this, the *Fredman–Saks bound* [10], that will be important to us.

The main part of this paper proves two theorems that can be viewed as generalisations of the Fredman–Saks bound. The lower bounds for planar point location and transitive closure follow from the first theorem, while the bound for parentheses matching follows from the second.

Much of the present paper can be enjoyed without knowledge of the proof of the Fredman–Saks bound; hence we present our results as a reduction to that result rather than modifying the original proof [10], trading elegance for (what we hope is) readability.

1.2 The Cell Probe Model

Our lower bounds work in the cell probe model [19], where the only resource is memory access—all computation is for free; we consider word size $O(\log n)$ for concreteness. Hence our bounds hold on all natural (and some unnatural) models of random access machines with logarithmic word size. For example, the cost or availability of operations like multiplication does not enter into the argument. Also, there are no assumptions on the the size of the memory or its organisation relative to the structure of the instance.

The cell probe model is so strong that no lower bound better than $\Omega(\log n/\log\log n)$ is known for *any* problem in Polynomial Time. This is discouraging in light of the fact that the best known algorithm for many dynamic problems is 'recompute from scratch.' However, recent breakthroughs in algorithms for random access machines [1, 2, 18] show that widely-held beliefs about the relevance *for real computers* of lower bounds in weaker models may be mistaken.

Unfortunately, cell probe lower bounds are often hard to come by and the range of general techniques is limited. We believe that the techniques of the present paper are widely applicable; we substantiate this claim by proving new lower bounds for several well-studied problems from various fields.

1.3 Prefix Parity

We use a result of Fredman and Saks [10] that gives a lower bound on the complexity of the *prefix parity* problem: given a vector $x_1, \ldots, x_n$ of bits, maintain a data structure that is able to react to the following operations for all $i = 1, \ldots, n$:

change(i): negate the value of x_i,
parity(i): return $\bigoplus_{j=1}^{i} x_j$, the parity of the first i elements.

The Fredman–Saks bound. *Let t_u denote the worst-case update time and let t_q denote the worst-case query time for any solution of the prefix parity problem. Then*

$$t_q \in \Omega\Big(\frac{\log n}{\log(t_u \log n)}\Big). \tag{1}$$

Especially, no algorithm can run faster than $\Omega(\log n / \log \log n)$ time per operation. Dietz [6] shows this bound to be tight.

We mention at this point that the Fredman–Saks bound holds for *amortised* complexity also. So do all our results; we claim this without proof and will not mention it again to keep the presentation simple.

2 Prefix Balancing

2.1 Signed Prefix Sum

To prove our lower bounds, we introduce the *signed prefix sum* problem. Given a vector $y_1, \ldots, y_n \in \{0, \pm 1\}^n$, maintain a data structure that is able to react to the following operations for all $i = 1, \ldots, n$:

change(i, a): let $y_i = a \in \{0, \pm 1\}$,
sum(i): return $\sum_{j=1}^{i} y_j$.

Obviously, the Fredman–Saks bound holds for signed prefix sum, since it is a generalisation of the prefix parity problem. The data structure of Dietz [6] can be used for an optimal $\Theta(\log n / \log \log n)$ implementation.

2.2 Range Reduction

We first show that signed prefix sum remains difficult even when the range of $\sum_{j \leq i} y_j$ is reduced.

Theorem 1. *Let t_u denote the worst-case update time and let t_q denote the worst-case query time for any solution of the signed prefix sum problem with the restriction that at all times during the updates,*

$$\left| \sum_{j=1}^{i} y_j \right| = O\left(\frac{\log n}{\log \log n} \right) \quad \text{for all } 1 \le i \le n. \tag{2}$$

Then (1) holds.

Proof. Let $x \in \{0,1\}^n$ be an instance of the prefix parity problem and assume that we have a solution to the signed prefix sum problem that works under the restriction (2). We construct an instance $y \in \{0,\pm 1\}^n$ to the latter such that $y_i = 0$ if and only if $x_i = 0$. Note that since $1 = -1 \bmod 2$ we can answer the query **parity**(i) by returning the parity of **sum**(i). To prove the desired lower bound we only have to keep the value of $\sum_{j \le i} y_j$ small. The rest of the proof explains how to construct y with this property—namely, how to choose values from $\{-1,+1\}$ for the nonzero elements.

Write

$$m = \left\lceil \frac{\log n}{\log \log n} \right\rceil$$

in the rest of the paper. We introduce sequences $w_1, \ldots, w_m$ such that w_1 is a subsequence of y and w_{k+1} is a subsequence of w_k. The sequences are defined as follows: w_1 contains exactly the nonzero entries of y. The elements of each sequence are either *single* or *coupled* with a neighbouring element. The singles in the kth sequence constitute the elements of w_{k+1}.

Note that every nonzero element of y is coupled at most once among all sequences. The values of these elements will be chosen from $\{+1,-1\}$ such that the sum of each couple is zero.

We will maintain a distance invariant: that there are at least $\log n$ elements between any two singles. This ensures that $|w_{k+1}| \le \lceil |w_k| / \log n \rceil$, so w_m contains at most a (single) element, which we will pair up with a dummy element y_{n+1} for simplicity.

Let us see how to maintain the invariant during updates. Whenever a bit in x is flipped, a nonzero element in y becomes zero or vice versa, which means that an element is inserted into or deleted from w_1.

insertions: Consider the case where a new element y_i is inserted into list w_k. If there are no singles among the nearest $2 \log n$ neighbours of y_i then we can insert y_i as a single in w_k and as a new element in w_{k+1}.

Otherwise, if there is a single y_j close to i, we have to change the coupling of elements in w_k. According to the invariant, all elements in the $\log n$ neighbourhood of y_j are coupled. We make new couples of these elements and y_j and y_i and remember to delete y_j from w_{k+1}.

deletions: Consider now the case where we want to delete y_i from w_k. If y_i is a single then we remove it and delete it from w_{k+1}. The case where y_i is coupled with some y_i' is handled as above, since deleting y_i corresponds to removing the couple and inserting y_i' as a single.

In both cases, the distance invariant is maintained, at most $O(\log n)$ are re-coupled and at most one element inserted into or deleted from w_{k+1}. Hence the update time for each **change** operation in the worst case is

$$t_u = O\Big(\frac{\log^2 n}{\log \log n} \cdot t\Big), \tag{3}$$

where t is the update time of the data structure for signed prefix sum.

Now for the query operation. We first explain how the values from $\{-1, +1\}$ are given to the nonzero element of y. The rule is straightforward and arbitrary: when a new couple is created, the leftmost element is assigned the value -1 and the rightmost $+1$.

To find $\sum_{j \le i} y_j$, first note that we can ignore couples $(y_i, y_{i'})$ with $i, i' \le j$, since their sum is zero. So we restrict our attention to elements y_i in couples $(y_i, y_{i'})$ with $i \le j < i'$. In every sequence w_k there can be at most one such couple (because elements are coupled with a neighbour in the same sequence), so the number of contributing y_i is at most m. This ensures that the range condition (2) holds and proves correctness. The bound on the query time follows from the Fredman–Saks bound. □

2.3 Planar Point Location

A classical problem in Computational Geometry is *planar point location*: given a subdivision of the plane, i.e. a partition into polygonal regions induced by the straight-line embedding of a planar graph, determine the region of query point $q \in \mathbb{R}^2$.

In the dynamic version, updates consist of insertion and deletion of vertices or (chains of) edges. An important restriction of the problem, for which our bound will apply, considers only *monotone* subdivisions, where the subdivision consists of polygons that are monotone (so no straight line crosses any polygon more than twice). Preparata and Tamassia [16] give an algorithm that runs in time $O(\log^2 n)$ per operation. Several other dynamic algorithms for this and other types of subdivisions have been found since, see [4] for a survey.

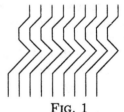

FIG. 1

To prove a lower bound for this problem we construct a monotone subdivision from the signed prefix sum instance $y \in \{0, \pm 1\}^n$. This is easier drawn than explained formally; Fig. 1 shows the subdivision corresponding to $y = (0, 0, +1, +1, -1, 0, +1, 0)$. There are 2 unbounded polygons at the sides and $2m$ strip-like ones with common sides and common top and bottom corners at infinity. Each of the strip-like polygons mimics the path described by y with $+1$ meaning 'go right' and -1 meaning 'go left.'

Now comes the only, but crucial, use of our range reduction (2): when y is changed, the subdivision can be updated in polylogarithmic time (given a fast data structure for planar point location) because it is so narrow.

To answer a sum query for the ith prefix, we query the names of the polygons that contain the points $(0,0)$ and $(0,i)$ (assuming some appropriate placement of the origin). The distance between these polygons is precisely the answer, so we can indeed implement a data structure for signed prefix sum. We conclude that (1) is a lower bound on the time per operation for planar point location in monotone subdivisions.

3 Binary Search

Using a simple binary search strategy, we can prove lower bounds for a variety of other problems. The cleanest application is for the majority function. This tells us a bit about the complexity of range searching as well. Following the same melody, we give lower bounds for a dynamic graph problem.

3.1 Prefix Majority

The *prefix majority* problem is defined in analogy with the prefix parity problem from Sect. 1.3; the query operation is

majority(i): return 'true' iff there are more 1s than 0s in the ith prefix.

We will show how to use Thm. 1 to prove a lower bound of

$$t_q = \Omega\Big(\frac{\log n}{\log\log^2 n}\Big), \qquad \text{if } t_u = \log^{O(1)} n \tag{4}$$

for any implementation, where t_u and t_q denote the update and query time, respectively. We know no better upper bound than $O(\log n / \log\log n)$ per operation (again, Dietz' data structure [6]), so the result leaves a double-logarithmic gap.

To see that (4) holds, let $y \in \{0, \pm1\}^n$ be an instance of signed prefix sum. We first construct an instance $x \in \{0,1\}^{2n}$ to the prefix majority problem in the obvious way:

$$-1 \mapsto 00, \qquad 0 \mapsto 01, \qquad +1 \mapsto 11. \tag{5}$$

The majority of a prefix of this instance is 1 if and only if the signed sum of the corresponding prefix in y is positive. This is the main idea.

To learn the *exact* values of y's prefixes we maintain $2m + 1$ bitstrings x_i, where $x_i = (11)^i x$ for positive i and $x_i = (00)^i x$ for negative i. We encourage the reader to check that this facilitates a binary search for the exact number of 1s in x's prefixes. The query time for this (and hence for the prefix sum of y) is $t_q \log m$, and since the update time is polylogarithmic if t_u is, the bound (4) follows from Thm. 1.

Note that while we still use the range reduction (2) to maintain our construction in polylogarithmic time during *updates* (as in the previous application), we now also use it to reduce the *query* time.

3.2 Range Searching

A fundamental algorithmic problem is *range searching*; we can put the above result in that framework. The problem is to maintain a set $S \subseteq \mathbb{R}^d$ (for our lower bound, $d = 1$ is hard enough) under the following operations:

insert(x): insert a point at coordinate $x \in \mathbb{R}^d$ into S,
delete(x): remove the point at $x \in \mathbb{R}^d$ from S,
report(R): how many points are in $R \cap S$, where R is a rectangle in $\mathbb{R}^d$.

The problem has been studied for many other query operations and our understanding of its complexity varies with the type of query. For *counting* (as above), the Fredman–Saks bound applies even in one dimension. On the other hand, the problem of *existential range queries* (return 'yes' iff $R \cap S$ is nonempty) is among the most interesting problems at the time of writing, see [14] for some results.

Our lower bound applies to versions of the problem where the query operation involves the majority function in some disguise. Here is one:

insert(x, c): insert $x \in R^d$ of colour $c \in \{\text{blue, red}\}$ into S,
delete(x): remove the point at x if it exists,
blue(R): are there more blue than red points in $R \cap S$?

This corresponds to asking questions like 'among the students aged 20 to 25, are there more males than females?'. Alternatively, in the monochromatic setting, we can ask: 'Are there more students aged 20 to 25 than 23 to 30?', reflected in the following query:

more(R_1, R_2): is $|R_1 \cap S| > |R_2 \cap S|$?

We leave it to the reader formalise this and show that (4) is a lower bound.

3.3 Upward Planar Graphs

A graph is planar if it can be embedded in the plane without crossing edges. A digraph is *upward planar* if it admits a planar embedding where all edges are directed upward, i.e. their projection on the y-axis is positive; such a graph is clearly acyclic.

There are planar dags that are not upward planar, like shown in Fig. 2.

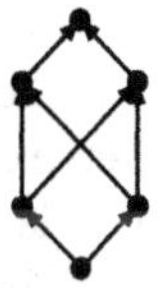

A digraph is a *source–sink* graph, or *st*-graph for short, if it has only one vertex with no incoming edges (the source s) and only one vertex with no outgoing edges (the sink t). It is well known that a graph is upward planar iff it is the subgraph of an acyclic planar *st*-graph that has s and t on the same face. Fig. 2 shows the last condition to be necessary. The survey [5] contains a recent list of references to other characterisations of these classes and many applications in graph drawing; see [17] for more applications.

FIG. 2

We give a lower bound of (4) for the *transitive closure*, i.e. for data structures that handle the following operations:

insert(u, v): insert an edge from vertex u to vertex v,
delete(u, v): delete the edge from u and v,
path(u, v): 'Is there a path from u to v?'

Our bound holds even under the severe restriction that at all times, the graph remains an upward planar st-graph (with the same embedding). The prize for this generality, compared to a related result [9, 12], is a double-logarithmic factor in the lower bound.

The construction is very similar to that for planar point location in Sect. 2.3. From an instance $y \in \{0, \pm 1\}^n$ of signed prefix sum, we construct a digraph $G = (V, E)$. The vertex set consists of the source s, the sink t, and $2m + 3$ vertices for each letter y_i:

$$V = \{ v_{ij} \mid 1 \leq i \leq n+1, -m-1 \leq j \leq m+1 \}.$$

The ith row is connected to its upper neighbour according to the value of y_i:

$$\{ (v_{ij}, v_{(i+1)j'}) \mid 1 \leq i \leq n, -m-1 \leq j \leq m+1 \},$$

$$\text{where } j' = \begin{cases} j + y_i, & \text{if } |j + y_i| \leq m+1, \\ m+1, & \text{if } j + y_i = m+2, \\ -m-1, & \text{if } j + y_i = -m-2. \end{cases}$$

For example, if y is $(0, 0, +1, +1, -1, 0, +1, 0)$ the edges look like Fig. 3(a). Note how the path starting in $(1, 0)$ (the middle vertex in the bottom row) mimics $s_i = \sum_{j \leq i} x_j$. Indeed, there is a path from $(1, 0)$ to $(i+1, u)$ for $1 \leq i \leq n$ and $-m \leq u \leq m$ if and only if $s_i = u$. We are going to use the transitive closure data structure to detect this.

First, we finish the construction by adding some more edges that have only technical significance and make sure that G is an st-graph. At the ends of the graph, $2m + 3$ edges connect s to the bottom row and $2m + 1$ edges connect the topmost row to t,

$$\{ (s, v_{1j}), (v_{j(n+1)}, t) \mid -m-1 \leq j \leq m+1 \}.$$

At the top- and bottommost rows, edges connect s to all vertices that would otherwise be sources:

$$\{ (s, v_{i(m+1)}) \mid y_{i-1} = -1 \} \cup \{ (s, v_{i(-m-1)}) \mid y_{i-1} = 1 \}.$$

From this we construct two graphs G_+ and G_-. In G_+, edges connect every vertex (u, v) with $1 \leq u \leq n$, $-m-1 \leq v \leq m$ to $(u, v+1)$. The other graph G_- is constructed symmetrically, with all (u, v) connected to $(u, v-1)$.

Figure 3(b) depicts it for our example. We have displaced the vertex rows slightly to make clear that all edges are directed upward. Arrows are removed for readability. The vertices at the bottom and top are s and t, respectively.

The desired property of G_+ is this: If $j = s_i$ then there is a path from v_{10} not only to v_{ij} but also to $v_{ij'}$ for any $j' \geq j$ but still none for $j' < j$. Likewise, in G_-, there is a path to $v_{ij'}$ for any $j' \leq j$ and none for $j' > j$. But now we can do a binary search; the rest of the proof is similar to Sect. 3.1.

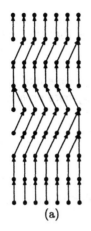 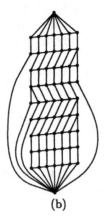

(a)   (b)

FIG. 3

4   Randomised Prefix Balancing

We return to the signed prefix sum problem and state and prove our second theorem. In this version, the time for a query is expressed in terms of the size of its answer.

For a quick motivation, assume that we have a data structure that can only check for zero, i.e. answer 'zero' iff $\sum_{j \leq i} y_j = 0$. Then we can use an exhaustive search strategy to solve signed prefix sum: (Assume for simplicity that the sum is positive.)

1. pad y with a number of 0s to the left,
2. change a padded 0 to -1 and query again,
3. repeat from 2 until we get the answer 'zero.'

Clearly, the number of iterations is exactly the number of -1s we used to balance the prefix sum down to zero, which in turn is the answer to the query. Theorem 2 allows us to give lower bounds for such a check-for-zero data structure.

Theorem 2. *Consider any solution to the signed prefix sum problem. For $1 \leq i \leq n$, let t_q^i denote the time for* **sum**(i) *and let t_u denote the worst-case time for any update. Then*

$$t_u = \Omega\left(\sqrt{\frac{\log n}{\log \log n}}\right), \qquad \text{if } t_q^i = O\left(t_u \cdot \left| \sum_{j=1}^i y_j \right|\right). \qquad (6)$$

This bound holds even with the restriction (2).

The proof uses the well-known fact that in a series of independent and fair coin flips, even though the difference between the number of heads and tails after the nth trail may be as big as n, the *expected* value is much smaller:

$$E\big(|\#\text{heads} - \#\text{tails}|\big) = \Theta(\sqrt{n}).$$

For a proof, solve Problem 1.6 of [15].

For this idea to work, we first have to observe that the Fredman–Saks bound works for *expected* query time as well.

Lemma 3. *Let t_u denote the worst-case update time and let t_q denote the expected query time for any solution of the prefix parity problem. Then*

$$t_q = \Omega\left(\frac{\log n}{\log(t_u \log n)}\right).$$

Sketch of proof. Equation (2) in Theorem 3 of [10] states the bound for q being the *worst-case* query time. This can be extended to expected time using Yao's Minimax principle. □

Proof of Theorem. We return to the proof of Theorem 1 and modify our scheme for giving values $\{-1, +1\}$ to the nonzero elements of y. The rule is quite straightforward: when a new couple is created, either the leftmost element is assigned the value -1 and the rightmost $+1$ or vice versa, depending on a fair coin toss.

But then, by Probability Theory, we have

$$E\left(\left|\sum_{j=1}^{i} y_j\right|\right) = \Theta(\sqrt{m}), \tag{7}$$

where the expectation is over the coin tosses used to determine the values of each couple.

Hence the expected time for a prefix parity query is

$$O\left(t_u \cdot \sqrt{\frac{\log n}{\log \log n}}\right).$$

The theorem now follows from the above lemma. □

4.1 Prefix Equality

Consider yet another relative to the prefix parity and majority problems, the prefix *equality* problem. The query operation is:

equal(i): return 'true' iff the number of 1s equals the number of 0s in the ith prefix.

We will show that

$$t = \Omega\left(\sqrt{\frac{\log n}{\log \log n}}\right) \tag{8}$$

is a lower bound on the worst-case time per operation for any implementation.

To see this, consider any algorithm for prefix equality with worst-case time t per operation. From an instance $y \in \{0, \pm 1\}^n$ of signed prefix sum we construct two strings $x_+, x_- = (01)^m x$, where $x \in \{0, 1\}^{2n}$ is constructed as in (5). For every signed prefix sum query we perform an exhaustive search by repeating the following until we get the answer 'true':

1. use **equal** to see if x_+ or x_- balance,
2. flip a 0 among the first $2m$ letters of x_+ to 1,
3. flip a 1 among the first $2m$ letters of x_- to 0.

The query time is $O(t \cdot \sum_{j \leq i} y_j)$ (we remember to change both strings back) and the update time is $2t$. The last theorem provides the stated bound on t.

The reader should now be able to show lower bounds of the same size for upward planarity testing or for planar point location where the query returns 'yes' iff two points are in the same polygon.

5 Parentheses Matching

The motivation for our last problem comes from modern editors. In many of them, a rudimentary syntax check is performed during editing, we focus on the feature of matching parentheses. Frandsen et al. [7] give polylogarithmic upper bounds for this problem; their lower bounds leave an exponential gap. Using the last theorem, we improve these bounds.

5.1 Dyck Languages

The language of *properly balanced parentheses* contains strings like ( ) and ( )(( )) but not)). The notion of balancedness also makes sense if we add more types of parentheses: ([])( ) balances but [ ) does not.

More formally, let $A = \{a_1, \ldots, a_k\}$ and $\bar{A} = \{\bar{a}_1, \ldots, \bar{a}_k\}$ be two disjoint sets of opening and closing symbols, respectively. For example, the pair $A = \{(, [, \mathbf{do}, \mathbf{if}\}$ and $\bar{A} = \{),], \mathbf{od}, \mathbf{fi}\}$ captures the nested structure of programming languages. The *one-sided Dyck language* D_k over $A \cup \bar{A}$ is the context-free language generated by the following grammar:

$$S \rightarrow SS \mid a_1 S \bar{a}_1 \mid \cdots \mid a_k S \bar{a}_k \mid \epsilon.$$

Closely related is the *two-sided Dyck language* D_k' over $A \cup \bar{A}$ defined by

$$S \rightarrow SS \mid a_1 S \bar{a}_1 \mid \bar{a}_1 S a_1 \mid \cdots \mid a_k S \bar{a}_k \mid \bar{a}_k S a_k \mid \epsilon.$$

This corresponds to two-sided cancellation, so now also)(and ( ][ ) balance, while [ ) still does not.

The two-sided Dyck language has an algebraic interpretation. If we identify $\bar{a}_i$ with a_i^{-1} and view concatenation as the product operator then $x \in D_k'$ if and only if x equals the identity in the free group generated by A. For example, $\bar{a}_1 a_2 \bar{a}_2 a_1 \in D_2'$ because $a_1^{-1} a_2 a_2^{-1} a_1$ evaluates to unity.

The Dyck languages bear the name of the German mathematician Walther von Dyck (1856–1934). They are covered in detail in Harrison's classical treatment [11].

5.2 The Membership Problem

We consider the problem of maintaining membership in D_k or D'_k of a string from $(A \cup \bar{A})^n$ dynamically. Given a vector $x \in (A \cup \bar{A})^n$ of even length, initially a_1^n, maintain x under the following operations for any Dyck language D:

change(i, a): change x_i to $a \in A \cup \bar{A}$,
member: return 'yes' if and only if $x \in D$.

Alternatively, we can use this set of updates for analysing the *word* problem for the free group. Here, the **member** query returns 'yes' if and only if $\prod_i x_i = 1$. (In this context, **product** or **identity** may be better names for the query.) However, we will refrain from distinguishing between the word problem for the free group and the membership problem for two-sided Dyck languages. Frandsen, Miltersen, and Skyum [8] study dynamic word problems for other monoids.

5.3 Interval Queries

We begin by showing that (8) is a lower bound for the two *single-letter* languages with a more powerful query:

interval(i, j): return 'yes' if $x_i \ldots x_j \in D$.

Let $y \in \{0, \pm 1\}^n$ be an instance of signed prefix sum. Construct an instance of the Dyck problem,

$$h(y_n)h(y_{n-1}) \ldots h(y_1) \, \bar{a}^{4n}$$

where

$$h(y_i) = \begin{cases} aaaa, & \text{if } y_i = +1, \\ aaa\bar{a}, & \text{if } y_i = 0, \\ a\bar{a}a\bar{a}, & \text{if } y_i = -1. \end{cases}$$

Note that for any i, the string $h(y_i) \ldots h(y_1)\bar{a}^{2(i+s)}$ balances if and only if $s = \sum_{j \leq i} y_j$. Therefore to answer a **sum** query, we check all intervals for $x = 0, -1, +1, -2, +2, \ldots$, until an interval balances. This takes time $O(t \cdot |s_i|)$ in the worst case, where t is the time for an **interval**-query. The bound follows from Theorem 2.

5.4 Lower Bound for Language Membership

We now show that for Dyck languages with *two or more* letters, (8) is a lower bound even for language membership, i.e. using the original **member**-query.

We first prove the claim for D'_2. We will use the **member** query for D'_2 to solve an instance of the problem from the last section.

Let $x \in \{a, \bar{a}\}^n$ be an instance of the interval problem for D'_1. Let

$$y = a\bar{a}x_1 a\bar{a}x_2 a\bar{a} \ldots a\bar{a}x_n a\bar{a}x^{\mathrm{R}}$$

be an instance of the membership problem and note $y \in D_2'$. To answer a query **interval**(i, j) we merely insert a matching pair of other parentheses in y at the corresponding place:

$$y' = a\bar{a}x_1a\bar{a}\ldots x_{i-1}bbx_i \ldots x_j\bar{b}\bar{b}x_{j+1}\ldots x^{\mathrm{R}},$$

where x^{R} denotes x reversed. It is easy to see that $y' \in D_2'$ iff $x_i \ldots x_j \in D_1'$. After the query, y' is changed back to y.

In the one-sided case, we have to extend both ends of the instance with parentheses to

$$y = a^{2n}a\bar{a}x_1a\bar{a}x_2a\bar{a}\ldots a\bar{a}x_na\bar{a}x^{\mathrm{R}}\bar{a}^2n,$$

just to make sure $y \in D_2$. The rest of the proof is the same.

Acknowledgements

The authors thank Gudmund Skovbjerg Frandsen and Peter Bro Miltersen for their co-operation.

References

1. Arne Andersson. Sublogarithmic searching without multiplications. In *Proc. 36th FOCS*, pages 655–663. IEEE Computer Society, 1995.
2. Arne Andersson, Torben Hagerup, Stefan Nilsson, and Rajeev Raman. Sorting in linear time? In *Proc 27thSTOC*, pages 427–436, 1995.
3. Paul Beame and Faith Fich, 1994. Personal communication, reported by Peter Bro Miltersen.
4. Yi-Jen Chiang and Roberto Tamassia. Dynamic algorithms in Computational Geometry. Technical Report CS-91-24, Dept. of Comp. Sc., Brown University, 1991.
5. Giuseppe Di Battista, Peter Eades, Roberto Tamassia, and Ioannis G. Tollis. Algorithms for drawing graphs: an annotated bibliography. Available via anonymous ftp from wilma.cs.brown.edu in /pub/papers/compgeo/gdbiblio.ps.Z, 1994.
6. Paul F. Dietz. Optimal algorithms for list indexing and subset rank. In *Proc. First Workshop on Algorithms and Data Structures (WADS)*, volume 382 of *Lecture Notes in Computer Science*, pages 39–46. Springer Verlag, Berlin, 1989.
7. Gudmund Skovbjerg Frandsen, Thore Husfeldt, Peter Bro Miltersen, Theis Rauhe, and Søren Skyum. Dynamic algorithms for the Dyck languages. In *Proc. 4th WADS*, volume 955 of *Lecture Notes in Computer Science*, pages 98–108. Springer, 1995.
8. Gudmund Skovbjerg Frandsen, Peter Bro Miltersen, and Sven Skyum. Dynamic word problems. In *Proc 34th FOCS*, pages 470–479, 1993.
9. Michael L. Fredman and Monika Rauch Henzinger. Lower bounds for fully dynamic connectivity problems in graphs. Manuscript, preliminary version in STOC 94.
10. Michael L. Fredman and Michael E. Saks. The cell probe complexity of dynamic data structures. In *Proc. 21st STOC*, pages 345–354, 1989.
11. Michael A. Harrison. *Introduction to Formal Language Theory*. Addison-Wesley, 1978.

12. P. B. Miltersen, S. Subramanian, J. S. Vitter, and R. Tamassia. Complexity models for incremental computation. *Theoretical Computer Science*, 130:203–236, 1994.

13. Peter Bro Miltersen. Lower bounds for union-split-find related problems on random access machines. In *Proc. 26th STOC*, pages 625–634. ACM, 1994.

14. Peter Bro Miltersen, Noam Nisan, Shmuel Safra, and Avi Wigderson. On data structures and asymmetric communication complexity. In *Proc. 27th STOC*, pages 103–111. ACM, 1995.

15. Rajeev Motwani and Prabhakar Raghavan. *Randomized Algorithms*. Cambridge University Press, 1995.

16. Franco P. Preparata and Roberto Tamassia. Fully dynamic point location in a monotone subdivision. *SIAM Journal of Computing*, 18(4):811–830, 1989.

17. Roberto Tamassia and Franco P. Preparata. Dynamic maintenance of planar digraphs, with applications. *Algorithmica*, 5:509–527, 1990.

18. Mikkel Thorup. On RAM priority queue. In *Proc 7th Ann. Symp. on Discrete Algorithms (SODA)*, pages 59–67, 1996.

19. Andrew Chi-Chih Yao. Should tables be sorted? *Journal of the ACM*, 28(3):615–628, July 1981.

Optimal Pointer Algorithms for Finding Nearest Common Ancestors in Dynamic Trees

Stephen Alstrup[1] and Mikkel Thorup[1]

Department of Computer Science, University of Copenhagen, Universitetsparken 1, DK-2100 Copenhagen, Denmark (e-mail: stephen,mthorup@diku.dk, www: http://www.diku.dk/~stephen,~mthorup)

Abstract. We consider the problem of finding the nearest common ancestor of two given nodes x and y (denoted by $nca(x, y)$) in a dynamic forest of rooted trees. Interspersed with nca-queries are on-line commands $link(x, y)$, where x but not necessarily y is a tree root. The effect of a command $link(x, y)$ is to combine the trees containing x and y by making y the parent of x. This problem was originally proposed by Aho, Hopcroft and Ullman (SIAM J. Comput. 5(1), 115-132, 1976). We present a pointer machine algorithm, which performs n $link$ and m nca in time $O(n + m \log \log n)$, matching a lower-bound by Harel and Tarjan (SIAM J. Comput. 13(2), 338-355, 1984). The previous best bound on a pointer machine was $O((n + m) \log n)$, due to Sleator and Tarjan (J. Comput. Syst. Sc. 26(3), 362-391, 1983).

1 Introduction

Aho, Hopcroft and Ullman [2] consider the following problem: Given a collection of rooted trees, answer queries of the form, "What is the nearest common ancestor (nca) of vertices x and y". They consider three different versions of the problem (1, 2 and 5 listed below), which are more or less dynamic depending upon whether the queries are all specified in advance and how much the trees change during the course of the queries. The following five problems are considered:

- **Problem 1 (off-line).** The collection of trees is static and the entire sequence of queries is specified in advance.
- **Problem 2 (static).** The collection of trees is static but the queries are given on-line, so each query must be answered before the next one is known.
- **Problem 3 (link root).** The queries are given on-line. Interspersed with the queries are on-line commands of the form $link\_root(x, y)$ where x and y are tree roots. The effect of a command $link\_root(x, y)$ is to combine the trees containing x and y by making y the parent of x.
- **Problem 4 (add leaf).** The queries are given on-line on a tree T. Interspersed with the queries are on-line commands of the form $add\_leaf(x, y)$ where y is any node in T and x is a new leaf. The effect of a command $add\_leaf(x, y)$ is to insert x as a new leaf in T by making y the parent of x.

- **Problem 5 (link).** The queries are given on-line. Interspersed with the queries are on-line commands of the form $link(x, y)$ where x but not necessarily y is a tree root. The effect of a command $link(x, y)$ is to combine the trees containing x and y by making y the parent of x.

The problems 1-5 have been investigated both for RAM [1] and pointer machines [9]. A pointer machine differs from a RAM by not allowing address arithmetic. This models the possibilities in many functional programming languages. Below n denotes the number of nodes in the collection of trees and m denotes the number of *nca*-queries. Notice that the number of nodes limits the number of tree operations *add_leaf*, *link* and *link_root*. For measuring time we use the *uniform cost measure* where all operations require constant time. Several papers improve and extend the results from [2]. The best known results for problems 1-5 are summarized in table 1.

	Pointer machine		RAM machine	
Problem	Algorithm	Time	Algorithm	Time
1. off-line	Tarjan [8]	$O((n+m)\alpha(n+m,n))$	Harel and Tarjan [6]	$O(n+m)$
2. static	Leeuwen and Tsakalidis [10]	$O(n+m\log\log n)$	Harel and Tarjan [6]	$O(n+m)$
3. link root	Leeuwen [12]	$O((n+m)\log\log n)$	Harel and Tarjan [6]	$O((n+m)\alpha(n+m,n))$
4. add leaf	Tsakalidis [11]	$O(n+m\log n)$	Gabow [4]	$O(n+m)$
5. link	Sleator and Tarjan [7]	$O((n+m)\log n)$	Gabow [4]	$O((n+m)\alpha(n+m,n))$
Optimal $O(n + m\log\log n)$ algorithms are given for problems 3-5 for pointer machine				

Table 1. Fastest algorithms 1996. All the algorithms use $O(n)$ space.

In this paper we give an $O(n+m\log\log n)$ algorithm for problem 5 for pointer machine, thereby improving the best known results for problems 3-5 for pointer machine. This matches a lower bound of $\Omega(\log\log n)$ per *nca*-query by Harel and Tarjan [6]. In section 2 we describe the overall scheme used for presenting our algorithms. In section 3 we derive an optimal algorithm for problem 4 by combining techniques from [2,4,5,6,11]. In section 4 the algorithm for problem 4 is used as a sub-routine for an optimal algorithm for problem 5.

2   A model for the algorithms

The algorithm in this paper follows a pointer machine version of the "Micro-MacroUniverse," as frequently used for RAM algorithms (see eg. [5]). The MicroMacroUniverse is build by partitioning the set of nodes from an original tree T into disjoint subsets, where each subset induces a subtree of T called a micro tree. The partitioning can be thought of as removing edges from T, leaving a forest of micro trees. The root from each micro tree is inserted in a macro tree. The macro tree contains an edge between two nodes, *iff* T has a path between the two nodes which does not contain any other micro tree roots. Thus, the macro tree is obtained by contracting all the micro trees. To maintain this structure we use three algorithms.

- A MacroAlgorithm to the macro tree which gives optimal nca-queries.
- A MicroAlgorithm to the micro trees which gives optimal tree operations.
- An optimal algorithm which combines the Micro- and MacroAlgorithm.

Notation : We denote the original trees T, the micro trees S and the macro trees U. If it not is clear from context in which tree an operation is used, subscripts are used; eg. $p_S(x)$ is the parent to x in the micro tree S. A node x in a micro tree has a pointer, $root_S(x)$, to the root in the micro tree to which it belongs. To decide nca_T we use an extended nca-operation, $nca*$, in the macro tree. Let $a = nca(x, y)$. For $v = x, y$ let a_v be the ancestor of v immediately preceding a; if $a = v$ then $a_v = a$. Now we define $nca * (x, y)$ as the triple (a, a_x, a_y). With these operations $nca_T(x, y)$ can be found in a MicroMacroUniverse as follows.

1. if $root_S(x) = root_S(y)$ then return $nca_S(x, y)$;
2. $(a, a_1, a_2) = nca *_U (root_S(x), root_S(y))$;
3. if $a = a_1$ then $x' := x$ else $x' := p_T(a_1)$;
4. if $a = a_2$ then $y' := y$ else $y' := p_T(a_2)$;
5. return $nca_S(x', y')$;

Algorithm 1

3 An optimal algorithm for the operation add leaf

In this section we present an optimal $O(n + m \log \log n)$ algorithm for add_leaf, where n is the number of nodes in the tree. Furthermore worst-case for each nca-query is $O(\log \log n)$. The previous best algorithm by Tsakalidis [11] has complexity $O(n + m \log h)$, where h is the height of the tree. We will use Tsakalidis algorithm as a subroutine (MicroAlgorithm) for our optimal algorithm and later we will use an extended version : Tsakalidis algorithm also supports $delete\_leaf$ in constant time and the nca-query is easily extended to a $nca*$-query [3].

Lemma 1. A MicroAlgorithm exists, which performs m $nca*$ and n add_leaf and $delete\_leaf$ in $O(n + m \log h)$-time. If k is the number of nodes in the tree at some point, the MicroAlgorithm uses $O(k)$ space.

Proof. See [3,11]. ☐

We also use a $O(n \log n + m \log \log n)$ MacroAlgorithm for n add_leaf and m $nca*$-queries, which is presented in subsection 3.1.
The Micro- and MacroAlgorithm together give an optimal algorithm as follows. The nodes in T have a field $size_S$, where $size_S(x)$ is the number of nodes in the micro tree with root x; if x is not a micro tree root then $size_S(x)$ is undefined. If a micro tree contains $l = 1 + \lceil \log n \rceil$ nodes it is denoted as full and otherwise as not

full[1]. When a new node x is inserted as a leaf with parent y ($add\_leaf(x,y)$), it is inserted in the same micro tree as the parent if the micro tree which y belongs to is not full ($size_S(root_S(y)) < l$)). Otherwise a new micro tree is created with the root x. In both cases the fields $size_S$ and $root_S$ are easily updated. Only root nodes from full micro trees are inserted in the macro tree. The micro tree root z is inserted when its micro tree become full ($size_S(z) = l$). Let r be the root in the original tree T. Then the macro tree U has edges $\{(v, root_S(p_T(v)))|v \in T\backslash\{r\} \wedge root_S(v) = v \wedge size_S(v) = l\}$. With this structure $nca_T(x, y)$ can be found using algorithm 1 except in cases where nodes are in not full micro trees; however if x is in a not full micro tree different from y's micro tree ($root_S(x) \neq root_S(y)$) then $nca(x, y)_T = nca_T(p_T(root_S(x)), y)$.

Theorem 2. *Given an $O(n+m \log h)$ MicroAlgorithm for n add_leaf and m nca where h is the height of the tree AND an $O(n \log n + m \log \log n)$ MacroAlgorithm for n add_leaf and m nca* we can construct an $O(n + m \log \log n)$ algorithm for n add_leaf and m nca.*

Proof. (sketch). An add_leaf command takes (amortized) constant time except for insertion in the macro tree; but only root nodes from full micro trees are inserted in a macro tree. Because full micro trees have size $l = 1 + \lceil \log n \rceil$ at most $\lfloor n/l \rfloor$ nodes are in a macro tree, which gives the complexity $O((n/l) \log(n/l)) = O(n)$. A nca-query can result in at most 6 constant time calls to $root_S$, an $O(\log \log n)$ query in a macro tree and a query in a micro tree. The query in a micro tree takes a time logarithmic to the height of the micro tree which is $l = O(\log n)$. □

3.1 MacroAlgorithm for the operation add leaf

In this section we present an $O(n \log n + m \log \log n)$ algorithm for n add_leaf and m $nca*$ in a tree T and show how to extend it to a MacroAlgorithm for $link$. In order to compute nca in a static tree (problem 2) Harel and Tarjan [6] use a secondary compressed C-tree. We use a similar tree modified for the dynamic algorithm. The C-tree contains the same nodes as T, but C is constructed such that its height is logarithmic to the number of nodes. The C-tree is constructed from T by classifying the edges in T as either heavy or light. If an edge $(v, p_T(v))$ is heavy then v is denoted as the heavy child of $p_T(v)$ and otherwise as a light child of $p_T(v)$. The heavy and light edges in T are chosen to meet the following conditions:

Condition 1 Each node in T which has a child, has exactly one heavy child.

Condition 2 A heavy child v to a node $p_T(v)$ is chosen such that for any other child z of $p_T(v)$ it is true that $(5/4) * size_T(z) < size_T(p_T(v))$, where $size$ is the number of descendants to a node.

---

[1] If the total number of nodes is not known in advance, then n is guessed to be a constant and each time the number of nodes extend the guess, we double the guess and reconstruct the structure.

The heavy edges in T partition the nodes in T on heavy paths such that each node belongs to exactly one heavy path (a leaf which is not a heavy child is a heavy path with one node). The node on a heavy path which is nearest the root of the tree is the *apex* node for the heavy path and $apex(v)$ is the *apex* node on the heavy path containing the node v. The tree C for the tree T with root r can now be described as the edges $C = \{(v, apex(p_T(v))|v \in T\backslash\{r\}\}$.

Lemma 3. *The height of C is $O(\log n)$.*

Proof. A path in C from a leaf v to the root contains all the light nodes from v to the root plus node v if it is light, hence $depth(v) \leq \lceil \log_{(5/4)} n \rceil$ by condition 2. □

The main idea to compute $nca *_T (x, y)$ is to use the C-tree to find the two nodes x' and y' which are respectively the first ancestor of x and y on the heavy path containing $apex(nca(x, y))$. To determine nca for two nodes on the same heavy path, we associate a d-label to each node, $d(v) \in \mathbb{Z}$, such that for any two nodes on the same heavy path, we have $d(w) < d(v)$ if the depth of w is less than the depth of v. Notice that the *apex* node for a node x is x if x is the root or a light child; otherwise it is $p_C(x)$. To maintain the C-tree we use the MicroAlgorithm (see lemma 1). An algorithm for computing $(b, b_1, b_2) = nca *_T (x, y)$

1. $(a, a_1, a_2) := nca *_C (x, y)$; {if $x \neq y$ then $a = apex(nca_T(x, y))$ }
2. if $(a = x)$ or $(a = y)$ then begin $b := a$; goto 6; end;
3. if $apex(a_1) \neq a$ then $a_1' := p_T(a_1)$ else $a_1' := a_1$; {$= x$}
4. if $apex(a_2) \neq a$ then $a_2' := p_T(a_2)$ else $a_2' := a_2$; {$= y$}
5. if $d(a_1') < d(a_2')$ then $b := a_1'$ else $b := a_2'$;
6. if $x = b$ then $b_1 := b$ else if $p_T(a_1) = b$ then $b_1 := a_1$ else $b_1 := heavychild(b)$;
7. if $y = b$ then $b_2 := b$ else if $p_T(a_2) = b$ then $b_2 := a_2$ else $b_2 := heavychild(b)$;

Algorithm 2

Lemma 4. *Given an $O(n+m \log h)$ MicroAlgorithm we can construct a MacroAlgorithm where each $nca*$ is bound by $O(\log \log n)$.*

Proof. Except from constant time operations a $nca*_T$-query is reduced to a $nca*_C$ query which has the complexity $O(\log h)$ (see lemma 1) and from lemma 3, $h = O(\log n)$ so $nca*_T$ is bound by $O(\log \log n)$. □

We now show how to maintain the structure when adding a leaf. The hard part is condition 2 – to make sure that the C-tree height is logarithmic to the number of nodes. To fulfill this it is necessary to check whether a light edge has to change to heavy. From the definition of the C-tree we have for a light child v that $size_T(v) = size_C(v)$. The field $size_C$ can easily be updated : Adding a leaf x to C we update $size_C$ with 1 for each of x's ancestors in C. Because C's hight is limited it takes $O(\log n)$ time. We cannot afford to check a light child each time it is updated but by condition 2 we only have to check a node when its

$size_C$ has doubled. The nodes in C get an extra field named $nextsize_C$ and each time $nextsize_C = size_C$ we check if the node should be heavy; if not we double $nextsize_C$. When checking if a node v should become heavy, we cannot rely on $size_C$ to determine $size_T$ for the heavy child of $p_T(v)$. Therefore the check is done by counting the descendants of the heavy child in T. For this purpose we need *left-* and *rightsibling* pointers to insert siblings in a double circular list. Algorithm for inserting a new leaf x.

1. Insert x in C. {and ensure condition 1 }
2. Update $size_C$ for all ancestors of $p_T(x)$ in C with $size_C(x)$. {=1, if x is a new leaf}.
3. Check if $p_T(x)$ have an ancestor in C except from the root where $size_C \geq nextsize_C$. If such a node exists the node w with least depth is chosen and the light edge $(w, p_T(w))$ is updated in the next steps.
4. Let $v = heavychild(p_T(w))$. {Because w is an *apex* its parent must have another heavy child}.
5. Check if $size_T(w) \geq 2 * size_T(v)$ by counting at most $\lceil size_C(w)/2 \rceil$ descendants of v.
6. If $size_T(w) \geq 2 * size_T(v)$ then remove the descendants of v and w in T from C with $delete\_leaf_C$ and make the edge $(w, p_T(w))$ heavy. The fields d, $size_C$ etc. of the removed nodes are updated and the nodes are inserted in C again using add_leaf_C.
7. Let z be that of the two nodes v and w which is light after step 6. Set $nextsize_C(z) = 2 * max\{nextsize_C(z), size_C(heavychild(p_T(z)))\}$.

Algorithm 3

Lemma 5. *The MacroAlgorithm has the complexity $O(n \log n + m \log \log n)$ for n add_leaf and m nca*.*

Proof. From lemma 4 we achieve the $O(\log \log n)$ bound for nca*. Next we consider the complexity of counting descendants in T and adding/removing leaves in C. Recall that the C-tree is maintained by the $O(n + m \log h)$ MicroAlgorithm (see lemma 1). Each time an edge $(w, p_T(w))$ is checked we have to count up to $\lceil size_C(w)/2 \rceil$ nodes and update at most $2 * size_T(w)$ nodes in T and C. Since w is a light child $size_C(w) = size_T(w)$, so the total cost is $O(size_T(w))$. Let m_0 be the root of T and let its children be $m_1, m_2 \cdots m_L$ where $size_T(m_1) \geq size_T(m_2) \geq \cdots \geq size_T(m_L)$. Set $size_T(m_0) = n$, $size_T(m_1) = \alpha$ and $\sum_{i=2}^{L} size_T(m_i) = \beta$, making $n = \alpha + \beta + 1$. Between two times a node is checked its size has at least been doubled and the last time a node m_i, $i > 1$, is checked its size is at most $size_T(m_i)$ and the last time node m_1 is checked its size is at most $4 * \beta$. This implies that the total amount of work for updating the children to m_0 is $O(\beta + \sum_{j=2}^{L} \sum_{i=1}^{\lfloor \log_2 size_T(m_j) \rfloor} 2^i) = O(\beta)$. Each of the trees $T^{m_2}, T^{m_3} \cdots T^{m_L}$ are at most half as big as the tree T^{m_0} and these trees contain β nodes which establishes the complexity $O(n \log n)$ for all updates in T. $\square$

3.2 MacroAlgorithm for the operation link

Given a detailed description of the MacroAlgorithm for *add_leaf* we now shortly show how to construct a $O(n \log n + m \log \log n)$ MacroAlgorithm for n link and m *nca**. We will use the same structure so we only show how to perform $link(x, y)$. Recall that x but not necessarily y is a tree root and notice that the root node α in the tree to which y belongs can be determined in $O(\log n)$ by following the path $y \cdots \alpha$ in C. If $size_C(x) < size_C(\alpha)$ we simply apply algorithm 3 (step 2-6) with the exception that if the tree is not updated then the nodes from C^x (x and its descendants) are inserted in the compressed tree C^α. Next we show how to proceed when $size_C(x) \geq size_C(\alpha)$. When a node is inserted in a C-tree a new node in the C-tree is created and pointers are set between the two nodes in the T-tree and the C-tree. Hence two T-nodes can in $O(1)$-time exchange nodes in the C-tree by moving only four pointers; let us call this operation an exchange operation. We are now able to use a variant of a technique from [4] to link two trees. The main idea is to let the path $x \cdots \alpha$ be one heavy path. This can be done in three steps. 1) Exchange pointers for node x and α, 2) Add node x to the compressed C-tree as a leaf to node α in the compressed tree and 3) Update and insert in C the former proper descendants to α. Step 3 can be done by d-labelling the nodes on the heavy path $P = y..\alpha$ with labels $d(x) - 1 \cdots d(x) - |P|$, inserting the nodes on the path in C by adding them as leaves to α and then updating (including d-labelling and insertion in C) these nodes proper descendants in a breadth-first manner.

Lemma 6. *The MacroAlgorithm has complexity $O(n \log n + m \log \log n)$ for n link and m nca*. Furthermore the root can be found from any node in constant time.*

Proof. Each time two trees are linked the smallest tree is updated and in the first case $(size_C(x) < size_C(\alpha))$ nodes from the greatest tree can be updated if an edge is checked. Updating the smallest trees takes $O(n \log n)$-time for n *link* and updating light edges does not exceed this complexity, by the proof of lemma 5. The root of T can be found using C. The easy proof of correctness is omitted. $\qquad\square$

4 An optimal algorithm for the operation link

In this section we describe an $O(n + m \log \log n)$ algorithm for n *link* and m *nca*. The algorithm uses MicroMacroUniverse model. As MacroAlgorithm we will use the $O(n \log n + m \log \log n)$ algorithm, for n *link* and m *nca** which is described in subsection 3.2. As MicroAlgorithm we will use the optimal algorithm from the previous section. This implies that the MicroAlgorithm used in this section performs n *add_leaf* and m *nca* in $O(n + m \log \log n)$-time. Using the optimal algorithm for *add_leaf* as a MicroAlgorithm for *link* it is not necessary to limit the size of the micro trees, so the only problem is to make sure that they are big enough, in order to limit the size of the macro trees. We solve the problem by partitioning the nodes in a tree in two levels such that a path from a node in level 1 to the root node contains only level 1 nodes. Removing the nodes in level 1 from a tree leaves a forest of trees, called the subtrees of the original tree. Each of the subtrees will be partitioned in micro trees and connected with a macro tree such that each of the subtrees in the forest is a single MicroMacroUniverse. For two nodes in the same subtree *nca* can be found by algorithm 1 in $O(\log \log n)$-time, so the only remaining problem for *nca* is a fast *nca*-algorithm for nodes in level 1. For this purpose we construct a LevelAlgorithm. The optimal algorithm is then constructed by using a slightly modified LevelAlgorithm on itself.

4.1 LevelAlgorithm

In this subsection an $O(n + m \log n)$ algorithm for n *link* and m *nca* is described. The nodes in a tree T in the forest of trees are partitioned in two levels:

Level 1 Level 1 contains up to n nodes. If a node is in Level 1, then so are all its ancestors. The nodes in level 1 are not inserted in any secondary structure but are marked as belonging to level 1. Level 1 may be empty.

Level 2 Removing the nodes in level 1 from a tree T leaves the nodes in level 2 as a forest of trees. Each of these trees will be denoted as subtrees of T and for a node x in level 2 $sub_T(x)$ is the root of the subtree. Each of the subtrees is treated in the following way : The nodes are partitioned in micro trees and the micro trees are maintained by the optimal algorithm for *add_leaf*. Each node in a micro tree S has a pointer $root_S$, which points to the root of the micro tree to which the node belongs. Each of the micro trees can contain up to n nodes and contains at least $l = 1 + \lceil \log n \rceil$ nodes. The micro tree root nodes are inserted in a macro tree U which is maintained by the MacroAlgorithm for *link* (see lemma 6).

First we describe how to decide *nca* in this universe and next how to *link* two trees. If two nodes x and y are in the same subtree ($sub_T(x) = sub_T(y)$, *iff* $root_U(root_S(x)) = root_U(root_S(y))$) then $nca(x, y)$ is found using algorithm 1. If they are not in the same subtree the problem is reduced to find *nca* for two nodes in level 1 (if one of the nodes, say x, are in level 2 then substitute it with $p_T(sub_T(x))$). Determining $nca(x, y)$ for two nodes in level 1 is done by travelling from each of the nodes to the root node. If the travelling contains at least $l = 1 + \lceil \log n \rceil$ nodes the nodes from level 1 are inserted in a new micro tree and the root is inserted in a new macro tree. When collecting the nodes in level 1 we also collect all roots from the subtrees in level 2 in a list L at the same time (because we have to collect nodes we need three more pointers : *leftsibling* and *rightsibling* pointers so siblings are in a double circular list and a *child* pointer in order to be able to reach the children of a node). Now it only remains to link all the macro trees to one macro tree, which is done by performing a $link_U(v, r)$ for each node v in L, where r is the root of T.

Lemma 7. *Except the time charged to link micro- and macro trees a nca query takes $O(\log n)$-time.*

Proof. Determination of *nca* for two nodes in the same subtree has the complexity $O(\log \log n)$ using algorithm 1. Determination of *nca* for two nodes in level 1 takes $O(\log n)$ if the nodes are not collected in a micro tree - if they are this time is charged to link micro- and macro trees. □

Now we describe how to *link*. Recall that $link(x, y)$ combines two trees by making x a child of y in the tree T (by setting the pointers p, *child*, *leftsibling* and *rightsibling*). To maintain the other trees, we split up in cases depending on which of the two levels the two nodes are in. If both nodes are in level 1 or x is in level 2 and y is in level 1, we are done. If both nodes are in level 2 we combine the macro trees to which they belong by the command $link_U(x, root_S(y))$ (x is root in a macro tree and y must belong to a micro tree which root is a node in another macro tree). The last case is when x is in level 1 and y in level 2. All the nodes from level 1 in T^x are inserted in the micro tree to which y belongs. They are simply added one by one using *add_leafs*. While inserting the nodes from level 1 in the micro tree we also collect the roots from the subtrees in T^x in a list L at the same time, these nodes are also the root nodes from the macro trees belonging to T^x which have to be linked below the node $root_S(y)$. This is done by the operation $link_U(v, root_S(y))$ for each node in L.

Lemma 8. *The LevelAlgorithm has complexity $O(n + m \log n)$ for n link and m nca.*

Proof. We have already argued (by lemma 7) that *nca* takes $O(\log n)$ unless the nodes are inserted in a micro tree. The *link* commands takes constant time except for updating the micro- and macro trees. We thus only have to prove that maintaining micro- and macro trees takes linear time. The nodes are only inserted once in a micro tree so this part takes $O(n)$-time using the optimal $O(n + m \log \log n)$ algorithm from the last section to maintain the micro trees (see theorem 2). The MacroAlgorithm has the complexity $O(n \log n + m \log \log n)$ for n *link* and m *nca*∗ (see lemma 6). Only root nodes from micro trees are inserted in a macro tree and a micro tree contains at least $l = 1 + \lceil \log n \rceil$ nodes so the number of nodes in macro trees is $O(n / \log n)$ giving the complexity $O(n)$ to maintain the macro trees. □

4.2 Combining

Now we are able to describe the optimal algorithm for *link*. The construction of the algorithm is done by using the LevelAlgorithm as follows. We maintain the same structure as in the last subsection but now the nodes in level 1 are inserted in a secondary structure which is maintained by the LevelAlgorithm. The LevelAlgorithm determines *nca* in $O(\log n)$ time so the remaining problem is to limit the number of nodes in level 1 to $O(\log n)$. When linking two nodes x and y, which are both in level 1, there is no direct path from y to the root so it is not possible to update the number of nodes in level 1 in constant time. To make a direct way to the root we could let the nodes in level 1 be in a set

(UNION-FIND) but this would give the complexity $O(n\alpha(n,n) + m\log\log n)$. Our method to remove the inverse Ackerman function is build on the following technique. The LevelAlgorithm used on nodes in level 1 is modified in such a way that a command to it will either respond normally or it will report that there are too many nodes. This modification can be done on the LevelAlgorithm as follows. When linking two macro trees we now check that the size of the two macro trees together does not exceed $\log n/\log\log n$. Because each node in a macro tree represent a micro tree with a least $\log\log n$ nodes a failure report from the LevelAlgorithm implies that level 1 contains at least $\log n$ nodes which again implies that there are enough nodes in level 1 to collect them in to a new micro tree.

Theorem 9. *We can construct an $O(n + m\log\log n)$ algorithm for n link and m nca.*

Proof. The only non-linear algorithm used by the LevelAlgorithm is the MacroAlgorithm with the the complexity $O(n\log n)$ for n link, but with the control instance there are at most $\log n/\log\log n$ nodes in one macro tree, and thereby we achieve the bound $O(n)$. □

The two algorithms given above offer different worst-case for on nca-query. Using UNION-FIND we get $O(\log n)$ and without $O(n)$. A third possibility is to use a technique from Gabow [4]. Given an algorithm with the complexity $O(f(n) + g(m))$ for m $nca*$ and n add_leaf and add_root^2 it is shown how to construct an $O(f(n)\alpha(L,n) + Lg(m))$ algorithm where the worst-case for one nca is $O(L\beta)$ where $O(\beta)$ is the worst-case for nca for the previous algorithm. In [3] it is shown how to construct an $O(n + m\log\log n)$ algorithm for m $nca*$ and n $link\_root$ and add_leaf where worst-case for each nca-query is $O(\log\log n)$. This gives three alternatives which are collected in table 2.

Amortized complexity for n link and m nca	Worst-case for one nca
$O(n + m\log\log n)$	$O(n)$
$O(n\alpha(n,n) + m\log\log n)$	$O(\log n)$
$O(n\alpha(L,n) + Lm\log\log n)$	$O(L\log\log n)$

Table 2. Three alternatives to *link*.

Acknowledgement. We thank Martin Appel and Peter W. Lauridsen for reading preprint of this paper and giving many good suggestions.

References

1. A.V. Aho, J.E. Hopcroft, and J.D. Ullman. *The design and analysis of computer algorithms.* Addison-Wesley, 1974.

---

^{2} The effect of the command $add\_root(x,y)$ where x is a single node and y is the root of a tree is the tree constructed by making x the parent of y.

2. A.V. Aho, J.E. Hopcroft, and J.D. Ullman. On finding lowest common ancestor in trees. *SIAM Journal on computing*, 5(1):115–132, 1976. See also STOC 1973.

3. S. Alstrup. Optimal algorithms for finding nearest common ancestors in dynamic trees. Technical Report 95-30, Department of Computer Science, University of Copenhagen, 1995.

4. H.N. Gabow. Data structure for weighted matching and nearest common ancestors with linking. In *Annual ACM-SIAM Symposium on discrete algorithms (SODA)*, volume 1, pages 434–443, 1990.

5. H.N. Gabow and R.E. Tarjan. A linear-time algorithm for a special case of disjoint set union. *Journal of computer and system sciences*, 30(2):209–221, 1985.

6. D. Harel and R.E. Tarjan. Fast algorithms for finding nearest common ancestors. *Siam J. Comput*, 13(2):338–355, 1984.

7. D.D. Sleator and R.E. Tarjan. A data structure for dynamic trees. *Journal of computer and system sciences*, 26(3):362–391, 1983. See also STOC 1981.

8. R.E. Tarjan. Applications of path compression on balanced trees. *Journal of the association for computing machinery (J.ACM)*, 26(4):690–715, 1979.

9. R.E. Tarjan. A class of algorithms which require nonlinear time to maintain disjoint sets. *Journal of computer and system sciences*, 18(2):110–127, 1979.

10. A.K. Tsakalides and J. van Leeuwen. An optimal pointer machine algorithm for finding nearest common ansectors. Technical Report RUU-CS-88-17, Department of Computer Science, University of Utrecht, 1988.

11. A.K. Tsakalidis. The nearest common ancestor in a dynamic tree. *Acta informatica*, 25(1):37–54, 1988.

12. J. van Leeuwen. Finding lowest common ancestors in less than logarithmic time. Unpublish technical report, 1976.

Neighborhood Graphs and Distributed $\Delta + 1$-Coloring

Pierre Kelsen

Max-Planck-Institut für Informatik

Saarbrücken, Germany

Abstract. A tantalizing open question in the theory of distributed computing asks whether a graph with maximum degree Δ can be colored with $\Delta + 1$ colors in polylog deterministic steps in the distributed model of computation. Linial introduced the notion of a t-neighborhood graph of a given graph G and showed that the chromatic number of this graph is a lower bound on the number of colors that G can be colored with in t steps of the distributed model. In this paper we show that the chromatic number of any t-neighborhood graph is at most $\Delta + 1$ for some $t = O(\log^3 n)$. This implies that current techniques for proving lower bounds on the distributed complexity of $\Delta + 1$-coloring are not strong enough to give a negative answer to the above open problem. The proof of this result is based on the analysis of a randomized algorithm for this problem using martingale inequalities. We also show that in a nonconstructive sense the $\Delta + 1$-coloring problem can be solved in polylog time for an infinite class of graphs including vertex-transitive graphs.

1 Introduction

In the distributed model of computation – distributed model for short – we are given a *communication graph* G. At each node of G sits a processor that may communicate with its neighbors through the edges of the communication graph. We assume that all processors are synchronized. In one time step each processor can do some local computation and exchange messages with each of its neighbors in the communication graph. Thus, after t time steps each processor has collected information about the nodes at distance at most t from itself. In order to allow nontrivial problems to be solved we need to have some symmetry-breaking rule. We follow the standard approach of assigning unique labels in the range $\{1, \ldots, n\}$ to the n processors (see e.g. [8]).

In this paper we consider the problem of coloring the vertices of a graph with maximum degree Δ with $\Delta+1$ colors so that no two adjacent vertices receive the same color. We are interested in distributed algorithms for this problem whose running time is at most polylogarithmic in the number of nodes of the network. The $\Delta + 1$-coloring problem is closely related to the maximal independent set (MIS) problem, i.e., the problem of computing a set of nodes that does not contain two adjacent nodes and that is not properly contained in another set with this property. In fact there is a well-known NC reduction from $\Delta + 1$-coloring to MIS (see [9]). This reduction cannot, however, be done efficiently in the distributed model. We give a brief survey of results regarding the distributed complexity of these problems.

Although much effort has been invested in these problems during the last ten years, little is known about the complexity of distributed $\Delta + 1$-coloring in the general case. If the degree of the communication graph is small, then a technique based on deterministic coin tossing ([6]) can be used to obtain fast algorithms for several problems including $\Delta + 1$-coloring ([7]) and MIS. An approach to extend this technique to arbitrary graphs makes use of so-called cluster decompositions: the idea is to decompose the communication graph into connected components of small diameter (clusters) so that the graph induced by the clusters has small chromatic number ([4]). Using this technique Awerbuch et al. ([4]) derived the first sublinear time distributed algorithms for the $\Delta + 1$-coloring problem and the MIS problem. By giving faster algorithms for computing a cluster decomposition Panconesi and Srinivasan ([12]) obtained somewhat faster algorithms for these problems. The resulting algorithms run in $n^{O(1/\sqrt{\log n})}$ time which is still significantly slower than polylogarithmic time.

In view of these rather weak upper bounds it is natural to investigate lower bounds for these problems. Linial ([8]) proved a $\Omega(\log^* n)$ lower bound on the complexity of $\Delta + 1$-coloring and MIS on a ring. This bound is tight because of earlier results of Cole and Vishkin ([6]). (Linial also gives a $O(\log^* n)$ time distributed algorithm for coloring a graph with $O(\Delta^2)$ colors; see [14] for further work along these lines.) Naor and Stockmeyer ([11]) investigate the class of problems that can be solved in constant time on graphs of bounded degree. Despite these efforts no nontrivial lower bound for $\Delta + 1$-coloring is known for graphs of arbitrary degree.

In this paper we study the complexity of $\Delta + 1$-coloring in the distributed model for two reasons. The first obvious reason for doing this is the rather large gap between lower and upper bounds for this problem for arbitrary graphs. Another reason is the potential for gaining insight into an outstanding open question in this area, namely the question whether derandomization is possible in the distributed model. Indeed all current derandomization techniques (see e.g. [2]) require central computation to be carried out in order to zero in on a good sample point. Such an approach would result in distributed algorithms running in time at least proportional to the diameter on the network. On the other hand fast and simple randomized algorithms are known for problems such as $\Delta + 1$-coloring ([9]) and MIS ([10, 1]). Having a derandomization technique that preserves locality would be of eminent interest since it would imply efficient distributed solutions for these problems and many other problems.

In this paper we study the $\Delta + 1$-coloring problem by examining the structure of neighborhood graphs. Informally a t-neighborhood graph represents the structure of the neighborhoods of radius t in the graph. The concept of neighborhood graph was first introduced by Linial ([8]) in connection with deriving lower bounds on the complexity of graphtheoretic problems in the distributed model. An important observation of Linial is that the chromatic number of the t-neighborhood graph of a graph G is a lower bound on the number of colors that G can be colored with in t steps in the distributed model. Indeed all nontrivial lower bounds for the distributed complexity of $\Delta + 1$-coloring can be expressed as lower bounds on the chromatic number of neighborhood graphs. The central result of this paper states that the t-neighborhood graph of any graph has chromatic number at most $\Delta + 1$ for some $t = polylog(n)$. Thus, the standard lower bound technique will not suffice to prove lower bounds above the polylog level for $\Delta + 1$-coloring. We prove this result by analyzing a probabilistic algorithm for $\Delta + 1$-coloring using martingale inequalities.

Our second result is based on extending the concept of neighborhood graphs to families of graphs. We are able show that in a certain nonconstructive sense an infinite family of graphs containing all vertex-transitive graphs can be $\Delta + 1$-colored in $O(\log^3 n)$ distributed steps.

This paper is organized as follows: in the next section we explain the basic terminology and notation. In section 3 we introduce neighborhood graphs and their relation to the $\Delta + 1$-coloring problem. In section 4 we give the main result of this paper and outline its proof. In section 5 we perform the analysis of the randomized algorithm on which the result from the previous section is based. In section 6 we prove the existence of a fast distributed $\Delta + 1$-coloring algorithm for an infinite class of graphs.

2 Preliminaries

Basic Notation and Definitions. We use $[q]$ to denote the set $\{1, \ldots, q\}$. For standard graph terminology the reader is referred to [5]. By $N_H(v)$ we denote the set of neighbors of v in H and by $deg_H(v)$ we denote their number. The quantity $\Delta(H)$ stands for the maximum degree of a vertex in H. As a general rule H may be omitted in the above quantities if H is clear from the context. A $\Delta + 1$-coloring of a graph G is an assignment of colors in $[\Delta + 1]$ so that no two adjacent vertices receive the same color.

Model of Computation. Our model of computation is the synchronous point-to-point communication network ([3]) – _distributed model_ for short. The distributed model is described by an undirected communication graph $G = (V, E)$ on n nodes. The nodes in G represent processors and the edges in the graph represent communication links over which adjacent processors may exchange messages. In one time step each processor may perform some local computation and exchange a message with each of its neighbors; we assume that each message has length $O(\log n)$. We assume that the processors in the graph have been assigned unique labels in the range $[n]$. Two complexity measures are commonly associated with this model: the _time complexity_ is the number of time steps required by the algorithm, and the _communication complexity_ is the total number of messages sent during the algorithm.

3 Neighborhood Graphs

We define the concept of a neighborhood graph first introduced by Linial ([8]). A _centered graph_ is a pair (H, v) where H is a graph and v is a (distinguished) vertex of H; we say that (H, v) is centered at v. Two centered graphs (H, v) and (H', v') are isomorphic if there exists a graph isomorphism from H to H' that maps v to v'. For $v \in V(G)$ let $S_t(v)$ denote the subgraph of G centered at v induced by the vertices in G that are at distance at most t from v; we call this subgraph the *t-neighborhood of* v. We construct the *t-neighborhood graph of* G, denoted by $N_t(G)$ as follows: the vertices of $N_t(G)$ are the centered graphs (H, v) with $V(H) \subseteq [n]$ that are isomorphic to some $S_t(v)$, $v \in G$; two vertices (H, v) and (H', w) are connected by an edge in $N_t(G)$ if there exists a bijective mapping $\lambda : [n] \to V$ and two adjacent vertices v and w in G such that $\lambda|V(H)$ (restriction of λ to $V(H)$) is an isomorphism from (H, v) to $S_t(v)$ and $\lambda|V(H')$ is an isomorphism from (H', w) to $S_t(w)$. Intuitively, it means that G can be labeled in such a way that the t-neighborhoods of v and w look like H and H', respectively.

An algorithm A running in t steps in the distributed model collects for each processor $v \in V$ information about the structure of the subgraph $S_t(v)$ and the labels of vertices in this subgraph. We may thus view algorithm A as a mapping from the vertices in $N_t(G)$ to the output domain. If A produces a valid coloring of the vertices in G, it induces a valid coloring of the vertices in $N_t(G)$ with the same number of colors. This is expressed in the following result first observed by Linial.

Lemma 1 *([8]) The chromatic number of* $N_t(G)$, $\chi(N_t(G))$, *is a lower bound on the number of colors* G *can be colored with in* t *steps in the distributed model. Therefore a* $\Delta + 1$*-coloring can be computed in* t *steps only if* $\chi(N_t(G)) \leq \Delta + 1$.

If we do not restrict the length of the messages exchanged nor the amount of local computation, then the converse of the result holds, i.e., a graph can be colored in t steps with $\chi(N_t(G))$ colors. We refer to this variant of the distributed model as the *strong distributed model*.

4   The Chromatic Number of Neighborhood Graphs

The main result of this paper is the following upper bound on the chromatic number of neighborhood graphs

Theorem 1 *For any graph* H *on* n *vertices we have* $\chi(N_t(H)) \leq \Delta(H) + 1$ *for some* $t = O((\log n^3))$.

Informally, we may interpret this result as saying that there exists an algorithm for coloring a known graph with unknown labeling in *polylog(n)* time. We remark that Linial's lower bounds ([8]) on the complexity of distributed $\Delta + 1$-coloring hold even if all vertices know the graph and only the labeling is unknown. An important consequence of theorem 1 is then that Linial's techniques (based on lemma 1) are not strong enough to rule out the existence of an algorithm that $\Delta + 1$-colors all graphs of maximum degree Δ in *polylog(n)* time – the central open question in this area.

The proof of theorem 1 is based on a careful analysis of the randomized distributed algorithm for $\Delta + 1$-coloring given below. A similar although simpler (and faster) randomized algorithm for this problem was given by Luby ([9]). We give a different algorithm here because we have to prove strong tail bounds on the performance of this algorithm (see lemma 2) - something we were not able to do for Luby's algorithm.

The quantity α is a suitable positive constant whose existence is established in theorem 2. We denote the label of a vertex v by $l(v)$.

1. Algorithm COLOR;
2. Initially all $v \in V$ are *active* and $avail(v) = \{1, \ldots, deg(v) + 1\}$;
3. for $i = 0$ to $\lceil \log n \rceil$ do
4.   for $\lceil \alpha (\log n)^2 \rceil$ iterations do
5.   all active vertices v in parallel do
6.   if $|avail(v)| \geq n/2^i$ then
7. v chooses a random color $col(v) \in avail(v)$;
8.   if $col(v) \neq col(w)$ for all active $w \in N(v)$ with $l(w) < l(v)$ then
9.   for all active $w \in N(v)$ do $avail(w) := avail(w) \backslash \{col(v)\}$;
10. v becomes inactive;
11.   endif;
12.   endif;
13.   endfor;
14. endfor.

Let σ_i denote the sequence of colors guessed by the vertex with label i in step 7 of COLOR until it becomes inactive. If a vertex v is active but does not participate in step 7 we let $col(v) = 0$. Let σ be the function that maps each label $i \in [n]$ to σ_i. The function σ uniquely describes a run of algorithm COLOR.

Let $X(\sigma)$ be the number of vertices that are active upon termination of COLOR. Note that $X(\sigma)$ may depend on the labeling of the vertices in G. The following theorem shows that all vertices are likely to be inactive when COLOR terminates, regardless of the labeling of G.

Theorem 2 *For some* $\alpha = O(1)$,

$$Pr[\exists \text{ labeling } \sigma \text{ of } G : X(\sigma) > 0] < 1/n^{\Theta(1)}.$$

This theorem implies theorem 1 as follows: for a fixed graph G, there exists a σ for which COLOR terminates with a valid $\Delta + 1$-coloring (all vertices inactive). Thus G can be colored with $\Delta + 1$ colors in $|\sigma|$ $(= O(\log^3 n))$ steps. Theorem 1 now follows with lemma 1.

The proof of theorem 2 depends on the following lemma whose proof will be given in the next section. Fix an execution of step 7 of COLOR. We say that an active vertex *fails* if it chooses the same color as an active neighbor of smaller label in step 7. (In particular it satisfies the condition in line 6.)

Lemma 2 *Fix a labeling of the vertices in G. Let T be the set of all vertices choosing a random color in step 7. Assume that for all $v, w \in T$ we have $|avail(v)| \geq |avail(w)|/2$. Then the probability that at least $30|T|/31$ vertices in T fail is at most $c^{|T|}$ for some constant $c < 1$ independent of T.*

With lemma 2 the proof of theorem 2 is now fairly straightforward.
Proof of theorem 2. Consider a fixed value $i = j$ for i in the outer for-loop.

We assume inductively that, at the start of this iteration of the for loop, all active vertices v satisfy $|avail(v)| \leq n/2^{j-1}$. Thus, the vertices choosing random colors during this iteration are exactly those active vertices that satisfy $n/2^j \leq |avail(v)| \leq n/2^{j-1}$. Let T denote the set of these vertices. Note that for any $v, w \in T$ we have $|avail(v)| \geq |avail(w)|/2$. Thus lemma 2 implies that at least $30|T|/31$ vertices in T fail in one execution of step 7 with probability less than $c^{|T|}$. The probability of that many vertices failing in $\beta \log n$ consecutive executions of step 7 is less than $c^{\beta|T| \log n}$ for any $\beta > 0$. Summing this probability over all possible labelings of T (there are at most $n^{|T|} = 2^{|T| \log n}$ labelings) yields a failure probability that is less than $1/n^{\Theta(1)}$ (for any $T \neq \emptyset$) if we choose a suitable constant β. Thus, with probability at least $1 - 1/n^{\Theta(1)}$ after $O(\log n)$ executions of step 7 fewer than $30|T|/31$ vertices in T are still active and satisfy $|avail(v)| \geq n/2^j$. Hence, with the same asymptotic probability after $O((\log n)^2)$ consecutive iterations of step 7 all vertices in T are either inactive or satisfy $|avail(v)| \leq n/2^j$. The claim of the theorem follows. QED

5 Proof of Lemma 2

Throughout this section we consider a fixed execution of step 7 of COLOR. Let k be the number of vertices choosing a random color in the current execution of step 7. In this section we prove that the probability that at least $30k/31$ vertices fail is roughly exponentially small in k (lemma 2). If the failure events were mutually independent for the k vertices, this would be easy to prove using elementary methods. Unfortunately the failure of one vertex may affect the probability of the failure of another vertex in a way that is difficult to quantify. We get around this problem by using tools from martingale theory. To make the exposition self-contained we briefly review the main definitions regarding martingales. The exposition here is based on [2]; for a more complete account the reader is referred to that source.

A sequence $X_0, X_1, \ldots, X_p$ is a *martingale* if $E[X_{i+1}|X_i] = X_i$ for $0 \leq i < p$. Fix a set $S = \{v_1, \ldots, v_p\}$ of p vertices in G. We define an *S-coloring* to be a function that maps each vertex $v \in S$ to a color in $avail(v)$. Let L be a real-valued function defined on S-colorings. For two S-colorings g and h we denote by $g \overset{i}{=} h$ the event "for all l, $1 \leq l \leq i$, $g(v_l) = h(v_l)$". We define the random variables $X_i(h)$ over the space of S-colorings by

$$X_i(h) = E[L(g)|g \overset{i}{=} h], \tag{1}$$

where g denotes a random S-coloring. The X_i's form a martingale ([2]). We refer to this martingale as the *color exposure martingale for* L. It measures the expectation of L conditional on the fact that some vertices have their color exposed. Note that $X_0(h) = E[L]$ and $X_p(h) = L(h)$. The following inequality is the basic result that we use for analyzing the behavior of the color exposure martingale.

Lemma 3 [2] *Let $\mu = E[L(g)]$. If*

$$|X_{i+1}(h) - X_i(h)| \leq 1 \tag{2}$$

for all h and i, $0 \leq i < p$, then for all $\lambda > 0$

$$Pr[L(g) > \mu + \lambda\sqrt{p}] < e^{-\lambda^2/2}.$$

The result will typically be used in the following form which is an immediate consequence of the previous lemma.

Corollary 1 *Let $\mu = E[L(g)]$. If*

$$|X_{i+1}(h) - X_i(h)| \leq c \tag{3}$$

for all h and i, $0 \leq i < p$, then for all $\lambda > 0$

$$Pr[L(g) > \mu + c\lambda\sqrt{p}] < e^{-\lambda^2/2}.$$

The following lemma will also be needed in the proof of lemma 2.

Lemma 4 *Let v be a vertex that chooses a random color at the current iteration of step 7 of COLOR. The probability that v fails is less than $29/30$.*

Proof. Let $a = |avail(v)|$. We note that the number of active neighbors of v is less than a. Fix a color $c \in avail(v)$. Each active neighbor w of v that chooses a random color at this step satisfies $|avail(w)| \geq a/2$ (assumption of lemma 2). Therefore, the probability that all active neighbors of v choose a color different from c is more than $(1 - 2/a)^a$. The latter quantity is greater than $1/30$ for $a \geq 3$. Since each active neighbor w of v satisfies $|avail(w)| \geq 2$, for $a = 2$ the probability is greater than $1/4$. The lemma follows. QED

Proof of lemma 2. Let $T = \{v_1, \ldots, v_k\}$ be the set of all vertices choosing a random color at the current execution of step 7 of COLOR with $l(v_1) < l(v_2) < \ldots < l(v_k)$ (where l is the fixed labeling assumed in the lemma). Let F denote the subset of vertices in T that fail. Note that F is a random variable that depends on the colors chosen by vertices in T. By lemma 4 the probability that a fixed $v \in T$ fails is less than $29/30$. Thus

$$E[F] < k29/30 \tag{4}$$

For analyzing the upper tail of F, we expose the vertices in increasing order of their labels and let $L(g) = |F|$ for a coloring g of the vertices in T. The corresponding color exposure martingale is defined as in equation 1, i.e., $X_i(h) = E[L(g)|g \stackrel{i}{=} h]$ where h denotes an arbitrary T-coloring.

We claim that the X_i's satisfy inequality 3 for some constant c. To see this, we write $X_i(h)$ as $X_i(h) = \sum_{j=1}^k q_i(h, v_j)$ where $q_i(h, v_j) = Pr[v_j \in F|g \stackrel{i}{=} h]$. Note that $q_i(h, v_j)$ depends only on colors of vertices v_r with $r \leq j$. For $j \in [i]$, we have $q_i(h, v_j) = q_{i+1}(h, v_j)$ since the colors of $v_1, \ldots, v_j$ are fixed by h. Furthermore $|q_{i+1}(h, v_{i+1}) - q_i(h, v_{i+1})| \leq 1$. Therefore

$$|X_{i+1}(h) - X_i(h)| \leq 1 + \sum_{j=i+2}^k |q_i(h, v_j) - q_{i+1}(h, v_j)|. \tag{5}$$

Now fix $j > i + 1$. If v_{i+1} is not a neighbor of v_j, then certainly $q_i(h, v_j) = q_{i+1}(h, v_j)$.

Henceforth assume that v_{i+1} is a neighbor of v_j. Let A_g denote the event "$g(v_j) = g(v_r)$ for $v_r \in N(v_j)$ with $1 \leq r \leq i$ or $i + 2 \leq r \leq j - 1$" and let B_g denote the event "$g(v_j) = g(v_{i+1})$". We have

$$q_i(h, v_j) = Pr[A_g \vee B_g|g \stackrel{i}{=} h].$$

Let $a = |avail(v_{i+1})|$. Since $|avail(v_j)| \geq a/2$ (by the assumption of the lemma) we have $Pr[B|g \stackrel{i}{=} h] \leq 2/a$, we get

$$Pr[A_g|g \stackrel{i}{=} h] \leq q_i(h, v_j) \leq Pr[A_g|g \stackrel{i}{=} h] + 2/a. \tag{6}$$

Similarly we obtain

$$Pr[A_g|g \stackrel{i\pm1}{=} h] \leq q_{i+1}(h, v_j) \leq Pr[A_g|g \stackrel{i\pm1}{=} h] + 2/a. \tag{7}$$

Now we observe that

$$Pr[A_g|g \stackrel{i\pm1}{=} h] = Pr[A_g|g \stackrel{i}{=} h]$$

because A_g does not depend on the color of v_{i+1}. Thus, from inequalities 6 and 7 we infer that

$$|q_i(h, v_j) - q_{i+1}(h, v_j)| \leq 2/a.$$

Since $v_{i+1} \in N(v_j)$ holds for at most a values of j, we obtain with inequality 5

$$|X_{i+1}(h) - X_i(h)| \leq 3$$

. By applying corollary 1 we see that

$$Pr[|F| > E[|F|] + 3\lambda\sqrt{k}] < e^{-\lambda^2/2}. \tag{8}$$

and thus

$$Pr[|F| > 30k/31] < e^{-\beta k}$$

for some constant β, as claimed. QED

6 Towards Uniform Algorithms

Theorem 1 guarantees the existence of a $\Delta + 1$-coloring algorithm for any fixed graph. More precisely it establishes the existence of a function σ that describes a "good" run of algorithm COLOR, i.e., a run in which the graph receives a valid $\Delta + 1$-coloring. This result is not quite satisfactory in two respects: first, it is nonconstructive in that it only proves the existence and does not provide an efficient (polynomial time, say) method for constructing such an algorithm; second the resulting algorithm is nonuniform in the sense that one may not be able to extend the algorithm so that it works for an arbitrary graph. Although we do not know at this point how to resolve the nonconstructive aspect of our result, we can do something about the nonuniformity. In this section we shall prove that there exists an algorithm that colors all graphs in an infinite class of graphs with $\Delta + 1$ colors in polylogarithmic time in the strong distributed model. The class of graphs includes vertex transitive graphs.

We extend the concept of a neighborhood graph (see section 2) to a class of graphs in the following way. Let $\mathcal{G}$ denote a (possibly infinite) class of graphs. Let $t = t(n)$ be an integer-valued function. We define the graph $N_t(\mathcal{G})$ as the union of the graphs $N_t(G)$, $G \in \mathcal{G}$, i.e., $V(N_t(\mathcal{G})) = \cup_{G \in \mathcal{G}} V(N_t(G))$ and $E(N_t(\mathcal{G})) = \cup_{G \in \mathcal{G}} E(N_t(G))$. Intuitively, $N_t(\mathcal{G})$ describes the structure of t-neighborhoods of graphs in $\mathcal{G}$.

Recall that a $\Delta + 1$-coloring algorithm for a fixed graph G yields a $\Delta + 1$-coloring of $N_t(G)$. A similar correspondence holds for algorithms on $\mathcal{G}$. Because a centered graph (H, v) may be a subgraph of graphs with varying maximum degrees, it will be convenient to restrict the class of coloring algorithms in the following way: define a *proper* $\Delta + 1$-coloring of a graph G to be a $\Delta + 1$-coloring that assigns to each node v a color in $[deg(v) + 1] = \{1, \ldots, deg(v) + 1\}$.

Define a *proper coloring* of $N_t(\mathcal{G})$ to be a coloring that assigns to each node (H, v) of $N_t(\mathcal{G})$ a color in $[deg_H(v) + 1]$. We now formulate the correspondence between coloring algorithms for $\mathcal{G}$ and colorings of $N_t(\mathcal{G})$. We remark that this result contains lemma 1 as a special case ($\mathcal{G} = \{G\}$).

Lemma 5 *An algorithm that produces a proper $\Delta + 1$-coloring for every graph $G \in \mathcal{G}$ in t time steps in the distributed model yields a proper coloring of $N_t(\mathcal{G})$. Conversely, a proper coloring of $N_t(\mathcal{G})$ implies the existence of an algorithm that computes a proper $\Delta + 1$-coloring for every graph in $\mathcal{G}$ in the strong model.*

We now describe an infinite family of graphs for which we can prove the existence of fast algorithm in the strong distributed model using lemma 5. Fix $t = t(n)$. Let $\mathcal{G}_t$ denote the class of graphs G with the property that all t-neighborhoods in G are isomorphic, i.e., for any two vertices v and w in G, $S_t(v)$ and $S_t(w)$ are isomorphic. The neighborhood graph for $\mathcal{G}_t$ has a simple structure as shown in the following theorem.

Theorem 3 *Any two nodes in the same connected component of $N_t(\mathcal{G}_t)$ are isomorphic as centered graphs. If t is unbounded, then each connected component of $N_t(\mathcal{G}_t)$ is finite. If a connected component is finite, then it is of the form $N_t(G)$*

for some $G \in \mathcal{G}_t$. If a component is infinite, then it is the union of an infinite sequence of graphs $N_t(G_1), N_t(G_2), \ldots$ where $N_t(G_i)$ is a subgraph of $N_t(G_{i+1})$.

Proof. By the definition of $N_t(\mathcal{G}_t)$ there is an edge between (H, v) and (H', w) only if these are isomorphic to t-neighborhoods of the same graph; by the definition of $\mathcal{G}_t$, (H, v) and (H', v) are then isomorphic. The first statement of the theorem follows.

Now consider a connected component C all of whose nodes are isomorphic to (H, v). If t is unbounded, then there is a maximum integer $p(H)$ such that there exists a graph in $\mathcal{G}_t$ on $p(H)$ vertices all of whose t-neighborhoods are isomorphic to (H, v). It follows that every node (H', w) in the component satisfies $V(H') \subseteq [p(H)]$. Hence C is finite.

For the last two statements of the theorem let C and $p(H)$ be defined as above. If C is finite, then $p(H)$ is finite. Let $G \in \mathcal{G}_t$ be a graph with $p(H)$ vertices all of whose t-neighborhoods are isomorphic to (H, v). Then $C = N_t(G)$. If C is infinite, then $p(H)$ is unbounded. Thus, there exists an infinite sequence of integers $0 < i_1 < i_2 < i_3 < \ldots$ so that for every i_j there exists a graph $G_j \in \mathcal{G}_t$ with i_j vertices all of whose t-neighborhoods are isomorphic to (H, v). It is not difficult to see that the graphs G_j satisfy the conditions stated in the theorem. QED

The following theorem is the main result of this section.

Theorem 4 *The graph $N_t(\mathcal{G}_t)$ has a proper coloring for some $t = O((\log n)^3)$. Thus, there exists an algorithm that produces a (proper) $\Delta + 1$-coloring for every graph in $\mathcal{G}_t$ in $O((\log n)^3)$ time steps in the strong distributed model.*

Proof. Let $t = \Omega(\log n)$, i.e., t is unbounded. By theorem 3 every connected component in $N_t(\mathcal{G}_t)$ is of the form $N_t(G)$ for some $G \in \mathcal{G}_t$. By theorem 1 $\chi(N_t(G)) \leq \Delta(G) + 1$ for $t = O((\log n)^3)$. In fact something stronger can be said. Because algorithm COLOR (section 4) produces a proper $\Delta + 1$-coloring, it follows from theorem 2 that $N_t(G)$ has a proper coloring for $t = O((\log n)^3)$. Note that the constant implied by 'O' does not depend on G. Thus $N_t(\mathcal{G}_t)$ has a proper coloring as claimed for some $t = O((\log n)^3)$. QED

A graph G is *vertex transitive* if, for any two vertices v and w in G, there is an automorphism of G (isomorphism from G onto itself) that maps v onto w. Informally, this means that G "looks the same" from any vertex. Clearly, any vertex transitive graph belongs to $\mathcal{G}_t$. We thus obtain the following immediate corollary of theorem 4.

Corollary 2 *There exists an algorithm that computes a $\Delta + 1$-coloring for any vertex transitive graph in $O((\log n)^3)$ time steps in the strong distributed model.*

Acknowledgment

The author wishes to thank Nick Pippenger for helpful discussions.

References

1. N. Alon, L. Babai, A. Itai, A fast randomized parallel algorithm for the maximal independent set problem, J. Algorithms 7, pp. 567-583, 1986.
2. N. Alon and J.H. Spencer, *The probabilistic method*, John Wiley& Sons, New York, 1992.
3. B. Awerbuch, Complexity of network synchronization, JACM, 32:804-823, 1985.
4. B. Awerbuch, A.V. Goldberg, M. Luby and S.A. Plotkin, Network decomposition and locality in distributed computation, Proceedings of the IEEE Symposium on Foundations of Computer Science, pages 364-369, 1989.
5. J.A. Bondy and U.S.R. Murty, *Graph theory with applications*, North-Holland, 1976.
6. R. Cole and U. Vishkin, Deterministic coin tossing with applications to optimal parallel list ranking, Inform. and Control, 70 (1986), pp. 32-56.
7. A.V. Goldberg, S. Plotkin and G.E. Shannon, Parallel symmetry-breaking in sparse graphs, SIAM J. Disc. Math, Vol. 1, No. 4, 1988.
8. N. Linial, Locality in distributed graph algorithms, SJC, 21: 193-201, 1992.
9. M. Luby, Removing randomness in parallel computation without a processor penalty, JCSS, 47:250-286, 1993.
10. M. Luby, *A simple parallel algorithm for the maximal independent set problem*, SIAM J. Computing, vol. 15, 1986, pp. 1036-1053.
11. M. Naor and L. Stockmeyer, What can be computed locally?, Proceedings of the 25th Annual ACM Symposium on the Theory of Computing, 1993.
12. A. Panconesi and A. Srinivasan, Improved distributed algorithms for coloring and network decomposition problems, Proceedings of the 24th Annual ACM Symposium on the Theory of Computing, 1992.
13. P. Raghavan, Probabilistic construction of deterministic algorithms: Approximating packing integer programs, *J. Comput. System Sci.*, 37:130-143, 1988.
14. M. Szegedy and S. Vishwanathan, Locality based graph coloring, Proceedings of the 25th Annual ACM Symposium on the Theory of Computing, 1993.

Communication Complexity of Gossiping by Packets*

Luisa Gargano   Adele A. Rescigno   Ugo Vaccaro

Dipartimento di Informatica ed Applicazioni,
Universita di Salerno,
84081 Baronissi (Sa), Italy

Abstract. This paper considers the problem of gossiping with packets of limited size in a network with cost function. We show that the problem of determining the minimum cost necessary to perform gossiping among a given set of participants with packets of limited size is NP-hard. We also give an approximate (with respect to the cost) gossiping algorithm. The ratio between the cost of an optimal algorithm and the approximate one is less than $1+2(k-1)/n$, were n is the number of nodes participating to the gossiping process and $k \leq n-1$ is the upper bound on the number of individual blocks of information that a packet can carry.
We also analyze the communication time and communication complexity, i.e., the product of the communication cost and time, of gossiping algorithms.

1 Introduction

In this paper we study the problem of gossiping in a weighted network with packets of limited size.

Gossiping (also called total exchange or all–to–all communication) in a communication network is the process of distribution of the informations known to each processor to every other processor of the system. This process of information dissemination is carried out by means of a sequence of message transmissions between nodes in the network.

Gossiping arises in a large class of computational problems, such as linear system solving, matrix manipulation, Discrete Fourier Transform, and sorting, where both input and output data are required to be distributed across the network [5, 17]. Due to the interesting theoretical questions it poses and its numerous practical applications, gossiping has been widely studied under various communication models [1, 3, 6, 7, 10, 12, 16, 17, 19, 20, 21]. Recent surveys paper collecting the latest results are [8], [13], [15], and [18].

The majority of the previous studies on gossiping has considered the case in which all the informations known to a processor at any given time during the execution of the gossiping protocol can be freely concatenated and the resulting

* Research partially supported by the Italian Ministry of University and of Scientific Research in the framework of the "Algoritmi, Modelli di Calcolo e Strutture Informative" project.

(longer) message can be transmitted in a constant amount of time, that is, it has been assumed that the time required to transmit a message is independent from its length. While this assumption is reasonable for short messages, it is clearly unrealistic in case the size of the messages becomes large. Notice that most of the gossiping protocols proposed in the literature require the transmission, in the last rounds of the execution of the protocol, of messages of size $\Theta(n)$, where n is the number of nodes in the network. Therefore, from the practical point of view it is important to have gossiping protocols that require only the transmission of *bounded* length messages between processors. In this paper we consider the problem of gossiping in weighted communication networks under the restriction that communicating nodes can exchange up to a fixed number k of elementary blocks of information at each round.

1.1 The Model

Consider a communication network modelled by a graph $H = (V, E)$ where the node set V represents the set of processors of the network and E represents the set of the communication lines between processors.

Each node in V taking part in the gossiping process will be called a *participant* and the set of participants will be denoted by $\mathcal{P}$. Without loss of generality, we suppose $\mathcal{P} = \{1, \ldots, n\}$. Formally the k-gossiping, or simply, the gossiping process can be defined as follows.

Gossiping. Each participant i, with $1 \leq i \leq n$, has a block of data $B(i)$. Each block has size b. The goal is to disseminate these blocks so that each processor gets all the blocks $B(1), \cdots, B(n)$. Blocks can be sent in packets containing up to k blocks each, where k is a parameter input to the gossiping algorithm.

We regard the set $\mathcal{P}$ as the node set of a complete digraph $K_{\mathcal{P}} = (\mathcal{P}, A_{\mathcal{P}})$, with $A_{\mathcal{P}} = \{(i, j) : i, j \in \mathcal{P}, i \neq j\}$. Each arc $(i, j) \in A_{\mathcal{P}}$ is labelled with the cost $c(i, j) > 0$ of sending a packet (of bounded size) along the interconnection network H from the participant i to the participant j, with $c(i, j) = c(j, i)$. The communication costs may differ from one arc to another; for example, the communication cost $c(i, j)$ may represent the *distance* between the participant i and the participant j in the interconnection network H.

Motivations to study the communication load of a gossiping algorithm by means of the weighted graph model vs the traditional study of the number of intersite packets are illustrated by the following example which shows that the number of intersite packets alone can be a poor measure of the load that the algorithm poses on the network. Consider the network given in Figure 1 (a), where the participants to the gossiping process are the square nodes numbered 1,2,3,4. Let $k = 2$, there are several ways to perform gossiping among the 4 participants using the minimum number of packets (containing up to 2 blocks each) sent from one participant to another, which is known to be 8 [2]. We consider here two of them which are illustrated in Figure 1 (b) and (c), respectively.

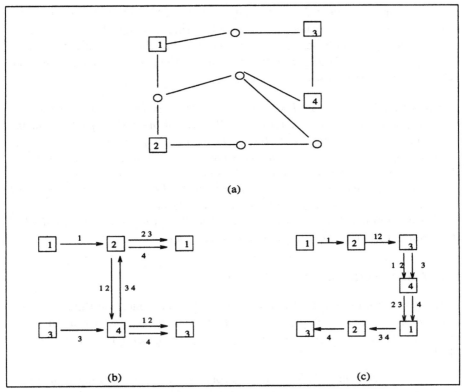

Figure 1

In the first algorithm the transmissions among participants are the following:

1 sends its block $B(1)$ to 2 and 3 sends $B(3)$ to 4;
2 sends $(B(1), B(2))$ to 4   and 4 sends $(B(3), B(4))$ to 2;
2 sends $(B(2), B(3))$ to 1   and 4 sends $(B(1), B(2))$ to 3;
2 sends $B(4)$ to 1   and 4 sends $B(4)$ to 3.

In the second algorithm the transmissions among participants are the following:

1 sends its block $B(1)$ to 2 which sends $(B(1), B(2))$ to 3;
3 sends $(B(1), B(2))$ to 4;
3 sends $B(3)$ to 4;
4 sends $(B(2), B(3))$ to 1;
4 sends $B(4)$ to 1;
1 sends $(B(3), B(4))$ to 2;
2 sends $B(4)$ to 3.

Both algorithms require a total of 8 packets transmissions. However, if we count the number of message transmissions made by the two algorithms between *adjacent* nodes in the network (assuming to choose always the shortest path to send a message from one participant to another), in the first case we have 15 message transmissions between adjacent nodes in the network while the second algorithm requires 20 message transmissions. Therefore, even though the two algorithms are equivalent from the point of view of the number of packets exchanged between participants, the second algorithm actually poses a larger load on the network. This is essentially due to the fact that the second algorithm uses longer paths or, abstracting from the structure of the graph and considering the associated cost graph, uses edges of greater cost.

Definition 1.1 *Given a set $\mathcal{P}$ of participants, the* communication cost *of a gossiping algorithm on $\mathcal{P}$ is the total cost of the arcs of the cost graph $K_{\mathcal{P}}$ that the algorithm uses to disseminate all the blocks among the participants.*

The communication time *of an algorithm is the interval of time necessary for the completion of the algorithm itself. We assume that to each arc $(i, j) \in A_{\mathcal{P}}$ it is associated a* travel time *$t(i, j)$ which represents the time needed for a packet originated at the participant i to reach the participant j.*

The communication complexity *of an algorithm is defined as the product of its communication cost and its communication time.*

1.2 Our Results and Related Works

In this paper we investigate the minimum cost, communication time and communication complexity of gossiping algorithms under the restriction that any packet from one participant to another can carry up to a fixed number k of blocks.

Recently, Wolfson and Segall gave a solution to the interesting problem of performing gossiping in weighted networks [21]. They show that the minimum cost of an algorithm that solves the gossiping problem is equal to 2·(*cost of a minimum spanning tree of $K_{\mathcal{P}}$*). Moreover, they propose an algorithm that achieves this bound and show that its communication time (resp. complexity) cannot be worse than the minimum possible communication time (resp. complexity) times a factor which is upper bounded by the number n of participants. The main concern of [21] was the *atomic commitment problem* in which any participant initially holds a bit and at the end of the protocol all participants have computed the AND of all the bits. In this scenario, only one-bit messages need to be exchanged. Therefore, Wolfson and Segall [21] do not consider the important issue of designing gossiping algorithms that require only transmissions of bounded length packets, which is our main concern here.

The problem of estimating the time necessary to perform gossiping with packets of limited size has recently received considerable attention in case of *uniform* cost function. In particular, this problem has been considered in [3] for the Full–Duplex 1–Port model, in [1, 6] for the Half–Duplex 1–Port model, and in [4] for the Full–Duplex All–Port model. The minimum number of calls necessary to perform gossiping with packets of limited size in the Half–Duplex communication model with uniform cost function has been considered in [2]. Analogous problems in bus networks have been considered in [9, 14].

The rest of the paper is organized as follows. In Section 2 we study the communication cost of gossiping algorithms. We show that the problem of gossiping with minimum cost and packets containing up to k blocks is an NP-hard problem for any $2 \leq k \leq n - 2$. Next, we give an approximate (with respect to the cost) gossiping algorithm and we prove that the ratio between the cost of the *optimal* cost algorithm (which is infeasible to find due to the NP-hardness of the associated decision problem) and the cost of our algorithm is upper bounded by $1 + 2(k - 1)/n$. We point out that our algorithm is asynchronous and efficient, the computation time at each participant is linear in the number of participants. We point out that the problem of gossiping with minimum communication cost is efficiently and exactly solvable for the extremal values $k = 1$ and $k = n - 1$. In particular, for $k = n - 1$ the problem was solved in [21]; we show in this paper that n times the cost of a minimum spanning tree of the cost graph $K_{\mathcal{P}}$ is necessary and sufficient to perform gossiping when $k = 1$.

In Section 3 we show that the ratio of the communication time of our gossiping algorithm to that of an optimal communication time algorithm is at most $\lceil (n-1)/k \rceil + n - 1$. We show that no better ratio than $\Omega(n)$ can be obtained for algorithms of cost within a constant factor from the minimum possible communication cost. Moreover, the communication complexity of our algorithm cannot be worse than the minimum communication complexity times a factor which is upper bounded by $n + 2k + n/k$. For $k = 1$ the communication complexity of our algorithm is at most a factor n larger than that of any algorithm optimal with respect of the communication complexity. It is worth to point out that, generally, the same algorithm cannot minimize both cost and time and that minimizing the communication complexity is a NP–complete problem even for the case of unbounded message length transmissions [21].

Due to space limits, all proofs are omitted.

2   Gossiping

The sequence of calls of a gossiping algorithm instance I can be represented by a labelled directed multigraph $G(I) = (\mathcal{P}, A)$ having as node set the set $\mathcal{P}$ of participants and as arc set the multiset A, where each arc (i, j) represents a packet transmission from i to j. Each arc has two labels: a *temporal* label that represents the temporal order in which calls are made and a *content* label that indicates the participants whose blocks are sent by participant i to participant j during the corresponding call. Our assumption on the packets size implies that each content label contains up to k elements.

An instance of a gossiping algorithm using packets of size at most k will be called a k–gossiping instance, or simply, a k–instance. A labelled multi–digraph G is called k–*multi-digraph* if $G = G(I)$ for some k–instance I.

The cost $cost(I)$ of the k–instance I (or equivalently, the cost $cost(G(I))$ of the associated k–multi–digraph $G(I)$) is then the sum of all arcs of $G(I)$, each added as many times as its multiplicity.

Example 2.1 *Let* $n = 4$ *and the cost graph given in Figure 2(a). Consider* $k = 2$, *and the 2–instance* I *consisting of the following calls*

At time 1 : participant 1 sends its block $B(1)$ *to 2 and*
  participant 3 sends its block $B(3)$ *to 4;*
At time 2: participant 2 sends the blocks $(B(1), B(2))$ *to 4 and*
  participant 4 sends the blocks $(B(3), B(4))$ *to 2;*
At time 3: participant 2 sends the blocks $(B(2), B(3))$ *to 1 and*
  participant 4 sends the blocks $(B(1), B(2))$ *to 3;*
At time 4: participant 2 sends the blocks $B(4)$ *to 1 and*
  participant 4 sends the blocks $B(4)$ *to 3.*

The 2–multi–digraph $G = G(I)$ *is shown in Figure 2(b); each arc has label* t/C, *where* t *is the time label and* C *is the content label of the arc. We have* $cost(I) = cost(G(I)) = 11$.

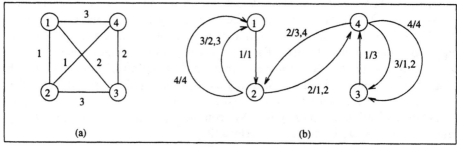

(a)   (b)

Figure 2

A path from i to j is called *ascending* if the sequence of temporal labels is strictly increasing when moving from i to j. An ascending path is called an i–*path* if the content label of each of its arcs contains participant i, that is, if the packet sent during the corresponding call carries the block of participant i.

It is immediate to see that a participant j receives the block of participant i in the gossiping algorithm instance I only if $G(I)$ contains an i–path from i to j. Therefore,

Lemma 2.1 *If* I *is a* k–*instance then* $G(I)$ *contains an* i–*path from* i *to* j, *for each pair of participants* $i, j \in \mathcal{P}$ *with* $i \neq j$.

2.1 Communication Cost

In this section we study the *minimum communication cost* of gossiping algorithms.

We first show that determining the minimum communication cost of a gossiping k–multi–digraph is NP-hard. To this aim consider the following associated decision problem.

MIN–COST–GOSSIPING
Instance: A set of participants $\mathcal{P}$, a cost graph $K_{\mathcal{P}}$, and bounds k and C;
Question: Is there a k–gossiping multi–digraph on $\mathcal{P}$ of cost $\leq C$?

For $k \geq n - 1$, it was shown in [21] how to solve the above problem efficiently. We will show the problem to be easy also for $k = 1$. However, for general values of k we have the following results on MIN–COST–GOSSIPING.

Theorem 2.1 *MIN–COST–GOSSIPING is NP-hard.*

Since finding a gossiping algorithm of minimum cost is computationally infeasible, we must relax our requirement for optimality and look for approximate (with respect to the cost) gossiping algorithm. To estimate the goodness of the algorithm we will propose, we first need to find a lower bound on the necessary communication cost of *any* gossiping algorithm.

2.2 Lower Bound on the Communication Cost

In order to prove the lower bound, let us first notice that since we are not concerned here with the communication time that is necessary to complete the gossiping instance, we can assume that no two calls are made at the same time. This implies that all the calls of the instance I (i.e., arcs of the associated multi–digraph $G(I)$) have different temporal labels. It is easy to see that we can always modify the temporal label $\ell(a)$ of each arc a in $G(I)$, in order to obtain new temporal labels, say $\ell'(a)$, so that $\ell'(a) \neq \ell'(a')$ for each $a \neq a'$ and, in order to preserve the ascending paths, $\ell'(a) < \ell'(a')$ whenever $\ell(a) < \ell(a')$. We stress that such an assumption does not influence the object of our analysis, that is, the arc multiset of $G(I)$.

Example 1 (continued) *In order to fullfill the above assumption we can modify the temporal labels of the graph in Figure 2(b) as shown in Figure 3. It is immediate to see that ascending paths are not influenced by such a time expansion.*

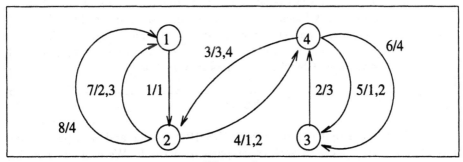

Figure 3

Let $cost(ST_{\min})$ represent the cost of a minimum spanning tree of the cost graph $K_{\mathcal{P}}$ and let $c_{\min} = \min c(i, j)$, where the minimum is taken over all $i, j \in \mathcal{P}$ with $i \neq j$. It is possible to show that

Theorem 2.2 *For any k–instance*

$$cost(I) \geq \frac{n}{k} cost(ST_{\min}) + \frac{k-1}{2} c_{\min}.$$

2.3   Gossiping algorithm

We give here a distributed gossiping algorithm GOSSIPING. We assume, as in other papers (see [21, 11]), that each participant knows the identity of all the other participants and the associated set of communication costs. The algorithm GOSSIPING$(c, \mathcal{P}, k)$ given in Figure 4 is executed by each participant; the spanning tree T is identical at all the participants, this will be the case if the construction procedures are identical at all participants.

The algorithm is asynchronous and does not require participants to know when the blocks of the other participants are ready nor the time packets take to travel between pairs of participant. Moreover, the amount of computation done by each participant is linear in the number of participants.

Given a tree T, for each edge $\{i, j\}$ in T we denote by $T_i(i, j)$ and $T_j(i, j)$ the subtrees of T, containing i and j respectively, resulting from T upon the removal of $\{i, j\}$.

GOSSIPING$(c, \mathcal{P}, k)$ /∗ executed at participant i, given
         a set of participants $\mathcal{P}$,
         a set of communication costs c, and
         a bound k on the number of blocks
         in each packet ∗/

1. Construct a minimum spanning tree T of the cost graph $K_{\mathcal{P}}$.
2. Wait until received at least k blocks (including the own block $B(i)$) or received from at least all neighbors but one.
3. For each neighbor j of i in T
     if $\ell \geq k$ blocks of participants in $T_i(i, j)$ remain to be sent to j then
         wait until k blocks of participants in $T_i(i, j)$ are ready and
         send to j a packet formed by k blocks of participants in $T_i(i, j)$
     if $\ell < k$ blocks of participants in $T_i(i, j)$ remain to be sent to j then
         send these ℓ blocks as soon as they are ready.

Figure 4

It is easy to see that the algorithm GOSSIPING ends and each participant $i \in \mathcal{P}$ knows the blocks of each other participant in $\mathcal{P}$. We evaluate now its communication cost.

Theorem 2.3 *The communication cost required by GOSSIPING(c, $\mathcal{P}$, k) is upper bounded by*

$$\left(\left\lceil\frac{n-1}{k}\right\rceil + 1\right) \cdot cost(ST_{\min}),$$

where $cost(ST_{\min})$ *represents the cost of the minimum spanning tree of the cost graph* $K_{\mathcal{P}}$.

Theorem 2.2 and Theorem 2.3 imply

Corollary 2.1 *The ratio between the cost of GOSSIPING(c, $\mathcal{P}$, k) and the cost of a minimum cost gossiping algorithm is upper bounded by* $1 + 2(k-1)/n$.

In case it is not possible to combine any number of blocks into a single packet, that is $k = 1$, from Corollary 2.1 we directly get that the above presented algorithm has optimal communication cost.

Corollary 2.2 *GOSSIPING(c, $\mathcal{P}$, 1) realizes gossiping with minimum possible communication cost equal to* $n \cdot cost(ST_{\min})$.

3   Communication complexity

The communication time of an instance I on a set $\mathcal{P}$ of participants is defined as the minimum time required to perform the calls in the order specified by temporal labelling of the associated multi-digraph $G(I)$ with respect to the set $\tau = \{\tau_i : i \in \mathcal{P}\}$, where τ_i is the time needed for i to have its block ready, and the set of travel times $t = \{t(i,j) : i, j \in \mathcal{P}, i \neq j\}$. Assuming that the values $t(i,j)$ satisfy the triangle inequality, the following lower bound on the gossiping time holds for each k (see [21])

$$time(I) \geq \max_{i,j \in \mathcal{P}}\{\tau_i + t(i,j)\}. \tag{1}$$

We consider now the communication time of the algorithm GOSSIPING(c, $\mathcal{P}$, k). Let I be the instance executed by the algorithm GOSSIPING(c, $\mathcal{P}$, k) and T be the spanning tree used in the algorithm GOSSIPING(c, $\mathcal{P}$, k). For each pair of participants i, j, denote by

$$\alpha(i,j) = (i_0 = i, i_1, \ldots, i_{d-1}, i_d = j)$$

the path from i to j in T and let $\delta_{i,j}$ denote the time it takes for the block $B(i)$ of participant i to reach participant j using the path $\alpha(i,j)$. Namely, $\delta_{i,j}$ represents the sum of the travel time $t(i_\ell, i_{\ell+1})$, for $\ell = 0, \ldots, d-1$, of each arc of the path $\alpha(i,j)$ plus the sum over all the participants i_ℓ, for $\ell = 0, \ldots, d-1$, of the time that $B(i)$ waits at participant i_ℓ before being sent to $i_{\ell+1}$. Then, the communication time of the algorithm GOSSIPING(c, $\mathcal{P}$, k) is

$$time(I) = \max_{i,j}\{\tau_i + \delta_{i,j}\}. \tag{2}$$

It is possible to prove the following result.

Theorem 3.1 *Denote by $I_{\min}$ a k–gossiping instance of minimum communication time on a set of n participants $\mathcal{P}$ and by I the instance executed by the algorithm GOSSIPING$(c, \mathcal{P}, k)$. Then*

$$\frac{time(I)}{time(I_{\min})} \leq \left\lceil \frac{n-1}{k} \right\rceil + n - 1.$$

In the case $k = 1$ we have the special situation in which each block travels as an individual packet and it is never blocked to wait for a node to get enough blocks to form a packet. This allows to specialize the arguments of the above Theorem 3.1 to prove that

Theorem 3.2 *Denote by $I_{\min}$ a 1–gossiping instance of minimum communication time on a set of n participants $\mathcal{P}$ and by I the instance executed by the algorithm GOSSIPING$(c, \mathcal{P}, 1)$. Then*

$$\frac{time(I)}{time(I_{\min})} \leq n.$$

Remark 3.1 Consider a set of n participant $\mathcal{P}$, a cost graph $K_{\mathcal{P}}$, the sets of travel times $t(i, j)$ and starting times τ_i, for $i, j \in \mathcal{P}$, and a parameter $k \geq 2$. Let I be a k–gossiping instance such that the ratio of $cost(I)$ to the minimum possible cost is upper bounded by a constant c_1, and $I_{\min}$ be a k–gossiping instance of minimum communication time. We want to prove that there exist values of starting times τ_i, travel time $t(i, j)$, and costs $c(i, j)$ such that $time(I)/time(I_{\min}) = \Omega(n)$. Indeed let $\tau_i = 0$, for $i = 1, \ldots, n$, $t(i, j) = 1$, and

$$c(i, j) = \begin{cases} 1 & \text{if } j = i + 1 \\ c_2 c_1 & \text{otherwise,} \end{cases}$$

for each pair of participants $i, j \in \mathcal{P}$ with $i \neq j$. For c_2 large enough any instance I, such that the ratio of $cost(I)$ to the minimum possible communication cost is upper bounded by the constant c_1, must use only the edges of the path

It is easy to see that for such an instance I it holds $time(I) = n - 1$ while, if our only concern is to minimize the communication time regardless of the communication cost, we have $time(I_{\min}) = 1$.

The communication complexity $comm(I)$ of an instance I is defined as $comm(I) = cost(I) \cdot time(I)$. We stress that minimizing the communication complexity is NP-complete even when k is unbounded [21].

By Theorems 3.1, 2.3, and 2.2 we can derive the following result.

Theorem 3.3 *Denote by $I_{\min}$ a k-gossiping instance of minimum communication complexity on a set of n participants $\mathcal{P}$ and by I the instance executed by the algorithm $GOSSIPING(c, \mathcal{P}, k)$. Then*

$$\frac{comm(I)}{comm(I_{\min})} \leq n\left(1 + \frac{1}{k}\right) + 2k.$$

In case $k = 1$ from Corollary 2.2 we have $cost(I) = cost(I_{\min})$; by Theorem 3.2 we get

Theorem 3.4 *Denote by $I_{\min}$ a 1-gossiping instance of minimum communication complexity on a set of n participants $\mathcal{P}$ and by I the instance executed by the algorithm $GOSSIPING(c, \mathcal{P}, 1)$. Then*

$$\frac{comm(I)}{comm(I_{\min})} \leq n.$$

References

1. A. Bagchi, E.F. Schmeichel, and S.L. Hakimi, "Parallel Information Dissemination by Packets", *SIAM J. on Computing*, 23 (1994), 355-372.
2. A. Bagchi, E.F. Schmeichel, and S.L. Hakimi, "Sequential Information Dissemination by Packets", *NETWORKS*, 22 (1992), 317–333.
3. J.–C. Bermond, L. Gargano, A. Rescigno, and U. Vaccaro, "Fast Gossiping by Short Messages", *SIAM J. on Computing*, to appear; an extended abstract appeared in: *Proceedings of ICALP '95*, Z. Fülöp and F. Gécseg (Eds.), Lectures Notes in Computer Science, vol. **944**, pp. 135–146, Springer-Verlag, 1995.
4. J.–C. Bermond, S. Perennes, and T. Kodate, "Gossiping in Cayley Graphs by Packets", in: *Proceedings of the 8-th French–Japanese Conference on Combinatorics and Computer Science*, Brest, July 1995.
5. D. P. Bertsekas, and J. N. Tsitsiklis, *Parallel and Distributed Computation: Numerical Methods*, Prentice–Hall, Englewood Cliffs, NJ, 1989.
6. K. Diks, A. Pelc, "Efficient Gossiping by Packets in Networks with Random Faults", SIAM J. Discrete Mathematics, 9 (1996).
7. S. Even and B. Monien, "On the number of Rounds Necessary to Disseminate Information", *Proc. 1st ACM Symp. on Parallel Algorithms and Architectures*, Santa Fe, NM (1989), 318–327.
8. P. Fraignaud, E. Lazard, "Methods and Problems of Communication in Usual Networks", *Discrete Applied Math.*, 53 (1994), 79–134.
9. S. Fujita, "Gossiping in Mesh–Bus Computers by Packets with Bounded Length", *IPS Japan SIGAL*, 36-6 (1993), 41–48.
10. L. Gargano, "Tighter Time Bounds on Fault–Tolerant Broadcasting and Gossiping", *NETWORKS*, 22 (1992), 469–486.
11. L. Gargano and A. A. Rescigno, "Communication Complexity of Fault–Tolerant Information Diffusion", *Proceeding of the 5th IEEE Symposium on Parallel and Distributed Computing (SPDP 93)*, Dallas, TX, 564-571, 1993.
12. R.W. Haddad, S. Roy, and A. A. Schäffer, "On Gossiping with Faulty Telephone Lines", *SIAM J. on Alg. Discr. Meth.*, 8 (1987), 439–445.

13. S. Hedetniemi, S. Hedetniemi, and A. Liestman, "A Survey of Gossiping and Broadcasting in Communication Networks", *NETWORKS*, 18 (1988), 129–134.

14. A. Hily and D. Sotteau, "Communications in Bus Networks", in: *Parallel and Distributed Computing*, M. Cosnard, A. Ferreira, and J. Peters (Eds.), Lectures Notes in Computer Science, 805, Springer – Verlag, (1994),197–206.

15. J. Hromkovič, R. Klasing, B. Monien, and R. Peine, "Dissemination of Information in Interconnection Networks (Broadcasting and Gossiping)", in: F. Hsu, D.-Z. Du (Eds.) *Combinatorial Network Theory*, Kluwer Academic Publishers, (1995) 125-212.

16. W. Knödel, "New Gossips and Telephons", *Discrete Math.*, 30 (1980), 151–156.

17. D. W. Krumme, K.N. Venkataraman, and G. Cybenko, "Gossiping in Minimal Time", *SIAM J. on Computing*, 21 (1992), 111–139.

18. A. Pelc, "Fault Tolerant Broadcasting and Gossiping in Communication Networks", *Technical Report* (1995), University of Quebec.

19. R. Ravi, "Rapid Rumour Ramification: Approximating the Minimum Broadcasting Time", *Proc. 35th Annual Symposium on Foundations of Computer Science (FOCS '94)*, (1994), 202–213.

20. Q. Stout and B. Wagar, "Intensive Hypercube Communication", *J. Parallel and Distr. Computing*, 10 (1990), 167–181.

21. O. Wolfson and A. Segall, "The Communication Complexity of Atomic Commitment and of Gossiping", *SIAM J. on Computing*, 20 (1991), 423–450.

Optimal Cost-Sensitive Distributed Minimum Spanning Tree Algorithm

Teresa Przytycka[1]
University of Maryland

Lisa Higham[2]
University of Calgary

Abstract. In a network of asynchronous processors, the cost to send a message can differ significantly from one communication link to another. Assume that associated with each link is a positive *weight* representing the cost of sending one message along the link and the cost of an algorithm executed on a *weighted* network is the sum of the costs of all messages sent during its execution. We present a distributed Minimum Cost Spanning tree algorithm that is optimal with respect to this cost measure.

1 Introduction

This paper presents an efficient *cost-sensitive*, asynchronous, distributed algorithm that finds a minimum spanning tree in a weighted connected network of processors.

A network of processors may cooperate to solve a problem by exchanging messages across communication channels. Such a network is naturally modelled as a connected, undirected graph with processors represented as vertices and communication channels represented as edges. For each channel, the cost of sending a message over that channel is captured by assigning a positive weight to the corresponding edge. Our goal is a distributed message-passing algorithm that determines a minimum spanning tree of the network.

The measure of the communication cost of an asynchronous distributed algorithm for finding a minimum spanning tree for a network has typically been the total number of messages sent. This measure assumes that the cost of sending a message along any link is equal to one. However, the network is weighted, and therefore it is more realistic to factor the edge weights into the communication complexity of the algorithm. Specifically, in "cost-sensitive analysis", as introduced by Awerbuch, Baratz and Peleg [2], the cost attributed to transmitting a message over a link is the edge weight of that link. The cost of a distributed

---

[1] Author's address: University of Maryland, Dept. of Computer Science, A.V. Williams Bldg., College Park, MD 20742. On leave from Odense University, Denmark. email: `przytyck@cs.umbc.edu`

[2] This research was carried out in part while visiting the University of Odense whose support is gratefully acknowledged, as well as that of the Natural Sciences and Engineering Research Council of Canada. Author's address: Computer Science Department, University of Calgary, Calgary, Alberta, T2N 1N4, Canada. email: `higham@cpsc.ucalgary.ca`

minimum spanning tree algorithm for a given weighted network is the maximum, over all message delay patterns, of the sum of the costs of all message traffic that occurs while executing the algorithm on that network.

Running an algorithm designed for an unweighted network on a weighted network will not, in general, be cost efficient. Let W be the sum of the weights of all edges of a weighted network containing N processors. The algorithm of Gallager, Humblet and Spira [7] has cost-sensitive complexity $\Omega(W \lg N)$. In fact, all other published minimum spanning tree algorithms have the same bound on weighted message complexity. The results of this paper show that this is not optimal. Let $\mathcal{G}(V, E)$ be a connected weighted undirected graph with total edge weight W. Let $\mathcal{S}(V, \hat{E})$ be a minimum spanning tree of G, and let n_i be the number of edges in S that have weight in $(2^{i-1}, 2^i]$. We present an algorithm for the distributed minimum spanning tree problem that has weighted message complexity $O((\sum_{n_i \geq 1} n_i 2^i \lg n_i) + W)$ on $\mathcal{G}$ [3]. We also show that this is asymptotically optimal even for rings.

The distributed minimum spanning tree problem has been well studied. Let $\mathcal{G}(V, E)$ be a connected undirected network of N processors and M edges, where each $e \in E$ has weight $w(e) \geq 1$ and total edge weight is W. The breakthrough algorithm of Gallager et. al. [7], denoted GHS, sends at most $5N \lg N + 2M$ messages each of size at most $O(\lg W)$, and has worst case time complexity $O(N \lg N)$. However, as pointed out above, the message cost in the cost-sensitive sense can be high. Several results followed that were based on the GHS algorithm but attempted to reduce the worst case time complexity [4, 1, 5, 10, 6]. All these algorithms remain expensive in the cost-sensitive sense.

In a paper that introduces the notion of cost-sensitive analysis, Awerbuch et. al. [2] claim without proof, that a variant of the Minimum Spanning Tree algorithm of Gallager, Humblet and Spira [7], has cost-sensitive communication complexity $O(S \lg N + W)$ where S is the weight of the minimum cost spanning tree and W is the total edge weight. Indeed, it is easy to see how a simple adaptation of GHS might achieve this result if large messages (polynomial in size of the graph and its edge weights) are used, but we see no straightforward variant that achieves this complexity with logarithmic size messages, as is typically assumed for distributed messages-passing settings.

Section 2 describes the model of computation, states the problem and establishes some terminology. Section 3 gives a high level description of distributed MST algorithms as well as presenting some observations on the problems that need to be overcome to convert GHS to an efficient cost-sensitive algorithm. The description of our algorithm is contained in Section 4. As shown in Section 5, the analysis for the cost-sensitive case requires completely different techniques from the analysis of those algorithms mentioned above. Finally, Section 6 comments on the proof that our algorithm is asymptotically optimal in the cost-sensitive sense, although the full proof is omitted because of space constraints.

---

[3] In this paper all logarithms are base 2 and are assumed to be *truncated logs* satisfying $\lg x = \max\{1, \log_2 x\}$.

2   Model, Problem and Terminology

A network of processors that communicate by exchanging messages is modelled as a connected, undirected graph with processors represented by vertices and communication links represented by edges. Each processor has a distinct identifier. We assume that communication is reliable but asynchronous. That is, all messages sent are eventually received uncorrupted, and messages travelling the same edge are received in the order in which they were sent. For each link, the cost of sending a message over that link is captured by assigning a weight greater than or equal to one, to the corresponding edge. We assume that each processor initially knows only the weight of each edge adjacent to it. There is no other topological knowledge available to the processors. In particular, processors do not know the size of the network. Without loss of generality, we may assume that all edge weights are distinct, since, if they are not, the identifiers of the endpoints of each link can be appended to the weight of the link in order to break ties, as suggested by Gallager et. al. [7].

We require a message-driven protocol for each node of the network such that for any possible pattern of finite message delays the processors eventually terminate having collectively identified a minimum spanning tree of their network. Upon termination, each processor has determined for each of its adjacent edges whether it is a tree or a non-tree edge. We also require that any message is constrained to have size $O(\lg W)$ bits where W is the total edge weight of the network.

Because the edge weights are distinct, the minimum spanning tree (MST) is unique so we can refer to *the* MST for a given network. A *fragment* of the MST is any connected set of nodes and edges in the MST. An edge is an *outgoing edge* of a fragment, f, if one of its endpoints is in f and one is not. An edge is *the minimum outgoing edge*, denoted $min\_out(f)$, of a fragment f, if it has the least weight of all outgoing edges of f.

3   Algorithm Overview and Intuition

A general strategy for building the MST is to start with fragments consisting of just single nodes. Each existing fragment, f, proceeds asynchronously, using an *edge-finding procedure*, to find $min\_out(f)$. When found, f attempts to combine with the neighbouring fragment, say f', that contains the other endpoint of $min\_out(f)$, using a *combining procedure*. All the published distributed algorithms for MST follow this general approach. However, care is needed in both procedures to ensure that the edge found is indeed outgoing, and to control the cost of the algorithm.

In the GHS algorithm, each fragment f has associated with it a value called *level(f)*, and contains a distinguished node called the *leader* that coordinates the edge-finding and combining procedures. In the combining procedure, a fragment that tries to connect to a fragment at a higher level is absorbed by the higher level fragment, accepting its leader and adopting its level. If the two fragments have the same level and the fragment on the other side of the link has attempted to connect over the same link then the two fragments form a new fragment with one of the endpoints of the connecting edge as a new leader and with level incremented by one. Otherwise, response to the request to connect is delayed until one of these conditions is met. These rules for combining fragments guarantee that the number of nodes in a fragment is always is at least $2^{level(f)}$, and hence there can be at most $\lg N$ levels.

In the edge-finding procedure, *test* messages are sent to determine whether a potential edge is outgoing. In GHS there is at most one accepted test message sent per node, per level. Also, an edge can carry a test message that will be rejected at most once in each direction for the entire duration of the algorithm. Since there can be at most $\lg N$ levels, the total number of test messages that have an accepting response is bounded by $O(N \lg N)$ and those that have a rejecting response is bounded by $O(M)$. Since the total number of other message types that are sent per level in a fragment is proportional to the fragment size, the total message count is $O(N \lg N + M)$.

In the cost-sensitive case we are charged for the cost of messages not just the number of messages. Hence the assurance of one successful test message per node per level is inadequate. Define the *weight of a fragment* to be the sum of the weights of the edges in the fragment. The most natural way to translate the GHS algorithm into a cost-sensitive algorithm would be to modify the definition of the level so that it reflects the weight of the fragment rather than the number of nodes in the fragment. However, this adaptation alone does not curb excessive cost. For example, it is possible that a node could repeatedly send a test message at successive levels over an expensive link. Also, even if a collection of nodes have relatively light untested edges, it may be that there are many of them making the total cost of such test messages too high. To address these types of problems we introduce extra machinery designed to prevent: (1) heavy edges from being probed prematurely, and (2) many edges from being probed simultaneously. We will use a careful cost balancing strategy to decide when to include a given edge in the search for the lightest outgoing edge. Delicate accounting will be used to show that these ideas, as implemented in the next section, are adequate to contain weighted message cost.

4   The Cost-Sensitive Algorithm — *weighted-MST*

Terminology: During the execution of *weighted-MST* each node marks its adjacent edges to be in one of three states: *branch, rejected* or *unlabelled*. A *branch* edge is an edge that has been determined to be an edge of the MST. A *rejected* edge is an edge that has been determined not to belong to the MST. When the algorithm terminates the *branch* edges are the edges of the minimum cost spanning tree. For each edge, e, denote the weight of e by $w(e)$. The *edge-phase* of e is $\lfloor \lg w(e) \rfloor$.

At each stage of the algorithm, the *branch* edges define a partition of the minimum spanning tree into a forest of connected component called *fragments*.

Each fragment f has a *level(f)*, a *phase(f)*, and a distinguished node denoted by *lead(f)*, called the *leader* of the fragment. The triple $(lead(f), level(f), phase(f))$ is the *identification* of the fragment f. The level of the fragment will provide an upper bound on the logarithm of its weight, and the phase of the fragment will provide a lower bound on the edge-phase of the lightest outgoing edge. We think of a fragment as a tree rooted at its leader. A *branch* is labelled by an adjacent node to be *inbound* (respectively, *outbound*) if it leads toward (respectively, away from) the fragment leader.

Each fragment that is in phase p and has weight bigger than 2^p is partitioned into connected *subfragments* each of weight $\Theta(2^p)$ and each having one node selected as the subfragment *chief*. If the weight of the whole fragment is less that 2^p, the fragment is one *underweighted* subfragment. The smallest connected subtree of a fragment that contains all subfragment chiefs is called the *chief tree* of the given fragment, and is also rooted at the leader of the fragment. Since the partition into subfragments is an edge partition, a node may be the chief of more than one subfragment. Each node maintains the identification of the fragment and subfragments to which it belongs.

Each node is in one of three states *sleeping*, *find*, or *found*. In addition, a non-sleeping node may be a leader of a fragment or a chief of one or more subfragments, or both or neither.

If T is a tree of processors and m is a message, a *broadcast of m on T* is a procedure that propagates the message m from the root of T to all the nodes of T. Each node that receive m from its parent, sends a copy of m to each of its children. Similarly, a *collect on T* is a procedure used to propagate information from the leaves of T to its root. Each node receives some information from each of its children, which it combines with its own, and then sends the result to its parent.

Initialization: Initially, all nodes are in the *sleeping* state and all edges are *unlabelled*. Execution begins asynchronously at nodes when they wake up either spontaneously or by receiving a message from an awakened neighbour. Upon wake-up each node v changes to state *find*, becomes the leader of the unpartitioned fragment containing only itself, having identification $(v, 0, 0)$, and begins executing the *edge_finding* procedure.

edge_finding **procedure:** This procedure, which may consist of several iterations, determines the lightest outgoing edge of a fragment. An iteration begins when the leader of a fragment with identification $(lead, \ell, p)$ broadcasts an INITIATE-FIND$(lead, \ell, p)$ message over the chief tree to all its subfragment chiefs (including itself). Upon receipt of the INITIATE-FIND message each chief enters the state *find* and executes the procedure *brute_force_find(ℓ, p)*. This procedure determines a *candidate edge*, which is the lightest outgoing edge that has edge-phase at most p, over all nodes in the subfragment, if such an edge exists and the minimum weight *unlabelled* edge otherwise. In the case that the candidate edge is determined to be outgoing, the path from the chief to this outgoing edge is also recorded by labelling each edge in the path with *best*. Details of the *brute_force_find* procedure will be described shortly. Once the candidate edge is determined for a subfragment, the subfragment chief changes to state *found* and participates in a collect on the chief tree that propagates a REPORT(A) message containing the weight A of the lightest candidate among all candidates. During the collect procedure each node marks as *best* that edge leading to the lightest candidate in its subtree. One iteration of the *edge_finding* procedure ends when the leader receives REPORT(A). The algorithm terminates if the leader learns from the REPORT messages that there are no remaining candidate edges in the entire fragment. An *edge_finding* iteration is *successful* if the leader learns of at least one candidate edge with weight $A \leq 2^p$. In this case the leader begins executing the *combining* procedure.

Otherwise, the weight A in the REPORT message delivered to the leader of the fragment, say f, by the collect satisfies $A > 2^p$ and the iteration of *edge_finding(ℓ, p)* is *unsuccessful*. In this case, however, $\lg A$ is a lower bound on the edge-phase of *min_out(f)*; so the leader updates *phase(f)* to $p' = \lg A$, and *level(f)* to $\ell' = \max\{\ell, p'\}$. Since the phase of f has increased, the partition of f into subfragments must be updated. Therefore, the leader initiates a depth-first search procedure, which broadcasts the new phase p' and repartitions f into subfragments of weight $\Theta(2^{p'})$ (or leaves f as one underweighted subfragment if it is not large enough to subdivide). After repartitioning its subfragments, the leader initiates another iteration of *edge_finding* by broadcasting INITIATE-FIND($lead, \ell', p'$).

***combining* procedure:**   This procedure is initiated by the leader after a successful iteration of *edge_finding(ℓ, p)*. In this case there is a path in the fragment with edges labelled with *best* directed from the leader to *min_out(f)*. The leader sends a CHANGE-LEADER message, which travels along this path to the node v in f adjacent to *min_out(f)*. This causes each node that receives the CHANGE-LEADER message to relabel its inbound edge to be outbound and set the new inbound edge to be the edge labelled *best*. Upon receipt of the CHANGE-LEADER message by v all inbound edges of f will form a fragment tree for f rooted at v, which becomes the new leader. Node v then sends a CONNECT($lead, \ell, p$) message along *min_out(f)*. Let *min_out(f)* $= (v, v')$, where v' belongs to some fragment f' and suppose v' has recorded $(lead', \ell', p')$ as the identification of its fragment f'. The following cases are possible:

1. $p' = phase(f)$ and $\ell' = level(f)$ and *min_out(f')* $=$ *min_out(f)*. Then v' will also send a CONNECT message along *min_out(f)* and the two fragments will form a new fragment of level $\ell' + 1$, and phase p' with a new leader, say v, which is that node adjacent to *min_out(f)* with the smallest identifier. Node v announces the new fragment identification to the nodes of the fragment by broadcasting an INITIATE-FIND(v, ℓ', p') message, which also serves to start the *edge_finding* procedure.

2. $p' = phase(f)$ and $l' > level(f)$. Then node v' of fragment f' responds with an ABSORB($lead', l', p'$) message, which is broadcast to all of f along the fragment tree of f. The ABSORB message causes each node of f to adopt the new identification $(lead', l', p')$. Thus f becomes part of f' and adopts its leader and level. The ABSORB message also carries the status (*find* or *found*)

of node v'. If the state propagated to fragment f is *find* then the nodes of f will participate in the *edge-finding* procedure of fragment f' with node v' considering the subtree rooted at v to be its descendants in the fragment tree for f'. (If the state of v' was *found* then the nodes of f cannot influence the search for $min\_out(f')$. This is because an outgoing edge of f' that is lighter than $< v, v' >$, and thus lighter than any outgoing edge from a node of f, must have already been determined.)

3. $(p' = phase(f)$ and $l' < level(f))$ or $(p' = phase(f)$ and $l' = level(f)$ but $min\_out(f') \neq min\_out(f))$. Then v' delays its response to v until $level(f')$ grows to satisfy one of the previous conditions. Note, that f' will keep growing without increasing its phase until it chooses $< v, v' >$ as its lightest outgoing edge.

4. $p' < phase(f)$. Then v' delays its response to v until $phase(f') = phase(f)$ when one of the previous conditions applies.

Note that only fragments in the same phase, say p, can combine, and when they do the new fragment remains in phase p. Thus the partition of the new fragment into subfragments can usually be inherited from the partition of the merged fragments. If each of these fragments has weight at least 2^p then the previous partitions of each of the old fragments is maintained, and the connecting edge of the newly formed fragment becomes an additional subfragment containing just this edge. If one fragment had weight smaller than 2^p, then the connecting edge is added to the underweighted fragment. If both fragments are underweighted, then the connecting edge and both previous fragments are contained in one new subfragment.

The *brute_force_find* procedure: This procedure may consist of several iterations. An iteration begins when a subfragment chief of fragment f broadcasts a FIND(ℓ, p) message to the nodes in its subfragment and collects a response SUB-REPORT(B, e) containing the lightest *unlabelled* edge $e = < v, v' >$ adjacent to its subfragment and its weight B. (The broadcast also causes recipient nodes to remove old *best* labels.) If e has edge-phase bigger than p the search is over and e becomes the candidate edge for the subfragment. Otherwise, the edge-phase of e is equal to p and the chief instructs the node v adjacent to edge e in the subfragment to send a TEST$(lead, \ell, p)$ message across e, in order to determine whether or not e is an outgoing edge of f. The response of node v' in fragment f' to the TEST message depends upon the identification of f' that v' has recorded. First, note that v is guaranteed to have its correct fragment identification, while the identification $(lead', \ell', p')$ stored in node v' may be out-of-date because the fragment f' may be in the process of changing its identification. However, if knowledge of v' is not current then $level(f')$ is strictly bigger than ℓ'. Therefore, if the identification stored by v and v' are the same, then v and v' are definitely in the same fragment so v' responds with a REJECT message. If the identification stored by v and v' are not the same, and $\ell' \geq level(f)$ then v and v' are guaranteed to be in different fragments so v' responds with an ACCEPT message. If $\ell' < level(f)$ then v' delays its response to the TEST message until one of the previous conditions is met when it can be certain that its possibly out-of-date information cannot lead to an erroneous reply. If e is not an outgoing edge, e is marked as *rejected* , and this information is returned to the subfragment chief, which initiates another iteration of *brute_force_find*. Iterations are repeated until either an outgoing edge of phase p is found or the lightest *unlabelled* edge of phase higher than p is reported.

Correctness: Correctness follows after establishing that fragments of *weighted-MST* always connect along minimum outgoing edges, and that *weighted-MST* cannot deadlock. The algorithm ensures that a node's response of ACCEPT to a TEST message over edge e from fragment f is possible only if e is outgoing from f, and furthermore all candidate edges in the current phase are so tested. Because phases only increase, the collect procedure ensures that $min\_out(f)$ is the minimum outgoing edge for f. Thus CONNECT messages are only sent over minimum outgoing edges. Now consider any stage of the algorithm when more than one fragment remains. Let edge $e = <v, v'>$ be the minimum weight spanning tree edge that has not yet been identified by any fragment. Suppose f with identification $(lead, \ell, p)$ and f' with identification $(lead', \ell', p')$ are the fragments containing v and v' respectively. Then both p and p' are less than or equal to edge-phase(e) since otherwise e would have already been tested and incorporated. While executing *edge_finding*, f and f' will each eventually increase their phases to be equal to edge-phase(e) until they each send a TEST across e. Case 4 of *combining* ensures that both fragments are in the same phase when responses are sent to the TEST message. Thus case 1 or case 2 must arise for one of f or f'. Hence, the fragments must merge forming a larger fragment, and ensuring no deadlock.

5 Weighted Message Cost of *weighted-MST*

Let $\mathcal{G}(V, E)$ be a network of processors with total edge weight W. Let T be the total weighted message cost of all INITIATE-FIND messages and all FIND messages sent in an execution of *weighted-MST* on $\mathcal{G}$.

Lemma 1. *The weighted message cost of weighted-MST is $O(T + W)$.*

Proof. The messages sent by *weighted-MST* are: (1) All broadcasts by fragment leaders over the chief trees of INITIATE-FIND messages and the corresponding collect of REPORT messages. (2) All broadcasts by subfragment chiefs to nodes in its subfragment of FIND messages and the corresponding collect of SUB-REPORT messages. (3) All CHANGE-LEADER messages. (4) All CONNECT messages. (5) All ABSORB messages. (6) All TEST messages. (7) All ACCEPT and REJECT messages. (8) All messages used to update the phase of a fragment and to repartition into subfragments.

Note that for each REPORT message there corresponds a unique INITIATE-FIND message that travelled the same edge; for each SUB-REPORT message there corresponds a unique FIND message that travelled the same edge; for each AC-CEPT or REJECT message there corresponds a unique TEST message that travelled the same edge. Also, each CHANGE-LEADER and ABSORB message can be matched with a unique INITIATE-FIND or FIND that travelled the same edge. Each CONNECT message sent on an edge e can be matched with the accepted TEST message that identified e as outgoing. Finally, the cost of the messages used to repartition a fragment and update its phase is no more than the cost of the previous iteration of *edge_finding*, which led to the repartitioning. Hence, it suffices to bound the weighted message cost of all INITIATE-FIND, FIND, and TEST messages. A TEST message is *rejected* if the response to it was a REJECT message; and it is *accepted* if the response to it was an ACCEPT message. An accepted TEST message is *wasted* if the tested edge is not the lightest outgoing edge as determined by the current iteration of *edge_finding*, and otherwise it is *non-wasted*. The total weighted message cost, C, of *weighted-MST* is of the order of the sum of the components: (1) C_1 = cost of rejected TEST messages, (2) C_2 = cost of wasted accepted TEST messages, (3) C_3 = cost of non-wasted accepted TEST messages, and (4) T.

Since an edge can carry at most one rejected TEST or non-wasted accepted TEST for the duration of the algorithm, $C_1 + C_3$ is dominated by W. If a fragment consists of only one subfragment, then there cannot be a wasted accepted TEST. Otherwise, each execution of *brute_force_find* on a subfragment s is responsible for at most one wasted accepted TEST. However, the edge-phase of each tested edge is equal to the phase of the fragment. So in this case the cost of the *brute_force_find* for s is at least of the same order as the weight of s which is the approximate cost of the wasted TEST message. □

Thus it remains to bound T. Let P be the maximum phase of an edge in E. Let n_i be the number of edges of the MST that are in phase i. Let w_i denote 2^{i+1}, which is the upper bound on the weight of an edge with edge-phase i.

Lemma 2. $T = O\left(\sum_{1 \le i \le P} w_i n_i \lg(n_i) + W\right)$.

Proof. Each execution of *brute_force_find* on a subfragment s of a fragment in phase p consists of one or more iterations where all but the last iteration results in sending one TEST on an edge with edge-phase p and receiving a REJECT in response. Since s was constructed to have weight approximately 2^p (or less if it is underweighted), and since an edge can be rejected only once, the total cost of all such iterations is of order W. Denote by R the remaining cost in T, consisting of the cost of FIND messages in the last iterations of executions of *brute_force_find*, plus the cost of all the INITIATE-FIND messages. The INITIATE-FIND and FIND messages that contribute to R in any iteration of *edge_finding* on a fragment f constitute one pass over the fragment tree, and hence have cost proportional to $w(f)$.

First consider unsuccessful iterations of the *edge_finding* procedure. Denote by $cand(f, p)$ the candidate edge that is reported by an unsuccessful iteration on a fragment f in phase p. Then the next iteration of *edge_finding* on f will have phase $p' = $ edge-phase$(cand(f, p))$ and edge $cand(f, p)$ will be tested (and never tested again). Hence, if $w(f) \le w(cand(f, p))$ then the cost in R due to this unsuccessful iteration can be attributed to $cand(f, p)$ and the cost of all such iterations absorbed in the term $O(W)$. The portion, say C, of R due to unsuccessful iterations of *edge_finding* that are not absorbed in the term $O(W)$ is therefore bounded by:

$$C = \sum_{1 \leq p \leq P \& \{ f \text{ is a fragment in phase } p \text{ s.t } w(cand(f,p)) < w(f)\}} w(f).$$

Since, after each unsuccessful iteration of edge-finding, the phase of the fragment increases, we need to compute, for each phase p, the maximum total weight of the fragments in phase p that satisfy $w(cand(f,p)) < w(f)$. The weight of all tree edges in fragments in phase p plus the weights of all minimum cost outgoing edges with edge-phase less than or equal to p of these fragments is bounded by $\sum_{i=1}^{p} n_i 2^{i+1}$. Let $d_p = \frac{\sum_{i=1}^{p} n_i 2^{i+1}}{2^p}$. If $d_p < 1$, then no fragment f in phase p can have weight bigger than $cand(f,p)$. If $d_p \geq 1$ then the total weight of the fragments with $w(cand(f,p)) < w(f)$ is bounded by $\sum_{i=1}^{p} n_i 2^{i+1}$. Thus we have $C = O(\sum_{p,d_p \geq 1} \sum_{i=1}^{p} n_i 2^i) = O(w_i n_i \lg n_i)$ where the last estimate was proved in [8] (see Appendix).

Now consider a successful iteration of *edge_finding* on a fragment f. If $w(f) \leq min\_out(f)$ then the cost in R due to this iteration can be attributed to $min\_out(f)$ and the cost of all such iterations absorbed in the term $O(W)$. The portion C' of R due to successful iterations of *edge_finding* that are not absorbed in the term $O(W)$ is therefore bounded by:

$$C' = \sum_{1 \leq l \leq L \& \{ f \text{ is a fragment s.t } level(f) = l, w(f) \geq min\_out(f)\}} w(f).$$

C' can be estimated in the similar way as C: If $d_l < 1$, then no fragment can satisfy the conditions under the sum. Otherwise, since $phase(f) \leq level(f)$ the total cost of edges that go from phase l to $l+1$ after a successful iteration is bounded by $\sum_{i=1}^{l} n_i 2^i$. Since after each successful *edge_finding* iteration the level of the fragment grows we have: $C' = O(\sum_{l,d_l \geq 1}^{L} \sum_{i=1}^{l} n_i 2^i) = O(w_i n_i \lg n_i)$. Thus $R = O(w_i n_i \lg n_i)$, and hence $T = O(w_i n_i \lg n_i + W)$. □

Lemmas 1 and 2 immediately yield:

Theorem 3. *Let $\mathcal{G}(V,E)$ be a network of processors with total edge weight W, and let n_i be the number of edges of the MST of $\mathcal{G}$ that are have edge-phase i. Then the weighted message cost of weighted-MST on $\mathcal{G}$ is $O(n_i 2^i \lg n_i + W)$.*

6 Optimality of *weighted-MST*

It has been shown [8] that given a multiset X of weights where n_i weight are in the interval $(2^{i-1}, 2^i]$ and a leader election algorithm A for unidirectional rings, there is a unidirectional ring $\mathcal{R}$ with edge weights equal to the multiset X such that the weighted message cost of A on $\mathcal{R}$ is $\Omega((\sum_{n_i \geq 1} n_i 2^i \lg n_i) + W)$. Also, Bolaender [3] established an $.346 n \lg n$ lower bound for the unweighted message complexity of a bidirectional ring. Both these results are adapted from that of Pachl *et.al.* [9]. The techniques can be combined and further adapted in a straightforward fashion to show that an leader election algorithm (and hence, any minimum spanning tree algorithm) for bidirectional rings must incur a weighted message cost of $\Omega((\sum_{n_i \geq 1} n_i 2^i \lg n_i) + W)$. Thus *weighted-MST* is asymptotically optimal even for rings.

References

1. B. Awerbuch. Optimal distributed algorithms for minimum weight spanning tree, counting, leader election and related problems. In *Proceedings of the Nineteenth Annual ACM Symposium on Theory of Computing*, pages 230–240, 1987.

2. B. Awerbuch, A. Baratz, and D. Peleg. Cost-sensitive analysis of communication protocols. In *Proc. 9th Annual ACM Symp. on Principles of Distributed Computing*, pages 177–187, 1990.

3. H. L. Bodlaender. A better lower bound for distributed leader finding in bidirectional asynchronous rings of processors. *Information Processing Letters*, 27(6):287–290, 1988.

4. F. Chin and H. F. Ting. An almost linear time and $O(n \lg n + e)$ messages distributed algorithm for minimum weight spanning tree. In *Proc. 26nd Annual Symp. on Foundations of Comput. Sci.*, pages 257–266, 1985.

5. M. Faloutsos and M. Molle. Optimal distributed algorithm for minimum spanning trees revisited. In *Proc. 14th Annual ACM Symp. on Principles of Distributed Computing*, pages 231–237, 1995.

6. E. Gafni. Improvements in the time complexity of two message-optimal election algorthms. In *Proc. 4th Annual ACM Symp. on Principles of Distributed Computing*, pages 175–184, 1985.

7. R. Gallager, P. Humblet, and P. Spira. A distributed algorithm for minimum weight spanning trees. *ACM Trans. on Prog. Lang. and Systems*, 5(1):66–77, 1983.

8. L. Higham and T. Przytycka. Asymptotically optimal election on weighted rings. In *Lecture Notes in Computer Science #824*, pages 207–218. Springer Verlag, 1994. SWAT94, revised version to appear in SIAM J. Comp.

9. J. Pachl, E. Korach, and D. Rotem. Lower bounds for distributed maximum finding. *J. Assoc. Comput. Mach.*, 31(4):905–918, 1984.

10. G. Singh and A. J. Bernstein. A highly asynchronous minimum spanning tree protocol. *Distributed Computing*, 8(3):151–161, 1995.

Appendix

Theorem 4. *Let $\mathcal{G}$ be a weighted graph with a unique minimum spanning tree S. Let n_i be the number of edges in S with edge-phase i. Let $w_i = 2^i$, and let L be the highest level value attained when executing weighted-MST on $\mathcal{G}$. Then $S = \sum_{\ell,d_\ell \geq 1}^{L} (\sum_{i=1}^{\ell} n_i 2^i) = O(w_i n_i \lg n_i)$*

Proof. Let $\hat{n}_i$ be the least integer that is a power of 2 and satisfies $\hat{n}_i \geq n_i$ and let $I = max\{i : n_i \geq 1\}$. Thus L (the number of levels until there is one fragment) is at most the minimum p satisfying $(\sum_{i=0}^{I} \hat{n}_i 2^i)/2^p \geq 1$. We will now show that $S = \sum_{p=0,d_p \geq 1}^{L} \sum_{i=0}^{p} \hat{n}_i 2^i \in O(\sum_{n_i \geq 1} \hat{n}_i 2^i \lg(\hat{n}_i + 1))$ which implies the theorem.

Let A be a $(L+1)$ by $(I+1)$ matrix defined by $A(p,i) = \hat{n}_i 2^{i-p}$ for $p \geq i$ and $A(p,i) = 0$ for $p < i$. Let $D_p = \sum_{i=0}^{p} A(p,i)$. Then each element of the summation S can be interpreted as the corresponding element of A multiplied by an appropriate scaling factor. Specifically, $S \leq \sum_{0 \leq p \leq L, D_p \geq 1, 0 \leq i \leq I} A(p,i) \cdot 2^p$.

Note that entries for any p such that $D_p < 1$ do not contribute to the sum S. Among the remaining entries of A we consider three types. Entries satisfying $A(p,i) \geq 1$ are called *whole entries* (denoted $\mathcal{W}$). Other entries are called *fractional* entries. Among fractional entries we distinguish *heavy* entries (denoted $\mathcal{H}$) and *light entries* (denoted $\mathcal{L}$) to be defined later.

Lemma 5. $\sum_{A(p,i) \in \mathcal{W}} A(p,i) 2^p \in O(\sum_{i=0}^{I} \hat{n}_i 2^i \lg(\hat{n}_i + 1))$.

Proof. For any fixed i and $p \geq i$, $A(p,i) \cdot 2^p = \hat{n}_i 2^i$. By definition, the largest entry in column i is $A(i,i) = \hat{n}_i$, and the smallest whole entry is $A(i + \lg \hat{n}_i, i) = 1$. Therefore there are $\lg \hat{n}_i + 1$ whole entries in column i, which, when multiplied by the corresponding scaling vector make up exactly those terms included in the summation $\sum_{i=0}^{I} \hat{n}_i 2^i \lg(\hat{n}_i + 1)$. □

Therefore, it remains to show that the contribution of the fractional elements in the summation S is of the same order.

For each i satisfying $\hat{n}_i > 0$, Let $level(i)$ be the number k satisfying $A(k,i) = 1$. That is, $level(i) = i + \lg \hat{n}_i$. Let $T_k = \{i : level(i) = k\}$ and $t_k = |T_k|$. A fractional entry $A(p,i)$ is called *heavy* if $p \leq level(i) + t_{level(i)}$. A fractional entry that is not heavy is called *light*.

The next claim states that the contribution of all heavy fractional elements to the sum S is of the same order as the contribution of whole elements.

Lemma 6. *For any k such that $T_k \neq \emptyset$*

$$\sum_{i \in T_k} \sum_{p=k+1}^{k+t_k} A(p,i) 2^p \leq 3 \sum_{i \in T_k} \hat{n}_i 2^i \lg \hat{n}_i$$

Proof. By definition of T_k, for all $i \in T_k$, $\hat{n}_i / 2^{k-i} = 1$. Thus $\hat{n}_i \cdot 2^i = 2^k$. So, $i, j \in T_k$ and $i \neq j$ implies $\hat{n}_i \neq \hat{n}_j$. Therefore, for all $i \in T_k$ the corresponding $\hat{n}_i$ are distinct and are powers of two. Hence:

$$\sum_{i \in T_k} \hat{n}_i \cdot 2^i \lg \hat{n}_i = 2^k \cdot \lg(\prod_{i \in T_k} \hat{n}_i) \geq 2^k \cdot \lg(2^0 \cdot \ldots \cdot 2^{t_k - 1}) > 2^k \cdot (t_k)^2/3$$

On the other hand, for any $i \in T_k$ and for any row p, $A(p, i) \cdot 2^p = n_i 2^i = 2^k$. Hence:

$$\sum_{i \in T_k} \sum_{p=k+1}^{k+t_k} A(p, i) \cdot 2^p = (t_k)^2 2^k < 3 \sum_{i \in T_k} \hat{n}_i \cdot 2^i \lg \hat{n}_i$$

$\square$

To complete the proof we estimate the contribution of light fractional elements. First we show the following claim:

Lemma 7. *For any* p

$$\sum_{i, A(p,i) \in \mathcal{L}} A(p, i) 2^p \in O(2^p).$$

Proof.

$$\sum_{i, A(p,i) \in \mathcal{L}} A(p, i) 2^p = \sum_{k, k+t_k < p} \sum_{i \in T_k} A(p, i) 2^p = \sum_{k, k+t_k < p} t_k 2^k$$

Since $k + t_k < p$ we have $t_k < p - k$ and thus the last sum is bounded by $\sum_{k=1}^{p-1}(p - k) 2^k \in O(2^p)$. $\square$

By claim 7, all light fractional entries that are in the same row as some whole entry, contribute to the sum S approximately the same amount as that whole entry. Thus we need to take care of light fractional entries that do not belong to the same row as a whole entry. Note that each row j that contains a whole entry can be directly followed by at most $\lg D_j$ rows that do not contain whole entries. (Any further row $p > j + \lg D_j$ that does not contain a whole entry has $D_p < 1$ and thus is not counted in the summation). By claim 7, the contribution of light fractional entries in all these rows is bounded by $\sum_{p=j+1}^{j+\lg D_j} 2^p \leq 2^{j+1+\lg D_j} \in O(D_j 2^j)$. Thus the contribution of light fractional entries that belong to a row that does not contain a whole entry is dominated by the contribution of the closest row that contains a whole entry. This concludes the proof of Theorem 4. $\square$

A Linear Time Algorithm for the Feasibility of Pebble Motion on Trees [*]

Vincenzo Auletta[1], Angelo Monti[2], Mimmo Parente[1], Pino Persiano[1]

[1] Dipartimento di Informatica ed Appl. "R.M. Capocelli", Università di Salerno, 84081 Baronissi, Italy.
[2] Dipartimento di Informatica e Sistemistica, Università "La Sapienza" di Roma

Abstract. We consider the following generalization of the popular "15 puzzle." Let T be a tree with n vertices and with $k < n$ distinct pebbles numbered $1, \cdots, k$ on distinct vertices. A move consists in transferring a pebble from its current position to an adjacent unoccupied vertex. We ask the following question: Is a given arrangement of pebbles reachable from another?

We present an algorithm that on input two arrangements of k pebbles on a tree with n vertices decides in time $O(n)$ whether the two arrangements are reachable from one another. We also give an algorithm that, on input two reachable configurations, return a sequence of moves that transforms one configuration into the other.

The pebble motion problem on trees has various applications including memory management in distributed systems, robot motion planning, and deflection routing.

1 Introduction

We consider the following generalization of the popular "15 puzzle" which we call the *Pebble Motion problem on a Tree* (PMT problem, in short). Let T be a tree with n vertices and with $k < n$ distinct pebbles numbered $1, \cdots, k$ on distinct vertices. A move consists in transferring a pebble from its current position to an adjacent unoccupied vertex. We ask the following question: Is a given arrangement of pebbles reachable from another by executing a sequence of moves?

The main contribution of this paper is a linear-time algorithm for deciding whether two arrangements of pebbles on a tree are reachable from one another.

The PMT problem has applications to several fields. We can think of the pebbles as indivisible packets of data that need to be moved from one site to another of a communication network without exceeding the capacities of the communication buffers of each site. Another application of the PMT problem is in the field of motion planning of independent robots. Here, each pebble represents a robot that has to be moved from one vertex to another of a system of tracks.

---

[*] Partially supported by Progetto MURST 40%, Algoritmi, Modelli di Calcolo e Strutture Informative. Part of this work was done while the last author was at International Computer Science Institute, Berkeley, CA, USA.

Due to its wide applicability, the problem of pebble motion has been studied in various contexts. Kornhauser, Miller, and Spirakis [2] proved that the decision problem for general graphs is decidable in polynomial time improving on an early work of Wilson [6] that considered only biconnected graphs and the case $k = n - 1$. Recently, Papadimitriou, Raghavan, Sudan and Tamaki [3] have considered a related problem where there is a distinguished pebble (called robot) that has to be moved from its position to a destination and $k - 1$ pebbles (called obstacles) that may end-up in any vertex of the graph. In [3] a simple feasibility criteria was given for trees. In [1] a $O(n^4)$ algorithm is given to find an optimal solution to the 1 Pebble Problem of [3]. Several optimality problems (i.e., where we ask the shortest sequence of moves to reach one arrangement from another) relative to pebble motion problem are believed to be computationally intractable. Goldreich proved that computing the shortest sequence of moves that solves an instance of a generalization of Loyd's famous 15-puzzle (this corresponds to the case in which $k = n - 1$) is NP-complete. This was later improved to the case in which the graph is a grid by Ratner and Warmuth [4].

The next theorem presents the main result of this paper.

Theorem [Informal statement] *It is possibile to decide in time $O(n)$ if a given arrangement of pebbles on a tree with n vertices can be transformed into another arrangement.*

Our algorithm improves on the previous algorithm of [2].

We next give an informal description of the linear-time algorithm for deciding feasibility of the PMT problem. We divide the presentation of the algorithm into three main conceptual steps.

In Section 2 we show that the feasibility of the PMT problem is equivalent to the feasibility problem of the *Pebble Permutation problem on a Tree* (the PPT problem). In the PPT problem, each pebble has to be moved to the original position of another pebble. In other words, the pebbles have to be permuted among themselves and thus an instance J of the PPT problem is simply a permutation. We give a linear time algorithm that on input an instance I of the PMT problem outputs an instance J of the PPT problem which is feasible if and only if I is feasible. In Section 3, we reduce the feasibility problem for the PPT problem to the problem of feasibility of exchanges between pairs of pebbles. Indeed we have that a permutation Π (representing an instance of the PPT problem) is feasible if and only if the exchanges $(i, \Pi(i))$ are feasible for $i = 1, \cdots, k$. An exchange (i, j) consists in exchanging the positions of the i-th and j-th pebble and moving back to their original position all other pebbles which have been moved for realizing the exchange. A linear-time algorithm for this task is then given in Section 4. In Section 5 we discuss some extensions of our main result.

Basic definitions and notation. The *Pebble Motion problem on a Tree* (in short the PMT problem) consists in deciding whether there exists a sequence of moves on a given tree T that takes each of k pebbles numbered $1, 2, \cdots, k$ from its source vertex to its destination vertex. No two pebbles start from the same source vertex. A *move* consists in taking a pebble from its current position to one of the adjacent vertices that is not occupied by another pebble. Thus, at any given time, each vertex of T hosts at most one pebble. A vertex hosting a pebble is said to be *occupied* while a vertex not hosting any pebble is said to be a *hole*.

We define a *configuration* on T as a sequence $\mathcal{U} = \langle u_1, u_2, \ldots u_k \rangle$ of vertices where u_i is the vertex hosting the i-th pebble. An *instance* of the PMT is described by a tree T and two configurations: the starting (or source) configuration $\mathcal{S} = \langle s_1, \cdots, s_k \rangle$ and the final (or destination) configuration $\mathcal{D} = \langle d_1, \cdots, d_k \rangle$. A *plan* P is a sequence of moves. A plan P of l moves applied to a configuration $\mathcal{U}$ results in a series of configurations $\mathcal{U}^0, \cdots, \mathcal{U}^l$, where $\mathcal{U}^0 = \mathcal{U}$ and configurations $\mathcal{U}^i$ and $\mathcal{U}^{i+1}$ differ exactly for the position of the pebble that has been moved by the i-th move of P. We say that a plan P solves, or realizes, an instance $I = (T, \mathcal{S}, \mathcal{D})$ if applying P to $\mathcal{S}$ we obtain a sequence of configurations leading to $\mathcal{D}$. An instance is *feasible* if there exists a plan that realizes it. The *feasibility problem* of PMT consists in deciding if for a given instance I there exists a plan solving I.

From now on we let T denote a given tree with n vertices and k be the number of pebbles. Without loss of generality, we assume that T is a rooted tree. For each vertex u we denote by T_u the subtree of T rooted in vertex u and by $F(u)$ the forest obtained from T by deleting vertex u. Moreover, for any forest F and any vertex v belonging to F we denote by $T(F, v)$ the subtree of F containing v. We let $path(u, v)$ be the unique path in T between vertices u and v.

In the rest of the paper, we use uppercase letters for configurations of pebbles and, given a configuration $\mathcal{U}$, we denote the i–th element of $\mathcal{U}$ by u_i, that is the position of pebble i in $\mathcal{U}$. Due to lack of space we omit some of the proofs.

2   The Pebble Permutation Problem

In this section we present a linear time reduction algorithm *Reduce* from the PMT problem to the simpler *Pebble Permutation Problem on a Tree*.

The *Pebble Permutation Problem on a Tree* (PPT problem, in short) is a special case of the PMT problem where the set of source vertices and the set of destination vertices coincide. Thus the problem consists in permuting the pebbles and an instance of the PPT problem is described by a tree T, a starting configuration $\mathcal{S} = \langle s_1, \cdots, s_k \rangle$ and a permutation Π on k objects. The destination of the i-th pebble that starts at s_i is the vertex $d_i = s_{\Pi(i)}$. In the following when T and $\mathcal{S}$ are clear from the context, we will speak of a plan of moves which realizes or solves the permutation Π, meaning that it solves the instance $(T, \mathcal{S}, \Pi)$.

Given an instance $I = (T, \mathcal{S}, \mathcal{D})$ of the PMT problem, the algorithm *Reduce* returns an instance $J = (T, \mathcal{S}, \Pi)$ of the Pebble Permutation Problem on a Tree such that J is feasible if and only if I is feasible. The computation of algorithm *Reduce* can be divided into two main phases:

Phase I. Construct a feasible instance $I' = (T, \mathcal{S}, \langle d_{i_1}, \cdots, d_{i_k} \rangle)$ of the PMT problem.

Phase II. Let Π be the permutation defined as $\Pi(j) = l$ if and only if $d_{i_l} = d_j$. Return the instance $J = (T, \langle d_{i_1}, \cdots, d_{i_k} \rangle, \Pi)$ of the PPT problem.

We next prove that, provided that I' is feasible, instance J computed by *Reduce* is feasible if and only if I is feasible. In the next subsection we show how I' is constructed and prove that the algorithm takes time $O(n)$ and that the instance I' is feasible.

Lemma 1. *Let I, I', and J be as above. Then, I is feasible if and only if J is feasible.*

Proof. Let P be a plan for I'. If the instance J of the PPT problem is feasible then a plan for the instance I of the PMT problem is obtained by concatenating P and the plan for J. On the other side, if I is feasible, then a plan for J is given by inverting the moves of P and executing them in the reverse order and then executing the plan for I.

2.1 Phase I of Algorithm *Reduce*

The algorithm computes a matching $((s_1, d_{i_1}), \cdots, (s_k, d_{i_k}))$ of source and destination vertices of I that naturally defines the instance I'.

The matching is computed in a bottom-up way starting from the leaves of T. To this aim, the algorithm constructs two lists for each vertex v of the tree: a list of source vertices S_v and a list of destination vertices D_v. Roughly speaking, the list S_v contains two kinds of elements: source vertices that belong to T_v and to which no destination has been assigned yet; and pairs (u_1, u_2) constituting a match of one source and one destination vertex. Instead, D_v is the list of all the destination vertices of the subtree T_v to which no source has been assigned yet. During the proof of correctness of the algorithm, we will use terms as front and tail of the list and expression as "vertex v is ahead of vertex u" or "vertex v is behind vertex u" with the obvious meaning. The algorithm uses a global counter ℓ to assign a label to each pair of the matching; the counter is not actually needed to compute the matching between source and destination vertices, but it is used to show that the resulting instance I' is feasible.

The lists relative to a leaf v are computed as follows. If v is both a source and a destination vertex, then the algorithm produces the triple (v, v, ℓ), increments the counter ℓ, and sets S_v and D_v equal to the empty list. If v is neither a source nor a destination then, again, both S_v and D_v are set equal to the empty list and no triplet is produced. Finally, if v is a source (resp., a destination) the list S_v (resp., D_v) contains v, the list D_v (resp., S_v) is empty, and no triplet is produced. Notice that, for the leaf v, at most one of the two lists is nonempty and, as we shall see, this invariant is maintained throughout the execution of the algorithm.

Now, consider an internal vertex v, let $v_1, \cdots, v_m$ be its children, and let S_{v_i} and D_{v_i} be the lists relative to vertex v_i, for $i = 1, \cdots, m$. Call S the list obtained by concatenating the lists S_{v_i} and D the list obtained by concatenating the lists D_{v_i}. If v is a source vertex then v is inserted in front of the list S. If

v is a destination vertex then we have to distinguish two cases: if S contains at least one single vertex, then the closest such vertex to the tail of S, call it u, is replaced with the pair (u, v); if the list S contains no single elements, then v is appended to the list D.

Once S and D have been constructed, the algorithm executes the following main loop until S is empty or D is empty and the front element of S is a single vertex:

Consider the front of the list S.

1. If the front of S consists of a single vertex u_1, then the algorithm extracts u_1 and the vertex u_2 at the front of D, produces the triplet (u_1, u_2, ℓ), and increments ℓ.
2. If the front of S is a pair (u_1, u_2) then the algorithm produces the triplet (u_1, u_2, ℓ) and increments ℓ;

At the end of the loop S_v is set equal to S and D_v is set equal to D.

We state the following easy to prove properties of the algorithm.

Lemma 2. *The following properties hold:*

1. *For each vertex v at most one of the lists S_v and D_v is non empty.*
2. *For each vertex v and each source vertex u of S, it holds that all the source vertices along $path(u, v)$ that belong to S are ahead of u.*
3. *For each vertex v and each destination vertex u of D, it holds that all the destination vertices along $path(u, v)$ that belong to D are behind u.*

In other words, property 2 above says that when a source vertex u gets to the front of S, then no other source vertex lying on $path(u, v)$ is still in S. Property 3 instead states that when a destination vertex u gets to the front of D, then no other destination vertex descendant of u is still in D.

To show that I' is feasible, we consider the plan *Plan* obtained by taking the triplets computed from the reduction algorithm in the order specified by the counter field and executing for each triplet (u_1, u_2, ℓ) the moves for moving a pebble from the source vertex u_1 to the destination vertex u_2. We claim that *Plan* realizes I'. The proof of this claim is based on the following two lemmas.

Lemma 3. *Let v be a vertex of T and suppose that the pair (u_1, u_2) is at the front of S. Then each source vertex s of T_{u_2} that is in S is part of a pair (s, d) and u_2 does not belong to $path(s, d)$.*

The correctness of the plan follows the following property of the triplets computed by *Reduce*.

Lemma 4. *For each triplet (u_1, u_2, ℓ) computed by Reduce it holds that all source vertices on $path(u_1, u_2)$ belong to a triplet with a counter field less than ℓ and all destination vertices on $path(u_1, u_2)$ belong to a triplet with a counter field greater than ℓ.*

We conclude with the following theorem.

Theorem 5. *Algorithm Reduce, on input an instance I of the PMT problem, computes in time $O(n)$ an instance J of the PPT problem that is feasible if and ony if I is feasible.*

Proof. By Lemma 1, to prove that the reduction algorithm works correctly it is sufficient to show that *Plan* realizes the instance I' computed in phase I of the algorithm. By Lemma 4 when *Plan* moves a pebble from u_1 to u_2 the path P is empty. In fact, all source vertices on P have no pebbles as they have already been moved; and no pebble has already been moved to a destination vertex on P. Therefore *Plan* is a feasible plan.

An analysis of the running time of the algorithm is derived from the observations that each of the k source and destination vertices is inserted into and removed from the lists exactly once and, aside from insertion and extraction operations, the algorithm spends constant time for each vertex.

3 Reducing Permutations to Exchanges

The algorithm for testing feasibility of an instance of the PPT problem is based on the concept of a *good decomposition* of a permutation.

Given two configurations $\mathcal{U}$ and $\mathcal{V}$ we define $\mathit{diff}(\mathcal{U}, \mathcal{V})$ as the number of pebbles that are at different vertices in $\mathcal{U}$ and $\mathcal{V}$. It is well known that any permutation Π can be decomposed as a product of exchanges of two elements. Let $(\pi_1, \pi_2, \cdots, \pi_l)$ be a decomposition of Π in exchanges and let $\mathcal{U}^j$ be the configuration obtained by applying the permutation $\Pi_j = \pi_1 \circ \pi_2 \circ \cdots \circ \pi_j$ to the initial configuration $\mathcal{S}$, for $j = 1, 2. \cdots, l$. We say that $(\pi_1, \pi_2, \cdots, \pi_l)$ is a *good decomposition* of Π if and only if for each j it holds that $\mathit{diff}(\mathcal{U}^j, \Pi(\mathcal{S})) < \mathit{diff}(\mathcal{U}^{j-1}, \Pi(\mathcal{S}))$. In other words, each exchange of a good decomposition of Π brings at least one pebble to its final destination. We say that the good decomposition $(\pi_1, \pi_2, \cdots, \pi_l)$ of Π is *feasible* if and only if for each j the permutation Π_j can be applied to $\mathcal{S}$.

We first prove that Π is feasible if and only if all the good decompositions of Π are feasible. Then, we show that the good decompositions of Π are feasible if and only if in the configuration $\mathcal{S}$ it is possible to exchange pebbles in vertices s_i and $s_{\Pi(i)}$, for $1 \leq i \leq k$, while leaving all the other pebbles in their original position. We would like to stress here that when we say that the other pebbles are left in their original positions this does mean that they are not moved at all, but rather that at the end of the sequence of moves they are back in their original positions.

Let us start by giving some definitions. We say that two configurations $\mathcal{U}$ and $\mathcal{V}$ are *reachable* from each other if there exists a permutation Π such that $\mathcal{V} = \Pi(\mathcal{U})$ and the instance $T, \mathcal{U}, \Pi$ is feasible. In particular, when Π consists only in the exchange of pebbles i and j we say that vertices u_i and u_j are *equivalent* with respect to $\mathcal{U}$, meaning that there is a plan that starting from the configuration $\mathcal{U}$ exchanges pebbles i and j leaving all the other pebbles in their originl positions. In the sequel, we simply say that two vertices are equivalent everytime the relative configuration is clear from the context. Given a move m which takes a pebble from vertex v_1 to vertex v_2, define $rev(m)$ as the move which takes a pebble from v_2 to v_1. Given a sequence of moves $H = (m_1, m_2, \ldots, m_h)$, define $rev(H)$ as the sequence $(rev(m_h), \ldots, rev(m_2), rev(m_1))$.

We start by proving that for each feasible instance $I = (T, \mathcal{S}, \Pi)$ of the PPT problem there exist two vertices s_i and $s_{\Pi(i)}$ in $\mathcal{S}$ that are equivalent. To this aim we consider a simpler version of the PPT problem, that we call the 1 Pebble problem, that consists in a configuration of k pebbles on a tree and requires to move one specified pebble from its initial position s to a given vertex t. No restriction is imposed to the positions where all the other pebbles are moved. An instance of the 1 Pebble problem is described by the quadruple $(T, \mathcal{U}, s, t)$.

Let P be a sequence of moves that solves the instance $(T, \mathcal{U}, s, t)$ of the 1 Pebble problem. We denote by R the set of vertices where the distinguished pebble is moved by the moves of P and denote by $\overline{R}$ the set of the remaining vertices of the tree. We say that P is a *simple plan* if and only if the following conditions hold:

- P does not contain any move from vertices of $\overline{R}$ to vertices of R;
- all moves from vertices of R to vertices of $\overline{R} \cap T(F(s), t)$ are executed before the distinguished pebble starts moving;
- the set $R \cap T(F(s), t)$ consists of vertices that either lie on the path $path(s, t)$ or are adjacent to this path.

Next Lemma states that for each instance of the 1-Pebble problem it can be given a simple plan that solves it.

Lemma 6. *For each instance $H = (T, \mathcal{U}, s, t)$ of the 1 Pebble problem there is a simple plan that solves H.*

Lemma 7. *Let $\mathcal{U} = \langle u_1, u_2, \ldots, u_k \rangle$ be a configuration of k pebbles in T and suppose that the paths $path(u_i, u_j)$ and $path(u_j, u_h)$ are not edge-disjoint. If there exists a sequence of moves P that moves pebble i to u_j and pebble j to u_h then vertices u_i and u_j are equivalent with respect to $\mathcal{U}$.*

Proof. Consider the first occurence in P of a configuration $\mathcal{V} = \langle v_1, \ldots, v_k \rangle$ such that the path from the position v_i of the i-th pebble to its destination u_j and the path from the position v_j of the j-th pebble to its destination u_h are edge disjoint. Denote by Q the sequence of moves which reaches configuration $\mathcal{V}$ from $\mathcal{U}$.

Consider now the following plan P' to exchange the i-th and the j-th pebble: first execute Q to reach configuration $\mathcal{V}$, then execute a sequence of moves to reach a configuration reachable from $\mathcal{V}$ where the pebbles i and j are exchanged (and all the other pebbles are in the same position as in $\mathcal{V}$), and finally execute $rev(Q)$. It can be easily seen that in the configuration obtained by applying this plan pebbles i and j are exchanged while all the other pebbles are in their original positions. It remains to prove that in $\mathcal{V}$ it is possible to exchange pebbles i and j. In the configuration of P just preceding $\mathcal{V}$, at least one pebble, say the j-th, is between v_i and u_j. Call y the vertex common to $path(v_i, v_j)$ and $path(u_j, v_j)$ and distinct from v_j, and let z and x be the vertices adjacent to y on $path(v_i, v_j)$

and on $path(u_j, v_j)$, respectively (see Figure 1). We show now that it is possible to reach a configuration in which pebble i is at vertex x, pebble j is at vertex v_j and y and z are unoccuppied and then observe that in this configuration vertices v_j and x are equivalent. Observe that, as the last move of Q takes pebble j from

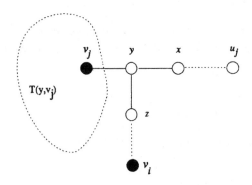

Fig. 1. The paths $path(v_i, v_j)$ and $path(u_j, v_j)$.

y to v_j, in configuration V vertex y does not contain any pebble. Moreover, if in V there is a pebble at x, then it has been moved to x after the pebble j has reached y; from this it follows that in $T(F(y), x)$ there is at least one empty vertex and hence x can be emptied by moving the pebble back into $T(F(y), u_j)$. Call W the configuration reached.

We observe that the problem of moving pebble i from vertex v_i to x can be seen as an instance of the 1 Pebble problem. Thus, by Lemma 6, there exists a simple plan R that, starting from W, moves pebble i from v_i to x. This is not enough for our purpose as R might move pebble j away from v_j and move some pebble to z (y is free when the i-th pebble reaches x). In fact, pebble j might be moved in order to let other pebbles enter the subtree $T(F(y), v_j)$; observe though that, by the properties of the simple plans, the pebbles distinct from the i-th that are moved to $T(F(y), v_j)$ come from vertices visited by pebble i during his trip from v_i to x and are moved before pebble i leaves v_i for the first time. On the other hand, v_j is the only vertex of $T(F(y), v_j)$ that pebble i could visit and we can find a simple plan R that does not move pebble i to v_j. In fact, pebble i is obliged to move in v_j only if, arriving to y vertex x is occupied by another pebble h, moved in x during the plan, that has to be moved to a vertex previously visited by pebble i. Let u be the vertex where pebble j is moved. It can be easily seen that the plan that moves pebble h to u and leaves pebble j in v_j is still a feasible plan that moves pebble i from v_i to x. We can thus modify R so that pebble j is first moved to x, then all pebbles that need to be moved are moved to $T(F(y), v_j)$, and, finally, pebble j is moved back to v_j. At the moment in which pebble i reaches x, z might be occupied. If this is so, then z must be occupied by a pebble h that was in x and was moved to z while i was standing in a vertex w adjacent to y other than x, v_j and z. In this case we modify R by moving pebble h to w while pebble i is in z and then moving pebble i from z to y and then from y to x.

The next lemma proves that for each feasible permutation Π, there exists an i such that the pebbles i and $\Pi(i)$ can be exchanged, leaving all other pebbles at their original position.

Lemma 8. *Let $I = (T, \mathcal{S}, \Pi)$ be a feasible instance of PPT. Then there exists i, $1 \le i \le k$, such that $i \ne \Pi(i)$ and the instance $I' = (T, \mathcal{S}, (i, \Pi(i)))$ is feasible too.*

Lemma 9. *The instance $I = (T, \mathcal{S}, \Pi)$ of PPT is feasible if and only if every good decomposition of Π is feasible.*

Finally, we can state the main result of this section.

Theorem 10. *The instance $I = (T, \mathcal{S}, \Pi)$ is feasible if and only if, for $1 \le i \le k$, the exchange $(i, \Pi(i))$ is feasible.*

4 The Algorithm for the PPT Problem

In this section we give a linear time algorithm *Verify* for testing the feasibility of an instance $J = (T, \mathcal{S}, \Pi)$ of the PPT problem. By Theorem 10, the algorithm *Verify* has to test only whether the vertices s_i and $s_{\Pi(i)}$ are exchangeable, for $i = 1, \cdots, k$. To this aim the algorithm partitions the vertices of $\mathcal{S}$ into equivalence classes such that two vertices s_l and s_k are equivalent if and only if the pebbles in s_l and s_k are exchangeable. We give a linear time algorithm that computes the equivalence classes of $\mathcal{S}$. For sake of clarity we assume that the tree T is binary, anyway all the arguments can be easily generalized.

Let $\mathcal{U} = \langle u_1, u_2, \ldots, u_k \rangle$ be a configuration of k pebbles on T. For a vertex u of $\mathcal{U}$ containing a pebble, let $seen(u)$ denote the set of vertices v containing a pebble and such that $path(u, v)$ is empty. We assume that for each vertex v the number of holes contained in each subtree of $T(v)$, the closest degree-3 vertex in each subtree, and, if v has a pebble, the set $seen(v)$ are known. All this information can be easily computed in time $O(n)$.

The algorithm that computes the equivalence classes works in a top-down way by labelling the vertices occupied by a pebble in such a way that two vertices are equivalent if and only if they have the same label. Let *class* be a global variable used to assign the labels to the vertices initialized to 1. The algorithm works as follows. It assigns the label *class* to the first vertex containing a pebble visited during the traversal and increments *class*. Then, for each labelled vertex u_i, it labels in constant time each vertex of $seen(u_i)$ which has not been labelled yet.

For sake of simplicity we assume that u_i has three adjacent vertices, x, y and z, and call T_x, T_y and T_z the subtrees of $F(u_i)$ that contain x, y and z, respectively (we remind the reader that $F(u_i)$ is the forest obtained by removing vertex u_i). The algorithm distinguishes three cases, depending on how many subtrees of $F(u_i)$ contain holes. If each subtree of $F(u_i)$ has at least one hole then all the vertices in $seen(u_i)$ are given u_i's label. Suppose, now, that only one subtree of $F(u_i)$, say T_z, is full (that is has no holes). Then z, that is the only vertex of $seen(u_i)$ belonging to T_z, is given the same label of u_i. Moreover, all the vertices in $seen(u_i)$ that belong to T_x are equivalent. If they are unlabelled, then take a vertex u_j from this set and tests if it is equivalent to u_i: if they are equivalent then all the vertices have the same label as u_i, otherwise the algorithm assigns to each of them the label $class$ and then increments $class$. The same steps are repeated for the set of vertices in $seen(u_i)$ that belong to T_y. Finally, suppose that only one subtree of $F(u_i)$, say T_x, has holes and assume that it has at least two holes (otherwise no pebble can be exchanged). As we shall see later, y and z are equivalent and have the same label. If they are both unlabelled, the algorithm tests if y and u_i are equivalent and assign to them either the same label of u_i or the label $class$ and then increments $class$. It remains to label the vertices of $seen(u_i)$ that belong to T_x. The algorithm tests if each of these vertices is equivalent to u_i and assigns the label of u_i to the vertices equivalent to u_i and $class$ to the others. Then, if at least a vertex has been assigned a label distinct from u_i, the variable $class$ is incremented. It is easy to see that this algorithm takes time $O(n)$ to label all the vertices containing a pebble. It remains to prove that it correctly computes the equivalence classes. Next we give necessary and sufficient conditions to exchange two vertices. The conditions are very natural and the proof of the theorem is omitted. In the sequel we denote by $C(F(u), v)$ the forest omprising all the trees of $F(u)$ distinct from $T(F(u), v)$.

Theorem 11. Let $\mathcal{U} = \langle u_1, u_2, \ldots, u_k \rangle$ be a configuration of the PPT problem and let u_i and u_j be vertices containing pebbles, and suppose that no pebble is contained in a vertex of $path(u_i, u_j)$. The vertices u_i and u_j are equivalent if and only if at least one of the two vertices (say u_i) that satisfies one of the following conditions:

- there exists a degree three vertex v on $path(u_i, u_j)$, distinct from u_i and u_j, such that the subtree not containing u_i and u_j has at least one hole;
- there exists a degree three vertex v in $C(F(u_i), u_j)$ such that the distance from u_i to v is d and $C(F(u_i), u_j)$ contains at least $d + 2$ holes;
- u_i is a degree three vertex and each subtree of $C(F(u_i), u_j)$ has at least one hole;
- u_i is a degree three vertex and the subtree $T(F(u_i), u_j)$ has at least one hole and one of the subtrees of $C(F(u_i), u_j)$ has at least two holes.

Lemma 12. Let $\mathcal{U} = \langle u_1, u_2, \ldots, u_k \rangle$ be a configuration of PPT and let u_i and u_l be vertices of $\mathcal{U}$ such that $path(u_i, u_l)$ contains only a vertex u_j with a pebble. Let T' be the tree of $F(u_j)$ not containing both u_i and u_l. If the vertices u_i and u_l are equivalent then either u_i is equivalent to u_j or T' has at least two holes.

Lemma 13. Let $\mathcal{U} = \langle u_1, u_2, \ldots, u_k \rangle$ be a configuration of PPT and let u_i and u_l be vertices of $\mathcal{U}$ such that $path(u_i, u_l)$ contains $r \geq 2$ vertices $u_{j_1}, \cdots, u_{j_r}$ other than u_i and u_l with pebbles. If the vertices u_i and u_l are equivalent then u_i is equivalent to u_{j_1} or to u_{j_2}.

By the above lemmas, the following corollary holds.

Corollary 14. *Let* $\mathcal{U} = \langle u_1, u_2, \ldots, u_k \rangle$ *be a configuration of PPT and let* u_i, u_j *and* u_l *be three vertices of* $\mathcal{U}$ *such that* $path(u_i, u_j)$ *is empty,* u_l *belongs to* $C(F(u_j), u_i)$ *and the subtree* $T(F(u_j), u_i)$ *has at least one hole. Then,* u_i *and* u_l *are equivalent if and only if they are both equivalent to* u_j.

Lemma 15. *Let* $\mathcal{U} = \langle u_1, u_2, \ldots, u_k \rangle$ *be a configuration of PPT. The algorithm Verify assigns the same label to two vertices of* $\mathcal{U}$ *if and only if they are equivalent.*

Proof's sketch: By Lemma 13 it is sufficient to prove that for each vertex u_j in $\mathcal{U}$ two vertices of $seen(u_j)$ have the same label if and only if they are equivalent. In fact let u_i and u_l be a pair of vertices such that u_i belongs to $seen(u_j)$ and u_l belongs to $C(F(u_j), u_i)$ but not to $seen(u_j)$; if u_i and u_l are equivalent then u_i is equivalent to u_j or to the only vertex of $seen(u_j)$ in $path(u_j, u_l)$.

Without loss of generality we assume that u_j has three adjacent vertices and call them x, y and z. Moreover, we call T_x, T_y and T_z the subtrees of $F(u_j)$ that contain x, y and z, respectively. We distinguish three cases, depending on the number of holes in $F(u_j)$.

If each of the three subtrees contains at least a hole, then, by Theorem 11, all the vertices of $seen(u_j)$ are equivalent to u_j and are correctly labelled with the same label as u_j.

Suppose, now, that a subtree of $F(u_j)$, say T_z, has all vertices occupied by pebbles while now T_x and T_y contain each some holes. The vertex z (the unique in T_z belonging to $seen(u_i)$) has the same label of u_i as the third condition of Theorem 11 holds. All the verteces in T_x (T_y respectively) have the same label since for every such pair the first condition of Theorem 11 holds. To determine these two labels (possibly equal), by Lemma 12 it is sufficient to test whether conditions of Theorem 11 hold for u_j and a witness vertex of $seen(u_i)$ belonging to T_x and T_y. If they are equivalent all the vertices of $seen(v)$ are equivalent, otherwise we assign a distinct label to the vertices of T_x and T_y.

Finally suppose that only one subtree of $F(u_j)$, say T_x, has holes and assume that it has at least two holes (if there is only one hole in T no vertices can be exchanged). By Lemma 12 y and z, that are the only vertices of $seen(u_j)$ in T_y and T_z, are equivalent and they have the same label. The vertices of $seen(u_j)$ in T_x can be divided into two sets. The vertices equivalent to u_j have the same label as u_j. By Theorem 11 all the vertices not equivalent to u_j are in the same equivalence class and, by Corollary 14, they are not equivalent to any vertex in $T(F(u_j), x)$.

5 Concluding Remarks

Obstacles. Our feasibility algorithm works also if not all pebbles have a destination (in which case they can be moved to any vertex in the tree). As a straightforward application, we obtain an $O(n)$ algorithm for the feasibility problem of the Tree Motion Planning Problem with k Robots (TMPR, in short) of [3].

Here, we have k_1 robots each having its own destination (these correspond to pebbles with destination) and k_2 obstacles (these correspond to pebbles with no destination). In [3] a simple feasibility criteria is given only for the case $k_1 = 1$ and they leave as an open question to study the problem for more than 1 robot (i.e, the case $k_1 > 1$).

Finding a plan for solving the problem. It can be easily seen that our algorithm can be adapted to output, for each feasible instance, also a plan that solves the instance in which case the algorithm stops in time $O(n + l)$ where l is the length of plan (a better running time can be obtained if a compact representation of the plan is sufficient; we omit details). An analysis of the algorithm shows that the plan output consists of $O(k^2(n - k))$ moves. The worst case is when $k = \alpha n$ $(0 < \alpha < 1)$, in which case the solution has $O(n^3)$ moves. In [2], it is claimed that all feasible instances admit an $O(n^2)$-move plan. We were unable to verify the claim. When $k = n - 1$ we are able to improve this bound by computing in time proportional to the size of the tree an optimal plan that has length $O(n)$.

Open problems. Next we list some problems that seems to be worth investigating. First of all, we would like to ask whether our algorithm can be generalized to general graphs thus giving a linear time feasibility algorithm for the pebble motion problem on graphs.

No much is known about the problem of computing the shortest plan on graphs. From a negative side it has been proved that the problem is NP-complete for $k = n - 1$ even when restricted to the grid [4]. However, the cases $k < n - 1$ have not been studied. Obtaining shortest plan for small k (i.e., $k = 2, 3, 4...$) is trivial but the complexity of the algorithm seems to be exponential with k.

On the positive side, algorithms for computing the shortest plan on trees have been given only by in [3] and [?] that considered the case of one pebble with destination and $k - 1$ pebbles without destination.

References

1. V. Auletta, D. Parente, G. Persiano, *Optimal Planning of Robot Motion on a Tree with Obstacles*, T.R. 18, Dip. Informatica ed Applicazioni, Univ. di Salerno, 1995.
2. D. Kornhauser, G. Miller, and P. Spirakis, *Coordinating pebble motion on graphs, the diameter of permutations groups, and applications*, in Proc. of 25-th IEEE Symp. on Found. of Comp. Sc., 241–250, 1984.
3. C. Papadimitriou, P. Raghavan, M. Sudan and H. Tamaki, *Motion Planning on a graph*, in Proc. of 35-th IEEE Symp. on Found. of Comp. Sc., 511–520, 1994.
4. D. Ratner and M. Warmuth, *The (n^2-1)-Puzzle and Related Relocation Problems*, Journal of Symbolic Computation, 10:111–137, 1990.
5. J.T. Schwartz, M. Sharir, and J. Hopcroft, *Planning, Geometry, and Complexity of Robot Motion*, Ablex, Norwood NJ, 1987.
6. R. M. Wilson, *Graph puzzles, homotopy, and the alternating group*, Journal of Comb. Theory Series B, 16, 86-94, 1974.

Linear-Time Heuristics for Minimum Weight Rectangulation

(Extended abstract)

Christos Levcopoulos   Anna Östlin

Department of Computer Science
Lund University, Box 118, S-221 00 Lund, Sweden

Abstract. We consider the problem of partitioning rectilinear polygons into rectangles, using segments of minimum total length. This problem is NP-hard for polygons with holes. Even for hole-free polygons no known algorithm can find an optimal partitioning in less than $O(n^4)$ time.
We present the first linear-time algorithm for computing rectangulations of hole-free polygons, within a constant factor of the optimum. We achieve this result by deriving a linear-time algorithm for producing rectangulations of histograms of length less than 2.42 times the optimum, and then solving the problem of producing a proper partition into histograms.

1 Introduction

The problem of partitioning rectilinear polygons into rectangles has various applications, eg. in construction of VLSI-circuits [12]. If the polygon contains holes, the problem is NP-hard [12]. If the polygon is hole-free an optimal partition can be computed in $O(n^4)$ time using dynamic programming [12].

To describe previous and new results we need the following definitions:

Let P be an isothetic polygon, i.e., all edges of the polygon are parallel to the x- or y-axis. A rectangulation of P is a set of segments which partition P into rectangles. An optimal rectangulation of P is a set of segments, of minimum total length, that rectangulate P, and its length is denoted by $M(P)$. The number of vertices of P is n, and the length of the perimeter of P is denoted by $p(P)$.

Lingas [10] showed that for polygons with holes a rectangulation of length $\leq \min(p(P)/2+4 \cdot M(P), 41 \cdot M(P))$ can be computed in $O(n^4)$ time. In [11] it is shown that for polygons without holes, a rectangulation of length $\leq O(p(P) \cdot \log n)$ can be computed in $O(n \log n)$ time.

The special case when the boundary of the polygon is a rectangle and all holes are points has also been studied. Even in this case it is NP-hard to find an optimal solution [4, 12]. In [4] it was also shown that in $O(n^2)$ time a rectangular partition of length $4.73 \cdot M(P)$ can be found. This result was later improved by giving an $O(n \log n)$ algorithm which produces the same partitions [7]. By modifying that algorithm an $O(n \log n)$ algorithm was obtained, which was shown to produce a rectangulation of any isothetic polygon P of length $\leq 6 \cdot p(P) + 12 \cdot M(P)$ [7].

In [4] also an $O(n^4)$ time algorithm was given, for rectangles with point-holes, achiving an approximation factor 3.

It has been shown that for arbitrary polygons a rectangulation of length $< 8 \cdot M(P)$ can be computed in $O(n^2)$ time [6]. In [6] it is also shown that, if P is a histogram, a rectangulation of length $< 2.42 \cdot M(P)$ can be computed in $O(n^2)$ time. This result is improved in this paper, Sect. 2, by reducing the time to $O(n)$. Using this result, we show that a rectangulation of any hole-free polygon of length $< 2.42 \cdot M(P)+p(P)$ can be computed in linear time. The second result presented in this paper, in Sect. 3, which builds on our first result, is a linear-time algorithm for finding a rectangulation of length $O(M(P))$, even if $M(P)$ is much smaller than $p(P)$, thus improving the previous $O(n \log n)$ time bound [7].

2 Rectangulating a Histogram in Linear Time

2.1 Preliminaries and Data Structures

An isothetic polygon without holes is a histogram iff it has some distinguished edge, called the *base*, such that the length of the base is equal to the total length of all other edges of the polygon which are parallel to the base, see Fig. 1.

In this section, we will assume w.l.o.g., that the base of the histogram is horizontal and that it is the edge with smallest y-coordinate.

To index the horizontal edges of a histogram we number all of them, except for the base, from 1 to $n/2-1$, from left to right. We call these numbers *e-indices*, Fig. 1. The edges retain the same e-index in sub-histograms as in the original histogram.

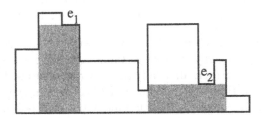

Fig. 1. A histogram where e_1 is too high, and e_2 is too low. The e-index for e_1 is 3, and the e-index for e_2 is 7 (i.e., $n/2 - 3$).

Definition 1. (From p. 27 in [8]) We say that a rectangle R is *thicker* than a rectangle R' iff the shortest side of R is longer than the shortest side of R'. A rectangle within P is called *maximal* (with respect to P) iff it is not properly included in any other rectangle lying within P. We say that it is a *thickest* rectangle within P iff there is no thicker rectangle lying within P.

Let S be a set of segments. We say that S is a *thickest-first* rectangular partition of P iff it consists of disjoint segments, lying within P and not overlapping with the boundary of P, and the rectangles into which P is partitioned by S can be drawn by the following procedure: If P is not a rectangle, then let R be any thickest maximal rectangle within P. Draw R, and continue recursively, in the same way, with the sub-polygons of P in the partition induced by R.

In [6] it is shown that a small modification of the idea of thickest-first partition results in an approximation algorithm, which for any histogram P, produces a rectangular partition of P of length $< 2.42 \cdot M(P)$. The algorithm works as follows: Start with transforming the histogram, by multiplying all y-coordinates with $\sqrt{2}$. Compute a thickest-first partition for the transformed histogram. Transform the segments produced by dividing with $\sqrt{2}$, to obtain a partition of the original histogram. This is called a $\sqrt{2}$-thickest-first partition.

Fact 2. *(Conclusion 2 in [6]) For any non-degenerated histogram P, it holds that every $\sqrt{2}$-thickest-first partition of P is of length $< (1 + \sqrt{2}) \cdot M(P)$.*

Definition 3. A *locally thickest* rectangle R in P is a maximal rectangle within P, which is not overlapped by any thicker rectangle R' lying within P.

Definition 4. Let e be a horizontal edge of a histogram P, and let R be the maximal rectangle within P whose perimeter includes e. If R overlaps with a thicker rectangle R' within P and R' is lower than R, then we say that e is *too high* in P. If R overlaps with a thicker rectangle R' within P and R' is higher than R, then we say that e is *too low* in P. See Fig. 1. If R does not overlap with any thicker rectangle in P, then we say that e is *exact* in P.

An important part of the algorithm used to find a thickest-first partition in linear time consists of computing k-reductions, defined below.

Definition 5. A *k-reduction* of a histogram P with n edges, is defined for all k, $4 < k < n/6$, as either a locally thickest rectangle of P or a histogram P' with m edges, $m < n - 4 \cdot k + 4$. Further, all locally thickest rectangles in P' are also locally thickest rectangles in P and the perimeter of P' consists of one connected part of the perimeter of P, all edges in P with e-index $[k_1..(n/2) - k_2]$, where $k_1, k_2 > k$, and at most four other edges which are not part of the perimeter of P, Fig. 2.

The data structure described below is used for getting certain information about the histogram in constant time. How this can be implemented is described after the definition.

Definition 6. An *array representation* of a histogram is a data structure where all horizontal edges, except for the base-edge and possibly the leftmost and the rightmost edge, are placed in an array, sorted from left to right. In addition, an array representation has two important properties:

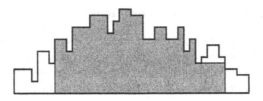

Fig. 2. Example of what a k-reduction may look like.

- Horizontal linking

  From every horizontal edge in the histogram there are links, into the open region of the histogram, to the first edges to the right and left encountered by an extension of the horizontal edge. For every horizontal edge e_i let l_i be the maximal line within the histogram including e_i. From e_i, there are links to the edges where the endpoints of l_i lie.

  For every line l_i, that includes more than one edge, and any two given edges on l_i, it is possible to find, in constant time, the longest connected part of l_i that is disjoint from the perimeter of the histogram.

- Finding the lowest edge

  The array representation includes also a data structure which makes it possible, for any two given edges with e-index e_1, respectively e_2, to decide, in constant time, which is the lowest edge with e-index $[e_1..e_2]$ in the array. If there are more than one such edge then one can also find, in constant time, the rightmost and leftmost of these edges.

An array representation can be built in linear time. For both data structures in the array representation (i.e. for horizontal linking and for finding the lowest segment), Cartesian trees can be used. The Cartesian tree was defined by Vuillemin, [13], as follows: for a sequence $x = \langle x_1, ..., x_n \rangle$, the Cartesian tree is a binary tree with root $x_i = \max(x_1, ..., x_n)$. The left subtree of x_i is the Cartesian tree for $\langle x_1, ..., x_{i-1} \rangle$ and x_i's right subtree is the Cartesian tree for $\langle x_{i+1}, ..., x_n \rangle$.

The Cartesian tree for a sequence of n elements can be computed in linear time [3]. The largest element between two given elements x_k and x_l is the root in the smallest subtree such that both x_k and x_l is included. We can find this root-element in $O(1)$ time [5].

In the data structure for finding the lowest edge, when more than one edge are lowest, we want to find the rightmost and the leftmost lowest edge. Therefore we build two Cartesian trees, where in the first one, for two edges with the same y-coordinate, the edge with smallest x-coordinate is treated as being lower, and in the second one, for edges with the same y-coordinate, the edge with largest x-coordinate is treated as being lower.

When the histogram is a k-reduction of the histogram which the array representation was originally built for, links to the outermost vertical edges may not end within the histogram.

2.2 Computing Thickest-First Partitions

Lemma 7. *Given the array representation for a histogram P and a horizontal edge e in P, it can be decided in $O(1)$ time if e is too low, too high or exact in P. If e is too low then a direction, left or right, can be computed in constant time, such that a locally thickest rectangle is located in that direction.*

Proof. By using the array representation it is easy to prove the lemma. The proof is omitted in this version, but can be found in [9]. □

To find a thickest-first partition we don't have to start with finding the thickest rectangle. It suffices to find a rectangle that is part of the thickest-first partition. Every locally thickest rectangle is part of the thickest-first partition, since no thicker rectangle overlaps. Following observation is therefore useful.

Lemma 8. *A locally thickest rectangle in P can be found in $O(\log n)$ time, where n is the number of edges in P.*

Proof. Divide the histogram into three parts, H_1, H_2 and H_3, with about equal number of edges in each part, where H_1 is the leftmost part, H_2 the middle part and H_3 the rightmost part. To simplify we write "1/3 of the edges", meaning "approximately 1/3". Find the lowest edge in each part and examine them. If any of the edges is exact in P, then we have found a locally thickest rectangle. If this is not the case, then at least one of the edges have to be too low in P, since there has to be some thickest rectangle in P. Depending on the lowest edge in H_2 there are two cases:

1. H_2's lowest edge is too low in P.
   We can, according to Lemma 7, decide whether a locally thickest rectangle is to the left or to the right of the lowest edge. We can replace all edges on the opposite side of the edge with a vertical edge and at least 1/3 of the edges are removed.
2. H_2's lowest edge is too high in P.
   We know that all edges in H_2 are too high in P. All the edges in H_2 can be replaced with a horizontal edge and at least 1/3 of the edges are removed.

The remainder of the histogram is a new histogram P', with fewer edges. We know that all locally thickest rectangles in P' also are locally thickest rectangles in P.

We continue recursively with P' and divide the histogram, in the same way as before, into three parts, H_1', H_2' and H_3'. P' consists of one or two connected parts of the perimeter of P. To avoid getting a histogram that, after many recursions, consists of several parts of the perimeter of P, we do not allow any split that results in a histogram that consists of three or more different parts of the perimeter of P. We can avoid this by only allowing edges from one connected part of the perimeter of P in each of H_1', H_2' and H_3'. If any part consists of edges from different parts of the perimeter of P, then we change the place for the split. We move the split to the right or to the left, depending on which case that results in the most balanced split, in such a way that no part consists of edges from different parts of the perimeter of P.

Now the problem arises that we can't guarantee that at least 1/3 of the edges are removed in each recursive step. The following cases may occur:

1. The middle part, H_2, consists of edges from different parts of the perimeter of P.
   (a) The edges in H_2 are replaced. We know that at least 1/6 (roughly) of the edges are removed, since the new split is done in such a way that it is as balanced as possible.
   (b) The edges in H_1 or H_3 are replaced. We know that at least 1/3 of the edges are removed.
2. One of the outermost parts, H_1 or H_3, consists of edges from different parts of the perimeter of P. Assume w.l.o.g. that it is H_1.
   (a) The edges in H_2 or H_3 are replaced. We know that at least 1/3 of the edges are removed.
   (b) The edges in H_1 are replaced. We know that in the next recursion step we are guaranteed that 1/3 of the edges are removed.

So, we know that at least 1/6 of the edges are removed in each recursion step. Continue until a locally thickest rectangle is found.

Each step takes constant time and the number of edges is reduced by a factor 1/6 in each step, which gives us a total time of $O(\log n)$. $\qquad\square$

Following lemma is only needed for showing Lemma 10.

Lemma 9. *Given the array representation of a histogram P and two horizontal edges in P, with e-index e_1, respectively e_2, where e_1 is too low in P, and e_2 is too high in P, $e_1 < e_2$, and the number of horizontal edges, from e_1 to e_2, inclusive, is k, one can find, in $O(\log k)$ time, either a locally thickest rectangle in P or an edge with e-index e_3, between e_1 and e_2, such that e_3 is too low in P and all edges between e_3 and e_2 are too high in P. Analogously this also holds when $e_1 < e_2$.*

Proof. Divide the edges $[e_1..e_2]$ in three parts, H_1, H_2 and H_3, with (about) equal number of edges in each part, where H_1 is the leftmost part, H_2 the middle part and H_3 the rightmost part. Find the lowest edge in each part. If any of these three edges is exact in P, then we have found a locally thickest rectangle. If this is not the case, then at least one of the three edges has to be too low in P.

Two cases may occur:

1. At least one of the too low edges has a locally thickest rectangle to the left. We can replace all edges to the right of this edge with a vertical edge, and we have a histogram with less than k edges, where we know that a locally thickest rectangle exists. According to Lemma 8 we can find a locally thickest rectangle in $O(\log n)$ time.

2. None of the too low edges has a locally thickest rectangle to the left (they all have locally thickest rectangles to the right).

Following three cases may occur:

(a) The lowest edge in H_3 is too low in P (independently of whether the lowest edges in H_1 and H_2 are too low or too high). Denote by e' the lowest edge in H_3.

(b) The lowest edge in H_2 is too low in P and the one in H_3 is too high (independently of whether the lowest edge in H_1 is too low or too high). Denote by e' the lowest edge in H_2.

(c) Only the lowest edge in H_1 is too low in P. Denote by e' the lowest edge in H_1.

In all three cases it holds that since there is a locally thickest rectangle to the right of e', we know that the edge e_3 can't be to the left of e'. We also know that all edges to the right of the third (H_1, H_2 or H_3) where e' lies (but to the left of e_2) are too high in P. Thus e_3 or an exact edge in P can be found to the right of e' and within the third where e' lies, and we can limit the search to this part, which consists of $k/3$ horizontal edges.

Continue recursively with the smaller number of edges, until e_3 or a locally thickest rectangle is found. Since two thirds of the remaining edges are excluded in each recursive step, the total time is $O(\log k)$. □

By k-reducing a histogram for growing k, we can find a rectangle that is part of a thickest-first rectangulation, or we can find a bounded part of the histogram where a locally thickest rectangle has to be. We therefore need the following lemma.

Lemma 10. *Given the array representation for a histogram P with n edges, and a constant k, $n>k>4$, one can, in $O(\log k)$ time, find a histogram P', such that P' is a k-reduction of P.*

Proof. If $k \geq n/6$ then it is possible, according to Lemma 8, to find a locally thickest rectangle in $O(\log n)=O(\log k)$ time.

If $k<n/6$ then do the following:

Divide the edges with e-index $[1..3 \cdot k]$ into three parts, H_1, H_2 and H_3, with k edges in each part, where H_1 is the leftmost part, H_2 the middle part and H_3 the rightmost part. Find for each part the lowest edge. If any of these edges is exact, then we have found a locally thickest rectangle. If this is not the case, then following three cases may occur:

1. All three lowest edges are too high in P.

Since all edges are too high, no edge above the lowest edge can be part of a locally thickest rectangle. We can replace all edges in H_1, H_2 and H_3 with one horizontal edge, which includes the lowest edge of the edges with e-index $[1..3 \cdot k]$. We have reduced P to a new histogram with $3 \cdot k$ fewer horizontal edges.

2. At least one of the lowest edges in H_2 and H_3 is too low in P (independently of whether the lowest edge in H_1 is too low).

   We can, according to Lemma 7, decide whether a locally thickest rectangle is to the right or to the left of the lowest edge in H_2 or H_3. Thus all edges on the opposite side can be replaced with a vertical edge. We have either reduced P to a new histogram with at least k fewer horizontal edges or we have a histogram with at most $3 \cdot k$ edges, where a locally thickest rectangle can be found in $O(\log 3 \cdot k) = O(\log k)$ time, according to Lemma 8.

3. Only the lowest edge in H_1 is too low in P.

   If there is a locally thickest rectangle to the left of the lowest edge in H_1 then we can replace all edges to the right with a vertical edge and we have a histogram with less than k edges, where we can find a locally thickest rectangle in $O(\log k)$ time, according to Lemma 8.

   If there is a locally thickest rectangle only to the right of the lowest edge in H_1, then we can replace all edges to the left of the lowest edge with a vertical edge and all edges in H_2 and H_3 can be replaced with a horizontal edge, since all these edges are too high. We get a histogram that doesn't fulfill the definition for a k-reduction, since we can get two separated parts of the perimeter of P. If we instead can find a precise edge which is in between the too high and the too low edges, then we can add edges in such a way that the new histogram fulfills the definition of a k-reduction. According to Lemma 9 we can find such an edge, or a locally thickest rectangle, in $O(\log k)$ time.

If a locally thickest rectangle has not been found then the corresponding procedure is performed, symmetrically, for the other side of the histogram, i.e. for the edges with e-index $[n/2 - 3 \cdot k .. n/2 - 1]$. $\qquad \square$

Theorem 11. *Given a histogram P, with n edges, a thickest-first partition can be computed in $O(n)$ time.*

Proof. Build an array-representation for P, which can be done in $O(n)$ time.

Make a k-reduction of P, denoted P_1, for $k = c$, where $c > 4$ is a constant. This takes $O(\log c)$ time, according to Lemma 10.

If P_1 isn't a locally thickest rectangle, then do a k-reduction of P_1, denoted P_2, for $k = 2 \cdot c$. Continue, in the same way, to create the k-reductions P_3, P_4, ... for $k = c \cdot 2^2, c \cdot 2^3, ...$ until a k-reduction P_i is found, where P_i is a locally thickest rectangle R, or until k becomes greater than the number of edges in the histogram. In the latter case a locally thickest rectangle can be found in $O(\log k)$ time, according to Lemma 8.

We denote the number of horizontal edges, except the base-edge, by n', where $n' = (n/2) - 1$.

In the worst case a minimum number of edges is removed in each k-reduction, that is k horizontal edges on each side. In the worst case, P_j consists of the edges with e-index $[(2^j - 1) \cdot c .. n' - (2^j - 1) \cdot c]$ in P.

Assume, w.l.o.g., that the rectangle R's perimeter includes a horizontal edge with e-index m' in P, where $m' < n' - m'$, i.e., there are more edges to the right of the edge than to the left. We know that for the edge with e-index m' in P it

holds that: $m'>(2^{i-1}-1)\cdot c>2^{i-2}\cdot c$ where i is the number of k-reductions done to find R. We can express the number of k-reductions, i, in m': $m'>(2^{i-2})\cdot c$, thus $i<\log m'$ when $c>4$. The total time, T_1, to find a rectangle is:
$$T_1 = O(\log c) + O(\log(2\cdot c)) + O(\log(2^2\cdot c)) + \ldots + O(\log(2^{i-1}\cdot c))$$
$$< O(\log^2 m') < O(\log^2 m)$$
where $m=2\cdot m'$ is the total number of edges to the left of the edge with e-index m', not only the horizontal.

We continue recursively in the same way with the resulting sub-histograms of P after R is cut off, until P is rectangulated. We get the following recurrence equation, which describes the total time complexity:
$$T(1) = 1$$
$$T(n) = T(m)+T(n-m)+O(\log^2(\min(m, n-m)))$$
$T(n)$ is maximized if m is greater than $n/3$ and less than $2\cdot n/3$. Thus, we obtain $T(n)\leq \sum_{i=1}^{\log n} 3\cdot 2^{i-1}\cdot O(\log^2 \frac{n}{2^{i-1}}) = O(n)$ $\qquad\square$

Theorem 12. *For any histogram P, with n edges, a rectangular partition of length $\leq 2.42\cdot M(P)$ can be computed in $O(n)$ time.*

Proof. Follows directly from Theorem 11 and Fact 2. $\qquad\square$

To be able to use this method for polygons we have to start by partitioning the polygon into histograms. That can be done in linear time. Following holds:

Fact 13. *(Theorem 3 in [8]) Any hole-free polygon P can be partitioned into histograms by producing line segments of total length $< p(P)$ in time $O(n)$, in such a way that all concave interior corners of the resulting histograms are also concave interior corners of P, and the total number of corners in the resulting figure is $O(n)$.*

Theorem 14. *For any hole-free polygon P, with n edges, a rectangular partition of length $\leq p(P)+2.42\cdot M(P)$ can be computed in $O(n)$ time.*

Proof. Partition the polygon into histograms, in $O(n)$ time, according to Fact 13, using segments of total length $p(P)$. Since there are no new concave interior corners created the length of the optimal rectangular partition of the figure isn't longer than $M(P)$. According to Theorem 12 a rectangular partition of the histograms of length $< 2.42 \cdot M(P)$ can be computed in $O(n)$ time. The total length of the partition is $< 2.42 \cdot M(P)+p(P)$. $\qquad\square$

3 When the Optimal Partition is Very Short

The result in the previous section can be used to approximate $M(P)$ when $M(P)$ isn't much smaller than $p(P)$. We are now going to describe how to deal with the case when $M(P)$ is much smaller than $p(P)$.

The intuition is that if $M(P)$ is sufficiently smaller than $p(P)$, then this implies that one or more rectangles in the partition induced by a minimum length rectangulation of P have the property that their boundary overlaps almost entirely with the perimeter of P. If the aspect ratio of such a rectangle is small, then it is "well-bounded" by the polygon (see definition below) from all directions. To deal with the case when the aspect ratio is big, the notion of a "pipe" was introduced, [7] (see definition below).

Definition 15. (From [7].)

Let P be a polygon, R an (isothetic) rectangle within P, and s the length of the shortest side of R. We say that R is a *well-bounded* rectangle of P iff there is no consecutive part of the perimeter of R of length $\geq s/2$ such that it doesn't touch the boundary of the polygon P. The rectangle R is a *pipe* iff it has the following properties:

1. there is no segment of length $\geq s/2$ which lies on a longer side of R and which doesn't touch the perimeter of P.
2. all four corners of R lie on the perimeter of P, and
3. it is not included in any other rectangle having the above properties.

Next we define critical rectangles of P as follows. Let R be a well-bounded rectangle of P. We say that R is a *critical rectangle* of P if and only if every well-bounded rectangle which overlaps with R, (if there is any) has some side which is shorter than the shortest side of R. Let P_2 be the remaining pieces of P after cutting off P all its critical well-bounded rectangles. The additional critical rectangles of P are exactly all pipes of P_2.

Following holds [7]: By first cutting off all well-bounded rectangles and then all pipes in a polygon P at most segments of length $O(M(P))$ are used. For the remaining of P, denoted by P', it holds that $M(P')=O(M(P))$, $p(P')=O(M(P))$.

We are now going to show that all well-bounded rectangles and all pipes, i.e. all critical rectangles, can be cut off in linear time. To find the critical rectangles in linear time we need a Voronoi diagram and a visibility graph.

The Voronoi diagram we need is the Voronoi diagram for a polygon according to the L_∞-metric. According to [2] the Voronoi diagram can be computed in $O(n)$ time, according to the L_2-metric, for a simple polygon, with n edges. This algorithm can also be used for other L_p-metrics according to [2].

Every vertex and isothetic edge in the Voronoi diagram corresponds to an isothetic rectangle in P. For every Voronoi vertex the corresponding (isothetic) rectangle is the maximal square, whose center lies on the vertex, and for every maximal isothetic segment consisting of Voronoi edges the interior of the corresponding rectangle equals the union of all maximal squares, whose centers lie on the edge. Let S be the set of all those rectangles. For every rectangle R in S and each side of R one link is created, from the corresponding Voronoi vertex or isothetic edge, to an edge of P overlapping with that side, if such an edge exists.

To be able to walk along the edges in the polygon, we create a visibility graph. The visibility is only orthogonal, that is, we can only see in vertical and horizontal directions. From every concave vertex in the polygon there are two

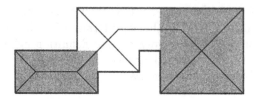

Fig. 3. A polygon and its Voronoi diagram. The shadowed rectangles correspond to a Voronoi vertex and an isothetic Voronoi edge respectively.

links, one in each direction, into the open region of the polygon, to the closest edge that is seen. This visibility graph can be computed in linear time [1].

To find the well-bounded critical rectangles in a polygon, we start with computing a set of $O(n)$ rectangles, of which all well-bounded critical rectangles are a subset.

Lemma 16. *Given the Voronoi diagram and the visibility graph for a polygon P, a set of $O(n)$ rectangles in P can be computed in $O(n)$ time, where the set of rectangles includes all well-bounded rectangles in P and for every point on the perimeter of P at most two rectangles in the set overlaps.*

Proof. Recall the set S of rectangles induced by the Voronoi diagram. By choosing all rectangles in S whose all four sides overlap with the perimeter of P, we obtain a set of rectangles including all well-bounded critical rectangles. This takes $O(n)$ time, since there are at most $O(n)$ isothetic edges and vertices in the Voronoi diagram.

For every point on the perimeter of P it holds that at most two rectangles in the set overlap since:

1. If two rectangles share one piece each of a side, and that piece, entirely or partly, overlaps with the perimeter of P, then one of the rectangles must have one side on which no part overlaps with the perimeter of P.
2. If two rectangles share one side entirely, and that side, entirely or partly, overlaps with the perimeter of P, then they can't be two different maximal rectangles and they don't correspond to two different isothetic edges or vertices in the Voronoi diagram.
3. If one side of a rectangle entirely overlaps with a part of another rectangle's side, and this part, entirely or partly, overlaps with the perimeter of P, then both these rectangles can overlap with the perimeter of P on all four sides. If both rectangles correspond to an isothetic edge in the Voronoi diagram then their common part has to be a square. If it wasn't a square then one of the rectangles must have a connected part of the perimeter, longer than its shortest side, which doesn't overlap with the perimeter of P, and then it can't correspond to an isothetic edge in the Voronoi diagram.

A third rectangle can't overlap with the perimeter of P in the same place, since it would overlap according to Case 1 or 2.

$\square$

Lemma 17. *Any well-bounded rectangle is overlapped by at most four other well-bounded rectangles, one in each corner.*

The proof of Lemma 17 can be found in the full version of this paper [9].

Lemma 18. *For any polygon P, all well-bounded critical rectangles in P can be found in $O(n)$ time.*

Proof. Compute the Voronoi diagram and the visibility graph for P, which can be done in $O(n)$ time. Compute a set of rectangles, according to Lemma 16. Since the rectangles in the set share sides with at most one other rectangle in every point that lies on the perimeter of P, we can walk around the perimeter of every rectangle in the set and see which rectangles that are well-bounded. This can be done by going through $O(n)$ links.

To decide which of the well-bounded rectangles are critical we do the following: Add edges on all well-bounded rectangles' horizontal sides, where these don't overlap with the perimeter of P. Compute a new visibility graph for visibility in vertical direction only. This can be done in $O(n)$ time. For every well-bounded rectangle R follow the links from every corner, towards the middle of R, see Fig. 4. Since each well-bounded rectangle overlaps at most four other well-bounded rectangles, according to Lemma 17, we find all well-bounded rectangles that R overlaps. When we know which well-bounded rectangles overlap R, then we know if R is critical or not. This takes $O(n)$ time since there are at most $O(n)$ well-bounded rectangles.

$\square$

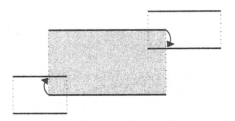

Fig. 4. A well-bounded rectangle overlaps at most four other well-bounded rectangles. These can be found by using a special visibility graph.

Lemma 19. *Let P_2 be the remaining parts of a polygon P after all well-bounded rectangles have been cut off. All pipes in P_2 can be found in $O(n)$ time.*

The proof of Lemma 19 is included in the full version of this paper [9].

As already mentioned all critical rectangles can be cut off by using segments of total length $O(M(P))$, and for the remaining polygon P' it holds that $p(P')=O(M(P))$ [7]. All critical rectangles can be found in $O(n)$ time, according to Lemmas 18 and 19. Thus, combining with Theorem 14 we obtain our final result:

Theorem 20. *A rectangular partition of a hole-free polygon, of length $O(M(P))$, can be computed in $O(n)$ time.*

References

1. Chazelle, B.: Triangulating a Simple Polygon in Linear Time. Proc. 31st Symp. on Foundations of Computer Science, pp. 220-230, 1990.
2. Chin, F., Snoeyink, J., Wang, C.A.: Finding the Medial Axis of a Simple Polygon in Linear Time. Proc., 6th International Symposium on Algorithms and Computation, ISAAC '95, Cairns, Australia, 1995. (LNCS 1006, Springer Verlag).
3. Gabow, H., Bentley, J., Tarjan, R.: Scaling and Related Techniques for Geometry Problems. Proc. 16th Annual ACM Symposium on Theory of Computing, pp. 135-143, April 1984.
4. Gonzalez, T, Zheng, S.Q.: Bounds for Partitioning Rectilinear Polygons. Proc. First ACM Symposium on Compuational Geometry, Baltimore, June 1985.
5. Harel, D.,Tarjan, R.E.: Fast Algorithms for Finding Nearest Common Ancestors. SIAM Journal of Computing, Vol. 13, No. 2, May 1984.
6. Levcopoulos, C.: Minimum Length and "Thickest-first" Rectangular partitions of Polygons. Proc. 20th Allerton Conf. on Comm. Control and Compt., Monticello, Illinois, 1982.
7. Levcopoulos, C.: Fast Heuristics for Minimum Length Rectangular Partitions of Polygons. In Proc. of the 2nd ACM Symp. on Comp. Geomety, pp. 100-108, 1986.
8. Levcopoulos, C.: Heuristics for Minimum Decompositions of Polygons. PhD dissertation no. 155, Linköping University, 1987.
9. Levcopoulos, C., Östlin, A.: Linear-Time Heuristics for Minimum Weight Rectangulation. Technical Report LU-CS-TR:96-165, Lund University, 1996.
10. Lingas, A.: Heuristics for Minimum Edge Length Rectangular Partitions of Rectilinear Figures. Proc. 6th GI-Conference, Dortmund, January 1983. (LNCS 145, Springer Verlag).
11. Levcopoulos, C., Lingas, A.: Bounds on the Length of Convex Partitions of Polygons. Proc. 4th Conference on Found. of Software Technology and Theoretical Computer Science, Bangalore, India, 1984. (LNCS 181, Springer Verlag).
12. Lingas, A., Pinter, R.Y., Rivest, R.L. Shamir, A.: Minimum Edge Length Partitioning of Rectilinear Polygons. Proc. 20th Allerton Conf. on Comm. Control and Compt., Monticello, Illinois, 1982.
13. Vuillemin, J.: A Unifying Look at Data Structures. Communications of the ACM, Vol. 23 (4), April 1980.

Visibility with Multiple Reflections

Boris Aronov[1*], Alan R. Davis[2], Tamal K. Dey[3**], Sudebkumar P. Pal[3***] and
D. Chithra Prasad[3]

[1] Computer and Information Science Department, Polytechnic University, Brooklyn,
NY 11201, USA, aronov@ziggy1.poly.edu.
[2] Division of Computer Science, Mathematics, and Science, St. Johns University,
Jamaica, NY 11439, USA, davisa@sjuvm.stjohns.edu.
[3] Department of Computer Science and Engineering, Indian Institute of Technology,
Kharagpur, India 721302, {dey,spp}@cse.iitkgp.ernet.in.

Abstract. We show that the region lit by a point light source inside a
simple n-gon after at most k reflections off the boundary has combinatorial complexity $O(n^{2k})$, for any $k \geq 1$. A lower bound of $\Omega((n/k)^{2k})$
is also established which matches the upper bound for any fixed k. A
simple near-optimal algorithm for computing the illuminated region is
presented, which runs in $O(n^{2k} \log n)$ time and $O(n^{2k})$ space for any
$k > 1$.

1 Introduction

Visibility-related problems have been extensively studied, in the diverse disci-
plines in which they naturally arise, in different ways. In computational geometry and associated research areas alone, O'Rourke [14] reports over 300 articles
related to various aspects of visibility. Visibility topics include, among others,
problems concerning computation, characterization, and realization of visibility graphs, art gallery problems, shortest path problems, and ray shooting and
hidden surface elimination (see, for example, [13, 14, 15, 16]).

Visibility is obviously intimately related to geometric optics, so that not only
the issue of direct (straight-line) visibility, but also of visibility with reflection
naturally occur here. Indeed, there is a large literature on geometric optics and
on the chaotic behavior of a reflecting ray of light or a bouncing billiard ball
(see, e.g., [7]). The field is very interesting and has accumulated a surprising
number of long-standing open problems, some of which are startlingly simple to
state [12]. For example, it is not known if every obtuse triangle admits a cyclic
billiard ball path. More closely related to the issues addressed in this paper is
the question: "Can any simple polygon bounded by mirrors be completely lit up

* Work on this paper by Boris Aronov has been supported by NSF grant CCR-92-
11541 and Sloan Research Fellowship.
** Tamal K. Dey acknowledges the support of NSF grant CCR-93-21799, USA and DST
grant SR/OY/E-06/95, India.
*** S. P. Pal acknowledges the support of a research grant from the Jawaharlal Nehru
Centre for Advanced Scientific Research, Bangalore, India.

by a single light bulb placed at an arbitrary point in its interior?" This question was first published in 1969 [11], and was finally settled only very recently [18].

Remarkably, there has been almost no investigation of visibility *with reflection* in the geometric complexity or algorithmic context. For example, reflection is a natural issue in computer graphics, where a common rendering technique is to trace the path of light arriving on each pixel of the screen, backwards through multiple reflections [4]. It is interesing to note, however, that most approaches for handling this problem, either query-based, or Z-buffer-based, deal with the problem one-reflection-at-a-time, solving, in affect, a series of direct visibility problems. In our paper we attempt to quantify cumulative effect of multiple reflections on the region visible from a point light source.

Direct visibility has been investigated extensively over the past several years, and a number of linear-time direct-visibility algorithms for simple polygons are known [6, 8]. In an earlier paper [1], we investigated the region visible from a point in a simple n-gon bounded by mirrors, when at most one reflection is permitted. We obtained a tight $\Theta(n^2)$ worst-case geometric complexity bound and described a simple $O(n^2 \log^2 n)$ algorithm for computing this set. In the current paper we investigate the case where at most k reflections are permitted. We are interested in both the worst-case complexity of the resulting lit region, and in an efficient algorithm for computing the region. We produce an $O(n^{2k})$ upper bound and an $\Omega((n/k)^{2k})$ worst-case lower bound on this complexity and construct an algorithm with $O(n^{2k} \log n)$ running time, for $k > 1$. The combinatorial complexity bound involves some careful analysis (it turns out that an upper bound of $O(n^{2k+1})$ is easy, but the proof of the stronger bound is more involved), while the algorithm uses a divide-and-conquer approach and follows almost immediately from previous analysis.

Among different notions of visibility, k-link visibility comes closest to what we study in this paper. Horn and Valentine introduced this concept, where a point y inside a given polygon is k-*link-visible* from another point x if there exists a k-link polygonal path between them inside the polygon [9]. Link visibility has been extensively studied since then; see for example [10, 17, 3]. However, in contrast to k-link visibility, we further restrict the path so that it may only turn at the boundary of the polygon and, moreover, must obey laws of geometric optics at reflection points. As a result, the two notions of visibility produce drastically different behavior.

The remainder of this paper is organized as follows. Section 2 presents some preliminary definitions. Sections 3 and 4 establish the upper and lower bounds, respectively. Finally, Sect. 5 describes a near-optimal algorithm that computes the visibility polygon with at most k reflections.

2 Preliminaries

Let $P \subset \Re^2$ be a simple n-gon with no three collinear vertices. Let $int(P)$ and $bd(P)$ denote the interior and the boundary of P, respectively. Two points in P are said to be 1-*visible* (or *directly visible*) if the interior of the line segment joining them lies in $int(P)$.

We consider visibility with reflection where the angle of incidence is equal to the angle of reflection. This type of reflection is termed *specular reflection* in computer graphics. For $k > 1$, a point y is said to be *k-visible* from a point x (under specular reflection), if there exist points $p_1, p_2, \ldots, p_{k-1}$ lying in the interiors of edges of P such that a ray emitted from x reaches y after $k - 1$ stages of specular reflection at $p_1, p_2, \ldots, p_{k-1}$, in this order. Since specular reflection at a vertex is not well defined, we disallow reflection at vertices of P. In Fig. 1, y is 2-visible from S and z is 4-visible from S.

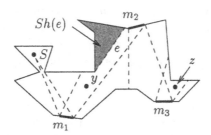

Fig. 1. Visibility under reflection

For a point $S \in P$, let $\mathcal{V}_0(S)$ denote the polygonal region consisting of points in P that are directly visible from S, and for $k \geq 1$, let $\mathcal{V}_k(S)$ denote the polygonal region consisting of points that are ℓ-visible from S, for some $\ell \leq k+1$. Informally, $\mathcal{V}_k(S)$ is the set of points that receive light from S after at most k reflections off the boundary of P. For $\ell > 1$, let D be an ℓ-visible point. By definition, there exist points $p_1, p_2, \ldots, p_{\ell-1}$ lying in the interiors of edges $e_1, e_2, \ldots, e_{\ell-1}$ of P, respectively, on the ℓ-link path from S to D. The maximal $(\ell - 1)$-visible portion of $e_{\ell-1}$ consisting of points lit up by rays reflected off edges $e_1, \ldots, e_{\ell-2}$, in this order, constitutes a *mirror* m at the $(\ell - 1)^{\text{st}}$ stage of reflection. All points of $\mathcal{V}_k(S)$ that are ℓ-visible to S through m, via the same sequence of reflections, constitute the *mirror visibility polygon*, $V(m)$, of that mirror. $V(m)$ is a relatively open subset of P since we assume that vertices of P absorb any light incident on them. As the light rays are reflected off edges $e_1, \ldots, e_{\ell-1}$, a corresponding sequence of virtual images of the source is also created. In the first stage, the light rays reflected off e_1 emerge (when extended backward) from a virtual image S^1 of $S^0 = S$ with respect to the mirror on e_1; S^1 is a reflection of S^0 in the line containing e_1. To define the sequence of virtual images, denote the virtual image with respect to the mirror on e_{i-1} for $1 < i \leq \ell$ by S^{i-1}. The next virtual image in the sequence S^i is the reflection of S^{i-1} through the mirror on e_i.

Let $\{m_1, m_2, \ldots, m_a\}$ be the set of all mirrors, up to stage k, in any order. Let $V_i = V(m_i)$. Slightly abusing the notation, we let m_0 represent a "dummy mirror" so that $\mathcal{V}_0(S) = V_0 = V(m_0)$ is the set of points directly visible from S in our collection $\{V_i\}$. Let the corresponding set of virtual images be $\{S^1, S^2, \ldots, S^a\}$ where S^i is created with respect to the mirror m_i.

As mentioned above, V_i is a polygonal relatively open subset of P. The edges of $bd(V_i)$ that lie inside P are called *shadow edges*. It is a straightforward, nevertheless crucial, observation that V_i has no vertex in $int(P)$. Let e be a shadow edge of V_i (see Fig. 1). P is divided by e into two sub-polygons with disjoint interiors. The interior of one of these two sub-polygons does not meet V_i. This portion of P, denoted $Sh(e)$, is called the *shadow* of e.

Clearly, $\mathcal{V}_k(S) = \cup_{i=0}^a V_i$. Put $\Delta_i = \cup_{j=0}^i V_j$, so that $\mathcal{V}_k(S) = \Delta_a$. The connected components of the complementary region $P \setminus \Delta_i$ are called *blind spots* of Δ_i. These are the regions of P that do not receive light when we consider mirror visibility polygons $V(m_0), V(m_1), \ldots, V(m_i)$. In particular, blind spots of Δ_a do not receive light after k stages of reflections, as a is the total number of (real) mirrors. The blind spots of Δ_i that are adjacent to $bd(P)$ are called *boundary blind spots* of Δ_i; the remaining blind spots are *interior*.

3 Upper Bound

We aim to prove that the complexity of $\mathcal{V}_k(S) = \Delta_a$ is $O(n^{2k})$. To estimate the size of $\mathcal{V}_k(S)$ we first show that there can be at most $O(n^{2k})$ blind spots in $\mathcal{V}_k(S)$. First we state several crucial properties of the mirror visibility polygons. We omit some of the proofs in this version.

Lemma 1. *Each V_i is a simple polygon with no more than n edges.*

Lemma 2. *There are $O(n^k)$ mirrors altogether if k stages of reflection are allowed.*

Lemma 3. *If e is a shadow edge of V_i, no other edge of V_i can lie in $\mathrm{Sh}(e)$.*

Lemma 4. *No segment contained in the interior of P can intersect the boundary of V_i more than twice.*

Lemma 5. *The region bounded by a simple closed curve contained in P cannot have any point of $bd(P)$ in its interior.*

Lemma 6. *If two mirror visibility polygons V_i, V_j intersect in such a way that each of two shadow edges e_1, e_2 of V_i intersects each of two shadow edges f_1, f_2 of V_j, then there are no other intersections between $bd(V_i)$ and $bd(V_j)$.*

To prove that there are only $O(n^{2k})$ blind spots in $\mathcal{V}_k(S)$, we add the mirror visibility polygons $V_0, V_1, \ldots, V_a$, one by one, and count the increase in the number of blind spots. Recall that, by definition, $\Delta_i = \Delta_{i-1} \cup V_i$ and $\mathcal{V}_k(S) = \Delta_a$. First we observe some important properties of blind spots. Each interior blind spot is convex and each boundary blind spot is bounded by a connected portion of $bd(P)$ and a convex chain formed by portions of intersecting shadow edges. The proof of this fact for the case of at most one reflection is given in [1]. It applies here as it only uses the fact that V_i's are polygonal and have no vertices in the interior of P.

The next property follows from lemma 3 and the fact that all lines containing the shadow edges of V_i must pass through the single image point S^i. We say that a segment s *cuts across* a blind spot if s crosses the boundary of the blind spot twice, if it is an interior blind spot, and crosses its bounding convex chain twice, if it is a boundary blind spot. The proof of the following lemma is straightforward for interior blind spots, and is more involved for boundary blind spots. We omit the proof in this version.

Lemma 7. *A blind spot in Δ_{i-1} can be cut across by at most two shadow edges of V_i.*

Blind spots of Δ_i are obtained by removing points of V_i from blind spots of Δ_{i-1}. Thus we have:

Corollary 8. *Any blind spot of Δ_{i-1} can generate at most two new interior blind spots in Δ_i as a result of overlapping with V_i.*

Lemma 9. *Let h_1, h_2 be two blind spots (interior or boundary) of Δ_{i-1} that are simultaneously intersected by a pair of shadow edges e and e' of V_i and such that no other blind spot intersects both e and e' between h_1 and h_2. Such an event can be charged to a pair (m_i, m_j) of mirrors, for some $j < i$, which is charged only once throughout the incremental construction of $V_k(S) = \Delta_a$ from Δ_0.*

Proof. Let e exit h_1 through the edge g. Consider the region Q bounded by the two convex chains of h_1, h_2 and the two portions of e and e' as in Fig. 2. By

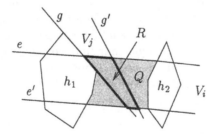

Fig. 2. A pair of shadow edges intersecting two blind spots

lemma 5, the interior of Q does not contain any point of $bd(P)$. Let $j < i$ be such that $g \subset bd(V_j)$. Since e enters another blind spot after entering V_j through g, it must exit V_j through another shadow edge, say g'. We claim that g and g' must intersect e'. Since Q cannot contain a boundary point of P, g and g' must exit Q through an edge other than e. These exit points cannot lie on the blind spot boundaries since the blind spots are contained in $P \setminus V_j$. Hence g, g' of V_j must intersect e and e' of V_i, and by lemma 6 no other edge of V_j can intersect V_i. This implies that V_i and V_j intersect in a quadrilateral R bounded by (portions of) two shadow edges e, e' of V_i and two shadow edges g, g' of V_j.

The event in question can be charged to the distinguished pair of mirrors (m_i, m_j), with $j < i$. This pair of mirrors cannot be charged for another pair of blind spots of Δ_{i-1}. Indeed, (h_1, h_2) is the only pair of blind spots that could have charged (m_i, m_j), as any other pair of blind spots meeting both e and e'

either would not have R between them, or would have another blind spot (h_1 or h_2) between them. □

We first count the number of interior blind spots that can be present in Δ_i. The number of boundary blind spots is determined separately. To count the interior blind spots in Δ_i, we enumerate them as they are generated throughout the incremental construction of Δ_i starting from Δ_0. For this we concentrate on a generic incremental step of constructing Δ_j from Δ_{j-1} by overlapping V_j on it for $1 \leq j \leq i$.

Let H^j denote the set of blind spots of Δ_{j-1}. We enumerate blind spots in H^j in successive steps and count the contributions of each group of blind spots to the increase of the number of *interior* blind spots during construction of $\Delta_j = \Delta_{j-1} \cup V_j$.

Step (i): First eliminate all blind spots from H^j that do not contribute to the increase in the number of interior blind spots as a result of the intersection with V_j. Let H_1^j denote the set of remaining blind spots.

Step (ii): Eliminate from H_1^j those boundary blind spots whose convex chains are intersected by only one edge of $bd(V_j)$. Each such edge intersects the convex chain of a boundary blind spot twice since otherwise the blind spot would have been eliminated in Step (i).

Since only one new interior blind spot is created from an existing boundary blind spot eliminated in step (ii), it is enough to count the total number of boundary blind spots eliminated in step (ii) for determining the number of new interior blind spots created from them. We charge the contributions of these boundary blind spots to the unique endpoints covered by interior of V_j. Since there are no more than n endpoints of shadow edges bounding every V_j, for each $j \leq i$, we have the following lemma:

Lemma 10. *At most ni boundary blind spots are eliminated in step (ii) over all V_j, $1 \leq j \leq i$.*

Now we proceed to count the other interior blind spots. Let H_2^j be the set of blind spots remaining after elimination step (ii) in Δ_{j-1}. The increase in the number of interior blind spots due to generation of new blind spots from H_2^j is bounded by the size of H_2^j, because each interior blind spot in H_2^j is replaced by at most two new interior blind spots; analogous statement holds for the new interior blind spots generated from boundary blind spots of Δ_j, see corollary 8.

Lemma 11. $\Sigma_{j=1}^i |H_2^j|$ *is at most* $\binom{i+1}{2} + 3ni$.

Proof. First, we prove that H_2^j has at most $j + 3n$ blind spots.

Due to eliminations in steps (i) and (ii), every interior blind spot and the convex chain of every boundary blind spot in H_2^j are intersected by exactly two edges of V_j. Consider the following planar graph G: Its nodes are the shadow edges of V_j that meet the boundary of at least one interior blind spot, or the convex chain of at least one boundary blind spot; recall that there are fewer than n such edges. The arcs of G correspond to blind spots of H_2^j—two nodes are adjacent if the corresponding shadow edges meet a common blind spot. We allow multiple arcs between two nodes, corresponding to multiple blind spots meeting the same pair of edges of V_j. G is clearly planar, as blind spots are disjoint and each meets exactly two edges of V_j. By Euler's formula, the number of arcs in G is proportional to the number of its nodes (fewer than n) plus the number of what we will refer to as *2-sided faces*, which are faces in the embedding of G bounded by two nodes (shadow edges) and two arcs connecting them (two consecutive blind spots). The 2-sided faces correspond exactly to events counted by the lemma 9. Thus the contribution of this quantity is at most j since m_j can be paired with at most j mirrors processed before it. By Euler's formula, the number of the arcs not incident to any 2-sided face is at most $3n$ proving the claim.

Summing over all H_2^j, $j = 1, \ldots, i$, we obtain the desired bound. $\square$

Lemma 12. Δ_{i-1} has at most $\binom{i+1}{2} + 5ni$ blind spots.

Proof. By the previous two lemmas there are $\binom{i+1}{2} + 4ni$ interior blind spots in Δ_{i-1}. Finally, since there are at most ni endpoints of shadow edges in i mirror visibility polygons, there are at most ni boundary blind spots in Δ_{i-1}. Summing the two estimates, we obtain the desired $\binom{i+1}{2} + 5ni$ bound. $\square$

Lemma 13. Δ_i has at most $O(i^2 + ni \log i)$ edges.

Proof. Divide the set of mirror visibility polygons into two subsets $M_1 = \{V_0, V_2, \ldots, V_{\lfloor i/2 \rfloor}\}$ and $M_2 = \{V_{\lfloor i/2 \rfloor + 1}, V_{\lfloor i/2 \rfloor + 2}, \ldots, V_i\}$. Let R_1, R_2 denote the polygonal regions obtained after taking the union of polygons in M_1 and M_2, respectively. According to lemma 11, R_1 and R_2 have $O(i^2 + ni)$ blind spots, since the argument can be applied to *any* ordering of the mirrors. We can think of the blind spots of R_1 (resp. R_2) as a collection of faces in the arrangement formed by the boundaries of the polygons in M_1 (resp. M_2). The blind spots of Δ_i are a subset of faces (marked) in the merged arrangement. Observe that we can adopt the following result here. Let $c(m, \ell)$ denote the complexity of m marked cells in an arrangement $A(L)$ of ℓ line segments. Let $L = L_1 \cup L_2$ where L_1 and L_2 have ℓ_1 and ℓ_2 segments, respectively. The combination lemma of [5] expresses the complexity of the marked faces in $A(L)$ in terms of the complexity of the marked faces in $A(L_1), A(L_2)$ and the effect of merging the two, as follows: $c(m, \ell) = c(m, \ell_1) + c(m, \ell_2) + O(m + \ell)$. For Δ_i we have $m = O(i^2 + ni)$ (lemma 11) and $\ell = O(ni)$. Denoting the worst-case complexity of blind spots in Δ_i as $f(i)$, over all possible orderings of the mirrors, we obtain the recurrence

$$f(i) = \begin{cases} 2f(i/2) + O(i^2 + ni), & \text{for } i > 1 \\ O(n), & \text{for } i = 1 \end{cases}$$

This recurrence solves to $O(i^2 + ni \log i)$. $\square$

Theorem 14. $\mathcal{V}_k(S)$ has combinatorial complexity $O(n^{2k})$, for any $k \geq 1$.

Proof. Recall that $\mathcal{V}_k(S) = \Delta_a$. Using lemma 13 and $a = O(n^k)$ we obtain an $O(n^{2k} + n^{k+1} \log n)$ bound for the complexity of $\mathcal{V}_k(S)$. For $k > 1$, the first term dominates the second and thus $V_k(S)$ has $O(n^{2k})$ edges. By a different argument we proved that $V_1(S)$ has $O(n^2)$ size in [1]. Combining these two results we obtain the desired bound for all $k \geq 1$. □

4 Lower Bound

In this section we construct a simple n-gon P and place a point source of light S so that the region $V_k(S)$ lit up with at most k reflections has combinatorial complexity $\Omega((n/k)^{2k})$. The construction can be carried out for any $k < n/c$, where $c > 1$ is an absolute constant.

The general plan is to have a series of k "convex mirrors" (CMs) each constructed of $N = \Theta(n/k)$ real flat mirrors. The first CM is directly lit by S and produces N beams overlapping in some area. The second CM is placed in that region and creates N^2 beams that all overlap in some region of positive area. The third CM is placed in that region etc. At this stage, after the $(k-1)$st CM, in the region covered by all N^{k-1} resulting beams, we place a modified version of a CM that produces N^k arbitrarily thin beams, many of which pairwise intersect. Since we arrange it so that no other light ray can reach the region in which the intersections occur, with fewer than $k+1$ reflections, this guarantees $\Omega(N^{2k})$ complexity of the region lit up with at most k reflections, thus proving the claim. The general layout is schematically depicted in Fig. 3, drawn not to scale. Details are provided below.

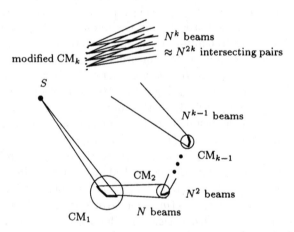

Fig. 3. Successive stages of reflection through "convex mirrors" create N^k thin beams many of which pairwise intersect

A "convex mirror": In order to implement the construction, the CM "gadget" which we will repeatedly use, is defined with parameter β determining its shape and γ determining its orientation.

GIVEN: A disk D which is lit by s *incoming* beams of light, i.e., each point of the disk will be lit by every beam, if no additional obstacles are erected to block the light. The rays are near-parallel, i.e., the range of directions of incoming light rays, over all beams and all points of the disk, is β, with $\beta N \ll \pi$. Each beam emanates from a point (its real or virtual source).

DESIRED: An N-mirror CM by which the incoming beams are reflected in such a way as to produce sN *outgoing* beams, all of which intersect at least in a disk D', and such that in D' the resulting beams are again near-parallel, i.e., the range of directions of the light rays arriving at D', over all beams and all points in D' is β', with $\beta' \to 0$ as $\beta \to 0$. Additionally, we want to guarantee that the ratio of the distance between D and D' to the size of the larger of the two disks is at least C, with $C \to \infty$ as $\beta \to 0$.

CONSTRUCTION: Without loss of generality, assume that the beams come from the left, nearly parallel to the x-axis. For definiteness, suppose that the disk is centered at the origin and that the directions from a point in D to a source of a beam are all in the range from $\pi - \beta$ to π. Construct the first mirror emanating from the origin at the angle of γ with positive x-axis. The second mirror will emanate from the right endpoint of the first at the angle of $\beta/2$ to the line containing it, or $\gamma + \beta/2$ to the positive x-axis. In general, mirror number i, for $i = 2, \ldots, N$, emanates from the rightmost endpoint of mirror $i - 1$ at the angle of $\beta/2$ to the line containing the $(i-1)$st mirror and thus at the angle of $\gamma + (i-1)\beta/2$ to the positive x-axis. Refer to Fig. 4.

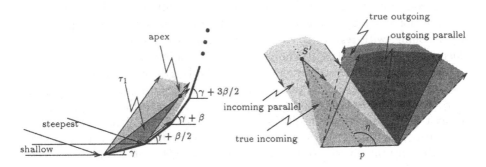

Fig. 4. A "convex mirror". Only one triangle is shown.

Fig. 5. Replacing parallel beams with real beams

The entire construction is scaled to fit in D. The relative sizes of the mirrors are specified below.

ANALYSIS: Using the ith mirror as a base, construct a triangle τ_i, as follows: Its third vertex ("apex") lies above the line containing the mirror. Its interior angle at the left endpoint of the base is $\gamma + (i-1)\beta/2$ and the interior angle at the right endpoint is $\pi - \gamma - (i+1)\beta/2$. The angle at the apex is obviously β. With this choice of angles, the left edge of τ_i overlaps the right edge of τ_{i-1}, for all $i = 2, \ldots, N$. We choose the lengths of the mirrors so that all N triangles share one apex, i.e., the triangles are scaled so that their overlapping edges coincide.

What is the significance of the triangles? For a moment, ignore the fact that the incoming beams originate from point light sources at a finite distance from D and regard them as parallel beams of light. We have s beams so that the most shallow one comes in parallel to the negative x-axis (as noted above, it cannot really come from that direction without contradicting our assumptions on the range of incoming light directions, but it will serve as a useful extreme case—clearly no beam can come from below the negative x-axis), the steepest one comes in at an angle at most β with the negative x-axis (again, let us assume it is exactly β for a moment) and the remaining beams lie in between. The reflection of the shallow beam off mirror i leaves at the angle of $2\gamma + (i-1)\beta$ and the steepest beam reflects at the angle of $2\gamma + i\beta$. So the former makes the angle of $\gamma + (i-1)\beta/2$ and the latter the angle of $\gamma + (i+1)\beta/2$ with the directed line containing the ith mirror. The two extreme reflected beams are parallel strips emanating from the ith mirror at the angles mentioned above and their intersection is easily checked to be exactly τ_i.

Now we address the approximations we have made: First of all, the reflection of any parallel beam that comes in at an intermediate angle will cover the triangle. Our second approximation was the assumption that the beams were parallel. Actually with the source placed at a finite distance inside the parallel beam, the non-parallel incoming beam would be contained inside this parallel beam. As a result the reflected beams will diverge slightly and thus the intersection of all beams will be slightly larger than τ_i, in that their interior angles at the mirrors will be slightly larger. See Fig. 5. A careful observation reveals that the directional spread of the sN beams (which are outgoing with respect to D and incoming with respect to the "output" disk D') is at most $(N+1)\beta$, and thus can be made arbitrarily small provided β is sufficiently small.

The size of D is no more than N times the length of the first mirror. The distance between D and D' is approximately the length of either lateral side of τ_i. Hence, by the theorem of sines, the ratio between the two quantities is at least (approximately) $\sin\gamma/(N\sin\beta) \approx \sin\gamma/(N\beta)$ and hence can be made arbitrarily large as $\beta \to 0$, provided that $\sin\gamma$ is bounded below by a positive absolute constant. In our construction below, $\gamma \approx \pi/4$, so the condition holds.

A global view: Start at the source S (refer to Fig. 3). Pick a disk D_1 visible to S. Put the first CM there. There is only one beam coming in to the first CM and N going out. The angular spread of the single incoming beam can be made less than δ, for any $\delta > 0$ of our choice, by shrinking D_1. The outgoing beams will overlap in a disk D_2. The spread among the beams in that disk will be at most $(N+1)\delta$. Put second CM in D_2. This produces N^2 beams overlapping in disk D_3 with angular spread bounded by $(N+1)^2\delta$. Repeat k times, getting N^k beams. This produces N^k beams overlapping in a common region ("target area"). The angular spread at the last CM will be at most $(N+1)^k\delta$. Putting $\delta = \pi/(10000(N+1)^k)$ ensures that angular spread in every CM is smaller than $\pi/10000$, which is sufficient to make all the CM constructions work as described—the definition of a CM assumed $\beta N \ll \pi$. We now modify CM_k in the following fashion. Pick a generic point on each of its N flat mirrors and temporarily replace each flat mirror by a "point-like mirror subsegment" with the same orientation. (We will arrange for these "point-like mirrors" to have a positive length below, but view them as line segments of zero length and specific orientation, for now.) This produces N fans of N^{k-1} reflected ray-like beams each. It is easy to check that roughly at least $\binom{N}{2} \cdot (N^{k-1})^2/4 = \Theta(N^{2k})$ of pairs of these rays intersect in the target area. Now, by the generic choice of point mirrors, each one can be expanded to positive length without reducing the complexity of the union of the reflected beams.

The only thing that remains is to arrange the mirrors and the source in a simple polygon so that no "unauthorized" ray can reach the target area with k or fewer reflections. Indeed such an arrangement is possible. We omit the details in this version. See figure 6.

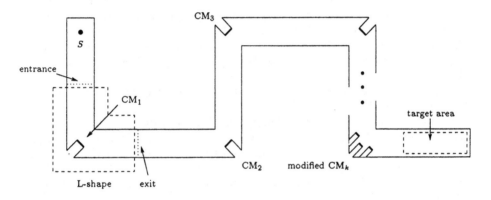

Fig. 6. Placement of mirrors in the polygon

5   Algorithm for computing $\mathcal{V}_k(S)$

We first compute $V_0(S)$ and all mirror visibility polygons V_i successively as follows. For computing the mirror visibility polygon V_i we first determine the image S^i of S with respect to the mirror m_i. Then considering the direct visibility polygon of S^i in the polygon $P \cup T$, T being the triangle formed by S^i and m_i, we can obtain V_i by any one of the known linear time algorithms [6, 8]. After computing all V_i's we apply a divide-and-conquer technique to compute the final visibility polygon $\mathcal{V}_k(S)$. Let $V' = V_0 \cup ... \cup V_{\lfloor \ell/2 \rfloor}$ and $V'' = V_{\lfloor \ell/2 \rfloor + 1} \cup ... \cup V_\ell$ be computed recursively. To compute $V = V' \cup V''$ we merge V' and V'' employing the sweep-line algorithm of Bentley and Ottmann [2]. By lemma 13 V', V'', V have only $O(\ell^2 + n\ell \log \ell)$ vertices and segments on their boundary. Thus sweeping takes $O(\ell^2 \log n + n\ell \log^2 n)$ time. The time $T(\ell)$ for this divide-and-conquer algorithm can be expressed as

$$T(\ell) = \begin{cases} 2T(\ell/2) + O(\ell^2 \log n + n\ell \log^2 n) & \text{for } \ell > 1 \\ O(n) & \text{for } \ell = 1 \end{cases}$$

which solves to $T(\ell) = O(\ell^2 \log n + n\ell \log^3 n)$. Putting $\ell = a = O(n^k)$ and observing that the required space remains bounded by the sizes of the unions of mirror visibility polygons, we get the following result.

Theorem 15. *The visibility polygon* $V_k(S)$ *can be computed in* $O(n^{2k} \log n + n^{k+1} \log^3 n)$ *time and* $O(n^{2k})$ *space, for any* $k \geq 1$.

References

1. B. Aronov, A. R. Davis, T. K. Dey, S. P. Pal, and D. C. Prasad. Visibility with reflection. *Proc. 11th ACM Symp. Comput. Geom.*, 1995, pp. 316–325.

2. J. L. Bentley and T. A. Ottmann. Algorithms for reporting and counting geometric intersections. *IEEE Trans. Comput.*, C-28:643–647, 1979.

3. H. N. Djidjev, A. Lingas, and J. Sack. An $O(n \log n)$ algorithm for computing the link center of a simple polygon. *Discr. Comput. Geom.*, 8(2):131–152, 1992.

4. J. Foley, A. van Dam, S. Feiner, J. Hughes, and R. Phillips. *Introduction to Computer Graphics*. Addison-Wesley, Reading, MA 1994.

5. H. Edelsbrunner, L. J. Guibas, and M. Sharir. The complexity and construction of many faces in arrangements of lines and of segments. *Discr. Comput. Geom.*, 5:161–196, 1990.

6. H. ElGindy and D. Avis. A linear algorithm for computing the visibility polygon from a point. *J. Algorithms*, 2:186–197, 1981.

7. E. Gutkin. Billiards in polygons. *Physica D*, 19:311–333, 1986.

8. L. J. Guibas, J. Hershberger, D. Leven, M. Sharir, and R. E. Tarjan. Linear-time algorithms for visibility and shortest path problems inside triangulated simple polygons. *Algorithmica*, 2:209–233, 1987.

9. A. Horn and F. Valentine. Some properties of l-sets in the plane. *Duke Math. J.*, 16:131–140, 1949.

10. Y. Ke. An efficient algorithm for link-distance problems. *Proc. 5th Annu. ACM Sympos. Comput. Geom.*, 1989, pp. 69–78.

11. V. Klee. Is every polygonal region illuminable from some point? *Amer. Math. Monthly*, 76:180, 1969.

12. V. Klee and S. Wagon. *Old and new unsolved problems in plane geometry and number theory*. Mathematical Association of America, 1991.

13. J. O'Rourke. *Art Gallery Theorems and Algorithms*. Oxford University Press, New York, NY 1987.

14. J. O'Rourke. Visibility. In *The CRC Handbook of Discrete & Computational Geometry*, Eds., J. E. Goodman and J. O'Rourke, CRC Press, to appear, 1997.

15. M. Pellegrini. Ray shooting and lines in space. In *The CRC Handbook of Discrete & Computational Geometry*, Eds., J. E. Goodman and J. O'Rourke, CRC Press, to appear, 1997.

16. T. C. Shermer. Recent results in art galleries. *Proc. IEEE*, 80(9):1384–1399, 1992.

17. S. Suri. On some link distance problems in a simple polygon. *IEEE Trans. Robot. Autom.*, 6:108–113, 1990.

18. G. W. Tokarsky. Polygonal rooms not illuminable from every point. *Amer. Math. Monthly*, 102:867–879, 1995.

A Fast Heuristic for Approximating the Minimum Weight Triangulation*

(Extended Abstract)

Christos Levcopoulos and Drago Krznaric

Department of Computer Science
Lund University, Box 118, S-221 00 Lund, Sweden.

1   Introduction

Minimizing the total length has been one of the main optimality criteria for triangulations and other kinds of partitions. Indeed, the *minimum weight triangulation* or MWT (i.e. a triangulation of minimum total edge length) has frequently been referred to as the "optimal triangulation". This triangulation has some good properties [1] and is e.g. useful in numerical approximation of bivariate data [23]. Its complexity is one of the most intriguing problems in computational geometry. No proof has yet been presented showing that it is NP-hard. On the other hand, no polynomial time heuristic for it was shown to guarantee even a constant approximation factor.

However, very recently we proved that what we called the *quasi-greedy triangulation* has length within a constant factor from the minimum [13]. A standard implementation of that heuristic using known results would yield a quadratic time algorithm. In this paper, we improve on this by describing an $O(n \log n)$ algorithm for quasi-greedy triangulation. Moreover, if the Delaunay triangulation is given, our algorithm runs in linear time.

The *minimum weight convex partition* (MWCP) problem has been shown to be NP-complete [7, 17]. By a MWCP we mean a set of non-crossing diagonals (i.e. without Steiner points) of minimum total length which includes the convex hull and partitions it into empty convex polygons. In [13] it was shown that, given the quasi-greedy triangulation, a convex partition of length within a constant factor from the MWCP can be computed in linear time. Thus from the results in this paper we also obtain a fast heuristic for approximating the MWCP.

The quasi-greedy triangulation is very closely related to the greedy triangulation (both are defined in the next section). In fact, we will describe an algorithm that, given the Delaunay triangulation, computes the greedy triangulation in linear time. This algorithm behaves in such a way that it is very easily adapted to yield an algorithm for the quasi-greedy triangulation. Consequently, we also present the first $O(n \log n)$ algorithm for greedy triangulation. (By using a substantially different approach, an attempt to develop an $O(n \log n)$ algorithm for greedy triangulation was done in [21]. Even if that approach could be corrected

---

* E-mail: {christos,drago}@dna.lth.se

and completed, it is not obvious how it could be modified to produce the quasi-greedy triangulation.)

Heuristics for MWT and MWCP were also developed by Plaisted and Hong [19], achieving approximation ratios $O(\log n)$ and 12, respectively. It is not known whether their heuristics can be implemented to run in time less than $O(n^2 \log n)$ [20]. No other polynomial time algorithm (except for the quasi-greedy method) has been proved to guarantee an approximation factor better than $O(\sqrt{n})$ (the $O(\sqrt{n})$ bound is due to the greedy triangulation [13]). However, for the minimum weight Steiner triangulation, in which additional vertices may be added, Eppstein [3] showed that it can be approximated within a constant factor. Other interesting results on the minimum weight triangulation problem appear in [4, 6, 8, 9, 14], and on the greedy triangulation in [2, 5, 16, 15, 21].

2 Definitions and our Approach

To simplify the presentation, we assume that no three points in our input point set S are collinear and that all diagonals of S have distinct length. The *greedy triangulation* of S is obtained by repeatedly producing a shortest possible edge that does not properly intersect any of the previously generated edges. To proceed we need the following definition. We say that a diagonal d of a PSLG G is *locally shortest* if there is no shorter diagonal within distance $2|d|$ from d. We define the *quasi-greedy triangulation* of S as the triangulation produced by the following algorithm:

Algorithm: Quasi-Greedy(S)
$G \leftarrow \{S, \emptyset\}$
while G is not a triangulation **do**
    let (v_1, u_1) be a locally shortest diagonal of G
    if all the following 6 conditions hold

    1. the diagonal (v_1, u_1) forms an empty triangle (v_1, u_0, u_1) with two edges in G,
    2. there is a diagonal (v_0, u_0) properly intersecting (v_1, u_1) and forming an empty triangle (v_0, v_1, u_0) with two edges in G,
    3. the angle $\angle v_1, u_0, u_1$ is > 135 degrees in the triangle (v_1, u_0, u_1),
    4. $|v_0, u_0| < 1.1|v_1, u_1|$,
    5. $|v_0, p| < 0.5|u_0, p|$, where p is the intersection of the straight-line extensions of (v_0, v_1) and (u_0, u_1), and
    6. there is an edge (u_1, u_2) in G such that (v_1, u_0, u_1, u_2) forms an empty quadrangle and the angle $\angle u_0, u_1, u_2$ in that quadrangle is > 180 degrees.

    then add the edge (v_0, u_0) to G
    else
        add the edge (v_1, u_1) to G
    end if
end while
return the triangulation G
end Quasi-Greedy

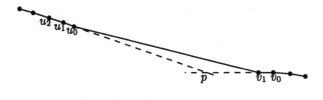

Fig. 1. An example of configuration for which all 6 conditions hold.

In this extended abstract we mainly describe an algorithm for the greedy triangulation. To ensure that it can easily be converted into one that computes the quasi-greedy triangulation, we preserve certain properties that are described in Section 8.

During the process of producing edges of the triangulation, given a diagonal which is shortest in a sufficiently large region around it, we show that there is only a constant number of concave chains in its vicinity, and a constant number of other vertices not belonging to these concave chains. This is formalized in Lemma 11. A main goal is therefore to handle such concave chains efficiently. This is done by partitioning them into short and slightly concave pieces, called "compvertices", as described in Section 5.

The easiest case of interacting concave chains is when we have to triangulate the area between two concave chains facing each other. We call this case "bipartite polygon". In Section 3 we describe a linear time algorithm for triangulating bipartite polygons. This specialized algorithm is also used as a subroutine by the main algorithm.

A special case of concave chains are isolated clusters of vertices whose convex hulls have been produced as greedy edges, but which still have no connections to other vertices via greedy edges. Such so-called "2-clusters" are helpful to organize the algorithm in a hierarchical way in order to avoid sorting of distances. Therefore, the 2-clustering ideas are shortly presented in Section 4.

Using the hierarchical decomposition of points into the well separated 2-clusters, we produce the greedy triangulation bottom-up in the hierarchy. The main step in the bottom up computation is, given a 2-cluster and the greedy triangulation of each of its children, to compute all greedy diagonals that connect the children of this 2-cluster. This main step is performed in phases, where in each phase all diagonals of approximately the same length (within a factor 1.2) are produced (Section 4.1). Some approximate sorting of closest neighbor distances between the children of a 2-cluster is implicit when assigning the children to various phases. However, this is done very simply in linear time because of a good bound on the ratio between the longest and the shortest such distance (Lemma 7). More details about how each phase operates are given in Section 6.

A first step of our algorithm is to compute the hierarchy of 2-clusters (Section 4), then to compute a kind of a threaded quadtree which is used in order to support the range queries made by our algorithm (Section 6.1). The first step can be done in $O(n)$ time given a Euclidean minimum spanning tree (EMST) [11], whereas the latter can be done in $O(n)$ time given the Delaunay triangulation [10]. (The Delaunay triangulation and EMST can be obtained from each other in $O(n)$ time according to [22] and [18], so we could start from either one.) After this preprocessing, our algorithm uses only the structure of 2-clusters and the threaded quadtree.

3 Greedy Triangulation Between Two Concave Chains

Definition 1. We say that a simple polygon P is *bipartite* if the vertices of P can be partitioned into two subsets, called *poles* of P, in such a way that each pole has the following two properties:

1. each vertex of the pole lies on the convex hull of the pole, and
2. the convex hull of the pole and the interior of P do not overlap.

It follows from the definition above that the vertices of each pole of a bipartite polygon P, if they are at least three, form a concave polygonal chain. Further, all internal diagonals of P connect vertices from opposite poles (this is why P is called bipartite).

Fig. 2. A normal and a not normal polygon.

A bipartite polygon is called *normal* if there is a unique partition of its vertices into poles. Further, a *fan* is a (not normal) bipartite polygon that can be partitioned into poles so that one of the poles contains only one vertex. This vertex is then called the *root* of the fan. If P is a fan, then there is only one way to triangulate it, namely by producing all diagonals incident to the root of the fan, which can be done trivially in linear time. If P is not normal then it is either a triangle, a quadrangle or a fan, or there is a convex vertex of P whose adjacent vertices on the perimeter of P are concave. In the last case, also depicted in Figure 2, all triangulations of P contain the diagonal connecting these two concave vertices, and the polygon resulting from producing this diagonal and cutting off the produced triangle is either a quadrangle, a fan, or a normal bipartite polygon. We can therefore assume in the continuation that the input bipartite polygon is normal. By a diagonal we will mean a diagonal internal to the polygon.

Definition 2. Let P be a normal bipartite polygon. The two edges of P that connect vertices of opposite poles are called the *walls* of P. For a vertex v of P, the *mate* of v, denoted by $m(v)$, is the closest vertex of P visible from v inside P and belonging to the pole that does not contain v. Next, a straight-line segment connecting two vertices v and v' of P is called an *anchor* of P if $m(v) = v'$ and $m(v') = v$. Finally, P is called *wall-anchored* if all anchors of P are walls of P.

The following observation can be easily shown.

Observation 3. *Let P be a normal bipartite polygon with poles V_1 and V_2. Then the following holds for every vertex v in V_1:*

(a) If v sees at least three vertices of V_2, then let $v_1, v_2, \ldots, v_k$ be the visible vertices of V_2 from v in clockwise order. Let d_i denote the distance from v to v_i, $1 \leq i \leq k$. Then for any integer i, $1 \leq i \leq k - 2$, if $d_i < d_{i+1}$ then it follows that $d_{i+1} < d_{i+2}$ and, symmetrically, if $d_{i+1} > d_{i+2}$ then $d_i > d_{i+1}$.

(b) If v' is another vertex of V_1, then $(v, m(v))$ does not properly intersect $(v', m(v'))$.

(c) No anchor of P is properly intersected by any shorter diagonal of P and, hence, if it is not a wall, it is a greedy diagonal of P.

Let P be a (normal) bipartite polygon. By using the above properties we can easily see that by scanning simultaneously the two poles of P, one in clockwise and the other in counterclockwise order, we can find for all vertices in one pole their corresponding mates in total linear time. By repeating the process symmetrically, we find the mates of the vertices in the other pole. Thus all anchors can also be computed in total linear time. Thereafter, all anchors which are diagonals are inserted into P, thus partitioning P into wall-anchored subpolygons. Hence, in the remainder it suffices to show how to triangulate wall-anchored polygons (and normal, as we have already assumed because of the trivial transformations).

For an anchor of a wall-anchored polygon P, let the *cutting diagonal* be the shortest diagonal that cuts from P a triangle edged by the anchor (which is by definition also a wall). We observe that the cutting diagonal is a greedy diagonal, because all diagonals that properly intersect it are longer by Property (a). Moreover, any normal subpolygon remaining after producing the cutting diagonal and cutting off the produced triangle is also wall-anchored (see [12] for a proof). Thus we can triangulate any wall-anchored polygon by repeatedly (as long as it is normal) producing a cutting diagonal and cut off one triangle. So we obtain the following lemma.

Lemma 4. *For any bipartite polygon P with n vertices, the greedy triangulation of P can be computed in time $O(n)$.*

4 Computing the Greedy Triangulation Hierarchically

We use the hierarchical clustering method from [11] to decompose the input set S into subsets for which the greedy triangulation can be computed locally. We define the *rectangular diameter* of a vertex set D, abbreviated rdiam(D), to be the diameter of the smallest enclosing rectangle with sides parallel to the coordinate axes.

Definition 5. *A subset D of S is a 2-cluster if the distance between vertices of D and vertices of $S - D$ is greater than $2 \cdot$ rdiam(D) or D equals S.*

It is easy to show that any two non-identical 2-clusters are either disjoint or one of them is a proper subset of the other. This property causes the 2-clusters to form in a natural way the following unique hierarchy.

Definition 6. The 2-*cluster tree* of S is a rooted tree whose nodes correspond to distinct 2-clusters, where the root corresponds to S and the leaves to single vertices in S. Let a be any internal node and let A be its corresponding 2-cluster. Then the children of a correspond to all 2-clusters C such that $C \subset A$ and there is no 2-cluster B such that $C \subset B \subset A$.

In the continuation we will by a 2-cluster also refer to its corresponding node of the 2-cluster tree and vice versa. Now, since the vertices in each 2-cluster D are closer to each other than to any vertex not in D, the convex hull of D belongs to the greedy triangulation of S. Thus we can compute the greedy triangulation of S by a depth-first search from the root of the 2-cluster tree, and computing the greedy triangulation of each 2-cluster locally when backtracking from it. In this way it is enough to consider the problem of greedy triangulating a 2-cluster D, given the greedy triangulation of each child of D.

A simple algorithm that computes the 2-cluster tree in $O(n)$ time from a EMST of S was presented in [11]. (It builds on the observation that there is a constant number of EMST edges connecting a 2-cluster with other 2-clusters.) As a byproduct of that algorithm, we receive for each 2-cluster D the shortest diagonal that has one endpoint in D and the other in a sibling of D. The following is another observation about 2-clusters that we use.

Lemma 7. (Lemma 3.3 in [11]) *For any 2-cluster D with $m \geq 2$ children, let l be the length of the shortest diagonal connecting two children of D, and let l' be the length of the longest diagonal connecting two children of D. Then the ratio between l' and l is less than 2^{2m-3}.*

4.1 Greedy Triangulation of a 2-Cluster

Let D be an arbitrary 2-cluster, and let $GT(D)$ be the set of all greedy diagonals of D that connect distinct children of D. To compute the greedy triangulation of D it is enough to compute the set $GT(D)$, since we may assume that the greedy triangulation of each child of D has been computed. Let l be the length of the shortest diagonal connecting any two children of D. We compute the greedy triangulation of D in a sequence $p_0, p_1, \ldots$ of phases. The objective of a phase p_i is to compute all greedy diagonals in $GT(D)$ of length in $[1.2^i l, 1.2^{i+1} l)$. By l_i, also called the *parameter* of phase p_i, we mean the number $1.2^i l$. By Lemma 7, if D has m children then $O(m)$ phases suffice to compute $GT(D)$.

Consider a child D' of D, and let d' be the shortest diagonal connecting D' with another child of D. Clearly, every greedy diagonal in $GT(D)$ with an endpoint in D' has length $\geq |d'|$. So D' can be ignored until we reach a phase at which we produce greedy diagonals of length $\geq |d'|$. Therefore, if i is the greatest integer such that $|d'| \geq l_i$, then D' is assigned to phase p_i. In this way we assign each child of D to a phase, and a child is kept idle until we reach the phase it is assigned to.

During the phases we augment a PSLG G (initially empty) in the following way. Before a phase p_i is executed, we augment G with the greedy triangulation of each child of D that has been assigned to phase p_i (so G may be unconnected). Then, during phase p_i, we augment G with each greedy edge produced by p_i. In this way, G becomes the greedy triangulation of D when the final phase terminates. A property of G is that none of its edges is longer than 1.2 times the length of its shortest diagonal (greedy diagonals are not necessarily computed by increasing length within a phase). Such a PSLG shall be called a *greedy PSLG*.

5 Grouping Vertices on Concave Chains

Definition 8. A *concave chain* of a greedy PSLG G is a maximal sequence $v_1, v_2, \ldots, v_m$ of at least three vertices (v_1 and v_m may be the same vertex but all others are distinct) such that for $k = 1, 2, \ldots, m-1$, (v_k, v_{k+1}) are edges of G, and for $k = 2, 3, \ldots, m-1$, v_{k-1}, v_k, v_{k+1} is a right turn and (v_k, v_{k+1}) is the next edge around v_k in clockwise order from (v_{k-1}, v_k).

Definition 9. An l-*compvertex* (compound vertex) of a greedy PSLG G is a subsequence $v_1, v_2, \ldots, v_m$ of a concave chain of G that satisfies the following properties:

1. the (straight-line) distance between v_1 and v_m is less than $\frac{l}{8}$, and
2. if we walk on the edges $(v_1, v_2), (v_2, v_3), \ldots, (v_{m-1}, v_m)$, then we do not change direction more than 45 degrees in total.

Thus the l-compvertices of G are not defined uniquely. However, we are merely interested in having a set of l-compvertices that satisfies certain properties, defined as follows.

Definition 10. A set C of l-compvertices of a greedy PSLG G is said to be *legal* if it satisfies the following properties:

1. if any two l-compvertices in C have a vertex in common, then this vertex is an endpoint of both l-compvertices,
2. any l-compvertex c in C is maximal in the sense that no vertex not belonging to an l-compvertex in C can be added to c to form another l-compvertex,
3. the set C is maximal in the sense that there is no l-compvertex of G disjoint from all l-compvertices in C, and
4. the set C is minimal in the sense that any two l-compvertices in C cannot be merged into a single l-compvertex.

Although there may be many different legal sets of l-compvertices in G, there are sufficient rules to decide whether a set of sequences of vertices of G is a legal set of l-compvertices. These rules enable the algorithm to compute efficiently a legal set of l_{i+1}-compvertices of G, having computed a legal set of l_i-compvertices, between any two phases p_i and p_{i+1}. An l-compvertex is represented by pointers to its first two and last two vertices. On the other hand, each vertex has a pointer to information concerning the (at most two) l-compvertices of which it is an endpoint. Using this structure, we can easily traverse any l-compvertex in constant time per vertex in the sequence (G is represented by a doubly connected edge list).

When a child D' of D which has been assigned to a phase p_i is added to G, the convex hull of D' consists of one concave chain (or a degenerated concave chain if D' has less than 3 vertices) and the interior of this concave chain has already been fully triangulated. Hence, a legal set of l_i-compvertices of D' is easy to find by performing one walk on the convex hull of D'. We observe that any legal set of l_i-compvertices of D' consists of at most a constant number of l_i-compvertices, since D' is contained in a rectangle of diameter less than $1.2 l_i / 2$.

Given a legal set C of l-compvertices of G, the remaining objects in our working data structure are pointers to vertices, called isolated vertices or isolvertices, which are defined below. Let v be a vertex of G. If all greedy triangles adjacent to v have been produced, then v is said to be *hidden*, otherwise we say that v is *manifest*. A manifest vertex v is called an *isolvertex* unless the following two conditions hold simultaneously: (i) there are vertices u and w such that u, v, w is a subsequence of an l-compvertex in C, and (ii) all greedy triangles incident to v and overlapping with the interior of the convex hull of u, v, w have been produced.

As our algorithm works, by inserting greedy edges in approximately increasing order according to their length, for any manifest vertex v there is at most a constant number of open regions in the immediate vicinity of v which are disjoint from produced greedy triangles and which are bounded by two edges incident to v. Therefore, we can easily keep track of each such open region at v, and remove them subsequently as they are included in greedy triangles. Thus when v is adjacent to no such open region, v becomes hidden and the pointer to v is removed from our working data structure.

A special case which we treat separately is when we have a small bipartite polygon defined as follows. A bipartite polygon P is called l-*bipartite* if, given a partition of its vertices into poles, the distance between any two vertices in the same pole is less than l.

Lemma 11. *Let G be any PSLG and let l be the length of the shortest diagonal of G. Assume that all l-bipartite polygons of G are fully triangulated, and that all edges of G that are not inside an l-bipartite polygon have length less than l. Then, given any legal set of l-compvertices of G, and any circle C of radius $O(l)$, C contains at most a constant number of l-compvertices and isolvertices of G.*

Proof. Is omitted in this short version but can be found in [12].

In the remainder of this paper, when we refer to an l_i-compvertex or isolvertex, we will mean one from some legal set of l_i-compvertices and isolvertices of the greedy PSLG G at a phase p_i. Further, when we say that two l-compvertices are connected by a diagonal, we will mean a diagonal that is disjoint from the back regions of both l-compvertices. The back region of an l-compvertex $v_1, v_2, \ldots, v_m$ is depicted in Figure 3.

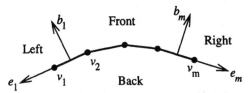

Fig. 3. The four regions of a compvertex. b_1 and b_m are semi-infinite parts of the bisectors of (v_1, v_2) and (v_{m-1}, v_m), whereas e_1 and e_m are semi-infinite parts of the straight-line extensions of (v_1, v_2) and (v_{m-1}, v_m).

We say that an l-compvertex c' is *slant* with respect to an l-compvertex c if c' has an endpoint v' such that all vertices of c are closer to v' than to any other vertex of c' (this means that no vertex of c lies in the front of c'). Finally, two l-compvertices c and c' are said to be *opposite* to each other if none of them is slant with respect to the other.

6 Computing a Phase p_i

In this section we describe the computation of a phase p_i, i.e. how all greedy diagonals in $\mathrm{GT}(D)$ of length in $[l_i, 1.2l_i)$ can be found, where D is a 2-cluster. To simplify the presentation, we will use the term *hypervertex* when we refer to either an l_i-compvertex or an isolvertex.

As an invariant we maintain for each pair of hypervertices the shortest diagonal between the pair if this diagonal exists and has length less than $1.2l_i$. Two hypervertices which are connected by such a short diagonal will be called an *interacting* pair. By $d_{min}(h, h')$ we denote the shortest diagonal between a pair (h, h') of hypervertices. All interacting pairs are kept in a pool. We define the *neighborhood* of an interacting pair (h, h') of hypervertices to be the set of all other interacting pairs (t, t') such that both t and t' have an endpoint within distance less than $5l_i$ from an endpoint of h or h' (the endpoints of an isolvertex are defined to be the isolvertex itself). The construction of the pool and neighborhoods are described in the following subsection.

Consider any pair (h, h') of hypervertices in the pool. Among all pairs (t, t') of hypervertices in the neighborhood of (h, h'), we call the one with shortest $d_{min}(t, t')$ for the *strongest* pair. If $d_{min}(h, h')$ is not longer than $d_{min}(t, t')$, where (t, t') is the strongest pair in the neighborhood of (h, h'), then it is easy to show that $d_{min}(h, h')$ is a greedy diagonal, and it is therefore produced. On the other hand, if $d_{min}(h, h')$ is longer than $d_{min}(t, t')$, then the pair (h, h') is pushed onto a stack and we try to produce $d_{min}(t, t')$ instead.

When a greedy edge between a pair (h, h') of hypervertices is produced, this edge may block the visibility between previously interacting pairs. Further, if the produced edge is incident to an l_i-compvertex, then this l_i-compvertex may be split into (at most) two new l_i-compvertices. So in the vicinity of (h, h'), we have to perform some updating of our working data structure. Among the pairs lying in the stack, only the one on top may be affected by these updates (because of the size of a neighborhood). The updates are further described in Section 6.2. The algorithm for a phase p_i is as follows, starting with an empty stack:

Phase p_i:
   loop
      if the stack is empty **then** remove from the pool any pair (h, h')
         else pop (h, h') from the stack
      endif
      let (t, t') be the strongest pair in the neighborhood of (h, h')
      if $d_{min}(t, t')$ is shorter than $d_{min}(h, h')$ **then**
         push (h, h') onto the stack
         push (t, t') onto the stack
      else
         produce the greedy diagonal $d_{min}(h, h')$
         update the data structure
      endif
      if both the stack and the pool are empty **then**
         exit loop
      endif
   endloop
end Phase p_i

6.1 Creating the Pool

For each hypervertex h, we compute the set N_h of all other hypervertices that have an endpoint within distance less than $5l_i$ from an endpoint of h. There is only a constant number of hypervertices in N_h by Lemma 11. We can therefore compute N_h in constant time by using the range searching technique developed in [10]. That technique builds basically on the construction of a threaded quadtree for S, which can be done in $O(n)$ time given the Delaunay triangulation of S. For more details we refer to [10].

Since there is only a constant number of hypervertices in N_h, we can in constant time find the set of all hypervertices that have both of their endpoints within distance $< (1.2 + 2/8)l_i = 1.45l_i$ from both endpoints of h (only these hypervertices may interact with h, since the distance between the endpoints of an l_i-compvertex is $< l_i/8$). For each of these hypervertices, say h', we compute the shortest diagonal (if it exists) between h and h'. If this diagonal has length $< 1.2l_i$ then the pair (h, h') is interacting and thus added to the pool. We will apply two different methods to compute the shortest diagonal between a pair of l_i-compvertices, depending on whether they are opposite or one of them is slant with respect to the other. Each of these two methods is described below.

Let c and c' be any pair of l_i-compvertices such that c' is slant with respect to c. Let $v_1, v_2, \ldots, v_m$ be the vertex sequence of c, and let v' be the endpoint of c' which is closest to the vertices of c. By the definition of slant compvertices, the shortest anchor of (c, c') connects v' with its mate among the vertices of c. If this anchor does not coincide with a produced greedy edge, then it is the shortest diagonal between c and c', otherwise the shortest diagonal forms a triangle with this anchor. To find the mate of v' we begin with $k = 1$ and proceed to larger k's. For each k we check each of the conditions, $|v', v_k| < |v', v_{k+1}|$ and $|v', v_{m-k+1}| < |v', v_{m-k}|$, until one of them holds. It follows from Observation 3 that the scan stops when the mate of v' has been found. (It is important to alternate the scan in this way, because it ensures that we do not consider more vertices than twice the number we would consider if we started from the best direction.)

The shortest diagonal between an isolvertex v' and an l_i-compvertex c can be found by the same technique as above, and to find the shortest diagonal between two isolvertices is trivial.

For a pair c and c' of opposite l_i-compvertices, the shortest diagonal between c and c' can be found as follows. For each vertex of one l_i-compvertex we compute its mate among the vertices of the other l_i-compvertex, thus computing all anchors of (c, c') (cf. Section 3). The shortest diagonal between c and c' is either the shortest anchor of (c, c') which does not coincide with a greedy edge connecting an endpoint of c and an endpoint of c', or it forms a triangle with such an edge. In this way we find the shortest diagonal between c and c' in linear time with respect to the number of vertices of c and c'.

6.2 Updates when a Greedy Edge is Produced

When a greedy edge e is produced, we first check whether e induces one or two l_i-bipartite polygons, in which case these polygons are triangulated in constant time per produced greedy edge as described in Section 3.

If e is incident to an l_i-compvertex c, then c may be split into (at most) two new l_i-compvertices. Further, the endpoints of e may become new isolvertices, and one or two isolvertices may become hidden (cf. Section 5). Also, previously interacting pairs do not longer interact if e blocks the visibility between them. Hence, when we produce e, we may also have to remove some interacting pairs from our working data structure and add some new interacting pairs. All these updates can be carried out in constant time due to the fact that there is only a constant number of hypervertices involved.

However, when we add new pairs of interacting hypervertices to our working data structure, we also have to compute the shortest diagonal between each pair. We do this as in the previous subsection except for pairs of opposite l_i-compvertices. For a pair (c, c') of opposite l_i-compvertices we instead maintain a data structure, which basically consists of all anchors between c and c' linked with vertices of c and c' in a special way. Using this structure, we can show that it is possible throughout the whole phase p_i to maintain the shortest diagonal between each pair consisting of interacting pieces of c and c' in total time $O(m)$, where m is the number of vertices in c and c'. For more details concerning this data structure we refer to [12].

7 The Running Time

The running time used by the algorithm to compute $GT(D)$ (all greedy diagonals connecting the children of a 2-cluster D) can be divided into various types of tasks. One task is finding shortest diagonals between interacting pairs, when those diagonals are incident to interior (non-endpoint) vertices of compvertices. For all other types of tasks, in each phase we use time linear with respect to the number of hypervertices active during the phase. Summing up over all phases, we can show that this is linear with respect to the number of diagonals in $GT(D)$. Concerning the former task, we use the ideas from Section 3 to keep the time linear with respect to the cardinality of $GT(D)$. Hence, since $GT(D)$ and $GT(D')$ are disjoint for two 2-clusters D and D', we get that the total time used to process all 2-clusters is $O(n)$. For a detailed run time analysis, we refer to [12].

8 Converting to Quasi-Greedy Triangulation

It is easy to convert our greedy triangulation algorithm into one that computes the quasi-greedy triangulation because the following three properties hold throughout the algorithm: (a) when our algorithm produces a diagonal d, then either it is produced within a bipartite polygon, or all other shorter diagonals within distance $2|d|$ from d are within bipartite polygons, (b) the mechanism for finding the next diagonal to be produced is not affected by whether we proceed by producing locally shortest or quasi-greedy diagonals, and (c) within a bipartite polygon, if the quasi-greedy diagonal is not the same as the shortest diagonal of the polygon, then it cuts off a triangle from the polygon. Hence, to compute the quasi-greedy triangulation we proceed according to the described greedy algorithm with the following exception: whenever the greedy algorithm is about to produce a diagonal d, we check whether the 6 conditions in the definition of the quasi-greedy triangulation hold. If so, then we produce the quasi-greedy diagonal crossing d.

References

1. G. Das and D. Joseph. Which triangulations approximate the complete graph. In *Proc. Inter. Symp. on Optimal Algorithms*, LNCS **401** (Springer, 1989) 168–183.
2. M. T. Dickerson, R. L. S. Drysdale, S. A. McElfresh, and E. Welzl. Fast greedy triangulation algorithms. *Proc. 10th ACM Symp. on Comp. Geom.* (1994) 211–220.
3. D. Eppstein. Approximating the minimum weight triangulation. *Disc. and Comp. Geom.* **11** (1994) 163–191.
4. P. D. Gilbert. New results in planar triangulations. Master's thesis, Univ. of Illinois, Urbana, 1979.
5. S. Goldman. A space efficient greedy triangulation algorithm. *Infor. Proc. Lett.* **31** (1989) 191–196.
6. L. Heath and S. Pemmaraju. New results for the minimum weight triangulation problem. *Algorithmica* **12** (1994) 533–552.

7. J. M. Keil. *Decomposing a Polygon into Simpler Components*. PhD thesis, Univ. of Toronto, Canada, 1983.

8. J. M. Keil. Computing a subgraph of the minimum weight triangulation. *Comp. Geom.: Theory & Appl.* **4** (1994) 13–26.

9. D. G. Kirkpatrick. A note on Delaunay and optimal triangulations. *Infor. Proc. Lett.* **10** (1980) 127–128.

10. D. Krznaric and C. Levcopoulos. Computing a threaded quadtree from the Delaunay triangulation in linear time. In *Proc. 7th CCCG* (1995) 187–192.

11. D. Krznaric and C. Levcopoulos. Computing hierarchies of clusters from the EMST in linear time. In *Proc. 15th FST&TCS*, LNCS **1026** (Springer, 1995) 443–455.

12. C. Levcopoulos and D. Krznaric. The greedy triangulation can be computed from the Delaunay in linear time. Tech. Rep. LU-CS-TR:94-136, Lund Univ., 1994.

13. C. Levcopoulos and D. Krznaric. Quasi-greedy triangulations approximating the minimum weight triangulation. In *Proc. 7th SODA* (1995) 392–401.

14. C. Levcopoulos and D. Krznaric. Tight lower bounds for minimum weight triangulation heuristics. *Infor. Proc. Lett.* **57** (1996) 129–135.

15. C. Levcopoulos and A. Lingas. Fast algorithms for greedy triangulation. *BIT* **32** (1992) 280–296.

16. C. Levcopoulos and A. Lingas. The greedy triangulation approximates the MWT and can be computed in linear time in the average case. In *Proc. ICCI*, LNCS **497** (Springer, 1991).

17. A. Lingas. *Advances in minimum weight triangulation*. PhD thesis, Linköping Univ., Sweden, 1983.

18. F. P. Preparata and M. I. Shamos. *Computational Geometry: An Introduction* (Springer, 1985).

19. D. A. Plaisted and J. Hong. A heuristic triangulation algorithm. *J. of Algorithms* **8** (1987) 405–437.

20. W. D. Smith. *Studies in Computational Geometry Motivated by Mesh Generation*. PhD thesis, Princeton Univ., 1989.

21. C. A. Wang. An optimal algorithm for greedy triangulation of a set of points. In *Proc. 6th CCCG* (1994) 332–338.

22. C. A. Wang and F. Chin. Finding the constrained Delaunay triangulation and constrained Voronoi diagram of a simple polygon in linear-time. In *Proc. 3rd ESA*, LNCS **979** (Springer, 1995) 280–294.

23. P. Yoeli. Compilation of data for computer-assisted relief cartography. In J. C. Davis and M. J. McCullagh, eds., *Display and Analysis of Spatial Data* (Wiley, 1975).

Neighbours on a Grid*

Andrej Brodnik[1] and J. Ian Munro[2]

[1] Luleå University, Luleå, Sweden; on leave from Institute of Mathematics, Physics, and Mechanics, Ljubljana, Slovenia
[2] University of Waterloo, Ontario, Canada

Abstract. We address the problem of a succinct static data structure representing points on an $M \times M$ grid ($M = 2^m$ where m is size of a word) that permits to answer the question of finding the closest point to a query point under the L_∞ or L_1 norm in constant time. Our data structure takes essentially minimum space. These results are extended to d dimensions under L_∞.

1 Introduction

Given a set of points, a query point, and a distance metric, the closest neighbour problem is that of determining the point of the set whose distance from the query point is minimal. If the query point is a member of the given set then it will be the solution, and if two or more points are of equal distance from the query point we choose one of them arbitrarily. This problem arises in many areas such as modeling of robot arm movements and integrated circuits layouts (cf. [26]). The problem has been heavily studied in the $\mathbb{R}^2$ contiguous domain where it is solved using Voronoi diagrams (cf. [29]). Furthermore, the problem can be generalized by considering the points as multidimensional records in which individual fields are drawn from an ordered domain (cf. [22]).

In this paper we describe an essentially *minimum space, constant time* solution to the *static* problem in a *discrete* $M \times M$ point universe under the L_∞ or L_1 norm. Our structure uses $M^2 + o(M^2)$ bits of memory, which differs from the information theoretic minimum by only the lower order term when a random half of the points are present. The solution is a combination of two approaches: under the first, the universe is represented by a bit map; and under the second, each point of the universe "knows" who is its closest neighbour – it has a pointer to the closest point. The advantage of the first approach is that it minimizes space required at the expense of query time. The second guarantees constant response time at the expense of space. We obtain advantages of both. Finally, we generalize the solution to d dimensional M^d-point universe (d is some predefined constant) under the L_∞ norm using $M^d + o(M^d)$ bits of space.

Our general approach is to divide the universe into regions we call *tiles* (cf. cells in [3, 4]) each covering dm ($m = \lg M$) discrete points of the universe. If any of the points in a tile are present, then we simply store a bit map representation of a tile; and if a tile is empty we store a *candidate* value. This value is the closest point in the entire set to the

---

* This work was done while the first author was a graduate student at the University of Waterloo and was supported in part by the NSERC of Canada, grant number A-8237, and the ITRC of Ontario. E-mail: Andrej.Brodnik@IMFM.Uni-Lj.SI and IMunro@UWaterloo.CA.

middle of the tile. Note that because of the choice of size of a tile, either option requires the same amount of space – dm bits. In this paper, we show that using appropriately shaped tiles the closest neighbour to any query point in a universe can be determined by inspecting constant number of tiles, while table lookup technique facilitates finding the closest element in a tile represented by a bit map.

The paper consists of three major parts: first we define the problem with some additional notation, and review the literature. The bulk of the paper deals with solutions to the problem in two dimensions. The final section explains how to extend the solution to one and d dimensions, and poses some open questions.

2 Definitions and Background

In general we deal with the set of points in d-dimensional space, $T = (x_1, \ldots, x_d)$ ($x_i \in \{0, \ldots, M-1\}$), where d is a predefined constant and coordinates are orthogonal. The distance between points $T_1 = (x_{1,1}, \ldots, x_{1,d})$ and $T_2 = (x_{2,1}, \ldots, x_{2,d})$ is measured by $\delta_f(T_1, T_2) = (\sum_{i=1}^{d} |(x_{1,i} - x_{2,i})^f|)^{\frac{1}{f}}$ for a real parameter $1 \leq f \leq \infty$ (cf. [26, p.222]). The parameter f also defines L_f, the *norm of the space*. The family of the distance functions defined this way satisfy the *triangle inequality*. Formally:

Definition 1. Let $\mathcal{N}$ ($|\mathcal{N}| = N$) be a subset of points from the universe $\mathcal{M} = [0 \ldots M]^d$. The *static closest neighbour* problem is to represent these points in a data structure so that given a query point, $T \in \mathcal{M}$, the closest member of $\mathcal{N}$, under norm L_f can be found efficiently.

Note if the query point is in the set $\mathcal{N}$, then it is its own closest neighbour, and if several points are the same distance from the query point any of them is a satisfactory answer.

In this paper we focus our attention on $f = \infty$ which, as the limit as $f \to \infty$, defines $\delta_\infty(T_1, T_2) = \max_{0 < i \leq d} |x_{1,i} - x_{2,i}|$. First, when $d = 1$ distance functions for all f are the same. Secondly, for two dimensional space ($d = 2$) Lee and Wong ([21]) proved, that search for the closest neighbour under L_∞ is computationally equivalent to search under L_1. However, direct use of their transformation increases the space, violating one of our key concerns. Therefore, we develop a solution for L_1 from scratch.

We use the extended random access machine model (ERAM) whose instruction set includes integer multiplication and division, and bitwise Boolean operations (cf. [6] and MBRAM in [14]). We assume that one register is large enough to store one coordinate of a point – it is m bits ($m = \lg M$) wide.

Our solutions consist of two parts: first we explain how to search for the closest neighbour in a small, b-point universe ($b = dm$), and second how to search in a big M^d-point universe ($M^d = 2^b$). Throughout the paper we assume that all divisions which define the size of a problem do not produce a remainder. It can be verified that by dropping this assumption, all algorithms and data structures remain correct, though the third order terms of the size of a data structure may change.

2.1 The Literature Background

Finding the closest element in a set to a query element is an important problem arising in many subfields of computer science, including computational geometry, pattern recognition, VLSI design, data compression and learning theory (cf. [11, 22, 26]). As noted, there are several versions of the problem. Clearly, the number of dimensions, d, the distance norm, typically L_2, L_1 or L_∞, and model of computation impact the appropriate choice of methods.

First consider continuous searching space (domain), $\mathbb{R}$. In a one-dimensional case all norms are equivalent. Under the comparison based model there is a simple logarithmic lower bound for the static problem, which is matched by a binary search algorithm. The same bound carries over to the dynamic problem, and is matched by any balanced tree algorithm (cf. [11]).

In two dimensions and under the Euclidean norm, L_2, the problem is also known as a *post-office* problem ([20]) and is related to the *point-location* problem (cf. [13]). The most common approach to solve it is to use Voronoi diagrams (cf. [29]) which gives, under the comparison based model, logarithmic deterministic running time using $O(N)$ words of memory (for logarithmic running time solutions see also [8, 9, 28]). Chang and Wu in [7] went outside the comparison based model. Using hashing they achieved constant running time at the cost of using, in the worst case, $O(N^2 + M)$ words. Under the same model Bentley et al. described constant expected time solution using $O(N)$ words of memory ([5]). All Voronoi diagram based approaches have similar bounds also under norms L_1 and L_∞, although the diagrams have different shapes ([21]). Yao in [29] reports that most deterministic solutions generalize to higher dimensions at the expense of using $O(N^{2^{d+1}})$ words, though there is no further discussion.

Unlike the static problem, there is no known efficient deterministic solution to the dynamic version in 2 or more dimensions. There are, however, expected poly-logarithmic time algorithms to maintain Voronoi diagrams under the comparison based model ([10]) and constant time probabilistic solutions under the random access machine model with integer division and multiplication (cf. [16, 27]). Both of these use $O(N)$ words.

Next consider a discrete domain upon which, in combination with a bounded universe, we concentrate in this work. The bounded discrete universe permits completely different data structures. For example, Karlsson ([18]), and Karlsson, Munro and Robertson ([19]) under a comparison based model, adapt the van Emde Boas et al. one-dimensional stratified trees ([15]) to two dimensions. Thus they achieve, in an $M \times M$ universe under norms L_1 and L_∞ a worst case run time of $O(\log^{(2)} M)$ using $O(N)$ words for the static problem, and for the dynamic problem a run time of $O(\log^{3/2} M)$ using $O(N \log M)$ words. On the other hand, Murphy and Selkow go outside the comparison based model and present a constant expected time probabilistic solution under L_∞ that uses $O(N)$ words of memory ([25]).

Finally, the only known lower bound under the cell probe model (cf. [24]) on the number of necessary bits for a data structure which would still allow constant query time in a bounded discrete universe is the trivial one, $\left\lceil \lg \binom{M}{N} \right\rceil$.

3 Preliminaries

3.1 Registers

The registers are m bits wide. Since in a d-dimensional universe d registers are necessary to store coordinates of an arbitrary point, we always consider d registers together. For convenience we use $b \equiv dm$ to denote the number of bits in such a grouping. We also assume b is a power of d. This simplifies the presentation, but alters only lower order terms in the space requirement. In two dimensions we view the grouping of b bits of a pair of registers as a *square register* (cf. double precision numbers):

Definition 2. A *square register* x_r consists of p rows and p columns of bits, where $p^2 = b$. The bit $x_r.b[i, j]$, for $0 \le i, j < p$, is positioned in the ith column of jth row, and the bit $x_r.b[0, 0]$ is the least significant bit of x_r. A square register with all bits set below its major (minor) diagonal is denoted by $P^{\backslash}$ ($P^{/}$).

Square registers are just a helpful logical abstraction – a different interpretation of a number ([6]). Thus a processor can perform all standard operations on them (e.g. shifts, bitwise Boolean operations, etc.). We will find it helpful to determine the extreme set bits in a square register, that is the left, the right, the top, and the bottom most set bit. If there is more than one extreme set bit in a certain direction (e.g. the left most), the ties are broken arbitrarily. In particular:

Theorem 3. *Using a fixed table of size $O(M^\epsilon)$, for any $0 < \epsilon \le 1$, we can find the extremal set bits of a square register in constant time.*

Proof. We divide the register into k pieces, all of the same shape in their geometric interpretation. Each $\frac{b}{k}$-bit piece is used as an index to a table. The corresponding table value gives the extremal bit, in each direction of the piece. Each table entry takes $4 \cdot (\lg b - \lg k)$ bits and there are $2^{\frac{b}{k}} = 2^{\frac{2m}{k}} = M^{\frac{2}{k}}$ entries. A search takes time $O(k)$. To satisfy the space constraint, and avoid lower order terms we set ϵ to a little less than $\frac{2}{k}$, that is k is a little more than $\frac{2}{\epsilon}$. $\qquad\qquad\square$

3.2 Geometry

The geometric background of this subsection provides a simple description of the area of the universe where the closest neighbour to the query point can lie. Though the background is essentially norm independent, it is most efficiently applied under the L_∞ and L_1 norms where the above mentioned area is small enough that it can be exhaustively searched. By a *circle* we mean a set of points that are equidistant from some central point under the norm that is being used. So, for example, under L_∞ a circle is a square aligned with the axes and under L_1 it has a diamond shape. For illustration of individual terms introduced in this section see Fig. 1. We divide (tile) the universe $\mathcal{M}$ into tiles with the following properties: they have to tile the plane in a regular pattern such that from the coordinates of a point we can efficiently compute the tile in which it lies; and if we put a circle with diameter m anywhere on a plane, it must lie in $O(1)$ tiles. Obviously there are many different tilings which satisfy the above conditions, but for the purpose of simplicity of explanation we choose to define:

Definition 4. A *tile* is a $p \times p$ square. The tiles sharing a common edge with a given tile are its *direct neighbours*.

For convenience, we number the direct neighbours of a tile $\mathcal{T}_0$ in a clockwise manner starting with $\mathcal{T}_1$ at the top. Hence, the direct neighbours of $\mathcal{T}_0$ are $\mathcal{T}_1$ through $\mathcal{T}_4$. Next:

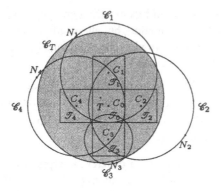
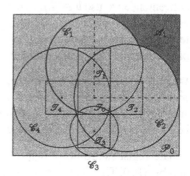

Fig. 1. Circle of candidates $\mathscr{C}_T$ with empty circles $\mathscr{C}_{1-4}$, and empty circles with the enclosing polygon $\mathscr{P}_0$ and the corner area $\mathscr{A}_1$.

Definition 5. Let C_x be the middle of a tile $\mathscr{T}_x$, then $\mathscr{C}_x$, the *empty circle* of $\mathscr{T}_x$, is the largest circle with centre C_x whose *interior* is empty. Thus, if N_x is the closest neighbour of C_x, N_x lies on the circumference of $\mathscr{C}_x$. Note that C_x need not be a point in the discrete domain.

Based on the tile definition and empty circles we define an *enclosing rectangle*:

Definition 6. Let $\mathscr{T}_0$ be a tile and let $\{\mathscr{C}_i\}$ be the empty circles of its respective direct neighbours. Then, $\mathscr{P}_0$, the *enclosing rectangle* of $\mathscr{T}_0$, is the smallest rectangle that has sides parallel to $\mathscr{T}_0$ and includes all empty circles.

A particularly interesting part of the plane is the area which is inside the enclosing rectangle, but outside the empty circles. In order to properly identify this area we define first a *wedge*:

Definition 7. Let $\mathscr{T}_0$ be a tile, and $\mathscr{P}_0$ its enclosing rectangle as above. Let $\mathscr{T}_i$ and $\mathscr{T}_j$ (where $j = (i \bmod 4) + 1$) be direct neighbours of $\mathscr{T}_0$. Further, draw lines from C_0 through C_i, and from C_0 through C_j. Then the rectangle defined by these two lines and sides of the enclosing rectangle is called a *wedge* of the enclosing rectangle.

Obviously, if we draw lines from C_0 through middles of all direct neighbours, we split $\mathscr{P}_0$ into 4 wedges. Inside the wedge we define a *corner area*:

Definition 8. Consider the wedge defined by direct neighbours $\mathscr{T}_i$ and $\mathscr{T}_j$ as above. Then the area that lies inside the wedge and outside empty circles of all direct neighbours is called a *corner area* $\mathscr{A}_i$.

Since the number of corner areas is at most the number of wedges, which is itself at most 4, it follows that:

Lemma 9. *There are at most 4 corner areas.*

The last term used in our discussion is the *circle of candidates*:

Definition 10. Let the point T lie on the tile $\mathcal{T}_0$ and let C_i $(0 < i \leq 4)$ be middle points of respective direct neighbours with their closest neighbours N_i. Further, among all points N_i, let N_x be the closest point to T. Then the circle $\mathcal{C}_T$ with centre at T and N_x on its circumference is called the *circle of candidates*.

Finally, based on Definition 10 and Definition 5, we can restrict the location of the closest neighbour of a given point:

Lemma 11. *Let T be a point on $\mathcal{T}_0$. Then the closest neighbour of T lies on the circumference or inside the circle of candidates $\mathcal{C}_T$, and outside the interior of the empty circles $\mathcal{C}_i$, where $0 < i \leq 4$.*

Lemma 11 concludes our brief geometrical excursion and hints at the idea behind our algorithm: compute empty circles of direct neighbours, compute the circle of candidates and search its intersection with the union of complements of empty circles. Later we will show, that under norm L_∞ the intersection lies inside corner areas, and that the corner areas are small enough that we can perform an exhaustive search on them.

4 When Circles are Squares: L_∞

We explore first the L_∞ norm. Under this norm, "circles" have a square shape.

4.1 The Small Universe

The small universe is a square containing order $b = 2m$ points. We represent it by a square register. We map the point $T = (x_1, x_2)$ to a bit $b[x_1, x_2]$ of the register and denote the point's presence or absence by setting the bit to 1 or 0 respectively.

The search algorithm is based on the idea of a search inside 4 distinct *search regions* (see Fig. 2):

Definition 12. Let $T = (x_1, x_2)$ be a query point, at which a *left border line* and a *right border line* with slopes $+45°$ and $-45°$ respectively, cross. These lines divide a plane into four *search regions* $\mathcal{R}_\uparrow$, $\mathcal{R}_\rightarrow$, $\mathcal{R}_\downarrow$, and $\mathcal{R}_\leftarrow$.

In order to search one region at a time, we eliminate points from other regions. This requires that we generate proper masks. These masks are square registers with all bits of $\mathcal{R}_\uparrow$ (respectively $\mathcal{R}_\rightarrow$, $\mathcal{R}_\downarrow$, and $\mathcal{R}_\leftarrow$) and none others set.

Lemma 13. *Let the left and right border lines cross at point $T = (x_1, x_2)$. Then we can generate masks for all four search regions in constant time using $O(m)$ bits of space.*

Proof. Each border line splits the plane into a positive and a negative half-plane, where the negative half-plane lies below the respective border line. In Fig. 2 the half-planes are denoted by $\mathcal{R}_{+\backslash}$, $\mathcal{R}_{-\backslash}$, $\mathcal{R}_{+/}$ and $\mathcal{R}_{-/}$.

It is easy to see that masks for half-planes $\mathcal{R}_{-\backslash}$ and $\mathcal{R}_{-/}$ can be generated in constant time by proper shifting of $P^\backslash$ and $P^/$ respectively. Finally, masks for the search regions can be computed using formulae: $\mathcal{R}_\downarrow = \mathcal{R}_{-\backslash} \wedge \mathcal{R}_{-/}, \mathcal{R}_\uparrow = \overline{\mathcal{R}_{-\backslash} \vee \mathcal{R}_{-/}}$, $\mathcal{R}_\leftarrow = \overline{\mathcal{R}_{-/}} \vee \mathcal{R}_\uparrow$, and $\mathcal{R}_\rightarrow = \overline{\mathcal{R}_{-\backslash}} \vee \mathcal{R}_\uparrow$. □

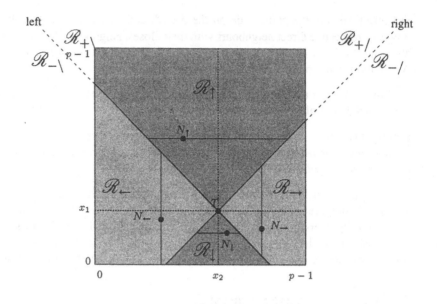

Fig. 2. Four search regions in a plane.

Using Lemma 13 we can easily prove:

Theorem 14. *Let the universe be a set of $b = 2m$ discrete points on a square grid and let $\mathcal{N}$ be some subset of this universe. Then there is an algorithm to find the closest neighbour to a query point in $\mathcal{N}$ under norm L_∞ in constant time using b bits for a data structure and $O(M^\epsilon)$ bits for internal constants.*

Internal constants in the text of the theorem are the constants used by the algorithm and thus they are the same for all possible sets.

Proof. As a data structure representing the set we use the obvious bit map stored in a b-bit square register. The search algorithm divides the plane into four search regions from Definition 12. It then determines the closest point to the query point T in each region. Because of the norm we are using this amounts, for $\mathcal{R}_\downarrow$ and $\mathcal{R}_\uparrow$, to finding the point in the row closest to T and, for $\mathcal{R}_\leftarrow$ and $\mathcal{R}_\rightarrow$, to finding the point in the closest column (see Fig. 2). Since the universe is represented by a square register, we can employ Theorem 3.   □

4.2   The Big Universe

Since the sides of a tile are parallel to the axes of the coordinate system, this also implies the orientation of an enclosing rectangle $\mathcal{P}_0$ to be parallel to the axes of the coordinate system. Further, the empty circles and the circle of candidates are also squares with sides parallel to coordinate axes. Thus, circles, tiles, and enclosing rectangles all have parallel sides. Finally, a tile contains $b = p \times p$ points.

The remaining entities of interest are the corner areas. Under the L_∞ norm, the corner areas have the following useful property:

Lemma 15. *Let $\mathcal{T}_0$ be some tile. Then there are at most four corner areas associated with $\mathcal{T}_0$, each of which lies on at most six tiles.*

Proof. By Lemma 9 there are at most four corner areas. Without loss of generality we confine our attention to $\mathcal{A}_1$ (see Fig. 3). Let a_1 and a_2 be the radii of $\mathcal{C}_1$ and $\mathcal{C}_2$ respectively. First, assume that either a_1 or a_2 is at least p and let the sides of $\mathcal{A}_1$ be of lengths u and v (see the left diagram in Fig. 3). Then, since the distance from C_2 to the top side of $\mathcal{P}_0$ is $v + a_2 = p + a_1$ and since the distance from C_1 to the right side of $\mathcal{P}_0$ is $u + a_1 = p + a_2$, $u + v = 2p$ and, consequently, $0 \le u, v \le 2p$. Furthermore, the area of $\mathcal{A}_1$ is $u \cdot v \le p^2 = b$. Thus, $\mathcal{A}_1$ lies on at most 6 tiles.

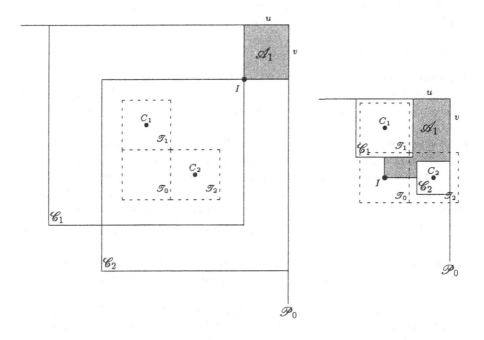

Fig. 3. The corner area $\mathcal{A}_1$ is limited by a distance between centres of empty circles $\mathcal{C}_1$ and $\mathcal{C}_2$.

On the other hand, if $a_1, a_2 \le p$, then $\mathcal{A}_1$ lies on both tiles adjacent to $\mathcal{T}_1$ and $\mathcal{T}_2$ (the right diagram in Fig. 3). It is not hard to verify that $\mathcal{A}_1$ lies on at most three other tiles and that this occurs when $p \ge a_1, a_2 \ge \frac{p}{2}$. $\qquad\square$

The most important consequence of Lemma 15 is that corner areas can be exhaustively searched in constant time using Theorem 14.

The next property relates the circle of candidates and the enclosing rectangle:

Lemma 16. *Under the norm L_∞, the circle of candidates lies inside the enclosing rectangle.*

Proof. Let the middle of tile $\mathcal{T}_0$ be point $C_0 = (0,0)$ and let $T = (x_T, y_T)$ be a query point where $-\frac{p}{2} < x_T, y_T < \frac{p}{2}$. By definition the radius of the circle of candidates is $r_T = \min_{1 \le i \le 4} \delta_\infty(T, N_i)$, where N_i are closest neighbours of middles of direct neighbours. Thus, we have to show, for all points U on the circumference of the enclosing rectangle $\mathcal{P}_0$, that $\delta_\infty(T, U) \ge r_T$.

Without loss of generality, we may assume that the closest point to T on the circumference is $W = (x_W, y_W)$ where $y_W = y_T$. By the definition of the enclosing polygon (Definition 6), x_W is either $-\delta_\infty(C_4, N_4) - p$ or $\delta_\infty(C_2, N_2) + p$. Again without loss of generality, we may assume $x_W = -\delta_\infty(C_4, N_4) - p$ and thus $\delta_\infty(T, W) = |x_T - p - \delta_\infty(C_4, N_4)| = |x_T - p| + \delta_\infty(C_4, N_4)$. However, since tile $\mathcal{T}_4$ is immediately to the left of $\mathcal{T}_0$, $C_4 = (-p, 0)$ and hence $\delta_\infty(T, C_4) = |x_T - p|$. Therefore, using a triangle inequality, we get $\delta_\infty(T, W) = \delta_\infty(T, C_4) + \delta_\infty(C_4, N_4) \ge \delta_\infty(T, N_4) \ge \min_{1 \le i \le 4} \delta_\infty(T, N_i) = r_T$. $\qquad\square$

We can now state:

Theorem 17. *Let the universe be the grid of $M \times M$ points and let $\mathcal{N}$ be some subset. Then there is an algorithm which finds the closest neighbour in $\mathcal{N}$ to a query point under the norm L_∞ in constant time using $M^2 + \frac{M^2}{2 \lg M} + O(M^\epsilon)$ bits of memory.*

Proof sketch. First, we tile universe with an $\frac{M}{p} \times \frac{M}{p}$ array of b-point tiles. With each tile there is associated a bit, which indicates whether the tile is nonempty. If the tile is nonempty it is represented by a bit map and if it is empty we store coordinates of the closest neighbour to the centre of the tile. Since the space needed for either of the stored entities is the same (b bits), the whole data structure occupies $(\frac{M}{p})^2 \cdot b + (\frac{M}{p})^2 = M^2 + \frac{M^2}{2 \lg M}$ bits. An additional $O(M^\epsilon)$ bits are used for the table to find extreme set bits.

Next, circles (empty and circle of candidates) are implicitly defined by the centre and a point on the circumference. Therefore, all circles can be constructed in constant time.

Finally, according to Lemma 11, to find the closest neighbour of T we search that part of interior of circle of candidates $\mathscr{C}_T$ which is outside empty circles $\mathscr{C}_1$, $\mathscr{C}_2$, $\mathscr{C}_3$, and $\mathscr{C}_4$. By Lemma 16, $\mathscr{C}_T$ lies inside the enclosing polygon, and thus it is sufficient to search the corner areas. According to Lemma 15, each corner area overlaps at most six tiles. Finally, by Theorem 14 each tile can be searched in constant time, and hence the closest neighbour can be found in constant time. $\qquad\square$

5 When Circles are Diamonds: L_1

Under L_1, the distance between $T_1 = (x_1, y_1)$ and $T_2 = (x_2, y_2)$ is defined as $\delta_1(T_1, T_2) = |x_1 - x_2| + |y_1 - y_2|$. The "circles" under this norm have a diamond shape; they are squares rotated $45°$ from the axes. Though the mapping

$$x' = x - y \qquad y' = x + y \tag{1}$$

of the point (x, y) under L_1 into the point (x', y') under L_∞ preserves the closest neighbourhood property (cf. [21]) and keeps all values integer, its straightforward application increases the domain to $2M \times 2M$ points and so quadruples the space bound of the data structure. Therefore, to achieve the space bound $M^2 + o(M^2)$ bits, we sketch a solution built from scratch:

Theorem 18. *Let the size of a universe be at most $M \times M$ points and let $\mathcal{N}$ be a subset. Then there is an algorithm which finds the closest neighbour in $\mathcal{N}$ to a query point under norm L_1 in constant time using $M^2 + \frac{M^2}{2m} + M \cdot \frac{2m+1}{\sqrt{m}} + O(M^\epsilon)$ bits of memory ($m = \lg M$).*

Proof sketch. The search itself employs ideas explained in Lemma 11 and used under L_∞. This time we tile the universe with diamonds (see above) which requires a few minor changes in some definitions, but keeps Lemmata 15 and 16 correct. As in Theorem 17, our data structure consists of an array of bit maps (or pointers) and an array of bits. Since this time the sides of a tile are not aligned with coordinate axes we have more tiles (the border ones are broken though) and thus a larger third order term in a space bound.

In contrast with L_∞ the bit map is stored in *two* m-bit registers. The points of a tile are mapped into registers using slightly modified mapping from the eq. (1): odd rows are mapped into one register and the even ones into the other register. This ensures the total number of bits in both registers is the same as the number of points in the tile. It also permits us to use Theorem 3 for search inside each register and thus inside a non-empty tile (for details see [6, § 5.4.3.]). □

6 Final Improvements and Generalizations

Obviously, Theorem 17 remains valid for the one-dimensional case with an appropriate change of tiles to line segments. Furthermore, using hyper-cuboidal registers (yet another interpretation of a number) and hyper-cubic tiling of d-dimensional space, we can extend the result also to higher dimensions under L_∞:

Theorem 19. *Let the d-dimensional universe be set of M^d points and let $\mathcal{N}$ be a subset of it. Then there is an algorithm which finds the closest neighbour in $\mathcal{N}$ of a query point under norm L_∞ by searching $O(d^2 \cdot 2^d) = O(1)$ tiles (each in $O(1)$ time) and using $M^d + \frac{M^d}{d \lg M} + O(M^\epsilon)$ bits of memory.*

The only aspect of the extension that requires care is keeping the number of tiles being searched down to $O(d^2 \cdot 2^d)$. A naive implementation searches $O(d^2 \cdot 6^d)$.

Further, by a simple replacement of the pointer to the closest point to the middle of the tile with a pointer to the tile on which this closest point lies we get:

Corollary 20. *Let the universe have dimensions $\{S_1, S_2, \ldots S_d\}$, where $0 < W = \prod_{i=1}^{d} S_i \leq dm \cdot 2^{dm+1}$, and let $\mathcal{N}$ be a subset of it. Then there is an algorithm which finds the closest neighbour in $\mathcal{N}$ of a query point under norm L_∞ in constant time using $W + \frac{W}{d \lg M} + O(M^\epsilon)$ bits of memory.*

In the described solution we use table lookup technique to find extreme set bits in square registers. This technique requires $O(M^\epsilon)$ bits of space. However, there is another algorithm which also finds extreme set bits under the same model in constant time, but it requires only $O(m)$ bits of memory (cf. [6, Theorem 4.3]). This algorithm employs the technique of performing many Boolean or small domain operations on a computer word in a single processor instruction. We call the technique *word-size parallelism* ([6, Chapter 4]) although the approach has been used by others without giving it a name. For example, computation of $\lfloor \lg x \rfloor$ ([17]), bitonic sorting ([1]), tight packing of fields ([2]) can all be considered specific instances of this technique. Replacing the table lookup technique with the above mentioned algorithm obviously decreases the last term in space requirements of our solutions.

In our solutions we side-stepped the problem of the data structure initialization. It can be seen that it takes $2d$ sweeps of the universe (cf. [12, 23]) and the time necessary to construct the table for search of extreme set bits. Since the time of one sweep is proportional to the number of tiles, the initialization takes time $O(\frac{M^d}{\log M} + M^\epsilon)$.

Finally, our approach does not seem to work under other norms L_f ($1 < f < \infty$, e.g. Euclidean L_2). Under these norms each corner area can lie on $\Theta(\frac{M}{\sqrt{b}})$ tiles, and thus, we can not exhaustively search all of them (Lemma 15 does not hold). Even adding $O(1)$ more empty circles does not improve the situation significantly. The reason the technique does not seem to work is the difference in curvatures of the circle of candidates and the empty circles. However, there remains the open question of how many tiles the discrete points of a corner areas can intersect. We conjecture that this number is also too large. It is possible to use more than four, but still a constant number, of empty circles and obtain an *approximate* solution. It remains open to be determined how good an approximation this gives.

References

1. S. Albers and T. Hagerup. Improved parallel integer sorting without concurrent writting. In *3rd ACM-SIAM Symposium on Discrete Algorithms*, pages 463–472, Orlando, Florida, 1992.
2. A. Andersson, T. Hagerup, S. Nilsson, and R. Raman. Sorting in linear time? In *27th ACM Symposium on Theory of Computing*, pages 427–436, Las Vegas, Nevada, 1995.
3. J.L. Bentley and J.H. Friedman. Data structures for range searching. *ACM Computing Surveys*, 11(4):397–409, 1979.
4. J.L. Bentley and H.A. Maurer. Efficient worst-case data structures for range searching. *Acta Informatica*, 13:155–168, 1980.
5. J.L. Bentley, B.W. Weide, and A.C. Yao. Optimal expected-time algorithms for closest-point problems. *ACM Transactions on Mathematical Software*, 6(4):563–580, December 1980.
6. A. Brodnik. *Searching in Constant Time and Minimum Space* (MINIMÆRES MAGNI MOMENTI SUNT). PhD thesis, University of Waterloo, Waterloo, Ontario, Canada, 1995. (Also published as technical report CS-95-41.).
7. C.-C. Chang and T.-C. Wu. A hashing-oriented nearest neighbor searching scheme. *Pattern Recognition Letters*, 14(8):625–630, August 1993.
8. B. Chazelle. An improved algorithm for the fixed-radius neighbor problem. *Information Processing Letters*, 16(4):193–198, May 13th 1983.
9. B. Chazelle, R. Cole, F.P. Preparata, and C. Yap. New upper bounds for neighbor searching. *Information and Control*, 68(1–3):105–124, 1986.

10. Y.-J. Chiang and R. Tamassia. Dynamic algorithms in computational geometry. *Proceedings of the IEEE*, 80(9):1412–1434, September 1992.

11. T.H. Cormen, C.E. Leiserson, and R.L. Rivest. *Introduction to Algorithms*. MIT Press, Cambridge, Massachusetts, 1990.

12. C.R. Dyer and A. Rosenfeld. Parallel image processing by memory-augmented cellular automata. *IEEE Transactions on Pattern Analysis and Machine Intelligence*, 3(1):29–41, January 1981.

13. H. Edelsbrunner. *Algorithms in Combinatorial Geometry*. EATCS Monographs in Theoretical Computer Science. Springer-Verlag, Berlin, 1987.

14. P. van Emde Boas. Machine models and simulations. In J. van Leeuwen, editor, *Handbook of Theoretical Computer Science*, volume A: Algorithms and Complexity, chapter 1, pages 1 – 66. Elsevier, Amsterdam, Holland, 1990.

15. P. van Emde Boas, R. Kaas, and E. Zijlstra. Design and implementation of an efficient priority queue. *Mathematical Systems Theory*, 10(1):99–127, 1977.

16. A. Faragó, T. Linder, and G. Lugosi. Nearest neighbor search and classification in $O(1)$ time. *Problems of Control and Information Theory*, 20:383 – 395, 1991.

17. M.L. Fredman and D.E. Willard. Surpassing the information theoretic bound with fusion trees. *Journal of Computer and System Sciences*, 47:424–436, 1993.

18. R.G. Karlsson. *Algorithms in a Restricted Universe*. PhD thesis, University of Waterloo, Waterloo, Ontario, Canada, 1984. (Also published as technical report CS-84-50.).

19. R.G. Karlsson, J.I. Munro, and E.L. Robertson. The nearest neighbor problem on bounded domains. In W. Brauer, editor, *Proceedings 12th International Colloquium on Automata, Languages and Programming*, volume 194 of *Lecture Notes in Computer Science*, pages 318–327. Springer-Verlag, 1985.

20. D.E. Knuth. *The Art of Computer Programming: Sorting and Searching*, volume 3. Addison-Wesley, Reading, Massachusetts, 1973.

21. D.T. Lee and C.K. Wong. Voronoi diagrams in L_1 (L_∞) metrics with 2-storage applications. *SIAM Journal on Computing*, 9(1):200–211, February 1980.

22. K. Mehlhorn. *Data Structures and Algorithms: Multi-dimensional Searching and Computational Geometry*, volume 3. Springer-Verlag, Berlin, 1984.

23. R. Miller and Q.F. Stout. Geometric algorithms for digitized pictures on a mesh-connected computer. *IEEE Transactions on Pattern Analysis and Machine Intelligence*, 7(2):216–228, March 1985.

24. P.B. Miltersen. Lower bounds for union-split-find related problems on random access machines. In *26th ACM Symposium on Theory of Computing*, pages 625–634, Montréal, Québec, Canada, 1994.

25. O.J. Murphy and S.M. Selkow. The efficiency of using k-d trees for finding nearest neighbors in discrete space. *Information Processing Letters*, 23(4):215–218, November 8th 1986.

26. F.P. Preparata and M.I. Shamos. *Computational Geometry*. Texts and Monographs in Computer Science. Springer-Verlag, Berlin, 2nd edition, 1985.

27. V. Ramasubramanian and K.K. Paliwal. An efficient approximation-elimination algorithm for fast nearest-neighbour search based on a spherical distance coordinate formulation. *Pattern Recognition Letters*, 13(7):471–480, July 1992.

28. R.F. Sproull. Refinements to nearest-neighbor searching in k-dimensional trees. *Algorithmica*, 6:579 – 589, 1991.

29. F.F. Yao. Computational geometry. In J. van Leeuwen, editor, *Handbook of Theoretical Computer Science*, volume A: Algorithms and Complexity, chapter 7, pages 343 – 389. Elsevier, Amsterdam, Holland, 1990.

On Two Dimensional Packing *

Yossi Azar[1], Leah Epstein[2]

[1] Dept. of Computer Science, Tel-Aviv University. ***
[2] Dept. of Computer Science, Tel-Aviv University. †

Abstract. The paper considers *packing of rectangles* into an infinite bin. Similar to the *Tetris game*, the rectangles arrive from the top and, once placed, cannot be moved again. The rectangles are moved inside the bin to reach their place. For the case in which rotations are allowed, we design an algorithm whose performance ratio is constant. In contrast, if rotations are not allowed, we show that no algorithm of constant ratio exists. For this case we design an algorithm with performance ratio of $O(\log \frac{1}{\epsilon})$, where ϵ is the minimum width of any rectangle. We also show that no algorithm can achieve a better ratio than $\Omega(\sqrt{\log \frac{1}{\epsilon}})$ for this case.

1 Introduction

In this paper we consider the problem of orthogonal packing. We are given a bin with a fixed width (assuming equal to 1, without loss of generality) and an unbounded height, and also a set of open oriented rectangles. The rectangles have to be placed in the bin with the bottom of the rectangle parallel to the bottom of the bin. The spaces occupied by different rectangles may not overlap. The original rectangle packing problem was first proposed in 1980, by Baker et al. [1]. They present an approximation algorithm that achieves a performance ratio of 3 for rectangles and 2 for squares. Coffman et al. [7] present various algorithms with better performance ratio, and in particular split fit that has ratio of 1.5. We discuss the version of the problem, in which each rectangle has to be placed before the next one arrives.

There are a few models, which differ in the allowed movements inside the bin. In the original two-dimensional packing problem, a rectangle could be placed directly in any free space of the size of the rectangle, and the concept of getting into a place was not discussed. In contrast, in our models, a rectangle arrives from the top (similar to the Tetris game), and should be moved continuously around only in the free space until it reaches its place, (see figure 1), and then cannot be moved again. Moreover, it is possible either to allow rotations or not.

---

* This work was submitted as part of the M.Sc. thesis of the second author.

*** E-Mail: azar@math.tau.ac.il. Research supported in part by Allon Fellowship and by the Israel Science Foundation administered by the Israel Academy of Sciences.

† E-Mail: lea@math.tau.ac.il.

If rotations are allowed, the rectangle may be rotated at any stage, and can be assigned on its side or on its bottom. If rotations are not allowed, the rectangle may only be moved with its bottom parallel to the bottom of the bin. It is also possible, to consider the integer case in which all widths and heights of rectangles are integers. In this case, the width of the bin is also an integer. We note that

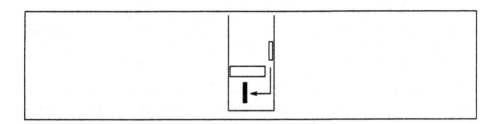

Fig. 1. The narrow rectangle moves continuously in the unoccupied space to its place.

our model in which the rectangles are not assigned directly, but should reach their place in a free space movement, makes on line packing difficult. (Since wide rectangles block those who follow them). One possible application for this model is loading trucks with boxes, since while loading a truck, it is impossible to put anything under a large box that has already been packed (see figure 2). Also, the integer model with free space movement and rotations resembles the well known Tetris game. The main difference between the game, and our models is the goal. Our goal is to minimize the total height used, and in the Tetris game, the goal is, roughly, to maximize the number of full rows. The cost of the

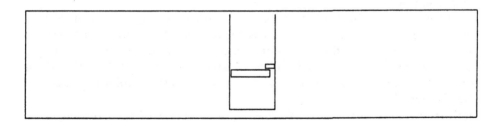

Fig. 2. The big rectangle blocks the smaller rectangle

algorithm is measured by the height of the packing, i.e. the maximum height, measured from the bottom of the bin, that is occupied by some rectangle. As usual, we try to compute the ratio between the cost of the on-line packing and the optimal off-line packing (the best packing that can be done for this sequence of rectangles).

The main results presented in this paper are as follows:

- A 4 competitive algorithm for the model with rotation.
- An $\Omega(\sqrt{\log \frac{1}{\epsilon}})$ lower bound for the model without rotation, for the case that the width is bounded below by ϵ or/and bounded above by $1 - \epsilon$. This implies that there is no competitive algorithm for the unbounded width case. Our lower bound holds for deterministic and randomised algorithms.
- An $O(\log \frac{1}{\epsilon})$ algorithm for the model without rotation for the case when widths are bounded below by ϵ or/and bounded above by $1 - \epsilon$.
- A 4 competitive algorithm for squares in both models. This immediately follows from the first result and the fact that squares do not change their form when rotated.

It is interesting to note that although the two main algorithms that we present (one without rotation, and one with rotation) are quite similar, there is a substantial difference in their analysis and performance.

We note that, Karloff [14], independently, provided a lower bound of $\Omega(\sqrt{\log \frac{1}{\epsilon}})$ for deterministic algorithms for the case where only up and down movements are allowed. It does not seem obvious to extend his bound for randomised algorithms or for algorithms with arbitrary movements.

Other related work. A special case of the problem considered in the model without rotations is, when all widths are equal. In fact this is equivalent to the list scheduling problem, that was first studied by Graham [12] and later in [2, 4, 11, 5, 15, 3].

In the case that all heights of the rectangles are equal it can be easily shown that the packing should consist of strips of that height. This problem is similar to the one-dimensional bin packing problem, since we can treat each strip as a bin. However the problems are not equivalent since full strips can block rectangles to reach other strips. Bin packing has been widely studied. Results on on-line bin packing appear in [13, 18, 16, 17]

The problem in which the rectangles are packed directly into bounded bins has been also studied. Here the goal is to minimize the number of bins. For the on-line version, constant competitive algorithms have been designed in [8]. Improvements and lower bounds on the constant appear in [8, 9, 6, 10, 17]. In both [10, 17] three dimensional packing of boxes into three dimensional bins is also considered.

Definitions and notations. We consider sequences σ of open rectangles r_i. The rectangles have to be packed into a bin of infinite height. Each rectangle, r_i has a width w_i (a real number between 0 and 1), and a height h_i (also real). The cost of the algorithm is measured by the maximum height, measured from the bottom of the bin, that is occupied by some rectangle of the packing. We denote the optimal off-line cost for the sequence by $C_{Opt}(\sigma)$, (or C_{Opt}, if the sequence is clear from the context). This is the smallest height that the sequence can occupy. The on-line algorithm's cost for σ is denoted by $C_{on}(\sigma)$, (or C_{on}). An on-line algorithm has competitive ratio cr if for all σ

$$C_{on} \le cr \cdot C_{Opt} + c_1$$

for some constant c_1. We also use the notation of $A(\sigma)$, which is the total area of the rectangles in σ i.e. $A(\sigma) = \sum_i w_i h_i$.

2 The Model With Rotations

We first discuss the model in which rotations are allowed. Here we obviously assume that both the width and the height of each rectangle is bounded by 1. The most natural thing to do is to rotate the rectangles and assign them on their wide side. Unfortunately, it can be shown that this method does not work well. In fact, our algorithm assigns the rectangles on their narrow side. Our algorithm divides the bin into horizontal strips, one on top of the other. Each strip will be used for a certain range of heights of rectangles. Let W and α be real constants: $0 < \alpha < 1$ and $0 < W < \frac{1}{2}$.

The Algorithm A: When a rectangle arrives, it is first rotated on its narrow side and then is placed as follows:

1. If the rectangle is a buffer (i.e the width after rotation is at least W), a new strip of height of the buffer is open for it and the buffer is placed into the strip to the left.
2. If the rectangle is not a buffer, it is placed into a strip with the height equal to that of the rectangle rounded up to the closest power of α. The algorithm checks if there is such a strip that is reachable by the rectangle and the total width of all the rectangles in this strip (including the new rectangle) does not exceed $1 - W$. If there is such a strip, the rectangle is assigned there, otherwise, a new strip is opened on top of all previous strips, and the rectangle is placed there to the left.

If a piece can reach some open strip of the suitable height, and can be placed there, it is placed into the lowest strip of this type, next to the pieces that are already there to the left. We call rectangles of width between W and $1 - W$ small buffers, and those of width between $1 - W$ and 1, large buffers. Note that only large buffers might block some future rectangles from getting into a suitable place since we try to assign only non-buffers in previous strips.

Theorem 1. *If we choose $W = \frac{1}{4}$ and $\alpha = \frac{2}{3}$, then the algorithm A is 4-competitive.*

Proof. Since all heights are bounded (the width and the height of the rectangle are bounded by 1), we allow an additive constant. We are going to show that $C_{on} \le 4 \cdot C_{Opt} + 3$. We define a strip as full, if the sum of the widths of the rectangles that were placed in it is at least $1 - 2W$, and non-full otherwise. We denote the subsequence of large buffers by $B_1, B_2, ..., B_k$. To prove the theorem it is enough to show that at least a fraction W of the area is occupied (except a height of $1/(1 - \alpha)$) and thus

$$C_{Opt} \ge A(\sigma) \ge W \cdot (C_{on} - \frac{1}{1 - \alpha}) .$$

We first consider strips in which small buffers were put. Since the width of buffers is at least W, those strips are at least W full. We ignore the first strip of each height that was ever opened, if it is non-full. The total height we ignore is bounded by $\sum_{i \geq 0} \alpha^i = 1/(1-\alpha)$. Consider the other non-full strips. We associate each non-full strip with a large buffer or full strip, depending on which of three ways a strip is opened:

- The first strip of a certain height (which we already considered).
- A large buffer blocks it from getting into a strip. We associate the strip with the highest buffer that blocked the rectangle, and caused the opening of the strip.
- A rectangle did not fit into the last strip of this height. The last strip must be full, otherwise any rectangle which is not a buffer would fit there. We associate the new strip with the last strip.

Note that for each buffer, there can be only one strip of each height associated with it, and for each full strip, only one non-full strip associated with it. Consider the full strips with no non-full strips associated with them. Those strips are at least α full in the height, and at least $1-2W$ full in the width. The occupied area is at least $\alpha(1-2W)$. We now compute the occupied area for the full strips with the non-full strips. If we put all the rectangles in one strip, the width would be at least $1-W$, since the rectangles did not fit into one strip together. The strip would be α full in the height, and the two strips together would be $\alpha(1-W)/2$ full, because of the second strip of the same height. As for the large buffers, each buffer was associated with a few strips, at most one of each height. Assume that the total height of those strips for a certain buffer is h, $0 \leq h \leq \frac{1}{1-\alpha}$ the height of the buffer is $h(B_i)$ and the width is $w(B_i)$. Since this is a large buffer, $1-W \leq w(B_i) \leq h(B_i) \leq 1$. The occupied height is $h + h(B_i)$ and the occupied area is at least $h(B_i)w(B_i) + \alpha \cdot h \cdot (1 - w(B_i))$, since the strips are at least α full in the height, and $1 - w(B_i)$ in the width (the rectangles in each one were blocked by the buffer). It is easy to check that for $W = \frac{1}{4}$ and $\alpha = \frac{2}{3}$ the occupied area is at least $\frac{1}{4}$ of the total area for each of the cases. This yields the competitive ratio of 4 which is actually the best ratio that can be achieved in this method.

3 The Lower Bound For The Model Without Rotations

In this section we provide a lower bound for the case of the problem in which the widths of the rectangles are bigger than ϵ, or all widths are less than $1 - \epsilon$ (or both).

Note that we allow to place rectangles in any free space, and not only above other rectangles, so that there is no gravity. If we enforced gravity, no algorithm can achieve a good competitive ratio since we can prove the following claim:

Claim 2. *Any algorithm for the model with gravity, no rotations, and when all rectangles are at least of width ϵ, is $\Omega(\frac{1}{\epsilon})$ competitive. This holds also if all widths are less than $1 - \epsilon$.*

Thus if we enforced gravity, the trivial algorithm which places the rectangles one on top of the other, would be optimal, for the case with minimum width ϵ.

We show that there is no constant competitive algorithm for the case without rotations (and without gravity). More precisely, we prove the following theorem:

Theorem 3. *Any on-line (deterministic or randomised) algorithm for this problem has a competitive ratio of at least $\Omega(\sqrt{\log \frac{1}{\epsilon}})$.*

Proof. We assume that $\epsilon \leq \frac{1}{16}$, otherwise the lower bound is constant. We first prove the deterministic lower bound. Later we show how to modify it for the randomised case.

We use a sequence which consists of rectangles with width between ϵ and $1-\epsilon$ and height between δ and 1 where $\delta \leq 1/\log \frac{1}{\epsilon}$. We show that for that sequence the off-line cost is 1, and the on-line cost is $\Omega(\sqrt{\log \frac{1}{\epsilon}})$, we call it a base sequence. By multiplying the heights by a constant, we can get any off-line cost, and thus get the lower bound even if we allow an additive constant. Moreover, the bound is correct even if the heights of the rectangles are bounded by 1 (or any other constant). To build the sequence, we repeat the base sequence several iterations, separating the iterations by a rectangle with width $1 - \frac{\epsilon}{2}$ and height δ. (Here we prove lower bound for $\frac{\epsilon}{2}$ instead of ϵ). Thus any rectangle that arrives after this rectangle can't be placed under this one, since the minimum width of rectangle is ϵ.

We can now introduce the base sequence. We define n such that $\epsilon = \frac{1}{2^n}$, which implies that $\delta \leq \frac{1}{n}$. To prove the lower bound consider the sequence of rectangles that consists of two types:

- Tall rectangles (with height $\frac{1}{4\sqrt{n}}$ and widths $2^{i-1}\epsilon$ for $i = 1$ to $\frac{n}{2}$)
- Buffers, (rectangles with height δ and widths $1 - 2^i\epsilon + \frac{\epsilon}{2}$)

The sequence consists of two types of phases. The ith phase, consists of $\frac{\sqrt{n}}{2}$ tall pieces of width $2^{i-1}\epsilon$, and one buffer of width either $1 - 2^i\epsilon + \frac{\epsilon}{2}$ or $1 - 2^{i-1}\epsilon + \frac{\epsilon}{2}$, which corresponds to type 1 or type 2 phase. We run the sequence until the completion of $\frac{n}{2}$ phases, or $\sqrt{n}$ phases of type 2, whatever happens first. We show that the off-line packing uses a maximum height of 1, and that the height required for any on-line algorithms is at least $\sqrt{\log \frac{1}{\epsilon}}/8$, the available space of the off-line algorithm is called a box. First, the off-line algorithm uses an 1×1 (height 1 and width 1) box. All the rectangles and buffers must be packed in this box. After each phase the on-line algorithm will have a smaller box available, (see figure 4).

The on-line algorithm is forced to put the buffer in such a way that no rectangle that arrives after this buffer can fit under the buffer hence for the on-line algorithm all the rectangles of one phase are above all the rectangles of the previous phase. Therefore the on-line algorithm may use at each phase width 1 to pack all rectangles of that phase. We call two rectangles overlapping, if it is possible to draw a horizontal line that intersects them both.

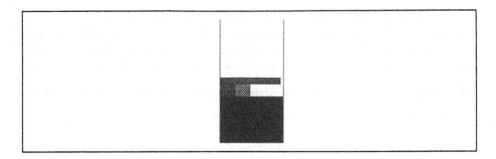

Fig. 3. The on-line packing at state 1

We build the sequence inductively. Assume we constructed the first i phases of the sequence, (i.e. chose the type of each phase). At phase i the $\frac{\sqrt{n}}{2}$ tall pieces arrive, and the type is chosen according to the way the on-line algorithm has placed them. There are two possible states.

1. If at least two current phase pieces overlap, (figure 3), then the phase becomes type 1 and a buffer of width of $1 - 2^i\epsilon + \frac{\epsilon}{2}$ arrives. The off-line places

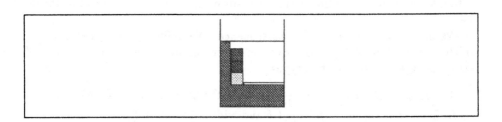

Fig. 4. The off-line packing at state 1

   all the pieces one on top of the other, and the buffer near them, as low as possible (see figure 4). Packing the rectangles like this, the off-line wastes height δ and width $2^{i-1}\epsilon$.
2. Otherwise, if no two current phase pieces overlap, then the phase becomes type 2 and   a buffer of width $1 - 2^{i-1}\epsilon + \frac{\epsilon}{2}$ arrives. The off-line places all the pieces in one row on the bottom of the available rectangle. The buffer is placed on top of them, to the left.   In this off-line packing the height wasted is $\frac{1}{4\sqrt{n}} + \delta$ and there is no wasted width.

Claim 4. *Assume that up to (including) phase i, there are j phases of type 2. Then the on-line has wasted height of at least $(i-j)/(4\sqrt{n})+j/8$ and the off-line has a free box of height $1 - \delta i - j/(4\sqrt{n})$ and width $1 - (2^i - 1)\epsilon$.*

Proof. omitted.

Recall that we run the sequence until the completion of $\frac{n}{2}$ phases or $\sqrt{n}$ type 2 phases, whatever happens first. Using Claim 4, it is easy to show that in both cases the on-line must have height of at least $\frac{\sqrt{n}}{8}$ and mxthe off-line algorithm can pack all the pieces in the box which completes the deterministic lower bound.

It is possible to modify the proof of the lower bound also for randomised algorithms. We omit the details.

4 Algorithms For The Model Without Rotations

As we proved in the last section, no constant competitive algorithm exists for the general problem, however we construct algorithms with competitive ratio which depends on the minimum width rectangle. In this section we present the algorithm for the case in which rotations are not allowed. The algorithm achieves competitive ratio of $O(\log \frac{1}{\epsilon})$ where ϵ is the minimum width of each rectangle. We also show how to change it for the case that the width of rectangles is bounded above by $1-\epsilon$ and not bounded below. Note that the heights of the rectangles are arbitrary and may be larger than 1. The algorithm uses horizontal strips, that are used for certain types of rectangles. Each strip is used for a certain range of heights, and a certain range of widths. An (i,j) strip is a strip that is used for rectangles of height h: $2^{j-1} < h \le 2^j$ and width w: $2^{-i-1} < w \le 2^{-i}$. (j is any integer, and i is a positive integer). The algorithm uses other separate strips for the rectangles of width at least $\frac{1}{4}$, those rectangles will be called buffers. Those strips are used only for buffers, one for each, and have the exact height of the buffer. We define a strip as available for a certain rectangle, if the rectangle can reach the strip (i.e. no buffer blocks the strip from the rectangle) and if after the rectangle is placed into the strip, the sum of all widths of the rectangles in the strip will not exceed $\frac{3}{4}$.

The Algorithm B: When a rectangle arrives it is classified and assigned as follows:

- If it is a buffer, a new strip of height of the buffer is opened for it, above all the previous strips, and the buffer is placed into this strip to the left.
- If it is a non-buffer, it is classified as an (i,j) rectangle for some i and j. If there exists an available (i,j) strip then we place it there to the left. Otherwise, we open a new strip of height 2^j, just above all previous strips, to be an (i,j) strip, and place the rectangle there, to the left.

Theorem 5. *The algorithm B is $O(\log \frac{1}{\epsilon})$ competitive, where ϵ is the minimum width of any rectangle.*

Substitute $\epsilon = 1/n$ to conclude the following:

Corollary 6. *For the integer case, the algorithm is $O(\log n)$ competitive, where n is the width of the bin.*

In order to prove Theorem 5 we assume without loss of generality that $\epsilon \le \frac{1}{16}$, (otherwise, the upper bound is constant). We define a strip as full, if the sum of widths of the rectangles placed there is at least $\frac{1}{2}$. We also define all buffer strips as full. We now can reduce the sequence σ to σ', so that there are no full strips for the on-line algorithm. We remove all rectangles that were placed into the full rows, but are not buffers. We also reduce the height of the buffers to zero, but we do not remove them. Those buffers remain in the sequence as one-dimensional buffers: they do not have height, but block the same rectangles as before the reduction from getting to strips.

Lemma 7. *If the competitive ratio of the reduced sequence σ' is $O(\log \frac{1}{\epsilon})$, so is the competitive ratio of the original sequence.*

Proof. omitted.

Note that since our algorithm keeps the width of all non-buffer strips below $\frac{3}{4}$, rectangles of different ranges of width are packed independently. We reduce the sequence further. For each i, we define σ_i to be the subsequence of all the buffers, and rectangles of width w: $2^{-i-1} < w \leq 2^{-i}$. Note that the same strips are opened for the rectangles in σ_i as in σ'.

Lemma 8. *If the algorithm is constant competitive on each such subsequence σ_i, then it is $O(\log \frac{1}{\epsilon})$ competitive on σ'.*

Proof. omitted.

Note that by the last reduction, the on-line algorithm has no full strips also for each σ_i.

Lemma 9. *For a subsequence σ_i of rectangles of widths w: $2^{-i-1} < w \leq 2^{-i}$, and one-dimensional buffers, the algorithm is 10 competitive.*

Proof. For this subsequence we can also omit all buffers of width $1 - 2^{-i}$ and less, since they cannot block any non-buffer rectangle from σ_i. We can also assume that there are no buffers wider than $1 - 2^{-i-1}$. If there are, we can treat all the rectangles between two wide buffers as the subsequence we are considering. Since those wide buffers block all subsequent rectangles, and force the off-line and the on-line begin a new packing, as if a new sequence has begun.

Consider the off-line packing for σ_i, and consider all remaining buffers: $Buf_1, ..., Buf_m$ (from the bottom of the packing to the top). (See figure 5). Recall that the buffers are one-dimensional and thus are assigned at some height in the bin. We denote by h_k the height that Buf_k was assigned by the off-line algorithm. Denote $h_0 = 0$, $h_{k+1} = C_{Opt}(\sigma_i)$, the bottom and the top are treated as buffers. Recall that two rectangles overlap, if it is possible to draw a horizontal line that intersects them both.

Consider all non-buffer rectangles, there are 3 types of possible packing for them at the off-line assignment:

1. A rectangle is considered "pioneer", if there was no *previous* rectangle that overlapped it.

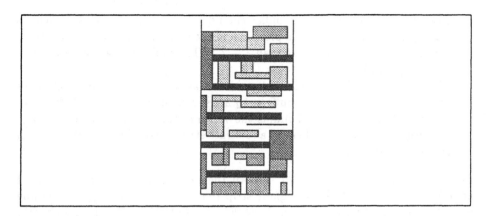

Fig. 5. The off-line packing for σ_i

2. The rectangle is not a pioneer, and was placed between two buffers, i.e. there exists k such that the top of the rectangle is not higher than h_{k+1}, and the bottom of the rectangle is not lower than h_k.

3. If the rectangle is not pioneer, and wasn't placed between buffers, then it must have been placed near some buffer.

We consider all strips that were opened for each type of rectangles by the on-line algorithm.

Claim 10. *The strips used for type 1 rectangles, occupy at most height of $2C_{Opt}(\sigma_i)$.*

Proof. omitted.

Claim 11. *The strips opened for type 2 rectangles, occupy at most height of $4C_{Opt}(\sigma_i)$.*

Proof. Denote by S_k the type 2 rectangles that were placed between Buf_k and Buf_{k+1} by the off-line. We first prove the following lemma.

Lemma 12. *The on-line algorithm opened at most one strip of each height in order to place the rectangles in S_k.*

Proof. By contradiction. Assume that two different strips of the same height were opened for the rectangles in S_k. Denote by r_1 and r_2 the two rectangles, that the two above strips were opened for. Since there are no full strips in the on-line packing, the second strip was opened since a buffer blocked r_2 from being placed at the same strip as r_1. This buffer arrived between r_1 and r_2 since all the buffers that arrived before r_1 were placed by the on-line algorithm below r_1.

We consider the place of this buffer in the off-line packing. Since r_1 is between two buffers, the buffer can not overlap r_1 in the packing and thus there are two possibilities for the off-line location of the buffer.

- The buffer is under r_1. The buffer should have passed near r_1 to reach its location. However, r_1 is not a pioneer and therefore any rectangle that passes near it must have width less than $1 - 2^{-i}$. The buffer has width of at least $1 - 2^{-i}$ which is a contradiction.
- The buffer is above r_1, The buffer is also above r_2, since both rectangles are between the same two buffers. r_2 arrived after the buffer and therefore its width is smaller than 1 minus the width of the buffer. Since the on-line algorithm assigns the buffers in a separate strip, it could not block r_2 which is a contradiction.

We continue the proof of Claim 11. All the rectangles in S_k have height of at most $h_{k+1} - h_k$. Thus the highest strip that may be opened by the on-line algorithm for those rectangles is at most $2(h_{k+1} - h_k)$. There is at most one strip for each height, so the total height of strips opened for the rectangles in S_k is $4(h_{k+1} - h_k)$. Summing for all k we get that the total height is $4C_{Opt}$, since

$$4 \sum_{k=0}^{m} (h_{k+1} - h_k) \le 4C_{Opt} .$$

Claim 13. *The strips used for type 3 rectangles, occupy at most height of* $4C_{Opt}(\sigma_i)$.

Proof. omitted.

Now we conclude the proof of Lemma 9. Note that there might be strips that were used for more than one type of rectangles. Nevertheless, by the three Claims, the total height occupied by the σ_i rectangles is at most $10C_{Opt}(\sigma_i)$, and thus the algorithm is 10 competitive.

The proof of Theorem 5 follows immediately from Lemmas
It is possible to show that the analysis it tight.

Claim 14. *The algorithm B is $\Omega(\log \frac{1}{\epsilon})$ competitive.*

We can modify algorithm B to somewhat more natural algorithm B' as follows. The strips of a certain height are used for all widths of rectangles (instead of a separate strip for each width), in a way similar to the algorithm in section 2. It is possible to prove the following theorem:

Theorem 15. *The algorithm B' is $\Theta(\log \frac{1}{\epsilon})$ competitive.*

Now we change the algorithm B to an algorithm C for the case that the width is not bounded below, but bounded above by $1 - \epsilon$. When a rectangle of width less than ϵ arrives, we define how to place it, otherwise we place it in the same way as in algorithm B or B'. We open special strips for those rectangles. When a narrow rectangle arrives, its height is rounded up to a negative power of 2. If there is a non-full strip of narrow rectangles, for this height, the rectangle is placed there. Otherwise, a new strip of this height is opened, and the rectangle is placed there. It is easy to prove the following theorem:

Theorem 16. *The algorithm C is $O(\log \frac{1}{\epsilon})$ competitive, where $1 - \epsilon$ is the maximum width of any rectangle.*

Acknowledgment: We would like to thank Howard Karloff for his helpful discussion.

References

1. B.S. Baker, E.G. Coffman,Jr , and R.L. Rivest. Orthogonal packings in two dimensions. In *The SIAM Journal of Computing*, pages 846–855, 1980.
2. Y. Bartal, A. Fiat, H. Karloff, and R. Vohra. New algorithms for an ancient scheduling problem. In *Proc. 24th ACM Symp. on Theory of Computing*, pages 51-58, 1992.
3. Y. Bartal, H. Karloff, Y. Rabani. A better lower bound for on-line scheduling. In *Information Processing Letters 50* pages 113-116, 1994.
4. B. Chen, and A. van Vliet. On the on-line scheduling algorithm RLS Report 9325/A, Econometric Institute, Erasmus University, Rotterdam. 1993.
5. B. Chen, A. van Vliet, and G.J. Woeginger. New lower and upper bounds for on-line scheduling. In *Operations Research Letters*, pages 222-230, 1994.
6. J. Csirik, J.B.G. Frenk, and M. Labbe. Two-dimensional rectangle packing: on-line methods and results. In *Discrete applied Mathematics 45*, pages 197-204, 1993.
7. E.G. Coffman,Jr , M.R. Garey, D.S. Johnson, and R.E. Tarjan. Performance bounds for level oriented two-dimensional packing Algorithms. In *The SIAM Journal of Computing*, pages 808-826, 1980.
8. D. Coppersmith, and P. Raghavan. Multidimensional on-line bin packing: algorithms and worst-case analysis. In *Operation Research Letters*, pages 17-20, 1989.
9. G. Galambos. A 1.6 lower bound for the two-dimensional on-line rectangle bin packing In *Acta Cybernetica*, pages 21-24, 1991.
10. G. Galambos, A. van Vliet. Lower bounds for 1-,2- and 3-dimensional on-line bin packing algorithms. In *Computing* , pages 281-297, 1994.
11. G. Galambos, and G.J. Woeginger. An on-line scheduling heuristic with better worst case than Graham's list scheduling. In *SIAM J. Comput. 22*, pages 349-355, 1993.
12. R.L. Graham. Bounds for certain multiprocessing anomalies. In *Bell System Tech J. 45*, pages 1563-1581, 1966.
13. D.S. Johnson, A. Demers, J.D. Ullman, M.R. Garey, and R.L. Graham. Worst-case performance bounds for simple one-dimensional packing algorithms. In *The SIAM Journal of Computing*, pages 299-325, 1974.
14. H. Karloff. Personal communication.
15. D.R. Karger, S.J. Phillips, and E. Torng. A better algorithm for an ancient scheduling problem. In *Proc. 5 Ann. ACM-SIAM symposium on Discrete Algorithms*, pages 132-140, 1994.
16. F. M. Liang. A lower bound for on-line bin packing. In *Information Processing letters*, pages 76-79, 1980.
17. A. van Vliet. Lower and upper bounds for on-line bin packing and scheduling heuristics. Ph.D. thesis. Thesis publishers, Amsterdam, 1995.
18. A. C. Yao. New algorithms for bin packing. In *Journal of the ACM*, pages 207-227, 1980.

Optimal Orthogonal Drawings of Triconnected Plane Graphs *

Therese C. Biedl

RUTCOR, Rutgers University, P.O. Box 5062, New Brunswick, NJ 08903,
therese@rutcor.rutgers.edu

Abstract. In this paper we produce orthogonal drawings of triconnected planar graphs where a planar embedding is given. Kant presented an algorithm to compute a small orthogonal drawing in linear time. In this paper, we will show that his algorithm in fact produces less bends than the bound shown. Moreover, with a small variation of the algorithm, the number of bends can be reduced even further, which also leads to lower bounds on the grid-size. Both bounds are optimal.

We also present a theorem that gives a bound on the grid-size of an orthogonal drawing, assuming that a bound on the number of bends is known. With the help of this theorem, we can prove bounds on the grid-size for the algorithm of Tamassia, which produces the minimum number of bends. No such bounds were known before.

1 Introduction

An orthogonal drawing of a graph is a drawing such that every vertex is drawn as a point in the plane, and every edge is drawn as a sequence of horizontal and vertical lines. Orthogonal graph drawings are an important tool for graph layout, since the minimum angle of 90° makes the drawings easily readable. Specific uses include Data Flow Diagrams and Entity Relationships Diagrams.

One approach to obtain "nice" orthogonal drawings is to start with a (non-orthogonal) drawing, planarize it by adding dummy-nodes for every crossing, and then to produce an orthogonal drawing of the obtained planar graph. Of course, this orthogonal drawing should have no crossing. Also, it should reflect the planar embedding, i.e. the order of the edges around each vertex, and the edges on the outer-face. Orthogonal drawings exist only if every vertex in the graph has at most four incident edges, such a graph is called a *4-graph*. On the other hand, every planar 4-graph with fixed planar embedding has an orthogonal drawing reflecting the embedding (e.g. with the algorithm of Tamassia [9]).

Two of the most important measurements of the quality of a drawing are the grid-size and the number of bends. Minimizing the number of bends is $\mathcal{NP}$-complete [6] if we need not have a planar drawing, or if we are allowed to choose the planar embedding. However, if as in our context the planar embedding is

---

* Some of these results were part of a diploma thesis written at TU Berlin. The author also wants to thank Goos Kant for useful discussions.

fixed, then minimizing the number of bends can be done with the algorithm of Tamassia [9]. The question whether a graph can be embedded in a grid of pre-scribed size is $\mathcal{NP}$-complete for non-planar drawings [8, 5], while to the problem is open for planar drawings.

Assume the given graph has n vertices and m edges. The algorithm by Tamassia takes $\mathcal{O}(n^2 \log n)$ time to compute the drawing with the minimum number of bends. Sometimes heuristics are preferred that work quickly (i.e. in linear time) and produce reasonable bounds. For biconnected graphs, there is such an algo-rithm which gives at most an $n \times n$-grid and $2n + 4$ bends [10, 11]. For graphs that are not biconnected, an algorithm was only recently presented that exactly reflects the planar embedding, it gives a $\frac{6}{5}n \times \frac{6}{5}n$-grid and $\frac{12}{5}n+2$ bends [1]. Kant gave an algorithm dealing with triconnected graphs, he achieved an $n \times n$-grid with $\frac{3}{2}n + 2$ bends [7].

In this paper we revisit this algorithm of Kant. We show that his algorithm produces only $\frac{4}{3}(m - n) + 4$ bends. Then, we give a variation of the algorithm, which works better if there are many vertices of degree 3. The number of bends is reduced to $2m - \frac{8}{3}n + 4$.

In order to show bounds on the grid-size of this algorithm, we prove another theorem. Assume that we are given a orthogonal drawing with b bends. Then the height and width each are at most $\frac{1}{2}b + 2n - m - 1$. Thus, we can show that the variation of the algorithm of Kant produces at most a grid of width and height $\frac{2}{3}n + 1$. It was shown by Biedl [3] that no algorithm can perform better, since there exists a triconnected graph that needs a $(\frac{2}{3}n+1) \times (\frac{2}{3}n+1)$-grid and $\frac{4}{3}n + 4$ bends in any plane orthogonal drawing.

The theorem relating the number of bends to the grid-size can also be used for the algorithm of Tamassia. Namely, since his algorithm achieves the optimal number of bends, this number cannot be bigger than the bound achieved by some other heuristic. With these bounds, we can then also achieve bounds on the grid-size of Tamassia's algorithm. No such bounds were known before.

Due to space restrictions, we have to severly shorten proofs and omit cases. A full version of this paper can be found in [2].

2 Definitions

Let $G = (V, E)$ be a 4-graph with n vertices and m edges. G is called a *k-graph* if every vertex has degree at most k; and *k-regular* if every vertex has degree k. We assume that G is *simple*, i.e. it has neither a multiple edge nor a loop. G is called *connected* if for any two vertices there is a path between them. It is called *k-connected* if after removing a set of $k - 1$ vertices the remaining graph is connected. A 2-connected graph is also called *biconnected*, a 3-connected graph is also called *triconnected*.

G is called *planar* if it can be drawn without crossing. A drawing of a planar graph without a crossing defines a circular ordering of the edges incident to a vertex v; this is called a *combinatorial embedding* of the graph. A planar drawing of a graph splits the plane into different components, called *faces*. The unbounded component is called the *outer-face*. A planar graph is called *plane* if both a combinatorial embedding and the outer-face is specified. In this paper we assume that all graphs are plane.

An *(orthogonal) drawing* of a plane graph G is an embedding of G such that all edges are drawn as sequences of horizontal and vertical line segments. Also, the orthogonal drawing should be planar and reflect the combinatorial embedding. If the drawing can be enclosed by a rectangle of *width* n_1 and *height* n_2, we call it a drawing with *grid-size* $n_1 \times n_2$ and *half-perimeter* $n_1 + n_2$.

The four grid-segments adjacent to a grid-point are called *ports* of the grid-point and denoted according to their direction as *top, bottom, right,* and *left*.

3 Relationship between bends and width

Theorem 1. *Assume we are given an orthogonal drawing Γ of G with b bends. Then the half-perimeter is at most $b + 2n - m - 2$, and the width and height each are at most $\frac{1}{2}b + 2n - m - 1$.*

Proof. Define $Top(\Gamma)$ to be the number of vertices of G where the top port is not used in Γ. Similarly, define $Bottom(\Gamma)$, $Right(\Gamma)$ and $Left(\Gamma)$. We claim that the width is at most $\frac{1}{2}(b + Top(\Gamma) + Bottom(\Gamma)) - 1$; and the height is at most $\frac{1}{2}(b + Left(\Gamma) + Right(\Gamma)) - 1$. We show only the claim on the width.

Consider a column. If it is used by a vertex, let u be the top-most vertex and w be the bottom-most vertex in this column ($u = w$ is possible). If the top port at u is used, then it must contain a bend, since there is no vertex above u in the column. So we either have a bend above u, or u contributes to $Top(\Gamma)$. Similarly, we either have a bend below w, or w contributes to $Bottom(\Gamma)$.

If the column is not used by a vertex, then it contains the vertical line of an edge (we assume that every column is used, otherwise we could reduce the width). There are two bends at the endpoints of this line.

So in all, this column contributes at least 2 to the expression $b + Top(\Gamma) + Bottom(\Gamma)$. Since no bends or unused ports belong to two columns, we have at most $\frac{1}{2}(b + Top(\Gamma) + Bottom(\Gamma))$ columns. The width is one less than the number of columns.

v has $4 - deg(v)$ unused ports, so $Top(\Gamma) + Bottom(\Gamma) + Right(\Gamma) + Left(\Gamma) = \sum_{v \in V}(4 - deg(v)) = 4n - 2m$. With this, we are done for the width and height. For the half-perimeter, we get a bound of $\frac{1}{2}(b + Top(\Gamma) + Bottom(\Gamma)) - 1 + \frac{1}{2}(b + Right(\Gamma) + Left(\Gamma)) - 1 = \frac{1}{2}(2b + 4n - 2m) - 2 = b + 2n - m - 2$.

4 Bounds for the algorithm by Tamassia

In this section, we show bounds obtained with the algorithm of Tamassia [9]. We do not describe the algorithm of Tamassia, the reader is referred to the original source. For our analysis, it suffices to know that it gives the optimum number of bends for an orthogonal drawing of a plane graph.

Theorem 2. *The algorithm of Tamassia [9] embeds every plane 4-graph within the following bounds:*

- *G triconnected: $(\frac{2}{3}n + 1) \times (\frac{2}{3}n + 1)$-grid and $2m - \frac{8}{3}n + 4$ bends.*
- *G biconnected: $(n + 1) \times (n + 1)$-grid and $2m - 2n + 4$ bends.*
- *G connected: $(\frac{5}{4}n - \frac{1}{2}) \times (\frac{5}{4}n - \frac{1}{2})$-grid, half-perimeter $\frac{12}{5}n$, and $\min\{2m - \frac{3}{2}n + \frac{1}{2}, m + \frac{2}{5}n + 2\}$ bends.*

Proof. Assume G is a biconnected plane graph. With the algorithm of Biedl and Kant [4], we can obtain a planar drawing with $2m - 2n + 4$ bends (this algorithm was designed for planar graphs only, but can be made to reflect the embedding). Let b be the number of bends achieved with the algorithm by Tamassia, so $b \leq 2m - 2n + 4$. Applying this to Theorem 1, we get a height and width of at most $\frac{1}{2}(2m - 2n + 4) + 2n - m - 1 = n + 1$.

The proof for the other cases is similar, where the bounds on the number of bends come from Lemma 10 and from another paper [1].

5 The algorithm by Kant revisited

In this section we consider the algorithm by Kant [7] for orthogonal drawings of triconnected plane graphs, and show improved bounds through a small variation.

5.1 The algorithm by Kant

For an ordering $\{v_1, \ldots, v_n\}$ of the vertices let $G(i)$ to be the graph induced by $\{v_1, \ldots, v_i\}$, and let its planar embedding be the one induced by G.

Definition 3. [7] Let G be a plane graph. An ordering $V = \{v_1, \ldots, v_n\}$ is called a *canonical ordering* if the following holds:

- (v_1, v_2) is an edge and belongs to the outer-face.
- v_n belongs to the outer-face and has at least three neighbors.
- For $3 \leq j \leq n - 1$, v_j is in the outer-face of $G(j - 1)$, and:
  - Either "v_j is a new vertex", i.e. v_j has at least two neighbors in $G(j-1)$ and at least one neighbor in $G - G(j)$. $G(j)$ is biconnected.
  - Or "v_j is part of a new chain", i.e. there exists i, k, $i \leq j \leq k$, such that for all $i < l < k$ v_l is adjacent to v_{l-1} and v_{l+1}, has no other neighbor in $G(k)$, and at least one neighbor in $G - G(k)$. Furthermore, v_i and v_k have each exactly one neighbor in $G(i - 1)$ and at least one neighbor in $G - G(k)$. $G(k)$ is biconnected.

The existence of a canonical ordering has been shown by Kant [7]. For a vertex v define the *incoming edges* to be the edges to neighbors with a smaller number, and, for a vertex that is part of a chain, also the incident edges of the chain. The other incident edges are called *outgoing*. Denote their number by $indeg(v)$ respectively $outdeg(v)$. Every vertex v_j, $3 \leq j \leq n - 1$ has $outdeg(v_j) \leq 2$, since we have a 4-graph, and since by definition $indeg(v_j) \geq 2$.

Assume $indeg(v) \geq 2$. The combinatorial embedding defines an ordering of the incoming edges of v, and we can distinguish the *right* and *left incoming edge*. If $indeg(v) \geq 3$ we also have one or two *middle incoming edges*. Similarly, for a vertex with $outdeg(v) = 2$, define the *left* and *right outgoing edge*.

For a new vertex v_j in the canonical ordering, the *leftvertex* and *rightvertex* are the endpoints of the left and right incoming edge. For a new chain $v_i, \ldots, v_k$, assume that after adding it the outer-face contains $v_i, \ldots, v_k$ in clockwise order. Then the *leftvertex* is the endpoint of the left incoming edge of v_i, and the *rightvertex* is the endpoint of the right incoming edge of v_k.

We will define a labelling for vertices with indegree 2. We mark v as *l (left)*, *r (right)*, or *u (up)*, which means the following: after embedding v there will be two ports free. One of these will be the top port, while the other is the right or the left port. The label describes whether it is preferable to have the right or the left port free after embedding the vertex. For a vertex of degree 3, the label also describes which of the free ports will be used for the outgoing edge.

These free ports cannot be always achieved. We then add an extra bend, so that the edge goes upward (see e.g. Figure 3(d)). An edge $e = (v_i, v_j)$, $i < j$ is said to *look upward*, if v_i is embedded, but v_j is not; and if either e uses the top port at v_i, or it obtained an extra bend when embedding v_i.

We defer the rather confusing precise definition of this labelling to later. We have the following invariants of the algorithm.

Invariant 1 *Assume* $indeg(v_j) \geq 3$, *and the edge* (v_i, v_j) *is a middle incoming edge of* v_j. *Then it looks upward at* v_i.

Invariant 2 *If* c_1 *is the leftvertex of a vertex or chain, then the edge from* c_1 *to this vertex or chain either looks upward, or uses the right port at* c_1.
If c_2 *is the rightvertex of a vertex or chain, then the edge from* c_2 *to this vertex or chain either looks upward, or uses the left port at* c_2.

We describe the algorithm in pictures. We compute only the ports used for each edge, the final coordinates can be found in linear time, see Kant [7].

Fig. 1. Drawing the first two vertices, for different degrees.

Following the steps of the canonical ordering, we either add a new vertex or a new chain. We know that the edge to the leftvertex goes to the right or looks upward; and the edge to the rightvertex goes to the left or looks upward (Invariant 2). This gives four possible cases, called RL, UL, RU, and UU. All middle incoming edges (if there are any) look upward (Invariant 1). We also have to distinguish by the degree of the vertex, and, for a vertex of indegree 2, by the label. See Figures 2 through 9.

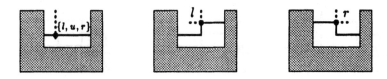

Fig. 2. Adding a vertex of indegree 2, case RL.

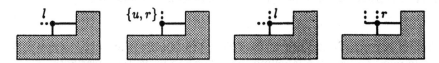

Fig. 3. Adding a vertex of indegree 2, case UL. The case RU is symmetric.

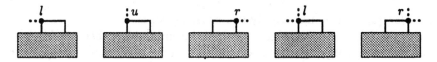

Fig. 4. Adding a vertex of indegree 2, case UU.

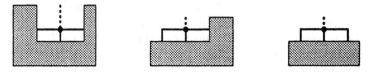

Fig. 5. Adding a vertex of indegree 3, for the cases RL, UL, and UU.

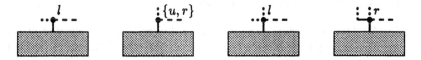

Fig. 6. Adding the first vertex of a chain, case UU or UL. The dashed line marks the edge to the second vertex of the chain, while dotted lines mark the outgoing edges. The last vertex of the chain is embedded symmetric.

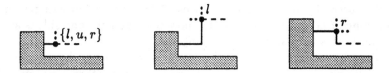

Fig. 7. Adding the first vertex of a chain, case RU or RL.

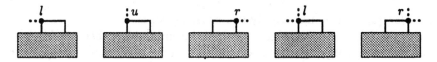

Fig. 8. Adding a vertex w_i, $i \neq 1, p$ of a chain $w_1, \ldots, w_p$.

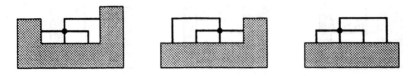

Fig. 9. Adding the last vertex v_n. If v_n has degree 3, then it is embedded as shown in Figure 5. Otherwise, we again distinguish the cases RL, UL, and UU.

Due to space restriction, the proof of the invariants has to be dropped. We will only mention here the labelling that allows to prove the invariants.

Definition 4. Assume we have v_i, $3 \leq i \leq n - 1$, with $indeg(v_i) = 2$.

- If $outdeg(v_i) = 4$, v_i has exactly two outgoing edges.
  - If the right outgoing edge is a middle incoming edge, then $mark(v_i) = l$.
  - If the left outgoing edge is a middle incoming edge, then $mark(v_i) = r$.
  - If both outgoing edges are right incoming edges, then $mark(v_i) = l$.
  - If both outgoing edges are left incoming edges, then $mark(v_i) = r$.
  - Otherwise, we mark v_i arbitrarily as either *left* or *right*.
- If $outdeg(v_i) = 3$, v_i has exactly one outgoing edge.
  - If the outgoing edge is right incoming, then $mark(v_i) = l$.
  - If the outgoing edge is left incoming, then $mark(v_i) = r$.
  - If the outgoing edge is middle incoming, then $mark(v_i) = u$.

5.2 Analysis of the number of bends

Definition 5. After embedding the ith vertex, let $up(i)$ be the number of edges which look upward, and let $b(i)$ be the number of bends. Also, let $n_3(i)$ be the number of vertices of degree 3 among the first i vertices. Finally, define the potential $\Phi(i) = 3b(i) + 2n_3(i) + up(i)$.

Lemma 6. *For $1 < i < n$ we have $\Phi(i) \leq 4i + 8$.*

Proof. We proceed by induction on the steps of the canonical ordering. Consider the embedding of v_1 and v_2. We have to show that the left hand side is at most 16, and can do this by distinguishing by $n_3(2)$.

Now consider adding either a chain or a vertex. For each, we do a case analysis, distinguishing by the degree of the vertex, and whether it was embedded with the case UU, UL, RU, or RL. We will present here only one (crucial) case, and must leave the rest to the reader. Assume that we add a new vertex v_i with $indeg(v_i) = 2$, $deg(v_i) = 3$ and we are in the case UU.

The two incoming edges of v_i looked upward before, but they are finished now. We may or may not create a new upward edge. Therefore, $up(i) \leq up(i)-1$. We add one new bend, so $b(i) = b(i)+1$. This gives $\Phi(i) = 3b(i)+2n_3(i)+up(i) \leq 3b(i-1)+3+2n_3(i-1)+2+up(i-1)-1 = \Phi(i-1)+4 \leq 4i+8$.

Lemma 7. *We have $\Phi(n) \leq 4n + 12$.*

Proof. $\Phi(n-1) \leq 4(n-1)+8 = 4n+4$ by the above lemma. So we only need to show that with adding the last vertex, $\Phi(.)$ increases by at most 8. This is done by distinguishing by $deg(v_n)$, and by the cases UU, UL, RU, and RL.

Lemma 8. *The number of bends in total is at most $\frac{4}{3}(m-n)+4$.*

Proof. Denote by n_3 the number of vertices of degree 3 in G. After the algorithm is finished, there is no upward edge left. So $up(n) = 0$, and the number of bends is $b(n) = \frac{1}{3}(\Phi(n) - 2n_3) \leq \frac{1}{3}(4n - 2n_3 + 12)$.

Every vertex in the graph has degree either 3 or 4. With the formula for degrees, we can compute $2m = \sum_{v \in V} deg(v) = 4(n - n_3) + 3n_3 = 4n - n_3$. So $2n_3 = 8n - 4m$, and the number of bends is $b(n) \leq \frac{1}{3}(4m - 4n + 12)$.

5.3 Improvement of the algorithm

The bound of Lemma 8 is optimal; there exists a triconnected plane 4-graph that has $m = 2n$ edges and needs $\frac{4}{3}n + 4$ bends [3]. The same graph also needs a width and height of $\frac{2}{3}n + 1$ in any drawing. If we try to get a bound on the height and width of Kant's algorithm by combining Lemma 8 with Theorem 1, we get a bound of $\frac{2}{3}n + (2n - m) + 1$. So this exceeds $\frac{2}{3}n + 1$, if $m < 2n$.

We will show in this subsection how with a change of the algorithm, we can achieve a bound on the bends that is better if the number of edges is small.

We show this by defining a stronger potential, namely, $\Psi(i) = 3b(i) + 3n_3(i) + up(i) = \Phi(i) + n_3(i)$. We want to show that Lemma 6 and 7 hold even if we replace Φ by Ψ. Case by case one checks that there is only one problematic situation: when we want to embed a vertex v_i with $indeg(v_i) = 2$, $deg(v_i) = 3$, $mark(v_i) = u$, and we are in the case UU. In this case, $\Psi(i+1) = \Psi(i) + 4 + 1$, and we say that "one unit of excess occurs at v_i."

In this case, while doing the layout we call the method RELABEL(v_i), which is shown in Figure 10. This method will either change $mark(v_i)$, or it will realize that the excess for v_i is compensated by some later vertex. Either way, after RELABEL(v_i) is finished, we embed v_i with the possibly changed label.

If the label of v_i is changed, then the outgoing edge of v_i does not look upward. Consequently, Invariant 1 is violated for x_1, i.e. the middle incoming edge need not look upward. We embed x_1 as shown in Figure 11. If (x_1, x_2) is middle incoming, then Invariant 1 is violated for x_2 as well. So the way the outgoing edge of v_i leaves v_i propagates to the outgoing edges of x_j, $j = 1, 2, \ldots$ We analyze different reasons why algorithm RELABEL(v_i) stopped.

1. We had a vertex x^*.
   (a) To embed x^* we used case UL, RU or RL. As can be checked case by case, $\Psi(.)$ increases by at most 2 if $x^* \neq v_n$; and by at most 6 if $x^* = v_n$. This reduction compensates for the excess incurred at v_i.
   (b) $x^* = v_n$, and $deg(v_n) = 3$. As can be checked case by case, $\Psi(.)$ increases by at most 6. This reduction compensates for the excess incurred at v_i.

RELABEL

Input: A vertex v_i in case UU, with $deg(v_i) = 3$, $indeg(v_i) = 2$ and $mark(v_i) = u$.

Output: A new $mark(v_i)$, or a vertex x^* that compensates for excess produced at v_i.

Set $j = 0$ and $x_0 = v_i$.

repeat

    Invariant: x_j is a vertex with $outdeg(x_j) = 1$; and its outgoing edge $e_j = (x_j, y_j)$ is middle incoming at y_j. All incoming edges of x_j look upward.

    if a predecessor $\neq x_j$ of y_j is not drawn yet, embed vertices until it is embedded.[2]

    if for embedding y_j we now have the case UL, RU, or RL, set $x^* = y_j$ and break.

    else /* for embedding y_j, we have the case UU */

        if $y_j = v_n$

            if $deg(v_n) = 3$, set $x^* = v_n$ and break.

            else let e'_j be the other middle incoming edge of v_n.

                if e'_j is marked, set $x^* = v_n$ and break.

                else if e_j is left of e'_j, set $mark(v_i) = r$, **else** set $mark(v_i) = l$.

                Mark e_j and break.

        else let $\bar{e}_j = (y_j, z_j)$ be the outgoing edge of y_j.

            if $\bar{e}_j$ is left incoming at z_j, set $mark(v_i) = r$, and break.

            if $\bar{e}_j$ is right incoming at z_j, set $mark(v_i) = l$, and break.

            else $\bar{e}_j$ is middle incoming. Set $x_{j+1} = y_j$, $j = j + 1$ and repeat.

Fig. 10. The algorithm RELABEL(v_i). During RELABEL$(.)$, we possibly mark an edge. This marking should be kept over repeated applications of RELABEL$(.)$.

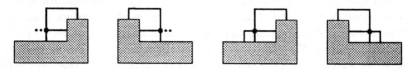

Fig. 11. The special embedding if the middle incoming edge does not look upward; for x_j with $outdeg(x_j) = 1$, and for v_n. $\Psi(.)$ increases by 4 for x_j, and by 6 for v_n.

2. We had a new label for v_i.

    (a) We stopped because $y_j = v_n$, and $deg(v_n) = 4$. From the invariant of RELABEL we know that e_j was middle incoming to v_n. If e'_j was marked, this must have happened during some previous call of RELABEL(v'_j), for some different vertex v'_j. Either way, one of the edges e_j, e'_j will be marked after RELABEL(v_j).

        The marked edge triggered a change of label of the vertex. This vertex was embedded differently, and the direction of its outgoing edge propagated to the direction of this incoming edge of v_n. The other edge was not marked, therefore the middle incoming edge looks upward, and for embedding v_n we have one of the cases UULU or URUU.

---

[2] More detailed: continue in the canonical ordering, and embed all those vertices $\neq x_j$ where all predecessors are embedded. It can be shown that eventually all other predecessors of y_j will be embedded.

We embed v_n as shown in Figure 11. This increases $\Psi(.)$ by at most 6. Therefore, v_n avoids the excess that would have been incurred at the vertex that triggered the marking of one edge. Also, it compensated for excess that might have been incurred at the vertex which tried to mark the other middle incoming edge.

(b) The edge $\bar{e}_j$ was left or right incoming to z_j. Assume it was left incoming, the other case is analogous. In this case we set $mark(v_i) = r$. So the outgoing edge of v_i used the right port at v_i. This propagates, so $\bar{e}_j$ used the right port at the other endpoint. Therefore, for z_j we are back to the "normal" case, all invariants hold again. Every vertex among $x_0, x_1, \ldots, z_j$ increased $\Psi(.)$ by at most 4. See also Figure 12. In this case we reduce the number of bends in the drawing.

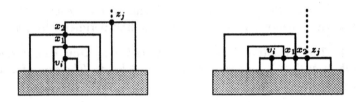

Fig. 12. The left incoming edge of z_j determines that the label of v_i is changed to r.

So the excess at v_i is either removed by changing the label, or it is compensated for by a later vertex. It can be shown that every vertex compensates as much as it has incoming edges that do not look upward. So the vertex compensates sufficiently for all vertices that use it, and we have proved the following.

Lemma 9. *With the changes through RELABEL, we have $\Psi(n) \leq 4n + 12$.*

Lemma 10. *The number of bends is at most $2m - \frac{8}{3}n + 4$.*

Proof. Denote by n_3 the number of vertices of degree 3. After the algorithm is finished, there is no upward edge. So $up(n) = 0$, and the number of bends is $b(n) = \frac{1}{3}(\Psi(n) - 3n_3) \leq \frac{1}{3}(4n - 3n_3 + 12)$. Since $2m = 4n - n_3$, we have $3n_3 = 12n - 6m$, and the total number of bends is $b(n) = \frac{1}{3}(6m - 8n + 12)$.

Lemma 11. *The half-perimeter is $m - \frac{2}{3}n + 2$, each side is at most $\frac{2}{3}n + 1$.*

Proof. We know that the number of bends b is at most $2m - \frac{8}{3}n + 4$. So by Theorem 1, the half-perimeter is at most $b + 2n - m - 2 \leq 2m - \frac{8}{3}n + 4 + 2n - m - 2 = m - \frac{2}{3}n + 2$. Each individual side is at most $\frac{1}{2}b + 2n - m - 1 \leq m - \frac{4}{3}n + 2 + 2n - m - 1 = \frac{2}{3}n + 1$.

The algorithm of Kant works in linear time, and all RELABEL steps together cost $\mathcal{O}(m)$ time, since we use every edge at most once.

Theorem 12. *There exists a linear time algorithm to draw any plane triconnected 4-graph in a $(\frac{2}{3}n + 1) \times (\frac{2}{3}n + 1)$-grid with at most $\frac{4}{3}n + 4$ bends.*

5.4   3-graphs

A triconnected 3-graph must by 3-regular, therefore it has $m = \frac{3}{2}n$ edges. For 3-graphs, Kant showed that his algorithm gives an $\frac{n}{2} \times \frac{n}{2}$-grid with $\frac{n}{2} + 1$ bends [7]. Applying the second algorithm, we obtain even better bounds.

Lemma 13. *For a 3-regular graph, we produce at most $\frac{n}{3} + 3$ bends.*

Proof. We have at most $2m - \frac{8}{3}n + 4$ bends, and with $m = \frac{3}{2}n$ therefore at most $\frac{n}{3} + 4$ bends. One extra unit can be saved since v_1, v_2, and v_n have degree 3.

The bound of $\frac{n}{3} + 3$ bends is almost optimal. Every triangle needs at least one bend. So if we construct a triconnected plane graph consisting of $\frac{n}{3}$ vertex-disjoint triangles, then it needs at least $\frac{n}{3}$ bends. For the grid-size, we get no improvement over the results by Kant. In fact, there exists a 3-graph that is drawn with either width $\frac{n}{2}$ or height $\frac{n}{2}$, depending on the chosen canonical ordering. But with Theorem 1 we can bound the half-perimeter by $\frac{5}{6}n + 1$.

Theorem 14. *There exists a linear time algorithm to draw any triconnected plane 3-graph in an $\frac{n}{2} \times \frac{n}{2}$-grid with at most $\frac{n}{3} + 3$ bends. The sum of width and height is at most $\frac{5}{6}n + 1$.*

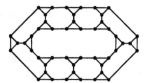

Fig. 13. Lower bounds for triconnected 3-graphs. The first graph needs $\frac{n}{3}$ bends, the second graph can be shown to need a width and height of $\frac{n}{3} + 1$.

6   Remarks and open problems

In this paper, we showed new and/or better bounds for the algorithms by Tamassia and Kant. The bounds for the algorithm by Tamassia are optimal for triconnected graphs. They are optimal up to a constant for biconnected graphs, and the half-perimeter and the number of bends are also almost optimal up to a constant for connected graphs (see [3] for lower bounds).

For the algorithm by Kant and its variation, we showed bounds that are likewise optimal. The same algorithm also performs well for 3-graphs, and for the bends is optimal up to a constant. We pose the following open problems:

- How should the canonical ordering be chosen? For different orderings we obtain different drawings, and the grid-size and the number of bends changes. What ways are there to choose a canonical ordering? Which ones are "best"?
- We did not find an example where Kant's algorithm exceeds a width and height of $\frac{2}{3}n + 1$; neither could we find an example where Kant's algorithm produces more than $2m - \frac{8}{3}n + 4$ bends. Do these two bounds always hold?

344

- Can the algorithm be transferred to non-planar graphs? There exists a canonical ordering for non-planar graphs (Kant, private communication). But how do markings have to be defined, and what invariants must be proven?

References

1. T. Biedl, Optimal Orthogonal Drawings of Connected Plane Graphs, *Rutcor Research Report* 11-96.[3]
2. T. Biedl, Optimal Orthogonal Drawings of Triconnected Plane Graphs, *Rutcor Research Report* 8-96.[3]
3. T. Biedl, New Lower Bounds for Orthogonal Graph Drawing, *Proc. Graph Drawing '95 (GD'95), Lecture Notes in Comp. Science 1027*, pp. 28-39. Also: *Rutcor Research Report* 19-95.[3]
4. T. Biedl, and G. Kant, A better heuristic for orthogonal graph drawings, *Proc. of the 2nd European Symp. on Algorithms (ESA 94), Lecture Notes in Comp. Science* 855, Springer-Verlag (1994), pp. 124–135. Also: *Rutcor Research Report* 12-95.[3]
5. M. Formann, and F. Wagner, The VLSI layout problem in various embedding models, *Graph-Theoretic Concepts in Comp. Science (16th WG'90)*, Springer-Verlag (1992), pp. 130–139.
6. A. Garg, and R. Tamassia, On the computational complexity of upward and rectilinear planarity testing, *Proc. Graph Drawing '94 (GD'94), Lect. Notes in Comp. Science* 894, Springer-Verlag (1994), pp. 286–297 .
7. G. Kant, Drawing planar graphs using the *lmc*-ordering, Extended Abstract in: *Proc. 33th Ann. IEEE Symp. on Found. of Comp. Science* 1992, pp. 101–110. Revised version to appear in *Algorithmica, special issue on Graph Drawing*.
8. M.R. Kramer, and J. van Leeuwen, The complexity of wire routing and finding minimum area layouts for arbitrary VLSI circuits. *Advances in Computer Research, Vol. 2: VLSI Theory*, F.P. Preparata (Ed.), JAI Press, Reading, MA, 1992, pp. 129–146.
9. R. Tamassia, On embedding a graph in the grid with the minimum number of bends, *SIAM J. Comp.* 16 (1987), pp. 421–444.
10. R. Tamassia, and I.G. Tollis, Efficient embedding of planar graphs in linear time, *Proc. IEEE Int. Symp. on Circuits and Systems* (1987), pp. 495–498.
11. R. Tamassia, and I.G. Tollis, Planar grid embedding in linear time, *IEEE Trans. Circ. Syst.* 36 (9), 1989, pp. 1230–1234.

[3] Rutcor Research Reports are available via anonymous FTP from *rutcor.rutgers.edu*, directory */pub/rrr*; or on the WWW at *http://rutcor.rutgers.edu/~rrr*.

For a comprised version of these four papers, see T. Biedl, *Orthogonal Graph Drawings, Algorithms and Lower Bounds*, Diploma Thesis TU Berlin, December 1996. Available on the WWW at *http://rutcor.rutgers.edu/~therese*.

Walking Streets Faster*

Alejandro López-Ortiz[1] and Sven Schuierer[2]

[1] Department of Computer Science, University of Waterloo, Waterloo, Ontario CANADA N2L
3G1, e-mail: `alopez-o@neumann.UWaterloo.ca`
[2] Institut für Informatik, Universität Freiburg, Am Flughafen 17, Geb. 051, D-79110
Freiburg, FRG, e-mail: `schuiere@informatik.uni-freiburg.de`

Abstract. A fundamental problem in robotics is to compute a path for a robot from its current
location to a given goal. In this paper we consider the problem of a robot equipped with an
on-board vision system searching for a goal g in an unknown environment.

We assume that the robot is located at a point s in a polygon that belongs to the well investigated class of polygons called *streets*. A *street* is a simple polygon where s and g are located
on the polygon boundary and the part of the polygon boundary from s to g is weakly visible
to the part from g to s and vice versa.

Our aim is to minimize the ratio of the length of the path traveled by the robot to the length
of the shortest path from s to g. In analogy to on-line algorithms this value is called the
competitive ratio. We present two strategies. Our first strategy, *continuous lad*, extends the
strategy *lad* which minimizes the Local Absolute Detour. We show that this extension results in
a 2.03-competitive strategy, which significantly improves the best known bound of 4.44 for this
class of strategies. Secondly, and most importantly, we present a hybrid strategy consisting of
continuous lad and the strategy *Move-in-Quadrant*. We show that this combination of strategies
achieves a competitive ratio of 1.73 which about halves the gap between the known $\sqrt{2}$ lower
bound for this problem and the previously best known competitive ratio of 2.05.

1 Introduction

Finding a path from a starting location to a goal within a given scene is an important problem
in robotics. A natural and realistic setting is to assume that the robot has only a partial
knowledge of its surroundings and that the amount of information available to the robot
increases as it travels and discovers its surroundings. For this purpose, the robot is equipped
with an on-board vision system that provides the visibility map of its local environment. The
robot uses this information to devise a search path for a visually identifiable goal located
outside the current visibility region. The quality of a search strategy is then evaluated under
the framework of competitive analysis for on-line searches, as introduced by Sleator and
Tarjan [13]. A search strategy is called *c-competitive* if the path traveled by the robot to
find the goal is at most c times longer than a shortest path. The parameter c is called the
competitive ratio of the strategy.

As can easily be seen, there is no strategy with a competitive ratio of $o(n)$ for scenes with
arbitrary obstacles having a total of n vertices [2] even if we restrict ourselves to searching
in a simple polygon. Therefore, the on-line search problem has been studied previously in
various contexts where the geometry of the obstacles is restricted [1, 2, 3, 9, 7, 10, 12].

Klein introduced the notion of a *street* as the first class of polygons which allow search
strategies with a constant competitive ratio even when the location of the goal is unknown [6].
In a street, the starting point s and the goal g are located on the boundary of the polygon
and the two polygonal chains from s to g are mutually weakly visible. Klein presents the
strategy *lad* for searching in streets which is based on the idea of minimizing the Local
Absolute Detour. He shows an upper bound on its competitive ratio of $1 + 3/2\pi$ (~ 5.71),
later improved to $1 + \pi/2 + \sqrt{1 + \pi^2/4}$ (~ 4.44) by Icking [5].

---

* This research is supported by the DFG-Project "Diskrete Probleme", No. Ot 64/8-1.

A strategy based on a different approach was presented by Kleinberg [7]. His strategy for searching in streets can be shown to have a competitive ratio of $2\sqrt{2}$ with a very simple analysis. A further improvement using ideas similar to Kleinberg's achieves a competitive ratio of $\sqrt{1 + (1 + \pi/4)^2}$ (~ 2.05) [8]; however, the analysis is significantly more complex. As the only known lower bound Klein presents a street where all strategies have a competitive ratio of at least $\sqrt{2}$ [6].

In this paper we present two strategies to traverse a street, one of which is an extension of the original approach presented by Klein. The first strategy presented, *continuous lad*, is shown to have a ~ 2.03 competitive ratio, which significantly improves the best known bound of 4.44 for this class of strategies. We then combine *continuous lad* with the strategy *Move-in-Quadrant* presented in [8], resulting in a hybrid strategy with a competitive ratio of 1.73. This new strategy halves the gap between the known $\sqrt{2}$ lower bound for this problem and the previously best known strategy of ~ 2.05.

The paper is organized as follows. In Section 2 we introduce the basic geometric concepts necessary for the rest of the paper. We also introduce a "High Level Strategy" as proposed by Klein [6] and state some results about search strategies that follow this High Level Strategy. In Section 3 we present the new strategy, *continuous lad*, and its analysis. In Section 4 we provide a new analysis of the strategy *Move-in-Quadrant* [8] and show how to combine *continuous lad* with *Move-in-Quadrant* to obtain a strategy with a performance guarantee of 1.73.

2 Preliminaries

Since we deal with point sets in the plane $I\!\!E^2$, we need the standard definitions of distance, norm, angle etc. for points. If p, q, and r are three points in the plane, then we denote the L_2-distance between p and q by $d(p, q)$, the line segment between p and q by $\overline{pq}$, and the counterclockwise angle between the line segment $\overline{qp}$ and the line segment $\overline{qr}$ at q by $\angle pqr$. If $\mathcal{P}$ is a path in $I\!\!E^2$, we denote its length by $\lambda(\mathcal{P})$. Furthermore, if p and q are two points on $\mathcal{P}$, then we denote the part of $\mathcal{P}$ from p to q by $\mathcal{P}(p, q)$.

A *simple polygon* is a simple, closed curve that consists of the concatenation of line segments, called the *edges* of the polygon, such that no two consecutive edges are collinear. The end points of the edges are called the *vertices* of the polygon.

We consider a simple polygon P in the plane with n vertices and a robot inside P which is located at a start point s on the boundary of P. The robot has to find a path from s to the goal g. We denote the shortest path from s to g by $sp(s, g)$.

The search of the robot is aided by simple vision (i.e. we assume that the robot knows the visibility polygon of its current location). Furthermore, the robot retains all the information seen so far (in memory) and knows its starting and current position. We are, in particular, concerned with a special class of polygons called *streets* first introduced by Klein [6].

Definition 1. [6] Let P be a simple polygon with two distinguished vertices, s and g, and let L and R denote the clockwise and counterclockwise, resp., oriented boundary chains leading from s to g. If L and R are mutually weakly visible, i.e. if each point of L sees at least one point of R and vice versa, then (P, s, g) is called a *street*.

The only available information to the robot is its *visiblity polygon* which is defined as the set of all points in P that are seen by the robot. It is denoted by $V(p)$ if the robot is located at point p. A *window* of $V(p)$ is an edge of $V(p)$ that does not belong to the boundary of P (see Figure 1a). A window w splits P into a number of subpolygons $P_1, \ldots, P_k$ one of which contains $V(p)$. We denote the union of the subpolygons that do not contain $V(p)$ by P_w.

The end point of a window w that is closer to p is called the *entrance point* of w. We assume that a window w has the orientation of the ray from p to entrance point of w. We say a window w is a *left window* if P_w is locally to the left of w w.r.t. the given orientation of w. A *right window* is defined similarly.

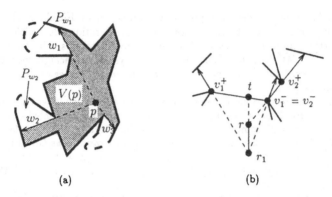

(a)   (b)

Fig. 1. (a): The visibility polygon $V(p)$ of p with left window w_1 and right windows w_2 and w_3. (b): As the robot moves to t the left extreme entrance point "jumps" from v_1^+ to v_2^+ and the robot moves directly to v_1^-.

Let p be the current location of the robot and $\mathcal{P}_{sp}$ the path the robot followed from s to p. We assume that the robot knows the part of P that can be seen from $\mathcal{P}_{sp}$, i.e. the robot maintains the polygon $V(\mathcal{P}_{sp}) = \bigcup_{q \in \mathcal{P}_{sp}} V(q)$. We say a window w of $V(p)$ is a *true window* w.r.t. $\mathcal{P}_{sp}$ if P_w is not contained in $V(\mathcal{P}_{sp})$. We say two (true) windows w_1 and w_2 are *clockwise consecutive* if the clockwise oriented polygonal chain of $V(p)$ between w_1 and w_2 does not contain a (true) window different from w_1 and w_2. *Counterclockwise consecutive* is defined analogously.

If w_0 is the window of $V(p)$ that is intersected the first time by $\mathcal{P}_{sp}$, then it can be shown that all left true windows are clockwise consecutive and all right true windows are counterclockwise consecutive from w_0 [6, 7, 8]. Hence, if left true windows exist, then there is a clockwise-most left true window in $V(p)$ which we call the *left extreme true window* and denote by w^+. The *right extreme true window* w^- is defined similarly. The entrance point v^+ (v^-) of w^+ (w^-) is called the *left (right) extreme entrance point of* $V(p)$. It can be easily shown that g is contained in either P_{w^+} or P_{w^-} and that either v^+ or v^- belongs to $sp(s,g)$ [6, 7, 8]. The angle $\angle v^- p v^+$ is called the *visibility angle of p* and denoted by $v_a(p)$.

The algorithms we propose all follow the same high level strategy as described by Klein [6]. The general idea is that the robot moves from one point that is known to lie on $sp(s,g)$ to a point on $sp(s,g)$ that is closer to g by a sequence of moves as described below.

Algorithm High Level Strategy
Input: a street (P, s, g) and a path $\mathcal{P}_{sr}$ from s to the current position of the robot r;
while v^+ and v^- are defined **and** g is not reached **do**
    Compute a path $\mathcal{P}_{rt}$ from r to some point t on $\overline{v^+v^-}$;
    Follow the path $\mathcal{P}_{rt}$ until one of the following events occurs:
    a) g becomes visible: the robot moves directly to g;
    b) P_{w^+} or P_{w^-} becomes visible: the robot moves to v^- if P_{w^+} is visible and to v^+ if P_{w^-} is visible;
    c) v^+ or v^- changes: Let r be the current robot position;
        1) **if** v^+ is on $\overline{rv^-}$ **or** v^- is on $\overline{rv^+}$ **then** move to v^+ or v^-, respectively (see Figure 1b);
        2) **else** Compute $V(r)$ and v^+ and v^- anew;
end while;

An example of how the robot moves is given in Figure 2a. The only detail left open by the

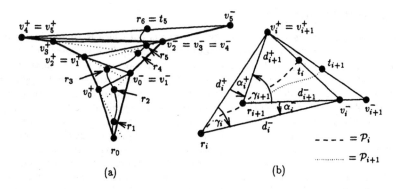

Fig. 2. (a) An example of the execution of the *High Level Strategy*. (b) r_{i+1} is the first point on $\mathcal{P}_i$ where the left or right extreme entrance point changes.

above description is what path $\mathcal{P}_{rt}$ to choose which is called a "low-level strategy" [6]. In the following we investigate two low-level strategies and analyse their performance.

2.1 Preliminary Results for Low-Level Strategies

A first observation about the high level strategy is that if one of the Cases a)–c1) occurs, then we know which of v^+ or v^- belongs to $sp(s,g)$. Hence, we assume in the following that the robot starts out at a point $r_0 \in sp(s,g)$ and encounters a number of events of Category c2) before it can finally decide which of the two extreme entrance points belongs to $sp(s,g)$. Each of these events corresponds to one point r_i, $i \geq 1$, at which new left and right extreme entrance points v_i^+ and v_i^- appear and a new path $\mathcal{P}_i$ from r_i to a point t_i on $\overrightarrow{v_i^+ v_i^-}$ is computed. Let d_i^+ be the distance of r_i to v_i^+ and d_i^- be the distance from r_i to v_i^-.

Given r_i, the point r_{i+1} is defined as the first point on $\mathcal{P}_i$ such that either the left or the right extreme entrance point of $V(r_{i+1})$ is different from v_i^+ or v_i^-, respectively (see Figure 2b). At the point r_{i+1} the robot computes a new target point and a new path $\mathcal{P}_{i+1}$.

We denote the angle $\angle r_i v_i^+ r_{i+1}$ by α_i^+ and the angle $\angle r_{i+1} v_i^- r_i$ by α_i^-. The angle $\angle v_i^- r_i v_i^+$ is denoted by γ_i. We can make the following elementary observation about the angles γ_{i+1} and γ_i.

Observation 2. $\gamma_{i+1} = \gamma_i + \alpha_i^+ + \alpha_i^-$.

Let $a_i^+ = d_i^+ - (d_{i+1}^+ - d(v_i^+, v_{i+1}^+))$ and $a_i^- = d_i^- - (d_{i+1}^- - d(v_i^-, v_{i+1}^-))$. Note that either $d(v_i^+, v_{i+1}^+) = 0$ or $d(v_i^-, v_{i+1}^-) = 0$. Furthermore, note that the distance of r_{i+1} to v_i^+ is $d_i^+ - a_i^+$ and the distance of r_{i+1} to v_i^- is $d_i^- - a_i^-$. Let $\mathcal{V}_i^+$ be the shortest path from r_0 to v_i^+, and $\mathcal{V}_i^-$ the the shortest path from r_0 to v_i^-.

If the distance to v_i^+ and v_i^- decreases monotonously as the robot travels on $\mathcal{P}_i$, for all $0 \leq i \leq k$, then the length of $\mathcal{V}_i^+$ or $\mathcal{V}_i^-$ can be expressed as d_i^+ plus the sum of the a_i^+ or d_i^- plus the sum of the a_i^-, respectively.

Lemma 3. *If, for all $0 \leq i \leq k$, $d(r_{i+1}, v_i^+) \leq d_i^+$ and $d(r_{i+1}, v_i^-) \leq d_i^-$, then we obtain, with the above definitions,*

$$\lambda(\mathcal{V}_i^+) = \sum_{j=0}^{i-1} a_j^+ + d_i^+ \quad and \quad \lambda(\mathcal{V}_i^-) = \sum_{j=0}^{i-1} a_j^- + d_i^-.$$

3 *lad* and Beyond

In this section we consider a new strategy *continuous lad* which is similar in spirit to the first strategy *lad* that was proposed to traverse streets [6]. The strategy *lad* is based on the idea of minimizing the local absolute detour. The importance of *lad*—apart from being the first strategy proposed—lies in the fact that it is the only strategy that uses a heuristic optimality criterion to guide the robot. All other strategies that have been presented have no comparable feature. The well-chosen heuristic and its excellent performance in practice make *lad* a very attractive strategy. Unfortunately, it seems that it is exactly this property that makes *lad* also extremely difficult to analyse. As mentioned before the best performance guarantee is $1 + \pi/2 + \sqrt{1 + \pi^2/4}$ (~ 4.44) which seems to be a very loose bound considering that the competitive ratio of the strategy observed in practice is less than 1.8 [6].

In the following we present a variant of *lad* which we call *continuous lad* that also follows the paradigm of minimizing the local absolute detour but whose analysis turns out to be much simpler and tighter.

3.1 The Strategy *lad*

We give a short description of the rationale behind *lad* as well as its definition, so as to stress both the differences and similarities between it and *continuous lad*.

If the robot has not been able to decide whether v_i^+ or v_i^- belongs to the shortest path from s to g after i steps, it chooses a new target point t_i on $\overline{v_i^+ v_i^-}$ and the line segment $\mathcal{P}_i = \overline{r_i t_i}$ to travel from its current position r_i to t_i. Let $\mathcal{Q}_i$ be the path of the robot from r_0 to r_i and recall that $\mathcal{V}_i^+$ is the shortest path from r_0 to v_i^+ and $\mathcal{V}_i^-$ the shortest path from r_0 to v_i^-. If v_i^+ lies on the shortest path from s to g, then the local absolute detour is given by the distance the robot travels from r_0 to v_i^+ which is $\lambda(\mathcal{Q}_i) + \lambda(\mathcal{P}_i) + d(t_i, v_i^+)$ minus the length of the shortest path $\lambda(\mathcal{V}_i^+)$ from r_0 to v_i^+. A similar statement holds if v_i^- belongs to $sp(s, g)$. Hence, the maximum local absolute detour is minimized if

$$\lambda(\mathcal{Q}_i) + \lambda(\mathcal{P}_i) + d(t_i, v_i^+) - \lambda(\mathcal{V}_i^+) = \lambda(\mathcal{Q}_i) + \lambda(\mathcal{P}_i) + d(t_i, v_i^-) - \lambda(\mathcal{V}_i^-) \qquad (1)$$

and the point t_i on $\overline{v_i^+ v_i^-}$ is given by

$$d(v_i^-, t_i) = \frac{\lambda(\mathcal{V}_i^-) - \lambda(\mathcal{V}_i^+) + d(v_i^+, v_i^-)}{2}. \qquad (2)$$

Note that $\lambda(\mathcal{V}_i^+) = \sum_{j=0}^{i} d(v_j^+, v_{j-1}^+)$ and $\lambda(\mathcal{V}_i^-) = \sum_{j=0}^{i} d(v_j^-, v_{j-1}^-)$ where we define $v_{-1}^+ = v_{-1}^- = r_0$.

3.2 The Strategy *continuous lad*

In the strategy *continuous lad* the robot also follows a path from r_i to t_i where t_i is determined by Equation 2; however, the robot does not move on a straight line segment. Instead, the robot travels along a path $\mathcal{P}_i$ from r_i to r_{i+1} such that every point r on $\mathcal{P}_i$ satisfies Equation 1 if we replace t_i by r and $\mathcal{P}_i$ by $\mathcal{P}_i(r_i, r)$. If the robot follows the strategy *continuous lad*, then $a_i^+ = a_i^-$ and the location of t_i is only determined by d_i^+ and d_i^-.

Lemma 4. *If the robot travels on a path* $\mathcal{P}_i$ *such that for all* $r \in \mathcal{P}_i$,

$$\lambda(\mathcal{Q}_i) + \lambda(\mathcal{P}_i(r_i, r)) + d(r, v_i^+) - \lambda(\mathcal{V}_i^+) = \lambda(\mathcal{Q}_i) + \lambda(\mathcal{P}_i(r_i, r)) + d(r, v_i^-) - \lambda(\mathcal{V}_i^-), \quad (3)$$

then $a_i^+ = a_i^- > 0$.

Proof: The proof is by induction on i. For $i = 0$, we have $\lambda(\mathcal{V}_0^+) = d(r_0, v_0^+)$ and $\lambda(\mathcal{V}_0^-) = d(r_0, v_0^-)$ and if we set $r = r_1$, then the above equation immediately yields

$$a_0^- = d(r_0, v_0^-) - d(r_1, v_0^-) = d(r_0, v_0^+) - d(r_1, v_0^+) = a_0^+.$$

Since the robot moves into the interior of the triangle (r_0, v_0^+, v_0^-) it is easy to see that $a_0^+ > 0$. So now assume the claim is true, for all $0 \leq i \leq k - 1$. Since $d(r_{i+1}, v_i^+) = d_i^+ - a_i^+ < d_i^+$, for all $0 \leq i \leq k - 1$, Lemma 3 holds and $\lambda(V_k^+) = \sum_{j=0}^{k-1} a_j^+ + d_k^+$. Similarly, we have $\lambda(V_k^-) = \sum_{j=0}^{k-1} a_j^- + d_k^-$. By the induction hypothesis $\sum_{j=0}^{k-1} a_j^+ = \sum_{j=0}^{k-1} a_j^-$ and the above equation again yields

$$a_k^- = d_k^- - d(r_{k+1}, v_k^-) = d_k^+ - d(r_{k+1}, v_k^+) = a_k^+.$$

$a_k^+ > 0$ can be seen as in the case $i = 0$. $\square$

Since $a_i^+ = a_i^-$, the path $\mathcal{P}_i$ is very easy to compute.

Corollary 5. *If the path $\mathcal{P}_i$ is chosen such that every point r on $\mathcal{P}_i$ satisfies Equation 3, then $\mathcal{P}_i$ is an arc of the hyperbola with foci v_i^+ and v_i^- that goes through r_i.*

If we choose a coordinate system with the origin at v_i^-, the x-axis going through v_i^+, $d(v_i^-, v_i^+) = 1$, and $d = d(v_i^-, t_i)$ computed according to Equation 2, then the x- and y-coordinate of the robot are given by

$$x = d + (2d - 1)a \quad \text{and} \quad y = 2\sqrt{d(1 - d)a(1 + a)}$$

where a is a parameter that decreases continuously from $a_i^+ - d(v_i^-, t_i)$ to 0.

3.3 Analysis of the Strategy *continuous lad*

In the following we assume that the robot travels on a path $\mathcal{P}_i$ such that, for all points r_{i+1} on $\mathcal{P}_i$ the distances a_i^+ and a_i^- are the same, i.e. $a_i^+ = a_i^- = a_i$. We analyse a step of the High-Level-Algorithm which consists of k consecutive events of Category c2) and one event in the Categories a)–c1).

We present two bounds for the length of the path connecting the points r_j, $0 \leq j \leq k$. The first bound gives a good approximation if the angle γ_i is small and the second bound approximates large angles.

Lemma 6. *If $a_i^+ = a_i^-$, then $d(r_i, r_{i+1}) \leq a_i^+ / \cos(\gamma_{i+1}/2)$.*

Proof: Let r_{i+1} be chosen such that $a_i^+ = a_i^-$. Consider the quadrilateral formed by r_i, u_i^+, u_i^-, and r_{i+1} as shown in Figure 3. The location of r_{i+1} is completely determined by the

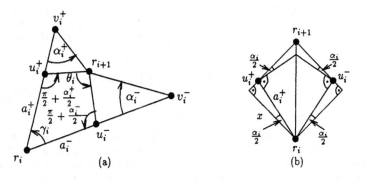

Fig. 3. (a) Illustrating the proof of Lemma 6. (b) Choosing γ_i.

angles α_i^+, α_i^-, and γ_i. The angle of the quadrilateral formed at u_i^+ is $(\pi + \alpha_i^+)/2$ and at u_i^- it is $(\pi + \alpha_i^-)/2$. Since $\alpha_i^+ + \alpha_i^- + \gamma_i = \gamma_{i+1}$, we can choose α_i^+ and α_i^- in order to maximize the distance of r_{i+1} to r_i. Let $\theta_i = \angle u_i^+ r_{i+1} u_i^-$. Note that $\theta_i = 2\pi - \gamma_i - (\pi + \alpha_i^+)/2 - (\pi + \alpha_i^-)/2 = \pi - \gamma_i - \alpha_i^+/2 - \alpha_i^-/2$.

Let $\delta_1 = \angle u_i^- u_i^+ r_{i+1}$ and $\delta_2 = \angle r_{i+1} u_i^- u_i^+$. Hence, $\delta_1 + \delta_2 = \pi - \theta_i$, where θ_i is fixed. Furthermore, we introduce a coordinate system such that the origin is located at u_i^+, $u_i^- = (1, 0)$, and r_i is located on the line $L = \{(x, y) \mid x = 1/2\}$. Let C be the circle that passes through u_i^-, r_{i+1}, and u_i^+ with center c. The path of all points with $\delta_1 + \delta_2 = \pi - \theta_i$ is the arc A of C from u_i^- to u_i^+ that contains r_{i+1} (see [11, Sec. 16, Th. 4]).

We claim that $d(r_i, r_{i+1})$ is maximal for $\delta_1 = \delta_2$. Let p be the topmost point of the arc A, i.e., $\delta_1 = \delta_2$ if $r_{i+1} = p$. We note that c is located on the line L. If c is above r_i, then the circle with center r_i and radius $d(r_i, p)$ contains C and, hence, p is the point with maximal distance to r_i.

Let q be the point $(1/2, 0)$. We claim that c is above r_i. In order to show this we compute $d(r_i, q)$ and $d(c, q)$. The angle $\angle q r_i u_i^+$ is obviously $\gamma_i/2$. Hence, $d(r_i, q) = 1/2 \cot(\gamma_i/2)$. By [11, Sec. 16, Th. 2] the angle $\angle u_i^- c u_i^+$ equals $2\pi - 2\theta_i = 2\gamma_i + \alpha_i^+ + \alpha_i^-$ and $d(c, q) = 1/2 \cot(\pi - \theta_i) = 1/2 \cot(\gamma_i + \alpha_i^+/2 + \alpha_i^-/2) < 1/2 \cot(\gamma_i/2) = d(r_i, q)$ as claimed.

Therefore, we can assume $\alpha_i^+ = \alpha_i^-$ and we have the configuration displayed in Figure 3. Since

$$\cos\left(\frac{\alpha_i^+}{2}\right) = \frac{x}{a_i^+} \quad \text{and} \quad \cos\left(\frac{\alpha_i^+ + \gamma_i}{2}\right) = \frac{x}{d(r_i, r_{i+1})},$$

we obtain

$$d(r_i, r_{i+1}) = \frac{\cos(\alpha_i^+/2) a_i^+}{\cos((\gamma_i + \alpha_i^+)/2)}.$$

With $(\alpha_i^+ + \gamma_i)/2 \le \gamma_{i+1}/2 < \pi/2$ and $\cos(\alpha_i^+/2) \le 1$ the claim follows. $\square$

For large angles we make use of the following observation.

Lemma 7. *If $a_i^+ = a_i^-$ and the angle at the robot position is γ_i, then*

$$d(r_i, r_{i+1}) \le \min\{\alpha_i^+ d_i^+, \alpha_i^- d_i^-\} + a_i.$$

Proof: We only show that $d(r_i, r_{i+1}) \le \alpha_i^+ d_i^+ + a_i$. Clearly, we have $d(r_i, r_{i+1}) \le d(r_i, u_i^+) + d(u_i^+, r_{i+1})$. Now $d(r_i, u_i^+) = a_i$ and $d(u_i^+, r_{i+1}) \le \alpha^+ d_i^+$ which proves the claim. $\square$

We now can analyse the competitive ratio of *continuous lad*. In the analysis we make use of the following lemma.

Lemma 8. *Let $r_i(t)$ denote the position of the robot at time t while traveling on $\mathcal{P}_i$ with $r_i(0) = r_i$ and $r_i(1) = t_i$. If the robot executes Strategy continuous lad, then the visiblity angle $v_\alpha(r_i(t))$ is a continuous and monotonically increasing function as the robot travels on $\mathcal{P}_i$.*

Proof: Let $\gamma(t) = v_\alpha(r_i(t))$. Since $d(r_i(t), v_i^+)$ and $d(r_i(t), v_i^-)$ both decrease monotonically and continuously with t, the angles $\alpha_i^+(t) = \angle r_i v_i^+ r_i(t)$ and $\alpha_i^-(t) = \angle r_i(t) v_i^- r_i$ are continuous and monotonically increasing functions of t. Therefore, $\gamma_i(t) = \gamma_i + \alpha_i^+(t) + \alpha_i^-(t)$ is also a continuous and monotonically increasing function of t. $\square$

Hence, if γ is an angle between γ_0 and γ_k, then there is one $0 \le i_0 \le k$ and one $0 \le t_0 \le 1$ with $\gamma_{i_0}(t_0) = \gamma$. We split the execution of the strategy into two parts. In the first part we consider the length of the path of the robot until the visibility angle equals $\gamma = \gamma_{i_0}(t_0)$ and in the second part we consider the length of the remaining path of the robot.

In order to analyse the competitive ratio of *continuous lad* we need to estimate the length of the path $\mathcal{P}_i$ which is the concatenation of parts of hyperbolas. Recall that if $\Lambda(\mathcal{P}_i)$ is the set of all finite sequences of points on $\mathcal{P}_i$ that occur in order, i.e. $\Lambda(\mathcal{P}_i) = \{(q_0, \ldots, q_m) \mid m \ge 1, q_j \in \mathcal{P}_i, \text{ for all } 0 \le j \le m, \text{ and } q_{j+1} \text{ occurs after } q_j \text{ on } \mathcal{P}_i\}$, then

$\lambda(\mathcal{P}_i) = \sup\{\sum_{j=0}^{m-1} d(q_j, q_{j+1}) \mid (q_0, \ldots, q_m) \in \Lambda(\mathcal{P}_i)\}$. We will make use of this definition to estimate the length of $\mathcal{P}_i$.

So consider a sequence $(q_0, \ldots, q_m) \in \Lambda(\mathcal{P}_i)$. Since we are interested in obtaining a supremum and adding points only increases $\sum_{j=0}^{m-1} d(q_j, q_{j+1})$, we can assume that $(r_0, \ldots, r_k)$ is a subsequence of $(q_0, \ldots, q_m)$. Furthermore, we assume that the point $\dot{r}_{i_0}(t_0) = q_{j_0}$ is also contained in $(q_0, \ldots, q_m)$. We define as before v_j^+ to be the left entrance point of $V(q_j)$, $d_j^+ = d(q_j, v_j^+)$, and $a_j^+ = d_j^+ - (d_{j+1}^+ - d(v_i^+, v_{i+1}^+))$. v_j^-, d_j^-, a_j^-, γ_j, etc. are defined analogously. Note that with the above definitions Lemmas 3 and 4 still hold which implies that Lemmas 6 and 7 hold as well.

So let $\mathcal{R}_m$ be the path connecting the points $q_0, \ldots, q_m$ by line segments. We now observe that if the angle γ_j at q_j is less than or equal to γ, i.e. $j \leq j_0$, then Lemma 6 yields that $d(q_{j-1}, q_j) \leq a_{j-1}/\cos(\gamma/2)$. Otherwise, Lemma 7 yields that $d(q_j, q_{j+1}) \leq \alpha_j^+ d_j^+ + a_j^+$ and $d(q_j, q_{j+1}) \leq \alpha_j^- d_j^- + a_j^-$. We obtain the following analysis of the length of $\mathcal{R}_m$ where we assume w.l.o.g. that $v_{m-1}^+ \in sp(s, g)$.

$$
\begin{aligned}
\sum_{j=0}^{m-1} d(q_j, q_{j+1}) + d_m^+ &= \sum_{j=0}^{j_0} d(q_j, q_{j+1}) + \sum_{j=j_0+1}^{m-1} d(q_j, q_{j+1}) + d_m^+ \\
&\leq \sum_{j=0}^{j_0} \frac{a_j^+}{\cos(\gamma/2)} + \sum_{j=j_0+1}^{m-1} (\alpha_j^+ d_j^+ + a_j^+) + d_m^+ \\
&\leq \sum_{j=0}^{j_0} \frac{a_j^+}{\cos(\gamma/2)} + \left(\lambda(\mathcal{V}_m^+) - \sum_{j=0}^{j_0} a_j^+\right) \sum_{j=j_0+1}^{m-1} \alpha_j^+ + \sum_{j=j_0+1}^{m-1} a_j^+ + d_m^+ \\
&\leq \frac{1}{\cos(\gamma/2)} \sum_{j=0}^{j_0} a_j^+ + (\pi - \gamma + 1)\left(\lambda(\mathcal{V}_m^+) - \sum_{j=0}^{j_0} a_j^+\right) \\
&\leq \max\{1/\cos(\gamma/2), \pi - \gamma + 1\}\lambda(\mathcal{V}_m^+)
\end{aligned}
$$

So let the angle γ be chosen such that the maximum of $\{1/\cos(\gamma/2), \pi - \gamma + 1\}$ is minimized, i.e., that $1/\cos(\gamma/2) = \pi - \gamma + 1$. By numerical evaluation we obtain that $\gamma \sim 2.111$. Hence, $(\pi - 2.111) + 1$ (~ 2.03) is an upper bound on the length of the path $\mathcal{R}_m$ that connects the points q_j by straight line segments. Since $(q_0, \ldots, q_m)$ is chosen arbitrarily from $\Lambda(\mathcal{P}_i)$, the supremum of $\{\sum_{j=0}^{m-1} d(q_j, q_{j+1}) \mid (q_0, \ldots, q_m) \in \Lambda(\mathcal{P}_i)\}$ is also bounded by 2.03.

Theorem 9. *The competitive ratio of the Strategy continuous lad is at most 2.03.*

A second interesting implication is that if we execute *continuous lad* until $\gamma(t) = \gamma$ and then switch to another strategy with competitve ratio c, then the competitive ratio of the combined strategy is $\max\{1/\cos(\gamma/2), c\}$. In particular, if $\gamma = \pi/2$, then we can execute *continuous lad* for small visibility angles without increasing the competitive ratio since $1/\cos(\pi/4) = \sqrt{2}$ is a lower bound for searching in streets.

Corollary 10. *The Strategy continuous lad is an optimal strategy in streets for which the visibility angle is at most $\pi/2$.*

4 Changing the Strategy

Since the robot can measure the visibility angle at its position, it is possible to change the strategy once a certain threshold is reached. We assume that the robot has encountered k events of Category c2) in *continuous lad* and then switches to a new strategy at point r_k.

In the following we consider the Strategy *Move-in-Quadrant* which was already presented in [8] but we provide a tighter analysis if the angle γ_k is larger than $\pi/2$.

In order to present the strategy we need the notion of a projection of a point. The *orthogonal projection* p' of a point p onto a line segment l is defined as the point of l that is closest to p.

Strategy Move-in-Quadrant
Input: A point r_k in P such that the angle $\gamma_k = \angle v_k^- r_k v_k^+$ is $\geq \pi/2$;
$i := k$;
while v_i^+ and v_i^- of $V(r_i)$ are defined **do**
    Move to the orthogonal projection r_{i+1} of r_k onto the line segment l_i from v_i^+ to v_i^-;
    Compute the points v_{i+1}^+ and v_{i+1}^- of the visibility polygon $V(r_{i+1})$ of r_{i+1};
    $i := i + 1$;
end while;

The correctness of the strategy has been proven in [8]. Note that the Strategy *Move-in-Quadrant* also follows the schema of the High-Level-Strategy except that events of Category c2) are replaced by events of Category c2'): $t_i = r_{i+1}$ is reached.

4.1 Analysis of the Strategy *Move-in-Quadrant*

In the following we assume that the Strategy *Move-in-Quadrant* has stopped after $m - k$ iterations. As before the shortest path goes either through v_i^+ or v_i^- [8].

Recall that γ_k is defined to be the angle $\angle v_k^- r_k v_k^+$ which we assume to be greater than or equal to $\pi/2$. We introduce a coordinate system where r_k is the origin and the angle δ_k^- between the x-axis and the line segment $\overline{r_k v_k^-}$ equals the angle δ_k^+ between the y-axis and the line segment $\overline{r_k v_k^+}$. We define $\delta_k = \delta_k^+ = \delta_k^-$.

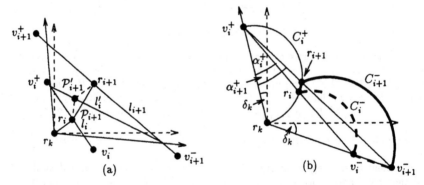

Fig. 4. (a) Introducing a new segment between l_i and l_{i+1}. (b) Case 2 if the robot moves from r_i to r_{i+1}.

Now suppose that we have arrived at point r_i and move to point r_{i+1} in the next iteration. To simplify the analysis, we consider the line segment l_i' from the intersection point of $v_i^+ v_i^-$ with the line through r_k and v_k^+ to the intersection point of $v_{i+1}^+ v_{i+1}^-$ with the line through r_k and v_k^- as shown Figure 4a.

The line segment l_i' is located between l_i and l_{i+1}. If we consider the path $\mathcal{P}_i'$ from r_k to r_i that visits the orthogonal projections of r_k onto the line segments l_j and l_j' in order, for $k \leq j \leq i$, then the length of $\mathcal{P}_i'$ is obviously greater than or equal to the length of $\mathcal{P}_i$. Furthermore, $\mathcal{P}_i$ and $\mathcal{P}_i'$ share the same start and end point. Hence, for the simplicity of exposition we assume in the following that v_i^+ and v_i^- are located on the line from r_k to v_k^+ and v_k^-, respectively, and that either $v_i^+ = v_{i+1}^+$ or $v_i^- = v_{i+1}^-$.

Let L_i be the length of the path $\mathcal{P}_i$ traveled by the robot from r_k to reach r_i; let α_i^- be the angle $\angle r_i v_i^- r_k$, and d_i^- the distance $d(r_k, v_i^-)$. Similarly, let α_i^+ be the angle $\angle r_k v_i^+ r_i$ and d_i^+ the distance $d(r_k, v_i^+)$. We define the angle α_i as $\min\{\pi/2 - \alpha_i^+, \pi/2 - \alpha_i^-\}$ and the distance d_i as $\min\{d_i^+, d_i^-\}$. Note that $\pi/2 - \alpha_i^+ + \pi/2 - \alpha_i^- = \gamma_k$ and, therefore, $\alpha_i^+ + \alpha_i^- + 2\delta_k = \pi/2$ or $\pi/2 - \alpha_i^+ = \alpha_i^- + 2\delta_k$ and $\pi/2 - \alpha_i^- = \alpha_i^+ + 2\delta_k$. In particular, $\alpha_i = \pi/2 - \alpha_i^+$ if and only if $d_i = d_i^+$.

Our approach to analyze our strategy is based on the idea of a potential function Q_i [8]. It is our aim to show that $L_i + Q_i \leq (\frac{\gamma_k}{2} + \cot \frac{\gamma_k}{2}) d_i$, for all $k \leq i \leq m$, where we define $Q_i = \alpha_i d_i$. So suppose the robot has reached the point r_i and $L_i \leq (\gamma_k/2 + \cot \gamma_k/2 - \alpha_i) d_i$ and d_i is equal to the distance between r_k and v_i^-. For simplicity of description we assume that the distance from r_k to v_i^+ is 1. For the distance d_i^- we obtain $d_i^- = \sin \alpha_i^+ / \cos(\alpha_i^+ + 2\delta_k)$. The robot moves now from r_i to r_{i+1}. We distinguish two cases.

Case 1 $\alpha_i^+ > \alpha_{i+1}^+$ or $\alpha_{i+1}^+ > \alpha_{i+1}^-$.
These two Cases can be analysed exactly as the Cases 1 and 3 the analysis of *Move-in-Quadrant* of [8].

Case 2 $\alpha_i^+ \leq \alpha_{i+1}^+ \leq \alpha_{i+1}^-$ (see Figure 4).
Hence, $d_{i+1} = \sin \alpha_{i+1}^+ / \cos(\alpha_{i+1}^+ + 2\delta_k)$. Note that r_{i+1} is on the circle C_i^+ with center at $c_i^+ = 1/2(-\sin \delta_k, \cos \delta_k)$ and radius $1/2$. The arc a_i^+ of C_i^+ from r_i to r_{i+1} has length $2(\pi/2 - \alpha_i^+ - (\pi/2 - \alpha_{i+1}^+))1/2$. Clearly, the line segment $\overline{r_i r_{i+1}}$ is shorter than the arc a_i^+. Hence,

$$L_{i+1} = L_i + d(r_i, r_{i+1}) \leq \left(\frac{\gamma_k}{2} + \cot \frac{\gamma_k}{2}\right) d_i - \alpha_i d_i + \alpha_{i+1}^+ - \alpha_i^+$$

We want to show that

$$\left(\frac{\gamma_k}{2} + \cot \frac{\gamma_k}{2} - \alpha_i\right) d_i + (\alpha_{i+1}^+ - \alpha_i^+) \leq \left(\frac{\gamma_k}{2} + \cot \frac{\gamma_k}{2} - \alpha_{i+1}\right) d_{i+1} \qquad (4)$$

or

$$\frac{\gamma_k}{2} + \cot \frac{\gamma_k}{2} \geq \frac{\alpha_{i+1} d_{i+1} - \alpha_i d_i + \alpha_{i+1} - \alpha_i}{d_{i+1} - d_i}$$

with $\gamma_k - \pi/2 \leq \alpha_i \leq \alpha_{i+1} \leq \pi/4 - \delta_k$. If we define $\beta_i = \alpha_{i+1} - \alpha_i = \alpha_{i+1}^+ - \alpha_i^+$ and

$$f(\alpha_i, \beta_i, \delta_k) = \frac{\beta_i + (\alpha_i^+ + \beta_i + 2\delta_k)\frac{\sin(\alpha_i^+ + \beta_i)}{\cos(\alpha_i^+ + \beta_i + 2\delta_k)} - (\alpha_i^+ + 2\delta_k)\frac{\sin \alpha_i^+}{\cos(\alpha_i^+ + 2\delta_k)}}{\sin(\alpha_i^+ + \beta_i)/\cos(\alpha_i^+ + \beta_i + 2\delta_k) - \sin \alpha_i^+ / \cos(\alpha_i^+ + 2\delta_k)},$$

then we want to prove that $f(\alpha, \beta, \delta) \leq \gamma/2 + \cot \gamma/2$, where $\gamma = \pi/2 + 2\delta$, for all $(\alpha, \beta, \delta) \in \Delta = \{(x, y, z) \mid x \geq 0, y \geq 0, z \geq 0, x + y + z \leq \pi/4\}$ since we assume that $\alpha_{i+1}^+ \leq \alpha_{i+1}^-$, i.e. $\alpha_{i+1}^+ \leq \pi/2 - \alpha_{i+1}^+ - 2\delta_k$ or $\alpha_i^+ + \beta_i + \delta_k \leq \pi/4$.

By considering the partial derivatives of f w.r.t. α it can be easily shown that f is monotone w.r.t. α and, therefore, $\max f(\alpha, \beta, \delta) = \max f(\pi/4 - \beta - \delta, \beta, \delta)$. If we define $g(\beta, \delta) = f(\frac{\pi}{4} - \beta - \delta, \beta, \delta)$, then

$$\frac{\partial}{\partial \beta}\left(\frac{\partial g}{\partial \beta}(\beta, \delta)\frac{1}{\cos 2\delta(\cos 2\beta - 1)}\right) = \sin(4\delta)\cos(2\beta) - 2\cos 2\delta \cos 2\beta - \sin 4\delta + \cos 2\delta$$

which is equal to 0 if and only if $\cos(2\beta) = 1$ or $\sin(4\delta)/2 = \cos 2\delta$, the latter of which only holds for $\delta = \pi/4$. Furthermore, since $0 \leq \beta \leq \pi/4$, the former holds only if $\beta = 0$. Therefore, we can see easily that $\frac{\partial}{\partial \beta}\left(\frac{\partial g}{\partial \beta}(\beta, \delta)\frac{1}{2}\frac{1}{\cos 2\delta(\cos 2\beta - 1)}\right) \leq 0$ and, thus, $\frac{\partial g}{\partial \beta}(\beta, \delta)/2(\cos 2\delta(\cos 2\beta - 1))$ is monotonically decreasing in β.

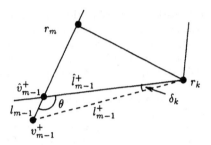

Fig. 5. Bounding the final competitive ratio.

It can be easily checked that $\lim_{\beta \to 0} \frac{\partial g}{\partial \beta}(\beta, \delta) = 0$ and, therefore, $\frac{\partial g}{\partial \beta}(\beta, \delta) \leq 0$, for all $0 \leq \beta \leq \pi/4 - \delta$. This in turn implies that g is monotonically decreasing in β and the maximum $\max_{(\alpha,\beta,\delta) \in \Delta} f(\alpha, \beta, \delta) = \max_{\beta \in [0,\pi/4-\delta]} g(\beta, \delta)$ is achieved for

$$\lim_{\beta \to 0} \frac{\pi}{4} + \delta + \frac{\beta}{2} + \frac{\beta \cos(\beta + 2\delta)}{2 \sin \delta} + \frac{\beta \cos \beta}{\sin \beta \cos 2\delta} - \frac{3\beta \sin(\beta + 2\delta)}{4 \sin \beta \cos 2\delta} + \frac{\beta \sin(\beta - 2\delta)}{4 \sin \beta \cos 2\delta} - \frac{\beta \cos(\beta + 4\delta)}{4 \sin \beta \cos 2\delta}$$

which yields $\pi/4 + \delta + \cot(\pi/4 + \delta)$ or, with $\gamma = \pi/2 + 2\delta$, $\gamma/2 + \cot(\gamma/2)$ as claimed.

4.2 The Final Ratio

In order to obtain the final competitive ratio for one step we have to take into account that the robot has to move to either v_{m-1}^+ or v_{m-1}^-. If v_m^- is undefined, then v_{m-1}^+ belongs to the shortest path from s to g. The above analysis provides an upper bound on the maximum distance the robot travels in order to reach $\hat{v}_{m-1}^+$ in Figure 5 which is located on the line through r_k and v_k^+.

Let l_{m-1} be the line segment between v_{m-1}^+ and $\hat{v}_{m-1}^+$ and θ the angle between $\hat{l}_{m-1}^+$ and l_{m-1}. The length of l_{m-1}^+ grows monotonically with θ if the lengths of $\hat{l}_{m-1}^+$ of l_{m-1} are fixed. Hence, the maximum ratio of $(c\lambda(\hat{l}_{m-1}^+) + \lambda(l_{m-1}))/\lambda(l_{m-1}^+)$ is achieved for the minimum angle θ which is $\theta = \gamma_k = \pi/2 + 2\delta_k$. Let the length of $\hat{l}_{m-1}^+$ be d_1 and the length of l_{m-1} be d_2. Hence, the maximum distance traveled by the robot from r_k to v_{m-1}^+ is bounded by

$$F(\delta_k) = \max \frac{c(\delta_k) d_1 + d_2}{\sqrt{d_1^2 + d_2^2 - 2 d_1 d_2 \cos(\frac{\pi}{2} + 2\delta_k)}}.$$

where $c(\delta) = \pi/4 + \delta + \cot(\pi/4 + \delta)$. This maximum is achieved if we set d_2 to the value $\max\{0, d_1(1 - c(\delta_k) \sin 2\delta_k)/(c(\delta_k) - \sin 2\delta_k)\}$ and yields a value of

$$F(\delta_k) = \frac{c(\delta_k) + \frac{1 - c(\delta_k) \sin 2\delta_k}{c(\delta_k) - \sin 2\delta_k}}{\sqrt{1 + \left(\frac{1 - c(\delta_k) \sin 2\delta_k}{c(\delta_k) - \sin 2\delta_k}\right)^2 + 2 \frac{(1 - c(\delta_k) \sin 2\delta_k) \sin 2\delta_k}{c(\delta_k) - \sin 2\delta_k}}}.$$

The same analysis applies if v_m^+ is undefined.

If we combine this with Lemma 6, we obtain the following upper bound on the distance traveled by the robot if the shortest path from s to g goes through v_{m-1}^+. Recall that $\mathcal{P}_i$ is the path the robot follows from point r_i to r_{i+1}, where we set $r_{m+1} = v_{m-1}^+$.

$$\sum_{j=0}^{m} \lambda(\mathcal{P}_i) = \sum_{j=0}^{k-1} \lambda(\mathcal{P}_i) + \sum_{j=k}^{m} d(r_j, r_{j+1}) \leq \frac{1}{\cos(\gamma_k/2)} \sum_{j=0}^{k} a_j^+ + F(\delta_k) \left(\lambda(\mathcal{V}_{m-1}^+) - \sum_{j=0}^{k} a_j^+\right)$$

$$\leq \max\left\{\frac{1}{\cos(\gamma_k/2)}, F(\delta_k)\right\} \lambda(\mathcal{V}_{m-1}^+)$$

with $\gamma_k = \pi/2 + 2\delta_k$. Again the minimum competitive ratio is achieved if both the terms in the maximum are equal. This yields a value of 1.91 radians for γ_k and a competitive ratio of ~ 1.73.

Theorem 11. *If a robot traverses a street using the Strategy continuous lad until the visibility angle is 1.91 radians and then switches to Strategy Move-in-Quadrant, then the competive ratio of the path traveled by the robot is at most 1.73.*

5 Conclusions

We have presented two strategies for a robot to search in streets if it is given the visibility map of its local surroundings. The strategies proposed use the same "high level strategy" as outlined by Klein [6]. In the strategy *continuous lad* the resulting path followed by the robot is a concatenation of parts of hyperbolas. Though the path generated by the strategy is fairly complicated its analysis turns out to be much simpler than the analysis of the similar strategy *lad*.

The strategy proposed has a relatively good competitive ratio of 2.03. Surprisingly, this strategy, combined with the previously best known 2.05-competitive strategy results in a hybrid strategy with a competitive ratio of 1.73.

Often the idealistic assumption that a robot can follow a precomputed path without deviation is violated by real life robots. An interesting open problem is, therefore, if it is possible for a robot to traverse a scene with a predetermined maximal navigational error per unit traversed at a predetermined competitive ratio. Also the gap between the lower bound of $\sqrt{2}$ and the upper bound of 1.73 for search strategies in streets is still significant and needs to be improved.

References

1. R. Baeza-Yates, J. Culberson and G. Rawlins. "Searching in the plane", *Information and Computation*, Vol. **106**, (1993), pp. 234-252.

2. A. Blum, P. Raghavan and B. Schieber. "Navigating in unfamiliar geometric terrain", *Proc. of 23rd ACM Symp. on Theory of Computing*, (1991), pp. 494-504.

3. K-F. Chan and T. W. Lam. "An on-line algorithm for navigating in an unknown environment", *International Journal of Computational Geometry & Applications*, Vol. **3**, (1993), pp. 227-244.

4. X. Deng, T. Kameda and C. Papadimitriou. "How to learn an unknown environment I: The rectilinear case", *Technical Report CS-93-04*, Dept. of Comp. Sci., York University, 1993. Also as *Proc. 32nd IEEE Symp. on Foundations of Comp. Sci.*, (1991), pp. 298-303.

5. Ch. Icking. Ph. D. Thesis, Fernuniversität Hagen, 1994.

6. R. Klein. "Walking an unknown street with bounded detour", *Computational Geometry: Theory and Applications* **1**, (1992), pp. 325-351.

7. J. Kleinberg. "On-line search in a simple polygon", *Proc. of 5th ACM-SIAM Symp. on Discrete Algorithms*, (1994), pp. 8-15.

8. A. Lopez-Ortiz and S. Schuierer. "Going home through an unknown street", Proc. of 4th Workshop on Data Structures and Algorithms, 1995, LNCS 955, pp. 135-146.

9. A. Lopez-Ortiz and S. Schuierer. "Simple, Efficient and Robust Strategies to Traverse Streets", Proc. 7th Canad. Conf. on Computational Geometry, 1995, pp. 217-222.

10. A. Mei and Y. Igarashi. "Efficient strategies for robot navigation in unknown environment" *Proc. of 21st Intl. Colloquium on Automata, Languages and Programming*, (1994).

11. E. Moise. "Elementary Geometry from an Advanced Standpoint", 2nd ed., Addison-Wesley, 1973.

12. C. H. Papadimitriou and M. Yannakakis. "Shortest paths without a map", *Theoretical Computer Science* **84**, (1991), pp. 127-150.

13. D. D. Sleator and R. E. Tarjan. "Amortized efficiency of list update and paging rules", *Communications of the ACM* **28**, (1985), pp. 202-208.

Safe and Efficient Traffic Laws for Mobile Robots

Sonne Preminger[1] [†] and Eli Upfal[12] [†] [‡]

[1] Weizmann Institute, Rehovot 76100, Israel.
[2] IBM Almaden Research Center, San Jose, CA 95120.

Abstract. The subject of this work is the design of traffic laws for safe and efficient operation of a large number of independent mobile robots in a common territory. The set of traffic laws must be small and simple, and it must allow each individual robot to perform its own movement tasks efficiently, while preventing possible collisions between different robots. We present a close to optimal solution for robots operating in a grid-like environment, significantly improving over previously published results.

1 Introduction

1.1 Motivation

Having several independent agents operating in a common environment gives rise to a variety of coordination and coexistence problems. A practical example is the domain of mobile robots in which the robots have to perform different tasks, while moving in a common territory. Each robot is independent, has its own control unit, and its list of locations it has to visit. Without coordination robots might block each other, causing long delays, or even collisions.

Large applications with complex moving patterns can not rely on one central control unit to direct all the robots and resolve all movement conflicts in real-time. Instead, one need to device a set of "traffic laws" that all robots must follow. The set of traffic laws must be small and simple to avoid large computing overhead in the individual robots. It must absolutely prevent any possibility of a collision, while allowing all the robots to reach their respected destinations is close to optimal time. Thus, central control is substituted by a distributed solution in which individual robots follow a common set of "traffic laws".

1.2 The Model

A *Multi Robot Grid System* consists on an $n \times n$ grid, and a set of m robots. Robots are placed in nodes of the grid. Only one robot may occupy a node at

---

[†] Work was supported in part by a grant from the Israeli Academy of Science. E-mail: son@wisdom.weizmann.ac.il, eli@wisdom.weizmann.ac.il.

[‡] Work at the Weizmann Institute supported in part by the Norman D. Cohen Professorial Chair of Computer Science, and a MINERVA grant.

a given time. Time is partitioned into steps. In one step a robot can traverse one grid edge, moving to a neighboring node on the grid. Edges of the grid are undirected, only one robot can traverse a given edge at any step. A *collision* occurs when two robots try to occupy the same node simultaneously, or when two robots try to traverse the same edge at the same step.

The grid represents the aisles between work locations. When a robot reaches its destination it leaves the grid and moves into a work location. For convenience we associate a robot destination with the grid node connected to that location.

A Multi Robot Grid Solution (MRG): is a set of laws such that for any initial locations of the robots on the grid and for any set of destinations, if all robots follow the laws, all robots eventually reach their respective destinations, and there are no collisions.

A multi robot grid solution is measured by its complexity, in particular the amount of communication it requires between the robots, and by its efficiency. Following the standard measure in packet routing, we avoid trivial cases by measuring the efficiency of a solution by the number of steps it requires to solve an arbitrary *1-relation*: no more than one robot is initially in any location, and no location is the destination of more than one robot in the system.

It is easy to construct a solution for an $n \times n$ grid that requires no communication between the robots and in which all robots reach their destinations in $O(n^2)$ steps. Simply connect the nodes of the grid by a directed Hamiltonian cycle. All robots move on the cycle till they reach their destinations. Our goal is to construct a significantly faster solution that is still simple and relies on minimum communication between the individual robots.

1.3 Related Work

Our work was motivated by the developing theory of *artificial social laws*. The goal of that theory is to formulate and study the requirements of systems in which multiple independent agents must coexist successfully in a common domain [5, 8, 9].

The MRG problem has been defined in [8, 9] as a paradigm for studying artificial social laws. Two solutions are presented. The first set of laws can control up to $\sqrt{n}$ robots on the $n \times n$ grid, it guarantees that any 1-relation with up to $\sqrt{n}$ robots takes $O(n)$ steps. The second set of laws gives an $O(n)$ solution for a special case of a 1-relation with up to n robots all initially located in the bottom row of the grid.

The MRG problem can be viewed as a variant of packet routing on a mesh with bounded buffers. However, known solutions to the packet routing problem (such as [4, 2]) do not translate to our model. The main difficulty is that in the MRG problem only one robot can occupy a node at any time, while in the various packet routing problems several packets can either reside in a node, or traverse a node simultaneously. While this difference between the models seems minor, it dictates a significantly different solution to the MRG problem.

1.4 Summary of Results

In the next section, we show that with absolutely no communication between the processors no set of laws can perform significantly better on the $n \times n$ grid than the trivial n^2 solution.

In section 3 we present a randomized solution that solves an arbitrary 1-relation with up to n^2 robots on an $n \times n$ grid in $O(n \log n)$ time. The amount of communication between the robots is minimal, a robot needs to know only about other robots at distance 2 or less. Note that the time it takes the robots to reach their destinations is within $O(\log n)$ of optimal.

2 Lower Bound on Solutions with No Communication

Theorem 1. *Any solution (deterministic or randomized) for the MRG problem that uses no communication between the processors requires $\Omega(n^2)$ steps on some 1-relation.*

Proof. (Sketch) Given a deterministic solution with no communication between the robots, the path taken by a robot, and the time it traverses any edge on the path, is completely determined by the robot's initial location and its destination (the fact that timing is determined by the input distinguishes our case from the standard packet routing analysis).

Define a directed *time graph* $H = (V, E)$. H has $n^2(n^2+1)$ vertices of the form (v, t), where v is a node of the grid, and $t = 0, ..., n^2$. Vertex (v, t) is connected in H to vertex $(w, t+1)$ if vertex v is connected to vertex w in the grid.

A route of a robot (including its timing) defines a path on the time graph H. A solution to the MRG problem is valid if for any 1-relation all paths on H are disjoint. The efficiency of the solution is measured by the longest path it defines on H. Using a counting argument similar to the one in [1, 6] we can show that if the path lengths are $o(N^2)$ then in most 1-relations there are at least two paths that collide. (See [7] for a complete proof.) □

3 A Randomized Solution for Arbitrary 1-Relations

3.1 The Routing Scheme

Our solution is based on 'marking' a set of circular *highways* on the grid. Robots moving on these highways have the right-of-way, and since the highways are circular, robots are never forced to stop, and there is no danger that a robot gets 'dead-ended'. To reach its destination a robot needs to switch highways. The crux of our algorithm is a limited communication based mechanism for 'switching' between highways. The analysis shows that the safe switching mechanism does not result is long delays.

To define the set of highways we partition the $n \times n$ grid into $n^2/(c \log n)^2$ disjoint squares, see figure 1 (the constant c is determined in the analysis).

We mark two disjoint highways in each square. The boundary of the square is marked as a circular *square's boundary* highway. A *snake cycle* connecting all the internal nodes of the square is marked as a second highway. The movement on the square boundary highway is in clockwise direction, movement on the snake cycle highway is in counter-clockwise direction.

c log n

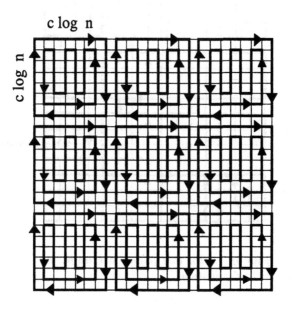

Fig. 1. *The set of highways.*

The *switching mechanism* : a robot can move from a node on one highway to a neighboring node on another highway only if there is no other robot that can reach that node or pass the same edge in that step. Note that this switching mechanism requires robots to 'know' only about robots at distance two or less.

The route of a robot from its initial location to its destination is partitioned into three phases (see figure 2):

In the *first phase* the robot moves on the internal snake cycle, from its initial location until it can switch to the boundary highway.

In the *middle phase* the movement is only on the squares' boundaries highways. Each robot chooses a random square as its *intermediate square*. The robot switches from one boundary highway to the next one, first on the row of boundary highways then on the column of boundary highways till it reaches the boundary highway of its random intermediate square. The robot then continues, again first on the row of boundary highways, then on the column till it reaches the boundary highway of the square that contains the robot's destination.

In the *last phase* the robot moves on the boundary highway until it can switch to the internal snake highway, then it moves on the internal snake until it reaches its destination.

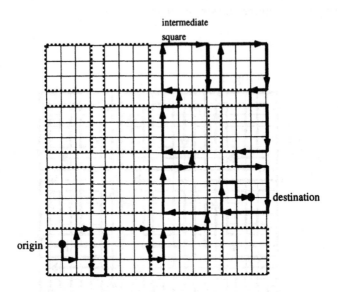

Fig. 2. *A typical path of a robot that follows our traffic law - from origin, through intermediate square, to destination.*

3.2 Analysis of a Special Case

We analyze first the performance of the above scheme on a special type of inputs. We say that a 1-relation is *good* if no square on the grid is a source or destination of more than $\alpha \log n$ robots. (Thus, a good 1-relation consists of up to $\frac{n^2}{(c \log n)^2} \alpha \log n$ robots, α is a constant that will be specified in the proof.)

Theorem 2. *Using the above routing scheme on an arbitrary good 1-relation, with probability at least $1 - \frac{1}{n^2}$ every robot reaches its destination within $16n + 2(c \log n - 2)^2$ steps.*

Proof. To simplify the analysis we assume first that the three routing phases do not overlap, all robots finish a given phase before any robot starts the next phase. We comment later on how to eliminate this assumption.

Proposition 3. *The first and last phases take $(c \log n - 2)^2$ steps each, for $\alpha < \frac{3}{2}c$.*

Proof. The length of the snake cycle highway in each square is $(c \log n - 2)^2$, there are $3(c \log n - 2)$ nodes of this snake that are continually adjacent to nodes of the boundary highway (the right, left and bottom edges). On its first cycle on the snake, the robot will travel on at least $3(c \log n - 2)/2$ such places continually. Since the 1-relation is good, only $\alpha \log n$ of the boundary highway nodes are occupied, where $\alpha < 3/2c$. Thus, there must be a step in which the robot can switch to the boundary highway within its first cycle. Similar arguments work for the last stage. □

We turn to analyze the middle phase. For the sake of the analysis we partition time into *rounds*, each round is a segment of $4c \log n$ steps. To simplify the analysis we assume w.l.o.g. that a robot does not switch between highways more than once in each round. Our goal is to show that w.h.p. all robots switch from one boundary highway to another once in each round. Since a robot needs to traverse at most $\frac{4n}{c \log n}$ squares through the phase, it implies that the phase terminates w.h.p. within $16n$ steps.

Proposition 4. *With probability at least* $1 - \frac{1}{n^2}$, *during all the first* $\frac{4n}{c \log n}$ *rounds of the middle phase:*

1. *Every robot that has not reached its destination square moves to the next boundary highway in its path;*
2. *No boundary highway has more than* $2\beta \log n$ *robots,*

for $\beta \geq max\{16\alpha, 28\}$, *and* $c > 5\beta$.

Proof. We define the following events (α specified as before):
$E_{orig} = \{$ at most $\alpha \log n$ robots are originating in every square$\}$,
$E_{dest} = \{$ at most $\alpha \log n$ robots are destined for every square$\}$,
$E_0 = E_{orig} \cap E_{dest}$ (notice that this event specifies exactly a good 1-relation),
$A_i = \{$ at round i all robots move to next boundary highway in their path$\}$,
$B_i = \{$ at end of round i there are at most $\beta \log n$ robots in every boundary highway$\}$, and
$E_i = \{A_i \cap B_i\}$.

In the following lemmas we show that

$$Prob\{ \bigcap_{i=0}^{\frac{4n}{c \log n}} E_i \} = Pr[E_{\frac{4n}{c \log n}} \mid \bigcap_{\frac{4n}{c \log n} - 1} E_i] \times Pr[E_{\frac{4n}{c \log n} - 1} \mid \bigcap_{i=0}^{\frac{4n}{c \log n} - 2} E_i] \times ... \times Pr[E_0]$$

$$\geq (1 - \frac{1}{n^3})^{\frac{4n}{c \log n}} \geq 1 - \frac{1}{n^2}$$

The first part of Proposition 4 follows since $A_i \subset E_i$. To prove the second part of the lemma we observe that at the end of each round there are at most $\beta \log n$ robots on each square boundary highway, (by B_i), during the round at most $\beta \log n$ robots will arrive (since at the end of the round the boundary has no more than $\beta \log n$ robots and a robot switches only one highway is each round), thus the maximum number of robots on a boundary highway during a round is $2\beta \log n$.

Lemma 5. *For every* $1 \leq t \leq \frac{4n}{c \log n}$, *if* $\bigcap_{i=0}^{t-1} E_i$ *occurs, then* A_t *also occurs.*

Lemma 6. *For every* $1 \leq t \leq \frac{4n}{c \log n}$, $Prob[B_t \mid \bigcap_{i=0}^{t-1} E_i] \geq 1 - \frac{1}{n^3}$.

Proof. (of Lemma 5)
Since $\bigcap_{i=0}^{t-1} E_i$ occurs, in particular we know that there were no more than $\beta \log n$ robots on each boundary highway at the end of round $t - 1$. Therefore during round t there are going be no more than $5\beta \log n$ robots on each boundary highway (robots from neighbor squares plus from the square itself). However, if $c > 5\beta$, and each robot has opportunity to switch into $c \log n$ places, then there will be at least one place to which the robot can switch. $\square$

Proof. (of Lemma 6)
To bound $Prob[B_t \mid \bigcap_{i=0}^{t-1} E_i]$, we should consider only the incoming robots to each boundary highway at round t. This is because by Lemma 5, the conditioning on $\bigcap_{i=0}^{t-1} E_i$ implies A_t, meaning that all the robots that were on the boundary highway at the beginning of round t, will move out of it during the round. We will prove that w.h.p. at the t-th round, the number of incoming robots to each boundary highway is not grater than $\beta \log n$.

We take some square (i, j), and define the event
$$B_t^{(i,j)} = \{ \text{at most } \beta \log n \text{ robots are arriving into square } (i, j) \text{ at round } t \}.$$
We now prove that $Prob[\overline{B}_t^{(i,j)} \mid \bigcap_{i=0}^{t-1} E_i] \leq \frac{1}{n^5}$. We consider separately robots that pass in (i, j) before passing their intermediate square, and robots that pass in (i, j) after the intermediate square. The proof is composed of the following claims,

Claim 1 *Define the event* $H_1 = \{$*number of robots passing in* (i, j) *at round* t *in their way from origin to intermediate square (including)* $\leq \frac{\beta}{2} \log n\}$, *then* $Prob[\overline{H}_1 \mid \bigcap_{i=0}^{t-1} E_i] \leq \frac{1}{n^6}$

Claim 2 *Define the event* $H_2 = \{$*number of robots passing in* (i, j) *at round* t *in their way from intermediate square to destination (including)* $\leq \frac{\beta}{2} \log n\}$, *then* $Prob[\overline{H}_2 \mid \bigcap_{i=0}^{t-1} E_i] \leq \frac{1}{n^6}$

Then, using these claims, and the facts that $B_t^{i,j} \supseteq H_1 \cap H_2$, and $B_t = \bigcap_{(i,j)} B_t^{(i,j)}$, we get $Prob[B_t \mid \bigcap_{i=0}^{t-1} E_i] \geq (1 - \frac{1}{n^5})^{n^2} \geq 1 - \frac{1}{n^3}$, which concludes Lemma 6.

Proof. (of Claim 1)
Define $D_t^{(i,j)} = \{$the set of all squares that are at distance of t squares from $(i,j)\}$.

Note that $|D_t^{(i,j)}| \leq \frac{2n}{c \log n}$. By the conditioning on $\bigcap_{i=0}^{t-1} E_i$, the robots that originate in the squares that belong to $D_t^{(i,j)}$ are the only robots that can arrive to (i,j) at time t in their way to their intermediate squares. We show that w.h.p. not too many robots that originate in $D_t^{(i,j)}$, pass in (i,j) before reaching their intermediate square. To use Chernoff bound we define the following Bernoulli variables

$$X_{(k,l),m}^{(i,j)} = \begin{cases} 1 \text{ if (i,j) is the t-th square in the path of the m'th robot} \\ \quad \text{originating in (k,l), and in this path (i,j) is passed} \\ \quad \text{before (or when) passing the intermediate square} \\ 0 \text{ otherwise (also if less than m robots originate in (k,l))} \end{cases}$$

for $1 \leq m \leq \alpha \log n$, $(k,l) \in D_t^{(i,j)}$.

The following sub-claims imply the claim:

Sub-claim 1 *Define the event* $C_{middle} = \{\sum_{(k,l) \in D_t^{(i,j)}, k \neq i,m} X_{(k,l),m}^{(i,j)} \leq \frac{3\beta}{8} \log n\}$.
Then $Prob[\overline{C}_{middle} \mid \bigcap_{i=0}^{t-1} E_i] \leq \frac{1}{n^6}$

Sub-claim 2 *Define the event* $C_{right} = \{\sum_{(k,l) \in D_t^{(i,j)}, l > j, k=i,m} X_{(k,l),m}^{(i,j)} \leq \frac{\beta}{16} \log n\}$.
Then $Prob[\overline{C}_{right} \mid \bigcap_{i=0}^{t-1} E_i] = 0$

Sub-claim 3 *Define the event* $C_{left} = \{\sum_{(k,l) \in D_t^{(i,j)}, l < j, k=i,m} X_{(k,l),m}^{(i,j)} \leq \frac{\beta}{16} \log n\}$.
Then $Prob[\overline{C}_{left} \mid \bigcap_{i=0}^{t-1} E_i] = 0$

Proof. (of Sub-claim 1)
Notice that $\forall (k,l) \in D_t^{(i,j)}, k \neq i, m$
$E[X_{(k,l),m}^{(i,j)} \mid \bigcap_{i=0}^{t-1} E_i] = Prob[$ a robot that starts in (k,l) has (i,j) in his path from origin to intermediate square$\mid \bigcap_{i=0}^{t-1} E_i] \leq \frac{c \log n}{n}$
Since the probability to choose an intermediate square that causes a path which passes in (i,j), is bounded by the probability to choose squares' row, since for robots that start in "middle" squares, the intermediate square has to be on the j-th column in order that the path will pass in (i,j). The choose of the intermediate square is done randomly. By summing up,
$$E[\sum_{(k,l) \in D_t^{(i,j)}, k \neq i,m} X_{(k,l),m}^{(i,j)}] \leq \frac{2n}{c \log n} \alpha \log n \frac{c \log n}{n} = 2\alpha \log n$$

All $X_{(k,l),m}^{(i,j)}$'s are independent, since they depend only on the choosing of the intermediate square, which is independent for different robots.
Therefore we can use the Chernoff bound [3] to get Sub-claim 1 for $\beta \geq max\{16\alpha/3, 16\}$.
$\square$

Proof. (of Sub-claims 2,3)
We show 2, proof of 3 is the same. At most $\alpha \log n$ robots originate in any square, therefore we get for $\beta > 16\alpha$

$$Prob[\textstyle\sum_{(k,l)\in D_t, l>j, k=i, m} X^{(i,j)}_{(k,l),m} \geq \tfrac{\beta}{16} \log n] \leq Prob[\sum X^{(i,j)}_{(k,l),m} > \alpha \log n] =$$
0

$\square$

Proof. (of Claim 2)

To evaluate how many robots pass in (i, j) at round t in their way from intermediate square to destination, we define the following Bernoulli variables

$$X^{(i,j)}_{(k,l),m} = \begin{cases} 1 \text{ if } (i,j) \text{ is the t-th square in the path of the m'th robot} \\ \quad \text{that has destination in } (k,l), \text{ and in this path } (i,j) \text{ is passed} \\ \quad \text{after passing the intermediate square} \\ 0 \text{ otherwise (also if less than m robots originate in } (k,l) \end{cases}$$

for $1 \leq m \leq \alpha \log n$, $(k, l) \in$ squares of the grid.

We evaluate separately the robots that have destinations in column j, and the rest of the robots. The following sub-claims imply the claim:

Sub-claim 4 *Define the event* $C_{middle} = \{\sum_{(k,l),l=j,m} X^{(i,j)}_{(k,l),m} \leq \tfrac{\beta}{4} \log n\}$.
Then $Prob[\overline{C}_{middle} \mid \bigcap_{i=0}^{t-1} E_i] \leq \tfrac{1}{2n^6}$

Sub-claim 5 *Define the event* $C_{rest} = \{\sum_{(k,l)l \neq j,m} X^{(i,j)}_{(k,l),m} \leq \tfrac{\beta}{4} \log n\}$.
Then $Prob[\overline{C}_{rest} \mid \bigcap_{i=0}^{t-1} E_i] \leq \tfrac{1}{2n^6}$

Proof. (of Sub-claim 4)

Notice that $\forall (k, l), l = j, m$

$E[X^{(i,j)}_{(k,l),m} \mid \bigcap_{i=0}^{t-1} E_i] = Prob[$ a robot that has destination in (k, l) has (i, j) t-th in his path and it is after the intermediate square$\mid \bigcap_{i=0}^{t-1} E_i] \leq \tfrac{4c \log n}{n}$

Since if you take a robot that is destined for (k,l), and consider its origin (v,w), it is easy to prove algebraically that for any possible square (i,j) and origin (v,w), there are at most $\tfrac{4n}{c \log n}$ intermediate squares (x,y) that can cause the robot 's path to pass in (i,j) at time t. In addition, intermediate squares are chosen at random from all the $\tfrac{n^2}{c^2 \log^2 n}$ squares.

By summing up over all the variables,

$$E[\textstyle\sum_{(k,l),l=j,m} X^{(i,j)}_{(k,l),m}] \leq \alpha \log n \tfrac{n}{c \log n} \tfrac{4c \log n}{n} = 4\alpha \log n$$

As in the previous case, all $X^{(i,j)}_{(k,l),m}$'s are independent, therefore by Chernoff bound [3] we get the sub-claim for $\beta \geq max\{16\alpha, 28\}$.

$\square$

Proof. (of Sub-claim 5)

Notice that $\forall (k, l), l \neq j, m$

$E[X^{(i,j)}_{(k,l),m} \mid \bigcap_{i=0}^{t-1} E_i] \leq \tfrac{2c^2 \log^2 n}{n^2}$

The reason is that the destination is not in the same column as (i,j), therefore, the intermediate square must be on the same row as (i,j) in order that the path will pass through (i,j). But in every row there are at most 2 intermediate squares that can cause the robot's path to pass in (i,j) at time t, and the intermediate squares are chosen randomly.

By summing up over all the variables,

$$E[\sum_{(k,l),l\neq j,m} X^{(i,j)}_{(k,l),m}] \leq \alpha \log n \frac{n^2}{c^2 \log^2 n} \frac{2c^2 \log^2 n}{n^2} = 2\alpha \log n$$

As in previous cases all $X^{(i,j)}_{(k,l),m}$'s are independent, therefore by Chernoff bound [3] we get the proof for $\beta \geq max\{8\alpha, 28\}$. □

We assumed so far that executions of the three phases do not overlap. To eliminate that assumption we notice that in the square boundary highways, all three phases can overlap, and in the internal snake highways, only the first and last phases can overlap. No more than $\alpha \log n$ robots use each of these highways on the first or last phases. The analysis showed that with high probability no more than $2\beta \log n$ robots use any of the square boundary highways in any step of the second phase. By fixing the length of these highways (fixing the constant c) to be large enough with respect to the constants α and β (e.g. $c > 2\alpha + 2\beta \geq 34\alpha$) the square boundary highways can accommodate robots from all the three phases together without degradation in total performance.

3.3 The General Solution

By adding random delays, we construct a solution that works for any 1-relation (up to n^2 robots) and w.h.p brings all robots to their destinations in $O(n \log n)$ time. The random delays partitioned the n^2 robots between $\frac{c^2}{\gamma} \log n$ stages (the constant γ is determined in the proof). Each stage takes $16n + 2(c \log n - 2)^2$ steps. W.h.p. the set of robots assigned to each stage defines a good 1-relation, thus by Theorem 2, with high probability the robots assigned to each stage reach their destination within that stage.

Theorem 7. *Given any 1-relation with up to n^2 robots, w.h.p. the general solution brings all robots to their destinations in $O(n \log n)$ steps.*

Proof. We need to show that the set of active robots in each stage defines a good 1-relation. There are a total of up to $(c \log n)^2$ robots initially placed in nodes of each square. Each robot chooses to be active at a given stage with probability $\frac{\gamma}{c^2 \log n}$, and the choices are independent. Using the Chernoff bound [3], the probability that in a given square at a given stage there are more than $\alpha \log n$ robots is bounded by n^{-7} when $\alpha \geq max\{\gamma, 7\}$. Therefore, at any stage, the probability that in some one of the $\frac{n^2}{(c \log n)^2}$ squares there are more than $\alpha \log n$ active robots is at most $\frac{n^2}{c^2 \log^2 n} \times \frac{1}{n^7} \leq \frac{1}{n^5}$.

Considering all stages, the probability that in any stage at any square there are at most $\alpha \log n$ robots is $\geq 1 - \sum_{stages} \frac{1}{n^5} = 1 - \frac{\frac{c^2}{\gamma} \log n}{n^5} \geq 1 - \frac{1}{2n^4}$ for sufficiently large n.

Using similar argument we show that with probability at least $1 - \frac{1}{2n^4}$ in all stages no square is the destination of more than $\alpha \log n$ robots. Thus, with probability $1 - \frac{1}{n^4}$ the set of active robots in all the stages define good 1-relations. By Theorem 2 the robots in each stage reach their destination within that stage with probability $1 - \frac{1}{n^2}$. Thus, with probability at least $1 - \frac{1}{n}$ all the n^2 robots reach their destinations in $O(n \log n)$ steps. □

3.4 Long Term Behavior

The traffic laws defined here guarantee that robots never collide. Their efficiency, however, is guaranteed only with high probability. Thus, if the scheme is used repeatedly, eventually some congestion will occur. If robots have an (approximate) common time, or if the system has some broadcast mechanism then the system can recover from bad states. Every $\Omega(n^2)$ step all robots switch to follow another set of laws. In the alternate set of laws all robots move on one directed Hamiltonian path connecting all the nodes of the grid. Following the alternate set of laws for n^2 steps clears the system from any congestion built up in the past. When the system switches back to the normal set of traffic laws, its state is independent of the past, and w.h.p. the system again operates efficiently.

References

1. A. Borodin and J.E. Hopcroft, Routing, merging, and sorting on parallel models of computation. *Jornal of Compumter and System Sciences* 30:130-145, 1985.
2. U. Feige and P. Raghavan, Exact Analysis of Hot-Potato Routing. In *proceedings of IEEE symposioum on foundations of computer science*, 553-562, 1992.
3. T. Hagerup and C. Rub, A guided tour of Chernoff bounds. *Information Processing Letters* 33, 305-308, 1989-90.
4. T. Leighton, Average case analysis of greedy routing algorithms on arrays. In *Proceedings of the 1990 ACM Symposium on Parallel Algorithms and Architectures*,p. 2-10, July 1990.
5. Y. Moses and M. Tennenholtz. On Computational aspects of artificial social systems. In *Proceedings of DAI-92*, 1992.
6. D. Peleg and E. Upfal, A time–randomness trade-off for oblivious routing. *SIAM Jurnal on Computing* 19:256-266, 1990.
7. S. Preminger, Complexity Analysis of Movement in Multi Robot System. *M.Sc. Thesis*, Departmant of Applied Mathematics, The Weizmann Institute of Science, 1995.
8. Y. Shoham and M. Tennenholtz, On traffic laws for mobile robots. In *First Conference on AI Planning Systems*, 1992.
9. Y. Shoham and M. Tennenholtz, On social laws for artificial agent societies: Off-line design. *Artificial Intelligence*, vol. 73, 1995.

Progress in Selection*

Mike Paterson

Department of Computer Science, University of Warwick, Coventry CV4 7AL, UK

Abstract. There has been recent progress in the selection problem, and in median-finding in particular, after a lull of ten years. This paper reviews some ancient and modern results on this problem, and suggests possibilities for future research.

1 Introduction

The *selection problem*, determining the kth largest out of a set of n elements, is a junior partner of the more fundamental sorting problem, but it has still been studied extensively over several decades.

Our focus will be on performing selection using a minimal number of comparisons in the worst case. Let $V_k(n)$ be the worst-case minimum number of pairwise comparisons required to find the kth largest out of n distinct elements. Of particular interest is finding the *median*, the $\lceil n/2 \rceil^{\text{th}}$ largest say. We denote $V_{\lceil n/2 \rceil}(n)$ by $M(n)$.

The worst-case comparison complexity of sorting is $n \log_2 n + O(n)$, and even the coefficient of the linear term has been fairly closely estimated. However for $V_k(n)$ we do not yet have an asymptotic value, except when $k = o(n)$, (and symmetrically, for $k - n = o(n)$). For finding the median, we currently know only a broad interval for the value of $M(n)$.

In this survey, I shall review some of the classic results in the quest to determine $V_k(n)$ and $M(n)$, report on some recent progress, and conjecture an asymptotic value for $M(n)$.

2 History

Credit for first raising the selection problem is often accorded to Charles Dodgson, who considered the proper allocation of the second and third prizes in tennis tournaments. Steinhaus proposed the problem of finding $V_2(n)$. The upper bound of $n + \lceil \log_2 n \rceil - 2$ was given by Schreier [22], but this was not shown to be the exact value until the proof by Kislitsyn [15]. Hadian and Sobel [10] gave an upper bound: $V_k(n) \leq n - k + (k-1)\lceil \log_2(n-k+2) \rceil$. This bound is asymptotically optimal for fixed k. A good account of early work in this area can be found in [16]. Successive improvements, for various ranges of k with respect to n, were

---

* This research was supported in part by the EU under contract 20244 (ALCOM-IT).

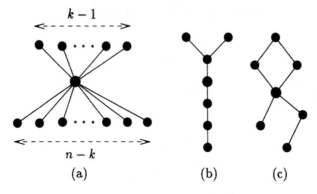

Fig. 1. (a) S_{n-k}^{k-1}; (b) and (c) both contain S_3^3.

made by Kirkpatrick [13, 14], Yap [25], Hyafil [11], Motoki [17], and Ramanan and Hyafil [20].

The classic paper by Blum, Floyd, Pratt, Rivest and Tarjan [2] in 1973 was the first to show that $M(n) = O(n)$, and therefore that finding the median is much easier than sorting. They gave an algorithm which requires at most about $5.43n$ comparisons, and introduced a technique which has been a basis of all subsequent improvements. In Section 3, I shall outline this technique, the improvements to $3n$ by Schönhage, Paterson and Pippenger [21], and the very recent further improvements by Dor and Zwick [5, 6, 7].

Blum et al. [2] were also the first to give a non-trivial lower bound for $M(n)$, and $V_k(n)$ when $k = \Omega(n)$. They showed that $M(n) \geq 3n/2 - O(1)$ and, more generally, that $V_k(n) \geq n + \min\{k, n - k\} - O(1)$, by using a simple adversary argument. This lower bound was successively improved by several authors (see [11, 13, 25, 18]), using more and more sophisticated adversaries and accounting schemes, and the coefficient was raised closer to 2.

A breakthrough came in 1985, with an elegant lower bound of $2n - o(n)$ by Bent and John [1]. It has taken a further ten years for this to be improved, by Dor and Zwick (again!) [5, 8]. In Section 4, I will review the adversary argument of Blum et al., and the use of a multitude of adversaries by Bent and John. I will also describe the subtle improvement in [5, 8].

Notation

We shall use the natural Hasse diagrams to describe partial orders. In our figures, the larger elements will be towards the top of the page. In the terminology of [21], a partial order which is composed of a *centre* element c together with u elements larger than c and v elements smaller than c is referred to as an S_v^u. The problem of selecting the kth largest element corresponds to constructing some S_{n-k}^{k-1} from a given set of n elements, i.e., determining some partial order which contains S_{n-k}^{k-1}. (See Figure 1(a).) For example, the partial orders in Figure 1(b),(c) both yield the median of seven elements.

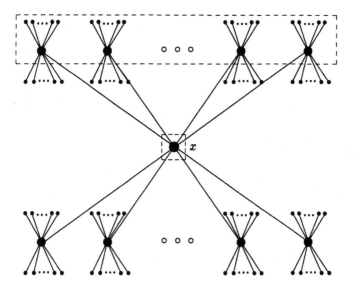

Fig. 2. Median of medians

3 Upper bounds

The general algorithmic technique introduced by Blum et al. is to generate many S_v^v's, for suitable v, and then to find the median x of the set of centre elements of the S_v^v's. The resulting partial order contains the partial order shown in Figure 2. The ranking of the element x with respect to the whole set is determined next. Suppose we are seeking the kth largest element. If the rank of x is k then we are finished. If not, then suppose without loss of generality that the rank of x is less than k. In this case, x and all the elements above x in the partial order (outlined in dashed boxes in Figure 2) may be discarded. These constitute more than a quarter of the elements. The algorithm proceeds with the appropriate selection problem from the remaining set. If the algorithm requires only a linear number of comparisons to discard a linear number of elements then a linear upper bound is assured. Blum et al. found it convenient to use C_{2v+1}'s, sorted chains of length $2v + 1$, as the S_v^v's in their algorithm and took v to be a small constant, seven. Finding the median of the centre elements was done by using the algorithm recursively. With some careful optimisation, they achieved an upper bound of $391n/72 \sim 5.43n$.

Note that, in this algorithm, a set of elements which is discarded consists of the top or bottom $v + 1$ elements from several C_{2v+1}'s, and they leave behind a residue of disconnected C_v's. Crucial to the performance of the algorithm is how economically the C_{2v+1}'s can be produced and how efficiently the returned C_v's can be recycled into new C_{2v+1}'s.

The balance of parameters used by Schönhage et al. [21] was very different. We took v to be rather large, so that the number of S_v^v's at any stage was $O(n^{3/4})$. The centres of the S_v^v's could therefore be kept in sorted order, and the

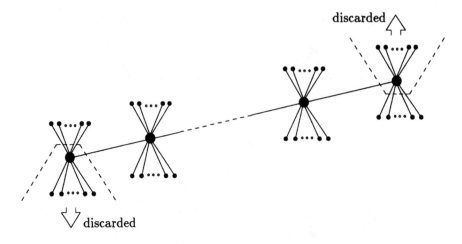

Fig. 3. Overall picture for SPP process.

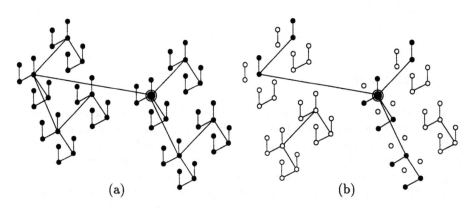

Fig. 4. (a) Hyperpair H_{011010}; (b) an S_7^7 produced by pruning

main part of the partial order maintained during the algorithm had the form shown in Figure 3.

The principal difference from the algorithm of Blum et al. was that whereas they produced S_v^v's (actually C_{2v+1}'s) in batches, we used a continuous production line. Much of the efficiency of our S_v^v factory arose from the nice properties of *hyperpairs*. Hyperpairs are built up recursively from smaller hyperpairs using symmetric comparisons. An illustration of the hyperpair H_{011010} is given in Figure 4(a). In (b) it is shown how an H_{011010} can be pruned to produce an S_7^7. Note also that the pieces pruned off are all in the form of smaller hyperpairs of various sizes. These are retained in the factory for recycling.

When the top or bottom parts of hyperpairs together with the central element are discarded during the algorithm, the remaining halves are returned to the factory for recycling. Unfortunately these are not themselves hyperpairs, so they are broken down to pairs and singletons, with a consequent loss in efficiency.

Dor and Zwick [5, 6, 7] introduce their *green* factories, which are able to recycle efficiently more of the debris from discarded S_v^v's. Instead of just pairs and singletons, they can recycle several larger partial order fragments. In [21], we describe a process where pairs and singletons are "grafted" onto structures to build S_v^v's more economically. Dor and Zwick show how to graft with a variety of different components, including even some 16-tuples, and they generalise hyperpairs to *hyperproducts*.

As a result of their many ingenious improvements, they achieve a median algorithm which requires at most $2.9423n$ comparisons. They also extend these techniques to the general selection problem to obtain improved bounds for $V_k(n)$.

4 Lower bounds

Many lower bound proofs for combinatorial algorithms such as selection can be usefully described in terms of an adversary, who "plays against" the algorithm by providing answers to the comparisons performed, in such a way that a fairly bad case is forced. The lower bound of $n + \min\{k - 1, n - k\} - 1$ given by Blum et al. [2] was proved in such a way.

Their adversary also provides some extra information to the algorithm from time to time, which may even assist the algorithm, but is chiefly provided to keep the state of the computation simple enough to deal with. As soon as any element has been declared the larger in two comparisons, the adversary tells the algorithm that this element is actually larger than the element being sought and so there is no need to carry out any further comparisons involving this element. Elements which are declared smaller in two comparisons are similarly eliminated. The partial order on the remaining candidates for selection consists always of only pairs and singletons. It is easy for the adversary to choose an outcome for each comparison involving a pair so that one element is eliminated, two comparisons are removed, and the simple form of the partial order is restored.

The adversary can continue with this "generous" strategy until either $k - 1$ elements have been declared too large or $n - k$ have been declared too small. At this point, the problem has been reduced to finding the maximum or minimum, respectively, of elements in the remaining r pairs or singletons. The adversary now keeps quiet and $r - 1$ further comparisons are required. It can be seen that at least $2 \min\{k - 1, n - k\} + \max\{k - 1, n - k\}$ comparisons are required overall, i.e., $n + \min\{k - 1, n - k\} - 1$ comparisons.

A sequence of improvements on this lower bound [19, 13, 25, 18] took the coefficient for medians from $3/2$ up to about 1.837. The new proofs introduced many new ideas and became more and more intricate, but were still based on a similar type of adversary argument. The components of the partial order retained at any time became larger and more varied: in [18] several hundred cases needed to be verified. Elaborate accounting systems were employed, e.g., "safe-boxes" and "joint accounts" in [25].

A different bounding method was introduced by Fussenegger and Gabow [9]. Instead of directly considering the depth of the decision tree of an algorithm, they count the number of leaves. The power of the method comes from showing that the decision tree has to contain many binary trees, each with a large number of leaves. If the leaves of the different included trees are disjoint, or at least do not overlap too much, then the decision tree must have many leaves and hence large depth. Although they were able to raise the lower bounds for some ranges of $V_k(n)$ and for other similar problems, they did not improve the lower bound in [2] for median-finding. A major improvement was made by Bent and John [1] in 1985, using this "leaf-counting" argument.

Any algorithm requires $j-1$ comparisons to find the largest (or the smallest) element from a set of size j. The corresponding decision tree will have at least 2^{j-1} leaves. Also, any algorithm for selecting the kth largest element x from a set of size n will need at least $n-1$ comparisons either involving x or between pairs of elements which are both above or both below x. A comparison between an element above x and an element below x will be called a *straddle*. Note that straddles do not contribute to the Hasse diagram of the final partial order for selection. So, to prove a lower bound of $n + m$, it would suffice to show that more than m straddles are sometimes made.

Bent and John use a multitude of adversaries in their lower bound proof for $V_k(n)$. Each adversary has its own special subset of elements A, where $|A| = k$. Up to a point, each adversary will answer comparison queries by using the rule that each element of A is above each element of the complement $\overline{A}$, i.e., $A > \overline{A}$. For other queries, of the form $A : A$ and $\overline{A} : \overline{A}$, both answers are valid and we regard the adversary as laying out a tree which branches at each such query. Unfortunately such simple adversaries are not strong enough to force a good bound – they need to be slightly malicious! When the algorithm is getting close to its goal of determining the minimum element of A, to return as the kth largest, the adversary is allowed to shift the goal-posts.

I will outline the proof of a lower bound which depends on some suitable parameter q. The full strategy for the adversary with special set A is described below. At any stage let $\mathrm{Min}A$ be the set of minimal elements in the partial order restricted to A, and let $\mathrm{Max}\overline{A}$ be the set of maximal elements in the partial order on $\overline{A}$.

Phase 1. Answer comparison queries according to the partial order $A > \overline{A}$. For comparisons of the type $A : A$ or $\overline{A} : \overline{A}$, follow both answers, creating a branching tree. Continue Phase 1 until $|\mathrm{Min}A| = q$. Now if $|\mathrm{Max}\overline{A}| < 2q$ then continue with Phase 2a, otherwise use Phase 2b.

Phase 2a. Continue as in Phase 1 until the end, when $|\mathrm{Min}A| = 1$.

Phase 2b. Choose an element $y \in \mathrm{Min}A$ such that the set $B(y)$ of elements in $\mathrm{Max}\overline{A}$ which have been compared with y is as small as possible. Let $A' = A\setminus\{y\}$, and answer the remaining comparison queries using the partial order $A' > \overline{A'}$.

Phase 1 requires $k-|\mathrm{Min}A|+n-k-|\mathrm{Max}\overline{A}|$ branching comparisons. Phase 2a requires a further $|\mathrm{Min}A|-1$ of these, giving a total of $n-|\mathrm{Max}\overline{A}|-1 \geq n-2q$.

For Phase 2b, the algorithm must find the maximum of the set $\overline{A'}$ in order to satisfy the adversary's strategy. At the beginning of Phase 2b, the maximal elements of $\overline{A'}$ are $y \cup (\mathrm{Max}\overline{A} \setminus B(y))$, and so Phase 2b requires at least $|\mathrm{Max}\overline{A}| - |B(y)|$ comparisons, giving a total of at least $n - q - |B(y)|$ comparisons. But if $|B(y)| > q$ then, by the choice of y, every element of $\mathrm{Min}A$ has been compared with at least $q + 1$ elements of $\mathrm{Max}\overline{A}$ by the end of Phase 1. If y were to be chosen as the kth largest element then the above comparisons already account for at least $(q - 1)(q + 1)$ straddles.

In summary, either there is a run of the algorithm producing $q^2 - 1$ straddles, and so at least $n + q^2 - 2$ comparisons, or else every adversary generates a binary tree with at least 2^{n-2q} leaves. Any leaf corresponds to a choice of a set A' for the $k - 1$ largest elements (together with a choice for the kth largest) and can be reached only by an adversary whose set A contains A', i.e., at most $n - k + 1$ of them. The number of different adversaries is $\binom{n}{k}$, so the decision tree must have at least $2^{n-2q}\binom{n}{k}/(n - k + 1)$ leaves. The choice $q = \sqrt{n}$ gives the bound

$$V_k(n) \geq n + \log \binom{n}{k} - O(\sqrt{n}).$$

In particular, Bent and John [1] prove $M(n) \geq 2n - O(\sqrt{n})$.

Dor and Zwick [5, 8] use a delicate argument to increase these lower bounds very slightly. They prove that $M(n) \geq (2 + \epsilon)n + o(n)$ for some $\epsilon > 2^{-40}$. Their proof follows the "leaf-counting" style of [9, 1]. Although they are not able to prove that the decision tree contains more leaves than did Bent and John [1], they can show that the tree is not balanced, so that some paths are longer than others. There is now a single powerful adversary which summarises the combined effect of the multitude of simple adversaries introduced above. Dor and Zwick look at the earlier stages of an algorithm when there are still many singletons remaining, and focus on the first and second comparisons in which each element is involved. They show by a careful analysis that in many comparisons the adversary can choose an outcome leading to a significantly larger number of leaves than the alternative. At times this adversary discards some of the sets A which it has been monitoring, and at other times it chooses an outcome leading to the smaller number of leaves. Overall however it comes out a little bit ahead using its subtle strategy. This gives the payoff of ϵ.

5 Future progress

For ten years, the upper and lower bound coefficients for $M(n)$ were sitting sedately at integers, with neither showing much inclination to approach the other. Now, thanks to Dor and Zwick [5, 6, 8], both coefficients have been given a nudge. Where are they heading? Which of them is nearer to the true value? Will the coefficient be semi-natural, such as 2.5, or rather unnatural, such as $\log_{4/3} 2$? The intricacy of the arguments in [5, 6, 8] makes it appear that there is no easy way to take large further steps without some substantially new approach.

Yao's Hypothesis

In [23], Frances Yao considered the problem of finding a (u, v)-*mediocre element*,

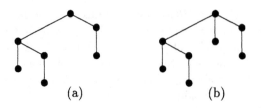

Fig. 5. Counter-example to generalised Yao's Hypothesis

from m elements, i.e., an element which is smaller than at least u elements and larger than at least v elements. This corresponds to constructing an S_v^u from m elements, where $m \geq u + v + 1$.

She defined $S(u, v, m)$ to be the worst-case minimum number of comparisons needed to find a (u, v)-mediocre element from a set of size m. Obviously, $S(u, v, m) \geq S(u, v, m')$ for $u + v + 1 \leq m \leq m'$. We have $V_k(n) = S(k - 1, n - k, n)$. Let $V_k^*(n) = \lim_{m \to \infty} S(k - 1, n - k, m)$, i.e., the cost of producing an S_{n-k}^{k-1} from arbitrarily many elements.

Yao observed that $V_1(n) = V_1^*(n)$ for all n. We define as *Yao's Hypothesis* the equation:

$$V_k(n) = V_k^*(n) \text{ for all } k, n. \tag{YH}$$

Yao proved in [23] that YH implies that $M(n) \leq 3n + o(n)$. An analogous proof in [21] showed that YH implies $M(n) \leq 2.5n + o(n)$.

To date, no counter-example to Yao's Hypothesis is known. Since the consequences of YH are so rewarding, it would be of great interest to resolve its truth.

The generalisation of YH from S_v^u's to arbitrary partial orders is known not to hold. The partial order (a) can be shown by an exhaustive analysis to require 8 comparisons when only 7 elements are present, whereas that shown in (b) requires only the obvious 7 comparisons.

Information theory methods

Information theoretic techniques provide a powerful tool to prove lower bounds for sorting and selection problems. In a typical application, a partial order π is assigned the weight $w(\pi)$, the number of its linear extensions, i.e., the number of total orders consistent with π. A further comparison $a : b$ yields one of the two extensions ($\pi \cup [a > b]$) or ($\pi \cup [a < b]$). Since $w(\pi \cup [a > b]) + w(\pi \cup [a < b]) = w(\pi)$, simple arguments show that the worst-case number of comparisons needed to sort a partial order π is at least $\log_2 w(\pi)$. Unfortunately, this technique is too weak for deriving useful bounds for selection. Since an S_v^u has weight $u!v!$, the information theoretic lower bound for $V_k(n)$ is only $\log_2(\binom{n}{k}k)$, which is at most $n + O(\log n)$.

For a variation on this technique which is more suitable for selection problems, we consider "bipartitions". A *bipartition* of the partial order π on the set X is a mapping g of the elements of X into $\{0, 1\}$ which is compatible with π, i.e., for all $x, y \in X$, if $x <_\pi y$ then $g(x) \leq g(y)$. Thus a bipartition of π is a partition of X into two sets $g^{-1}(1)$, the *up-set*, and $g^{-1}(0)$, the *down-set*, such that no element of the up-set is below an element of the down-set in π.

6 Partition measures

Let $P(\pi)$ be the set of bipartitions of π, and $p(\pi) = |P(\pi)|$. We will use the notation $P(\pi, a/b)$ for the set of bipartitions g of π such that $g(a) = 1$ and $g(b) = 0$, and similarly the notations $P(\pi, b/a)$, $P(\pi, ab/)$, and $P(\pi, /ab)$ for the other three cases where $(g(a), g(b)) = (0, 1), (1, 1), (0, 0)$, respectively. The cardinalities of these sets are represented analogously using "p" in place of "P". Note that $p(\pi) = p(\pi, a/b) + p(\pi, b/a) + p(\pi, ab/) + p(\pi, /ab)$.

The effect of a comparison is not now to give a splitting of $P(\pi)$ into two disjoint sets, as it was for linear extensions. Instead, we find

$$P(\pi \cup [a > b]) = P(\pi, a/b) \cup P(\pi, ab/) \cup P(\pi, /ab),$$

and

$$P(\pi \cup [a < b]) = P(\pi, b/a) \cup P(\pi, ab/) \cup P(\pi, /ab).$$

This has the advantage for lower bounding that we can hope that p decreases more slowly per comparison than did w. Indeed the following theorem holds.

Theorem 1. *For any partial order π, and elements $a, b \in X$,*

$$\max\{p(\pi \cup [a > b]), \ p(\pi \cup [a < b])\} \geq \frac{3}{4} \, p(\pi).$$

Proof. For convenience, we denote $p(\pi), p(\pi, a/b), p(\pi, b/a), p(\pi, ab/), p(\pi, /ab)$ by $p, p_{10}, p_{01}, p_{11}, p_{00}$, respectively. The theorem is equivalent to showing that $\min\{p_{01}, p_{10}\} \leq p/4$.

I will prove below that $p_{10}p_{01} \leq p_{11}p_{00}$. The theorem follows quickly, since

$$
\begin{aligned}
\left(\sqrt{p_{01}} + \sqrt{p_{10}}\right)^2 &= p_{01} + p_{10} + 2\sqrt{p_{10}p_{01}} \\
&\leq p_{01} + p_{10} + 2\sqrt{p_{11}p_{00}}, \text{ since } p_{10}p_{01} \leq p_{11}p_{00}, \\
&\leq p_{01} + p_{10} + p_{11} + p_{00}, \\
&\qquad \text{since the geometric mean is at most the arithmetic mean,} \\
&= p.
\end{aligned}
$$

Hence, $\min\{\sqrt{p_{01}}, \sqrt{p_{10}}\} \leq \frac{1}{2}\left(\sqrt{p_{01}} + \sqrt{p_{10}}\right) \leq \frac{1}{2}\sqrt{p}$, i.e., $\min\{p_{01}, p_{10}\} \leq \frac{1}{4}p$.

Finally, to prove that $p_{10}p_{01} \leq p_{11}p_{00}$, I give an explicit injective map F from $P(\pi, a/b) \times P(\pi, b/a)$ into $P(\pi, ab/) \times P(\pi, /ab)$. Any $h \in P(\pi) \times P(\pi)$ partitions X into four subsets $H_{i,j}$, where $i, j \in \{0, 1\}$, where $H_{i,j} = \{x \in X : h(x) = (i, j)\}$. These sets have the property that if $x \in H_{10}$ and $y \in H_{01}$ then x and y are unrelated in π. Note that if $h \in P(\pi, a/b) \times P(\pi, b/a)$ then $a \in H_{10}$ and $b \in H_{01}$, while for $h \in P(\pi, ab/) \times P(\pi, /ab)$ we have $a \in H_{10}$ and $b \in H_{10}$.

We regard the partial order as a directed graph on X, and h assigns labels $10, 01, 11, 00$ to the vertices. Vertex a has label 10, and b has label 01. Let

C_b be that weakly connected component of the vertices labelled 01 which contains b. The map $F : P(\pi, a/b) \times P(\pi, b/a) \to P(\pi, ab/) \times P(\pi, /ab)$ is defined by specifying the four sets $H'_{10}, H'_{01}, H'_{11}, H'_{00}$ corresponding to $h' = F(h)$. Let $H'_{10} = H_{10} \cup C_b$, $H'_{01} = H_{01} \setminus C_b$, $H'_{11} = H_{11}$, and $H'_{00} = H_{00}$. With respect to h', C_b is now the weakly connected component of the vertices labelled 10 which contains b. Therefore the mapping F is invertible and so injective, as required to complete the proof. □

Some extensive generalisations of this result have been given by J. Daykin [3]. (See also [4] for related results.)

Under this new measure for partial orders, an adversary can guarantee an outcome for each comparison such that the new p-value is at least 3/4 of the previous p-value. What are the applications? Disappointingly, the resulting bound for median-finding is very weak. For the initial, empty, partial order, p is 2^n, while, finally, we have $p\left(S^{\lceil n/2 \rceil - 1}_{\lfloor n/2 \rfloor}\right) \geq \Theta(2^{\lceil n/2 \rceil})$. The lower bound is therefore

$$M(n) \geq \log_{4/3}(2^{\lfloor n/2 \rfloor}) \sim 1.2n.$$

I shall suggest a possible alternative approach below. But first, for a small non-trivial result using the p-measure, here is a lower bound for an approximate sorting problem. Say that a set is *k-nearly sorted* if it is partially ordered so that, for any rank r, the number of elements which could possibly have rank r in the sorted order is at most k.

Theorem 2. *The worst-case number of comparisons required to k-nearly sort a set of n elements is at least $(n - k - O(\log n)) \log_{4/3} 2$.*

Proof. For any k-nearly sorted partial order π on n elements, $p(\pi) = O(n2^k)$, since the up-sets of any given cardinality r differ only with respect to the at-most-k elements of possible rank r. Our bipartition-counting technique gives a lower bound of about

$$\log_{4/3}(2^n/(n2^k)) = (n - k - O(\log n)) \log_{4/3} 2. \qquad \square$$

For comparison, the linear extension counting measure w yields a bound of $\log_2(n!/k^n) = n(\log_2(n/k) - O(1))$. For small k, the latter bound is better, but for $k > n/12$ the new bound is higher. For example:

Corollary 3. *To $n/8$-nearly sort n elements requires at least $2.1n - O(1)$ comparisons in the worst case.*

Equipartitions

In an attempt to tune our information-theoretic measure to be more sensitive to median-finding, let us now define an *equipartition* to be a bipartition where the up-set is of size $\lceil n/2 \rceil$. Let $Q(\pi)$ be the set of equipartitions compatible with π, and let $q(\pi) = |Q(\pi)|$. For median-finding, we have initially $q = \binom{n}{\lceil n/2 \rceil}$, for the empty partial order, and finally $q = 1$ for an $S^{(\lceil n/2 \rceil - 1)}_{\lfloor n/2 \rfloor}$. If we could establish for the q-measure the analogous result to Theorem 1, we would have a lower bound of about $n \log_{4/3} 2 \sim 2.41n$. We will see however that the analogous result does *not* hold.

We may view Theorem 1 as an affirmation that the probabilities of a and b being in the up-set of a random bipartition (under a suitable distribution) are either positively correlated or independent, i.e.,

$$\frac{p(\pi, a/)}{p(\pi)} \frac{p(\pi, b/)}{p(\pi)} \leq \frac{p(\pi, ab/)}{p(\pi)}$$

or, equivalently,

$$(p_{11} + p_{10})(p_{11} + p_{01}) \leq p_{11}(p_{10} + p_{01} + p_{11} + p_{00}).$$

Under the restriction to *equi*partitions, there is an extra slight tendency toward negative correlation: if a is in the up-set then there is less room up there for b. This effect is extreme in the limiting case of a partial order π where only a and b remain as candidates for the median, the remaining $\lceil n/2 \rceil - 1$ elements of the up-set being determined. In this case, $q(\pi, ab/) = q(\pi, /ab) = 0$, and a factor of $1/2$ (as opposed to $3/4$) results from the comparison $a : b$.

What can we hope to achieve? The measure p has the good $3/4$ ratio property, but is ill-matched to the median problem; the measure q fits the median problem well but fails to satisfy the ratio property. One approach would be to design a compromise measure between p and q, which retains enough of the good properties of each to be useful. For example, it could count all bipartitions, but assign a greater weight the more balanced the partition. An alternative approach is to retain the measure q, but try to show that ratios close enough to $3/4$ could be guaranteed for a sufficiently long initial phase to yield good bounds.

7 Conclusion

We have taken a quick tour of some old and new results in median-finding and selection problems. As Dor and Zwick [5, 6, 7, 8] have broken through the long-standing upper and lower barriers, the time seems ripe for a new leap forward.

I have proposed some speculative new approaches for lower bounds. In the same vein, it would seem that an algorithm might do very well by choosing, where possible, pairs of elements to compare which are each roughly equally likely to lie in the top or bottom halves of the ordering and which are reasonably independent. If this were achievable, the algorithm might come close to reducing the equipartition measure by a factor of $3/4$ per comparison. My ambitious guess with which I close is therefore the following.

Conjecture 1 *The worst-case number of comparisons required to find the median of n elements is asymptotic to $n \log_{4/3} 2 \sim 2.4094 \cdots n$.*

Acknowledgements

I am grateful to Dorit Dor and Uri Zwick for their helpful contributions to this paper.

References

1. S. W. Bent and J. W. John. Finding the median requires $2n$ comparisons. In *Proc. 17th ACM Symp. on Theory of Computing*, 1985, 213–216.

2. M. Blum, R. W. Floyd, V. R. Pratt, R. L. Rivest, and R. E. Tarjan. Time bounds for selection. *J. Comput. Syst. Sci.*, 7, 1973, 448–461.

3. J. W. Daykin. Inequalities for the number of monotonic functions of partial orders. *Discrete Mathematics*, 61, 1986, 41–55.

4. D. E. Daykin, J. W. Daykin, and M. S. Paterson. On log concavity for order-preserving maps of partial orders. *Discrete Mathematics*, 50, 1984, 221–226.

5. D. Dor. *Selection Algorithms*. PhD thesis, Tel-Aviv University, 1995.

6. D. Dor and U. Zwick. Selecting the median. In *Proc. 6th Annual ACM-SIAM Symp. on Discrete Algorithms*, 1995, 28–37.

7. D. Dor and U. Zwick. Finding the αn^{th} largest element. *Combinatorica*, 16, 1996, 41–58.

8. D. Dor and U. Zwick. Median selection requires $(2+\epsilon)n$ comparisons. Technical Report 312/96, April 1996, Department of Computer Science, Tel Aviv University.

9. F. Fussenegger and H. N. Gabow. A counting approach to lower bounds for selection problems. *J. ACM*, 26, 1978, 227–238.

10. A. Hadian and M. Sobel. Selecting the tth largest using binary errorless comparisons. *Colloquia Mathematica Societatis János Bolyai*, 4, 1969, 585–599.

11. L. Hyafil. Bounds for selection. *SIAM J. on Computing*, 5, 1976, 109–114.

12. J. W. John. *The Complexity of Selection Problems*. PhD thesis, University of Wisconsin at Madison, 1985.

13. D. G. Kirkpatrick. Topics in the complexity of combinatorial algorithms. Tech. Rep. 74, Dept. of Computer Science, University of Toronto, 1974.

14. D. G. Kirkpatrick. A unified lower bound for selection and set partitioning problems. *J. ACM*, 28, 1981, 150–165.

15. S. S. Kislitsyn. On the selection of the kth element of an ordered set by pairwise comparisons. *Sibirsk. Mat. Zh.*, 5, 1964, 557–564. (In Russian.)

16. D. E. Knuth. *Sorting and Searching*, volume 3 of *The Art of Computer Programming*. Addison-Wesley, Reading, MA, 1973.

17. T. Motoki. A note on upper bounds for the selection problem. *Inf. Proc. Lett.*, 15, 1982, 214–219.

18. J. I. Munro and P. V. Poblete. A lower bound for determining the median. Technical Report Research Report CS-82-21, University of Waterloo, 1982.

19. V. Pratt and F. F. Yao. On lower bounds for computing the ith largest element. In *Proc. 14th IEEE Symp. on Switching and Automata Theory*, 1973, 70–81.

20. P. V. Ramanan and L. Hyafil. New algorithms for selection. *J. Algorithms*, 5, 1984, 557–578.

21. A. Schönhage, M. S. Paterson, and N. Pippenger. Finding the median. *J. Comput. Syst. Sci.*, 13, 1976, 184–199.

22. J. Schreier. On tournament elimination systems. *Mathesis Polska*, 7, 1932, 154–160. (In Polish.)

23. F. F. Yao. On lower bounds for selection problems. Technical Report MAC TR-121, M.I.T., 1974.

24. C. K. Yap. New upper bounds for selection. *Comm. ACM*, 19, 1976, 501–508.

25. C. K. Yap. New lower bounds for medians and related problems. Computer Science Report 79, Yale University, 1976.

Probabilistic Ancestral Sequences and Multiple Alignments

Gaston H. Gonnet and Steven A. Benner
Informatik

Organic Chemistry
E.T.H.
Zurich, Switzerland

Abstract

An *evolutionary configuration* (EC) is a set of aligned sequences of characters (possibly representing amino acids, DNA, RNA or natural language). We define the probability of an EC, based on a given phylogenetic tree and give an algorithm to compute this probability efficiently. From these probabilities, we can compute the most likely sequence at any place in the phylogenetic tree, or its probability profile. The probability profile at the root of the tree is called the probabilistic ancestral sequence. By computing the probability of an EC, we can find by dynamic programming alignments over two subtrees. This gives an algorithm for computing multiple alignments. These multiple alignments are maximum likelihood, and are a compatible generalization of two sequence alignments.

1 Introduction

In our view the main contribution of this paper is to introduce the computation of probabilities of a given evolutionary configuration (EC), that is a phylogenetic tree with sequences at its leaves, based on a Markovian model of evolution. From this probabilities, we can compute the probability profile at any internal node or internal branch of the phylogenetic tree, and when these are computed at the root of the tree, we call them *probabilistic ancestral sequences* (PAS). The ability to compute probabilities of particular configurations, allows us to use a dynamic programming (DP) algorithm to align two subtrees. By starting from the leaves and working towards the root of the tree with this procedure, we construct a multiple alignment of all the sequences.

The problem of computing multiple alignments is a difficult one. All of the existing algorithms [7, 2, 5, 11, 14, 19, 16, 12, 1, 13] are either heuristic, or require exponential time. The algorithm here described is the first one to work in polynomial time and to be founded on an accepted model of evolution. These methods can be applied to DNA, RNA, natural language or any other similar problem. We will denote by Σ the alphabet over which these sequences are built. All of our algorithms work for arbitrary alphabets. In this paper, all the examples are on proteins. This particular case can be summarized as being over an alphabet of 20 symbols, the letters $\Sigma = $ `ACDEFGHIKLMNPQRSTVWY`.

This paper will not discuss how to construct the phylogenetic trees, this subject falls beyond our present scope. The algorithms we describe assume we start with the sequences and a phylogenetic tree.

1.1 Definitions

Mutation model. The evolution between sequences can be modelled by mutation matrices. A mutation matrix, denoted by M, describes the probabilities of amino acid mutations for a given period of evolution.

$$Pr\{\text{amino acid } i \longrightarrow \text{amino acid } j\} = M_{ji}$$

This corresponds to a model of evolution in which amino acids mutate randomly and independently from one another but according to some predefined probabilities depending on the amino acid itself. This is a Markovian model of evolution and while simple, it is one of the best models.

Intrinsic properties of amino acids, like hydrophobicity, size, charge, etc. can be modelled by appropriate mutation matrices. Dependencies which relate one amino acid characteristic to the characteristics of its neighbours are not possible to model through this mechanism.

Amino acids appear in nature with different frequencies. These frequencies are denoted by f_i and correspond to the steady state of the Markov process defined by the matrix M. I.e. the vector f is any of the columns of M^∞ or the eigenvector of M whose corresponding eigenvalue is 1 ($Mf = f$).

This model of evolution is symmetric, i.e. the probability of having an i which mutates to a j is the same as starting with a j which mutates into an i. This symmetry means

$$f_i M_{ji} = f_j M_{ij}$$

PAM distance. In the definition of mutation, we use the matrix M which implies certain amount of mutation. For all our work it is important to quantify mutation. We will use the terminology introduced by Dayhoff et al. [6] where amount of mutation is measured in PAM units.

A 1-PAM mutation matrix describes an amount of evolution which will change, on the average, 1% of the amino acids. In mathematical terms this is expressed as a matrix M such that

$$\sum_{i \in \Sigma} f_i (1 - M_{ii}) = 0.01$$

The diagonal elements of M are the probabilities that a given amino acid does not change, so $(1 - M_{ii})$ is the probability of mutating away from i.

If we have a probability or frequency vector p, the product Mp gives the probability vector or the expected frequency of p after an evolution equivalent to 1-PAM unit. Or, if we start with amino acid i (a probability vector which contains a 1 in position i and 0s in all others) M_{*i} (the ith column of M) is the corresponding probability vector after one unit of random evolution. Similarly, after k units of evolution (what is called k-PAM evolution) a frequency vector p will be changed into the frequency vector $M^k p$. Notice that chronological time is not linearly dependent on PAM distance. Evolution rates may be very different for different species and different proteins.

Phylogenetic tree. A phylogenetic tree is a representation of evolution. In our case, since we are interested in amino acid sequences, these trees normally describe the evolution of the species where the sequences are found. All the phylogenetic trees are based on a model or theory of evolution. The model of evolution which we consider here is a simple model based on ancestor sequences mutating into descendant sequences where no parallel evolution or horizontal transfers will be considered.

We will assume that we do not have any sequence information corresponding to the internal nodes of the phylogenetic tree. This is the normal situation. All the sequence information is at the leaves. Our phylogenetic trees are always binary (each internal node has degree 3), that is to say, every internal node corresponds to a splitting point in the phylogeny.

In our case, the leaves of the phylogenetic tree are the sequences from present day species. The internal nodes of the tree represent the points of divergence where two different branches of evolution arose. The root of the tree represents the nearest (latest) common ancestor of all the species considered. For example Figure 1 is a phylogenetic tree where 1, 2, ..., 5 represent the present-day sequences, W represents the nearest common ancestor of 1 and 2, X is the nearest common ancestor of 4 and 5 and O, the root of the tree, represents the nearest common ancestor of all the sequences.

We are interested in trees with branches which measure amount of evolution in PAM units. We call this an evolutionary phylogenetic tree (EPT). There is no obvious constraint between the distances from the root to the leaves, as it is well known that similar proteins in different species may evolve at different rates.

In Figure 1, if lengths mean amount of evolution, we could say that 3 evolved more from O than 2 and 4. Since we assume that all these descended from a common ancestor, we can also say that 3 evolved more rapidly (mutated more rapidly) than 2 and 4, since in the same amount of time it evolved more.

When the ancestral sequences (O, Y, X and W) are not available for analysis, as it is usually the case, we have to infer their existence and location from the present-day sequences 1, 2, ..., 5. Phylogenetic trees derived only from the information on the leaves are normally called dendrograms.

The evolution from O to Y will be modelled by a mutation matrix M^{d_Y}, where d_Y is the PAM distance between O and Y; the evolution from O to 1 by $M^{d_{O1}} = M^{d_Y + d_W + d_1}$, etc. The exponent d_{ij} denotes the distance between node i and node j. d_i (with a single index) denotes the distance between node i and its parent.

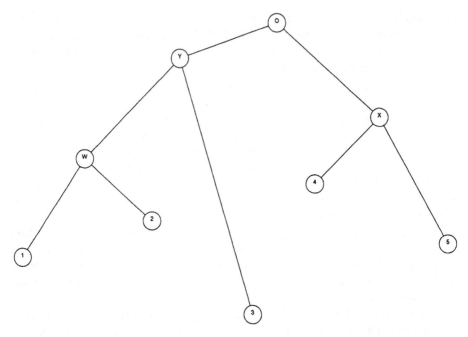

Figure 1: Example of an EPT with 5 leaf nodes

Dayhoff matrices. Dayhoff et al. [6] presented a method for estimating the matrix M from the observation of 1572 accepted mutations between 34 super-families of closely related sequences. Their method was pioneering in the field. Nowadays we are able to estimate M by more accurate and better founded methods [8, 4].

A Dayhoff matrix (in honour of Margaret O. Dayhoff) is a matrix, computed from a 250-PAM mutation matrix, used for the standard dynamic programming method of sequence alignment. The Dayhoff matrix entries are related to M^{250} by

$$D_{ij} = 10 \log_{10} \frac{(M^{250})_{ij}}{f_i}$$

Sequence alignment. Aligning sequences is the process of associating some positions of each sequence with a position of the other sequence. This association preserves the order of the sequences. E.g.

```
VNRLQQNIVSL_____EVDHKVANYKPQVEPFGHGPIFMATALVPGLYLGVPWF
VNRLQQSIVSLRDAFNDGTKLLEELDHRVLNYKPQANPFGNGPIFMVTAIVPGLHLGAPWF
```

Unassociated positions are called *insertions* (or their counterpart *deletions*). Aligning protein sequences by dynamic programming (DP) using Dayhoff matrices is equivalent to finding the alignment which maximizes the probability that the two sequences evolved from an ancestral sequence as opposed to being random sequences. More precisely, we are comparing two events

a) that the two sequences are independent of each other, and hence an arbitrary position with amino acid i aligned to another arbitrary position with amino acid j has the probability equal to the product of the individual frequencies

$$Pr\{i \text{ and } j \text{ are independent}\} = f_i f_j$$

b) that the two sequences have evolved from some common ancestral sequence after t units of evolution.

$$
\begin{aligned}
Pr\{i \text{ and } j \text{ descended from } x\} &= \sum_x f_x Pr\{x \to i\} Pr\{x \to j\} \\
&= \sum_x f_x (M^t)_{ix} (M^t)_{jx} \\
&= \sum_x f_j (M^t)_{ix} (M^t)_{xj} \\
&= f_j (M^{2t})_{ij} = f_i (M^{2t})_{ji}
\end{aligned}
$$

We use $\sum_i$ as a shorthand for $\sum_{i \in \Sigma}$, that is a sum over all symbols of the alphabet. The entries of the Dayhoff matrix are the logarithm of the quotient of these two probabilities.

$$D_{ij} = 10 \log_{10} \left(\frac{Pr\{i \text{ and } j \text{ descended from } x\}}{Pr\{i \text{ and } j \text{ are independent}\}} \right)$$

Since DP maximizes the sum of the similarity measure, DP maximizes the sum of the logarithms or maximizes the product of these quotients of probabilities. As a conclusion, DP finds the alignment which maximizes the probability of having evolved from a common ancestor (a maximum likelihood alignment) against the null hypothesis of being independent. This makes aligning sequences using Dayhoff matrices a soundly based algorithm.

Multiple sequence alignment. A multiple sequence alignment, or multiple alignment, is a generalization of the case of 2 sequences to k sequences. Instead of relating the sequences by a single parent, we have an EPT which describes the parent-descendant relations. Dynamic programming is no longer applicable in practice, it requires exponential space and time in k. The following is an example of a multiple sequence alignment with $k = 5$ for the sequences described in the earlier examples.

```
1    FKQCCWNSLP____RGLSNVALVYQEFMAKCRGESENLQLVTALVINLPSMA
2    SMFRQCIWNSLS____HGLPETAPIYQPLKARCRGVSENLQLVTEIIINLPTLC
3    SLWCQCIKASLPLKVIRGTPEVAPLYDQLEQVCRSENQ____VSEIVAKFASLC
4    TMFKMCLWNALP____RGLPEVAPVYRPLKARCRGDSENLQLCAERLVNLPELC
5    AILRSCIWNLLP____RGLPEAAPIYEPLKARLRGESENYKLVTEIIMTLPSLC
```

Probabilistic ancestral sequence. A probabilistic ancestral sequence (PAS) is like a protein sequence where each position, instead of an amino acid, has a vector of dimension $|\Sigma|$ describing the probability of each amino acid being in that position. A PAS is normally associated to an EPT and to a particular place in this tree. It is normally most interesting to compute the PAS at divergence points or at the root of the EPT. E.g. find the PAS for the common ancestor of all mammals.

2 Probability of an evolutionary configuration

In this section we will describe how to compute the probability of an evolutionary configuration (EC), that is the probability of a particular alignment of sequences according to a given EPT.

First we should notice that our model of evolution treats each position independently of its neighbours. Hence the probability of an EC will be the product of the probabilities for each of the aligned positions. For each aligned position we have an EPT with one amino acid at each leaf. (We consider the special case of indels later). The tree in Figure 2 represents a slice of the EC at position 4 where sequence 1 has a K, sequence 2 has an R, etc. In this case, the amino acids placed at nodes W, X and Y are the unknown amino acids at the divergence points.

How to compute this probability efficiently. Let O be the point which identifies the root of the EPT. To compute the probability of a given position, we use the same idea as Dayhoff et al. [6] i.e. sum over all possible unknown

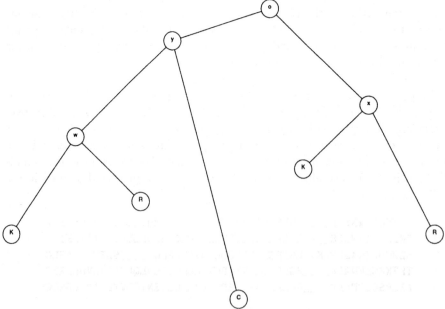

Figure 2: EPT slice at position 4 of the aligned sequences

amino acids o, w, x and y and evaluate all the mutation probabilities.

$$Pr\{EC\} = \sum_o f_o \sum_x M_{xo}^{dx} M_{Kx}^{d_4} M_{Rx}^{d_5} \sum_y M_{yo}^{dy} M_{Cy}^{d_3} \sum_w M_{wy}^{dw} M_{Kw}^{d_1} M_{Rw}^{d_2}$$

The interpretation of each part of the product is simple. For each branch between $U \to V$ we will have a term of the form M_{vu}^{dv}, for each unknown internal amino acid at node U we will have a sum for all its possibilities ($\sum_u$) and for the root we have the sum of each possible amino acid times its natural frequency of occurrence. Lower case letters denote the particular amino acid at a given position, e.g. x is the amino acid in a given position of sequence X. The upper case K, R and C indicate the known amino acids at the leaves.

As written, this formula is very expensive to compute, it requires $|\Sigma|^{k-1}$ products, where k is the number of sequences. We can reorganize this summation by the introduction of new vectors T^X and S^X for each internal or external node X. The value of the vector depends on the position of the root of the tree and it is computed as follows

- if X is an external leaf, i.e. a known amino acid, x

$$T_i^X = \begin{cases} 1 & i = x \\ 0 & i \neq x \end{cases}$$

$$S^X = M^{dx} \cdot T^X = M_{*x}^{dx}$$

(i.e. S^X is just the xth column of M^{dx}).

- if X is an internal node, then it is a ternary node. Let Y and Z be the adjacent nodes whose subtrees do not include the root of the tree (away from the root). Then

$$T_i^X = \left(\sum_y M_{yi}^{dy} T_y^Y \right) \left(\sum_z M_{zi}^{dz} T_z^Z \right) = S_i^Y \cdot S_i^Z$$

$$S_i^X = \sum_x M_{xi}^{dx} T_x^X$$

$$S^X = \left(M^{dx} \right)' T^X$$

These recursive definitions can be used if we do the computation from the leaves towards the root. Each S corresponding to an internal node requires $|\Sigma|^2$ multiplications, and each T requires $|\Sigma|$ multiplications. For k sequences, each of length m, this requires $m(k-1)|\Sigma|(|\Sigma|+1)$ multiplications ($420m(k-1)$ for proteins), which is not inexpensive, but perfectly feasible.

The computation of the probability of the EC is done with the two immediate descendants of the root, call them X and Y.

$$Pr\{EC\} = \sum_i f_i \left(\sum_x M_{xi}^{dx} T_x^X\right) \left(\sum_y M_{yi}^{dy} T_y^Y\right) = \sum_i f_i T_i^O = f \cdot T^O$$

The PAS at the root of the tree can be computed as follows: for each amino acid at the root compute the probability of such a configuration

$$Pr\{aa\ i\ \text{at the root}\} = \text{PAS}_i = \left(\sum_x M_{xi}^{dx} T_x^X\right) \left(\sum_y M_{yi}^{dy} T_y^Y\right) = T_i^O$$

where X and Y are the descendants of the root. These are probabilities of the entire EC, to find the relative probabilities for each amino acid the PAS is normalized to sum 1, i.e.

$$\text{PAS} = T^O / \sum_i T_i^O$$

Independence of the position of the root. It can be shown that the probability of an EC is independent of where we place the root of the tree. This is a direct consequence of the symmetry of the evolution model mentioned in 1.1. To prove this, we first show that the probabilities are not affected if we move the root along the edge liking its two descendants (X and Y). The length of the branch from X to Y will remain constant, we will just change d_X and d_Y so that $d_X + d_Y = d_{XY} = $ constant. The probability of the EC is

$$\sum_i f_i \left(\sum_x M_{xi}^{dx} T_x^X\right) \left(\sum_y M_{yi}^{dy} T_y^Y\right)$$

Moving the summations around and using the symmetry relation of f and M and noticing that the summation in i gives a matrix product, we obtain

$$\sum_y \sum_x T_y^Y T_x^X \sum_i f_i M_{yi}^{dy} M_{xi}^{dx} = \sum_y \sum_x T_y^Y T_x^X f_y (M^{dx+dy})_{yx}$$

and the formula is independent of d_X and d_Y, only depends on their sum. By continuity, this can be extended to any position within the EPT. Consequently for the purposes of evaluating the probability of a particular EC, we can place the root wherever it is most convenient.

3 Probabilistic Dynamic Programming and Multiple Alignments

The standard DP algorithm for aligning two sequences [15, 18, 10], requires that we estimate a cost of matching any two individual positions. This is done by the method described in the introduction or by completely empirical *cost/similarity* functions which assign some value to the alignment of each pair of amino acids.

The DP algorithm for aligning sequences can be viewed as an algorithm which takes as parameter such a cost/similarity function,

$$C \; : \; \{\Sigma \cup \phi\} \times \{\Sigma \cup \phi\} \to \Re$$

and produces an alignment which maximizes the sum of the C function applied to all aligned pairs[1].

We will use DP over partially built multiple alignments and the C function will be derived from the probability of an EC. We call this aligning algorithm *probabilistic dynamic programming*.

More precisely, our DP algorithm works over two partial multiple alignments. A partial multiple alignment is a multiple alignment of all the sequences of a subtree of the EPT. Hence a partial multiple alignment is identified by an internal node and a direction in the EPT. E.g. node Y has as descendants the sequence 3 and the node W; node W has sequences 1 and 2 as descendants. The partial multiple alignment for node Y is:

```
1      FKQCCWNSLP____RGLSNVALVYQEFMAKCRGESENLQLVTALVINLPSMA
2      SMFRQCIWNSLS____HGLPETAPIYQPLKARCRGVSENLQLVTEIIINLPTLC
3      SLWCQCIKASLPLKVIRGTPEVAPLYDQLEQVCRSENQ____VSEIVAKFASLC
```

For each subtree X and its partial multiple alignment we also compute the T^X and S^X vectors. The C function for this algorithm will be derived from the probability of alignment of two slices of a multiple alignment under the same ancestor. In essence, this is exactly the same idea as in Dayhoff [6], extended so that we can compute the probabilities of alignments not just with two descendant sequences, but with two subtrees of descendants.

The C function is the logarithm of the quotient of probabilities, or

$$C(Y, Z) = 10 \log_{10} \left(\frac{Pr\{Y \text{ and } Z \text{ are descendants of } x\}}{Pr\{Y\}Pr\{Z\}} \right)$$

(The factor 10 is retained for purely historical reasons, it was used first by Dayhoff et al. Any constant factor can be used without any material effect.) Using the T and S vectors this becomes

$$C(Y, Z) = 10 \log_{10} \left(\frac{\sum_x f_x \left(\sum_y M_{yx}^{d_Y} T_y^Y \right) \left(\sum_z M_{zx}^{d_Z} T_z^Z \right)}{(f \cdot T^Y)(f \cdot T^Z)} \right)$$

$$= 10 \log_{10} \frac{\sum_x f_x S_x^Y S_x^Z}{(f \cdot T^Y)(f \cdot T^Z)}$$

At this point, we are using DP to align the two subtrees rooted at Y and Z.

---

[1] This algorithm has been well described in the literature. Finding the cost of the best alignment, and producing the aligned sequences can be done with $m_A m_B$ evaluations of C and $O(\min(m_A, m_B))$ storage for sequences A and B with lengths m_A and m_B.

Hence we still do not have a correspondence between each position of Y and each position of Z. That is why we have to use the sum $\sum_x f_x S_x^Y S_x^Z$ in C. Once that we have found the alignment of Y and Z, then we can compute T^X and S^X for the node we have just joined, the parent of Y and Z.

The cost of each computation of C is $O(|\Sigma|)$ multiplications. The cost of one probabilistic DP alignment is $O(m^2|\Sigma|)$ and the cost of the entire process (including the computation of S and T) is $O(mk|\Sigma|(|\Sigma| + m))$.

The alignment at the root of the EPT is the multiple alignment of all the sequences. Notice that for two sequences, this algorithm coincides exactly with DP using Dayhoff matrices, so this presents a continuous generalization of the 2-sequence algorithm.

Normalization. For any node Y, multiplying S^Y and T^Y by an arbitrary constant k_1 has no effect on the dynamic programming algorithm. (Both S^Y and T^Y have to be multiplied by the same constant so that the equation $S^Y = (M^{d_Y})' T^Y$ is preserved). This can be readily verified from the definition of the cost function for DP, $C(Y, X)$ above. Similarly, the PAS are not altered by such multiplication, as the last step normalizes the probabilities to add to 1. It is then advantageous to normalize the T and S vectors to prevent underflows which are very likely to occur for large multiple alignments. This independence from a constant factor also comes handy for indels.

Indels. Insertions/deletions are handled in the same way they would be handled by the standard DP algorithms [15, 10]. The cost of a deletion is known to depend on the PAM distance of the aligned sequences [3] and there exist approximations to compute them based on the distance alone. In case DP chooses an indel, one of the subtrees is viewed as having had a deletion and this deletion has to be propagated to the entire aligned subtree. If X is a node with descendants Y and Z, and DP chooses Y to be an insertion, i.e. Y is not aligned to anything, then T^X and S^X are computed as

$$T^X = S^Y Pr\{\text{deletion of } Z\}$$

and

$$S^X = (M^{d_X})' T^X$$

as usual. This corresponds to computing the EC when all the Z subtree is missing. Since multiplying T^X and S^X by a constant has no effect (as discussed above), we can simply ignore $Pr\{\text{deletion of } Z\}$ and use $T^X = S^Y$.

4 Conclusions

This algorithm computes maximum likelihood multiple alignments given the sequences and their EPT. A maximum likelihood alignment under a Markovian model of evolution is a very desirable type of alignment, as it has well understood properties. This algorithm was implemented in Darwin between 1990 and 1991. It went through several (some major) revisions until about 1993 and it has been in use by the community since then. This is one of the rare cases where the algorithm had a successful service life *before* being published. It can be used through the Web (`http://cbrg.inf.ethz.ch/`) or by e-mail to (`cbrg.inf.ethz.ch`) from an automatic Darwin server. The server handles about 800 requests per month, of which about 34% involve multiple alignments. So far the feedback from users has been very positive.

A more formal evaluation of this algorithm is required. This has been done with a technique where we generate random EPTs and randomly mutate the sequences. From the resulting mutated sequences at the leaves of the tree we try to reconstruct the multiple alignment. It is easy to verify the accuracy, as we know the correct alignment by construction. The comparisons were done for this and several other algorithms available to us. These results and the description of the methodology exceed the scope of the paper and will be available in [9].

One problem affects the quality of these multiple alignments. The results are dependent on a correct EPT, which is not always available. Minor errors in the EPT are of little consequence, unless they straddle incorrectly a point where an indel occurred. This causes the same indel to be in separate subtrees of the EPT. The above algorithm will handle this by repeating the indel. As a result the two indels may not match. Heuristics to try to fix this problem include weighting the indels in a special way in the subtrees, but have not been entirely successful. It should be noted that if the EPT is correct then the algorithm described here will work correctly.

References

[1] L. Allison and C.S. Wallace. The posterior probability distribution of alignments and its application to parameter estimation of evolutionary trees and to optimization of multiple alignments. *J. Molecular Evolution*, 39:418–430, 1994.

[2] Lachlan H. Bell, John R. Coggins, and James E. Milner-White. Mix'n'match: an improved multiple sequence alignment procedure for distantly related proteins using secondary structure predictions, designed to be independent of the choice of gap penalty and scoring matrix. *Protein Engineering*, 6(7):683–690, 1993.

[3] Steven A. Benner, Mark A. Cohen, and Gaston H. Gonnet. Empirical and structural models for insertions and deletions in the divergent evolution of proteins. *J. Molecular Biology*, 229:1065–1082, 1993.

[4] Steven A. Benner, Mark A. Cohen, and Gaston H. Gonnet. Amino acid substitution during functionally constrained divergent evolution of protein sequences. *Protein Engineering*, 7(11), 1994.

[5] Humberto Carillo and David. Lipman. The multiple sequence alignment problem in biology. *SIAM J. Appl. Math.*, 48(5):1073–1082, 1988.

[6] Margaret O. Dayhoff, R. M. Schwartz, and B. C. Orcutt. A model for evolutionary change in proteins. In Margaret O. Dayhoff, editor, *Atlas of*

Protein Sequence and Structure, volume 5, pages 345–352. National Biochemical Research Foundation, Washington DC, 1978.

[7] Adam Godzik and Jeffrey Skolnick. Flexible algorithm for direct multiple alignment of protein structures and sequences. *CABIOS*, 10(6):587–596, 1994.

[8] Gaston H. Gonnet, Mark A. Cohen, and Steven A. Benner. Exhaustive matching of the entire protein sequence database. *Science*, 256:1443–1445, 1992.

[9] Gaston H. Gonnet and Chantal Korostensky. Evaluation measures of multiple sequence alignments. In preparation, 1996.

[10] O. Gotoh. An improved algorithm for matching biological sequences. *J. Mol. Biol.*, 162:705–708, 1982.

[11] Sandeep K. Gupta, John Kececioglu, and Alejandro A. Schaffer. Improving the practical space and time efficiency of the shortest-paths approach to sum-of-pairs multiple sequence alignment. *J. Computational Biology*, 1996. To appear.

[12] Xiaoqiu Huang. On global sequence alignment. *CABIOS*, 10(3):227–235, 1994.

[13] Charles E. Lawrence, Stephen F. Altschul, Mark S. Boguski, Jun S. Liu, Andrew F. Neuwald, and John C. Wootton. Detecting subtle sequence signals: A gibbs sampling strategy for multiple alignment. *Science*, 262:208–214, October 1993.

[14] David J. Lipman, Stephen F. Altschul, and John D. Kececioglu. A tool for multiple sequence alignment. *Proc. Natl. Acad. Sci. USA*, 86:4412–4415, June 1989.

[15] S. B. Needleman and C. D. Wunsch. A general method applicable to the search for similarities in the amino acid sequence of two proteins. *J. Mol. Biol.*, 48:443–453, 1970.

[16] Gregory D. Schuler, Stephen F. Altschul, and David J. Lipman. A workbench for multiple alignment construction and analysis. *PROTEINS: Structure, Function, and Genetics*, 9:180–190, 1991.

[17] Peter H. Sellers. On the theory and computation of evolutionary distances. *SIAM J Appl. Math.*, 26(4):787–793, Jun 1974.

[18] Temple F. Smith and Michael S. Waterman. Identification of common molecular subsequences. *J. Mol. Biol.*, 147:195–197, 1981.

[19] J.D. Thompson, D.G. Higgins, and T.J Gibson. Clustal w: improving the sensitivity of progressive multiple sequence alignment through sequence weighting, positions-specific gap penalties and weight matrix choice. *Nucleic Acids Research*, 22:4673–4680, 1994.

Efficient Algorithms for Lempel-Ziv Encoding

(Extended Abstract)

Leszek Gąsieniec[1] * Marek Karpinski[2] ** Wojciech Plandowski[3] *** Wojciech Rytter[3] †

[1] Max-Planck Institut für Informatik, Im Stadtwald, Saarbrücken D-66123, Germany.
[2] Dept. of Computer Science, University of Bonn, D-53117, Bonn, Germany.
[3] Instytut Informatyki, Uniwersytet Warszawski, Banacha 2, 02–097 Warszawa, Poland.

Abstract. We consider several basic problems for texts and show that if the input texts are given by their Lempel-Ziv codes then the problems can be solved deterministically in polynomial time in the case when the original (uncompressed) texts are of exponential size. The growing importance of massively stored information requires new approaches to **algorithms for compressed texts without decompressing.** Denote by $LZ(w)$ the version of a string w produced by **Lempel-Ziv encoding** algorithm. For given compressed strings $LZ(T)$, $LZ(P)$ we give **the first known deterministic polynomial time algorithms** to compute *compressed representations* of the set of all **occurrences of the pattern** P in T, all **periods** of T, all **palindromes** of T, and all **squares** of T. Then we consider several classical language recognition problems:
• **regular language recognition:** given $LZ(T)$ and a language L described by a regular expression, test if $T \in L$,
• **extended regular language recognition:** given $LZ(T)$ and a language L described by a LZ-compressed regular expression, test if $T \in L$, the alphabet is unary,
• **context-free language recognition:** given $LZ(T)$ and a language L described by a context-free grammar, test if $T \in L$, the alphabet is unary.
We show that the first recognition problem has a polynomial time algorithm and the other two problems are $\mathcal{NP}$-hard.
We show also that the LZ encoding can be computed *on-line* in **polynomial time delay and small space** (i.e. proportional to the size of the compressed text). Also the compressed representation of a pattern-matching automaton for the compressed pattern is computed in polynomial time.

---

* On leave from Institute of Informatics, Warsaw University, ul. Banacha 2, 02–097, Warszawa, Poland. WWW: `http://zaa.mimuw.edu.pl/~lechu/lechu.html`, Email:`leszek@mpi-sb.mpg.de`

** This research was partially supported by the DFG Grant KA 673/4-1, and by the ESPRIT BR Grant 7097 and the ECUS 030. Email:`marek@cs.uni-bonn.de`

*** Supported partially by the grant KBN 8T11C01208. Email:`wojtekpl@mimuw.edu.pl`

† Supported partially by the grant KBN 8T11C01208. Email:`rytter@mimuw.edu.pl`

1 Introduction

In the algorithmics of textual problems only recently the problems related to compressed objects were investigated ([2], [3], [1] and [9]). The *compressed string-matching* problem has been already investigated in [2], [3], [1], however only for the case when the text is compressed but the pattern is **not** compressed. The LZ compression (see [14]) gives a very natural way of representing a string and it is a practically successful method of text compression. Many classical algorithmic problems in the compressed setting requires efficient solution for equality testing problem. The randomized, based on finger-printing approach, version of the equality testing algorithm was already presented in [8]. In this paper we focus on **deterministic** algorithms for problems dealing with *LZ*-compressed strings. The first of them is the **Fully Compressed Matching Problem**:

   Instance: a compressed pattern $LZ(P)$ and a compressed text $LZ(T)$

   Question: does P occur in T? If "yes" then report the first occurrence, the exact number of all occurrences and a compressed set of all occurrences.

The set $S = Occ(P, T)$ of all occurrences of P in T could be of exponential size with respect to $|LZ(T)|$ and by *computing* S we mean constructing its **compressed representation**: a data structure in which the size $|S|$ and the first element of S are given, and we can test for the membership in S in time $O(n \log n)$, in case of pattern matching, and in $O(n \log n \log \log U)$ in case of palindromes and squares, where $U = |T|$.

   The size of the problem is $n + m$, where $n = |LZ(T)|$ and $m = |LZ(P)|$. Assume for simplicity that $m \leq n$, and $|P| \leq |T|$ then n determines the size of the input strings and U determines the total size of the uncompressed strings. Note that in general U can be exponential with respect to n, and any algorithm which decompresses the pattern P or the text T would work in exponential time!

   We consider the same version of the LZ algorithm as in [6] (this is called LZ1 in [6]). Intuitively, LZ algorithm compresses the text because it is able to discover some repeated subwords. We consider here the version of LZ algorithm without *self-referencing* but our algorithms can be extended to the general self-referential case. Assume that Σ is an underlying alphabet and let w be a string over Σ. The factorization of w is given by a decomposition: $w = c_1 f_1 c_2 \ldots f_k c_{k+1}$, where $c_1 = w[1]$ and for each $1 \leq i \leq k$ $c_i \in \Sigma$ and f_i is the longest prefix of $f_i c_{i+1} \ldots f_k c_{k+1}$ which appears in $c_1 f_1 c_2 \ldots f_{i-1} c_i$. We can identify each f_i with an interval $[p, q]$, such that $f_i = w[p..q]$ and $q \leq |c_1 f_1 c_2 \ldots f_{i-1} c_{i-1}|$. If we drop the assumption related to the last inequality then it occurs a *self-referencing* (f_i is the longest prefix which appears before but not necessarily terminates at a current position). We assume that this is not the case.

Example. The factorization of a word $aababbabbaabbabbabba\#$ is given by the sequence: $c_1 f_1 c_2 f_2 c_3 f_3 c_4 f_4 c_5 = a\ a\ b\ ab\ b\ abb\ a\ ababbabba\ \#$. After identifying each subword f_i with its corresponding interval we obtain the LZ encoding of the string. Hence $LZ(aababbabbababbabb\#) = a[1,1]b[1,2]b[4,6]a[2,10]\#$.

The key concepts in our algorithms are *periodicity* and *linearly-succinct* representations of exponentially many periods. The concept of periodicity appears in many advanced string algorithms, it is naturally related to LZ compression, since the high compression ratio is achieved when there are many repetitions in the text and repetitions are closely related to the periodicity.

Denote $Periods(w) = \{p : p$ is a period of $w\}$. A set of integers forming an arithmetic progression is called here *linear*. We say that a set of positive integers from $[1 \ldots U]$ is *linearly-succinct* iff it can be decomposed in at most $\lfloor \log_2(U) \rfloor + 1$ linear sets. The following lemma was shown in [9].

Lemma 1. LINEARLY-SUCCINCT SETS LEMMA
The set $Periods(w)$ is linearly-succinct.

In this paper the terms *linearly-succinct* and *compressed* representations have different meanings, however each *linearly-succinct* set has a *compressed* representation.

Observation. The set of all occurrences of a given pattern in a compressed text T is not necessarily linearly-succinct, even if the pattern is a single letter.

In [9] and [12] the compressed strings were considered in terms of context-free grammars (grammars, in short) generating single words. We can prove:

Lemma 2. *For each string w given in LZ-compressed form we can construct a context-free grammar generating w of size $O(n^2)$, where $n = |LZ(w)|$.*

Proof. We omit the proof. □

In this paper we consider more compact and more useful abstraction of *LZ*-encodings in terms of *composition systems*. The *composition system approach* reduces the complexity considerably compared with context-free grammars. The *composition systems* (introduced here) are variations of straight line programs and context-free grammars. Introduce the set $VAR(S)$ of *variables* of a composition system S. The variables correspond to the subwords f_i (to intervals $[i,j]$ in the LZ encoding of a given word w). The value of each variable is a string over Σ. Denote by $Y_{[i]}$ and $Z^{[i]}$ the prefix of length i of Y and the suffix of length i of Z. Denote by $\cdot$ the operation of concatenation. The **composition system** S is a sequence of *composition rules* of the form: $X = Y^{[i]} \cdot Z_{[j]}$, $X = Y \cdot Z$ or $X = a$, where $a \in \Sigma$. Each variable appears exactly once on the left side of a composition rule. It is called *the rule* for this variable. The rule for a variable occurs before all rules in which this variable is on their right sides. The variables whose compositions are of the form $X = a$ are called *atomic*. The values of atomic variables are the constants which appear on the right sides. The value of the last variable of the composition system S is the value of S and is denoted by $val(S)$.

Example. We have $val(S) = val(G) = abbababababba$ in the following composition system S:

$$A = a; \; B = b; \; C = A \cdot B; \; D = B \cdot C; \; E = C \cdot D; \; F = D^{[2]} \cdot E_{[4]}; \; G = E \cdot F.$$

Lemma 3. *For each string w given in LZ-compressed form and a subword v of w we can construct a composition system generating v of size $O(n \cdot \log(n))$, where $n = |LZ(w)|$, for each variable A the word $val(A)$ is a subword of w.*

Proof. The proof will be given in the full version of the paper. □

Fact 4 *Testing for an occurrence of pattern $\mathcal{P}$ in text $\mathcal{T}$ can be reduced to the following problem:*
* *for two composition systems $\mathcal{P}$, $\mathcal{T}$ decide whether there is a variable X in the system $\mathcal{T}$ such that*
* *$val(\mathcal{P})$ is a subword of $val(X)$.*

For a given string w generated by a composition system $\mathcal{S}$ we consider the **bracket structure** of w with respect to $\mathcal{S}$. The bracket structure appears if we replace each composition rule $X = Y^{[i]} \cdot Z_{[j]}$ by $X = (\ Y^{[i]} \cdot Z_{[j]}\ )$, where (and) are new terminal symbols. In this way inside the text w many pairs of brackets will appear, each of them associated with a variable. The brackets define the family $\mathcal{F}$ of intervals in w, each interval is associated with a variable, consider only intervals which are decomposed into two intervals (according to a composition of the composition system). The point of the decomposition is called the **cut**. Our compressed representations of objects in w are related to the bracket structure, for example the set of all occurrences of the pattern is represented as a set of occurrences for each interval in $\mathcal{F}$. An occurrence is **associated with** an interval τ iff τ is the smallest interval in $\mathcal{F}$ containing the pattern P and the pattern *overlaps* the cut of τ. The first crucial point is that the number of *essentially different* intervals in $\mathcal{F}$ is only linear, since they correspond to n variables, though $|\mathcal{F}|$ can be exponential. The second crucial point is that the set of occurrences *associated with* a given interval in $\mathcal{F}$ forms a single arithmetic progression. Moreover for each position i it is easy to find an interval with which i is (possibly) *associated* by traversing *top-down* the generation tree of w. Then we test if i is in an arithmetic progression of positions *associated with* a given interval. The height of the tree is at most n. This approach gives the membership algorithms working in linear time with respect to n.

2 Fully Compressed String-Matching

Our auxiliary problem is that of checking if a part of the pattern P occurs at a given position i in T. The **Compressed Equality Testing** problem is described here as follows.

> **Instance:** a compressed pattern $LZ(P)$, a compressed text $LZ(T)$ and integers i, j, i', j'
>
> **Question:** does $P[i..j] = T[i'..j']$? If "no" then find the first **mismatch**.

Assume we have two composition systems $\mathcal{S}_1$, $\mathcal{S}_2$ with n_1, n_2 variables, respectively. The key point of our algorithm is to consider relations between some parts of the words which are values of variables in these composition systems. For the

convenience we sometimes identify the name of the variable with its value.
The main object in our algorithm is an information that two parts of some variables are equal: $A[p..q] = B[p'..q']$, where $p = 1$ or $q = |A|$ or $p' = 1$ or $q' = |B|$. Such information is stored in objects called here the *equality-items* (*items*, in short). There are three types of *items*:

1. *overlap items*: $OV(A, B, i)$ means that $B[1..i]$ is a suffix of A (in other words $A^{[i]} = B_{[i]}$);
2. *suffix items*: $SU(A, B, i, k)$ means that $A[i..k]$ is a suffix of B;
3. *prefix items*: $PR(A, B, i, k)$ means that $A[i..k]$ is a prefix of B.

We distinguish also another type of items: *subword items*. These are the prefix (suffix) items in the case when the whole word B is considered as its prefix (suffix). The items will be denoted by small greek letters α, β, γ, possibly with subscripts. The sets of items will be denoted by capital greek letters. Each item corresponds to equality of two subwords, the item is **valid** iff this equality is satisfied. The set Γ of items is valid iff each item in Γ is valid. The *size* of an item is the length of the text which "takes part" in the equality. If the item is of type $OV(A, B, i)$ then the equality concerns the prefix $B_{[i]}$ and the suffix $A^{[i]}$, both of length i. Hence $size(OV(A, B, i)) = i$. The sizes of other types of items are defined similarly. The items of size one are called **atomic items**. The validity of atomic items is rather simple. Two sets Γ_1 and Γ_2 of items are equivalent (we write $\Gamma_1 \equiv \Gamma_2$) iff validity of Γ_1 is equivalent to validity of Γ_2. The basic operation in our equality-test algorithm is $SPLIT(\alpha)$, where α is an item. The value of this operation is a set of one or two items: α is split into "smaller" items. The operation satisfies: $\{\alpha\} \equiv SPLIT(\alpha)$. The operation $SPLIT$ can be defined formally in a similar way as in [12]. We describe only how overlap items are split, other types of items are split similarly. Assume $A, B \in VAR(S_1) \cup VAR(S_2)$. Assume our item α is $OV(A, B, i)$, (which means $A^{[i]} = B_{[i]}$) and the composition rule related to A is: $A = C^{[p]} \cdot D_{[q]}$.

Case 1: $i \le q$. Now $A^{[i]} = B_{[i]}$ corresponds to $(D_{[q]})^{[i]} = B_{[i]}$. Thus $SPLIT(\alpha) = \{PR(D, B, q - i + 1, q)\}$.

Case 2: $i > q$. Now $A^{[i]} = B_{[i]}$ is equivalent to $C^{[i-q]} = B_{[i-q]}$ and $(B_{[i]})^{[q]} = D_{[q]}$, and $SPLIT(\alpha) = \{OV(C, B, i - q), PR(B, D, i - q + 1, i)\}$.

Assume that in each $SPLIT$ exactly one variable (the longer one) is *decomposed*. The variables participating in $SPLIT$ are different (one from system S_1, another from S_2). Assume X, Y are the last variables in composition systems S_1, S_2, respectively. The equality-test checks if $val(X) = val(Y)$.

The item $\alpha_0 = OV(X, Y, |X|)$ is called the *starting item*. Hence, if $|X| = |Y|$, then the equality-test problem is reduced to the validity problem for the starting item. The structure of the algorithm is:

> *Initially:* $\Gamma = \{\alpha_0\}$
> **invariant1:** $\Gamma \equiv \{\alpha_0\}$.
> **invariant2:** $|\Gamma|$ is polynomial.
> *Finally:* Γ consists only
>   of *atomic* items.

Assume Δ is a set of overlap items. We use the operation $Compact(\Delta)$. Essentially this operation works similarly as in [12]. The operation removes from Δ some number of overlap items and possibly inserts other overlap items (related to the same variables as removed items).

Assume that for each atomic item α holds the equality $SPLIT(\alpha) = \{\alpha\}$. Let $\Delta_{A,B}$ be the set of overlap items of the type $OV(A, B, *)$. This set is represented by the largest overlap and set of periods in a prefix of B, since other overlaps correspond to shifts of B on itself. However such set of periods can be represented by a set of $\log U + 1$ size due to Lemma 1. The overlaps correspond to periods and due to Lemma 1 we can choose only $\log U + 1$ number of items of a given type $OV(A, B, *)$. We have quadratic number of pairs of variables, hence the upper bound for $|Compact(\Delta)|$ is $O((n_1 + n_2)^2 \log U)$.

> **ALGORITHM** *EQUALITY_TEST* ;
> $\Gamma := \{ \alpha_0 \}$;
> **while** Γ contains a non-atomic item **do**
> $\Gamma' := \emptyset$;
>   **for each** $\alpha \in \Gamma$ **do** $\Gamma' := \Gamma' \cup SPLIT(\alpha)$;
> $\Gamma := Compact(\Gamma')$;
> **if** all items in Γ are valid **then return** *true*
>   **else return** *false*

The operation *Compact* satisfies:
$$\Delta \equiv Compact(\Delta) \text{ and } |Compact(\Delta)| \leq c \cdot (n_1 + n_2)^2 \log U,$$
for a constant c.

If $\Gamma = \Delta_1 \cup \Delta_2$, where Δ_1 is the set of overlap items in Γ and Δ_2 is the set other items then define
$$Compact(\Gamma) = Compact(\Delta_1) \cup \Delta_2.$$
It can be proved that $|\Gamma| \leq c \cdot (n_1 + n_2)^3 \log U$ and this implies the following theorem (the details are omitted).

Theorem 5. *The Compressed Equality Testing problem can be solved in time* $O((n \log n)^4 \log^2 U)$.

We will now describe how to apply the *Compressed Equality Testing* in pattern matching algorithm. Denote by $Eq(m)$ the time complexity of equality test algorithm for two compressed texts of size m. Denote $ArithProg(i, p, k) = \{i, i + p, i + 2p, \ldots, i + kp\}$, so it is an arithmetic progression of length $k + 1$.

Its description is given by numbers i, p, k written in binary representation. Our pattern matching algorithm deals with a polynomial number of arithmetic progressions representing periods or overlaps.

Denote by $Solution(p, V, W)$ any position $i \in V$ such that $i + j = p$ for some $j \in W$. In case there is no such position i then $Solution(p, V, W) = 0$. Moreover let $\#Solution(p, V, W)$ be the number of such is.

Lemma 6. APPLICATION OF EUCLID'S ALGORITHM
Assume that two linear sets $V, W \subseteq [1 \ldots U]$ are given by their descriptions. Then for a given number $c \in [1 \ldots U]$ we can compute $Solution(c, V, W)$ and $\#Solution(c, V, W)$ using $\log^2(U)$ arithmetic operations.

We show only how to find an occurrence of the pattern, the number of occurrences can be computed by applying Lemma 6 during the second phase of the algorithm. Let us fix the pattern $P = val(\mathcal{P})$. Let $val(X_i)$ be a string of length K and j be any position in this string. Define $Pre(j, i)$ to be the lengths of subwords of $val(X_i)$ that end at position j in $val(X_i)$ and that are prefixes of P. Similarly, denote by $Suf(j, i)$ the lengths of subwords of $val(X_i)$ that begin at position j in $val(X_i)$ and that are suffixes of P. Formally: $Pre(j, i) = \{1 \le i \le j \ : \ X_i[j - i + 1..j]$ is a a a prefix of $P \}$.
$Suf(j, i) = \{j \le i \le K \ : \ X_i[j..j + i - 1]$ is a suffix of $P \}$. Observe that these tables depend on the pattern P, however it is convenient to assume further that P is fixed.

Lemma 7. *Let $X_i = X_j \cdot X_k$, then P occurs in X_i iff P occurs in X_j or P occurs in X_k, or $Solution(|P|, Pre(|X_j|, j), Suf(1, X_k)) \ne 0$.*

Let $X_1, X_2, \ldots, X_m$ be a sequence of variables that appear in consecutive rules of the composition system $\mathcal{T}$ defining the text T. By Lemma 3 $m = O(n \log n)$.

Let k be the first position in $Prefs(j, i)$, then all the other positions in $Prefs(j, i)$ are of the form $k + p'$, where p' is a period of $P[1..k]$. Hence Lemma 1 implies directly the following fact.

Lemma 8. *The sets $Suffs(j, i)$ and $Prefs(j, i)$ are linearly-succinct.*

Let the composition rule for a variable X_k be of the form $X_k = X_i^{[s]} \cdot X_{j[t]}$. Then for each position b in the word $val(X_k)$ denote by $Pred[b, X_k]$ the position $|val(X_i)| - s + b$ in the word X_i if $1 \le b \le s$ and the position $b - s$ in the word X_j if $b > s$. These positions are associated with corresponding variables. If the composition rule for a variable X_k is of the form $X_k = a$ then $Pred[b, X_k]$ is undefined. The function $Pred$ (predecessor) defines a partial order "to be a predecessor" between pairs (position in $val(X_k)$, variable X_k).

We are now able to give a sketch of the whole structure of the algorithm. In the first phase of the algorithm in each word $val(X_k)$ at most $2m$ positions are being distinguished. They are called **finger** and are denoted by $Finger(X_k)$. They correspond to *informers* in [6]. The positions in $Finger(X_k)$ are those predecessors of end-positions of variables that are in the word $val(X_k)$. Clearly, for a fixed k, in the set $Finger(X_k)$ there are at most two predecessors of end-positions of one variable, so that there are at most $2m$ positions in the set $Finger(X_k)$.

Lemma 9. *The sets $Finger(X_k)$ can be computed in $O(n^2)$ time.*

ALGORITHM *SECOND_PHASE* ;
   for $i := 1$ **to** n **do**
      for each informer b in X_i **do**
         compute $Prefs(b, i)$ and $Suffs(b, i)$;
         test for an occurrence using Lemma 6 and Lemma 7

The values of $Prefs(b, i)$ and $Suffs(b, i)$ are computed as follows. Let c be the cut of $val(X_k)$. First, the values of $Prefs(c, k)$ and $Suffs(c, k)$ are computed. Then for each arithmetic sequence in those sets we compute the set of **maximal pattern prefixes** which start in the positions of the sequence. As it is proved in [9] such set can be represented in constant space and it is enough to compute such prefixes only for three positions of the sequence. Given a position i in $val(X_k)$ the length of the maximal pattern prefix which starts at i in $val(X_k)$ can be computed by **binary search** using $\log |val(X_k)|$ times the **equality test** procedure. Then the sets $Prefs(b, k)$ and $Suffs(b, k)$ are computed. For each finger b we put to $Prefs(b, k)$, for $b \leq c$ the prefixes from $Prefs(Pred[b, k])$ which are shorter than b, and, for $b > c$, the set $Prefs(Pred[b - c, k])$ and the parts of sequences from $Prefs(c, k)$ for which the maximal prefixes extend over b. Similarly we compute the sets $Suffs(b, k)$. The time complexity is dominated by computing maximal prefixes. Computing one prefix is done in $O(Eq(m) \log U)$ time where m is the size of the composition system generated from the LZ-code. There are at most $m \log U$ prefixes to compute. This gives the total time complexity $O(m \log^2 U \cdot Eq(m))$. Since $m = O(n \log n)$, we have:

Theorem 10. *The Fully Compressed Matching Problem can be solved in time $O(n \log n \log^2 U \cdot Eq(n \log n))$.*

As a side effect of our pattern-matching algorithm we can compute the set of all periods for strings with short description.

Theorem 11. *Assume $\mathcal{P}$ is a compressed pattern. Then the compressed representation of the set $Periods(\mathcal{P})$ can be computed in $O(n \log n \log^2 U \cdot Eq(n \log n))$ time. The representation consists (in this case) of $\log U$ number of linear sets.*

Proof. Use our string-matching algorithm with the pattern $\mathcal{P} = val(\mathcal{S})$ and the text $\mathcal{T} = val(\mathcal{S})$ ignoring the occurrence of the pattern at position 1. As a side effect we compute all suffixes of $\mathcal{T}$ which are prefixes of $\mathcal{P}$. This determines all periods. □

3 Compressed Palindromes and Squares

Our algorithms for compressed **palindromes** and **squares** use ideas from [4]: palindromes are searched using **periodicities** implied by sequences of many palindromes which are *close to each other* and searching of squares is reduced to multiple application of **pattern-matching**.

First we consider a data structure for palindromes, consider only even length palindromes (the algorithms for odd length palindromes are similar). Let $w[i..j]$ be a subword of w which is a palindrome. This palindrome is **centered in position** $(i+j)/2$ in w and its **radius** is $(j-i)/2$. Let $Radius[1..|w|]$ be an array of radii of palindromes, this means that the entry $Radius[i]$ contains the maximal radius of a palindrome centered in i. The array $Radius$ is a representation of all even length palindromes inside a word. Indeed, $w[i..j]$ is an even palindrome iff (i+j) is odd and $Radius[(i+j-1)/2] > (j-i-1)/2$. A compressed representation of the array $Radius$ is called here a **pal-structure**. A palindrome which is a prefix (suffix) of a word is called *initial* (*final*) palindrome. Denote by $InitPal(w, i)$ ($FinPal(w, i)$) the set of initial palindromes in $w[i+1..|w|]$ (final palindromes in $w[1..i]$). We say that a palindrome **covers** a given position i iff i is inside this palindrome. In other words, the palindrome of radius r centered in j covers i iff $j - r < i \leq j + r$.

Lemma 12. *The sets $InitPal(w, i)$ and $FinPal(w, i)$ are both linearly-succinct. Moreover, if $i_1 > i_2 > \ldots > i_k$ is a set of positions in $InitPal(w, i)$, then the sequence $\{i_s\}$ can be divided in $O(\log |w|)$ blocks of arithmetic sequences.*

The **pal-structure** consists of sequences of numbers which are assigned to variables in a composition system. Let A be a variable and let the rule for A be $A = E^{[r]} F_{[s]}$. Denote by $LeftPal(A)$ ($RightPal(A)$) the set of centers of palindromes which cover r and that are not in $FinPal(A, |A|)$ ($InitPal(A, 1)$) and that are to the left (right) of r. Formally, $LeftPal(A) = \{j : j < r < j + Radius[j], j \notin FinPal(A, |A|)\}$. Clearly, $LeftPal(A) \subseteq FinPal(E^{[r]})$ and $RightPal(A) \subseteq \{r + i : i \in InitPal(F_{[s]})\}$. The pal-structure consists of the sets $LeftPal(A)$, $RightPal(A)$, for each variable A. Each arithmetic sequence in $LeftPal(A)$ and $RightPal(A)$ is equipped with the values of $Radius$ for the first, last and some other element of the sequence.

Theorem 13.
(A) The compressed representation of all palindromes in the compressed text can be computed in $O(n \log n \log^2 U \cdot Eq(n \log n))$ time.
(B) Given a position i and the compressed representation of all palindromes, the value of $Radius[i]$ can be computed in $O(n \log n \log \log U)$ time.

Proof. To appear in the full version of the paper. □

Theorem 14. *The compressed representation of the set of all squares in the compressed text can be computed in $O(n^2 \log^2 n \log^3 U \cdot Eq(n \log n))$ time.*

Proof. To appear in the full version of the paper. □

4 Compressed Language Recognition Problems

For a given regular expression describing the language R and a context-free grammar G generating a language L we can construct a grammar generating the language $L \cap R$. The construction proves also the following theorem (we omit details in this version).

Theorem 15. *The following problem has a polynomial time algorithm: given $LZ(T)$ and a language L described by a regular expression, test if $T \in L$.*

Proof. First, the encoding $LZ(T)$ is transformed into a context-free grammar G which generates the language $L' = \{T\}$. Then a context-free grammar for the language $L' \cap L$ is constructed. Finally, the language $L' \cap L$ is tested for the emptiness. All steps can be accomplished in polynomial time. This completes the proof. $\square$

The problem becomes *computationally infeasible* if we allow exponentiation in regular expressions. Such expressions are called here *extended regular expressions*. Consequently, the problem is $\mathcal{NP}$-hard for context-free grammars.

Theorem 16. *The following two problems are $\mathcal{NP}$-hard:*
(1) given $LZ(T)$ and a language L described by an extended regular expression, test if $T \in L$, the expression does not contain empty string and the alphabet is unary,
(2) given $LZ(T)$ and a language L described by a context-free grammar, test if $T \in L$, the alphabet is unary.

Proof. Part (2) is a consequence of part (1). The proof of part (1) is a reduction from the SUBSET SUM problem defined as follows:

Input instance: Finite set $A = \{a_1, a_2, \ldots, a_n\}$ of integers and an integer K. The size of the input is the number of bits needed for the description.

Question: Is there a subset $A' \subseteq A$ such that the sum of the elements in A' is exactly K?

The problem SUBSET SUM is $\mathcal{NP}$-complete, see [7]. The LZ code for the string $P = 1^K$ is of size $O(\log K)$. The SUBSET SUM problem is reduced to the membership:
$$P \in (1^{a_1} \cup \varepsilon) \cdot (1^{a_2} \cup \varepsilon) \cdots (1^{a_n} \cup \varepsilon).$$

The empty string ε can be easily eliminated by replacing each ε and 1^{a_i} by a single letter 1 and by 1^{a_i+1}, respectively, and concatenating P with 1^n. This completes the proof. $\square$

5 Two Applications of Our Compressed Representation

At the end we show two applications of our compressed representations.

Lemma 17. *Assume $a \in \Sigma$ and we have a compressed representation of the set of occurrences of the pattern P in T, then we can compute the compressed set of all occurrences of Pa in $O(n^2 \log^2 n)$ time.*

Proof. Recall, that the compressed representation of a set of occurrences of a pattern P in T is a composition system representing T and additionally for each variable X in the system one arithmetic sequence of those occurrences of P in X which cover the cut of X. We show how to modify the sequences to obtain the sequences for the pattern Pa. Let $a_1 < a_2 \ldots < a_k$ be such a sequence. Then we check whether the occurrences of P at a_1 and a_k can be extended to occurrences of Pa. This can be done in $O(m)$ time where m is the size of the composition system for P ($m = O(n \log n)$). If the occurrence of P at a_1 cannot be extended by a then no occurrence of P at a_i, for $i < k$, can be extended by a. If the occurrence of P at a_1 can be extended by a then all occurrences of P at a_i, for $i < k$, can be extended by a. This allows to construct a part of the sequence for Pa. To obtain the final sequence we have to check whether there is an occurrence of Pa which sticks to the cut of a variable. This can be done in $O(m)$ time. This completes the proof. □

Theorem 18. *For a given text T, its code $LZ(T)$ can be computed on-line with $O(n^2 \log^2 n)$ delay using $O(n \log n)$ space.*

Proof. It is enough to show how to compute in the claimed complexities a code $LZ(Sa)$ given a code $LZ(S)$ for a string S. Let $c_1 f_1 \ldots c_k f_k$ be the LZ-factorization of S. Then the factorization for Sa is either $c_1 f_1 \ldots c_k f_k'$ where $f_k' = f_k a$ (if $f_k a$ occurs inside S), or $c_1 f_1 \ldots c_k f_k a$ (if $f_k a$ does not occur inside S). If we keep the compressed representation of the set of occurrences of the last factor f_k inside S then by Lemma 17 the code $LZ(Sa)$ and the set of occurrences of the last LZ-factor of Sa can be computed in $O(n^2 \log^2 n)$ time and $O(n \log n)$ space. This completes the proof. □

We can compute the compressed representations of the table $Next$ from the Knuth-Morris-Pratt algorithm, see [5], and of the pattern-matching automaton. This gives another application of our data structure.

Theorem 19. *The compressed representation $\mathcal{A}$ of the pattern-matching automaton (of size polynomial on n) for a compressed pattern P can be constructed in polynomial time in $LZ(P)$. The constructed automaton works with the delay $O(n \log n \cdot \log U)$.*

6   Concluding Remarks

We proved that the membership problem for extended regular expressions and for context-free grammars are $\mathcal{NP}$-hard if an input word is compressed. An open problem is the membership in $\mathcal{NP}$. The same problem for regular grammars is in $\mathcal{P}$. The important open problems are the complexity of the membership problem for deterministic context-free grammars. If the first problem is in $\mathcal{P}$ then parsing of compressed programs can be done polynomially with respect to the size of the compressed program.

Our method yields the first polynomial time algorithm for the **LZ Fully Compressed Matching Problem** and other classical problems for texts. An interesting open problem remains on improving running time and storage requirements of our algorithms.

This is the first approach on polynomial-time deterministic algorithms for *fully* compressed versions of problems on texts.

Our algorithms mostly make sense for highly compressed texts, an open problem is to adjust them to the case when the compression is small. Of course if there is no compression then the standard algorithms (for noncompressed texts) work, but in the case of small compression it seems that a hybrid of these standard algorithms and algorithms presented here would be more efficient.

References

1. A. Amir, G. Benson and M. Farach, *Let sleeping files lie: pattern-matching in Z-compressed files*, in *SODA'94*.
2. A. Amir, G. Benson, *Efficient two dimensional compressed matching*, Proc. of the *2nd IEEE Data Compression Conference* 279-288 (1992).
3. A. Amir, G. Benson and M. Farach, *Optimal two-dimensional compressed matching*, in *ICALP'94*.
4. A. Apostolico, D. Breslauer, Z. Galil, Optimal parallel algorithms for periods, palindromes and squares, in *ICALP'92*, pp. 296-307.
5. M. Crochemore and W. Rytter, *Text Algorithms*, Oxford University Press, New York (1994).
6. M. Farach and M. Thorup, *String matching in Lempel-Ziv compressed strings*, in STOC'95, pp. 703-712.
7. M.R. Garey and D.S. Johnson, *Computers and Intractability: A Guide to the Theory of NP-Completeness*. W.H. Freeman (1979).
8. L. Gąsieniec, M. Karpiński, W. Plandowski and W. Rytter, *Randomized Efficient Algorithms for Compressed Strings: the Finger-Print Approach*, to appear in proceedings of the 7th Combinatorial Pattern Matching, Laguna Beach (1996).
9. M. Karpinski, W. Rytter and A. Shinohara, *Pattern-matching for strings with short description*, in *Combinatorial Pattern Matching*, 1995.
10. D. Knuth, *The Art of Computing, Vol. II: Seminumerical Algorithms*. Second edition. Addison-Wesley, 1981.
11. A. Lempel and J. Ziv, *On the complexity of finite sequences*, IEEE Trans. on Inf. Theory 22, 75-81 (1976).
12. W. Plandowski, *Testing equivalence of morphisms on context-free languages*, ESA'94, Lecture Notes in Computer Science 855, Springer-Verlag, 460–470 (1994).
13. J. Storer, *Data compression: methods and theory*, Computer Science Press, Rockville, Maryland, 1988.
14. J. Ziv and A. Lempel, *A universal algorithm for sequential data compression*, IEEE Trans. on Inf. Theory vo. IT–23(3), 337–343, 1977.

The Deterministic Complexity of Parallel Multisearch*

(Extended Abstract)

Armin Bäumker[1]   Wolfgang Dittrich[1]   Andrea Pietracaprina[2]

[1] Department of Mathematics and Computer Science and Heinz Nixdorf Institute,
University of Paderborn, Paderborn, Germany
[2] Dipartimento di Matematica Pura e Applicata, Via Belzoni 7, Università di
Padova, Padova, Italy

Abstract. Given m ordered segments that form a partition of some universe (e.g., a 2D strip), the multisearch problem consists of determining, for a set of n query points in the universe, the segments they belong to. We present the first parallel deterministic scheme that efficiently solves the problem in the case $m \geq n$. The scheme is designed on the BSP* model, a variant of Valiant's BSP that rewards blockwise communication, and uses a suitable redundant representation of the data. Both computation and communication complexities are studied as functions of the redundancy. In particular, it is shown that optimal speed-up can be achieved using logarithmic redundancy. We also prove a lower bound on the communication requirements of any multisearch scheme realized on a distributed memory machine.

1   Introduction

Multisearch is a fundamental problem that arises in several application fields. In general terms, it can be regarded as the problem of performing a number of search processes on a given data structure, such as a set of ordered items, a balanced tree or a graph. For concreteness, we adopt the definition given in [BDM96]. Let $\mathcal{S} = \{\sigma_1, \sigma_2, \ldots, \sigma_m\}$ be a set of m ordered segments forming a partition of a given universe (e.g., a strip in 2D). The segments are ordered in the sense that there exists an elementary operation that compares a *point* q in the universe with a segment σ_i and establishes whether $q \in \sigma_i$, or $q \in \bigcup_{j=1}^{i-1} \sigma_j$ or $q \in \bigcup_{j=i+1}^{m} \sigma_j$. A *multisearch problem* consists of determining, for a set of n points (*queries*), the segments they belong to. The multisearch problem has a large number of important applications in fields such as computational geometry, vision and pattern recognition, among others, and it naturally arises

* This research was supported, in part, by the ESPRIT III Basic Research Programme of the EC under contract No. 9072 (project GEPPCOM), and in part by DFG-Sonderforschungsbereich 376 "Massive Parallelität: Algorithmen, Entwurfsmethoden, Anwendungen". Part of the work was done while the third author was visiting the Heinz Nixdorf Institute, Paderborn, Germany.

in the parallel implementation of several data structures (see [ADM+91] for a more complete list of applications).

In the sequential setting, a straightforward binary search yields a simple and optimal multisearch algorithm running in $\Theta(n \log m)$ time. In parallel, while such strategy can be easily implemented on a CREW-PRAM, attaining optimal speed-up, the development of efficient multisearch algorithms that do not rely on the concurrent-read capability constitutes a real challenge. Indeed, the problem appears already quite complicated for the EREW-PRAM because of the congestion arising when several queries need to be compared with the same sequence of segments. The congestion problem is even worse on more realistic machines where the memory is partitioned into modules accessed through a network, since both the modules and the network become bottlenecks for accessing the shared data.

The aim of this paper is to study the worst-case complexity of parallel multisearch by developing upper and lower bounds on the computation and communication time required to perform it on the BSP*, a variant of Valiant's BSP. A *Bulk Synchronous Parallel* machine, or $BSP(p, g, L)$, consists of p processors each provided with a local memory and communicating through a network of *bandwidth* g and *latency* L [Val90]. The computation of such a machine is organized as a sequence of *supersteps*. In a superstep the processors operate independently performing local computation and generating a number of point-to-point messages. At the end of the superstep, the messages are delivered to their destinations and a global barrier synchronization is enforced. If each processor performs at most w local operations and sends/receives at most h messages, the superstep requires $\max\{w, L\}$ *computation time* and $\max\{gh, L\}$ *communication time*.

The adoption of few parameters (bandwidth and latency) to specify the communication capabilities of a parallel machine allows BSP to retain the simplicity and generality of powerful abstractions, such as the PRAM, while taking into account the limitations of real machines based on specific architectures. For these reasons, BSP is rapidly emerging as a framework for general purpose parallel computation. In [BDM96], a variant of the BSP, called $BSP*(p, g, L, B)$, is presented, which introduces an additional parameter B to denote the *minimum message size* needed to fully exploit the bandwidth of the router. In BSP*, a superstep where at most h messages of size at most s are sent/received by any processor is charged $\max\{gh\lceil\frac{s}{B}\rceil, L\}$ communication time [BDM96]. This feature is meant to reward blockwise communication and, as shown by the experimental results reported in [BDM96], it enhances the descriptiveness of the model with respect to actual machines.

1.1 Previous Work

A number of parallel algorithms for multisearch are known in the literature. Most of these algorithms deal with the case $m = O(n)$, which appears to be easier than the case of large m because, intuitively, it causes less congestion. In [RS94], an optimal randomized algorithm for the EREW-PRAM is presented. The algorithm runs in time $O(\log n)$, with high probability, using n processors, and can be adapted to run on the butterfly, as well. Deterministic algorithms are given in [ADM+91] and [AF94], which require time $O(\log n (\log \log n)^3)$ on an n-node hypercube, and time $O(\sqrt{n})$ on an $\sqrt{n} \times \sqrt{n}$ mesh, respectively. On the Coarse Grained Multiprocessor (a model somewhat similar to BSP), [DFR93] show that multisearch can be performed in optimal $O((n/p) \log n)$ time if $p \leq \sqrt{n}$ processors are used. The case $m \geq n$ is studied in [Ran92] where a randomized algorithm is given that achieves optimal speed-up on a p-processor butterfly for $n = p \log p$ queries and m polynomial in p. Recently, Bäumker et al. [BDM96] studied the multisearch problem on the BSP* obtaining 1-optimal algorithms, that is, algorithms that require $(1+o(1))\frac{n \log m}{p}$ computation time and $o(1)\frac{n \log m}{p}$ communication time. In particular, they present a 1-optimal deterministic algorithm for the case $m \leq n$, with $n = \Omega(p \log^2 n)$, and a 1-optimal randomized algorithm for the case $n < m < 2^p$, with $n = \Omega(p \log^3 n)$. Both results hold for wide ranges of BSP* parameters. For the case $m = \omega(n)$ no efficient deterministic algorithms are known in the literature.

1.2 New Results

In this paper, we present a deterministic scheme that performs multisearch on the BSP*(p, g, L, B) for $m = \omega(n)$ segments. The scheme is a modification of the one in [BDM96] and employs a redundant representation of the segments in order to achieve efficient worst-case performance without resorting to randomization. In particular, each segment is replicated into r copies stored in a suitable data structure. The value r is called the *redundancy* of the scheme. Our results are summarized by the theorems below and hold under the following assumptions: $n = \Omega(p^{1+\epsilon})$, with $\epsilon = \Omega(1)$; $m = \omega(n)$; and $B, L \leq (n/p)^\eta$, with $\eta > 0$ a sufficiently small constant.

Theorem 1. *For any $r = o(\log m)$, there exists a multisearch scheme for the BSP*(p, g, L, B) which uses redundancy r and is able to answer any set of n queries in computation time $O(\frac{n \log m}{p} r(\frac{m}{n^\alpha p^{1-\alpha}})^{2/r})$ and communication time $O(\frac{n \log m}{p} \frac{rg}{B \log n}(\frac{m}{n^\alpha p^{1-\alpha}})^{2/r})$, for some constant $\alpha < 1$.*

A specialized scheme can be devised if $r = \Theta(\log m)$, attaining better performance.

Theorem 2. *There exists a multisearch scheme for the BSP*(p, g, L, B) which uses redundancy $r = \Theta(\log m)$ and is able to answer any set of n queries in computation time $O(\frac{n \log m}{p} \frac{r}{\log n})$ and communication time $O(\frac{n \log m}{p} \frac{rg}{B \log n})$. If $\epsilon > 1$, the communication time becomes $O(\frac{n \log m}{p} \frac{g}{B \log n})$.*

Note that if m is polynomial in n and either $g = o(B \log n / \log m)$ or $g = o(B \log n)$ and $\epsilon > 1$, the above scheme is c-optimal for some constant c, i.e., it takes $(c + o(1))\frac{n \log m}{p}$ computation time and $o(1)\frac{n \log m}{p}$ communication time.

The above results provide the first non-trivial worst-case upper bounds for parallel multisearch in the case $m = \omega(n)$. A natural question is whether the redundancy used in our schemes is truly needed to achieve efficient performance. We tackle the question by proving a lower bound on the amount of communication required for performing multisearch on any p-processor distributed-memory machine, expressed as a function of m, n, p and the redundancy r. The lower bound argument assumes that the answer to a query is based exclusively on the outcomes of individual comparisons between the query and the segments, and that each query or segment can be communicated in a single word. Also, it uses a slightly more general notion of redundancy, defined as the average number of copies per segment available in the processors' memories.

Theorem 3. *Let $1 \leq r \leq \min\{p/24, \log(m/6n)/6\}$. For any deterministic multisearch scheme designed on a p-processor distributed-memory machine, which uses redundancy r, the maximum number of words that need to be communicated from/to a processor in order to answer n queries is*

$$T_{\text{comm}} = \Omega \left(\min \left\{ \frac{n}{r}, \frac{n}{p} \left(\frac{m}{n} \right)^{\frac{1}{6r}} \right\} \right) .$$

The lower bound indicates that $\Omega(\log(m/n)/\log\log m)$ redundancy is needed to reduce the communication requirements to $O(n \log m/p)$. This implies that when m is polynomial in n the redundancy used by the scheme of Theorem 2 is only a factor $\log\log m$ away from optimal. Moreover, the behavior of the communication time achieved by the scheme of Theorem 1, as a function of the redundancy, is qualitatively similar to that indicated by the lower bound.

The rest of the paper is organized as follows. Section 2 describes the data structure used to store the segments and how it is distributed among the processors' memories. Section 3 presents a number of BSP* primitives and the implementation of two protocols for accessing the data structure. The algorithm is presented in Section 4 where Theorems 1 and 2 are proved. Finally, Theorem 3 is proved in Section 5.

2 The Redundant Search Tree

In our multisearch scheme the m segments are organized in a *Redundant Search Tree (RST)*, which is precomputed and stored in the local memories of the BSP* processors. The RST is essentially a complete binary search tree over the segments, which is conceptually partitioned into complete subtrees with $d - 1 = (n/p)^\alpha$ nodes, where α is a suitable constant $0 < \alpha < 1$. By regarding each subtree as a *supernode*, the tree appears as a d-ary tree with $\log m/\log d$ levels[3] and $M = \Theta(m/d)$ supernodes, with each supernode of size $\Theta(d)$. Let U denote the set of supernodes and V the set of BSP* processors. Each supernode is replicated into r copies stored by distinct processors. The distribution of the copies among the processors is governed by a bipartite graph $G = (U, V)$ with suitable expansion properties, which is defined below.

---

[3] Unless otherwise specified, all the logarithms are taken to the base 2.

Let $G = (U, V)$ be a bipartite graph with $|U| = M$ and $|V| = p$. We say that G is r-*regular* if every node of U has degree r and every node of V has degree Mr/p. In the rest of the paper, we make use of the following notations. Let $u \in U$, $S \subseteq U$, $v \in V$ and $Q \subseteq V$ denote arbitrary nodes or subsets of U and V. $\Gamma(u) \subseteq V$ denotes the set of neighbors of u, and $\Gamma(S)$ the set $\bigcup_{u \in S} \Gamma(u)$. $E(u)$ (resp., $E(v)$) denotes the set of edges adjacent to u (resp., v) and $E(S) = \bigcup_{u \in S} E(u)$ (resp., $E(Q) = \bigcup_{v \in Q} E(v)$). Let $E \subseteq E(S)$. E is a k-*bundle* for S if $|E| = k|S|$ and $|E \cap E(u)| = k$, for every $u \in S$. If $k = 1$, E is called a *target set* for S. The quantity $\max_{v \in V} |E \cap E(v)|$ is called the *congestion* of E. $\Gamma^E(S)$ denotes the set $\{v \in \Gamma(S) : E(v) \cap E \neq \emptyset\}$. Let $\mu = \lfloor r/2 \rfloor + 1$.

Definition 4. G has (c, δ)-*expansion*, for some $c > 0$ and $0 < \delta < 1$, if for any subset $S \subseteq U$, with $|S| \leq p/r$, and any μ-bundle E for S, $|\Gamma^E(S)| > cr|S|^{1-\delta}$.

Lemma 5 [PP95]. *Let* $\beta = \log M / \log p$. *There is a constant* b *such that for every* $r > b\beta \log \beta$ *there exists an* r-*regular bipartite graph* $G = (U, V)$, *with* $|U| = M$ *and* $|V| = p$, *which has* (c, δ)-*expansion with* $c = \Theta(1)$ *and* $\delta = (\beta - 1)/\mu$. *Moreover, every random* r-*regular graph exhibits such expansion with high probability.*

From now on, we assume that the copies of the RST supernodes are distributed among the BSP* processors by an r-regular graph $G = (U, V)$ with (c, δ)-expansion where $c = \Theta(1)$ and $\delta = (\log(M/p)/(\mu \log p)$. Specifically, the copies of a supernode $u \in U$ are stored by those processors at the endpoints of the edges of $E(u)$. As will be apparent later, the performance of our multisearch algorithm heavily relies on the ability to select a target set of low congestion for any arbitrary subset $S \subseteq U$.

2.1 Selection of Target Sets

Let $S \subseteq U$, with $|S| \leq p/r$. A target set T for S of congestion at most $K = (2/c)|S|^\delta$ can be constructed using the following procedure.

        Procedure 1
        $T := \emptyset$; $R := S$;
        while $R \neq \emptyset$ do
          $Q := \{v \in \Gamma(R) : |E(R) \cap E(v)| \geq K\}$;
          mark all edges in $E(R) \cap E(\Gamma(R) - Q)$;
          for each $u \in R$ add one marked edge, if any, to T;
          $R := R - \{u \in R : |E(u) \cap T| = 1\}$
        end.

The following lemma can be proved by means of a standard argument based on the expansion of G. The details will be provided in the full version of this paper.

Lemma 6. *Procedure 1 produces a target set* T *of congestion* $(2/c)|S|^\delta$ *for* S. *Moreover, at the beginning of the* i-*th iteration of the* while *loop* $|R| \leq |S|/2^{i-1}$, *for* $i \geq 1$.

Consider now a *weighted set* $S \subseteq U$ where an integral weight $w(u)$ is attached to every edge in $E(u)$, for $u \in S$. Let T be a target set for S and define W_v^T to be the sum of the weights of the edges in $T \cap E(v)$. We define the *weight* of T as $\max_{v \in V} W_v^T$. Note that when all $w(u)$'s are equal to 1, the notion of weight coincides with that of congestion. The following algorithm constructs a target set for S of low weight. Let $Z = 1 + \max\{w(u) : u \in S\}$ and $N = \sum_{u \in S} w(u)$. Define $\Psi_i = \{u \in S : 2^i \leq w(u) < 2^{i+1}\}$, $0 \leq i < \log Z$, and let $\ell_i = \lceil |\Psi_i|/(p/r) \rceil$.

Algorithm W1
For $0 \leq i < \log Z$, partition Ψ_i into $\Psi_i(1), \Psi_i(2), \ldots, \Psi_i(\ell_i)$, with $|\Psi_i(j)| \leq p/r$;
Run Procedure 1 on each $\Psi_i(j)$, in parallel, to produce a target set $T_i(j)$;
$T := \bigcup_{i=0}^{\log Z - 1} \bigcup_{j=1}^{\ell_i} T_i(j)$
end.

Theorem 7. *The set T computed by Algorithm W1 is a target set for S of weight*
$$O\left(\left(\frac{N}{p/r} + Z\right)(p/r)^\delta\right).$$

Proof. By Lemma 6, the congestion of each $T_i(j)$ is at most $(2/c)(p/r)^\delta$. Each edge in $T_i(j)$ contributes a weight at most 2^{i+1} to its endpoint in V. Since $N \geq \sum_{i=0}^{\log Z - 1} 2^i |\Psi_i|$, we have that the weight of T is at most $\sum_{i=0}^{\log Z - 1} 2^{i+1} \ell_i \frac{2}{c} (p/r)^\delta = O((\frac{N}{p/r} + Z)(p/r)^\delta)$.

If G is highly expanding, i.e., $\delta = O(1/\log p)$, target sets of smaller congestion/weight can be obtained, as shown in the next subsection.

2.2 Selection of Target Sets in Highly Expanding Graphs

Suppose that G has (c, δ)-expansion, with $c < 1$ constant and $\delta = O(1/\log p)$, which requires $r = \Theta(\log(M/p))$. Assume also that r is odd and note that $\mu = \lfloor r/2 \rfloor + 1$ is such that $r - \mu + 1 = \mu$. Consider a set $S \subseteq U$ of size $|S| \leq cp$. A target set T for S of congestion at most $4/c$ can be constructed using the following procedure. Let $\tau = \lceil |S|/(p/r) \rceil \leq \lceil cr \rceil$.

Procedure 2
Partition S into $S_1, S_2, \ldots, S_\tau$, with $|S_i| \leq p/r$;
$Q := V$;
for $i := 1$ to τ do
$S_i' := \{u \in S_i : |E(u) \cap E(Q)| \geq \mu\}$;
Let $E = E(S_i') \cap E(Q)$;
Select from E a target set T_i of congestion $2/c$ for S_i';
$Q := Q - \Gamma^{T_i}(S_i')$;
Select a target set T' of congestion $2/c$ for $S - \bigcup_{i=1}^\tau S_i'$;
$T := T_1 \bigcup \cdots \bigcup T_\tau \bigcup T'$
end.

Theorem 8. *Procedure 2 produces a target set T of congestion $4/c$ for S.*

Proof (sketch). Apply Procedure 1 to determine each T_i, imposing that the edges of T_i be chosen from a subset E of $E(S_i')$. Since E contains a μ-bundle for S_i', it can be easily seen that Lemma 6 carries through with no modifications, yielding congestion $2/c$ for each T_i. Since $\Gamma^{T_i}(S_i') \cap \Gamma^{T_j}(S_j') = \emptyset$, for $i \neq j$, the combined congestion of the T_i's is still $2/c$. By using the expansion of G we can prove that $|S - \bigcup_{i=1}^{r} S_i'| \leq p/r$, therefore Procedure 1 can be employed again to determine T', which adds an extra $2/c$ term to the congestion of T.

Let $S \subseteq U$ be weighted, with weights $\{w(u) : u \in S\}$. Proceeding as in the previous subsection, we determine a target set T of low weight for S. Let Z, N and Ψ_i, for $0 \leq i \leq \log Z$, be as before, and define $\ell_i = \lceil |\Psi_i|/(cp) \rceil$.

Algorithm W2
For $0 \leq i < \log Z$, partition Ψ_i into $\Psi_i(1), \Psi_i(2), \ldots, \Psi_i(\ell_i)$, with $|\Psi_i(j)| \leq cp$;
Run Procedure 2 on each $\Psi_i(j)$, in parallel, to produce a target set $T_i(j)$;
$T := \bigcup_{i=0}^{\log Z - 1} \bigcup_{j=1}^{\ell_i} T_i(j)$
end.

Theorem 9. *Algorithm W2 determines a target set T for S of weight $O(\frac{N}{p} + Z)$.*

Proof. The proof is similar to that of Theorem 7.

Note that when all weights are 1, algorithm W2 can be employed as a general protocol for accessing data from a redundant representation of a shared read-only memory in a p-processor distributed-memory machine. The protocol ensures minimum congestion at the processors.

3   BSP* Implementation

Consider a BSP*(p, g, L, B). The following results are proved in [BDM96].

Fact 1 *Consider $n \geq p$ vectors of size ℓ evenly distributed among the processors. If $\ell \geq BL \log p$, the prefix sums of the k-th components of the vectors, for every $1 \leq k \leq \ell$, can be computed in communication time $O(g\ell/B)$ and computation time $O(n\ell/p)$.*

Fact 2 *Consider n integer keys in $[0, \text{poly}(n/p)]$ evenly distributed among the processors. If $n \geq p^{1+\epsilon}$, with $\epsilon > 0$ constant, and if $B, L \leq (n/p)^\eta$, for a sufficiently small constant $\eta > 0$, then the keys can be sorted in communication time $O(gn/(pB))$ and computation time $O(n/p)$.*

An *h-relation* is defined as a permutation of at most hp items where each processor is source or destination of at most h items.

Fact 3 *Let $h \geq p^\epsilon$, with $\epsilon > 0$ constant. If $B, L \leq h^\eta$, for a sufficiently small constant $\eta > 0$, an h-relation can be performed in communication time $O(gh/B)$ and computation time $O(h)$.*

We now present the BSP* implementation of W1 and W2, which are key components of our multisearch algorithm. Let $S \subseteq U$ be a weighted set and let Z, N and Ψ_i, $0 \le i < \log Z$, be defined as before. The Ψ_i's are called *weight classes*. Suppose that a *request* for each $u \in S$ is issued by some processor and that a processor issues at most N/p requests. We want to construct a target set for S of weight C, where $C = O((\frac{N}{p/r} + Z)(p/r)^\delta)$ when W1 is applied, and $C = O(\frac{N}{p} + Z)$ when W2 is applied. The edges in the target set will be returned to the processors issuing the corresponding requests.

Implementation of W1. First the requests are sorted by weight class. Within each weight class Ψ_i, $\ell_i = \lceil |\Psi_i|/(p/r) \rceil$ *groups*, namely $\Psi_i(1), \Psi_i(2), \ldots, \Psi_i(\ell_i)$, are created, with $|\Psi_i(j)| \le p/r$. Then, Procedure 1 is executed in parallel on each $\Psi_i(j)$ as follows. For each request u, r packets are created, with each packet carrying the name of the processor originating the request (OR), the group of the request (GR), the endpoint in V of a distinct edge of $E(u)$ (DEST), and a flag (F) initially set to 0. The r packets relative to the same request are called *companions*. The following steps are executed until at least one packet for each request has its flag set to 1.

1. Sort all packets with F=0 by the ordered pair (GR,DEST);
2. For each pair (GR,DEST), if there are at most C packets corresponding to it, then set their flags to 1;
3. Unsort the packets and eliminate all packets with F=0 that have a companion with F=1.

At the end, the surviving packets (all of them with F=1) are sent to the origins and one packet for each request is (arbitrarily) selected. We have

Lemma 10. *If $N = p^{1+\epsilon}$, with $\epsilon > 0$ constant, and $B, L \le (n/p)^\eta$, for some small constant η, Algorithm W1 can be implemented on the BSP*(p, g, L, B) in computation time $O(rN/p)$ and communication time $O(grN/(pB))$. If $\epsilon \ge 1$, the communication time becomes $O(gN/(pB))$.*

Proof. The complexity of the algorithm is dominated by the sortings of the packets. Initially, we have at most Nr/p packets per processor and, by Lemma 6, the number of packets to be sorted decreases geometrically at each iteration. The lemma follows by employing the BSP* primitives quoted before. Note that if $\epsilon \ge 1$ each group can be handled by a single processor, requiring only $O(gN/(pB))$ communication time to create the groups and using radix sort for the sortings.

Implementation of W2. Algorithm W2 is similar to W1 except for the fact that each weight class Ψ_i is partitioned into $\ell_i = |\Psi_i|/(cp)$ groups of size cp each, and the target set for each group is determined using Procedure 2. Its implementation in BSP* can be obtained by suitably modifying that of W1. The details will be provided in the full version of this paper, together with the proof of the following lemma.

Lemma 11. *Let* $r = \Theta(\log(M/p))$. *If* $N = p^{1+\epsilon}$, *with* $\epsilon > 0$ *constant, and* $B, L \leq (n/p)^{\eta}$, *for some small constant* η, *Algorithm W2 can be implemented on the BSP**(p, g, L, B)$ *in computation time* $O(rN/p)$ *and communication time* $O(grN/(pB))$. *If* $\epsilon \geq 1$, *the communication time becomes* $O(gN/(pB))$.

4 The Multisearch Algorithm

The structure of our multisearch algorithm is similar to the one of [BDM96], but randomness is avoided by exploiting the redundant representation of the segments. Suppose that m segments are organized in the RST defined in Section 2, and that n queries are initially assigned to the processors of the BSP*(p, g, L, B), with each processor in charge of n/p queries. We assume $n = \Omega(p^{1+\epsilon})$, with $\epsilon = \Omega(1)$; $m = \omega(n)$ and $B, L \leq (n/p)^{\eta}$, with $\eta > 0$ a sufficiently small constant. The idea is to let each query flow down the unique path that leads from the root of the RST to the supernode holding its segment, visiting one level at a time. However, the access to the supernodes visited in each level must be carefully scheduled in order to minimize the amount of work and communication performed by each processor.

Recall that the RST is a complete d-ary tree of height $h = \log m / \log d$ containing $M = \Theta(m/d)$ supernodes, where $d = (n/p)^{\alpha}$, for a suitable positive constant $\alpha < 1$. The supernodes are replicated into r copies each, distributed among the processors according to a bipartite graph G with $(\Theta(1), \delta)$ expansion, where $\delta = \log(M/p)/(\mu \log p)$. For a supernode u, we define the *job at* u (J_u) to be the set of queries visiting u. *Executing a job* means determining, for each query in the job, the supernode it has to visit next. Note that if the query finds its segment within the supernode, the query is answered and its path ends. If w is a child of u, then J_w is called a *successor job* of J_u and $J_w \subseteq J_u$. If u is on level i of the RST, then J_u is a *job on level* i. Let $t = (n/p)^{\alpha'}$, with $\alpha < \alpha' < 1$. (We refer the reader to [BDM96] for the actual values of α and α'.) We call *small jobs* those jobs of size less than t, and *large jobs* those jobs of size at least t.

The multisearch algorithm is organized in two *phases*. Phase 1 consists of a sequence of h *rounds*, where Round i executes the large jobs on level i and creates their successor jobs, for $1 \leq i \leq h$ (no successor jobs are created in the last round). The following invariant is maintained through all rounds. At the beginning of Round i, the jobs on level i are *balanced*, i.e., each processor holds at most n/p queries, and *ordered*, i.e., the queries of each job are distributed among consecutive processors. Processors holding queries from the same job form a *group* and the first processor of a group is its *leader*. The execution of Round i follows the lines of its analogous in Algorithm ManyQueries of [BDM96]: each supernode corresponding to a large job on level i is fetched by the corresponding group leader and broadcast to the other processors in the group, which execute the job for the queries they hold. However, in our case the actual copy to be fetched, for each supernode, must be selected. This is done by letting each group leader issue a request for the corresponding supernode. Weight 1 is associated with each request. (Note that the total weight is $O(\frac{n}{t})$ and that each processor issues $O(\frac{n}{pt})$ requests.) Then, algorithm W1 is executed to determine a target set for the requests, that is, to select a copy for each requested supernode. Unlike the algorithm in [BDM96], possible small jobs on level $i+1$ generated in Round i, are temporarily frozen in the hosting processors and will be processed in Phase 2. By combining the analysis in [BDM96] with the result of Lemma 10, we can prove the following lemma.

Lemma 12. *Phase 1 requires computation time $O(\frac{n}{p}\log m)$ and communication time $O(g\frac{n\log m}{pB\log d})$.*

In Phase 2, all queries belonging to small jobs left behind by the previous phase are answered. The queries flow along their paths down the RST level by level until each query is answered. However, fetching the appropriate supernode for executing each job would be too costly because of the possibly large number of small jobs. Instead, as done in [BDM96], we select, for each small job, a copy of the corresponding supernode and send the small job to the processor storing this copy, which will execute it. The following sequence of steps is iterated until all queries are answered.

1. For each small job, a request for the corresponding supernode is issued by the processor holding the job. A weight equal to the job size is associated with each request. (Note that the total weight is $O(n)$ and that each processor issues $O(n/p)$ requests.) For these requests a target set of low weight is determined by executing W1, if $r = o(\log(M/p))$, and W2, if $r = \Theta(\log(M/p))$.
2. Each job is sent to the processor that holds the selected copy of the corresponding supernode.
3. Each processor executes the jobs it has received, possibly answering some of the queries, and creates the successor jobs. The successor jobs are then returned to the senders.

Lemma 13. *If $r = o(\log(M/p))$, Phase 2 is executed in $O(\frac{n\log m}{p}r(\frac{p}{r})^{\delta})$ computation time and $O(g\frac{n\log m}{p\log d}\frac{r}{B}(\frac{p}{r})^{\delta})$ communication time. If $r = \Theta(\log(M/p))$ and $0 < \epsilon < 1$, then Phase 2 requires computation time $O(\frac{n\log m}{p\log d}(r+\log d))$ and communication time $O(g\frac{n\log m}{pB\log d}r)$. Finally, if $r = \Theta(\log(M/p))$ and $\epsilon \geq 1$, the communication time becomes $O(g\frac{n\log m}{pB\log d})$.*

Proof. The sequence of steps in Phase 2 is iterated at most h times. Step 1 determines a target set of weight $C = O(\frac{n}{p}(\frac{p}{r})^{\delta}r)$, when W1 is applied (i.e., $r = o(\log(M/p))$), and of weight $C = O(\frac{n}{p})$, when W2 is applied (i.e., $r = \Theta(\log(M/p))$). The computation and communication times required by such step are obtained from Lemmas 10 and 11, by substituting N for n. In Step 2, sending the jobs to the appropriate processors can be accomplished in communication time $O(gC/B)$ and computation time $O(C)$ (Fact 3). Finally, Step 3 needs computation time $O(C\log d)$ and communication time $O(gC/B)$.

Note that $\left(\frac{p}{r}\right)^\delta = O((\frac{m}{n^\alpha p^{1-\alpha}})^{1/\mu})$, $\log d = \Theta(\log n)$ and $\log(M/P) = \Theta(\log m)$. Then, Theorems 1 and 2 stated in the introduction are immediate consequences of Lemmas 12 and 13.

5 Lower Bound

In this section, we present a lower bound on the amount of communication required for performing multisearch on any p-processor distributed-memory machine where the only storage available is constituted by the processors' local memories. Let S be a set of m ordered segments and consider a multisearch scheme for S. Without loss of generality, we assume that for each segment $\sigma \in S$ a certain number r_σ of copies are initially available in distinct processors. We also assume that the algorithm employed by the scheme to answer a set of n queries satisfies the following conditions: (1) Initially, each processor is in charge of n/p queries; (2) The answer to a query is based exclusively on the outcomes of individual comparisons between the query and the segments.

The lower bound does not account for the complexity of the initial distribution of the copies of the segments among the processors, however it does account for any movement or replication of the copies made during the execution of the algorithm. We define $r = \sum_{\sigma \in S} r_\sigma/m$ as the *redundancy* of the scheme, that is, the average number of copies per segment initially available. Let us partition S into $m/3$ *intervals* $I_1, I_2, \ldots, I_{m/3}$, where each I_j consists of three consecutive segments in the given ordering. Let σ_j denote the central segment in I_j, $1 \le j \le m/3$. Consider a set of n indices $1 \le j_1 < j_2 < \ldots < j_n \le m/3$ and a set of n query points $q_1, q_2, \ldots, q_n$, where q_k belongs to σ_{j_k}. It is easy to see that, in order to answer q_k correctly, q_k has to be compared with at least one segment in I_k. In other words, in order to answer correctly all queries, n comparisons between distinct queries and distinct segments are needed.

Lemma 14. *There exists a set of n distinct intervals such that all of the copies of their segments are stored in the local memories of $p' \le \max\left\{12r, p\left(\frac{6n}{m}\right)^{\frac{1}{6r}}\right\}$ processors.*

Proof. We say that an interval is *sparse* if there is a total of at most $6r$ copies of its segments. Note that there are at least $m/6$ sparse intervals, otherwise the non-sparse ones would account for a total of more than mr copies, which is impossible. By means of a standard counting argument (e.g., see [PP95, Lemma 1]), it can be shown that there exist n sparse intervals and p' processors storing all copies of their segments.

Let T_{comm} denote the maximum number of words communicated from/to any processor in order to answer n queries, in the worst case. (We assume that a segment or a query can be represented using a constant number of words.)

Theorem 15. *For any multisearch scheme with redundancy r, with $1 \le r \le \min\left\{\frac{p}{24}, \frac{\log(m/6n)}{6}\right\}$, $T_{comm} = \Omega\left(\min\left\{\frac{n}{r}, \frac{n}{p}\left(\frac{m}{n}\right)^{\frac{1}{6r}}\right\}\right).$*

Proof. Consider a set of n query points belonging to the middle segments of n distinct intervals chosen according to Lemma 14. As argued before, each query has to be compared with at least one segment in the corresponding interval. By the lemma, the copies of the segments in the chosen intervals are stored by a set V' of $p' \leq \max\left\{12r, p\left(\frac{6n}{m}\right)^{\frac{1}{6r}}\right\}$ processors. Note that when r is in the stated range, $p' \leq p/2$ and, therefore, at least $(p - p')n/p = \Theta(n)$ queries are initially assigned to processors outside V'. In order to answer these queries, at least $\Theta(n)$ words have to be exchanged between processors in V' and processors outside V', therefore $T_{\text{comm}} = \Omega(n/p')$, which proves the theorem.

References

[ADM+91] M.J. Atallah, F. Dehne, R. Miller, A. Rau-Chaplin, and J.J. Tsay. Multisearch techniques for implementing data structures on a mesh-connected computer. In *Proc. of the 3rd ACM Symp. on Parallel Algorithms and Architectures*, pages 204–214, 1991.

[AF94] M.J. Atallah and A. Fabri. On the multisearch problem for hypercubes. In *Proc. of Parallel Architectures and Languages Europe (PARLE 94)*, 1994.

[BDM96] A. Bäumker, W. Dittrich, and F. Meyer auf der Heide. Truly efficient parallel algorithms: 1-optimal multisearch for and extension of the BSP model. Technical Report tr-rsfb-96-008, Department of Mathematics and Computer Science, University of Paderborn, 1996. See also *Proc. of the 3rd ESA*, 1995, pages 17–30.

[DFR93] F. Dehne, A. Fabri, and A. Rau-Chaplin. Scalable parallel computational geometry for coarse-grained multicomputers. In *Proc. of the ACM Conference on Computational Geometry*, 1993.

[PP95] A. Pietracaprina and G. Pucci. The complexity of deterministic PRAM simulation on Distributed Memory Machines. Technical Report GEPPCOM-II-23, DEI Università di Padova, Padova, Italy, 1995. See also *Proc. of the 2nd ESA*, 1994, pages 391–400.

[Ran92] A.G. Ranade. Maintaining dynamic ordered sets on processors networks. In *Proc. of 4rd ACM Symp. on Parallel Algorithms and Architectures*, pages 127–137, 1992.

[RS94] J.H. Reif and S. Sen. Randomized algorithms for binary search and load balancing on fixed connection networks with geometric applications. *SIAM Journal on Computing*, 23(3):633–651, June 1994.

[Val90] L.G. Valiant. A bridging model for parallel computation. *Communications of the ACM*, 33(8):103–111, August 1990.

Priority Queues on Parallel Machines

Gerth Stølting Brodal*

BRICS**, Computer Science Department, Aarhus University,
Ny Munkegade, DK-8000 Århus C, Denmark.

Abstract. We present time and work optimal priority queues for the CREW PRAM, supporting FINDMIN in constant time with one processor and MAKEQUEUE, INSERT, MELD, FINDMIN, EXTRACTMIN, DELETE and DECREASEKEY in constant time with $O(\log n)$ processors. A priority queue can be build in time $O(\log n)$ with $O(n/\log n)$ processors and k elements can be inserted into a priority queue in time $O(\log k)$ with $O((\log n + k)/\log k)$ processors. With a slowdown of $O(\log \log n)$ in time the priority queues adopt to the EREW PRAM by only increasing the required work by a constant factor. A pipelined version of the priority queues adopt to a processor array of size $O(\log n)$, supporting the operations MAKEQUEUE, INSERT, MELD, FINDMIN, EXTRACTMIN, DELETE and DECREASEKEY in constant time.

1 Introduction

The construction of priority queues is a classical topic in data structures. Some references are [1, 2, 6, 7, 8, 9, 19, 20]. A historical overview of implementations can be found in [13]. Recently several papers have also considered how to implement priority queues on parallel machines [3, 4, 5, 11, 15, 16, 17, 18]. In this paper we focus on how to achieve optimal speedup for the individual priority queue operations known from the sequential setting [16, 17]. The operations we support are all the commonly needed priority queue operations from the sequential setting [13] and the parallel insertion of several elements at the same time [3, 15].

MAKEQUEUE Creates and returns a new empty priority queue.

INSERT(Q, e) Inserts element e into priority queue Q.

MELD(Q_1, Q_2) Melds priority queues Q_1 and Q_2. The resulting priority queue is stored in Q_1.

FINDMIN(Q) Returns the minimum element in priority queue Q.

EXTRACTMIN(Q) Deletes and returns the minimum element in priority queue Q.

---

* Supported by the Danish Natural Science Research Council (Grant No. 9400044). This research was done while visiting the Max-Planck Institut für Informatik, Saarbrücken, Germany. E-mail: **gerth@daimi.aau.dk**.

** Basic Research in Computer Science, a Centre of the Danish National Research Foundation.

DELETE(Q, e) Deletes element e from priority queue Q provided a pointer to e is given.

DECREASEKEY(Q, e, e') Replaces element e by e' in priority queue Q provided $e' \leq e$ and a pointer to e is given.

BUILD($e_1, \ldots, e_n$) Creates a new priority queue containing elements $e_1, \ldots, e_n$.

MULTIINSERT($Q, e_1, \ldots, e_k$) Inserts elements $x_1, \ldots, x_k$ into priority queue Q.

We assume that elements are taken from a totally ordered universe and that the only operation allowed on elements is the comparison of two elements that can be done in constant time. Throughout this paper n denotes the maximum allowed number of elements in a priority queue. We assume w.l.o.g. that n is of the form 2^k. This guarantees that $\log n$ is an integer.[1] Our main result is:

Theorem 1. *On a CREW PRAM priority queues exist supporting* FINDMIN *in constant time with one processor, and* MAKEQUEUE, INSERT, MELD, EXTRACTMIN, DELETE *and* DECREASEKEY *in constant time with* $O(\log n)$ *processors.* BUILD *is supported in time* $O(\log n)$ *with* $O(n/\log n)$ *processors and* MULTIINSERT *in time* $O(\log k)$ *with* $O((\log n + k)/\log k)$ *processors.*

Table 1 lists the performance of different implementations adopting parallelism to priority queues. Several papers consider how to build heaps [7] optimally in parallel [4, 5, 11, 18]. On an EREW PRAM an optimal construction time of $O(\log n)$ is achieved in [18] and on a CRCW PRAM an optimal construction time of $O(\log \log n)$ is achieved in [5].

An immediate consequence of the CREW PRAM priority queues we present is that on an EREW PRAM we achieve the bounds stated in Corollary 2, because the only bottleneck in the construction requiring concurrent read is the broadcasting of information of constant size, that on an $O(\log n / \log \log n)$ processor EREW PRAM requires time $O(\log \log n)$. The bounds we achieve matches those of [3] for k equal one and those of [14]. See Table 1.

Corollary 2. *On an EREW PRAM priority queues exist supporting* FINDMIN *in constant time with one processor, and supporting* MAKEQUEUE, INSERT, MELD, EXTRACTMIN, DELETE *and* DECREASEKEY *in time* $O(\log \log n)$ *with* $O(\log n / \log \log n)$ *processors. With* $O(n / \log n)$ *processors* BUILD *can be performed in time* $O(\log n)$ *and with* $O((k + \log n)/(\log k + \log \log n))$ *processors* MULTIINSERT *can be performed in time* $O(\log k + \log \log n)$.

That a systolic processor array with $\Theta(n)$ processors can implement a priority queue supporting the operations INSERT and EXTRACTMIN in constant time is parallel computing folklore, see Exercise 1.119 in [12]. Recently Ranade et al. [17] showed how to achieve the same bounds on a processor array with only $O(\log n)$ processors. In Sect. 5 we describe how the priority queues can be modified to allow operations to be performed via pipelining. As a result we get an implementation of priority queues on a processor array with $O(\log n)$

---

[1] All logarithms in this paper are to the base two.

Model	[16] EREW	[14] EREW^2	[15] CREW	[3] EREW	[17] Array	This paper CREW
FINDMIN	1	$\log \log n$	1	1	1	1
INSERT	$\log \log n$	$\log \log n$	–	–	1	1
EXTRACTMIN	$\log \log n$	$\log \log n$	–	–	1	1
MELD	–	$\log \log n$	$\log \frac{n}{k} + \log \log k$	$\log \log \frac{n}{k} + \log k$	–	1
DELETE	–	$\log \log n$	–	–	–	1
DECREASEKEY	–	$\log \log n$	–	–	–	1
BUILD	$\log n$	–	$\frac{n}{k} \log k$	$\log \frac{n}{k} \log k$	–	$\log n$
MULTIINSERT	–	–	$\log \frac{n}{k} + \log k$	$\log \log \frac{n}{k} + \log k$	–	$\log k$
MULTIDELETE	–	–	$\log \frac{n}{k} + \log \log k$	$\log \log \frac{n}{k} + \log k$	–	–

Table 1. Performance of different parallel implementations of priority queues.

processors, supporting the operations MAKEQUEUE, INSERT, MELD, FINDMIN, EXTRACTMIN, DELETE and DECREASEKEY in constant time. This extends the result of [17].

The priority queues we present in this paper do not support the operation MULTIDELETE, that deletes the k smallest elements from a priority queue (where k is fixed [3, 15]). However, a possible solution is to apply the k-bandwidth idea used in [3, 15], by letting each node contain k elements instead of one. If we apply the idea to the data structure in Sect. 2 we get the time bounds in Theorem 3, improving upon the bounds achieved in [15], see Table 1. We omit the details and refer the reader to [15].

Theorem 3. *On a CREW PRAM priority queues exist, supporting* MULTI-INSERT *in time* $O(\log k)$, MULTIDELETE *and* MELD *in time* $O(\log \log k)$, *and* BUILD *in time* $O(\log k + \log \frac{n}{k} \log \log k)$.

2 Meldable priority queues

In this section we describe how to implement the priority queue operations MAKEQUEUE, INSERT, MELD, FINDMIN and EXTRACTMIN in constant time on a CREW PRAM with $O(\log n)$ processors. In Sect. 3 we describe how to extend the repertoire of priority queue operations to include DELETE and DE-CREASEKEY.

The priority queues in this section are based on heap ordered binomial trees [19]. Throughout this paper we assume a one to one mapping between tree nodes and priority queue elements.

Binomial trees are defined as follows. A binomial tree of *rank* zero is a single node. A binomial tree of rank $r > 0$ is achieved from two binomial trees of rank $r - 1$ by making one of the roots a son of the other root. It follows by induction that a binomial tree of rank r contains exactly 2^r nodes and that a node of rank

---

[2] The operations DELETE and DECREASEKEY require the CREW PRAM and require amortized time $O(\log \log n)$.

r has exactly one son of each of the ranks $0, \ldots, r-1$. Throughout this section a tree denotes a heap ordered binomial tree.

A priority queue is represented by a forest of binomial trees. In the following we let the largest ranked tree be of rank $r(Q)$, we let $n_i(Q)$ denote the number of trees of rank i and we let $n_{\max}(Q)$ denote the value $\max_{0 \leq i \leq r(Q)} n_i(Q)$. We require that a priority queue satisfies the constraints:

$\mathbf{A_1}$: $n_i(Q) \in \{1, 2, 3\}$ for $i = 0, \ldots, r(Q)$, and
$\mathbf{A_2}$: the minimum root of rank i is smaller than all roots of rank larger than i.

It follows from $\mathbf{A_2}$ that the minimum root of rank zero is the minimum element.

A priority queue is stored as follows. Each node v in a priority queue is represented by a record consisting of:

e : the element associated to v,
r : the rank of v, and
L : a linked list of the sons of v in decreasing rank order.

For each priority queue Q an array $Q.L$ is maintained of size $1 + \log n$ of pointers to linked lists of roots of equal rank. By $\mathbf{A_1}$, $|Q.L[i]| \leq 3$ for all i. Notice that the chosen representation for storing the sons of a node allows two nodes of equal rank to be linked in constant time by one processor. The required space for a priority queue is $O(n)$.

Two essential procedures used by our algorithms are the procedures PAR-LINK and PARUNLINK in Fig. 1. In parallel PARLINK for each rank i links two trees of rank i to one tree of rank $i + 1$, if possible. By requiring that the trees of rank i that are linked together are different from $\min(Q.L[i])$, $\mathbf{A_2}$ does not become violated. Let $n_i'(Q)$ denote the value of $n_i(Q)$ after performing PAR-LINK. If $n_i(Q) \geq 3$ before performing PARLINK then $n_i'(Q) \leq n_i(Q) - 2 + 1$, because processor i removes two trees of rank i and processor $i-1$ adds at most one tree of rank i. Otherwise $n_i'(Q) \leq n_i(Q) + 1$. This implies that $n_{\max}'(Q) \leq \max\{3, n_{\max}(Q) - 1\}$. The equality states that if the maximum number of trees of equal rank is larger than three, then an application of PARLINK decreases this value by at least one. The procedure PARUNLINK unlinks the minima of all $Q.L[i]$. All $n_i(Q)$ at most increase by one except for $n_0(Q)$ that can increase by two. Notice that the new minimum of $Q.L[i]$ is less than or equal to the old minimum of $Q.L[i+1]$. This implies that if $\mathbf{A_2}$ is satisfied before performing PARUNLINK then $\mathbf{A_2}$ is also satisfied after the unlinking. Notice that PARLINK and PARUNLINK can be performed on an EREW PRAM with $O(\log n)$ processors in constant time if all processors know Q.

The priority queue operations can now be implemented as:

MAKEQUEUE The list $Q.L$ is allocated and in parallel all $Q.L[i]$ are assigned the empty set.

INSERT(Q, e) A new tree of rank zero containing e is created and added to $Q.L[0]$. To avoid $n_{\max}(Q) > 3$, PARLINK(Q) is performed once.

```
Proc PARLINK(Q)
  for p := 0 to log n − 1 pardo
    if n_p(Q) ≥ 3 then
      Link two trees from Q.L[p] \ min(Q.L[p]) and
      add the resulting tree to Q.L[p + 1]

Proc PARUNLINK(Q)
  for p := 1 to log n pardo
    if n_p(Q) ≥ 1 then
      Unlink min(Q.L[p]) and add the resulting two trees to Q.L[p − 1]
```

Fig. 1. Parallel linking and unlinking binomial trees.

```
Proc FINDMIN(Q)                        Proc MAKEQUEUE
  return min(Q.L[0])                     Q := new-queue
                                         for p := 0 to log n pardo Q.L[p] := ∅
Proc INSERT(Q, e)                        return Q
  Q.L[0] := Q.L[0] ∪ {new-node(e)}
  PARLINK(Q)                           Proc EXTRACTMIN(Q)
                                         e := min(Q.L[0])
Proc MELD(Q_1, Q_2)                      Q.L[0] := Q.L[0] \ {e}
  for p := 0 to log n pardo              PARUNLINK(Q)
    Q_1.L[p] := Q_1.L[p] ∪ Q_2.L[p]      PARLINK(Q)
  do 3 times PARLINK(Q_1)                return e
```

Fig. 2. CREW PRAM priority queue operations.

MELD(Q_1, Q_2) First $Q_2.L$ is merged into $Q_1.L$ by letting processor p set $Q_1.L[p]$ to $Q_1.L[p] \cup Q_2.L[p]$. The resulting forest satisfies $n_{max}(Q_1) \leq 6$. Performing PARLINK(Q_1) three times reestablishes A_1.

FINDMIN(Q) The minimum element in priority queue Q is $min(Q.L[0])$.

EXTRACTMIN(Q) First the minimum element $min(Q.L[0])$ is removed. Performing PARUNLINK once guarantees that A_2 is satisfied, especially that the new minimum element is contained in $Q.L[0]$, because the new minimum element was either already contained in $Q.L[0]$ or it was the minimum element in $Q.L[1]$. Finally PARLINK performed once reestablishes A_1.

A pseudo code implementation for a CREW PRAM based on the previous discussion is shown in Fig. 2. Notice that the only part of the code requiring concurrent read is to "broadcast" the values of Q, Q_1 and Q_2 to all the processors. Otherwise the code only requires an EREW PRAM. From the fact that PARLINK and PARUNLINK can be performed in constant time with $O(\log n)$ processors we get:

Theorem 4. *On a CREW PRAM priority queues exist supporting* FINDMIN *in constant time with one processor, and* MAKEQUEUE, INSERT, MELD *and* EXTRACTMIN *in constant time with* $O(\log n)$ *processors.*

3 Priority queues with deletions

In this section we extend the repertoire of supported priority queue operations to include DELETE and DECREASEKEY. Notice that DECREASEKEY(Q, e, e') can be implemented as DELETE(Q, e) followed by INSERT(Q, e').

The priority queues in this section are based on heap ordered trees defined as follows. A rank zero tree is a single node. A rank r tree is a tree where the root has exactly five sons of each of the ranks $0, 1, \ldots, r-1$. A tree of rank r can be created by linking six trees of rank $r-1$ by making the five larger roots sons of the smallest root.

The efficiency we achieve for DELETE and DECREASEKEY is due to the concept of *holes*. A hole of rank r in a tree is a location in the tree where a son of rank r is missing.

We represent a priority queue by a forest of trees with holes. Let $r(Q), n_i(Q)$ and $n_{\max}(Q)$ be defined as in Sect. 2. We require that:

B$_1$: $n_i(Q) \in \{1, 2, \ldots, 7\}$, for $i = 1, \ldots, r(Q)$,
B$_2$: the minimum root of rank i is smaller than all roots of rank larger than i,
B$_3$: at most two holes have equal rank.

Temporary while performing MELD we allow the number of holes of equal rank to be at most four. The requirement that a node of rank r has five sons of each of the ranks $0, \ldots, r-1$ implies that at least one son of each rank is not replaced by a hole. This implies that the subtree rooted at a node has at least size 2^r and therefore the largest possible rank is at most $\log n$.

A priority queue is stored as follows. Each node v of a tree is represented by a record consisting of:

e : the element associated to v,
r : the rank of v,
f : a pointer to the father of v, and
L : an array of size $\log n$ of pointers to linked lists of sons of equal rank.

For each priority queue Q two arrays $Q.L$ and $Q.H$ are maintained of size $1 + \log n$. $Q.L$ contains pointers to linked lists of trees of equal rank and $Q.H$ contains pointers to linked lists of "holes" of equal rank. More precisely $Q.H[i]$ is a linked list of nodes such that for each missing son of rank i of node v, v appears once in $Q.H[i]$. By B$_1$ and B$_3$, $|Q.L[i]| \leq 7$ and $|Q.H[i]| \leq 2$ for all i. Notice that the space required is $O(n \log n)$. By using worst case constant time extendible arrays to store the required arrays such that $|v.L| = v.r$, the space requirement can be reduced to $O(n)$. For simplicity we in the following assume that $|v.L| = \log n$ for all v.

The procedures PARLINK and PARUNLINK have to be modified such that linking and unlinking involves six trees and such that PARUNLINK catches holes to be removed from $Q.H$. PARLINK now satisfies $n'_{\max}(Q) \leq \max\{7, n_{\max}(Q) - 5\}$, and PARUNLINK $n'_i(Q) \leq n_i(Q) + 5$ for $i > 0$ and $n'_0(Q) \leq n_0(Q) + 6$.

We now describe a procedure FixHoles that reduces the number of holes similar to how ParLink reduces the number of trees. The procedure is constructed such that processor p takes care of holes of rank p. The work done by processor p is the following. If $|Q.H[p]| < 2$ the processor does nothing. Otherwise it considers two holes in $Q.H[p]$. Recall that all holes have at least one real tree node of rank p as a brother. If the two holes have different fathers, we swap one of the holes with a brother of the other hole. This makes both holes have the same father f. By choosing the largest node among the two holes' brothers as the swap node we are guaranteed to satisfy heap order after the swap.

There are now two cases to consider. The first case is when the two holes have a brother b of rank $p+1$. Notice that b has at least three sons of rank p because we allowed at most four holes of rank p. We can now cut off b and all sons of b of rank p. By assigning b the rank p we only create one hole of rank $p+1$. We can now eliminate the two original holes by replacing them with two previous sons of b. At most four trees remain to be added to $Q.L[p]$. The second case is when f has rank $p+1$. Assume first that $f \neq \min(Q.L[p+1])$. In this case the subtree rooted at f can be cut off without violating B_2. This creates a new hole of rank $p+1$. We can now cut off all sons of f that have rank p and assign f the rank p. This eliminates the two holes. At most four trees now need to be added to $Q.L[p]$. Finally there is the case where $f = \min(Q.L[p+1])$. By performing ParUnlink and ParLink once the two holes disappear. To compensate for the created new trees we finally perform ParLink once.

The priority queue operations can now be implemented as follows.

MakeQueue Allocate a new priority queue Q and assign the empty set to all $Q.L[i]$ and $Q.H[i]$.

Insert(Q, e) Create a tree of rank zero containing e and add this tree to $Q.L[0]$. Perform ParLink(Q) once to reestablish B_1. Notice that Insert does not affect the number of holes in Q.

Meld(Q_1, Q_2) Merge $Q_2.L$ into $Q_1.L$, and $Q_2.H$ into $Q_1.H$. We now have $|Q_1.L| \leq 14$ and $|Q_1.H[i]| \leq 4$ for all i. That B_2 is satisfied follows from that Q_1 and Q_2 satisfied B_2. Performing ParLink(Q_1) twice followed by FixHoles(Q_2) twice reestablishes B_1 and B_3.

FindMin(Q) Return $\min(Q.L[0])$.

ExtractMin(Q) First perform FindMin and then perform Delete on the found minimum.

Delete(Q, e) Let v be the node containing e. Remove the subtree with root v. If this creates a hole then add the hole to $Q.H$. Merge $v.L$ into $Q.L$ and remove all appearances of v from $Q.H$. Notice that only for $i = v.r$, $\min(Q.L[i])$ can change and this only happens if e was $\min(Q.L[i])$. Unlinking $\min(Q.L[i])$ for $i = v.r + 1, \ldots, r(Q)$ reestablishes B_2. Finally perform ParLink twice to reestablish B_1 and FixHoles once to reestablish B_3.

DecreaseKey(Q, e, e') Perform Delete(Q, e) followed by Insert(Q, e').

A pseudo code implementation for a CREW PRAM based on the previous discussion is shown in Fig. 3. Notice that the only part of the code that requires

---

Proc MAKEQUEUE
  $Q := new\text{-}queue$
  for $p := 0$ **to** $\log n$ **pardo**
    $Q.L[p], Q.H[p] := \emptyset$
  return Q

Proc FINDMIN(Q)
  return $\min(Q.L[0])$

Proc INSERT(Q, e)
  $Q.L[0] := Q.L[0] \cup \{new\text{-}node(e)\}$
  PARLINK(Q)

Proc MELD(Q_1, Q_2)
  for $p := 0$ **to** $\log n$ **pardo**
    $Q_1.L[p] := Q_1.L[p] \cup Q_2.L[p]$
    $Q_1.H[p] := Q_1.H[p] \cup Q_2.H[p]$
  do 2 times PARLINK(Q_1)
  do 2 times FIXHOLES(Q_1)

Proc DECREASEKEY(Q, e, e')
  DELETE(Q, e)
  INSERT(Q, e')

Proc EXTRACTMIN(Q)
  $e :=$ FINDMIN(Q)
  DELETE(Q, e)
  return e

Proc DELETE(Q, e)
  $v :=$ the node containing e
  if $v.f \neq$ NIL **then**
    $Q.H[v.r] := Q.H[v.r] \cup \{v.f\}$
    $v.f.L[v.r] := v.f.L[v.r] \setminus \{v\}$
  for $p := 0$ **to** $\log n$ **pardo**
    for $u \in v.L[p]$ **do** $u.f :=$ NIL
    $Q.L[p] := Q.L[p] \cup v.L[p]$
    $Q.H[p] := Q.H[p] \setminus \{v\}$
  for $p := 0$ **to** $\log n$ **pardo**
    if $n_p(Q) \geq 1$ **and** $p > v.r$ **then**
      $Q.H[p-1] := Q.H[p-1] \setminus \min(Q.L[p])$
      Unlink $\min(Q.L[p])$ and
      add the resulting trees to $Q.L[p-1]$
  do 2 times PARLINK(Q)
  FIXHOLES(Q)

Fig. 3. CREW PRAM priority queue operations.

concurrent read is the "broadcasting" of the parameters of the procedures and $v.r$ in DELETE. The rest of the code does very local computing, in fact processor p only accesses entries p and $p \pm 1$ of arrays, and that these local computations can be done in constant time with $O(\log n)$ processors on an EREW PRAM.

Theorem 5. *On a CREW PRAM priority queues exist supporting* FINDMIN *in constant time with one processor, and* MAKEQUEUE, INSERT, MELD, EXTRACT-MIN, DELETE *and* DECREASEKEY *in constant time with* $O(\log n)$ *processors.*

4 Building priority queues

In this section we describe how to perform BUILD$(x_1, \ldots, x_n)$ for the priority queues in Sect. 3. Because our priority queues can report a minimum element in constant time and that there is lower bound of $\Omega(\log n)$ for finding the minimum of a set of elements on a CREW PRAM [10] we have an $\Omega(\log n)$ lower bound on the construction time on a CREW PRAM. We now give a matching upper bound on an EREW PRAM.

First a collection of trees is constructed satisfying B_1 and B_3 but not B_2. We partition the elements into $\lfloor (n-1)/6 \rfloor$ blocks of size six. In parallel we now construct a rank one tree from each block. The remaining 1–6 elements are stored in $Q.L[0]$. The same block partitioning and linking is now done for the rank one trees. The remaining rank one trees are stored in $Q.L[1]$. This process continues until no tree remains. There are at most $O(\log n)$ iterations because each iteration reduces the number of trees by a factor six. The resulting forest satisfies B_1 and B_3. It is easy to see that the above construction can be done in time $O(\log n)$ with $O(n/\log n)$ processors on an EREW PRAM.

To establish B_2 we $\log n$ times perform ParUnlink followed by ParLink. By induction it follows that in the ith iteration all $Q.L[j]$ where $j \geq \log n - i$ satisfy B_2. This finishes the construction of the priority queue. The last step of the construction requires time $O(\log n)$ with $O(\log n)$ processors. We conclude that:

Theorem 6. *On an EREW PRAM a priority queue containing n elements can be constructed optimally with $O(n/\log n)$ processors in time $O(\log n)$.*

Because $\text{Meld}(Q, \text{Build}(x_1, \ldots, x_k))$ implements the priority queue operation $\text{MultiInsert}(Q, x_1, \ldots, x_k)$ we have the corollary below. Notice that k does not have to be fixed as in [3, 15].

Corollary 7. *On a CREW PRAM MultiInsert can be performed in time $O(\log k)$ with $O((\log n + k)/\log k)$ processors.*

5 Pipelined priority queue operations

The priority queues in Sect. 2, 3 and 4 require the CREW PRAM to achieve constant time per operation. In this section we address how to perform priority queue operations in a pipelined fashion. As a consequence we get an implementation of priority queues on a processor array of size $O(\log n)$ supporting priority queue operations in constant time. On a processor array we assume that all requests are entered at processor zero and that output is generated at processor zero too [17].

The basic idea is to represent a priority queue by a forest of heap ordered binomial trees as in Sect. 2, and to perform the operations sequentially in a loop that does constant work for each rank in increasing rank order. This approach then allows us to pipeline the operations. We require that a forest of binomial trees representing a priority queue satisfies:

C_1 : $n_i(Q) \in \{1, 2\}$, for $i = 1, \ldots, r(Q)$,
C_2 : the minimum root of rank i is smaller than all roots of rank larger than i.

Notice that C_1 is stronger than A_1 in Sect. 2. Sequential implementations of the priority queue operations are shown in Fig. 4. We assume a similar representation as in Sect. 3. The pseudo code uses the following two procedures similar to those used in Sect. 2.

Link(Q, i) Links two trees from $Q.L[i] \setminus \min(Q.L[i])$ to one tree of rank $i + 1$ that is added to $Q.L[i + 1]$, provided $i \geq 0$ and $|Q.L[i]| \geq 3$.

```
Proc MakeQueue                              Proc Delete(Q, e)
    Q := new-queue                              v := the node containing e
    for p := 0 to log n do Q.L[p] := ∅          for i := 0 to v.r - 1 do
    return Q                                        Move v.L[i] to Q.L[i]
                                                    Link(Q, i)
Proc FindMin(Q)                                 r, f := v.r, v.f
    return min(Q.L[0])                          Remove node v
                                                while f ≠ nil do
Proc Insert(Q, e)                                   if f.r = r + 1 then
    Q.L[0] := Q.L[0] ∪ {new-node(e)}                    f.r := f.r - 1
    for i := 0 to log n do Link(Q, i)                   Move f to Q.L[r] and
                                                        f := f.f
Proc Meld(Q₁, Q₂)                                   else
    for i := 0 to log n do                              Unlink f.L[r + 1] and add
        Q₁.L[i] := Q₁.L[i] ∪ Q₂.L[i]                    one tree to f.L[r] and
    do 2 times Link(Q₁, i)                              one tree to Q.L[r]
                                                    Link(Q, i)
Proc DecreaseKey(Q, e, e')                          r := r + 1
    Delete(Q, e)                                for i := r to log n do
    Insert(Q, e')                                  Unlink(Q, i + 1)
                                                   do 2 times Link(Q, i)
Proc ExtractMin(Q)
    e := FindMin(Q)
    Delete(Q, e)
    return e
```

Fig. 4. A sequential implementation allowing pipelining.

Unlink(Q, i) Unlinks the tree min$(Q.L[i])$ and adds the resulting two trees to
$Q.L[i - 1]$, provided $i \geq 1$ and $|Q.L[i]| \geq 1$.

Each of the priority queue operations can be viewed as running in steps
$i = 0, \ldots, \log n$. Step i only accesses, creates and destroys nodes of rank i and
$i + 1$. Notice that requirement C_1 implies that Meld only has to perform Link
two times for each rank, whereas the implementation of Meld in Fig. 2 has to do
the corresponding linking three times. Otherwise the only interesting procedure
is Delete. Procedure Delete proceeds in three phases. First all sons of the
node to be removed are cut off and moved to $Q.L$. In the second phase the hole
created is eliminated by moving it up thru the tree by unlinking the brother node
of the hole's current position or unlinking the father node of the hole. Finally
the third phase reestablishes C_2 in case phase two removed min$(Q.L[i])$ for some
i. This phase is similar to the last for loop in the implementation of Delete in
Fig. 3.

The pseudo code given in Fig. 4 assumes the same representation for nodes
as in Sect. 3. To implement the priority queues on a processors array a representation is required that is distributed among the processors. The canonical
distribution is to let processor p store nodes of rank p.

The representation we distribute is the following. Assume that the sons of a node are ordered from right-to-left in increasing rank order (this allows us to talk about the leftmost and rightmost sons of a node). A node v is represented by a record with the fields:

e : the element associated to v,
r : the rank of v,
left, right : pointers to the left and right brothers of v,
leftmost-son : a pointer to the leftmost son of v,
f : a pointer to the father of v, if v is the leftmost son. Otherwise NIL.

The array $Q.L$ is replaced by linked lists. Finally an array *rightmost-son* is maintained that for each node stores a pointer to the rank zero son of the node or to the node itself if it has rank zero. Notice that this representation only has pointers between nodes with rank difference at most one.

It is straightforward to modify the code given in Fig. 4 to this new representation. The only essential difference is when performing DELETE. The first rank zero son of v to be moved to $Q.L$ is found by using the array *rightmost-son*. The succeeding sons are found by using the *left* pointers.

On a processor array we let processor p store all nodes of rank p. In addition processor p stores $Q.L[p]$ for all priority queues Q. The array *rightmost-son* is stored at processor zero. The "locations" that DELETE and DECREASEKEY refer to are now not the nodes but the corresponding entries in the *rightmost-son* array.

With the above described representation step i of an operation only involves information stored at processors $\{i-1, i, i+1, i+2\}$ (processor $i-1$ and $i+2$ because back pointers have to be updated in the involved linked lists) that can be accessed in constant time. This immediately allows us to pipeline the operations, such that we for each new operation perform exactly four steps of each of the previous operations. Notice that no latency is involved in performing the queries: The answer to a FINDMIN query is known immediately.

Theorem 8. *On a processor array of size $O(\log n)$ each of the operations* MAKE-QUEUE, INSERT, MELD, FINDMIN, EXTRACTMIN, DELETE *and* DECREASE-KEY *can be supported in constant time.*

References

1. Gerth Stølting Brodal. Fast meldable priority queues. In *Proc. 4th Workshop on Algorithms and Data Structures (WADS)*, volume 955 of *Lecture Notes in Computer Science*, pages 282–290. Springer Verlag, Berlin, 1995.
2. Gerth Stølting Brodal. Worst-case efficient priority queues. In *Proc. 7th ACM-SIAM Symposium on Discrete Algorithms (SODA)*, pages 52–58, 1996.
3. Danny Z. Chen and Xiaobo Hu. Fast and efficient operations on parallel priority queues (preliminary version). In *Algorithms and Computation: 5th International Symposium, ISAAC '93*, volume 834 of *Lecture Notes in Computer Science*, pages 279–287. Springer Verlag, Berlin, 1994.

4. Paul F. Dietz. Heap construction in the parallel comparison tree model. In *Proc. 3rd Scandinavian Workshop on Algorithm Theory (SWAT)*, volume 621 of *Lecture Notes in Computer Science*, pages 140–150. Springer Verlag, Berlin, 1992.

5. Paul F. Dietz and Rajeev Raman. Very fast optimal parallel algorithms for heap construction. In *Proc. 6th Symposium on Parallel and Distributed Processing*, pages 514–521, 1994.

6. James R. Driscoll, Harold N. Gabow, Ruth Shrairman, and Robert E. Tarjan. Relaxed heaps: An alternative to fibonacci heaps with applications to parallel computation. *Communications of the ACM*, 31(11):1343–1354, 1988.

7. Robert W. Floyd. Algorithm 245: Treesort3. *Communications of the ACM*, 7(12):701, 1964.

8. Michael L. Fredman, Robert Sedgewick, Daniel D. Sleator, and Robert E. Tarjan. The pairing heap: A new form of self–adjusting heap. *Algorithmica*, 1:111–129, 1986.

9. Michael L. Fredman and Robert Endre Tarjan. Fibonacci heaps and their uses in improved network optimization algorithms. In *Proc. 25rd Ann. Symp. on Foundations of Computer Science (FOCS)*, pages 338–346, 1984.

10. Joseph JáJá. *An Introduction to Parallel Algorithms*. Addison-Wesley, 1992.

11. C. M. Khoong. Optimal parallel construction of heaps. *Information Processing Letters*, 48:159–161, 1993.

12. F. Thomson Leighton. *Introduction to Parallel Algorithms and Architectures: Arrays, Trees, Hypercubes*. Morgan Kaufmann, 1992.

13. Kurt Mehlhorn and Athanasios K. Tsakalidis. Data structures. In J. van Leeuwen, editor, *Handbook of Theoretical Computer Science, Volume A: Algorithms and Complexity*. MIT Press/Elsevier, 1990.

14. Maria Cristina Pinotti, Sajal K. Das, and Vincenzo A. Crupi. Parallel and distributed meldable priority queues based on binomial heaps. In *Int. Conference on Parallel Processing*, 1996.

15. Maria Cristina Pinotti and Geppino Pucci. Parallel priority queues. *Information Processing Letters*, 40:33–40, 1991.

16. Maria Cristina Pinotti and Geppino Pucci. Parallel algorithms for priority queue operations. In *Proc. 3rd Scandinavian Workshop on Algorithm Theory (SWAT)*, volume 621 of *Lecture Notes in Computer Science*, pages 130–139. Springer Verlag, Berlin, 1992.

17. A. Ranade, S. Cheng, E. Deprit, J. Jones, and S. Shih. Parallelism and locality in priority queues. In *Proc. 6th Symposium on Parallel and Distributed Processing*, pages 490–496, 1994.

18. Nageswara S. V. Rao and Weixiong Zhang. Building heaps in parallel. *Information Processing Letters*, 37:355–358, 1991.

19. Jean Vuillemin. A data structure for manipulating priority queues. *Communications of the ACM*, 21(4):309–315, 1978.

20. J. W. J. Williams. Algorithm 232: Heapsort. *Communications of the ACM*, 7(6):347–348, 1964.

Binary Search Trees: How Low Can You Go?

Rolf Fagerberg*

Department of Mathematics and Computer Science, Odense University
DK-5230 Odense M, Denmark

Abstract. We prove that no algorithm for balanced binary search trees performing insertions and deletions in amortized time $O(f(n))$ can guarantee a height smaller than $\lceil \log(n+1) + 1/f(n) \rceil$ for all n. We improve the existing upper bound to $\lceil \log(n+1) + \log^2(f(n))/f(n) \rceil$, thus almost matching our lower bound. We also improve the existing upper bound for worst case algorithms, and give a lower bound for the semi-dynamic case.

1 Introduction

The smallest possible height of a binary search tree of n nodes is $\lceil \log(n+1) \rceil$. There is an abundance of schemes for keeping the height within some constant factor of this optimum while inserting and deleting in logarithmic time. For instance, in AVL-trees [1], the constant factor is 1.44, in red-black trees [12], it is 2, etc. A natural question to ask is: Can we do better than a constant factor? Or, more fundamentally: *What is the smallest height maintainable with a given update time?*

In a paper from 1976 [16], Maurer et al. present a search tree, the k-neighbor tree, with a maximal height of $c \cdot \log(n)$, where c can be chosen arbitrarily close to 1. The update time is $O(\log n)$, with the constant depending on c. Amazingly, no further progress on the problem seems to have been made until around 1990, when Lai and Andersson addressed it in their theses [3, 13] and in resulting papers [2, 4, 5, 6, 14], some of which are with additional collaborators. They give a series of schemes for maintaining height $\lceil \log(n+1) \rceil + 1$, using amortized $O(\log^2 n)$ rebalancing work per update for the simplest, improving to $\Theta(1)$ for the most complicated. Andersson also gave worst case solutions achieving this height in $O(\log n)$ time per update [2, 3]. Clearly, these results are sufficient for all practical purposes.

However, they do not answer the fundamental question above. Spending linear time per update, we can guarantee optimal height for all n by rebuilding the entire tree after each update. By an observation in [13], this time is also necessary, even in the amortized sense. Thus, we cannot hope to get optimal height,

---

* E-mail address: rolf@imada.ou.dk. Supported by the Danish National Science Research Council (grant no. 11-0575) and by the ESPRIT Long Term Research Programme of the EU under project no. 20244 (ALCOM-IT). Part of this research was done while visiting the Department of Computer Science, University of Waterloo, Canada.

if we want update times more reasonable than linear. The height guaranteed in the results by Andersson and Lai is of the form

$$\lceil \log(n+1) + \epsilon \rceil \ , \tag{1}$$

for arbitrary $\epsilon > 0$. When $\epsilon < 1$, this expression is optimal for the first integers n above $2^k - 1$ for any k, and optimal plus one for the last before $2^{k+1} - 1$. By first order approximation to the logarithm function,[2] we see that ϵ is proportional the fraction of integers n for which the height is non-optimal.

The height (1) can be maintained with amortized $O(\log \log^2(n)/\epsilon + 1/\epsilon^2)$ rebalancing work per update,[3] by a result sketched in [6] (a detailed exposition is given in [13]). This implies that in $O(f(n))$ amortized time per update, the height (1) with $\epsilon(n) = 1/\sqrt{f(n)}$ can be maintained (for functions $f \in \Omega(\log \log^4 n)$). Lai poses [13] as an open question whether a smaller ϵ can maintained.

In this paper, we show that $\epsilon(n) = \log^2(f(n))/f(n)$ is possible in $O(f(n))$ amortized time. Perhaps more interesting, we also show a lower bound of $\epsilon(n) \in \Omega(1/f(n))$ for all algorithms using $O(f(n))$ amortized time per update. Thus, we give an almost exact answer to the question asked in the beginning of this section. Note that here, as in the rest of the paper, time refers to the *update time*, i.e. the amount of restructuring needed, and does not include the search for a key. Of course, the most interesting case is $f(n) = \log(n)$, as this is the search time.

The best existing worst case algorithm [2, 3] maintains the height (1) in $O(\log(n)/\epsilon)$ time. Thus, for logarithmic update times only constant ϵ is possible. We also improve the upper bounds in this case, showing how to get $\epsilon(n) = 1/\sqrt{f(n)}$ in $O(f(n))$ worst case time. This gives a partial answer to an open question in [6].

Finally, our lower bound result can also be applied to the maintenance of optimal height in the semi-dynamic case, i.e. under insertions only. The best upper bound is obtained by Andersson in his thesis [3], where he showed how to insert in amortized $O(\log^2 n)$ time. We prove that $\Omega(\log n)$ is necessary.

2 Lower Bounds

In this section, we prove the lower bounds stated in the introduction. These follow as corollaries to our main result, Theorem 1. First, we note that any integer n can be uniquely written as $(2^k - 1)(1 - \epsilon)$ for some integer k and some $0 \leq \epsilon < 1/2$.

---

[2] Considering tangents to the graph of $\log(x)$ at points a and b, it is easy to see that $\log(a) + i/(b \ln(2)) \leq \log(a + i) \leq \log(a) + i/(a \ln(2))$ for $a \leq b$ and $0 \leq i \leq b - a$. This and similar observations will be used throughout the paper under the name *first order approximations*.

[3] By $\log \log^k n$ we mean $(\log \log(n))^k$.

Theorem 1. *Let T be a binary search tree of $n = (2^k - 1)(1 - \epsilon)$ nodes, where k is an integer and $0 < \epsilon < 1/2$, and let T have optimal height. Then there exists an insertion such that any binary search tree of optimal height on the new set of nodes must contain $\Omega(1/\epsilon)$ edges which are not in T.*

Here, we identify nodes and keys, and we say that two edges differ if at least one of their endpoints differs.

We prove Theorem 1 at the end of this section. In the first corollary below, we restrict ourselves to functions in $O(n)$ that are not too ill-behaved.[4] The following definition suits our needs: Define $\mathcal{F}$ as the set of non-decreasing functions $f \in O(n)$, for which there exists an integer m such that $f(m) \geq 2$, and such that $f(n + 1) \leq 2f(n)$ for all $n > m$.

Corollary 2. *For any function $f \in \mathcal{F}$, no algorithm maintaining a binary search tree under insertions and deletions with amortized $o(f(n))$ restructuring work per update can guarantee a height of $\lceil \log(n + 1) + 1/f(n) \rceil$ for all n.*

Proof. Consider an algorithm maintaining height $h(n) = \lceil \log(n + 1) + 1/f(n) \rceil$. Let k be any integer such that $f(2^k - 1) \geq 2$. Choose the largest n between $2^k - 1$ and $2^{k+1} - 1$ such that $h(n)$ and $h(n + 1)$ both are equal to the optimal height $k + 1$. As $h(n + 2)$ is non-optimal, we know that $\log(n + 3) + 1/f(n + 2) > k + 1$. By first order approximation, we have $k + 1 \geq \log(2^{k+1} - i) + i/(\ln(2)2^{k+1})$. So for i defined by $n + 3 = 2^{k+1} - i$, we know that $1/f(n + 2) > i/(\ln(2)2^{k+1})$. From this it follows that $n = (2^{k+1} - 1)(1 - \epsilon)$ for $\epsilon \in O(1/f(n + 2))$, which, due to the definition of $\mathcal{F}$, is the same as $O(1/f(n))$. By Theorem 1, an insertion into any tree of size n can be made, requiring $\Omega(f(n))$ time. Alternating insertions and deletions proves the result. □

Corollary 3. *No algorithm maintaining a binary search tree under insertions with amortized $o(\log n)$ restructuring work per insertion can guarantee optimal height for all n.*

Proof. Consider any algorithm maintaining optimal height, and consider, for any k, the time for inserting 2^k elements while increasing the size from $2^k - 1$ to $2^{k+1} - 1$. The equation $(2^{k+1} - 1)(1 - \epsilon) = (2^k - 1) + i$ has the solution $\epsilon = (2^k - i)/(2^{k+1} - 1)$. By Theorem 1, we can force the algorithm to use time proportional to

$$(2^{k+1} - 1) \sum_{i=0}^{2^k - 1} 1/(2^k - i) = (2^{k+1} - 1) \sum_{i=1}^{2^k} 1/i.$$

Thus, n insertions into an empty tree take $\Omega(n \log n)$ time. □

---

[4] We only need to consider $f \in O(n)$, as $\lceil \log(n + 1) + 1/f(n) \rceil = \lceil \log(n + 1) \rceil$ for n large enough, when $f \in \omega(n)$ (by first order approximation).

In the rest of this section, we prove Theorem 1.

We are, for some k and some ϵ between 0 and $1/2$, given a tree T of size $n = (2^k - 1)(1 - \epsilon)$ and optimal height k. Denoting the n keys, in increasing order, by $x_1, x_2, \ldots, x_n$, we will first point out a gap (x_i, x_{i+1}) into which the insertion should be, and then prove that any tree of optimal height on this new set of keys has at least $\Omega(1/\epsilon)$ edges which are not in T.

As the tree has height k, the nodes of the tree can be seen as members of an array of length $2^k - 1$ by a mapping ψ defined by sending node v into the entry of index i if a node in v's position would have rank i in the perfect tree on $2^k - 1$ nodes. The figure below shows a tree of 10 nodes and its corresponding array version $\psi(T)$. Throughout the proof, we will think of nodes as existing both places, and use phrases like "the index of the root" with the obvious meaning. Note that $x_1, x_2, \ldots, x_n$ must appear in $\psi(T)$ in order for any T. Only their spacing can vary.

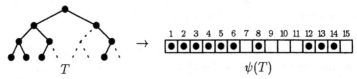

To determine the gap into which we will insert, we use a variation (actually, a dual) of a rather fundamental lemma on density, given in [8]. For completeness, we give a proof here, although it follows the same lines as in [8]. We let $[a; b]$ denote the integers $a, a+1, \ldots, b$, and define its length l by $l([a; b]) = b - a + 1$.

Lemma 4. *For any integers a and b, and any subset S of $[a; b]$, there exists $i \in [a; b]$ such that for all integers s, t with $a \leq s \leq i \leq t \leq b$, we have*

$$\frac{|S \cap [s; t]|}{l([s; t])} \leq 2 \frac{|S|}{l([a; b])}.$$

Proof. Assume not for some a, b and S. Then all $i \in [a; b]$ have a surrounding interval I_i with more than $2 \cdot l(I_i) \cdot |S|/l([a; b])$ elements from S. If any $s \in S$ is contained in more than two such intervals, keep only the two reaching farthest to the left and the right, respectively. Summing $|S \cap I_i|$ for the remaining intervals counts the points in S at most twice, but as the intervals still cover $[a; b]$, their total length is at least $l([a; b])$. Hence, by assumption, this sum is greater than $2|S|$, which is a contradiction. □

Using $S = \{ j \mid \psi(T)[j] \text{ empty} \}$, we get a *dense index* i in $\psi(T)$ with the property that the density of empty entries is at most 2ϵ in any surrounding segment of the array. If $\epsilon \geq 1/16$, Theorem 1 is obvious (the lower bound is $\Omega(1)$), so for the rest of the proof we assume $\epsilon < 1/16$. Then any segment of less than 8 entries surrounding $\psi(T)[i]$ has less than one (i.e. zero) empty entry, hence $\psi(T)[i]$ and its two neighboring entries certainly are non-empty. We insert the new key into the gap between the keys in $\psi(T)[i]$ and one of these neighbors.

Now consider any tree T' of optimal height on this new set of keys. In T, we color red all edges not in T', and remove some of these as described below.

This breaks the tree into pieces, and we will prove the existence of $\Theta(1/\epsilon)$ such pieces, hence of that many red edges. As counting the edges from T which are not in T' is equivalent to counting the edges from T' which not in T, this will prove Theorem 1.

The red edges that we remove are found by the following recursive procedure: We let $\{T\}$ be the initial set of trees. For each tree in the set, we locate the first red edge (if any) on its leftmost path and on its rightmost path and remove these, thereby enlarging the set of trees. This continues recursively, until we have a set $\{S_1, S_2, \ldots, S_m\}$ of trees where no leftmost or rightmost path has a red edge. The figure below exemplifies the process. Red edges are dotted.

Viewed in $\psi(T)$, the trees produced will constitute non-overlapping segments of keys in the array, and the boundary of each segment is the leftmost and the rightmost key in the corresponding tree. Inside each of the trees, there may still be red edges left. However, due to the inorder ordering, any subtree produced by removing red edges from a tree in the final set above must still be a subtree of this tree, when the pieces are combined to form T'. In terms of $\psi(T)$, the alteration of these edges can only move keys around inside each segment, not out of its boundary.

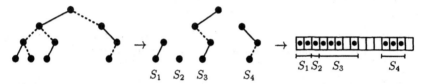

We now have two possibilities; namely Case I: The gap into which we insert falls between two segments, and Case II: The gap is spanned by some segment. In Case II, if the red edges inside the tree S corresponding to this segment *by themselves* are sufficient to get optimal height after the insertion, we start our dissection procedure all over. We substitute for T the tree rooted by the lower node of the highest red edge on the path from the leaf under which we are inserting to the root of S (the red edges inside *this* tree must be sufficient), and disregard the rest of the trees. This can only happen a finite number of times, since the new T is lower than the old. Thus, in Case II, we may without loss of generality assume that the root of S *must* appear at least one level higher in T'.

We analyze Case I first. Let $S_1, \ldots, S_{l-1}, S_l, \ldots, S_m$ be the segments in $\psi(T)$, where the the insertion point falls between S_{l-1} and S_l. In $\psi(T')$, the same segments appear. The distance between their endpoints may have grown or shrunk (if the corresponding tree moves vertically from T to T'), they may have slid around in the array (if the corresponding tree moves horizontally from T to T'), and their interior may have been altered (by the effect of the remaining red edges). However, they must appear in the same order and contain the same number of keys.

In $\psi(T')$, between the right endpoint of S_{l-1} and the left endpoint of S_l, there is now room for the new key. Assume without loss of generality that the left endpoint of S_l has moved to the right. By the following lemma, the index of the root of S_l must have moved to the right, too.

Lemma 5. *Let i be the dense index in $\psi(T)$, and let $\epsilon \leq 1/16$. Let S be a segment to the right of i in $\psi(T)$, and let its leftmost endpoint have index α and its root have index β. If, in $\psi(T')$, its left endpoint has moved to the right, but its root has not, then $l([\alpha; \beta]) \leq 3/8 \cdot l([i; \beta])$.*

Proof. As the index of the left endpoint and the index of the root have moved closer to each other, the root must be on a lower level in T' than in T. This means that in $\psi(T)$, approximately half of the entries in $[\alpha; \beta]$ must be empty. In the worst case, α and β can be neighboring entries of even index with one empty entry in between, so we at least can guarantee one empty entry for each two non-empty in $[\alpha; \beta]$. By the properties of index i, there are at most $2\epsilon \cdot l([i; \beta]) \leq l([i; \beta])/8$ empty entries in $[\alpha; \beta]$, hence at most three times as many entries in total. □

Consider the first segment S_{l+r} to the right of S_l whose root has *not* moved to the right. If its left endpoint has not moved to the right either, we let j be the index in $\psi(T)$ of this left endpoint, otherwise, we let j be the index in $\psi(T)$ of its root. If no such segment exists, we let j be the last index in the array. The next lemma is simple, but crucial:

Lemma 6. *If a segment S contains s keys, and the index of its root changes from $\psi(T)$ to $\psi(T')$, then this change is at least of size $s/2$.*

Proof. The root has height at least $h = \lceil \log(s+1) \rceil$ in T as well as in T'. Hence, its index is always a multiple of $2^{h-1} \geq s/2$. □

The interval $[i; j]$, where i is the dense index, spans the segments $S_l, \ldots, S_{l+(r-1)}$ in $\psi(T)$ as well as in $\psi(T')$. By Lemma 4, it contains at most $2\epsilon \cdot l([i; j])$ empty entries. Hence, none of the segments $S_l, \ldots, S_{l+(r-1)}$ can have a root that changes its index by more than this amount, as movement of an element inside a fixed array can be seen as the passing of empty entries past the element. By Lemma 6, the maximum number of keys in any of these segments is $4\epsilon \cdot l([i; j])$. But of the more than $(1 - 2\epsilon) \cdot l([i; j]) \geq 7/8 \cdot l([i; j])$ keys in $[i; j]$, at most $3/8 \cdot l([i; j]) + 1$ do not belong to any of the segments $S_l, \ldots, S_{l+(r-1)}$, by Lemma 5 (plus one, because i may not belong to S_l). Hence, there are $\Omega(1/\epsilon)$ segments. This proves Theorem 1 in Case I.

In Case II, we argue very similarly. Let $S_1, \ldots, S_l, \ldots, S_m$ be the segments in $\psi(T)$, with the insertion point spanned by S_l. As discussed above, we may assume that in T', the root of S_l must be at least one level higher than in T. Hence, its index must move. Assume without loss of generality that it moves to the right, and let S_{l+r} be the first segment to the right of S_l whose root does not move to the right. Let i' be the left endpoint of S_l in $\psi(T)$, and define j as above. Then $[i'; j]$ contains the dense index and spans the roots of the segments $S_l, \ldots, S_{l+(r-1)}$ in $\psi(T)$ as well as in $\psi(T')$. Proceeding as above proves Theorem 1 in Case II.

3 New Upper bounds

In this section, we prove the new upper bounds described in the introduction. As these results are mostly of theoretical importance, we only give the main ideas. Furthermore, as we build on the techniques in [2, 5], we assume some familiarity with these.

3.1 Amortized Complexity

We now show how to maintain the height (1) with $\epsilon(n) = \log^2(f(n))/f(n)$ in amortized $O(f(n))$ work per update. We first consider insertions only, then explain how to handle deletions at the end.

Like in [5], we use a two-layered structure. The top is a binary search tree maintained by the $O(\log^2(n)/\epsilon)$ amortized time algorithm from [5] (to which we refer for a description). The leaves in this top tree are themselves trees of a smaller size, maintained by the same type of algorithm. As in [5], we denote them *buckets*.

In [5], when a bucket grows to a certain maximum size, it is split. Only then an insertion in the top tree occurs, hence the time for carrying it out can be amortized over the insertions that made the bucket grow. However, in order to guarantee the desired height, it is necessary to reset some parameters by a global rebuilding each $\epsilon^2 n$ updates. This is amortized $\Theta(1/\epsilon^2)$ work, making $\epsilon(n) = 1/\sqrt{f(n)}$ best possible in $O(f(n))$ time.

Our improvement is achieved by controlling the size of the buckets more carefully, removing the need for the global rebuilding above. Instead of splitting large buckets (which halves their size), we will distribute some of their keys into neighboring smaller buckets in such a way that the buckets always are of size at least $(1 - \epsilon/4)\Delta$, and at most $(1 - \epsilon/8)\Delta$. Here, Δ is a power of two between $2^4 \cdot \max\{1/\epsilon, \log^2(n)\}$ and $2^8 \cdot \max\{1/\epsilon, \log^2(n)\}$. The value of Δ is changed by global rebuilding when necessary to ensure this. Amortized, the time for that is negligible. In the definition of Δ, $\log^2(n)$ is the essential part – the $1/\epsilon$ only appears because our interval of allowed bucket sizes would otherwise vanish for $\epsilon(n) \in o(1/\log^2(n))$.

Lemma 7. *Let ϵ be a real number between 0 and 1/4. If the algorithm for the top tree uses $\epsilon' = \epsilon/2$ and the algorithm for the buckets uses $\epsilon'' = \epsilon/8$, then the height of the entire tree is at most $\lceil \log(n + 1) + \epsilon \rceil$, for n sufficiently large.*

Proof. By first order approximation to the logarithm function, we have $-2x < \log(1 - x) < -5x/4$ for $0 \leq x \leq 1/4$, as well as $\log(n+1) < \log(n)+2/n$. There are at most $n/((1-\epsilon/4)\Delta)$ buckets, hence at most $n/((1-\epsilon/4)\Delta)-1$ nodes in the top tree. As $\log(\Delta)$ is an integer, the height of the top tree is bounded by

$$\lceil \log(n/((1 - \epsilon/4)\Delta))) + \epsilon/2 \rceil < \lceil \log(n) - \log(\Delta) + \epsilon/2 + \epsilon/2 \rceil$$
$$= \lceil \log(n + 1) + \epsilon \rceil - \log(\Delta).$$

The height of the buckets is bounded by $\lceil \log((1 - \epsilon/8)\Delta + 1) + \epsilon/8 \rceil$, hence, for n large enough, by $\lceil \log(\Delta) - (\epsilon/8)(5/4) + \epsilon/8 \rceil = \log(\Delta)$. Thus, the total height is as asserted. $\qquad\qquad\square$

To decide *how* to redistribute the keys when a bucket overflows, we also use the $O(\log^2(n)/\epsilon)$ amortized time algorithm from [5], but in a special way.

First of all, as mentioned in the introduction, if we use a constant ϵ very close to 1, any tree maintained by the algorithm has optimal height for all but a small fraction of n's close to the next power of two.

Furthermore, in the algorithm, the only rebalancing operation used is *partial rebuilding*, i.e. the rebuilding of subtrees to perfect balance (the size of left and right subtree differ by at most one for any node), and the task of the algorithm is to decide when and where to rebuild. In trees maintained in this way, only the lowest level is incomplete, for the n's where the height is optimal. When a height violation occurs, the partial rebuilding can be viewed as the even redistribution of the occupied slots on some segment of the lowest level (hence, it can be seen as a *smooth list labeling algorithm*—see [8, 10, 18] for more on this).

In our tree, we group the buckets into groups of size $\Theta(1/\epsilon)$, and use the algorithm on each group with a small, constant ϵ (unrelated to the global ϵ), in a way to be described now.

We divide the allowed bucket sizes into three intervals, I_1, I_2, and I_3, as follows:

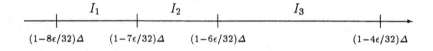

We think of buckets with size in $I_1 \cup I_2$ as the empty slots – and buckets with size in I_3 as the occupied slots – on the lowest level of an imaginary tree of optimal height, having $\Theta(1/\epsilon)$ nodes. When a bucket changes size from a value in $I_1 \cup I_2$ to a value in I_3, we see it as an insertion at an empty slot in the imaginary tree, and when a bucket overflows, we see it as an insertion at an occupied slot. When the algorithm from [5] decides to make a partial rebuilding in the imaginary tree, we rebuild the corresponding buckets, together with the subtree of the top tree that they span. We make the overflowing bucket lose $\epsilon\Delta/32$ keys, make a bucket with size in $I_1 \cup I_2$ receive this number of keys, and keep all other sizes in such a way that afterwards, the distribution of buckets with size in I_3 again follows the distribution of occupied slots in the rebuilt imaginary tree.

When half of the buckets in a group have reached a size in I_3 (corresponding to a halfway filled lowest level in the imaginary tree), we reset the group by creating $\Theta(1)$ new buckets and rebuilding the old in such a way that all sizes are in I_1, corresponding to empty slots. Finally, when a group has doubled in size, it is split in two.

To make the correspondence with the imaginary tree work, the group size should actually be exactly a power of two. However, this is easily achieved by conceptually "padding" the group with imaginary full buckets. We never need more imaginary buckets than real buckets to get to a power of two. Thus, after resetting the group, at least half of the slots on the lowest level in the imaginary tree are empty, and just before the next resetting of the group, at least one fourth are empty. Hence, a sufficiently small, constant ϵ in the algorithm maintaining the imaginary tree will keep the height of this tree optimal all the time.

We now calculate the work for an insertion. For brevity, we only consider the case $\epsilon(n) \in \Omega(1/\log^2(n))$, i.e. the case $\Delta \in \Theta(\log^2(n))$. The calculations in the other case are very similar.

Each invocation of the algorithm from [5] on a group of buckets rebuilds amortized $O(\log^2(1/\epsilon))$ buckets, hence makes $O(\Delta \log^2(1/\epsilon))$ work. However, by the choice of the intervals I_1, I_2, and I_3, it always takes at least $\epsilon\Delta/32$ insertions for a bucket to change status from empty to occupied, or from occupied to overflowing. Thus, amortized over all insertions, the redistribution work is $O(\log^2(1/\epsilon)/\epsilon)$.

The actual insertion in a bucket takes amortized $O(\log^2(\Delta)/\epsilon) = O(\log\log^2(n)/\epsilon)$ time. It take $\Theta(\epsilon\Delta/\epsilon) = \Theta(\Delta) = \Theta(\log^2 n)$ insertions before a new bucket is created. Hence, the amortized $O(\log^2(n)/\epsilon)$ work for inserting in the top tree and the $O(\Delta/\epsilon)$ work for resetting the group is amortized $O(1/\epsilon)$ work per insertion. The amortized work for splitting a group is even lower.

Thus, the height (1) can be maintained in amortized $O(\log^2(1/\epsilon)/\epsilon + \log\log^2(n)/\epsilon)$ time, when only considering insertions. However, deletions are easy to handle by simply marking nodes as deleted, employing the above scheme with an ϵ half the desired value, and each $\Theta(\epsilon n)$ updates rebuild the entire structure, removing marked nodes. This is amortized $\Theta(1/\epsilon)$ work, and it is easy to verify (again, by first order approximation to the logarithm function) that the height is bounded by (1) with the desired ϵ. Thus, we have:

Theorem 8. *For any $f \in \Omega(\log n)$, there is an algorithm for maintaining binary search trees of height $\lceil \log(n+1) + \log^2(f(n))/f(n) \rceil$ in amortized time $O(f(n))$ per update.*

We remark that the restriction $f \in \Omega(\log n)$ is not essential. By recursion, i.e. by using the above scheme itself for doing updates in the buckets, the second term in $O(\log^2(1/\epsilon)/\epsilon + \log\log^2(n)/\epsilon)$ can be lowered arbitrarily, hence the above restriction can too (one level of recursion gives $f \in \Omega(\log\log n)$, for instance).

We also note that deletions can be handled directly, without marking nodes. The idea is to express the size of a bucket as $(1 - 6\epsilon/32)\Delta + i - d$, where i is the number of insertions into the bucket since it was last rebuild, and d is the number of deletions. We maintain $i, d \in [0\,;\,2\epsilon\Delta/32]$ by dividing *this* interval into three sub-intervals I_1, I_2, and I_3, and running *two* versions of the algorithm from [5] on each group of buckets, one for the i's and one for the d's.

3.2 Worst Case Complexity

In [3], Andersson (elaborating on the result in [2]) presents a tree maintaining height (1) in *worst case* time $O(\log(n)/\epsilon)$. The most relevant bound on the update time in search trees is logarithmic, as this is the time spent on searching. In this case, the result above only allows constant ϵ, in contrast to the amortized results in section 3.1 and [6], where $\epsilon(n) \in o(1)$ is possible. The problem with using the techniques of these results in a worst case setting is that several consecutive insertions each can trigger $\omega(\log n)$ work on the top tree (e.g. when buckets are split).

Here, we indicate how to adapt an idea employed in [7] and [15] to the present setting, enabling us to sustain $\epsilon(n) \in o(1)$ in logarithmic worst case time. The idea is simple: Split buckets with regular intervals, and spread the resulting work on the top tree incrementally over the updates between the splits.

As in [7], the following lemma, versions of which are proved independently in [9] and [15], will allow us to control the size of the buckets. It concerns a combinatorial game on n real variables $x_1, x_2, \ldots, x_n$, all initially zero. The game consists of a possible infinite number of rounds of the following form: First, some non-negative values $a_1, a_2, \ldots, a_n$ are chosen subject to the constraint $\sum_{i=1}^{n} a_i \leq 1$, then x_i are set to $x_i + a_i$ for all i, and finally, some variable x_i of maximal value is set to zero. The choices for each round are independent.

Lemma 9 [9, 15]. *In the game above, no set of choices can bring the value of any x_i above $H_{n-1} + 1$, no matter how many rounds are played.*

Here, H_k designates the kth harmonic number $\sum_{i=1}^{k} 1/i$, which is in $\Theta(\log k)$.

We again employ a two-layered structure, now with the top tree as well as the buckets being trees of the type from [3] (to which we refer for a description). When the buckets are created, we make them have size $(1 - \epsilon/4)\Delta$, where Δ is a power of two in $\Theta(\log^2 n)$. We will only consider the case $\epsilon(n) \in \omega(1/\log(n))$, so there is no problem of $\epsilon\Delta$ tending to zero.

Each $c\epsilon \log(n)$ updates, we split the largest bucket in two, for some constant c. For a bucket B, we denote its size s_B, and define $x_B = \max\{0, s_B - (1-\epsilon/4)\Delta\}$. Splitting bucket B will certainly set x_B to zero, if no bucket ever contains more than $(1-\epsilon/8)\Delta$ elements. But this is exactly what Lemma 9 tells us, if we choose c small enough: Using a "unit" of $c\epsilon \log(n)$ in the lemma (i.e. using the constraint $\sum_{i=1}^{n} a_i \leq c\epsilon \log(n)$), we get that no x_B is ever greater than $c\epsilon \log(n)(H_{n-1}+1)$, which is in $O(c\epsilon\Delta)$.

In summary, by an appropriate choice of c we can ensure that the buckets start out having size $(1 - \epsilon/4)\Delta$, and that they never have size larger than $(1 - \epsilon/8)\Delta$. If we, as in [5], rebuild the entire tree each $\epsilon^2 n/32$ updates, we can prove the following:

Lemma 10. *Let ϵ be a real number between 0 and 1/4. If the algorithm for the top tree uses $\epsilon' = \epsilon/2$ and the algorithm for the buckets uses $\epsilon'' = \epsilon/8$, then the height of the entire tree is at most $\lceil \log(n + 1) + \epsilon \rceil$, for n sufficiently large.*

Proof. The proof is a mixture of the proofs of Lemma 7 and the height bound in [5, Theorem 6], and is omitted. □

We note that the updates in the top tree after a bucket split, as well as the global rebuilding, must be done incrementally, a by now standard technique first described in [17]. The basic idea is to have two copies of the data structure. Updates are done on one copy, while the other is being restructured. An amount of restructuring work is done for each update, such that the total restructuring task is finished in half the number N of updates necessary to trigger a restructuring of the first copy. Information about the updates made on the first copy during the restructuring is kept, such that after the restructuring, they can be performed on the second copy. During this, further updates occur on the first copy, which afterwards need to be performed on the second one, etc. However, if two kept updates are performed on the second copy for each new update on the first, the second copy will ready to use before N updates have been done in total, at which point the copies are switched around. Hence, there is always a valid copy of the data structure.

In our case, we need more copies, because we have several independent restructuring tasks (the trees from [3] already have one), but the same principle applies.

The $O(\log(n)/\epsilon)$ work for inserting in the top tree after a bucket split is done incrementally over $\Theta(\epsilon \log n)$ updates, and thus constitutes $O(1/\epsilon^2)$ work per update. The global rebuilding is also done incrementally, and constitutes $\Theta(1/\epsilon^2)$ work per update. Updates in the buckets are $O(\log(\Delta)/\epsilon) = O(\log\log(n)/\epsilon)$ work. The bucket to be split can be found by maintaining a priority queue whose elements are lists of (pointers to) buckets of equal size. There are at most Δ such lists, hence the time used on the priority queue is $O(\log\log n)$. Finally, it is a not-too-hard exercise to give an algorithm for dividing a tree of the type from [3] into two trees of approximately equal size in $O(\log^2(n)/\epsilon)$ time, where n is the size of the tree. Thus, the splitting of a bucket can be done in $O(\log\log^2(n)/\epsilon)$ time. The sum of all these time bounds is $O(1/\epsilon^2 + \log\log^2(n)/\epsilon)$. Hence, we have proven the theorem below for functions f between $\log\log^4(n)$ and $\log^2(n)$. For functions in $\Omega(\log^2 n)$, the original algorithm in [3] proves it.

Theorem 11. *For any $f \in \Omega(\log\log^4 n)$, there is an algorithm for maintaining binary search trees of height $\lceil \log(n+1) + 1/\sqrt{f(n)} \rceil$ in worst case time $O(f(n))$ per update.*

4 Open Problems

In this paper, we did not obtain completely matching upper and lower bounds on the $\epsilon(n)$ in (1) maintainable with a given update time $O(f(n))$. An obvious open problem is to close this gap. Another interesting question is whether there is any difference between the amortized and the worst case complexity. We conjecture that our lower bound is tight in both cases.

We also leave a gap between upper and lower bounds in the semi-dynamic case. Again, we believe the lower bound to be tight (this will follow if the lower bound in the fully dynamic case is tight, by a technique in [5]).

Finally, it is an open question, also raised in [11], whether a height of $\lceil \log(n+1) \rceil + O(1)$ can be maintained in $\Theta(1)$ worst case rebalancing time.

As mentioned in the introduction, an amortized solution is given in [6]. Worst case time $O(\log^* n)$ seems possible by using the idea in section 3.2 recursively like in [6], but the need for several copies (due to the use of incremental rebuilding) at each level of the recursion prevents $\Theta(1)$ time.

References

1. G. M. Adel'son-Vel'skiĭ and E. M. Landis. An Algorithm for the Organisation of Information. *Dokl. Akad. Nauk SSSR*, 146:263–266, 1962. In Russian. English translation in *Soviet Math. Dokl.*, 3:1259-1263, 1962.
2. A. Andersson. Optimal bounds on the dictionary problem. In *Proc. Symp. on Optimal Algorithms, Varna*, volume 401 of *LNCS*, pages 106–114. Springer-Verlag, 1989.
3. A. Andersson. *Efficient Search Trees*. PhD thesis, Department of Computer Science, Lund University, Sweden, 1990.
4. A. Andersson, C. Icking, R. Klein, and T. Ottmann. Binary search trees of almost optimal height. *Acta Informatica*, 28:165–178, 1990.
5. A. Andersson and T. W. Lai. Fast updating of well-balanced trees. In *SWAT'90*, volume 447 of *LNCS*, pages 111–121. Springer-Verlag, 1990.
6. A. Andersson and T. W. Lai. Comparison-efficient and write-optimal searching and sorting. In *ISA'91*, volume 557 of *LNCS*, pages 273–282. Springer-Verlag, 1991.
7. P. F. Dietz and R. Raman. A constant update time finger search tree. *Information Processing Letters*, 52, 1994.
8. P. F. Dietz, J. I. Seiferas, and J. Zhang. A tight lower bound for on-line monotonic list labeling. In *SWAT'94*, volume 824 of *LNCS*, pages 131–142. Springer-Verlag, 1994.
9. P. F. Dietz and D. D. Sleator. Two algorithms for maintaining order in a list. In *19th STOC*, pages 365–372, 1987.
10. P. F. Dietz and J. Zhang. Lower bounds for monotonic list labeling. In *SWAT'90*, volume 447 of *LNCS*, pages 173–180. Springer-Verlag, 1990.
11. R. Fleischer. A simple balanced search tree with O(1) worst-case update time. In *ISSAC'93*, volume 762 of *LNCS*, pages 139–146. Springer-Verlag, 1993.
12. L. J. Guibas and R. Sedgewick. A Dichromatic Framework for Balanced Trees. In *19th FOCS*, pages 8–21, 1978.
13. T. Lai. *Efficient Maintenance of Binary Search Trees*. PhD thesis, Department of Computer Science, University of Waterloo, Canada., 1990.
14. T. Lai and D. Wood. Updating almost complete trees or one level makes all the difference. In *STACS'90*, volume 415 of *LNCS*, pages 188–194. Springer-Verlag, 1990.
15. C. Levcopoulos and M. H. Overmars. A balanced search tree with O(1) worst-case update time. *Acta Informatica*, 26(3):269, 1988.
16. H. A. Maurer, T. Ottmann, and H.-W. Six. Implementing dictionaries using binary trees of very small height. *Information Processing Letters*, 5, 1976.
17. M. H. Overmars. *The Design of Dynamic Data Structures*. Springer, Berlin, 1983.
18. J. Zhang. *Density Control and On-Line Labeling Problems*. PhD thesis, Department of Computer Science, University of Rochester, New York, 1993.

Boolean Analysis of Incomplete Examples

Endre Boros[1], Toshihide Ibaraki[2] and Kazuhisa Makino[2]

[1] RUTCOR, Rutgers University, P.O. Box 5062, New Brunswick, NJ 08903, USA
boros@rutcor.rutgers.edu
[2] Department of Applied Mathematics and Physics
Graduate School of Engineering, Kyoto University, Kyoto 606, Japan
{ibaraki,makino}@kuamp.kyoto-u.ac.jp

Abstract. As a form of knowledge acquisition from data, we consider the problem of deciding whether there exists an extension of a partially defined Boolean function with missing data $(\tilde{T}, \tilde{F})$, where $\tilde{T}$ (resp., $\tilde{F}$) is a set of positive (resp., negative) examples. Here, "$*$" denotes a missing bit in the data, and it is assumed that $\tilde{T} \subseteq \{0, 1, *\}^n$ and $\tilde{F} \subseteq \{0, 1, *\}^n$ hold. A Boolean function $f : \{0, 1\}^n \longrightarrow \{0, 1\}$ is an extension of $(\tilde{T}, \tilde{F})$ if it is true (resp., false) for the Boolean vectors corresponding to positive (resp., negative) examples; more precisely, we define three types of extensions called consistent, robust and most robust, depending upon how to deal with missing bits. We then provide polynomial time algorithms or prove their NP-hardness for the problems under various restrictions.

1 Introduction

The knowledge acquisition in the form of Boolean logic has been intensively studied in the recent research (e.g., [4, 6, 10]): given a set of data, represented as a set T of binary "true n-vectors" (or "positive examples") and a set F of "false n-vectors" (or "negative examples"), establish a Boolean function (extension) f, such that f is true (resp., false) in every given true (resp., false) vector; i.e., $T \subseteq T(f)$ and $F \subseteq F(f)$, where $T(f)$ (resp., $F(f)$) denotes the set of true vectors (resp., the set of false vectors) of f. A pair of sets (T, F) is called a *partially defined Boolean function (pdBf)*.

For instance, data x represent the symptoms to diagnose a disease, e.g., x_1 denotes whether temperature is high ($x_1 = 1$) or not ($x_1 = 0$), and x_2 denotes whether blood pressure is high ($x_2 = 1$) or not ($x_2 = 0$), etc. Establishing an extension f, which is consistent with the given data, amounts to finding a logical diagnostic explanation of the given data. Therefore, this may be considered as a form of knowledge acquisition from given examples. It is evident that the problem

* This research was partially supported by ONR (Grants N00014-92-J-1375 and N00014-92-J-4083), and the Scientific Grants in Aid by the Ministry of Education, Science and Culture of Japan. The visit of the first author to Kyoto University was made possible by Grant 06044112 of the Ministry of Education, Science and Culture of Japan. The third author is supported by Research Fellowships of the Japan Society for the Promotion of Science for Young Scientists.

is closely related to learning theory [1, 11], in which a systematic improvement of the obtained extensions is also taken into account.

Unfortunately, the real-world data might not be complete. As for the above examples, for some data x, temperature might not be measured, that is, it is not known whether $x_1 = 0$ or 1, which is represented as $x_1 = *$. For another instance, we have a battery of 45 biochemical tests for carcinogenicity. However, we do not usually apply all tests, since all tests cannot be checked in a laboratory or some tests are very expensive. When a test is not applied, we say that the test result is *missing*. A set of data $(\tilde{T}, \tilde{F})$, which includes the missing results, is called a *partially defined Boolean function with missing data (pBmd)*, where $\tilde{T}$ (resp., $\tilde{F}$) $\subseteq \{0, 1, *\}^n$ denotes the set of "positive examples" (resp., "negative examples") of such vectors. To cope with such situations, we introduce in this paper three types of complete Boolean functions called *consistent*, *robust* and *most robust* extensions, respectively. More precisely, given a pBmd $(\tilde{T}, \tilde{F})$, (i) a consistent extension (CE) is a Boolean function f such that, for every $\tilde{a} \in \tilde{T}$ (resp., $\tilde{F}$), there is a 0-1 vector a obtained from $\tilde{a}$ by fixing missing data appropriately, for which $f(a) = 1$ (resp., $f(a) = 0$) holds, (ii) a robust extension (RE) is a Boolean function f such that, for every $\tilde{a} \in \tilde{T}$ (resp., $\tilde{F}$), any 0-1 vector a obtained from $\tilde{a}$ by fixing missing data arbitrarily satisfies $f(a) = 1$ (resp., $f(a) = 0$), and (iii) a most robust extension (MRE) is a Boolean function f which is a robust extension of a pBmd (T', F'), where (T', F') is obtained from $(\tilde{T}, \tilde{F})$ by fixing a smallest set of missing bits appropriately (the remaining missing bits in $T' \cup F'$ are assumed to take arbitrary values). All of these extensions provide logical explanations of a given pBmd $(\tilde{T}, \tilde{F})$ with varied freedom given to the missing bits in $\tilde{T}$ and $\tilde{F}$. By definition, if $(\tilde{T}, \tilde{F})$ has a robust extension f, it is also a most robust extension and is a consistent extension, and if $(\tilde{T}, \tilde{F})$ has a most robust extension f, it is a consistent extension. In case of most robust and consistent extensions, they also provide information such that some missing data must take certain values if $(\tilde{T}, \tilde{F})$ can have a consistent extension.

In this paper, we study the problems of deciding the existence of these extensions for a given pBmd $(\tilde{T}, \tilde{F})$, under various restrictions, mainly from the view point of their computational complexity. We obtain computationally efficient algorithms in some cases, and prove NP-completeness in some other cases, as summarized in Table 1, where $AS(a)$ denotes the set of missing bits in a vector a.

Table 1. Summary of complexity results.

Restrictions	RE	CE	MRE
$|AS(a)| \leq 1$ for all $a \in \tilde{T} \cup \tilde{F}$	P	P	P
$|AS(a)| \leq 2$ for all $a \in \tilde{T} \cup \tilde{F}$	P	NPC	NPH
General case	P	NPC	NPH

P: Polynomial, NPC: NP-complete, NPH: NP-hard

2 Partially Defined Boolean Functions with Missing Data

A *Boolean function*, or a *function* in short, is a mapping $f : \mathbf{B}^n \mapsto \mathbf{B}$, where $\mathbf{B} = \{0, 1\}$, and $V \in \mathbf{B}^n$ is called a *Boolean vector* (or a *vector* in short). If $f(V) = 1$ (resp., 0), then V is called a *true* (resp., *false*) vector of f. The set of all true vectors (resp., false vectors) is denoted by $T(f)$ (resp., $F(f)$).

A *partially defined Boolean function* (*pdBf*) is defined by a pair of sets (T, F) such that $T, F \subseteq \mathbf{B}^n$. A function f is called an *extension* (or a *theory*) of the pdBf (T, F) if $T \subseteq T(f)$ and $F \subseteq F(f)$. Obviously, a pdBf (T, F) has an extension if and only if $T \cap F = \emptyset$.

To handle missing components, we introduce set $\mathbf{M} = \{0, 1, *\}$, and interpret the asterisk components $*$ of $v \in \mathbf{M}^n$ as missing bits. For a vector $v \in \mathbf{M}^n$, let $ON(v) = \{j \mid v_j = 1, j = 1, 2, \ldots, n\}$ and $OFF(v) = \{j \mid v_j = 0, j = 1, 2, \ldots, n\}$. For a subset $\tilde{S} \subseteq \mathbf{M}^n$, let $AS(\tilde{S}) = \{(v, j) \mid v \in \tilde{S}, j \in V \setminus (ON(v) \cup OFF(v))\}$ be the collection of all missing bits of the vectors in $\tilde{S}$. If $\tilde{S}$ is a singleton $\{v\}$, we shall write simply $AS(v)$ instead of $AS(\{v\})$. Clearly, $\mathbf{B}^n \subseteq \mathbf{M}^n$, and $v \in \mathbf{B}^n$ if and only if $AS(v) = \emptyset$. Let us consider binary assignments $\alpha \in \mathbf{B}^Q$ to subsets $Q \subseteq AS(\tilde{S})$ of the missing bits. For a vector $v \in \tilde{S}$ and an assignment $\alpha \in \mathbf{B}^Q$, let v^α denote the vector obtained from v by replacing the $*$ components belonging to Q by the binary values assigned to them by α, i.e.,

$$v_j^\alpha = \begin{cases} v_j & \text{if } (v, j) \notin Q \\ \alpha(v, j) & \text{if } (v, j) \in Q. \end{cases}$$

For vectors $v, w \in \mathbf{M}^n$, we shall write $v \approx w$ if there exists an assignment $\alpha \in \mathbf{B}^{AS(\{v, w\})}$ for which $v^\alpha = w^\alpha$ holds, and we say that v is *potentially identical* with w.

A *pdBf with missing data* (or in short *pBmd*) is a pair $(\tilde{T}, \tilde{F})$, where $\tilde{T}, \tilde{F} \subseteq \mathbf{M}^n$. To a pBmd $(\tilde{T}, \tilde{F})$ we always associate the set $AS = AS(\tilde{T} \cup \tilde{F})$ of its missing bits. A function f is called a *robust extension* of the pBmd $(\tilde{T}, \tilde{F})$ if

$$f(a^\alpha) = 1 \text{ and } f(b^\alpha) = 0 \text{ for all } a \in \tilde{T}, b \in \tilde{F} \text{ and for all } \alpha \in \mathbf{B}^{AS}.$$

We first consider the problem of deciding the existence of a robust extension of a given pBmd $(\tilde{T}, \tilde{F})$.

ROBUST EXTENSION (RE)
Input: A pBmd $(\tilde{T}, \tilde{F})$, where $\tilde{T}, \tilde{F} \subseteq \mathbf{M}^n$.
Question: Does $(\tilde{T}, \tilde{F})$ have a robust extension?

It may happen that a pBmd $(\tilde{T}, \tilde{F})$ has no robust extension, but it has an extension if we change some (or all) $*$ bits to appropriate binary values. A function f is called a *consistent extension* of pBmd $(\tilde{T}, \tilde{F})$, if there exists an assignment $\alpha \in \mathbf{B}^{AS}$ for which $f(a^\alpha) = 1$ and $f(b^\alpha) = 0$ for all $a \in \tilde{T}$ and $b \in \tilde{F}$. In other words, a pBmd $(\tilde{T}, \tilde{F})$ is said to have a consistent extension if, for some assignment $\alpha \in \mathbf{B}^{AS}$, the pdBf $(\tilde{T}^\alpha, \tilde{F}^\alpha)$ defined by $\tilde{T}^\alpha = \{a^\alpha \mid a \in \tilde{T}\}$ and $\tilde{F}^\alpha = \{b^\alpha \mid b \in \tilde{F}\}$ has an extension. This leads us to the following decision problem.

CONSISTENT EXTENSION (CE)
Input: A pBmd $(\tilde{T}, \tilde{F})$, where $\tilde{T}, \tilde{F} \subseteq \mathbf{M}^n$.
Question: Does $(\tilde{T}, \tilde{F})$ have a consistent extension?

It may also happen that not all missing bits are necessary to be specified in order to have a robust extension. An assignment $\alpha \in \mathbf{B}^Q$ for a subset $Q \subseteq AS$ is called a *robust assignment* if the resulting pBmd $(\tilde{T}^\alpha, \tilde{F}^\alpha)$ has a robust extension. We are interested in finding a robust assignment with the smallest size $|Q|$.

MOST ROBUST EXTENSION (MRE)
Input: A pBmd $(\tilde{T}, \tilde{F})$, where $\tilde{T}, \tilde{F} \subseteq \mathbf{M}^n$.
Output: NO if $(\tilde{T}, \tilde{F})$ does not have a consistent extension; otherwise a
robust assignment $\alpha \in \mathbf{B}^Q$ for a subset $Q \subseteq AS$, which minimizes $|Q|$.

It follows from definition that if RE or CE are NP-complete, then MRE is NP-hard, and conversely, if MRE is solvable in polynomial time, then both RE and CE are polynomially solvable.

Let us add that we shall also consider various restricted variants of the above problems, in which the input pBmd $(\tilde{T}, \tilde{F})$ is restricted to satisfy the following condition for a given k:

$$|AS(a)| \le k, \text{ for every } a \in \tilde{T} \cup \tilde{F}.$$

3 Robust and Consistent Extensions

Theorem 1. *Problem* RE *can be solved in polynomial time.*

Proof. It is easy to see that a pBmd $(\tilde{T}, \tilde{F})$ has a robust extension if and only if there exists an index j such that $a_j \ne b_j$ and $\{a_j, b_j\} = \{0, 1\}$ (i.e., either $a_j = 0$ and $b_j = 1$, or $a_j = 1$ and $b_j = 0$) for every pair of $a \in \tilde{T}$ and $b \in \tilde{F}$. Obviously, this can be checked in $O(n|T||F|)$ time. □

Let us note next that CE can be trivially solved if $|AS(a)| > 0$ holds for all $a \in \tilde{T} \cup \tilde{F}$, since in this case $(\tilde{T}, \tilde{F})$ always has a consistent extension f. Indeed, let us consider an assignment $\alpha \in \mathbf{B}^{AS}$ such that $|ON(a^\alpha)|$ is odd for all $a \in \tilde{T}$, and $|ON(b^\alpha)|$ is even for all $b \in \tilde{F}$, and let f be the parity function for which $f(v) = 1$ if and only if $|ON(v)|$ is odd. Problem CE becomes more complicated when not all input vectors have missing bits, although it remains polynomially solvable if each input vector contains at most one missing bit.

Theorem 2. *Problem* CE *can be solved in polynomial time for a pBmd $(\tilde{T}, \tilde{F})$ for which every $a \in \tilde{T} \cup \tilde{F}$ satisfies $|AS(a)| \le 1$.*

Proof. Let j_a be the index of the $*$ in each vector $a \in \tilde{T} \cup \tilde{F}$ (i.e., $AS(a) = \{(a, j_a)\}$), if any. Then $(\tilde{T}, \tilde{F})$ has a consistent extension if and only if (i) there is no pair of $a \in \tilde{T}$ and $b \in \tilde{F}$ such that $a, b \in \mathbf{B}^n$ and $a = b$, and (ii) there is an assignment $\alpha \in \mathbf{B}^{AS}$ satisfying the conditions

$$\alpha(a, j_a) \neq b_{j_a} \quad \text{if } a \notin \mathbf{B}^n \text{ and } b \in \mathbf{B}^n \tag{1}$$

$$\alpha(b, j_b) \neq a_{j_b} \quad \text{if } a \in \mathbf{B}^n \text{ and } b \notin \mathbf{B}^n \tag{2}$$

$$\alpha(a, j_a) \neq b_{j_a} \text{ or } \alpha(b, j_b) \neq a_{j_b} \quad \text{if } a, b \notin \mathbf{B}^n \text{ and } j_a \neq j_b \tag{3}$$

$$\alpha(a, j_a) \neq \alpha(b, j_b) \quad \text{if } a, b \notin \mathbf{B}^n \text{ and } j_a = j_b \tag{4}$$

for every pair of $a \in \tilde{T}$ and $b \in \tilde{F}$ with $a \approx b$. Obviously, condition (i) can be checked in $O(n|\tilde{T}||\tilde{F}|)$ time. To check (ii), let us observe that each of the conditions (1)–(4) can equivalently be represented as clauses in the variables $\alpha(v, j)$ for $(v, j) \in AS$. Namely, (1) and (2) can be represented by linear clauses, (3) by a clause containing two variables, and (4) by the conjunction of two clauses, each of which contains two variables. E.g. (4) is equivalent with the condition

$$1 = (\alpha(a, j_a) \vee \alpha(b, j_b))(\overline{\alpha(a, j_a)} \vee \overline{\alpha(b, j_b)}).$$

In total, we have a 2-SAT problem containing at most $2|\tilde{T}||\tilde{F}|$ clauses, which is solvable in time linear in its input size (see e.g., [2]). This shows that problem CE can be solved in $O(n|\tilde{T}||\tilde{F}|)$ time. $\qquad \square$

Example 1. Let us define $\tilde{T}, \tilde{F} \subseteq \{0,1\}^3$ by

$$\tilde{T} = \begin{cases} a^{(1)} = (1,1,*) \\ a^{(2)} = (0,0,1) \\ a^{(3)} = (0,1,*) \\ a^{(4)} = (*,0,0) \end{cases}, \quad \tilde{F} = \begin{cases} b^{(1)} = (1,1,1) \\ b^{(2)} = (0,*,1) \\ b^{(3)} = (*,0,0) \end{cases}.$$

Then we have the following 2-SAT:

$$\overline{\alpha(a^{(1)}, 3)}\, \alpha(b^{(2)}, 2)\, \overline{(\alpha(a^{(3)}, 3) \vee \alpha(b^{(2)}, 2))}\, (\alpha(a^{(4)}, 1) \vee \alpha(b^{(3)}, 1))$$

$$\overline{(\alpha(a^{(4)}, 1) \vee \alpha(b^{(3)}, 1))} = 1.$$

For this, the assignment $\alpha \in \mathbf{B}^{AS}$ given by $\alpha(a^{(1)}, 3) = \alpha(a^{(3)}, 3) = \alpha(a^{(4)}, 1) = 0$ and $\alpha(b^{(2)}, 2) = \alpha(b^{(3)}, 1) = 1$, is a satisfying solution. $\qquad \square$

In general, however, we have the following negative result (see [5]).

Theorem 3. *Problem* CE *is NP-complete, even if* $|AS(a)| \leq 2$ *holds for all* $a \in \tilde{T} \cup \tilde{F}$.

4 Most Robust Extensions

As Theorem 3 implies that MRE is NP-hard even if $|AS(a)| \leq 2$ for all $\tilde{T} \cup \tilde{F}$. Therefore, we only consider the case in which

$$|AS(a)| \leq 1 \text{ for all } a \in \tilde{T} \cup \tilde{F},$$

and show that it can be solved in polynomial time.

Let us remark first that any assignment $\alpha \in \mathbf{B}^{AS}$ for which $(\tilde{T}^{\alpha}, \tilde{F}^{\alpha})$ has an extension must satisfy the conditions (i) and (ii) in the proof of Theorem 2. Hence, some components of such an α may be forced to take a unique binary value by conditions (1) and (2). Let us assume therefore that we fix all such asterisks $*$ in advance, and let us consider only conditions (3) and (4) in the sequel.

Let us define next a bipartite graph

$$
\begin{aligned}
&G_{AS} = (V, E), \\
&V = AS(\tilde{T}) \cup AS(\tilde{F}), \text{ and} \\
&E = \{(q, r; \alpha) \,|\, q = (a, i) \in AS(\tilde{T}), r = (b, j) \in AS(\tilde{F}), \\
&\qquad \text{there exists an assignment } \alpha \in \mathbf{B}^{\{q,r\}} \text{ such that } a^{\alpha} = b^{\alpha}\},
\end{aligned}
\tag{5}
$$

where the label $c(e)$ of each edge $e = (q, r; c(e))$, as defined in (5), is called the *configuration* of e. If there are more than one assignments $\alpha \in \mathbf{B}^{\{q,r\}}$ for some $q \in AS(\tilde{T})$ and $r \in AS(\tilde{F})$, for which $a^{\alpha} = b^{\alpha}$ (this occurs if $q = (a, i)$ and $r = (b, j)$ satisfy $i = j$), then the graph G_{AS} has parallel edges corresponding to such different configurations. Let us note that, since $|AS(a)| \le 1$ holds for all $a \in \tilde{T} \cup \tilde{F}$, every pair of $q = (a, i) \in AS(\tilde{T})$ and $r = (b, j) \in AS(\tilde{F})$ has at most two assignments $\alpha \in \mathbf{B}^{\{q,r\}}$ such that $a^{\alpha} = b^{\alpha}$.

Example 2. Let us define $\tilde{T}, \tilde{F} \subseteq \{0, 1\}^{6}$ by

$$
\tilde{T} = \left\{ \begin{aligned}
a^{(1)} &= (*, 1, 1, 1, 1) \\
a^{(2)} &= (1, 1, 1, 1, *) \\
a^{(3)} &= (1, 1, 1, *, 1) \\
a^{(4)} &= (1, 1, *, 1, 1) \\
a^{(5)} &= (1, *, 0, 1, 0)
\end{aligned} \right\}, \quad
\tilde{F} = \left\{ \begin{aligned}
b^{(1)} &= (1, *, 1, 1, 1) \\
b^{(2)} &= (1, 1, 1, 1, *) \\
b^{(3)} &= (1, 1, *, 1, 0) \\
b^{(4)} &= (1, 1, 0, 1, *)
\end{aligned} \right\}.
$$

Then the graph G_{AS} is given in Figure 1. Although the configurations of edges are not indicated, they are easy to find out. For example, the edge $e = (a^{(1)}, b^{(1)})$ has $c(e) = (a_1^{(1)} = 1, b_2^{(1)} = 1)$, and the parallel edges $e' = (a^{(2)}, b^{(2)})$ and $e'' = (a^{(2)}, b^{(2)})$ have $c(e') = (a_5^{(2)} = 0, b_5^{(2)} = 0)$ and $c(e'') = (a_5^{(2)} = 1, b_5^{(2)} = 1)$, respectively. $\square$

Lemma 4. *Given a pBmd $(\tilde{T}, \tilde{F})$, an assignment $\beta \in \mathbf{B}^{Q}$ for a subset $Q \subseteq AS$ is a robust assignment of $(\tilde{T}, \tilde{F})$ (i.e., $(\tilde{T}^{\beta}, \tilde{F}^{\beta})$ has a robust extension) if and only if, for every edge $e = (q, r; \alpha)$ of G_{AS}, we have either $q = (a, i) \in Q$ and $a^{\beta} \ne a^{\alpha}$, or $r = (b, j) \in Q$ and $b^{\beta} \ne b^{\alpha}$, or both.*

Proof. Let us first show the only-if-part. Let f be a robust extension of $(\tilde{T}^{\beta}, \tilde{F}^{\beta})$, and let $e = (q, r; \alpha)$ be an edge of G_{AS}. We can assume, without loss of generality that $q = (a, i) \in AS(\tilde{T})$.

Let us assume that either $q \notin Q$ or $a^{\beta} = a^{\alpha}$. Let us show first that $f(a^{\alpha}) = 1$. Indeed, if $q = (a, i) \notin Q$, then $(a^{\beta})^{\alpha} = a^{\alpha}$, and since $\beta \in \mathbf{B}^{Q}$ is a robust

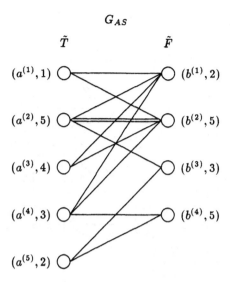

Fig. 1. The graph G_{AS} of the pBmd $(\tilde{T}, \tilde{F})$ in Example 2.

assignment, $f(a^\alpha) = 1$ must hold. On the other hand, if $a^\beta = a^\alpha$, then obviously $f(a^\alpha) = f(a^\beta) = 1$ must hold, since $a \in \tilde{T}$.

We then show that $f(a^\alpha) = 1$ implies $r = (b, j) \in Q$ and $b^\beta \neq b^\alpha$. If $r \notin Q$, then $(b^\beta)^\alpha = b^\alpha = a^\alpha$, and hence $f(a^\alpha) = f(b^\alpha) = 0$ by $b \in \tilde{F}$, which is a contradiction. Similarly $b^\beta = b^\alpha$ leads to the same contradiction. Hence $r \in Q$ and $b^\beta \neq b^\alpha$ must hold.

To prove the if-part, assume that $\beta \in \mathbf{B}^Q$ for a subset $Q \subseteq AS$ is not a robust assignment of $(\tilde{T}, \tilde{F})$. Then, by the definition of robustness, we have a pair of vectors $a \in \tilde{T}$ and $b \in \tilde{F}$ such that $a^\beta \approx b^\beta$. Then the edge $e = (q, r; \alpha)$ with $q = (a, i)$ and $r = (b, j)$ does not satisfy the statement of the lemma. □

For a vector $d \in \mathbf{B}^n$, let $E(d)$ denote the set of edges $e = (q, r; \alpha) \in E$ with $a^\alpha = b^\alpha = d$, where $q = (a, i)$ and $r = (b, j)$ Then $E = \cup_d E(d)$. Let us define a *coherent domain* $D(d)$ as the set of vertices incident to some edges of $E(d)$, and let D_0 denote the set of isolated vertices (i.e., incident to no edge $e \in E$). (Vertices in D_0 do not belong to any coherent domain.) In the following discussion, we only consider nonempty coherent domains. Figure 2 shows all nonempty coherent domains of the graph G_{AS} of $(\tilde{T}, \tilde{F})$ in Example 2.

Lemma 5. *Every coherent domain $D(d) \subseteq V$ of G_{AS} induces a complete bipartite subgraph of G_{AS}.*

Proof. Take any pair $q = (a, i) \in AS(\tilde{T})$ and $r = (b, j) \in AS(\tilde{F})$ that satisfy $q, r \in D(d)$. Then there exist assignments $\alpha \in \mathbf{B}^{\{q\}}$ and $\beta \in \mathbf{B}^{\{r\}}$ such that $d = a^\alpha = b^\beta$. We concatenate these assignments to have an assignment $\gamma = (\alpha, \beta) \in \mathbf{B}^{\{q,r\}}$ for which $a^\gamma = b^\gamma = d$, implying that there is an edge $(q, r) \in E(d)$. □

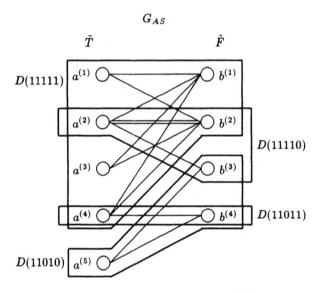

Fig. 2. Coherent domains of the graph G_{AS} of $(\tilde{T}, \tilde{F})$ in Example 2.

Lemma 6. *Let $D(d)$ and $D(d')$ be two coherent domains of G_{AS}, where $d, d' \in \mathbf{B}^n$ and $d \neq d'$. If $D(d) \cap D(d') \neq \emptyset$, then $\| d - d' \| = 1$ holds, where $\| x \| = \sum_{i=1}^{n} |x_i|$.*

Proof. Let $q = (a, i) \in D(d) \cap D(d')$. Then there exist two assignments $\alpha, \beta \in \mathbf{B}^{\{q\}} (= \{0,1\})$ such that $a^\alpha = d$ and $a^\beta = d'$. Since $|AS(a)| \leq 1$ is assumed, $\| d - d' \| = 1$ is implied. □

Lemma 7. *Let $D(d)$ and $D(d')$ be two coherent domains of G_{AS}, where $d, d' \in \mathbf{B}^n$ and $d \neq d'$. Then $|D(d) \cap D(d')| \leq 2$ holds. Furthermore, if $D(d) \cap D(d') = \{q, r\}$, then the graph G_{AS} has two parallel edges between q and r.*

Proof. If $q = (a, i), r = (b, j) \in D(d) \cap D(d')$, then by assigning 0 and 1 to q and r, each of a and b can become both d and d'. Since $\| d - d' \| = 1$ by Lemma 6, this can only happen if the vectors a and b are identical, missing the same component $i = j$. Therefore $|D(d) \cap D(d') \cap AS(\tilde{T})| \leq 1$ and $|D(d) \cap D(d') \cap AS(\tilde{F})| \leq 1$, and hence $|D(d) \cap D(d')| \leq 2$. Finally, if $D(d) \cap D(d') = \{q, r\}$, where $q = (a, i) \in AS(\tilde{T})$ and $r = (b, j) \in AS(\tilde{F})$, then $q = r$ implies that there are two assignments $\alpha, \beta \in \mathbf{B}^{\{q, r\}}$ such that $a^\alpha = b^\alpha = d$ and $a^\beta = b^\beta = d'$, i.e. the graph G_{AS} has two parallel edges between q and r. □

Let us now color the edges of G_{AS} by "yellow" and "blue", so that all edges of a set $E(d)$ have the same color, and every pair of sets $E(d)$ and $E(d')$ with $D(d) \cap D(d') \neq \emptyset$ has different colors. We call such a two coloring *alternating*. The following lemma shows that an alternating coloring is always possible. Furthermore, it can be uniquely completed after fixing a color of a set $E(d)$ in each connected component of G_{AS}.

Lemma 8. *Let $D(d^{(0)}), D(d^{(1)}), \ldots, D(d^{(l)})$ denote a cycle of coherent domains such that $d^{(i-1)} \neq d^{(i)}$ and $D(d^{(i-1)}) \cap D(d^{(i)}) \neq \emptyset$ hold for all $i = 1, 2, \ldots, l-1$, and $D(d^{(l)}) = D(d^{(0)})$. Then l is even.*

Proof. Lemma 6 tells that $\| d^{(i-1)} - d^{(i)} \| = 1$ holds for all $i = 1, 2, \ldots, l-1$. Since $\| d^{(0)} - d^{(l)} \| = 0$ is even, l must be even. $\qquad\square$

Finally, let us orient the edges of G_{AS} according to a given alternating coloring, as follows. Every yellow edge (q, r) is oriented from $q \in AS(\tilde{T})$ to $r \in AS(\tilde{F})$, and every blue edge (q, r) is oriented from $r \in AS(\tilde{F})$ to $q \in AS(\tilde{T})$. Let G'_{AS} denote the resulting directed graph. E.g. Figure 3 shows the directed graph G'_{AS} corresponding to the pBmd $(\tilde{T}, \tilde{F})$ of Example 2. Let us observe that every directed path of this graph is alternating in colors, and every alternating undirected path is either forward directed or backward directed.

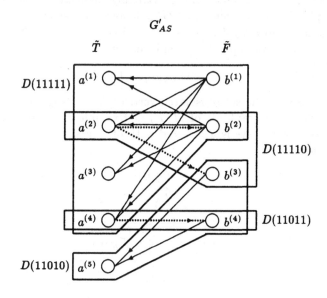

Fig. 3. The directed graph G'_{AS} of $(\tilde{T}, \tilde{F})$ in Example 2.

The next lemma characterizes a robust assignment by a directed path of G'_{AS}.

Lemma 9. *Let $(\tilde{T}, \tilde{F})$ be a pBmd, and let $q^{(0)} \xrightarrow{e_1} q^{(1)} \xrightarrow{e_2} q^{(2)} \ldots q^{(l-1)} \xrightarrow{e_l} q^{(l)}$ be a directed path in G'_{AS}. Then $\beta \in \mathbf{B}^Q$ for $Q \subseteq AS$ is a robust assignment if and only if the following properties hold, where $q^{(i)} = (a^{(i)}, j_i)$ and $\alpha_i = c(e_i)$ for all i.*

(i) *If $q^{(0)} \notin Q$ or $(a^{(0)})^\beta = (a^{(0)})^{\alpha_1}$, then $q^{(i)} \in Q$ and $(a^{(i)})^\beta \neq (a^{(i)})^{\alpha_i}$ hold for all $i = 1, 2, \ldots, l$.*

(ii) If $q^{(l)} \notin Q$ or $(a^{(l)})^\beta = (a^{(l)})^{\alpha_l}$ for some $l > 0$, then $q^{(i)} \in Q$ and $(a^{(i)})^\beta \neq (a^{(i)})^{\alpha_{i+1}}$ hold for all $i = 0, 1, \ldots, l - 1$.

Proof. We first prove the only-if-part. For condition (i), we first consider $e_1 = (q^{(0)}, q^{(1)})$. By Lemma 4, $q^{(0)} \notin Q$ or $(a^{(0)})^\beta = (a^{(0)})^{\alpha_1}$ implies that $q^{(1)} \in Q$ and $(a^{(1)})^\beta \neq (a^{(1)})^{\alpha_1}$. Now, since $e_1 = (q^{(0)}, q^{(1)}) \in E(d)$ and $e_2 = (q^{(1)}, q^{(2)}) \in E(d')$ have different colors, we must have $d \neq d'$ and $q^{(1)} \in D(d) \cap D(d')$, and hence $\| d - d' \| = 1$ by Lemma 6. Therefore, $(a^{(1)})^\beta \neq (a^{(1)})^{\alpha_1} (= d)$ implies $(a^{(1)})^\beta = (a^{(2)})^{\alpha_2} (= d')$, and hence $q^{(2)}$ satisfies $(a^{(2)})^\beta \neq (a^{(2)})^{\alpha_2}$ by Lemma 4. This assignment can proceed in a similar manner to $q^{(i)}$, $i = 2, 3, \ldots, l$. Case (ii) is similar to (i).

Conversely, if conditions (i) and (ii) hold, then, by Lemma 4, $\beta \in \mathbf{B}^Q$ is a robust assignment. □

Let C_i, $i = 1, 2, \ldots, s$, denote all the strongly connected components of this directed graph G'_{AS}. Furthermore, let G^*_{AS} denote the transitive closure of G'_{AS} (i.e., (s, t) is an arc in G^*_{AS} if there is an s-t directed path in G'_{AS}), and let G_0 denote the directed subgraph of G^*_{AS} induced by

$$W = \cup_{i \text{ s.t. } |C_i| = 1} C_i. \tag{6}$$

It is easy to see that the set of isolated vertices D_0 in G_{AS} satisfies $D_0 \subseteq W$. Figure 4 contains the graph G_0 of $(\tilde{T}, \tilde{F})$ in Example 2, where, for simplicity, arcs (u, v), for which there is a directed path of length at least 2 from u to v, are not indicated.

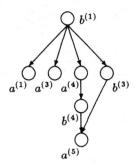

Fig. 4. The graph G_0 corresponding to G'_{AS} of $(\tilde{T}, \tilde{F})$ in Example 2.

Lemma 10. Let $(\tilde{T}, \tilde{F})$ be a pBmd, let $\alpha \in \mathbf{B}^Q$ for some $Q \subseteq AS$ be a robust assignment, and let C_i and W be defined as above. Then the following two conditions hold:

(i) $C_i \subseteq Q$ for all C_i with $|C_i| > 1$, and
(ii) $W \setminus Q$ is an antichain in G_0 (i.e., for any pair of $q, r \in W \setminus Q$, there is no directed path from q and r in G_0, and vice versa).

Proof. Consider a robust assignment $\alpha \in \mathbf{B}^Q$. Assume $q \in C_i \setminus Q$ for some C_i with $|C_i| > 1$. Then there is a directed cycle $q^{(0)} (= q), q^{(1)}, q^{(2)}, \ldots, q^{(l)} (= q)$ of length $l > 1$ in G'_{AS}, and $q \notin Q$ implies $q \in Q$ by Lemma 9, which is a contradiction. Hence condition (i) holds. To prove condition (ii), let us assume that for some pair of $q, r \in W \setminus Q$, there exists a directed path from q and r in G'_{AS}. This is again a contradiction since $q \notin Q$ implies $r \in Q$ by Lemma 9. □

Lemma 11. *Let $(\tilde{T}, \tilde{F})$ be a pBmd, and let $S \subseteq W$ be any maximal antichain in G_0. Then for $Q = AS \setminus S$, there is a robust assignment $\alpha \in \mathbf{B}^Q$ of $(\tilde{T}, \tilde{F})$.*

Proof. For $Q = AS \setminus S$, we shall construct a robust assignment $\alpha \in \mathbf{B}^Q$. In the following, we shall consider the directed graph G'_{AS}, and let us note that, by definition, S is also an antichain in G'_{AS}. Lemma 9 tells that, starting from a vertex $q \in S$ (i.e., $q \notin Q$), a robust assignment β for all vertices t which are either reachable from q or reachable to q is uniquely determined, unless the following cases of conflicts are encountered.

(i) For $q, r \in S$, there is a vertex t for which there are two directed paths $P_1 = q^{(0)} (= q) \to q^{(1)} \to \cdots \to q^{(k)} (= t)$ and $P_2 = r^{(0)} (= r) \to r^{(1)} \to \cdots \to r^{(l)} (= t)$ such that $t^\alpha \neq t^{\alpha'}$, where $\alpha = c(q^{(k-1)}, t)$ and $\alpha' = c(r^{(l-1)}, t)$.

(ii) For $q, r \in S$, there is a vertex t for which there are two directed paths $P_1 = q^{(0)} (= t) \to q^{(1)} \to \cdots \to q^{(k)} (= q)$ and $P_2 = r^{(0)} (= t) \to r^{(1)} \to \cdots \to r^{(l)} (= r)$ such that $t^\alpha \neq t^{\alpha'}$, where $\alpha = c(t, q^{(1)})$ and $\alpha' = c(t, r^{(1)})$.

If one of these conflicts occurs, Lemma 9 tells that t must be assigned in different ways, and hence we cannot construct an appropriate robust assignment β.

However, we now show that none of these conflicts can occur. Let us consider case (i) only, since case (ii) can be analogously treated. Now $t^\alpha \neq t^{\alpha'}$ implies $(q^{(k-1)}, s) \in E(d)$ and $(r^{(l-1)}, s) \in E(d')$ for some $d \neq d'$. Thus $(q^{(k-1)}, t)$ and $(r^{(l-1)}, t)$ have different colors, since $D(d) \cap D(d') \neq \emptyset$. By the rule of orienting edges (yellow edges are oriented from $AS(\tilde{T})$ to $AS(\tilde{F})$, and blue edges are oriented from $AS(\tilde{F})$ to $AS(\tilde{T})$), this means that one of $(q^{(k-1)}, t)$ and $(r^{(l-1)}, t)$ is oriented towards t, and the other is away from t, a contradiction to the assumption in (i).

Let us denote by R the set of all vertices $t \notin S$ such that either t is reachable from some $q \in S$ or some $q \in S$ is reachable from t. The above argument shows that a robust assignment β for R is uniquely determined by Lemma 9. Finally, we consider an assignment $\gamma \in \mathbf{B}^{AS \setminus (S \cup R)}$. By the maximality of S, every vertex $t \in AS \setminus (S \cup R)$ has an incoming arc $e = (r, t) \in E(d)$. Therefore, determine the robust assignment β of this t so that $t^\beta = d$ holds. This is well-defined because all incoming arcs to t belong to the same $E(d)$ by the definition of G'_{AS}. It is easy to see that the resulting β over AS is in fact a robust assignment. □

Lemmas 10 and 11 tell that problem MRE is equivalent to the problem of finding a maximum antichain of G_0. Since G_0 is acyclic, we can find such an antichain in polynomial time by Dilworth's theorem (see e.g. [8]). Hence, we have shown the following theorem.

Theorem 12. *Problem* MRE *can be solved in polynomial time for a pBmd* $(\tilde{T}, \tilde{F})$ *in which all* $a \in \tilde{T} \cup \tilde{F}$ *satisfy* $|AS(a)| \leq 1$.

5 Discussion

From the view point of knowledge acquisition, it is interesting to consider extensions for restricted classes of Boolean functions, because some structural information that justifies such restrictions might be available beforehand. In this case, however, even the problem of deciding whether there is an extension or not for a given pdBf (T, F) may not be trivial, depending on the class of functions at hand. This problem and the problem of finding an extension with a minimum number of errors are extensively discussed in [4] for such classes as positive (i.e., monotone) functions, Horn functions, functions with k-DNF and/or h-term-DNF, threshold functions, regular functions, read-once functions, self-dual functions, decomposable functions and so on. This direction is further pursued in [5] to consider the problems RE, CE and MRE of this paper, assuming that a pBmd $(\tilde{T}, \tilde{F})$ is given.

References

1. Angluin, D.: Queries and concept learning. Machine Learning **2** (1988) 319-342
2. Apswall, B., Plass, M.F., Tarjan, R.E.: A linear-time algorithm for testing the truth of certain quantified Boolean formulas. Information Processing Letters **8** (1979) 121-123
3. Boros, E., Hammer, P. L., Hooker, J. N.: Predicting cause-effect relationships from incomplete discrete observations. SIAM Journal on Discrete Mathematics **7** (1994) 531-543
4. Boros, E., Ibaraki, T., Makino, K.: Error-free and best-fit extensions of a partially defined Boolean function. RUTCOR Research Report RRR 14-95, Rutgers University (1995)
5. Boros, E., Ibaraki, T., Makino, K.: Extensions of partially defined Boolean functions with missing data. RUTCOR Research Report RRR 06-96, Rutgers University (1996)
6. Crama, Y., Hammer, P. L., Ibaraki, T.: Cause-effect relationships and partially defined boolean functions. Annals of Operations Research **16** (1988) 299-326
7. Dechter, R., Pearl, J.: Structure identification in relational data. Artificial Intelligence **58** (1992) 237-270
8. Ford, L. R., Fulkerson, D. R.: Flows in Networks. Princeton University Press (1962)
9. Garey, M. R., Johnson, D. S.: Computers and Intractability. Freeman, New York (1979)
10. Quinlan, J. R.: Induction of decision trees. Machine Learning **1** (1986) 81-106
11. Valiant, L. G.: A theory of the learnable. Communications of the ACM **27** (1984) 1134-1142

Author Index

Springer-Verlag and the Environment

We at Springer-Verlag firmly believe that an international science publisher has a special obligation to the environment, and our corporate policies consistently reflect this conviction.

We also expect our business partners – paper mills, printers, packaging manufacturers, etc. – to commit themselves to using environmentally friendly materials and production processes.

The paper in this book is made from low- or no-chlorine pulp and is acid free, in conformance with international standards for paper permanency.

Lecture Notes in Computer Science

For information about Vols. 1–1026

please contact your bookseller or Springer-Verlag